Business Forecasting
With
ForecastX™

Sixth Edition

J. Holton Wilson
Central Michigan University

Barry Keating
University of Notre Dame

John Galt Solutions, Inc.
Chicago

Mc
Graw
Hill

Boston   Burr Ridge, IL   Dubuque, IA   Madison, WI   New York   San Francisco   St. Louis
Bangkok   Bogotá   Caracas   Kuala Lumpur   Lisbon   London   Madrid   Mexico City
Milan   Montreal   New Delhi   Santiago   Seoul   Singapore   Sydney   Taipei   Toronto

BUSINESS FORECASTING: WITH FORECASTX™
International Edition 2009

Exclusive rights by McGraw-Hill Education (Asia), for manufacture and export. This book cannot
be re-exported from the country to which it is sold by McGraw-Hill. This International Edition is
not to be sold or purchased in North America and contains content that is different from its North
American version.

Published by McGraw-Hill/Irwin, a business unit of The McGraw-Hill Companies, Inc., 1221
Avenue of the Americas, New York, NY, 10020. Copyright © 2009, 2007, 2002, 1998, 1994, 1990
by The McGraw-Hill Companies, Inc. All rights reserved. No part of this publication may be
reproduced or distributed in any form or by any means, or stored in a database or retrieval system,
without the prior written consent of The McGraw-Hill Companies, Inc., including, but not limited
to, in any network or other electronic storage or transmission, or broadcast for distance learning.
Some ancillaries, including electronic and print components, may not be available to customers
outside the United States.

10 09 08 07 06 05 04
20 15 14 13 12 11
CTF   ANL

When ordering this title, use ISBN 978-007-127609-2 or MHID 007-127609-2

Printed in Singapore

www.mhhe.com

To Eva, Ronnie, and Clara
To Maryann, John, Ingrid, Vincent,
Katy, Alice, Casey, and Jill Keating

Preface

The sixth edition of *Business Forecasting* with ForecastX™ builds on the success of the first five editions. While a number of significant changes have been made in this sixth edition, it remains a book about forecasting methods for managers, forecasting practitioners, and students who will one day become business professionals and have a need to understand practical issues related to forecasting. Our emphasis is on authentic learning of the forecasting methods that practicing forecasters have found most useful. *Business Forecasting* with ForecastX™ is written for students and others who want to know how forecasting is really done.

The major change to the sixth edition of the text is a new chapter on data mining as a tool in business forecasting. As with the fifth edition, we again use the ForecastX™ software as the tool to implement the methods described in the text. This software is included on a CD with each copy of the text and has been made available through an agreement with John Galt Solutions, Inc. Every forecasting method discussed in the text can be implemented with this software (the data mining techniques, however, require separate software). Based on our own experiences and those of other faculty members who have used the fifth edition, we know that students find the ForecastX™ software easy to use, even without a manual or other written instructions. However, we have provided a brief introduction to the use of ForecastX™ at the end of each relevant chapter. There is also a User's Guide on the CD with the software for those who may want more extensive coverage, including information on advanced issues not covered in the text, but included in the software.

John Galt Solutions provides us with the ForecastX software that does contain proprietary algorithms, which in some situations do not match exactly with the results one would get if the calculations were done "by hand." Their methods, however, have proven successful in the marketplace as well as in forecast competitions.

We are confident that faculty and students will enjoy using this widely adopted, commercially successful software. However, the text also can be used without reliance on this particular package. All data files are provided on the student CD in Excel format so that they can be easily used with almost any forecasting or statistical software. As with previous editions, nearly all data in the text is real, such as jewelry sales, book store sales, and total houses sold. In addition, we have continued the use of an ongoing case involving forecasting sales of The Gap, Inc., at the end of each chapter to provide a consistent link. Additionally, a number of excellent sources of data are referenced in the text. These are especially useful for student projects and for additional exercises that instructors may wish to develop.

Comments from the Field by forecasting practitioners provide quick insights into issues and problems faced daily by individuals who are actively engaged in the forecasting process. These offer a practical perspective from the "real world" to help students appreciate the relevance of the concepts presented in the text.

Today, most business planning routinely begins with a sales forecast. Whether you are an accountant, a marketer, a human resources manager, or a financial analyst, you will have to forecast something sooner or later. This book is designed to lead you through the most helpful techniques to use in any forecasting effort. The examples we offer are, for the most part, based on actual historical data, much like that you may encounter in your own forecasts. The techniques themselves are explained as procedures that you may replicate with your own data.

The Online Learning Center accompanying the book includes all data used in the text examples and chapter-ending problems. In addition, Excel sheets with suggested answers to these problems are on this Web site.

The authors would like to thank the students at the University of Notre Dame and Central Michigan University for their help in working with materials included in this book during its development. Their comments were invaluable in preparing clear expositions and meaningful examples for this sixth edition. Comments from students at other universities both in the United States and elsewhere have also been appreciated. It has been particularly gratifying to hear from students who have found what they learned from a course using this text to be useful in their professional careers.

The final product owes a great debt to the inspiration and comments of our colleagues, especially Professors Thomas Bundt of Hillsdale College, and Tunga Kiyak at Michigan State University. In addition, we would like to thank the staff at John Galt Solutions for facilitating our use of the ForecastX™ software. We also thank Professor Eamonn Keogh at the University of California, Riverside, for sharing with us his illuminating examples of data mining techniques.

Adopters of the first five editions who have criticized, challenged, encouraged, and complimented our efforts deserve our thanks. The authors are particularly grateful to the following faculty and professionals who used earlier editions of the text and/or have provided comments that have helped to improve this sixth edition.

Paul Altieri
Central Connecticut State University

Peter Bruce
Statistics.com

Margaret M. Capen
East Carolina University

Thomas P. Chen
St. John's University

Ronald L. Coccari
Cleveland State University

Lewis Coopersmith
Rider University

Ali Dogramaci
Rutgers, the State University of New Jersey

Farzad Farsio
Montana State University

Robert Fetter
Yale University

Benito Flores
Texas A & M University

Kenneth Gaver
Montana State University

Rakesh Gupta
Adelphi University

Joseph Kelley
California State University, Sacramento

Thomas Kelly
BMW of Canada

Eamonn Keogh
University of California, Riverside

Krishna Kool
University of Rio Grande

John Mathews
University of Wisconsin, Madison

Joseph McCarthy
Bryant College

Elam McElroy
Marquette University

Rob Roy McGregor
University of North Carolina, Charlotte

John C. Nash
University of Ottawa

Thomas Needham
US Bancorp

Nitin Patel
Massachusetts Institute of Technology

Gerald Platt
San Francisco State University

Melissa Ramenofsky
University of Southern Alabama

Helmut Schneider
Louisiana State University

Stanley Schultz
Cleveland State University

Nancy Serafino
United Telephone

Galit Shmueli
University of Maryland

Donald N. Stengel
California State University, Fresno

Kwei Tang
Louisiana State University

Dick Withycomb
University of Montana

We are especially grateful to have worked with the following publishing professionals on our McGraw-Hill/Irwin book team: Dick Hercher, Rebecca Mann, Rhonda Seelinger, Lori Hazzard, Joanne Mennemeier, Debra Sylvester, and Balaji Sundararaman.

We hope that all of the above, as well as all new faculty, students, and business professionals who use the text, will be pleased with the sixth edition.

J. Holton Wilson
Holt.Wilson@cmich.edu

Barry Keating
Barry.P.Keating.1@nd.edu

Brief Contents

Contents

Introduction to Business Forecasting

I believe that forecasting or demand management may have the potential to add more value to a business than any single activity within the supply chain. I say this because if you can get the forecast right, you have the potential to get everything else in the supply chain right. But if you can't get the forecast right, then everything else you do essentially will be reactive, as opposed to proactive planning.

Al Enns, Director of Supply Chain Strategies, Motts North America, Stamford, Connecticut[1]

INTRODUCTION

If you are reading this text as part of the course requirements for a college degree, consider yourself fortunate. Many college graduates, even those with degrees in business or economics, do not ever study forecasting, except as a sidelight in a course that has other primary objectives. And yet, we know that forecasting is an essential element of most business decisions.

The need for personnel with forecasting expertise is growing.[2] For example, Levi Strauss only started its forecast department in 1995 and within four years had a full-time forecasting staff of thirty. Many people filling these positions have had little formal training in forecasting and are paying thousands of dollars to attend educational programs. In annual surveys conducted by the Institute of Business Forecasting it has been found that there are substantial increases in the staffing of forecasters in full-time positions within American companies.

---

[1] Sidney Hill, Jr., "A Whole New Outlook," *Manufacturing Systems* 16, no. 9 (September 1998), pp. 70–80.

[2] Chaman L. Jain, "Explosion in the Forecasting Function in Corporate America," *Journal of Business Forecasting,* Summer 1999, p. 2.

AT&T WIRELESS SERVICES ADDRESSES CAPACITY PLANNING NEEDS

AT&T Wireless Services is one of the largest wireless carriers in the United States, offering voice, aviation communications, and wireless data services over an integrated, nationwide network.

AT&T Wireless sought to redefine its forecasting process, as the company had been using many different data sources—including Oracle 8—combined with a judgmental process to estimate its future demand. AT&T Wireless needed to find an integrated solution that would automate its sales forecasting process to more effectively manage the deployment and utilization of its infrastructure. The chosen solution would also need to be easily integrated with AT&T's existent sales forecasting process.

After searching for a solution that could be used to enhance its existing judgmental process by accounting for marketing promotions, sales events, and other market factors, AT&T Wireless decided to implement a scalable solution comprising John Galt Solutions' ForecastX Wizard product family. John Galt provided AT&T Wireless with documentation and working examples that enabled the company to visualize and validate the benefits of ForecastX immediately and throughout the implementation process. The examples and help that John Galt extended provided AT&T with the background the company needed to answer its questions.

John Galt's ForecastX gave AT&T powerful front-end analytical capabilities to utilize batch forecasting—an automated process that generates forecasts according to a schedule determined by the parties responsible for forecasting within AT&T Wireless. Users simply adjust their parameters and set the Batch Scheduler, and the program runs without further user intervention. At current staffing levels, AT&T Wireless can support its capacity planning needs, thanks to a framework and tools that will allow analysts to focus their attention on business issues. Using ForecastX, the company can quantify the costs and benefits that will be obtained from its infrastructure investments.

Source: http://www.johngalt.com/customers/success.shtml.

QUANTITATIVE FORECASTING HAS BECOME WIDELY ACCEPTED

We might think of forecasting as a set of tools that helps decision makers make the best possible judgments about future events. In today's rapidly changing business world such judgments can mean the difference between success and failure. It is no longer reasonable to rely solely on intuition, or one's "feel for the situation," in projecting future sales, inventory needs, personnel requirements, and other important economic or business variables. Quantitative methods have been shown to be helpful in making better predictions about the future course of events,[3] and a number of sophisticated computer software packages have been developed to make these methods accessible to nearly everyone. In a recent survey it was found that about 80 percent of forecasting is done with quantitative methods.[4]

[3] J. Holton Wilson and Deborah Allison-Koerber, "Combining Subjective and Objective Forecasts Improves Results," *Journal of Business Forecasting* 11, no. 3 (Fall 1992), pp. 12–16.

[4] Chaman Jain, "Benchmarking Forecasting Models," *Journal of Business Forecasting* 26, no. 4 (Winter 2007–08), p.17.

Sophisticated software such as ForecastX make it relatively easy to implement quantitative methods in a forecasting process. There is a danger, however, in using canned forecasting software unless you are familiar with the concepts upon which the programs are based.

This text and its accompanying computer software (ForecastX) have been carefully designed to provide you with an understanding of the conceptual basis for many modern quantitative forecasting models, along with programs that have been written specifically for the purpose of allowing you to put these methods to use. You will find both the text and the software to be extremely user-friendly. After studying the text and using the software to replicate the examples we present, you will be able to forecast economic and business variables with greater accuracy than you might now expect. But a word of warning is appropriate. Do not become so enamored with quantitative methods and computer results that you fail to *think* carefully about the series you wish to forecast. In the evolution of forecasting over the last several decades there have been many changes, but the move to more quantitative forecasting has been the most dramatic. This has been due primarily to the availability and quality of data and to the increased accessibility of user-friendly forecasting software.[5] Personal judgments based on practical experience and/or thorough research should always play an important role in the preparation of any forecast.

> Personal judgments based on practical experience and/or thorough research should always play an important role in the preparation of any forecast.

FORECASTING IN BUSINESS TODAY

Forecasting in today's business world is becoming increasingly important as firms focus on increasing customer satisfaction while reducing the cost of providing products and services. Six Sigma initiatives and lean thinking are representative of moves in this direction. The term "lean" has come to represent an approach to removing waste from business systems while providing the same, or higher, levels of quality and output to customers (business customers as well as end users).[6] One major business cost involves inventory, both of inputs and of final products. Through better forecasting, inventory costs can be reduced and wasteful inventory eliminated.

Two professional forecasting organizations offer programs specifically aimed at increasing the skills and abilities of business professionals who find forecasting an important part of their job responsibilities. The International Institute of Forecasters (IIF) offers "Forecasting Summits" at which professional forecasters share ideas with others and can participate in various tutorials and workshops designed to enhance their skills (see www.forecasting-summit.com). With the leadership of

---

[5] Barry Keating et al., "Evolution in Forecasting: Experts Share Their Journey," *Journal of Business Forecasting* 25, no. 1 (Spring 2006), p. 15.

[6] Kenneth B. Kahn and John Mello, "Lean Forecasting Begins with Lean Thinking on the Demand Forecasting Process," *Journal of Business Forecasting* 23, no. 4 (Winter 2004–05), pp. 30–32, 40.

Len Tashman, in 2005 the IIF started a new practitioner-oriented journal, *Foresight: The International Journal of Applied Forecasting,* aimed at forecast analysts, managers, and students of forecasting.

The Institute of Business Forecasting (IBF) offers a variety of programs for business professionals where they can network with others and attend seminars and workshops to help enhance their forecasting skills (see www.ibf.org). Examples include the "Demand Planning and Forecasting Best Practices Conference," "Supply Chain Forecasting Conference," and "Business Forecasting Tutorials." The IBF also provides programs that lead to two levels of certifications in forecasting and publishes a journal that focuses on applied forecasting issues (*The Journal of Business Forecasting*).

Both IIF and IBF offer forecast certification programs. IIF offers three levels of certification as a Certified Professional Demand Forecaster (CPDF); see www.cpdftraining.org. IBF offers two levels of certification as a Certified Professional Forecaster (CPF); see www.ibf.org/certjbf.cfm. Both organizations present a variety of workshops and training sessions to prepare business professionals for certification. After completing this course you will have a good knowledge base to achieve certification from these organizations.

Business decisions almost always depend on some forecast about the course of events. Virtually every functional area of business makes use of some type of forecast. For example:

1. Accountants rely on forecasts of costs and revenues in tax planning.
2. The personnel department depends on forecasts as it plans recruitment of new employees and other changes in the workforce.
3. Financial experts must forecast cash flows to maintain solvency.
4. Production managers rely on forecasts to determine raw-material needs and the desired inventory of finished products.
5. Marketing managers use a sales forecast to establish promotional budgets.

Because forecasting is useful in so many functional areas of an organization it is not surprising that this activity is found in many different areas. Consider the following survey results concerning where one sample of forecasters resides within their organizations:[7]

Marketing/Logistics/Sales	29%
Operations/Production	27%
Forecasting Department	19%
Finance	7%
Strategic Planning	6%
Other	12%

[7] Chaman Jain, "Benchmarking Forecasting Processes," *Journal of Business Forecasting* 26, no. 4 (Winter 2007–08), p.12.

The sales forecast is often the root forecast from which others, such as employment requirements, are derived.

The sales forecast is often the root forecast from which others, such as employment requirements, are derived. As early as the mid-1980s a study of large American-operated firms showed that roughly 94 percent made use of a sales forecast.[8] The ways in which forecasts are prepared and the manner in which results are used vary considerably among firms.

As a way of illustrating the application of forecasting in the corporate world, we will summarize aspects of the forecasting function in eight examples. In these examples you may see some terms with which you are not fully familiar at this time. However, you probably have a general understanding of them, and when you have completed the text, you will understand them all quite well.

Krispy Kreme

During summer 1937 the first Krispy Kreme doughnuts were sold in Winston-Salem, North Carolina. Since that time the company has grown and spread well beyond the borders of North Carolina. As we entered the current century, Krispy Kreme's operations had expanded to a point that it recognized the need for a new multiple forecasting system to provide information related to production requirements based on demand forecasts and to provide financial forecasts.[9] It identified three major drivers of its business: new stores, new off-premises customers that make Krispy Kreme products available through retail partners, and seasonal factors. For new stores, forecast models were developed for the opening week through sales 18 months out. Sales are related to such factors as general population growth, brand awareness, foot traffic, and display locations. Each month a series of conference calls with market operators are used to gather information for the forecasting models. Meetings with executive-level managers are also held on a monthly basis to communicate forecast information. This process has led to forecasts with errors of only plus or minus 1 percent.

Bell Atlantic

At Bell Atlantic, the forecasting process begins with the collection of historical data on a monthly basis.[10] These data are saved for both service classifications and geographic regions. The Demand Forecasting Group at Bell Atlantic developed a data warehouse so that the data can be shared and integrated across the entire corporation. In preparing forecasts, subjective forecasting methods are used along with time-series methods, and regression modeling based on economic, demographic, and other exogenous variables. The forecasts are continually monitored and compared with actual results monthly and annually to ensure that Bell Atlantic meets customer needs.

---

[8] Wilson and Allison-Koerber, pp. 12–16.

[9] Brad Wall, "Evolution in the Forecasting Process at Krispy Kreme," *Journal of Business Forecasting* 21, no. 1 (Spring 2002), pp. 15–16.

[10] Sharon Harris, "Forecasting with Demand Forecasting Group Database at Bell Atlantic," *Journal of Business Forecasting,* Winter 1995–96, p. 23.

Columbia Gas

Columbia Gas of Ohio (Columbia) is a large natural gas utility that delivers over 300 billions of cubic feet (BCF) of natural gas annually.[11] Columbia develops two kinds of forecasts, which it refers to as the Design Day Forecast and the Daily Operational Forecast. The former is used to determine gas supply, transportation capacity, storage capacity, and related measures. This forecast is used primarily for supply and capacity planning. Over a seven-year period the average mean absolute percentage error in its Design Day Forecast was 0.4 percent.

The Daily Operational Forecast is used primarily to ensure that supplies are in balance with demand over five-day spans. As would be expected, the average errors for these shorter term forecasts have been higher at about 3 percent. The forecasts are based to a large degree on regression models (see Chapters 4 and 5) in which demand is a function of such variables as current-day temperatures, previous-day temperatures, wind speed, and day of the week.

Segix Italia

Segix Italia is a pharmaceutical company in Italy that produces products that are sold domestically and are exported to countries in Europe, such as Belgium, Holland, Germany, and England, as well as to African, South American, Asian, and Middle Eastern countries.[12] The forecasting function at Segix is housed within the marketing group, and forecasts are reviewed by the marketing director and the sales director, both of whom may make subjective adjustments to the forecasts based on market forces not reflected in the original forecasts. The forecasts are prepared monthly for seven main prescription drug products. The monthly forecasts are then aggregated to arrive at annual forecasts. These forecasts are used to develop targets for sales representatives.

Pharmaceuticals in Singapore

In this example we look at some survey results related to forecasting by pharmaceutical firms in Singapore.[13] The survey included many well-known firms, such as Glaxo Wellcome, Bayer, Pfizer, Bristol-Myers Squibb, and others. Respondent forecasters were from across business areas such as management marketing, finance, and operations. The primary uses of forecasts were found to be allocation of corporate resources for human resources planning, and for promotions, strategic planning, and setting sales quotas. Both quantitative methods and personal judgments were found to be important in the development of forecasts.

[11] H. Alan Catron, "Daily Demand Forecasting at Columbia Gas," *Journal of Business Forecasting* 19, no. 2 (Summer 2000), pp. 10–15.

[12] Anna Maria Rosati, "Forecasting at Segix Italia: A Pharmaceutical Company," *Journal of Business Forecasting*, Fall 1996, pp. 7–9.

[13] Louis Choo, "Forecasting Practices in the Pharmaceutical Industry in Singapore," *Journal of Business Forecasting* 19, no. 2 (Summer 2000), pp. 18–20.

Fiat Auto

Top management at Fiat considers the forecasting function as an essential aspect of its decision-making process.[14] Midway through the 1990s Fiat was selling over 2 million vehicles annually and employed some 81,000 people in Italy and about another 38,000 overseas. All functional areas in the company make use of the forecasts that are prepared primarily in the Planning, Finance, and Control Department and in the Product Strategy Department. Macroeconomic data such as gross domestic product, the interest rate, the rate of inflation, and raw-material prices are important inputs in Fiat's forecasting process. At Fiat forecasts are first prepared for total sales of vehicles, engines, and gears, and then broken down to specific stockkeeping units (SKUs). Sales are measured by orders rather than shipments because its system is customer-driven.

Brake Parts, Inc.

Brake Parts, Inc. (BPI), is a manufacturer of replacement brake parts for both foreign and domestic cars and light trucks.[15] It has nine manufacturing plants and seven distribution centers in the United States and Canada. Overall, BPI has roughly 250,000 stockkeeping units at various distribution locations (SKULs) to forecast. The development and implementation of a multiple forecasting system (MFS) has saved BPI over $6 million per month, resulting from sales not being lost due to stockouts. The MFS at BPI uses up to 19 time-series forecasting techniques, such as a variety of exponential smoothing methods, and causal regression models in tandem. Forecasts are first developed with a time-series method, and then the errors, or residuals, are forecast using regression. The two forecasts are then added together and provided to management in a form that allows management to make subjective adjustments to the forecasts.

Forecasts are evaluated using three measures: percent error (PE), mean absolute percent error (MAPE), and year-to-date mean absolute percent error (YTD MAPE). The first two of these are common error measures, but the third is somewhat unique. The YTD MAPE is used to give management a feeling for how each forecast is performing in the most current time frame. The PE and MAPE contain errors that may have occurred at any time in the historical period and thus may not reflect how well the method is working currently.

Some Global Forecasting Issues: Examples from Ocean Spray Cranberries

Sean Reese, a demand planner at Ocean Spray Cranberries, Inc., has summarized some issues that are particularly salient for anyone involved in forecasting in a global environment. First, units of measurement differ between the United States and most other countries. Where the U.S. uses such measures as ounces, pounds,

[14] Anna Maria Rosati, "Forecasting at Fiat Auto," *Journal of Business Forecasting,* Spring 1996, pp. 28–29.
[15] John T. Mentzer and Jon Schroeter, "Multiple Forecasting System at Brake Parts, Inc.," *Journal of Business Forecasting,* Fall 1993, pp. 5–9.

quarts, and gallons, most other countries use grams, kilograms, milliliters, and liters. Making appropriate conversions and having everyone involved understand the relationships can be a challenge.[16] Second, seasonal patterns reverse between the northern and southern hemispheres, so it makes a difference whether one is forecasting for a northern or southern hemisphere market. Third, such cultural differences as preference for degree of sweetness, shopping habits, and perception of colors can impact sales. The necessary lead time for product and ingredient shipments can vary a great deal depending on the geographic regions involved. Further, since labels are different, one must forecast specifically for each country rather than the system as a whole. Consider, for example, two markets that may at first appear similar: the United States and Canada. These two markets use different units of measurement, and in Canada labels must have all information equally in both French and English. Thus, products destined to be sold in one market cannot be sold in the other market, so each forecast must be done separately.

These examples illustrate the role forecasting plays in representative firms. Similar scenarios exist in thousands of other businesses throughout the world and, as you will see in the following section, in various nonbusiness activities as well.

FORECASTING IN THE PUBLIC AND NOT-FOR-PROFIT SECTORS

The need to make decisions based on judgments about the future course of events extends beyond the profit-oriented sector of the economy. Hospitals, libraries, blood banks, police and fire departments, urban transit authorities, credit unions, and a myriad of federal, state, and local governmental units rely on forecasts of one kind or another. Social service agencies such as the Red Cross and the Easter Seal Society must also base their yearly plans on forecasts of needed services and expected revenues.

Brooke Saladin, working with the research and planning division of the police department in a city of about 650,000 people, has been effective in forecasting the demand for police patrol services.[17] This demand is measured by using a call-for-service workload level in units of hours per 24-hour period. After a thorough statistical analysis, five factors were identified as influential determinants of the call-for-service work load (W):

POP   a population factor
ARR   an arrest factor
AFF   an affluence factor
VAC   a vacancy factor
DEN   a density factor

[16] Sean Reese, "Reflections of an International Forecaster," *Journal of Business Forecasting* 22, no. 4 (Winter 2003–04), pp. 23, 28.

[17] Brooke A. Saladin, "A Police Story with Business Implications and Applications," *Journal of Business Forecasting* 1, no. 6 (Winter 1982–83), pp. 3–5.

The following multiple-regression model was developed on the basis of a sample of 40 cruiser districts in the city:

$$W = 5.66 + 1.84\text{POP} + 1.70\text{ARR} - 0.93\text{AFF} + 0.61\text{VAC} + 0.13\text{DEN}$$

Using the remaining 23 cruiser districts to test this model, Saladin found that "the absolute error in forecasting workload ranged from 0.07827 to 1.49764, with an average of 0.74618."[18] This type of model is useful in planning the needs for both personnel and equipment.

In Texas, the Legislative Budget Board (LBB) is required to forecast the growth rate for Texas personal income, which then governs the limit for state appropriations. The state comptroller's office also needs forecasts of such variables as the annual growth rates of electricity sales, total nonagricultural employment, and total tax revenues. Richard Ashley and John Guerard have used techniques like those to be discussed in this text to forecast these variables and have found that the application of time-series analysis yields better one-year-ahead forecasts than naive constant-growth-rate models.[19]

Dr. Jon David Vasche, senior economist for the California Legislative Analysis Office (LAO), is involved with economic and financial forecasting for the state. He has noted that these forecasts are essential, since the state's budget of over $70 billion must be prepared long before actual economic conditions are known.[20] The key features of the LAO's forecasting approach are:

1. *Forecasts of national economic variables.* The Wharton econometric model is used with the adaptations that reflect the LAO's own assumptions about such policy variables as monetary growth and national fiscal policies.
2. *California economic submodel.* This model forecasts variables such as trends in state population, personal income, employment, and housing activity.
3. *State revenue submodels.* These models are used to forecast the variables that affect the state's revenue. These include such items as taxable personal income, taxable sales, corporate profits, vehicle registrations, and cash available for investment.
4. *Cash-flow models.* These models are used to forecast the flow of revenues over time.

In developing and using forecasting models, "the LAO has attempted to strike a balance between comprehensiveness and sophistication on the one hand, and flexibility and usability on the other."[21] LAO's success is determined by how

---

[18] Ibid., p. 5.

[19] Richard Ashley and John Guerard, "Applications of Time-Series Analysis to Texas Financial Forecasting," *Interfaces* 13, no. 4 (August 1983), pp. 46–55.

[20] Jon David Vasche, "Forecasting Process as Used by California Legislative Analyst's Office," *Journal of Business Forecasting* 6, no. 2 (Summer 1987), pp. 9–13; and "State Demographic Forecasting for Business and Policy Applications," *Journal of Business Forecasting,* Summer 2000, pp. 23–30.

[21] Jon David Vasche, "Forecasting Process," pp. 9, 12.

accurately it forecasts the state's revenues. In the three most recent years reported, the "average absolute value of the actual error was only about 1.6 percent."[22] Errors of 5 percent or more have occurred when unanticipated movements in national economic activity have affected the state's economy.

A multiple-regression forecasting model has been developed to help forecast a hospital's nursing staff requirements.[23] This model forecasts the number of patients that need to be served and the nature of care required (e.g., pediatric or orthopedic) for each month, day of the week, and time of day. Such models have become very valuable for directors of nursing personnel in determining work schedules.

In a study of a hospital that holds over 300 beds, we have found that the forecasting methods discussed in this text are effective in forecasting monthly billable procedures (BILLPROC) for the hospital's laboratories.[24] The primary purpose of producing monthly forecasts is to help laboratory managers make more accurate staffing decisions in the laboratory. Also, an accurate forecast can help in controlling inventory costs and in providing timely customer service. This can streamline operations and lead to more satisfied customers.

For preparing short-term forecasts of billable procedures, two models are used: a linear-regression model and Winters' exponential-smoothing model. The linear-regression model is based on inpatient admissions, a time index, and 11 monthly dummy variables to account for seasonality. The second model is a Winters' exponential smoothing that incorporates a multiplicative seasonal adjustment and a trend component.

The root-mean-squared error (RMSE) is used to evaluate the accuracy of forecast models at the hospital. The first annual forecast, by month, of billable procedures for the laboratory prepared with these quantitative methods provided good results. The linear-regression model provided the most accurate forecast, with an RMSE of 1,654.44. This was about 3.9 percent of the mean number of procedures per month during that year. The Winters' model had a higher RMSE of 2,416.91 (about 5.7 percent of the mean number of procedures per month). For the entire fiscal year in total, the forecast of the annual number of laboratory procedures resulted in an error of only 0.7 percent.

FORECASTING AND SUPPLY CHAIN MANAGEMENT

In recent years there has been increased attention to supply chain management issues. In a competitive environment businesses are forced to operate with maximum efficiency and with a vigilant eye toward maintaining firm cost controls, while continuing to meet consumer expectations in a profitable manner. To be

[22] Ibid., p. 12.

[23] F. Theodore Helmer, Edward B. Opperman, and James D. Suver, "Forecasting Nursing Staffing Requirements by Intensity-of-Care Level," *Interfaces,* June 1980, pp. 50–55.

[24] J. Holton Wilson and Steven J. Schuiling, "Forecasting Hospital Laboratory Procedures," *Journal of Medical Systems,* December 1992, pp. 269–79.

successful, businesses must manage relationships along the supply chain more fully than ever before.[25] This can be aided by effectively using the company's own sales organization and making forecasting an integral part of the sales and operations planning (S&OP) process.[26]

We can think of the supply chain as encompassing all of the various flows between suppliers, producers, distributors (wholesalers, retailers, etc.), and consumers. Throughout this chain each participant, prior to the final consumer, must manage supplies, inventories, production, and shipping in one form or another. For example, a manufacturer that makes cellular phones needs a number of different components to assemble the final product and ultimately ship it to a local supplier of cellular phone services or some other retailer. One such component might be the leather carrying case. The manufacturer of the carrying case may have suppliers of leather, clear plastic for portions of the case, fasteners, dyes perhaps, and possibly other components. Each one of these suppliers has its own suppliers back one more step in the supply chain. With all of these businesses trying to reduce inventory costs (for raw materials, goods in process, and finished products), reliability and cooperation across the supply chain become essential.

Forecasting has come to play an important role in managing supply chain relationships. If the supplier of leather phone cases is to be a good supply chain partner, it must have a reasonably accurate forecast of the needs of the cellular phone company. The cellular phone company, in turn, needs a good forecast of sales to be able to provide the leather case company with good information. It is probably obvious that, if the cellular phone company is aware of a significant change in sales for a future period, that information needs to be communicated to the leather case company in a timely manner.

To help make the entire supply chain function more smoothly, many companies have started to use collaborative forecasting systems in which information about the forecast is shared throughout the relevant portions of the supply chain. Often, in fact, suppliers have at least some input into the forecast of a business further along the supply chain in such collaborative forecasting systems.[27] Having good forecasts at every stage is essential for efficient functioning of the supply chain.

At the beginning of the text, at the very start of page 1, you read the following quote from Al Enns, director of supply chain strategies, at Motts North America:

> I believe that forecasting or demand management may have the potential to add
> more value to a business than any single activity within the supply chain. I say this

> To help make the entire supply chain function more smoothly, many companies have started to use collaborative forecasting systems in which information about the forecast is shared throughout the relevant portions of the supply chain.

---

[25] See, for example, David Simchi-Levi, Philip Kaminsky, and Edith Simchi-Levi, *Designing and Managing the Supply Chain* (New York: Irwin/McGraw-Hill), 2000.

[26] Tony Alhadeff, "Engaging the Sales Organization for a Better Forecast," *Journal of Business Forecasting* 23, no. 1 (Spring 2004), pp. 7–10.

[27] Many forecasting software packages facilitate collaborative forecasting by making the process Web-based so that multiple participants can potentially have access to, and in some cases input into, the forecast process.

because *if you can get the forecast right, you have the potential to get everything else in the supply chain right.* But if you can't get the forecast right, then everything else you do essentially will be reactive, as opposed to proactive planning.[28]

Daphney Barr, a planning coordinator for Velux-America, a leading manufacturer of roof windows and skylights, has similarly observed that:

Demand planning is the key driver of the supply chain. Without knowledge of demand, manufacturing has very little on which to develop production and inventory plans while logistics in turn has limited information and resources to develop distribution plans for products among different warehouses and customers. *Simply stated, demand forecasting is the wheel that propels the supply chain forward* and the demand planner is the driver of the forecasting process.[29]

These are two examples of the importance business professionals are giving to the role of forecasting.

There is another issue that is partially related to where a business operates along the supply chain that is important to think about when it comes to forecasting. As one gets closer to the consumer end of the supply chain, the number of items to forecast tends to increase. For example, consider a manufacturer that produces a single product that is ultimately sold through discount stores. Along the way it may pass through several intermediaries. That manufacturer only needs to forecast sales of that one product (and, of course, the potentially many components that go into the product). But assume that Wal-Mart is one of the stores that sells the product to consumers throughout the United States. Just think of the tens of thousands of stockkeeping units (SKUs) that Wal-Mart sells and must forecast. Clearly the methods that the manufacturer considers in preparing a forecast can be much more labor intensive than the methods that Wal-Mart can consider. An organization like Wal-Mart will be limited to applying forecasting methods that can be easily automated and can be quickly applied. This is something you will want to think about as you study the various forecast methods discussed in this text.

COLLABORATIVE FORECASTING

The recognition that improving functions throughout the supply chain can be aided by appropriate use of forecasting tools has led to increased cooperation among supply chain partners. This cooperative effort, designed by the Voluntary Interindustry Commerce Standards Association (VICS), has become known as Collaborative Planning Forecasting and Replenishment (CPFR).[30] CPFR involves coordination, communication, and cooperation among participants in the supply chain.

[28] Sidney Hill, Jr., "A Whole New Outlook," *Manufacturing Systems* 16, no. 9 (September 1998), pp. 70–80. (*Emphasis* added.)

[29] Daphney P. Barr, "Challenges Facing a Demand Planner: How to Identify and Handle Them," *Journal of Business Forecasting* 21, no. 2 (Summer 2002), pp. 28–29. (*Emphasis* added.)

[30] Lisa H. Harrington, "Retail Collaboration: How to Solve the Puzzle," *Transportation and Distribution,* May 2003, pp. 33–37.

In the simplest form the process is as follows: A manufacturer that produces a consumer good computes its forecast. That forecast is then shared with the retailers that sell that product to end-use consumers. Those retailers respond with any specific knowledge that they have regarding their future intentions related to purchases based on known promotions, programs, shutdowns, or other proprietary information about which the manufacturer may not have had any prior knowledge. The manufacturer then updates the forecast including the shared information. In this way the forecast becomes a shared collaborative effort between the parties.

Some benefits of collaborative forecasting include:

1. *Lower inventory and capacity buffers.* The producer can push the forecast throughout the supply chain resulting in a better match of inventories for all participants.
2. *Fewer unplanned shipments or production runs.* When buyers of the product have swings in their purchasing cycles, sellers find themselves having to rush material to warehouses. These unplanned shipments usually carry a premium price.
3. *Reduced stockouts.* If buyers are ready to buy and the seller doesn't have the product, buyers will seek alternative means of meeting their needs. This will always have a negative impact on the seller due to lost sales and lower customer satisfaction.
4. *Increased customer satisfaction and repeat business.* Buyers know that they sometimes have unusual demand cycles. If the seller can respond quickly to these cycles, buyers will be that much more satisfied with the producer.
5. *Better preparation for sales promotions.* Promotions are special demand situations. No one wants to promote products that cannot be supplied. Meeting the needs of promotions is another positive input for customer service.
6. *Better preparation for new product introductions.* New product launches can be very tricky as sellers attempt to establish the supply chain. Meeting the needs of new product launches can maximize launch timing and increase speed to market.
7. *Dynamically respond to market changes.* Sometimes markets change based on external factors (popular culture, governmental controls, etc.). Being able to respond dynamically to these special cases without overstocking or understocking is critical.[31]

With so much to gain, it's no wonder that there are many companies that have successfully implemented collaborative forecasting partnerships. Examples include Wal-Mart, Target, Kmart, Sears, EMD Chemicals, Whirlpool, Fuji Photo Film, and Goodyear. Companies that have adopted collaborative forecasting programs have generally seen very positive results. For example, True Value

---

[31] "The Improved Demand Signal: Benefiting from Collaborative Forecasting," *PeopleSoft White Paper Series,* January 2004, 5 pages. Accessed February 9, 2005. http://www.peoplesoft.com/media/en/pdf/white_paper/improved_demand_signal_wp_0104.pdf.

found that service levels to stores improved by between 10 and 40 percent, while inventory levels decreased 10 to 15 percent.[32]

The value of information sharing has been documented in many studies. Consider one such study of a small- to midsized retailer with about $1 billion in annual sales. This retailer operates at more than 20 locations each with multiple retail outlets including department stores, mass-merchandisers, and convenience stores. As a result of sharing information in the supply chain the retailer achieved supply chain savings at the two biggest locations of about 15 percent and 33 percent.[33]

To effectively use CPFR, a company must be prepared to share information using electronic data transfer via the Internet. A number of software developers offer programs that are designed to create that data link between parties. It is this link to electronic data and the use of the Internet that is the first hurdle companies must overcome when considering CPFR. A company needs to be committed to an electronic data platform including available hardware, software, and support staff. Depending on the size of the company and the complexity of the integration, the amount of resources can vary greatly.

One of the most interesting problems to consider when establishing a collaborative relationship is how to deal with a nonparticipant. That is, if a manufacturer sells to two customers—one that enters the collaborative relationship and one that doesn't—are they both entitled to the benefits that result? At the center of the issue is the preferential delivery of goods to the customer with the collaborative relationship. If that customer is guaranteed first delivery of goods over the nonparticipating customer, then the nonparticipant bears nearly all the risk of stockouts.

Companies with this dilemma have responded in several different ways. Some companies pass cost savings and reduced price structuring to all their customers. Some provide preferential delivery and pricing to the collaborative partner alone. Others simply attempt to drive out the costs of excess inventory and stockouts while keeping their price structuring the same for all customers.[34]

In a collaborative environment there is a lot of information that flows between the two parties. Most of the time, information resides in public forums (computer servers) with only a software security system protecting it from outsiders. Collaborative forecasting does run the risk of loss of confidentiality to outsiders. Production forecasts can often be tied to production capacity, which is very critical information, especially to competitors.

Other information surrounding product launches and special promotions is also very sensitive and could be at risk. Securing this information and ensuring that it doesn't become public knowledge add to the importance of the job of the software administrator. Information breaches could be an oversight as well. With

---

[32] Peter A. Buxbaum, "Psyched Up," *Operations & Fulfillment,* Mar. 1, 2003. Accessed February 9, 2005. http://www.opsandfulfillment.com/warehouse/fulfillment_psyched.

[33] Tonya Boone and Ram Ganeshan, "The Value of Information Sharing in the Retail Supply Chain: Two Case Studies," *Foresight,* 9 (Spring 2008), pp.12–17.

[34] Srinivasan Raghunathan, "Interorganizational Collaborative Forecasting and Replenishment Systems and Supply Chain Implications," *Decision Sciences* 30, no. 4 (Fall 1999), pp. 1053–71.

forecasts and production information flowing so freely, parties on either side of the collaboration might inadvertently mistake sensitive information for common knowledge. At the very least, the issue of confidentiality must be addressed between the parties, and proper measures should be put in place to ensure all parties are satisfied that their interests are protected.

COMPUTER USE AND QUANTITATIVE FORECASTING

In today's business environment computers are readily available to nearly everyone. There was a time when only very large business enterprises had the resources to spend on computer systems, and within those businesses, access to the computer's power was limited. Today things are quite different. The cost of large-scale computer systems has dropped significantly, and microcomputers have made computer technology available to virtually any business professional interested in utilizing it. As early as 1966 a study reported that 68 percent of the companies surveyed used computers in preparing forecasts.[35] In 1986 a survey of economists found that over 93 percent used a computer in developing forecasts.[36] A similar study of marketing professionals found that about 87 percent were using computers in forecasting. Just over 30 percent of the marketing professionals surveyed who use a computer in developing forecasts relied solely on a personal computer.[37] It is clear that personal computers are currently the primary computational tool for the preparation of forecasts.

The widespread availability of computers has contributed to the use of quantitative forecasting techniques, many of which would not be practical to carry out by hand. Most of the methods described in this text fall into the realm of quantitative forecasting techniques that are reasonable to use only when appropriate computer software is available. A number of software packages, at costs that range from about $100 to many thousands of dollars, are currently marketed for use in developing forecasts. You will find that the software that accompanies this text will enable you to apply the most commonly used quantitative forecasting techniques to data of your choosing.

The use of personal computers in forecasting has been made possible by rapid technological changes that have made these desktop (or laptop) computers very fast and capable of storing and processing large amounts of data. User-friendly software makes it easy for people to become proficient in using forecasting programs in a short period of time. Dr. Vasche has said in this regard that "reliance on such PC systems has given state economists added flexibility in their forecasting work. By minimizing use of mainframe computers, it has also reduced the state's

---

[35] Spyros Makridakis, Steven C. Wheelwright, and Victor E. McGee, *Forecasting: Methods and Applications,* 2nd ed., (New York: John Wiley & Sons, 1983), p. 782.

[36] Barry Keating and J. Holton Wilson, "Forecasting: Practices and Teachings," *Journal of Business Forecasting* 6, no. 3 (Winter 1987–88), p. 12.

[37] J. Holton Wilson and Hugh G. Daubek, "Marketing Managers Evaluate Forecasting Methods," *Journal of Business Forecasting* 8, no. 1 (Spring 1989), p. 20.

costs of preparing forecasts."[38] The same is true in most business situations as well. The dominance of PC forecasting software is clear at the annual meetings of the major forecasting associations. At these meetings various vendors of PC-based forecasting software packages display and demonstrate their products.

The importance of quantitative methods in forecasting has been stressed by Charles W. Chase, Jr., who was formerly director of forecasting at Johnson & Johnson Consumer Products, Inc., and now is Business Enablement Manager for SAS Institute, Inc. He says, "Forecasting is a blend of science and art. Like most things in business, the rule of 80/20 applies to forecasting. By and large, forecasts are driven 80 percent mathematically and 20 percent judgmentally."[39]

QUALITATIVE OR SUBJECTIVE FORECASTING METHODS

Quantitative techniques using the power of the computer have come to dominate the forecasting landscape. However, there is a rich history of forecasting based on subjective and judgmental methods, some of which remain useful even today. These methods are probably most appropriately used when the forecaster is faced with a severe shortage of historical data and/or when quantitative expertise is not available. In some situations a judgmental method may even be preferred to a quantitative one. Very long range forecasting is an example of such a situation. The computer-based models that are the focal point of this text have less applicability to such things as forecasting the type of home entertainment that will be available 40 years from now than do those methods based on expert judgments. In this section several subjective or judgmental forecasting methods are reviewed.

Sales Force Composites

The sales force can be a rich source of information about future trends and changes in buyer behavior. These people have daily contact with buyers and are the closest contact most firms have with their customers. If the information available from the sales force is organized and collected in an objective manner, considerable insight into future sales volumes can be obtained.

Members of the sales force are asked to estimate sales for each product they handle. These estimates are usually based on each individual's subjective "feel" for the level of sales that would be reasonable in the forecast period. Often a range of forecasts will be requested, including a most optimistic, a most pessimistic, and a most likely forecast. Typically these individual projections are aggregated by the sales manager for a given product line and/or geographic area. Ultimately the person responsible for the firm's total sales forecast combines the product-line and/or geographic forecasts to arrive at projections that become the basis for a given planning horizon.

[38] Vasche, "Forecasting Process," p. 12.
[39] Charles W. Chase, Jr., "Forecasting Consumer Products," *Journal of Business Forecasting* 10, no. 1 (Spring 1991), p. 2.

While this process takes advantage of information from sources very close to actual buyers, a major problem with the resulting forecast may arise if members of the sales force tend to underestimate sales for their product lines and/or territories.[40] This behavior is particularly likely when the salespeople are assigned quotas on the basis of their forecasts and when bonuses are based on performance relative to those quotas. Such a downward bias can be very harmful to the firm. Scheduled production runs are shorter than they should be, raw-material inventories are too small, labor requirements are underestimated, and in the end customer ill will is generated by product shortages. The sales manager with ultimate forecasting responsibility can offset this downward bias, but only by making judgments that could, in turn, incorporate other bias into the forecast. Robin Peterson has developed a way of improving sales force composite forecasts by using a prescribed set of learned routines as a guide for salespeople as they develop their forecasts.[41]

These sets of learned routines are referred to as *scripts,* which can serve as a guide in developing an essentially subjective forecast. An example of a hypothetical script adapted from Peterson's work follows:

Review data on gross domestic product.

Review forecasts of gross domestic product.

Review industry sales data for the preceding year.

Review company sales data for the preceding year.

Review company sales forecasts for the previous years.

Survey key accounts concerning their purchasing plans.

Review last year's sales data in the salesperson's territory.

Review the employment situation in the salesperson's territory.

Do a simple trend projection of sales in the salesperson's territory.

Examine competitors' actions in the salesperson's territory.

Gather internal data about the company's promotional plans.

Gather internal data about the company's product introduction plans.

Gather internal data about the company's customer service plans.

Gather internal data about the company's credit-granting plans.

Check to see if there are planned changes in the company's pricing structure.

Evaluate the pricing practices of competitors.

Track the company's sales promotions.

Track the competitors' sales promotions.

A script such as this can be developed, based on interviews with successful salespeople concerning procedures they have used in preparing their forecasts.

[40] Robin T. Peterson, "Sales Force Composite Forecasting—An Exploratory Analysis," *Journal of Business Forecasting* 8, no. 1 (Spring 1989), pp. 23–27.

[41] Robin T. Peterson, "Improving Sales Force Composite: Forecasting by Using Scripts," *Journal of Business Forecasting,* Fall 1993, pp. 10–14.

Surveys of Customers and the General Population

In some situations it may be practical to survey customers for advanced information about their buying intentions. This practice presumes that buyers plan their purchases and follow through with their plans. Such an assumption is probably more realistic for industrial sales than for sales to households and individuals. It is also more realistic for big-ticket items such as cars than for convenience goods like toothpaste or tennis balls.

Survey data concerning how people feel about the economy are sometimes used by forecasters to help predict certain buying behaviors. One of the commonly used measures of how people feel about the economy comes from a monthly survey conducted by the University of Michigan Survey Research Center (SRC). The SRC produces an Index of Consumer Sentiment (ICS) based on a survey of 500 individuals, 40 percent of whom are respondents who participated in the survey six months earlier and the remaining 60 percent new respondents selected on a random basis. This index has its base period in 1966, when the index was 100. High values of the ICS indicate more positive feelings about the economy than do lower values. Thus, if the ICS goes up, one might expect that people are more likely to make certain types of purchases.

Jury of Executive Opinion

The judgments of experts in any area are a valuable resource. Based on years of experience, such judgments can be useful in the forecasting process. Using the method known as the *jury of executive opinion,* a forecast is developed by combining the subjective opinions of the managers and executives who are most likely to have the best insights about the firm's business. To provide a breadth of opinions, it is useful to select these people from different functional areas. For example, personnel from finance, marketing, and production might be included.

The person responsible for making the forecast may collect opinions in individual interviews or in a meeting where the participants have an opportunity to discuss various points of view. The latter has some obvious advantages such as stimulating deeper insights, but it has some important disadvantages as well. For example, if one or more strong personalities dominate the group, their opinions will become disproportionately important in the final consensus that is reached.

The Delphi Method

The Delphi method is similar to the jury of executive opinion in taking advantage of the wisdom and insight of people who have considerable expertise about the area to be forecast. It has the additional advantage, however, of anonymity among the participants. The experts, perhaps five to seven in number, never meet to discuss their views; none of them even knows who else is on the panel.

The Delphi method can be summarized by the following six steps:

1. Participating panel members are selected.
2. Questionnaires asking for opinions about the variables to be forecast are distributed to panel members.
3. Results from panel members are collected, tabulated, and summarized.

4. Summary results are distributed to the panel members for their review and consideration.
5. Panel members revise their individual estimates, taking account of the information received from the other, unknown panel members.
6. Steps 3 through 5 are repeated until no significant changes result.

Through this process there is usually movement toward centrality, but there is no pressure on panel members to alter their original projections. Members who have strong reason to believe that their original response is correct, no matter how widely it differs from others, may freely stay with it. Thus, in the end there may not be a consensus.

The Delphi method may be superior to the jury of executive opinion, since strong personalities or peer pressures have no influence on the outcome. The processes of sending out questionnaires, getting them back, tabulating, and summarizing can be speeded up by using advanced computer capabilities, including networking and e-mail.[42]

Some Advantages and Disadvantages of Subjective Methods

Subjective (i.e., qualitative or judgmental) forecasting methods are sometimes considered desirable because they do not require any particular mathematical background of the individuals involved. As future business professionals, like yourself, become better trained in quantitative forms of analysis, this advantage will become less important. Historically, another advantage of subjective methods has been their wide acceptance by users. However, our experience suggests that users are increasingly concerned with how the forecast was developed, and with most subjective methods it is difficult to be specific in this regard. The underlying models are, by definition, subjective. This subjectivity is nonetheless the most important advantage of this class of methods. There are often forces at work that cannot be captured by quantitative methods. They can, however, be sensed by experienced business professionals and can make an important contribution to improved forecasts. Wilson and Allison-Koerber have shown this dramatically in the context of forecasting sales for a large item of food-service equipment produced by the Delfield Company.[43] Quantitative methods reduced errors to about 60 percent of those that resulted from the subjective method that had been in use. When the less accurate subjective method was combined with the quantitative methods, errors were further reduced to about 40 percent of the level when the subjective method was used alone. It is clear from this result, and others, that there is often important information content in subjective methods.

The disadvantages of subjective methods were nicely summarized by Charles W. Chase, Jr., when he was with Johnson & Johnson Consumer Products, Inc. He stated that "the disadvantages of qualitative methods are: (1) they are almost

---

[42] See, for example, Bernard S. Husbands, "Electronic Mail System Enhances Delphi Method," *Journal of Business Forecasting* 1, no. 4 (Summer 1982), pp. 24–27.

[43] Wilson and Allison-Koerber, "Combining Subjective and Objective Forecasts," p. 15.

always biased; (2) they are not consistently accurate over time; (3) it takes years of experience for someone to learn how to convert intuitive judgment into good forecasts."[44]

NEW-PRODUCT FORECASTING

Quantitative forecasting methods, which are the primary focus of this text, are not usually well suited for predicting sales of new products, because they rely on a historical data series for products upon which to establish model parameters. Often judgmental methods are better suited to forecasting new-product sales because there are many uncertainties and few known relationships. However, there are ways to make reasonable forecasts for new products. These typically include both qualitative judgments and quantitative tools of one type or another. One way to deal with the lack of known information in the forecasting of new products is to incorporate a modified version of the Delphi method. This was done by Ken Goldfisher while he worked in the Information Services Division of the Nabisco Foods Group. Goldfisher has also found some relatively simple quantitative methods, such as moving averages, to be helpful in developing new-product forecasts at Nabisco.[45]

Using Marketing Research to Aid New-Product Forecasting

Various market research activities can be helpful in new-product forecasting. Surveys of potential customers can provide useful preliminary information about the propensity of buyers to adopt a new product. Test-market results and results from the distribution of free samples can also provide estimates of initial sales. On the basis of predictions about the number of initial innovators who will buy a product, an S-shaped market-penetration curve can be used to forecast diffusion of the new product throughout the market.

Terry Anderson has described a process for new-product forecasting at Howmedica that is based on various judgmental factors.[46] It begins with an estimate of the total number of customers, based on a consensus within the marketing and sales groups. A customer usage rate is derived based on experience with past new introductions. Inventory requirements are also included in making projections.

Whitlark, Geurts, and Swenson have used customer purchase intention surveys as a tool to help prepare forecasts of new products.[47] They describe a three-step

[44] Charles W. Chase, Jr., "Forecasting Consumer Products," p. 4.

[45] Ken Goldfisher, "Modified Delphi: A Concept for New Product Forecasting," *Journal of Business Forecasting* 11, no. 4 (Winter 1992–93), pp. 10–11; and Ken Goldfisher and Colleen Chan, "New Product Reactive Forecasting," *Journal of Business Forecasting* 13, no. 4 (Winter 1994–95), pp. 7–9.

[46] Anderson, "Demand Forecasting at Howmedica," pp. 2–3.

[47] David B. Whitlark, Michael D. Geurts, and Michael J. Swenson, "New Product Forecasting with a Purchase Intention Survey," *Journal of Business Forecasting* 10, no. 3 (Fall 1993), pp. 18–21.

TABLE 1.1
**Probabilities
Assigned to
Purchase-Intention
Categories**

Source: Adapted from Whitlark
et al., p. 20.

Intention-to-Purchase Category	Three-Month Time Horizon	Six-Month Time Horizon
Definitely will buy	64%	75%
Probably will buy	23	53
Might or might not buy	5	21
Probably will not buy	2	9
Definitely will not buy	1	4

process that starts with the identification of a demographic profile of the target market, then the probability of purchase is estimated from survey data, and finally a forecast is developed by combining this probability with information on the size of the target market. A sample of consumers from the target market is asked to respond to an intent-to-purchase scale such as: definitely will buy; probably will buy; might or might not buy; probably will not buy; and definitely will not buy. Probabilities are then assigned to each of the intention-to-buy categories, using empirical evidence from a longitudinal study of members of the target market covering a length of time comparable to the length of time for the proposed forecast horizon. An example of these probabilities for a three- and a six-month time horizon is shown in Table 1.1. Note that the probabilities of purchase increase as the time horizon increases.

Applying this method to two products produced good results. For the first product the three-month forecast purchase rate was 2.9 percent compared with an actual purchase rate of 2.4 percent. In the six-month time horizon the forecast and actual rates were 15.6 percent and 11.1 percent, respectively. Similar results were found for a second product. In the three-month horizon the forecast and actual percents were 2.5 percent versus 1.9 percent, while in the six-month forecast horizon the forecast was 16.7 percent and the actual was 16.3 percent.

The Product Life Cycle Concept Aids in New-Product Forecasting

The concept of a product life cycle (PLC), such as is shown in Figure 1.1, can be a useful framework for thinking about new-product forecasting. During the introductory stage of the product life cycle, only consumers who are classified as "innovators" are likely to buy the product. Sales start low and increase slowly at first; then, near the end of this stage, sales start to increase at an increasing rate. Typically products in this introductory stage are associated with negative profit margins as high front-end costs and substantial promotional expenses are incurred.

As the product enters the growth stage of the life cycle, sales are still increasing at an increasing rate as "early adopters" enter the market. Eventually in this stage the rate of growth in sales starts to decline and profits typically become positive. Near the end of the growth stage, sales growth starts to level off substantially as the product enters the maturity stage. Here profits normally reach the maximum

FIGURE 1.1
A Product Life Cycle Curve

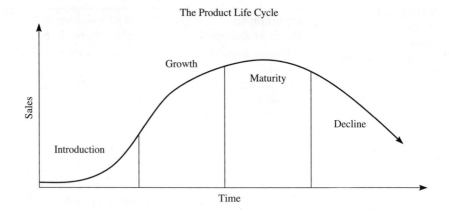

The Product Life Cycle

level. Businesses often employ marketing strategies to extend this stage as long as possible. However, all products eventually reach the stage of decline in sales and are, at some point, removed from the market (such as Oldsmobile cars, which had been in the automobile market for a century).

This notion of a product life cycle can be applied to a product class (such as personal passenger vehicles), to a product form (such as sport utility vehicles), or to a brand (such as Jeep Cherokee—whose life cycle ended after many years and was replaced with the Jeep Liberty). Product life cycles are not uniform in shape or duration and vary from industry to industry. The Jeep example illustrates a relatively long life cycle. For high-tech electronic products, life cycles may be as short as six to nine months. An example would be a telephone that has a design based on a movie character.

The forecasting approach that is best will vary depending on where a product or product class is in the life cycle. Once the mid-to-late growth stage is reached, there is probably sufficient historical data to consider a wide array of quantitative methods. The real forecasting problems occur in the introductory stage (or in the preintroductory product development stage). Here the forecaster finds traditional quantitative methods of limited usefulness and must often turn to marketing research techniques and/or qualitative forecasting techniques.

Analog Forecasts

The basic idea behind the analog method is that the forecast of the new product is related to information that you have about the introduction of other similar products in the past.[48] Suppose that you work for a toy company that sells toys to children in the 4-to-14 age group. Two years ago for the Christmas season you introduced a toy that was based on a popular animated Christmas movie. The

---

[48] See, for example, Scott E. Pammer, Duncan K. H. Fong, and Steven F. Arnold, "Forecasting the Penetration of a New Product—A Bayesian Approach," *Journal of Business & Economic Statistics* 18, no. 4 (October 2000), pp. 428–35; and David A. Aaker, V. Kumar, and George S. Day, *Marketing Research* (New York: John Wiley & Sons, 2001), pp. 628–39.

This example shows the new product curve for VCR sales in the United States. Both unit sales and market penetration are illustrated. One might expect high definition DVD player/recorders to follow a similar trend.

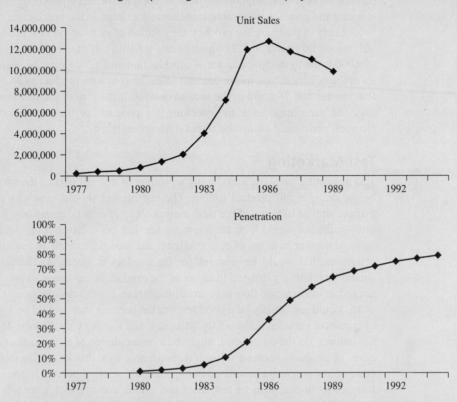

Year	Unit Sales	Household Penetration	Year	Unit Sales	Household Penetration
1977	225000		1986	12685000	0.36
1978	402000		1987	11700000	0.487
1979	478000		1988	10998000	0.58
1980	804000	0.011	1989	9843000	0.646
1981	1330000	0.02	1990		0.686
1982	2030000	0.031	1991		0.719
1983	4020000	0.055	1992		0.75
1984	7143000	0.106	1993		0.771
1985	11912000	0.208	1994		0.79

Source: http://www.bassmodelinstitute.org/NPF/D/D_47.aspx.

percentage of total market households that purchased that product was 1.3 percent, 60 percent of potential toy stores stocked the product, and your company spent $750,000 on promotions. Now you have a new toy to bring to market this Christmas season, and you need some estimate of sales. Suppose that this new product appeals to a narrower age range such that the likely percentage of households that would purchase the product is 1.1 percent, and that you can expect comparable promotional support as well as comparable acceptance by retailers in stocking the product. Assuming that the only change is the percentage of households likely to purchase the product, the relation of sales of the new product to the old one would be 1.1 ÷ 1.3 (which equals 0.84615). If the previous product sold 100,000 units in the first quarter of introduction and 120,000 in the second quarter of introduction, you might forecast sales for your new product as 84,615 in the first quarter and 101,538 in the second quarter. If the size of the relevant population, the percentage of stores stocking the product, or the promotional effort changes, you would adjust the forecast accordingly.

Test Marketing

Test marketing involves introducing a product to a small part of the total market before doing a full product rollout. The test market should have characteristics that are similar to those of the total market along relevant dimensions. For example, usually we would look for a test market that has a distribution similar to the national market in terms of age, ethnicity, and income, as well as any other characteristics that would be relevant for the product in question. The test market should be relatively isolated in terms of the product being tested to prevent product and/or information flow to or from other areas. For example, Kansas City, Missouri, would not usually be a good test market because there would be a good deal of crossover between Kansas City, Missouri, and Kansas City, Kansas. Indianapolis, Indiana, on the other hand, might be a better choice of a test market for many types of products because it has a demographic mix that is similar to the entire country and is relatively isolated in the context discussed here.[49] Suppose we do a test market in one or more test cities and sell an average of 1.7 units per 10,000 households. If, in the total market, there are 100 million households, we might project sales to be 17,000 units ([1.7 ÷ 10,000] × 100,000,000 = 17,000). The cost of doing a local rollout is far less than a national rollout and can provide significant new information.

Product Clinics

The use of product clinics is a marketing research technique in which potential customers are invited to a specific location and are shown a product mockup or prototype, which in some situations is essentially the final product. These people

---

[49] A small sample of stores can also be selected for this purpose as reported in Marshall Fisher and Kumar Rajaram, "Accurate Retail Testing of Fashion Merchandise: Methodology and Application," *Marketing Science* 19, no. 3 (Summer 2000), pp. 266–78.

are asked to "experience the product," which may mean tasting a breakfast cereal, using a software product, or driving a test vehicle. Afterwards they are asked to evaluate the product during an in-depth personal interview and/or by filling out a product evaluation survey. Part of this evaluation would normally include some measure of likelihood to purchase the product. From these results a statistical probability of purchase for the population can be estimated and used to predict product sales. The use of in-home product evaluations is a similar process. A panel of consumers is asked to try the product at home for an appropriate period of time and then is asked to evaluate the product, including an estimate of likelihood to purchase.

Type of Product Affects New-Product Forecasting

All products have life cycles and the cycles have similar patterns, but there may be substantial differences from one product to another. Think, for example, about products that are fashion items or fads in comparison with products that have real staying power in the marketplace. Fashion items and products that would be considered fads typically have a steep introductory stage followed by short growth and maturity stages and a decline that is also very steep.

High-tech products often have life cycles that are relatively short in comparison with low-technology products. It has been found that "high-technology businesses show a significant preference for data-less, qualitative, internal judgment forecasting methods" in comparison with low-technology businesses, which are more likely to use external sources such as surveys of consumer-buying intentions.[50]

The Bass Model for New-Product Forecasting

The Bass model for sales of new products, first published in 1969, is probably the most notable model for new-product forecasting. Its importance is highlighted by the fact that it was republished in *Management Science* in December 2004.[51] This model gives rise to product diffusion curves that look like those illustrated in Figure 1.2. The Bass model was originally developed for application only to durable goods. However, it has been adapted for use in forecasting a wide variety of products with short product life cycles, and new products with limited historical data.

The model developed by Bass is:

$$S_t = pm + (q - p)*Y_t - (q/m)*Y_t^2$$

[50] Gary S. Lynn, Steven P. Schnaars, and Richard B. Skov, "Survey of New Product Forecasting Practices in Industrial High Technology and Low Technology Businesses," *Industrial Marketing Management* 28 (November 1999), pp. 565–71.

[51] Frank M. Bass, "A New Product Growth Model for Consumer Durables,"*Management Science* 50, no. 12S (December 2004), pp. 1825–32. See also Gary Lilien, Arvind Rangaswamy, and Christophe Van den Bulte, "Diffusion Models: Managerial Applications and Software," ISBM Report 7-1999, Institute for the Study of Business Markets, Pennsylvania State University. Available at http://www.ebusiness.xerox.com/isbm/dscgi/ds.py/Get/File-89/7-1999.pdf.

FIGURE 1.2   Examples of New-Product Diffusion Curves

These examples of new-product diffusion curves are from http://www.andorraweb.com/bass, a Web site where you can find such curves for many different products.

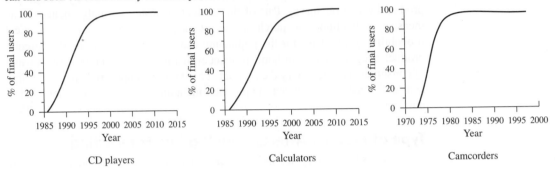

CD players   Calculators   Camcorders

Where:

S_t = Sales at time period t.

p = Probability of initial purchase at time $t = 0$. This reflects the importance of innovators and is called the coefficient of innovation.

m = Number of initial purchases of product over the life cycle (excludes replacement purchases).

q = Coefficient of imitation representing the propensity to purchase based on the number of people who have already purchased the product.

Y_t = Number of previous buyers at time t.

The values for p, q, and m can be estimated using a statistical tool called *regression analysis,* which is covered in Chapters 4 and 5 of this text. The algebraic form for the regression model is:

$$S_t = a + bY_{t-1} + cY_{t-1}^2$$

From the regression estimates for a, b, and c the values of p, q, and m can be derived. Note that:

$$a = pm$$
$$b = q - p$$
$$c = -q/m$$

Bass shows that:

$$p = a/m \quad q = -mc \quad \text{and} \quad m = (-b \pm [b^2 - 4ac]^{0.5})/2c$$

Getting the estimates of the three parameters in the Bass model is the difficult part. If the product is entirely new and in a prelaunch stage, we might gather data

FIGURE 1.3

A Typical PLC for a Short-Lived Product

An initial product launch is followed by a sharp decline, then a more modest drop in sales, and finally a steeper drop to the end of the PLC. (Data are in the c1t2 file.)

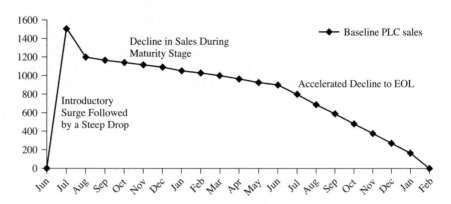

for an analogous product for which a sales history is known, such as a previous model of a cell phone. Once the product has been launched, knowing even four or five values of sales we can get preliminary estimates of the parameters. As a sales history develops, these estimates can be refined.[52]

Forecasting Sales for New Products That Have Short Product Life Cycles

In an age of rapid change there are many products that have short product life cycles (PLC). This is especially true of high-tech products for which technological change and/or marketing strategies make products obsolete relatively quickly. Cell phones would be a good example. New cell phones with a variety of enhancements seem to appear almost weekly. Such products may have a life cycle of perhaps 12 to 24 months, which means that there is little time to gather historical data upon which to base a forecast. It also means that the initial forecasts are exceptionally important because there is less time to recover from either over- or underprojecting sales.

The life cycle for this type of situation may look something like that shown in Figure 1.3. Upon introduction, sales are typically high then drop quickly, level out to a slower rate of decline for some period, followed by a more rapid drop to the end of the product's life cycle (EOL). We illustrate this in Figure 1.3 for a product with a 20-month PLC. The data shown in such a graph can frequently be developed by looking at the historic PLC for similar products, such as past generations of cell phones.[53]

---

[52] If you go to http://www.andorraweb.com/bass, you can experiment with altering the coefficients of innovation and imitation (*p* and *q*) and observe how the changes affect the shape of the new-product diffusion curve. You can find other examples and Excel programs at http://www.bassmodelinstitute.org.

[53] The work of Burress and Kuettner at Hewlett-Packard provides a foundation for this example. See Jim Burress and Dorothea Kuettner, "Forecasting for Short-Lived Products: Hewlett-Packard's Journey," *Journal of Business Forecasting* 21, no. 4 (Winter 2002–03), pp. 9–14.

Suppose that we know that there has been a seasonal pattern for similar products in the past. Based on this knowledge, a natural bump to sales can be expected during the back-to-school period in August and September, followed by increased buying during the holiday season, and another bump when people get tax returns in March. Based on knowledge from past product introductions, the seasonal indices are estimated to be:

August, 1.15
September, 1.10
November, 1.10
December, 1.30
March, 1.05

You will see how such seasonal indices are computed later in the text. A complete list of the seasonal indices (SI) for this product are shown in Table 1.2.

We can also incorporate the marketing plans for the product into the PLC forecast. Suppose that the marketing mix for the product calls for a skimming introductory price followed by a price cut three months after the product launch. This price cut is expected to increase sales by 15 percent the first month of the cut (October, in our example), followed by 10 and 5 percent increases in the following two months (November and December), after which time the market has fully adjusted to the price drop. A similar price cut is planned for the following July to help prop up sales as the life cycle moves into a more rapid rate of decline. Typically a price cut this late in the PLC has less effect, as can be seen in Table 1.2.

In addition, two promotional campaigns are planned for the product: one designed to promote the product as a holiday gift, and the other to communicate the benefits to students of having the product as the school year gets under way. The holiday promotion is expected to have a 10 percent lift in both the first November and December and a 5 percent lift the next holiday season. The back-to-school promotion is expected to add 5 percent to sales the first August and September and 4 percent at the beginning of the following school year.

These seasonal and marketing mix constructs are used to adjust the baseline new-product life cycle as illustrated in Table 1.2. The baseline forecast is first multiplied by the seasonal indices, then by the factors representing the expected effect of each part of the marketing mix. Additional marketing mix relationships, such as distribution and awareness strategies, could be included in a similar manner.

The sales forecast based on the seasonal adjustment (the column headed "After SI Adj") is found by multiplying the baseline forecast by the seasonal indices (SI). The baseline forecast and the seasonally adjusted forecast are shown in the top of Figure 1.4. Each subsequent adjustment for marketing mix elements is done in a similar manner until the final adjusted forecast is developed. This final forecast is shown in the right-hand column of Table 1.2. The baseline and final adjusted forecast are shown in the bottom graph of Figure 1.4.

TABLE 1.2 Modifying a Baseline Forecast for a Product with a Short PLC (c1t2)

The baseline forecast for each month is multiplied by the seasonal index for that month (SI) as well as by factors that represent the percentage change in sales expected from other factors such as price cut (P) or various promotional strategies (H and S). The influence of factors such as SI, P, H, and S could be additive if they are expressed in number of units rather than as a percent adjustment.

Month	Baseline PLC Sales	SI	Price Cut (P)	Holiday Promotion (H)	School Promotion (S)	After SI Adj	After SI & P Adj	After SI, P, & H Adj	After SI, P, H, & S Adj
Jun	0	0.80	1.00	1.00	1.00	0.00	0.00	0.00	0.00
Jul	1,500	0.80	1.00	1.00	1.00	1,200.00	1,200.00	1,200.00	1,200.00
Aug	1,200	1.15	1.00	1.00	1.05	1,380.00	1,380.00	1,380.00	1,449.00
Sep	1,170	1.10	1.00	1.00	1.05	1,287.00	1,287.00	1,287.00	1,351.35
Oct	1,140	0.90	1.15	1.00	1.00	1,026.00	1,179.90	1,179.90	1,179.90
Nov	1,110	1.10	1.10	1.10	1.00	1,221.00	1,343.10	1,477.41	1,477.41
Dec	1,080	1.30	1.05	1.10	1.00	1,404.00	1,474.20	1,621.62	1,621.62
Jan	1,050	0.65	1.00	1.00	1.00	682.50	682.50	682.50	682.50
Feb	1,020	0.70	1.00	1.00	1.00	714.00	714.00	714.00	714.00
Mar	990	1.05	1.00	1.00	1.00	1,039.50	1,039.50	1,039.50	1,039.50
Apr	960	0.85	1.00	1.00	1.00	816.00	816.00	816.00	816.00
May	930	0.80	1.00	1.00	1.00	744.00	744.00	744.00	744.00
Jun	900	0.80	1.00	1.00	1.00	720.00	720.00	720.00	720.00
Jul	795	0.80	1.10	1.00	1.00	636.00	699.60	699.60	699.60
Aug	690	1.15	1.05	1.00	1.04	793.50	833.18	833.18	866.50
Sep	585	1.10	1.00	1.00	1.04	643.50	643.50	643.50	669.24
Oct	480	0.90	1.00	1.00	1.00	432.00	432.00	432.00	432.00
Nov	375	1.10	1.00	1.05	1.00	412.50	412.50	433.13	433.13
Dec	270	1.30	1.00	1.05	1.00	351.00	351.00	368.55	368.55
Jan	165	0.65	1.00	1.00	1.00	107.25	107.25	107.25	107.25
Feb	0	0.70	1.00	1.00	1.00	0	0	0	0

FIGURE 1.4

Adjusted Baseline Forecasts

The upper graph shows the new-product life cycle baseline forecast adjusted only for seasonality (S). The bottom graph shows the baseline forecast and the forecast after adjustment for seasonality, and marketing mix strategies including pricing (P), a holiday promotion (H), and a back-to-school promotion (S).   (c1t2)

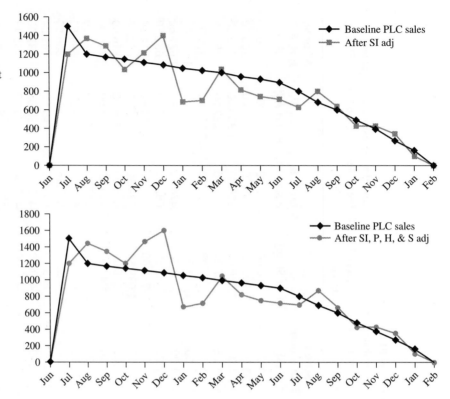

TWO SIMPLE NAIVE MODELS

The simplest of all forecasting methods is to assume that the next period will be identical to the present. You may have used this method today in deciding what clothes to wear. If you had not heard a professional weather forecast, your decision about today's weather might be based on the weather you observed yesterday. If yesterday was clear and the temperature was 70°F, you might assume today to be the same. If yesterday was snowy and cold, you might expect a similar wintry day today. In fact, without evidence to suggest otherwise, such a weather forecast is quite reasonable. Forecasts based solely on the most recent observation of the variable of interest are often referred to as "naive forecasts."

In this section we will use such a method, and a variation on it, to forecast the monthly value of the University of Michigan Index of Consumer Sentiment (UMICS). For this example we use data from January 2006 through December 2006. These data are given and shown graphically in Figure 1.5. In both forms of presentation you can see that the UMICS varied considerably throughout this period, from a low of 79.1 in May 2006 to a high of 93.6 in October 2006. The fluctuations in most economic and business series (variables) are usually best seen

FIGURE 1.5   **University of Michigan Index of Consumer Sentiment—UMICS**   (c1f5)

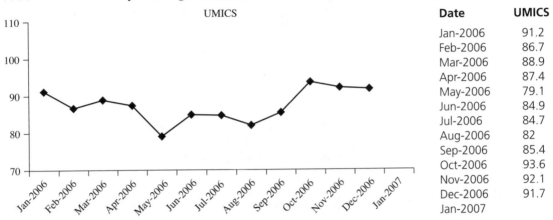

Date	UMICS
Jan-2006	91.2
Feb-2006	86.7
Mar-2006	88.9
Apr-2006	87.4
May-2006	79.1
Jun-2006	84.9
Jul-2006	84.7
Aug-2006	82
Sep-2006	85.4
Oct-2006	93.6
Nov-2006	92.1
Dec-2006	91.7
Jan-2007	

after converting the data into graphic form, as you see in Figure 1.5. You should develop the habit of observing data in graphic form when forecasting.

The simplest naive forecasting model, in which the forecast value is equal to the previous observed value, can be described in algebraic form as follows:

$$F_t = A_{t-1}$$

where F_t represents the forecast value for time period t and A_{t-1} represents the observed value one period earlier $(t - 1)$. In terms of the UMICS data we wish to forecast, the model may be written as:

$$\text{UMICSF}_t = \text{UMICS}_{t-1}$$

where UMICSF_t is the University of Michigan Index of Consumer Sentiment naive forecast number 1 at time period t and UMICS_{t-1} is the observed University of Michigan Index of Consumer Sentiment one period earlier $(t - 1)$. We call this *Naive forecast 1* because we will very shortly look at another naive forecast. This first naive forecast was done using Excel. The results are shown in Table 1.3 along with measures of how well the model did. These measures will be discussed shortly.

Note that each forecast value simply replicates the actual value for the preceding month. These results are presented in graphic form in the upper graph of Figure 1.6, which clearly shows the one-period shift between the two series. The forecast for every month is exactly the same as the actual value for the month before.

We might argue that in addition to considering just the most recent observation, it would make sense to consider the direction from which we arrived at the latest observation. If the series dropped to the latest point, perhaps it is reasonable to assume some further drop. Alternatively, if we have just observed an increase, it may make sense to factor into our forecast some further increase. Such adjustments can be made in a second naive forecasting model, which includes some proportion

TABLE 1.3 Two Naive Forecasts of the University of Michigan Index of Consumer Sentiment (c1t3&f6)

Using seven measures of forecast error, Naive forecast1 was better than Naive forecast2 on all of the seven measures.

Date	UMICS	Naive Forecast1	Error	Sq Error	Abs Error	% Error	% Abs Error
Jan-2006	91.2						
Feb-2006	86.7	91.2	-4.5	20.25	4.5	-0.052	0.052
Mar-2006	88.9	86.7	2.2	4.84	2.2	0.025	0.025
Apr-2006	87.4	88.9	-1.5	2.25	1.5	-0.017	0.017
May-2006	79.1	87.4	-8.3	68.89	8.3	-0.105	0.105
Jun-2006	84.9	79.1	5.8	33.64	5.8	0.068	0.068
Jul-2006	84.7	84.9	-0.2	0.04	0.2	-0.002	0.002
Aug-2006	82	84.7	-2.7	7.29	2.7	-0.033	0.033
Sep-2006	85.4	82	3.4	11.56	3.4	0.040	0.040
Oct-2006	93.6	85.4	8.2	67.24	8.2	0.088	0.088
Nov-2006	92.1	93.6	-1.5	2.25	1.5	-0.016	0.016
Dec-2006	91.7	92.1	-0.4	0.16	0.4	-0.004	-0.004
Jan-2007		91.7					

MSE = 19.855
RMSE = 4.456
ME = 0.045
MAE = 3.518
MPE = -0.001
MAPE = 0.041
Theil's U = 1.00

Number of times best: 6

Date	UMICS	Naive Forecast2	Error	Sq Error	Abs Error	% Error	% Abs Error
Jan-2006	91.2						
Feb-2006	86.7						
Mar-2006	88.9	84.45	4.45	19.803	4.45	0.050	0.050
Apr-2006	87.4	90	-2.6	6.76	2.6	-0.030	0.030
May-2006	79.1	86.65	-7.55	57.003	7.55	-0.095	0.095
Jun-2006	84.9	74.95	9.95	99.003	9.95	0.117	0.117
Jul-2006	84.7	87.8	-3.1	9.61	3.1	-0.037	0.037
Aug-2006	82	84.6	-2.6	6.76	2.6	-0.032	0.032
Sep-2006	85.4	80.65	4.75	22.563	4.75	0.056	0.056
Oct-2006	93.6	87.1	6.5	42.25	6.5	0.069	0.069
Nov-2006	92.1	97.7	-5.6	31.36	5.6	-0.061	0.061
Dec-2006	91.7	91.35	0.35	0.1225	0.35	0.004	0.004
Jan-2007		91.5					

MSE = 29.523
RMSE = 5.434
ME = 0.455
MAE = 4.745
MPE = 0.004
MAPE = 0.055
Theil's U = 1.22

Number of times best: 0

FIGURE 1.6

Two Forecasts of the University of Michigan Index of Consumer Sentiment

Naive forecast1 is simply the previous actual value of the index. That is: $UMICSF_t = UMICS_{t-1}$. The naive forecast2 takes into account the change between previous periods. It is:

$$UMICSF2_t = UMICS_{t-1} + .5 (UMICS_{t-1} - UMICS_{t-2})$$

See Table 1.3 for the calculated values for each forecast. (c1t3&f6)

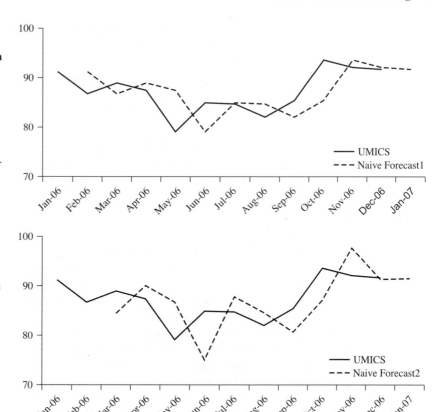

of the most recently observed rate of change in the series. In general algebraic terms the model becomes

$$F_t = A_{t-1} + P(A_{t-1} - A_{t-2})$$

where F_t is the forecast for period t, A_{t-1} is the actual observation at period $t - 1$, A_{t-2} is the observed value at period $t - 2$, and P is the proportion of the change between periods $t - 2$ and $t - 1$ that we choose to include in the forecast.

Applying this second naive model to the University of Michigan Index of Consumer Sentiment data, we have

$$UMICSF2_t = UMICS_{t-1} + P(UMICS_{t-1} - UMICS_{t-2})$$

where $UMICSF2_t$ represents the modified naive forecast for time period t; $UMICS_{t-1}$ and $UMICS_{t-2}$ are the observed indices one and two periods earlier, respectively; and P is the fraction of the most recent change in the index that is now included in our forecast. This is illustrated with $P = 0.5$ in Table 1.3.

Let us look closely at the circled value in Table 1.3 to help you see the exact calculations that are involved in developing this forecast. To get the forecast for March 2006 (denoted as MAR06), we take the observed value for February 2006 (Feb-06) and adjust it by including some information from the most recent trend.

(For illustrative purposes we have used one-half of that recent change, but we could try other values to see whether improved forecasts are possible.) Thus, the forecast for MAR04 is:

$$\text{UMICSF2}_{\text{MAR06}} = \text{UMICS}_{\text{FEB06}} + 0.5(\text{UMICS}_{\text{FEB06}} - \text{UMICS}_{\text{JAN06}})$$
$$= 86.7 + .5(86.7 - 91.2)$$
$$= 86.7 + .5(-4.5)$$
$$= 86.7 - 2.25$$
$$= 84.45$$

The values for this second naive forecast are shown in graphic form in the lower graph of Figure 1.6, along with the actual values for each month.

EVALUATING FORECASTS

You have now looked at two alternative forecasts of the University of Michigan Index of Consumer Sentiment. Which forecast is best depends on the particular year or years you look at. For example, the first model did a better job of forecasting the index for April-06, whereas the second model did a better job for May-06. See Table 1.3 for the entire set of forecasts.

It is rare to find one model that is always best for any given set of business or economic data.

In retrospect it is easy to say which forecast was better for any one period. However, it is rare to find one model that is always best for any given set of business or economic data. But we need some way to evaluate the accuracy of forecasting models over a number of periods so that we can identify the model that generally works the best. Among a number of possible criteria that could be used, seven common ones are the mean error (ME), the mean absolute error (MAE), the mean percentage error (MPE), the mean absolute percentage error (MAPE), the mean-squared error (MSE), the root-mean-squared error (RMSE), and Theil's U.

To illustrate how each of these is calculated, let

$$A_t = \text{Actual value in period } t$$
$$F_t = \text{Forecast value in period } t$$
$$n = \text{Number of periods used in the calculation}$$

1. The mean error is calculated as:

$$\text{ME} = \frac{\Sigma(A_t - F_t)}{n}$$

2. The mean absolute error is then calculated as:

$$\text{MAE} = \frac{\Sigma|A_t - F_t|}{n}$$

3. The mean percentage error is calculated as:

$$\text{MPE} = \frac{\Sigma[(A_t - F_t)/A_t]}{n}$$

4. The mean absolute percentage error is calculated as:

$$\text{MAPE} = \frac{\Sigma |(A_t - F_t)/A_t|}{n}$$

5. The mean-squared error is calculated as:

$$\text{MSE} = \frac{\Sigma (A_t - F_t)^2}{n}$$

6. The root-mean-squared error is:

$$\text{RMSE} = \sqrt{\frac{\Sigma (A_t - F_t)^2}{n}}$$

7. Theil's U can be calculated in several ways, two of which are shown here.

$$U = \sqrt{\Sigma (A_t - F_t)^2} \div \sqrt{\Sigma (A_t - A_{t-1})^2}$$

$$U = \text{RMSE (model)} \div \text{RMSE (no-change model)}$$

The no-change model used in calculating Theil's U is the basic naive forecast model described above, in which $F_t = A_{t-1}$.

For criteria one through six, lower values are preferred to higher ones. For Theil's U a value of zero means that the model forecast perfectly (no error in the numerator). If $U < 1$, the model forecasts better than the consecutive-period no-change naive model; if $U = 1$, the model does only as well as the consecutive-period no-change naive model; and if $U > 1$, the model does not forecast as well as the consecutive-period no-change naive model.

The values for these measures, for both forecasts of the University of Michigan Index of Consumer Sentiment, are shown in Table 1.3. From these results we see that for all seven measures the first forecast is the more accurate forecast. Often you can expect mixed results, in which no one model performs best as measured by all seven measures.

Mean error (ME) and mean percentage error (MPE) are not often used as measures of forecast accuracy because large positive errors ($A_t > F_t$) can be offset by large negative errors ($A_t < F_t$). In fact, a very bad model could have an ME or MPE of zero. ME and MPE are, however, very useful as measures of forecast bias. A negative ME or MPE suggests that, overall, the forecasting model overstates the forecast, while a positive ME or MPE indicates forecasts that are generally too low.

The other measures (MAE, MAPE, MSE, RMSE, and Theil's U) are best used to compare alternative forecasting models for a given series. Because of different units used for various series, only MAPE and Theil's U should be interpreted across series. For example, a sales series may be in thousands of units, while the prime interest rate is a percentage. Thus, MAE, MSE, and RMSE would be lower for models used to forecast the prime rate than for those used to forecast sales.[54]

[54] Brian P. Mathews and Adamantios Diamantopoulos, "Towards a Taxonomy of Forecast Error Measures," *Journal of Forecasting*, August 1994, pp. 409–16.

Throughout this text we will focus on root-mean-squared error (RMSE) to evaluate the relative accuracy of various forecasting methods. The RMSE is easy for most people to interpret because of its similarity to the basic statistical concept of a standard deviation, and it is one of the most commonly used measures of forecast accuracy.

All quantitative forecasting models are developed on the basis of historical data. When measures of accuracy, such as RMSE, are applied to the historical period, they are often considered measures of how well various models fit the data (i.e., how well they work "in sample"). To determine how accurate the models are in actual forecasts ("out of sample"), a holdout period is often used for evaluation. It may be that the best model "in sample" may not hold up as the best "out of sample."[55] Terry Anderson, of Howmedica, has said, "We often test models for their accuracy by preparing expost forecasts (forecasts for which actuals are known). This helps us in selecting an appropriate model."[56]

USING MULTIPLE FORECASTS

When forecasting sales or some other business or economic variable, it is usually a good idea to consider more than one model. We know it is unlikely that one model will always provide the most accurate forecast for any series. Thus, it makes sense to "hedge one's bets," in a sense, by using two or more forecasts. This may involve making a "most optimistic," a "most pessimistic," and a "most likely" forecast. In our example of forecasting the University of Michigan Index of Consumer Sentiment, using the two naive models described in previous sections, we could take the lowest forecast value in each month as the most optimistic, the highest as the most pessimistic, and the average value as the *most likely*. The latter can be calculated as the mean of the two other forecast values in each month. That is:

In making a final forecast, we again stress the importance of using well-reasoned judgments based on expertise regarding the series under consideration.

$$\text{Most likely forecast} = \frac{\text{UMICSF1} + \text{UMICSF2}}{2}$$

This is the simplest way to combine forecasts.

The purpose of a number of studies has been to identify the best way to combine forecasts to improve overall accuracy.[57] After we have covered a wider array of forecasting models, we will come back to this issue of combining different forecasts (see Chapter 8). For now, we just want to call attention to the

---

[55] Pamela A. Texter and Peg Young, "How Accurate Is a Model That Fits Best the Historical Data?" *Journal of Business Forecasting* 8, no. 4 (Winter 1989–90), pp. 13–16; and Spyros Makridakis, "Accuracy Measures: Theoretical and Practical Concerns," *International Journal of Forecasting,* December 1993, pp. 527–29.

[56] Anderson, "Demand Forecasting at Howmedica," p. 4.

[57] For example, see Wilson and Allison-Koerber, "Combining Subjective and Objective Forecasts."

desirability of using more than one method in developing any forecast. In making a final forecast, we again stress the importance of using well-reasoned judgments based on expertise regarding the series under consideration.

SOURCES OF DATA

The quantity and type of data needed in developing forecasts can vary a great deal from one situation to another. Some forecasting techniques require only the data series that is to be forecast. These methods include the naive methods discussed in previous sections as well as more sophisticated time-series techniques such as time-series decomposition, exponential smoothing, and ARIMA models, which will be discussed in subsequent chapters of this text. On the other hand, multiple-regression methods require a data series for each variable included in the forecasting model. This may mean that a large number of data series must be maintained to support the forecasting process.

The most obvious sources of data are the internal records of the organization itself. Such data include unit product sales histories, employment and production records, total revenue, shipments, orders received, inventory records, and so forth. However, it is surprising how often an organization fails to keep historical data in a form that facilitates the development of forecasting models. Often, monthly and/or quarterly data are discarded after three or four years. Thus, models that depend on such data may be difficult to develop. Another problem with using internal data is getting the cooperation necessary to make them available both in a form that is useful and in a timely manner. As better information systems are developed and made available through computer technology, internal data will become even more important and useful in the preparation of forecasts.

For many types of forecasts the necessary data come from outside the firm. Various trade associations are a valuable source of such data, which are usually available to members at a nominal cost and sometimes to nonmembers for a fee. But the richest sources of external data are various governmental and syndicated services.

You will find a wealth of data available on the Internet.[58] Using various search engines you can uncover sources for most macroeconomic series that are of interest to forecasters.

FORECASTING TOTAL HOUSES SOLD

In each chapter of the text where new forecasting techniques are developed, we will apply at least one of the new methods to preparing a forecast of total houses sold (THS). As you will see, there is a fair amount of variability in how well different methods work for this very important economic series. The data we will

---

[58] We encourage students to explore the data available on http://www.economagic.com.

FIGURE 1.7

Total Houses Sold (THS)

This graph shows THS in thousands of units per month from January 1978 through July 2007. (c1f7)

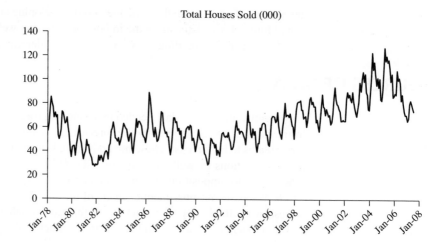

Total Houses Sold (000)

be using are shown graphically in Figure 1.7. As you see from the graph, we have monthly THS from January 1978 through July 2007. The data represent sales in thousands of units and have not been seasonally adjusted.

In this chapter we apply a modified naive model to forecast total houses sold. The model is:

$$\text{THSF}_t = \text{THS}_{t-12}$$

where THSF_t is the forecast of sales for time t and THS_{t-12} is the actual sales 12 months earlier. As seen in Table 1.4, the level of sales for December 2006 was 71. Thus, our forecast for December 2007 is 71.

Table 1.4 and Figure 1.8 show how this naive model worked for the last year. The root-mean-squared error for this modified naive model for the period from August 2006 through July 2007 is 21.01.

FIGURE 1.8

Total Houses Sold (THS) with Naive Forecast

In this example the naive forecast is modified to be the actual sales 12 months earlier. $\text{THSF} = \text{THS}_{(t-12)}$ (c1t4&f8)

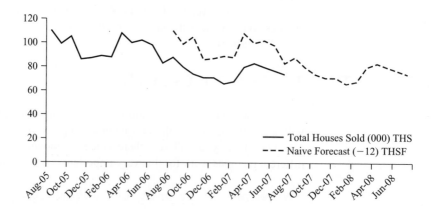

——— Total Houses Sold (000) THS
--- Naive Forecast (−12) THSF

TABLE 1.4
Total Houses Sold (THS) with Naive Forecast (c1t4&f8)
In this example the naïve forecast is modified to be the actual sales 12 months earlier.
$THSF = THS_{(t-12)}$

Date	Total Houses Sold (000) THS	Naive Forecast (−12) THSF	Error	Squared Error	
Aug-05	110				
Sep-05	99				
Oct-05	105				
Nov-05	86				
Dec-05	87				
Jan-06	89				
Feb-06	88				
Mar-06	108				
Apr-06	100				
May-06	102				
Jun-06	98				
Jul-06	83				
Aug-06	88	110	−22	484	
Sep-06	80	99	−19	361	
Oct-06	74	105	−31	961	MSE = 441.25
Nov-06	71	86	−15	225	
Dec-06	71	87	−16	256	RMSE = 21.01
Jan-07	66	89	−23	529	
Feb-07	68	88	−20	400	
Mar-07	80	108	−28	784	
Apr-07	83	100	−17	289	
May-07	80	102	−22	484	
Jun-07	77	98	−21	441	
Jul-07	74	83	−9	81	
Aug-07		88			
Sep-07		80			
Oct-07		74			
Nov-07		71			
Dec-07		71			
Jan-08		66			
Feb-08		68			
Mar-08		80			
Apr-08		83			
May-08		80			
Jun-08		77			
Jul-08		74			

OVERVIEW OF THE TEXT

Business Forecasting has been organized in such a way that by working consecutively through the text, you will gradually develop a sophisticated forecasting capability. In this first chapter you have been given an introduction to business forecasting that has included naive models and some introduction to forecasting new products. Figure 1.9 shows the various methods you will learn as you complete the text.

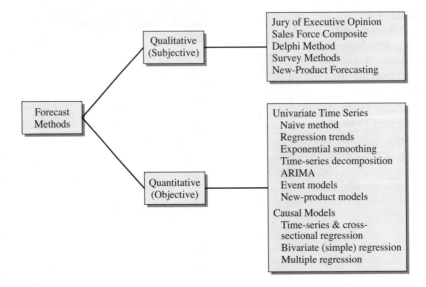

FIGURE 1.9
An Overview of the Forecast Methods Covered in This Text

The second chapter provides a discussion of data exploration through visualization, an overview of model-selection criteria, and a review of some statistical concepts that will be helpful as you learn about additional forecasting methods.

Chapter 3 presents moving-average and exponential smoothing techniques. These methods are widely used, quite simple from a computational standpoint, and often very accurate. Chapter 4 provides an explanation of simple linear-regression analysis and its applications to business forecasting. Both simple trend models and simple two-variable causal models are presented. In Chapter 5 the simple regression model is expanded to include more than one independent variable. Multiple-regression models are applied to specific forecasting problems, and a method for accounting for seasonality is presented.

Classical time-series decomposition, discussed in Chapter 6, provides accurate forecasts for many series. In addition, it can be used to develop seasonal indices that help identify the degree of seasonality in the data. These indices can also be used to deseasonalize the data series. ARIMA forecasting models are presented in Chapter 7.

Chapter 8 contains a discussion of alternative methods for combining individual forecasts to take advantage of information contained in different methods to improve forecast accuracy. In Chapter 9, a new chapter in this edition, we present data mining as another useful forecasting tool. Often businesses have huge amounts of data that can be used to predict sales or other outcomes but the data are not amenable to standard forecasting methods. Data mining is a tool that has evolved to help us deal with such situations.

Chapter 10 focuses on how to select appropriate forecasting methods for a particular situation and how to establish an effective forecasting process. The

N. Carroll Mohn, Manager of Field Services, European Community Group, in the Corporate Marketing Research Department of The Coca-Cola Company.

WHY TRY TO FORECAST?

Forecasts are critical inputs to a wide range of business decision-making processes. From letters, teaching forecasting, managing the function, and consulting work, I know that many people are striving to get a practitioner's grasp of the subject—some feeling for the applied state of the art and its science.

As forecasters, at one time or another, we have to ask ourselves why we should try to forecast in the first place. First, the power of forces such as economics, competition, markets, social concerns, and the ecological environment to affect the individual firm is severe and continues growing. Secondly, forecast assessment is a major input in management's evaluation of different strategies at business decision-making levels. Thirdly, the inference of *no* forecasting is that the future either contains "no significant change" or there is ample time to react "after the fact."

Forecasting is far too important to the organization not to have appropriate management and resource backing. Each firm must develop its own *explicit* forecast system so that alternative courses of action can be identified.

We can see the future coming if we know what to look for because many things often progress in an astonishingly orderly manner over time. This consistent progress provides a basis for forecasting. At the same time, many things respond to needs, opportunities, and support resources. If these driving forces can be identified, we believe future progress can be forecast.

Source: Adapted from an address given at the Fourth Annual Conference of the International Association of Business Forecasters, Philadelphia, September 1989.

role of judgments based on experience with the series to be forecast is stressed once more.

At the end of each chapter you will find suggested readings that will provide additional insight into the topics covered. In addition, a set of exercises in each chapter will help you validate your understanding of the material. Many of these exercises will also help you to become proficient in the use of the ForecastX™ software.

Integrative Case

Forecasting Sales of The Gap

PART 1: BACKGROUND OF THE GAP AND ITS SALES

Throughout the text we will be using The Gap sales in an integrative case at the end of each chapter. In these cases, concepts from the chapter will be applied to this sales series. In this chapter we will apply concepts as well as provide an overview of the company.

THE GAP: AN INTRODUCTION

Few retailers have accomplished what The Gap has. The Gap has managed to successfully market its retail stores and the apparel it carries. In 1992, The Gap was the number two clothing brand in America, and in 1994 it placed in the top 25 of the 50 most recognizable brands in the United States. There are only two private-brand retailers that achieved this coveted brand image for their stores' products: Victoria's Secret and The Gap. While many other retailers, such as The Limited, lost strong brand images, The Gap continued to redefine its strategy and managed to maintain market dominance. By the end of 1995, The Gap operated over 1,500 stores in its four domestic divisions, which include The Gap, GapKids, Banana Republic, and the Old Navy Clothing Co. The Gap's fifth division, its International Division, operated 164 stores by the end of 1995 in countries such as Canada, the United Kingdom, France, Germany, and Japan.

The first Gap store was opened in 1969 by founder Donald Fisher, who decided to open a store after he had a problem exchanging a pair of Levi's jeans that were an inch too short. He felt that there was a need for a store that would sell jeans in a full array of sizes. He opened his first store in San Francisco, which advertised that it had "four tons" of Levi's. The store was an instant success, and The Gap stores were on their way to national prominence. Levi's were the mainstay of The Gap's business, and due to Levi Strauss & Co.'s fixed pricing, Fisher maintained a 50 percent margin on the sales of these jeans. This changed in 1976, however, when the Federal Trade Commission prohibited manufacturers from dictating the price that retailers could charge for their products. There was suddenly massive discounting on Levi's products, which drastically cut The Gap's margins. Fisher recognized the need to expand his product offerings to include higher-margin items, and therefore began to offer private-label apparel.

In 1983, Fisher recruited Millard Drexler as president, with his objective being to revamp The Gap. Drexler did this by liquidating its existing inventories and focusing on simpler, more classic styles that offered the consumer "good style, good quality, good value." The Gap started to design its own clothes to fit into this vision. The Gap already had formed strong relationships with manufacturers from its earlier entry into the private-label business. This enabled it to monitor manufacturing closely, which kept costs low and quality high. The Gap's strategy didn't end with high-quality products. Drexler paid equally close attention to the visual presence of the stores. He replaced the old pipe racks and cement floors with hardwood floors and attractive tables and shelves with merchandise neatly folded, which made it easier for the customers to shop. As new merchandise came in, store managers were given detailed plannograms, which told them precisely where the items would go. With this control, Drexler ensured that each Gap store would have the same look, and would therefore present the same image to the customer.

The Gap capitalized on these same concepts as it entered the kids' clothing market. The idea originated after Drexler was disappointed with the lack of selection he found while shopping for his own child. Drexler organized a meeting with his employees who had children to discuss their thoughts about the children's clothing market. Their mutual frustration with the selection of children's clothing triggered the idea for GapKids. Drexler and his team believed that they could use the same merchandising principles that made The Gap a success and apply them to the children's clothing market. GapKids was launched in 1986, and was a success in its first year of operation with sales of $2 million.

Drexler's retailing prowess also became evident when he turned around the poor performance of the Banana Republic division. In 1983, The Gap bought Banana Republic, which featured the then-popular safari-style clothing. This trend toward khakis had been brought on by the popularity of movies such as *Raiders of the Lost Ark* and *Romancing the Stone*. By 1987, Banana Republic's sales had reached $191 million. Then the safari craze ended, and this once popular division lost roughly $10 million in the two years that followed. Banana Republic was repositioned as a more upscale Gap, with fancier decor as well as more updated fashions that offered a balance between sophistication and comfort. By 1992, the chain was once again profitable, with about $300 million in sales.

Although these other Gap divisions had grown and prospered, the traditional Gap stores began to falter in the early 1990s. Coupled with the effects of a retailing recession, their strong emphasis on basic styles had made them a target of competition. The market became flooded with "Gap-like" basics. Other retailers were also mimicking their presentation strategy, and started folding large-volume commodity items such as jeans, T-shirts, and fleece, some selling them at substantially lower prices. Drexler and his team recognized that several major changes were taking place in the retailing environment, and they needed to identify ways to respond to this competition if they were to continue to grow.

One way The Gap responded to increasing competition was to revise its merchandise mix. Customers were shifting away from the basics toward more fashion items, in gender-specific styles. To respond to this trend, The Gap took advantage of aggressive changes already under way in its inventory management programs, which gave it faster replenishment times. This enabled The Gap to reduce its inventories in basics by as much as 40 percent, giving it more room for hot-selling, high-profit items. In addition to shifting to more fashion, The Gap also fine-tuned its product mix so that merchandise would be more consistent between stores.

Another way that The Gap responded to increased competition and changing retailing trends was by entering into strip malls. This move has been facilitated in part by the reduction of available spaces in large malls. As fewer spaces became available, retailers wishing to expand have had to explore other possible options. Many strip centers have been upgraded in response to this trend, and retailers found that they could offer their customers easier access to stores and more convenient parking than they could in their traditional mall locations. With carefully placed geographic locations, retailers also discovered that they could often do the same volume that they could in the large malls. Additionally, strip-center rents are substantially lower than those of their mall counterparts. Their common charges are sometimes a mere 25 percent of what they would be in a typical large mall.

As other retailers and discounters found success by knocking off The Gap's classic styles and its presentation standards, The Gap responded by entering the "discount" market itself in 1993, with the transformation of 48 of its lowest-performance stores into "Gap Warehouse" stores. By doing so, The Gap capitalized on the new surge of price-conscious consumers. Gap Warehouse stores offer Gap-type styles at prices about 30 percent lower than The Gap apparel.

Its success with this discount concept led to the launch of the Old Navy Clothing Co. in April 1994, which targeted consumers in households with incomes between $20,000 and $50,000, who make about one-half of the nation's $150 billion apparel purchases each year. Old Navy stores carry a different assortment of apparel than traditional Gap stores. They differentiated themselves from The Gap stores by offering alternative versions of basic items, with different fabric blends that enable them to charge lower retail prices. In fact, 80 percent of their assortment retailed at $22 or less. There are other ways in which The Gap differentiates its Old Navy stores from its traditional Gap stores, however. To help keep costs down, it also scaled down the decor of these stores, with serviceable concrete floors and shopping carts instead of the hardwood floors found in The Gap. It is venturing away from The Gap's traditional means of advertising for these new stores and is offering more short-term promotions. Old Navy stores are further positioning themselves as one-stop-shopping stores by offering clothing for the whole family in one location.

In August 2005 Gap launched "Forth and Towne." Forth and Towne was a retail experiment targeted at female Baby Boomers. Stores featured uniquely located dressing rooms with three-way mirrors, adjustable lighting, and "style consultants" to assist customers with purchasing decisions. Forth and Towne was not well received by the market. In February 2007 Gap announced that it would close all 19 of the concept stores. In 2006 Gap launched "piperlime.com" an online only retail shoe store. Piperlime.com features men's and women's shoes from over 100 brands as well as insights from "fashion experts." Time will reveal if Piperlime will be as successful as other ventures like Old Navy, or will suffer the same fate as Forth and Towne.

With its current mix of stores, The Gap has successfully carved out a position for itself in every retail clothing category. Table 1.5 shows the distribution of store types. Although there have been some hurdles along the way, The Gap has proven that it has the ability to respond to changes in the retail environment and has, therefore, managed to stay in the race. This is evidenced by the increased quarterly sales shown in Table 1.6 and the graphic in Figure 1.10.

Table 1.6 also has a modified naive forecast for The Gap sales using a four-quarter lag.

TABLE 1.5

The Gap Store Count

Source: http://www.gapinc.com/ public/Investors/inv_ re_storecount.shtml (click on Historical Store Count by country).

Stores	Quarter 4, 2007
Gap North America	1,249
Banana Republic North America	555
Old Navy North America	1,059
Forth & Towne	0
International	304
Total	**3,167**

TABLE 1.6
The Gap Sales and a Modified Naive Forecast
(Forecast = Sales [−4])
(c1t6&f10)

The Gap sales data are in thousands of dollars by quarter. The months indicated in the date columns represent the middle month in The Gap's financial quarter. For example, the first quarter in its fiscal year includes February, March, and April.

Date	Gap Sales (000)	Gap Sales Modified Naive Forecast	Date	Gap Sales (000)	Gap Sales Modified Naive Forecast
Mar-85	$ 105,715		Mar-95	$ 848,688	$ 751,670
Jun-85	120,136		Jun-95	868,514	773,131
Sep-85	181,669		Sep-95	1,155,930	988,346
Dec-85	239,813		Dec-95	1,522,120	1,209,790
Mar-86	159,980	$ 105,715	Mar-96	1,113,150	848,688
Jun-86	164,760	120,136	Jun-96	1,120,340	868,514
Sep-86	224,800	181,669	Sep-96	1,383,000	1,155,930
Dec-86	298,469	239,813	Dec-96	1,667,900	1,522,120
Mar-87	211,060	159,980	Mar-97	1,231,186	1,113,150
Jun-87	217,753	164,760	Jun-97	1,345,221	1,120,340
Sep-87	273,616	224,800	Sep-97	1,765,939	1,383,000
Dec-87	359,592	298,469	Dec-97	2,165,479	1,667,900
Mar-88	241,348	211,060	Mar-98	1,719,712	1,231,186
Jun-88	264,328	217,753	Jun-98	1,904,970	1,345,221
Sep-88	322,752	273,616	Sep-98	2,399,900	1,765,939
Dec-88	423,669	359,592	Dec-98	3,029,900	2,165,479
Mar-89	309,925	241,348	Mar-99	2,277,734	1,719,712
Jun-89	325,939	264,328	Jun-99	2,453,339	1,904,970
Sep-89	405,601	322,752	Sep-99	3,045,386	2,399,900
Dec-89	545,131	423,669	Dec-99	3,858,939	3,029,900
Mar-90	402,368	309,925	Mar-00	2,731,990	2,277,734
Jun-90	404,996	325,939	Jun-00	2,947,714	2,453,339
Sep-90	501,690	405,601	Sep-00	3,414,668	3,045,386
Dec-90	624,726	545,131	Dec-00	4,579,088	3,858,939
Mar-91	490,300	402,368	Mar-01	3,179,656	2,731,990
Jun-91	523,056	404,996	Jun-01	3,245,219	2,947,714
Sep-91	702,052	501,690	Sep-01	3,333,373	3,414,668
Dec-91	803,485	624,726	Dec-01	4,089,625	4,579,088
Mar-92	588,864	490,300	Mar-02	2,890,840	3,179,656
Jun-92	614,114	523,056	Jun-02	3,268,309	3,245,219
Sep-92	827,222	702,052	Sep-02	3,644,956	3,333,373
Dec-92	930,209	803,485	Dec-02	4,650,604	4,089,625
Mar-93	643,580	588,864	Mar-03	3,352,771	2,890,840
Jun-93	693,192	614,114	Jun-03	3,685,299	3,268,309
Sep-93	898,677	827,222	Sep-03	3,929,456	3,644,956
Dec-93	1,060,230	930,209	Dec-03	4,886,264	4,650,604
Mar-94	751,670	643,580	Mar-04	3,667,565	3,352,771
Jun-94	773,131	693,192	Jun-04	3,720,789	3,685,299
Sep-94	988,346	898,677	Sep-04	3,980,150	3,929,456
Dec-94	1,209,790	1,060,230	Dec-04	4,898,000	4,886,264
			Mar-05	3,626,000	3,667,565
RMSE = 294,790.08			Jun-05	3,716,000	3,720,789
RMSE as % of average = 15,77			Sep-05	3,860,000	3,980,150

(continued on next page)

TABLE 1.6
(continued)

Date	Gap Sales (000)	Gap Sales Modified Naive Forecast
Dec-05	$4,821,000	$4,898,000
Mar-06	3,441,000	3,626,000
Jun-06	3,716,000	3,716,000
Sep-06	3,856,000	3,860,000
Dec-06	4,930,000	4,821,000
Mar-07	3,558,000	3,441,000
Jun-07		3,716,000
Sep-07		3,856,000
Dec-07		4,930,000
Mar-08		3,558,000

FIGURE 1.10
The Gap Sales in Thousands of Dollars and a Modified Naive Forecast
The data are quarterly so a four-quarter lag was used for a modified naive forecast.
(c1t6&f10)

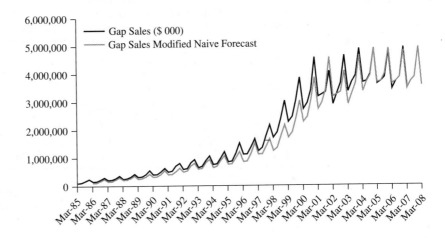

Case Questions

1. Based on the tabular and the graphic presentations of The Gap sales data, what do you think explains the seasonal pattern in its sales data?
2. Using a modified naive forecasting method, such as the one used for total houses sold in this chapter, make a forecast of The Gap sales for the four quarters from June 2006 through March 2007. Based on inspection of the graph of The Gap sales, what is your expectation in terms of forecast accuracy?
3. Calculate the RMSE for your forecast of those four quarters, given that the actual sales were as shown in Table 1.6.

Solutions to Case Questions

Data are in the c1 Gap file.

1. The seasonal pattern is one in which sales typically have a small increase from the first to the second quarter, followed by a considerable increase in the third quarter and yet another large increase in the fourth quarter. The third quarter increase is related to back-to-school buying, while the increase in the fourth quarter is caused by the Christmas shopping season.

2. The model would be: GAPF = GAPSALES(−4). GAPF represents the forecast values, while GAPSALES(−4) is the actual value four periods earlier. An inspection of The Gap sales series would lead us to expect that a naive forecasting model with a lag of four periods would pick up the seasonality as well as the recent flattening of the trend in The Gap sales. This can be seen in the graph of actual and predicted values in Figure 1.10.

3. The actual and predicted values for June 2006 through March 2007 are shown below. The RMSE for these four quarters is: RMSE = 79,878.1. This is about a 2.0 percent error, based on the average quarterly sales for the year (4,015,000).

Date	Gap Sales (000)	Gap Sales Modified Naive Forecast	Error	Squared Error
Jun-05	$3,716,000	na		
Sep-05	3,860,000	na		
Dec-05	4,821,000	na		
Mar-06	3,441,000	na		
Jun-06	3,716,000	$3,716,000	0	0
Sep-06	3,856,000	3,860,000	$−4,000	$ 16,000,000
Dec-06	4,930,000	4,821,000	109,000	11,881,000,000
Mar-07	3,558,000	3,441,000	117,000	13,689,000,000

Jun-06 to Mar-07 Mean = 4,015,000

MSE = 6,396,500,000
RMSE = 79,978.1
RMSE as % of Mean = 2.0

The RMSE for the entire March-85 through March-07 period was 294,790,08, or 15.77% of the mean. One reason the RMSE was higher in the historic period is that the increasing trend in the sales series from the mid-1990s through about 2002 meant that simply using a four-quarter lag to forecast resulted in consistently larger errors during that time. However, the recent flattening in sales made this less important for the June 2006 to March 2007 forecast.

Case References

Arlen, Jeffrey. "Gap Knocks Off Gap." *Discount Store News,* Sept. 6, 1993, p. A8.

——. "It's a Trend." *Discount Store News,* Sept. 6, 1993, p. A5.

Cuneo, Alice. "Gap Floats Lower-Price Old Navy Stores." *Advertising Age,* July 25, 1994, p. 36.

Edelson, Sharon. "Strip Centers: The Chain Reaction." *WWD,* Aug. 9, 1995, p. 9.

Mitchell, Russell. "A Bit of a Rut at The Gap." *BusinessWeek,* Nov. 30, 1992, p. 100.

PFIZER HARNESSES JOHN GALT FOR OPTIMIZED SALES FORECASTING

Pfizer Inc. (formerly Warner Lambert & Pfizer Inc.) is a research-based, global pharmaceutical company, which discovers and develops innovative, value-added products that improve the quality of life of people around the world and help them enjoy longer, healthier, and more productive lives. The company has three business segments: health care, animal health, and consumer health care. Pfizer products are available in more than 150 countries.

Warner Lambert, Mexico—also now Pfizer—formed its consensus forecast (CF) team to define a process to generate comprehensive and accurate unconstrained forecasts that would improve the stock-turn rate and reduce returns. The company needed a solution that could be rolled out across the entire enterprise to collect data from key stakeholders within the newly defined area. The CF team installed John Galt Solutions' ForecastX Wizard software to support its process, and engendered positive results.

The company's demand department uses the software to forecast sales at the SKU level for up to 18 months at a time. According to the department: "We have a broad base of seasonal products that are subject to the effects of several promotions and particular events. Event modeling has proven to be the most useful functionality for obtaining accurate forecasts. The results have been very satisfactory. Warner Lambert has been very pleased with ForecastX. ForecastX provided a very user-friendly, affordable, well-supported, and fast option for our sales forecasting needs."

But the positive report on John Galt ForecastX did not end there: "It functions very well as a strong sales forecasting tool that is also very easy to use," observed the Warner Lambert Demand Department. "The fact that you don't have to be an expert in statistics is excellent. Everybody understands how to use it and how to manipulate the data."

Source: http://www.johngalt.com/customers/success. shtml.

——. "The Gap: Can the Nation's Hottest Retailer Stay on Top?" *BusinessWeek,* March 9, 1992, p. 58.

——. "The Gap Dolls Itself Up." *BusinessWeek,* March 21, 1994, p. 46.

——. "A Humbler Neighborhood for The Gap." *BusinessWeek,* Aug. 16, 1993, p. 29.

Mui, Ylan Q. "Gap to Close Forth & Towne Stores," *Washington Post,* Tuesday, Feb. 27, 2007, p. D01. Available at: http://www.washingtonpost.com/wp-dyn/content/article/2007/02/26/AR2007022601357.html.

Popiel, Leslie A. "Old Navy Store Is Gap's Answer to the Penny-Pinching Shopper." *Christian Science Monitor,* Oct. 28, 1994, p. 8.

Street, Pamela. "Old Navy Fills Off-Price Gap for The Gap." *Daily News Record,* March 31, 1994, p. 3.

The Gap, Inc., Annual Reports.

Wilson, Marianne. "The Magic of Brand Identity." *Chain Store Age Executive,* Feb. 1994, p. 66.

http://www.gapinc.com

http://www.gapinc.com/Public/About/abt_faq.shtml

http://money.cnn.com/2005/02/23/news/fortune500/Gap/?cnn5yes

http://www.piperlime.com

http://profile.canadianretail.com/gap/

JOHN GALT PARTIAL CUSTOMER LIST

The ForecastX software that accompanies your text is from John Galt Solutions Incorporated. Below is a partial list of their customers. A more complete list can be found on their Web site: www.johngalt.com. You can see from this list that John Galt's forecasting software is widely used in the business community.

Automotive
Hyundai
Kawasaki
Monroe Muffler/Brake
PepBoys
Volkswagen

Consumer Goods
Gillette
Hartz Mountain
Hasbro Inc
Kitchenaid
Leatherman Tool Group
L'Oreal
Mattel Inc
Nintendo of America

Technology
America Online
ITT Aerospace Controls
Microsoft Corporation
PeopleSoft
Toshiba

Financial
American Express
Bank One
Capital One
Discover Financial Services
Fidelity Investments
TIAA-CREF
Visa International

Food Services
Alaska Brewing Co.
Baskin-Robbins
Dean Foods
Domino's Pizza
Keebler Company
Starbucks Coffee

Retail
The Container Store
Dockers Khakis

IKEA North American Services
JC Penney
Levis
Liquor Control Board of Ontario
Yankee Candle Co.

Shipping
FedEx
United Parcel Services

Energy/Utilities
BP Amoco
Commonwealth Edison
Duquesne Light Company
Nova Scotia Power & Light

Telecommunications
AT & T Wireless
Bell Canada
Bell South
SBC Communications
Nextel Communications

Pharmaceutical & Health Care
Abbott Laboratories
Baxter International
Biogen
Blue Cross Blue Shield
Eli Lilly Deutschland
GlaxoSmithKline
Novartis AG
Pfizer
Wyeth

Transportation
Royal Caribbean Cruise Lines
Ryder Trucks
Yellow Freight

Manufacturing
Adams Golf
3M Canada
Callaway Golf
Corning

DuPont
Hyundai
In-Sink-Erator
John Deere and Company
Lockheed Martin
Maytag Corp
Remington Arms Corporation
Shell Chemical.

Government
United States Air Force
United States Marine Corps
United States Army
California Dept. of Health
Oregon Dept. of Justice

Universities
Auburn University
Babson College
California State University
Central Michigan University
DePaul University
Drexel University
Duke University
Elon University
Meredith College
Oakland University
Portland State University
Rider University
Southern Illinois University
Suffolk University
University of Alabama
University of California
University of Idaho
University of Massachusetts
University of Notre Dame
University of Southern California
University of Texas
Western Illinois University
Wright State University

AN INTRODUCTION TO FORECASTX 7.0

ForecastX™ is a family of forecasting tools capable of performing the most complex forecast methods and requires only a brief learning curve that facilitates immediate, simple, and accurate operation regardless of user experience.

FORECASTING WITH THE FORECASTX WIZARD™

The following provides a brief description of some features of the ForecastX Wizard™ and how to use them while forecasting. A complete manual can be found in the "Wizard 7.0 Users Guide.pdf" file which is in the Help subfolder of the ForecastX folder within the Programs folder (or wherever you have installed the software).

> Open the "c1 Gap sales new.xls" spreadsheet that is on the CD that came with your book.

> When the spreadsheet opens, click in any cell that contains data.

> Click the ForecastX Wizard™ icon ⟨🔘 Forecast⟩ to start the Wizard.

USING THE FIVE MAIN TABS ON THE OPENING FORECASTX SCREEN

Use the Gap sales data you have opened and follow the directions in the following screen shots to get a first look at how ForecastX works.

The Data Capture Tab

This tab appears when you first start ForecastX.

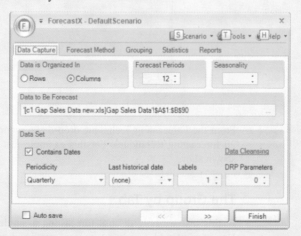

The purpose of the Data Capture screen is to tell ForecastX™ about your data.

When the ForecastX Wizard™ captures your data, the Intelligent Data Recognizer determines the following:

a. *Organization:* Indicates whether the data is in rows or columns.

b. *Data to Be Forecast:* Specifies the range of the data to be forecasted.

c. *Dates:* Specifies whether the data has dates, and the seasonal feature of the dates.

d. *Labels:* Indicates the number of descriptive labels in the data.

e. *Paras (Parameters):* Indicates the number of DRP (Distribution Resource Planning) fields in your data. For the purposes of this text you will not need to use this functionality.

f. *Seasonality:* Either you can select the seasonality of the data, or allow ForecastX™ to determine it. These fields must follow the labels information in your underlying data.

g. *Forecast:* Set the number of periods to forecast out into the future.

Forecast Method Tab

The ForecastX Wizard™ allows you to select individual forecasting techniques and their parameters. Selections include time series, promotional, regression, and growth curve models. To select a Forecasting Technique:

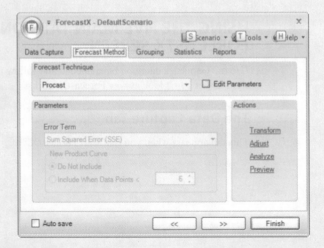

From the Forecasting Technique drop-down menu, select a particular method from over 20 forecasting techniques. For this example just leave the default method "Procast" as shown above.

The Group by Tab

In this text we only discuss forecasting a single series so you will not need this tab. However, should you want to forecast product groups see the "Wizard 7.0 Users Guide.pdf" file.

The Statistics Tab

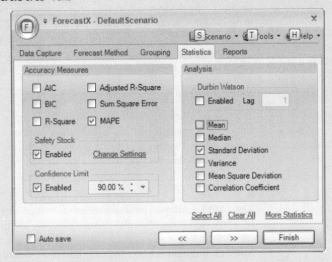

The ForecastX Wizard™ allows you to select statistical analyses to include on the Audit Trail report. ForecastX™ supports more than 40 statistics from both descriptive and accuracy measurement categories. For this example just use the defaults as shown above.

The More Statistics option offers advanced statistics for seasoned statisticians. The Root Mean Squared Error (RMSE) and the statistics for regression models are located in this dialog box. To access the Advanced Statistics dialog, click the More Statistics button on the Statistics screen.

The Report Tab

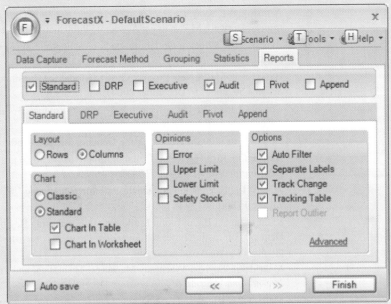

The ForecastX Wizard™ offers five report choices with specific options for each. Checking any of the report boxes in the upper grouping of check boxes automatically includes it in the output. You may check more than one if desired. Each type of report will have its own workbook, but may contain several series within one workbook. Here we only discuss the most commonly used report tabs. Detailed information about all these tabs can be found in the "Wizard 7.0 Users Guide.pdf" file.

Standard Report

The Standard Report is built for speed and handling of large volumes of data. It produces a side-by-side report listing the actual values compared to the forecasted values. It also includes selected statistics and a few common statistics: Mean Absolute Percentage Error (MAPE), R-Squared Value, and Standard Deviation.

Audit Trail Report

The Audit Trail Report produces the most detailed analysis of the forecast. Those who need to justify their forecasts with statistics generally use the Audit Trail report.

Note: **Throughout the text you may find some situations in which the standard calculations that we show do not match exactly with the ForecastX results. This is because they, at times, invoke proprietary alterations from the standard calculations. The results are always very close but sometimes do not match perfectly with "hand" calculations.**

Suggested Readings and Web Sites

Adams, F. Gerard. *The Business Forecasting Revolution*. New York: Oxford University Press, 1986.

Armstrong, J. Scott. "Forecasting for Environmental Decision Making." In *Tools to Aid Environmental Decision Making*, eds. V. H. Dale and M. E. English. New York: Springer-Verlag, 1999, pp. 192–225.

Armstrong, J. Scott. *Principles of Forecasting: A Handbook for Researchers and Practitioners*. Norwell, MA: Kluwer Academic Publishers: The Netherlands, 2001.

Aviv, Y. "The Effect of Collaborative Forecasting on Supply Chain Performance." *Management Science* 47, no. 10 (2001), pp. 1326–43.

Bass, Frank M. "A New Product Growth Model for Consumer Durables." *Management Science* 50, no. 125 (December 2004), pp. 1825–32.

Chase, Charles W., Jr. "Forecasting Consumer Products." *Journal of Business Forecasting* 10, no. 1 (Spring 1991), pp. 2–6.

Goodwin, P. (2008) "Predicting the Demand for New Products," *Foresight,* 9, pp. 8–10.

Harrington, Lisa H. "Retail Collaboration: How to Solve the Puzzle." *Transportation and Distribution,* May 2003, pp. 33–37.

Jain, C. L. "Forecasting at Colgate-Palmolive Company." *Journal of Business Forecasting* 11, no. 1 (Spring 1992), pp. 16–20.

Kahn, Kenneth B.; and John Mello. "Lean Forecasting Begins with Lean Thinking on the Demand Forecasting Process." *Journal of Business Forecasting* 23, no. 4 (Winter 2004–05), pp. 30–40.

Makridakis, Spyros. "Accuracy Measures: Theoretical and Practical Concerns." *International Journal of Forecasting,* December 1993, pp. 527–29.

Mathews, Brian P.; and Adamantios Diamantopoulos. "Towards a Taxonomy of Forecast Error Measures." *Journal of Forecasting,* August 1994, pp. 409–16.

Meade, N. "Evidence for the Selection of Forecasting Methods." *Journal of Forecasting* 19, no. 6 (2000), pp. 515–35.

Mead, N.; and T. Islam (2006) "Modeling and Forecasting the Diffusion of Innovation—A 25-Year Review," *International Journal of Forecasting*, 22, pp. 519–45.

Mentzer, John T.; and Jon Schroeter. "Multiple Forecasting System at Brake Parts, Inc." *Journal of Business Forecasting* 14, no. 3 (Fall 1993), pp. 5–9.

Moriarty, Mark M.; and Arthur J. Adams. "Management Judgment Forecasts, Composite Forecasting Models, and Conditional Efficiency." *Journal of Marketing Research,* August 1984, pp. 239–50.

Morwitz, V. G.; J. H. Steckel; and A. Gupta (2007) "When Do Purchase Intentions Predict Sales?" *International Journal of Forecasting*, 23, pp. 347–64.

Rosati, Anna Maria. "Forecasting at Segix, Italia: A Pharmaceutical Company." *Journal of Business Forecasting* 17, no. 3 (Fall 1996), pp. 7–9.

Shore, H.; and D. Benson-Karhi (2007) "Forecasting S-Shaped Diffusion Processes Via Response Modeling Methodology," *Journal of the Operational Research Society*, 58, pp. 720–28.

Van Vught, F. A. "Pitfalls of Forecasting: Fundamental Problems for the Methodology of Forecasting from the Philosophy of Science." *Futures,* April 1987, pp. 184–96.

Wilson, J. Holton; and Deborah Allison-Koerber. "Combining Subjective and Objective Forecasts Improves Results." *Journal of Business Forecasting* 11, no. 3 (Fall 1992), pp. 12–16.

Wilson, J. Holton; and Steven J. Schuiling. "Forecasting Hospital Laboratory Procedures." *Journal of Medical Systems,* December 1992, pp. 269–79.

http://www.andorraweb.com/bass
http://www.bassmodelinstitute.org
http://www.economagic.com
http://www.forecasters.org
http://www.forecastingprinciples.com
http://www.johngalt.com

Exercises

1. Write a paragraph in which you compare what you think are the advantages and disadvantages of subjective forecasting methods. How do you think the use of quantitative methods relates to these advantages and disadvantages?

2. Suppose that you work for a U.S. senator who is contemplating writing a bill that would put a national sales tax in place. Because the tax would be levied on the sales revenue of retail stores, the senator has asked you to prepare a forecast of retail store sales for year 8, based on data from year 1 through year 7. The data are:

(c1p2)

Year	Retail Store Sales
1	$1,225
2	1,285
3	1,359
4	1,392
5	1,443
6	1,474
7	1,467

     a. Use the first naive forecasting model presented in this chapter to prepare a forecast of retail store sales for each year from 2 through 8.

     b. Prepare a time-series graph of the actual and forecast values of retail store sales for the entire period. (You will not have a forecast for year 1 or an actual value for year 8.)

     c. Calculate the root-mean-squared error for your forecast series using the values for year 2 through year 7.

3. Use the second naive forecasting model presented in this chapter to answer parts (*a*) through (*c*) of Exercise 2. Use $P = 0.2$ in preparing the forecast. Which model do you think works the best? Explain why. (c1p3)

4. Suppose that you work for a major U.S. retail department store that has outlets nationwide. The store offers credit to customers in various forms, including store credit cards, and over the years has seen a substantial increase in credit purchases. The manager of credit sales is concerned about the degree to which consumers are using credit and has started to track the ratio of consumer installment credit to personal income. She calls this ratio the credit percent, or CP, and has asked that you forecast that series for year 8. The available data are:

(c1p2)	Year	CP
	1	12.96
	2	14.31
	3	15.34
	4	15.49
	5	15.70
	6	16.00
	7	15.62

     a. Use the first naive model presented in this chapter to prepare forecasts of CP for years 2 through 8.

     b. Plot the actual and forecast values of the series for the years 1 through 8. (You will not have an actual value for year 8 or a forecast value for year 1.)

     c. Calculate the root-mean-squared error for your forecasts for years 2 through 7.

5. Go to the library and look up annual data for population in the United States from 1981 through 2004. One good source for such data is the *Economic Report of the President*, published each year by the U.S. Government Printing Office. This series is also available at a number of Internet sites, including http://www.economagic.com.

     Plot the actual data along with the forecast you would get by using the first naive model discussed in this chapter. (c1p5)

6. Pick a corporation you are interested in and go to the library or check online to find annual reports for that company. Look at five consecutive annual reports and find the firm's total revenue for each of those years. Plot the firm's actual revenue along with the forecast of revenue you would get by using the first naive model discussed in this chapter.

7. CoastCo Insurance, Inc., is interested in developing a forecast of larceny thefts in the United States. It has found the following data:

(c1p8)	Year	Larceny Thefts*	Year	Larceny Thefts*
	1	4,151	10	7,194
	2	4,348	11	7,143
	3	5,263	12	6,713
	4	5,978	13	6,592
	5	6,271	14	6,926
	6	5,906	15	7,257
	7	5,983	16	7,500
	8	6,578	17	7,706
	9	7,137	18	7,872

*Data are in thousands.

Plot this series in a time-series plot and make a naive forecast for years 2 through 19. Calculate the RMSE and MAD for years 2 through 18. On the basis of these measures and what you see in the plot, what do you think of your forecast? Explain.

8. As the world's economy becomes increasingly interdependent, various exchange rates between currencies have become important in making business decisions. For many U.S. businesses, the Japanese exchange rate (in yen per U.S. dollar) is an important decision variable. This exchange rate (EXRJ) is shown in the following table by month for a two-year period:

(c1p9)	Period	EXRJ	Period	EXRJ
	Year 1		Year 2	
	M1	127.36	M1	144.98
	M2	127.74	M2	145.69
	M3	130.55	M3	153.31
	M4	132.04	M4	158.46
	M5	137.86	M5	154.04
	M6	143.98	M6	153.70
	M7	140.42	M7	149.04
	M8	141.49	M8	147.46
	M9	145.07	M9	138.44
	M10	142.21	M10	129.59
	M11	143.53	M11	129.22
	M12	143.69	M12	133.89

Prepare a time-series plot of this series, and use the naive forecasting model to forecast EXRJ for each month from year 1 M2 (February) through year 3 M1 (January). Calculate the RMSE for the period from year 1 M2 through year 2 M12.

The Forecast Process, Data Considerations, and Model Selection

INTRODUCTION

In this chapter we will outline a forecasting process that is a useful guide to the establishment of a successful forecasting system. It is important that forecasting be viewed as a process that contains certain key components. This process includes the selection of one or more forecasting techniques applicable to the data that need to be forecast. This selection, in turn, depends on the type of data that are available. In selecting a forecasting model, one should first evaluate the data for trend, seasonal, and cyclical components.

In evaluating a data series for its trend, seasonal, and cyclical components, it is useful to look at the data in graphic form. In this chapter we evaluate data for the U.S. population, total houses sold, disposable personal income, and The Gap sales to see which time-series components exist in each. This chapter also includes a review of statistics and an introduction to the use of autocorrelation coefficients, which can provide useful information about the underlying components in a time series.

THE FORECAST PROCESS

The forecast process begins with recognizing the need to make decisions that depend on the future—and unknown—value(s) of some variable(s). It is important for managers who use forecasts in making decisions to have some familiarity with the methods used in developing the forecast. It is also important for the individuals involved in developing forecasts to have an understanding of the needs of those who make decisions based on the forecasts. Thus, good communication among all involved with forecasting is paramount.

There are a variety of ways in which we could outline the overall for
process. We have found the sequence shown below to be a useful paradigm.

1. Specify objectives.
2. Determine what to forecast.
3. Identify time dimensions.
4. Data considerations.
5. Model selection.
6. Model evaluation.
7. Forecast preparation.
8. Forecast presentation.
9. Tracking results.

This flow of relationships in the forecasting process will be discussed in more detail in Chapter 10, after a base of understanding of quantitative forecasting
methods has been established.

It may seem obvious that the forecasting process should begin with a clear
statement of objectives that includes how the forecast will be used in a decision
context. Objectives and applications of the forecast should be discussed between
the individual(s) involved in preparing the forecast and those who will utilize the
results. Good communication at this phase will help ensure that the effort that
goes into developing the forecast results in improved decision outcomes.

The second step of the process involves specifying explicitly what to forecast.
For a traditional sales forecast, you must decide whether to forecast unit sales or
dollar sales. Should the forecast be for total sales, or sales by product line, or sales
by region? Should it include domestic sales, export sales, or both? A hospital may
want to forecast patient load, which could be defined as admissions, discharges,
patient-days, or acuity-days. In every forecasting situation, care must be taken to
carefully determine exactly what variable(s) should be forecast.

Next, two different issues that relate to the time dimensions of the forecast need
to be considered. One of these dimensions involves the length and periodicity of
the forecast. Is the forecast needed on an annual, a quarterly, a monthly, a weekly,
or a daily basis? In some situations an even shorter time period may be necessary,
such as in forecasting electricity demand for a generating facility. The second time
dimension to be considered is related to the urgency of the forecast. If there is little time available before the forecast is needed, the choice of methods that can be
used will be limited. When forecasting is established as an ongoing process, there
should be ample time to plan for the use of any forecasting technique.

The fourth element of the forecasting process involves a consideration of the
quantity and the type of data that are available. Some data may be available inter-
nally, while other data may have to be obtained from external sources. Internal
data are often the easiest to obtain, but not always. Sometimes data are not re-
tained in a form useful for a particular forecast. It is surprising how frequently we
find that data are kept only on an annual basis rather than for shorter periods such
as quarterly or monthly. Similarly, we often run into situations where only dollar

alues are available rather than units. External data are available from a wide variety of sources, some of which were discussed in Chapter 1. Most external sources provide data in both printed and electronic form.

Model selection, the fifth phase of our forecasting process, depends on a number of criteria, including:

1. The pattern exhibited by the data
2. The quantity of historic data available
3. The length of the forecast horizon

Table 2.1 summarizes how these criteria relate to the quantitative forecasting methods that are included in this text. While all of these criteria are important, the first is the most important. We will discuss the evaluation of patterns in data and model selection in greater detail after completing our review of the forecasting process.

The sixth phase of the forecasting process involves testing the models on the specific series that we want to forecast. This is often done by evaluating how each model works in a retrospective sense. That is, we see how well the results fit the historic data that were used in developing the models. Measures such as the root-mean-squared error (RMSE) are typically used for this evaluation. We often make

TABLE 2.1   A Guide to Selecting an Appropriate Forecasting Method*

Forecasting Method	Data Pattern	Quantity of Historical Data (Number of Observations)	Forecast Horizon
Naive	Stationary	1 or 2	Very short
Moving averages	Stationary	Number equal to the periods in the moving average	Very short
Exponential smoothing			
Simple	Stationary	5 to 10	Short
Adaptive response	Stationary	10 to 15	Short
Holt's	Linear trend	10 to 15	Short to medium
Winters'	Trend and seasonality	At least 4 or 5 per season	Short to medium
Bass model	S-curve	Small, 3 to 10	Medium to long
Regression-based			
Trend	Linear and nonlinear trend with or without seasonality	Minimum of 10 with 4 or 5 per season if seasonality is included	Short to medium
Causal	Can handle nearly all data patterns	Minimum of 10 per independent variable	Short, medium, and long
Time-series decomposition	Can handle trend, seasonal, and cyclical patterns	Enough to see two peaks and troughs in the cycle	Short, medium, and long
ARIMA	Stationary or transformed to stationary	Minimum of 50	Short, medium, and long

* The methods presented in this table are the most commonly used techniques. There are many other methods available, most of which are included in the ForecastX™ software that accompanies this text.

Fit refers to how well the model works retrospectively. *Accuracy* relates to how well the model works in the forecast horizon.

a distinction between *fit* and *accuracy* in evaluating a forecast model. *Fit* refers to how well the model works retrospectively. *Accuracy* relates to how well the model works in the forecast horizon (i.e., outside the period used to develop the model). When we have sufficient data, we often use a "holdout" period to evaluate forecast accuracy. For example, suppose that you have 10 years of historic quarterly sales data and want to make a two-year forecast. In developing and evaluating potential models, you might use just the first eight years of data to forecast the last two years of the historical series. RMSEs could then be calculated for the two holdout years to determine which model or models provide the most accurate forecasts. These models would then be respecified using all 10 years of historic data, and a forecast would be developed for the true forecast horizon. If the models selected in phase 6 did not yield an acceptable level of accuracy, you would return to step 5 and select an alternative model.

Phase 7, forecast preparation, is the natural result of having found models that you believe will produce acceptably accurate results. We recommend that more than one technique be used whenever possible. When two, or more, methods that have different information bases are used, their combination will frequently provide better forecasts than would either method alone. The process of combining forecasts is sufficiently important that Chapter 8 is devoted to this topic.

The eighth phase of the forecasting process involves the presentation of forecast results to those who rely on them to make decisions. Here, clear communication is critical. Sometimes technicians who develop forecasts become so enamored with the sophistication of their models that they focus on technical issues rather than on the substance of the forecast. In both written and oral presentations, the use of objective visual representations of the results is very important.[1]

Finally, the forecasting process should include continuous tracking of how well forecasts compare with the actual values observed during the forecast horizon. Over time, even the best of models are likely to deteriorate in terms of accuracy and need to be respecified, or replaced with an alternative method. Forecasters can learn from their mistakes. A careful review of forecast errors may be helpful in leading to a better understanding of what causes deviations between the actual and forecast series.

TREND, SEASONAL, AND CYCLICAL DATA PATTERNS

The data that are used most often in forecasting are time series. For example, you might have sales data by month from January 1970 through December 2005, or you might have the number of visitors to a national park every year for a 30-year period, or you might have stock prices on a daily basis for several years. These would all be examples of time-series data.

Such time series can display a wide variety of patterns when plotted over time. Displaying data in a time-series plot is an important first step in identifying

[1] An excellent discussion of how to present information in graphic form can be found in Edward R. Tufte, *The Visual Display of Quantitative Information* (Cheshire, CT: Graphics Press, 1983).

various component parts of the time series. A time series is likely to contain some, or all, of the following components:

Trend

Seasonal

Cyclical

Irregular

Let us first define and discuss each of these in general terms, and then we will look at several specific data series to see which components we can visualize through graphic analyses.

Data are considered *stationary* when there is neither a positive nor a negative trend.

The *trend* in a time series is the long-term change in the level of the data. If, over an extended period of time, the series moves upward, we say that the data show a positive trend. If the level of the data diminishes over time, there is a negative trend. Data are considered *stationary* when there is neither a positive nor a negative trend (i.e., the series is essentially flat in the long term).

A *seasonal* pattern occurs in a time series when there is a regular variation in the level of the data that repeats itself at the same time each year.

A *seasonal* pattern occurs in a time series when there is a regular variation in the level of the data that repeats itself at the same time each year. For example, ski lodges in Killington, Vermont, have very regular high occupancy rates during December, January, and February (as well as regular low occupancy rates in the spring of the year). Housing starts are always stronger in the spring and summer than during the fall and winter. Retail sales for many products tend to peak in November and December because of holiday sales. Most university enrollments are higher in the fall than in the winter or spring and are typically the lowest in the summer. All of these patterns recur with reasonable regularity year after year. No doubt you can think of many other examples of time-series data for which you would expect similar seasonal patterns.

A *cyclical* pattern is represented by wavelike upward and downward movements of the data around the long-term trend. Cyclical fluctuations are of longer duration and are less regular than are seasonal fluctuations. The causes of cyclical fluctuations are less readily apparent as well. They are usually attributed to the ups and downs in the general level of business activity that are frequently referred to as *business cycles*.

The *irregular* component of a time series contains the fluctuations that are not part of the other three components. These are often called *random* fluctuations. As such, they are the most difficult to capture in a forecasting model.

To illustrate these components, let us analyze three specific sets of data. One of these is a monthly series for the population in the United States (POP), which is an important driver for many types of business activities. POP tends to increase at a fairly constant linear rate. The second series is monthly data for total houses sold (THS), which is also important for many businesses to forecast since it drives so many other types of sales (such as drapes, furniture, appliances, etc.). THS has a lot of seasonality, some upward trend, and a cyclical component. The third series is disposable personal income (DPI, in billions of dollars), which also has a positive trend, but the trend is slightly nonlinear with DPI increasing at an increasing rate. DPI is also sometimes referred to as a prime mover because income is the revenue

FIGURE 2.1

Total Population of the U.S. in Thousands
The upper graph shows the U.S. population growth from January 1948 through April 2008. The bottom graph illustrates how closely a linear trend approximates the actual population growth. (c2f1)

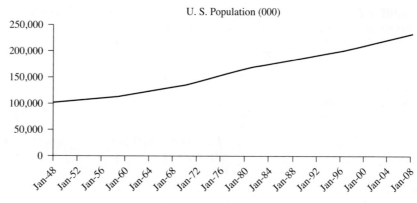

U. S. Population (000)

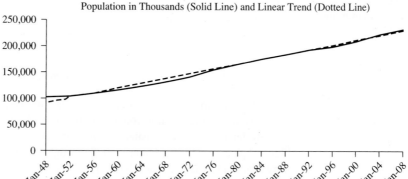

Population in Thousands (Solid Line) and Linear Trend (Dotted Line)

source for personal consumption. The integrative case at the end of this chapter involves a similar evaluation of the sales of The Gap stores.

Figure 2.1 shows a times-series plot of population on a monthly basis starting with January 1948 and ending with April 2008. From a visual inspection of this graph, it is fairly easy to see that there has been a positive trend to POP over the period shown. The long-term trend is shown by the lighter straight line in Figure 2.1. (In later chapters, you will learn how to determine an equation for this long-term trend line.) You see that population is nonstationary. Because POP is nonstationary, some models would not be appropriate in forecasting POP (see Table 2.1). Later in this chapter we will show one method that could be used to transform population to a stationary series.

Total houses sold (THS) is plotted in Figure 2.2 for the period from January 1978 through July 2007. Probably the most striking feature of this visualization of the THS data is the regular and sharp upward and downward movements that repeat year after year. This indicates a seasonal pattern, with housing sales reaching a peak in the spring of each year. Overall, there also appears to be some upward trend to the data and some cyclical movement as well.

The straight line in Figure 2.2 shows the long-term trend in the THS series. The third line, which moves above and below the long-term trend but is smoother than the plot of THS, is what the THS series looks like after the seasonality has been removed. Such a series is said to be "deseasonalized," or "seasonally adjusted"

FIGURE 2.2

Total Houses Sold by Month in Thousands: January 1978 through July 2007

The thin line shows the actual values of houses sold. The dark dashed straight line shows the long-term linear trend of total houses sold while the gray wave-like line shows the cyclical nature of home sales over time. (c2f2)

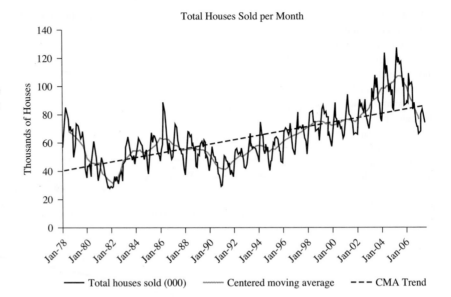

(SA). By comparing the deseasonalized series with the trend, the cyclical nature of houses sold becomes clearer. You will learn how to deseasonalize data in Chapter 6.

Now let us turn to a visual analysis of disposable personal income (DPI). Figure 2.3 shows DPI for January 1978 through June 2007. Clearly, there is an upward trend in the data, and it is a trend that appears to be accelerating slightly (i.e., becoming increasingly steep). You will learn to forecast such nonlinear trends later in this text. There does not appear to be a cyclical component to the series, and there is no seasonality. You can see in the top graph of Figure 2.3 that the linear trend would underforecast DPI beyond June 2007. However, the quadratic (nonlinear) trend in the lower graph provides a better basis for forecasting.

DATA PATTERNS AND MODEL SELECTION

The pattern that exists in the data is an important consideration in determining which forecasting techniques are appropriate.

As discussed earlier in this chapter, the pattern that exists in the data is an important consideration in determining which forecasting techniques are appropriate. On the basis only of the pattern of data, let us apply the information in Table 2.1 to determine which methods might be good candidates for forecasting each of the three specific series just discussed and plotted in Figures 2.1 through 2.3.

For POP, which has a trend but no cycle and no seasonality, the following might be most appropriate:

Holt's exponential smoothing
Linear regression trend

Total houses sold (THS) has a trend, seasonality, and a cycle. Therefore, some likely candidate models for forecasting THS would include:

Winters' exponential smoothing
Linear regression trend with seasonal adjustment

FIGURE 2.3

Disposable Personal Income in the U.S.
The dark line in the upper graph shows the actual DPI (in billions of dollars) from January 1978 through June 2007, while the lighter line in the upper graph shows a linear trend for DPI. The bottom graph illustrates how a quadratic trend approximates the actual DPI more accurately than the linear trend. (c2f3)

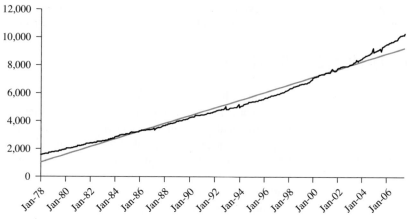

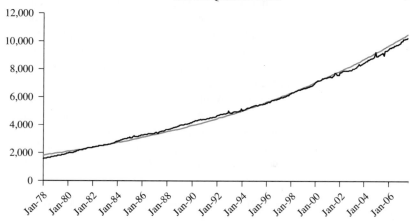

Causal regression
Time-series decomposition

The existence of a cycle component would suggest that the latter two may be the best candidates.

For disposable personal income (DPI), there is a nonlinear trend, with no seasonality and no cycle. Thus, the models most likely to be successful are:

Nonlinear regression trend
Causal regression
Holt's exponential smoothing

In subsequent chapters of the text, we will return to these series from time to time as examples. By the time you finish with the text, you will be able to develop good forecasts for series that exhibit a wide variety of data patterns. After a review of some statistical concepts, we will return to an evaluation of data patterns that goes beyond the simple, yet powerful, visualization of data and that will be of additional help in selecting appropriate forecasting techniques.

A STATISTICAL REVIEW[2]

The approach that we will take in this discussion is more intuitive than theoretical. Our intent is to help you recall a small part of what is normally covered in an introductory statistics course. We begin by discussing descriptive statistics, with an emphasis on measures of central tendency and measures of dispersion. Next we review two important statistical distributions. These topics lead to statistical inference, which involves making statements about a population based on sample statistics. We then present an overview of hypothesis testing and finish with a discussion of correlation.

Descriptive Statistics

We often want to use numbers to describe one phenomenon or another. For example, we might want to communicate information concerning the sales of fast-food restaurants in a community. Or we might want to describe the typical consumption of soft drinks in U.S. households. Or we might want to convey to someone the rate at which sales have been increasing over time. All of these call for the use of descriptive statistics.

When we want to describe the general magnitude of some variable, we can use one or more of several *measures of central tendency*. The three most common measures of central tendency are the mean, median, and mode. To grasp each of these measures, let us consider the data in Table 2.2. These data represent 25 consecutive months of computer sales for a small office-products retailer. The

TABLE 2.2
Twenty-Five Consecutive Months of Total Sales   (c2t2)

Month	Sales	Month	Sales
1	3	14	4
2	4	15	7
3	5	16	3
4	1	17	4
5	5	18	2
6	3	19	5
7	6	20	7
8	2	21	4
9	7	22	5
10	8	23	2
11	1	24	6
12	13	25	4
13	4		

[2] Students with a good statistical background may be able to skip this section.

mode is the response that occurs most frequently. If you count the number of times each value for sales is found in Table 2.2, you obtain the following results:

Sales	Number of Occurrences
1	2
2	3
3	3
4	6
5	4
6	2
7	3
8	1
13	1
Total	25

Since the largest number of occurrences is 6 (for sales of four computers), the mode is 4.

The *median* is the value that splits the responses into two equal parts when they are arrayed from smallest to largest. In this set of data, the median is 4. This is shown in the following diagram:

Responses Arrayed from Low to High

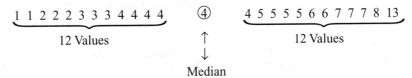

There are 12 numbers to the left of the circled 4, and 12 numbers to the right. When there are an even number of observations, the median is the midpoint of the two center values. For example, in the series 1, 4, 6, 10, the median is 5. Note that the median may be a number that is not actually in the data array.

The *mean* is the arithmetic average of all the numbers in the data set. To find the mean, add up all the values and divide by the number of observations. If the set of numbers is a population, rather than a sample, the mean is designated by the Greek mu (μ). It is calculated as:

$$\mu = \sum_{i=1}^{N} X_i/N$$

where the subscript i is used to identify each X value and

$$\sum_{i=1}^{N} X_i$$

means the sum of all the values of X_i, in which i ranges from 1 to N. X is simply a shorthand way of representing a variable. For the data in Table 2.2, $X_3 = 5$ and

$X_{15} = 7$. N represents the total number of elements, or observations, in the population. In this case $N = 25$. Adding up all 25 values, we get:

$$\sum X = 115$$

Note that we have dropped the subscript here. This will often be done to simplify the notation. The population mean is then:

$$\mu = \sum X/N = 115/25 = 4.6$$

If the data represent a sample (i.e., a portion of the entire population), the mean is designated $\overline{X}$ and the number of elements in the sample is designated n. Thus, a sample mean is:

$$\overline{X} = \sum_{i=1}^{n} X_i/n$$

If the data in Table 2.2 represented a sample of months, the mean would be calculated as:

$$\overline{X} = \sum X/n = 115/25 = 4.6$$

All three of these measures of central tendency provide some feel for what we might think of as a "typical case." For example, knowing that the median and mode for sales are both 4 and the mean is 4.6 gives you an idea about what is a typical month's sales.

These sales data are plotted over time in Figure 2.4, along with the trend line. You see in this plot that sales fluctuate around a nearly flat trend. Thus, this sales series is stationary.

We have seen that for the data in Table 2.2, the mean is 4.6, and both the mode and the median are 4.0. Note that the mean is above both of the other measures of central tendency. This can result when there is one relatively large value (in this example, the 13). That large value pulls up the mean but has little or no effect on the median or mode. Without that observation the median and mode for this example would still be 4, but the mean would be 4.25 ($4.25 = 102/24$).

FIGURE 2.4

Sales and Sales Trend
(c2f4)
For this sales series, the trend is almost perfectly flat, so that the data are stationary. Note that the level of the trend line is fairly close to the sample mean of 4.6.

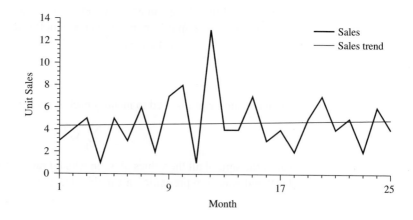

Let us now consider dispersion in data. A measure of dispersion tells us something about how spread out (or dispersed) the data are. Such information helps us to gain a clearer picture of the phenomenon being investigated than we get by looking just at a measure of central tendency. Look, for example, at the following two data sets marked *A* and *B*:

A:	18	19	20	21	22
B:	0	10	20	30	40

In both cases the mean and median are 20. (Since no value occurs more frequently than the others, there is no mode.) However, the two data sets are really very different. Measures of dispersion can be helpful in conveying such a difference.

The simplest measure of dispersion is the *range,* which is the difference between the smallest value and the greatest value. In Table 2.2 the smallest value is 1 (observations 4 and 11); the greatest is 13 (observation 12). Thus,

$$\text{Range} = \text{Greatest value} - \text{Smallest value}$$
$$= 13 - 1$$
$$= 12$$

For the two data sets *A* and *B* just given, the range for *A* is 4 and the range for *B* is 40.

Think for a moment about the different perception you get from the following two statements:

"The data set *A* has a mean of 20 and a range of values equal to 4, from 18 to 22."

"The data set *B* has a mean of 20 and a range of values equal to 40, from 0 to 40."

You can see how much your perception is affected by knowing this measure of dispersion in addition to the mean.

Two other measures of dispersion, the variance and the standard deviation, are probably the ones that are most used. The standard deviation is a measure of the "average" spread of the data around the mean. Thus, it is based on the mean and tells us how spread out the data are from the mean. The variance is the square of the standard deviation.

The calculation of sample and population standard deviations and variances can be shown in the shorthand of mathematical expressions as follows (let X_i represent the *i*th observation):

	For a Sample	For a Population
Standard deviation	$S = \sqrt{\dfrac{\sum(X_i - \bar{X})^2}{n - 1}}$	$\sigma = \sqrt{\dfrac{\sum(X_i - \mu)^2}{N}}$
Variance	$S^2 = \dfrac{\sum(X_i - \bar{X})^2}{n - 1}$	$\sigma^2 = \dfrac{\sum(X_i - \mu)^2}{N}$

For the computer sales data in Table 2.2, the calculations of the standard deviation and variance are illustrated in Table 2.3. Note that the sum of the unsquared differences between each observation and the mean is equal to zero. This is always true. Squaring the differences gets around the problem of offsetting positive and negative differences. The standard deviation for the sales data is (assuming the data represent a sample) 2.582 units around a mean of 4.6. That is, the "average" spread around the mean is 2.582. The corresponding variance is 6.667 "units squared." You can see that the interpretation of the variance is a bit awkward. What is a "squared computer"? Because of this squaring of the units of measurement,

TABLE 2.3

Calculation of the Standard Deviation and Variance for the Computer Sales Data (Assuming a Sample) (c2t3)

Observation Number	Computer Sales (X_i)	$(X_i - \bar{X})$	$(X_i - \bar{X})^2$
1	3	−1.6	2.56
2	4	−0.6	0.36
3	5	0.4	0.16
4	1	−3.6	12.96
5	5	0.4	0.16
6	3	−1.6	2.56
7	6	1.4	1.96
8	2	−2.6	6.76
9	7	2.4	5.76
10	8	3.4	11.56
11	1	−3.6	12.96
12	13	8.4	70.56
13	4	−0.6	0.36
14	4	−0.6	0.36
15	7	2.4	5.76
16	3	−1.6	2.56
17	4	−0.6	0.36
18	2	−2.6	6.76
19	5	0.4	0.16
20	7	2.4	5.76
21	4	−0.6	0.36
22	5	0.4	0.16
23	2	−2.6	6.76
24	6	1.4	1.96
25	4	−0.6	0.36
Total	115	0.0	160.00

$$\text{Mean} = \bar{X} = \frac{\Sigma X_i}{n} = \frac{115}{25} = 4.6$$

$$\text{Variance} = S^2 = \frac{\Sigma(X_i - \bar{X})^2}{n - 1} = \frac{160}{25 - 1} = 6.667$$

$$\text{Standard deviation} = S = \sqrt{\frac{\Sigma(X_i - \bar{X})^2}{n - 1}} = \sqrt{\frac{160}{24}} = \sqrt{6.667} = 2.582$$

the variance is less useful in communicating dispersion than is the standard deviation. In statistical analysis, however, the variance is frequently far more important and useful than the standard deviation. Thus, both are important to know and understand.

Look back at the two small data sets *A* and *B* referred to earlier. For both sets the mean was 20. Assuming that these are both samples, the standard deviations are:

For *A*: $S = 1.58$
For *B*: $S = 15.8$

You see that knowing both the mean and the standard deviation gives you a much better understanding of the data than you would have if you knew only the mean.

The Normal Distribution

Many statistical distributions are important for various applications. Two of them—the normal distribution and Student's *t*-distribution—are particularly useful for the applications in forecasting to be discussed in this text. In this section we will describe the normal distribution. We will consider the *t*-distribution in a later section.

The normal distribution for a continuous random variable is fully defined by just two characteristics: the mean and the variance (or standard deviation) of the variable. A graph of the normal distribution has a bell shape such as the three distributions shown in Figure 2.5.[3] All such normal distributions are symmetrical around the mean. Thus, 50 percent of the distribution is above the mean and 50 percent is below the mean. It follows that the median must equal the mean when the distribution is normal.

In Figure 2.5, the top graph represents the normal curve for a variable with a population mean of 4 and a standard deviation of 2. The middle graph is for a variable with the same mean but a standard deviation of 3. The lower graph is for a normal distribution with a mean of 6 and a standard deviation of 2. While each is unique, the three graphs have similar shapes, and they have an important common feature: for each of these graphs the shaded area represents roughly 68 percent of the area under the curve.

This brings us to an important property of all normal curves. The area between one standard deviation above the mean and one standard deviation below the mean includes approximately 68 percent of the area under the curve. Thus, if we were to draw an element at random from a population with a normal distribution, there is a 68 percent chance that it would be in the interval $\mu \pm 1\sigma$. This 68 percent is represented by the shaded areas of the graphs in Figure 2.5.

---

[3] Technically, these are probability density functions, for which the area under the curve between any two points on the horizontal axis represents the probability of observing an occurrence between those two points. For a continuous random variable, the probability of any particular value occurring is considered zero, because there are an infinite number of possible values in any interval. Thus, we discuss only probabilities that values of the variable will lie between specified pairs of points.

FIGURE 2.5

Three Normal Distributions

The top and middle distributions have the same mean but different standard deviations. The top and bottom distributions have the same standard deviation but different means.

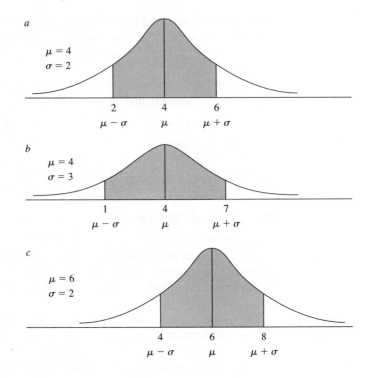

If you remember that the normal distribution is symmetrical, you will realize that 34 percent must be in the shaded area to the left of the mean and 34 percent in the shaded area to the right of the mean. Since the total area to the right (or left) of the mean is 50 percent, the area in either tail of the distribution must be the remaining 16 percent (these are the unshaded regions in the graphs in Figure 2.5).

If you extend the range to plus or minus two standard deviations from the mean, roughly 95 percent of the area would be in that interval. And if you go out three standard deviations in both directions from the mean, over 99.7 percent of the area would be included. These concepts can be summarized as follows:

$\mu \pm 1\sigma$ includes about 68% of the area

$\mu \pm 2\sigma$ includes about 95% of the area

$\mu \pm 3\sigma$ includes over 99% of the area

These three rules of thumb are helpful to remember.

In Figure 2.5 you saw three similar yet different normal distributions. How many such distributions are there? There may be billions of them. Every variable or measurement you might consider could have a different normal distribution. And yet any statistics text you look in will have just one normal distribution. The reason for this is that every other normal distribution can be transformed easily into a *standard* normal distribution called the Z-distribution. The transformation is simple:

$$Z = \frac{X - \mu}{\sigma}$$

In this way any observed value (X) can be standardized to a corresponding Z-value. The Z-value measures the number of standard deviations by which X differs from the mean. If the calculated Z-value is positive, then X lies to the right of the mean (X is larger than μ). If the calculated Z-value is negative, then X lies to the left of the mean (X is smaller than μ).

The standard normal distribution is shown in Table 2.4. Note that it is centered on zero. For every value of X there is a corresponding value for Z, which can be found by using the transformation shown in the preceding equation. For example, let us calculate the Z-values that correspond to $X = 40$ and to $X = 65$ assuming a standard deviation of 10:

$$Z = \frac{X - \mu}{\sigma}$$

For $X = 40$, $Z = \dfrac{40 - 50}{10} = -1$

For $X = 65$, $Z = \dfrac{65 - 50}{10} = 1.5$

Through this process every normal variable can be transformed to the standard normal variable Z.

The normal distribution provides a background for many types of data analysis. However, it is not typically appropriate for work with sample data, and in business we almost always have sample data. When working with sample data, we use the *t*-distribution.

The Student's *t*-Distribution

When the population standard deviation is not known, or when the sample size is small, the Student's *t*-distribution should be used rather than the normal distribution. The Student's *t*-distribution resembles the normal distribution but is somewhat more spread out for small sample sizes. As the sample size becomes very large, the two distributions become the same. Like the normal distribution, the *t*-distribution is centered at zero (i.e., has a mean of zero) and is symmetrical.

Since the *t*-distribution depends on the number of degrees of freedom (df), there are many *t*-distributions. The number of degrees of freedom appropriate for a given application depends on the specific characteristics of the analysis. Throughout this text, we will specify the value for df in each application. Table 2.5 has a *t*-distribution for 29 different degrees of freedom plus infinity. The body of this table contains *t*-values such that the shaded area in the graph is equal to the subscript on *t* at the top of each column, for the number of degrees of freedom (df) listed along the left.

TABLE 2.4 The Standard Normal Distribution*

Source: Adapted from Owen P. Hall, Jr., and Harvey M. Adelman, *Computerized Business Statistics* (Homewood, Ill.: Richard D. Irwin, 1987), p. 91.

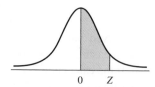

0   Z

Z	.00	.01	.02	.03	.04	.05	.06	.07	.08	.09
0.0	.0000	.0040	.0080	.0120	.0160	.0199	.0239	.0279	.0319	.0359
0.1	.0398	.0438	.0478	.0517	.0557	.0596	.0636	.0675	.0714	.0753
0.2	.0793	.0832	.0871	.0910	.0948	.0987	.1026	.1064	.1103	.1141
0.3	.1179	.1217	.1255	.1293	.1331	.1368	.1406	.1443	.1480	.1517
0.4	.1554	.1591	.1628	.1664	.1700	.1736	.1772	.1808	.1844	.1879
0.5	.1915	.1950	.1985	.2109	.2054	.2088	.2123	.2157	.2190	.2224
0.6	.2257	.2291	.2324	.2357	.2389	.2422	.2454	.2486	.2518	.2549
0.7	.2580	.2612	.2642	.2673	.2704	.2734	.2764	.2794	.2823	.2852
0.8	.2881	.2910	.2939	.2967	.2995	.3023	.2051	.3078	.3106	.3133
0.9	.3159	.3186	.3212	.3238	.3264	.3289	.3315	.3340	.3365	.3389
1.0	.3413	.3438	.3461	.3485	.3508	.3531	.3554	.3577	.3599	.3621
1.1	.3643	.3665	.3686	.3708	.3729	.3749	.3770	.3790	.3810	.3830
1.2	.3849	.3869	.3888	.3907	.3925	.3944	.3962	.3980	.3997	.4015
1.3	.4032	.4049	.4066	.4082	.4099	.4115	.4131	.4147	.4162	.4177
1.4	.4192	.4207	.4222	.4236	.4251	.4265	.4279	.4292	.4306	.4319
1.5	.4332	.4345	.4357	.4370	.4382	.4394	.4406	.4418	.4429	.4441
1.6	.4452	.4463	.4474	.4484	.4495	.4505	.4515	.4525	.4535	.4545
1.7	.4554	.4564	.4573	.4582	.4591	.4599	.4608	.4616	.4625	.4633
1.8	.4641	.4649	.4656	.4664	.4671	.4678	.4686	.4693	.4699	.4706
1.9	.4713	.4719	.4726	.4732	.4738	.4744	.4750	.4756	.4761	.4767
2.0	.4772	.4778	.4783	.4788	.4793	.4798	.4803	.4808	.4812	.4817
2.1	.4821	.4826	.4830	.4834	.4838	.4842	.4846	.4850	.4854	.4857
2.2	.4861	.4864	.4868	.4871	.4875	.4878	.4881	.4884	.4887	.4890
2.3	.4893	.4896	.4898	.4901	.4904	.4906	.4909	.4911	.4913	.4916
2.4	.4918	.4920	.4922	.4925	.4927	.4929	.4931	.4932	.4934	.4936
2.5	.4938	.4940	.4941	.4943	.4945	.4946	.4948	.4949	.4951	.4952
2.6	.4953	.4955	.4956	.4957	.4959	.4960	.4961	.4962	.4963	.4964
2.7	.4965	.4966	.4967	.4968	.4969	.4970	.4971	.4972	.4973	.4974
2.8	.4974	.4975	.4976	.4977	.4977	.4978	.4979	.4979	.4980	.4981
2.9	.4981	.4982	.4982	.4983	.4984	.4984	.4985	.4985	.4986	.4986
3.0	.49865	.4987	.4987	.4988	.4988	.4989	.4989	.4989	.4990	.4990
4.0	.49997									

* Z is the standard normal variable. Other variables can be transformed to Z as follows:

$$Z = \frac{X - \mu}{\sigma}$$

For $Z = 1.96$, the shaded area in the distribution is 0.4750 (found at the intersection of the 1.9 row and the .06 column).

TABLE 2.5
Student's
*t***-Distribution***

Source: Adapted from Owen
P. Hall, Jr., and Harvey M.
Adelman, *Computerized Business Statistics* (Homewood, Ill.:
Richard D. Irwin, 1987), p. 93.

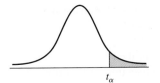

t_α

df	$t_{.100}$	$t_{.050}$	$t_{.025}$	$t_{.010}$	$t_{.005}$
1	3.078	6.314	12.706	31.821	63.657
2	1.886	2.920	4.303	6.965	9.925
3	1.638	2.353	3.182	4.541	5.841
4	1.533	2.132	2.776	3.747	4.604
5	1.476	2.015	2.571	3.365	4.032
6	1.440	1.943	2.447	3.143	3.707
7	1.415	1.895	2.365	2.998	3.499
8	1.397	1.860	2.306	2.896	3.355
9	1.383	1.833	2.262	2.821	3.250
10	1.372	1.812	2.228	2.764	3.169
11	1.363	1.796	2.201	2.718	3.106
12	1.356	1.782	2.179	2.681	3.055
13	1.350	1.771	2.160	2.650	3.012
14	1.345	1.761	2.145	2.624	2.977
15	1.341	1.753	2.131	2.602	2.947
16	1.337	1.746	2.120	2.583	2.921
17	1.333	1.740	2.110	2.567	2.898
18	1.330	1.734	2.101	2.552	2.878
19	1.328	1.729	2.093	2.539	2.861
20	1.325	1.725	2.086	2.528	2.845
21	1.323	1.721	2.080	2.518	2.831
22	1.321	1.717	2.074	2.508	2.819
23	1.319	1.714	2.069	2.500	2.807
24	1.318	1.711	2.064	2.492	2.797
25	1.316	1.708	2.060	2.485	2.787
26	1.315	1.706	2.056	2.479	2.779
27	1.314	1.703	2.052	2.473	2.771
28	1.313	1.701	2.048	2.467	2.763
29	1.311	1.699	2.045	2.462	2.756
Inf.	1.282	1.645	1.960	2.326	2.576

*The *t*-distribution is used for standardizing when the population standard deviation is unknown and the sample standard
deviation is used in its place.

$$t = \frac{\overline{X} - \mu}{s/\sqrt{n}}$$

To learn how to read the *t*-table, let us consider three examples. First, what value of *t* would correspond to 5 percent of the area in the shaded region if there are 15 degrees of freedom? To answer this, go to the row for 15 degrees of freedom, then to the column that has .050 for the subscript on *t*. The *t*-value at the intersection of that row and column is 1.753. Second, if there are 26 degrees of freedom and the *t*-value is 2.479, how much area would be in the shaded region? Looking across the row for 26 degrees of freedom, we see that 2.479 is in the column for which *t* is subscripted with .010. Thus, 1 percent of the area would be in that tail.

For our third example, consider the following question: If there are 85 degrees of freedom, what value of *t* would be associated with finding 97.5 percent of the area in the unshaded portion of the curve? For any number of degrees of freedom greater than 29, we would use the infinity (Inf.) row of the table. If we want 97.5 percent in the clear area, then 2.5 percent must be in the shaded region. Thus, we need the column for which *t* is subscripted with .025. The *t*-value at the intersection of this row and column is found to be 1.960. (Note that this is the same as the *Z*-value for which 2.5 percent would be in the tail, or 0.4750 is in the shaded section of the normal distribution shown in Table 2.4.)

While *t*-tables are usually limited to four or five areas in the tail of the distribution and perhaps 30 levels for degrees of freedom, most statistical software incorporates the equation for the *t*-distribution and will give exact areas, given any *t*-value and the appropriate number of degrees of freedom. *We will rely on the t-distribution extensively in Chapters 4 and 5 as part of the evaluation of statistical significance in regression models.*

From Sample to Population: Statistical Inference

We are usually much less interested in a sample than in the population from which the sample is drawn. The reason for looking at a sample is almost always to provide a basis for making some inference about the whole population. For example, suppose we are interested in marketing a new service in Oregon and want to know something about the income per person in the state. Over 3.5 million people live in Oregon. Clearly, trying to contact all of them to determine the mean income per person would be impractical and very costly. Instead we might select a sample and make an inference about the population based on the responses of the people in that sample of Oregon residents.

A sample statistic is our best point estimate of the corresponding population parameter. While it is best, it is also likely to be wrong. Thus, in making an inference about a population it is usually desirable to make an interval estimate.

For example, an interval estimate of the population mean is one that is centered on the sample mean and extends above and below that value by an amount that is determined by how confident we want to be, by how large a sample we have, and by the variability in the data. These elements are captured in the following equation for a confidence interval:

$$\mu = \overline{X} \pm t(s/\sqrt{n})$$

The ratio $s/\sqrt{n}$ is called the standard error of the sample mean and measures dispersion for sample means. The *t*-value is determined from Table 2.5 after choosing the number of degrees of freedom ($n - 1$ in this case), and the level of confidence we desire as reflected by the area in the shaded tail of the distribution.

If we want a 95 percent confidence interval that is symmetrical around the mean, we would want a total of 5 percent in the two extreme tails of the distribution. Thus, 2.5 percent would be in each tail. The following diagram will help you see this:

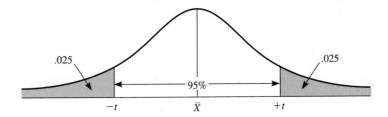

The *t*-value that would correspond to 2.5 percent in each tail can be determined from Table 2.5, given the appropriate number of degrees of freedom. Several examples follow:

Number of Degrees of Freedom	t-Value for 95% Confidence Interval
5	2.571
10	2.228
20	2.086
50	1.960
100	1.960

Suppose that a sample of 100 responses gives a mean of $25,000 and a standard deviation of $5,000. Our best point estimate for the population mean would be $25,000, and a 95 percent confidence interval would be:

$$\mu = 25{,}000 \pm 1.96(5{,}000/\sqrt{100})$$
$$= 25{,}000 \pm 980$$

that is,

$$24{,}020 \le \mu \le 25{,}980$$

See if you can correctly find the endpoints for a 90 percent confidence interval given this same set of sample results.[4]

---

[4] The lower bound is $24,177.5; the upper bound is $25,822.5. Notice that at this lower confidence level the value of *t* is smaller (other things equal) and thus the confidence interval is narrower.

Hypothesis Testing

Frequently we have a theory or hypothesis that we would like to evaluate statistically. For example, we might hypothesize that the mean expenditure on entertainment in some city is equal to the national average for all age groups. Or we may theorize that consumption of soft drinks by retired people is less than the national level. Or we may want to evaluate the assumption that women professionals work more than the standard 40-hour work week. All of these can be evaluated by using an appropriate hypothesis testing procedure.

The process begins by setting up two hypotheses, the null hypothesis (designated H_0:) and the alternative hypothesis (designated H_1:). These two hypotheses should be structured so that they are mutually exclusive and exhaustive. For example, if we hypothesize that the mean expenditure on entertainment by people in some city is different from the national average, the null and alternative hypotheses would be (let μ_0 = the national average and μ = this city's population mean):

Case I
$$\begin{cases} H_0: & \mu = \mu_0 \\ \text{i.e., } H_0: & \text{The city mean equals the national mean.} \\ H_1: & \mu \neq \mu_0 \\ \text{i.e., } H_1: & \text{The city mean is not equal to the national mean.} \end{cases}$$

If we theorize that the consumption of soft drinks by retired people is *less* than the national average, the null and alternative hypotheses would be (let μ_0 = the national average and μ = the mean for retired people):

Case II
$$\begin{cases} H_0: & \mu \geq \mu_0 \\ \text{i.e., } H_0: & \text{The mean for retired people is greater than or} \\ & \text{equal to the national average.} \\ H_1: & \mu < \mu_0 \\ \text{i.e., } H_1: & \text{The mean for retired people is less than the} \\ & \text{national average.} \end{cases}$$

If we want to evaluate the assumption that women professionals work *more* than the standard 40-hour work week, the null and alternative hypotheses would be (let μ_0 = the standard work week and μ = the mean for professional women):

Case III
$$\begin{cases} H_0: & \mu \leq \mu_0 \\ \text{i.e., } H_0: & \text{The mean for professional women is less than} \\ & \text{or equal to the standard.} \\ H_1: & \mu > \mu_0 \\ \text{i.e., } H_1: & \text{The mean for professional women is greater} \\ & \text{than the standard.} \end{cases}$$

In each of these cases the null and alternative hypotheses are mutually exclusive and exhaustive.

In statistical hypothesis testing, the approach is to see whether you find sufficient evidence to reject the null hypothesis. If so, the alternative is found to have

The process begins by setting up two hypotheses, the null hypothesis (designated H_0:) and the alternative hypothesis (designated H_1:). These two hypotheses should be structured so that they are mutually exclusive and exhaustive.

TABLE 2.6
Type I and Type II Errors

Statistical Decision	The Truth	
	H_0: Is True	H_0: Is Not True
Reject H_0:	Type I error	No error
Fail to Reject H_0:	No error	Type II error

support. For questions of the type we are considering, this is done by using a *t*-test. To perform a *t*-test, we must first determine how confident we want to be in our decision regarding whether or not to reject the null hypothesis. In most business applications a 95 percent confidence level is used. A measure that is closely related to the confidence level is the significance level for the test. The significance level, often denoted α (alpha), is equal to 1 minus the confidence level. Thus, a 95 percent confidence level is the same as a 5 percent significance level. The significance level is the probability of rejecting the null hypothesis when in fact it is true.

In testing hypotheses, there are four possible outcomes, two of which are good and two of which are bad. These are summarized in Table 2.6. If we reject H_0: when in fact it is true, we have what is termed a *type I error*. The other possible error results when we fail to reject a null hypothesis that is in fact incorrect. This is a *type II error*. These two errors are related in that by reducing the chance of a type I error we increase the chance of a type II error and vice versa. Most of the time, greater attention is given to type I errors. The probability of making a type I error is determined by the significance level (α) we select for the hypothesis test. If the cost of a type I error is large, we would use a low α, perhaps 1 percent or less.

Hypothesis tests may be one- or two-tailed tests. When the sign in the alternative hypothesis is an unequal sign ($\neq$), the test is a two-tailed test. Otherwise, a one-tailed test is appropriate. For a two-tailed test the significance level (α) is split equally into the two tails of the distribution. For a one-tailed test the entire significance level (α) goes in the one tail of the distribution that is indicated by the direction of the inequality sign in the alternative hypothesis. Consider the three situations described a few paragraphs back. These are summarized in the following diagrams, which show where the significance level would be (a 5 percent significance level is used in all three cases).

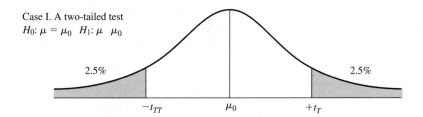

Case I. A two-tailed test
$H_0: \mu = \mu_0$ $H_1: \mu \neq \mu_0$

2.5%   2.5%

$-t_{TT}$ μ_0 $+t_T$

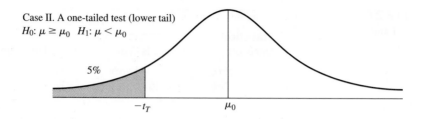

Case II. A one-tailed test (lower tail)
$H_0: \mu \geq \mu_0$ $H_1: \mu < \mu_0$

5%

$-t_T$ μ_0

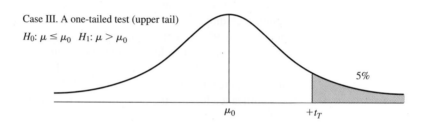

Case III. A one-tailed test (upper tail)
$H_0: \mu \leq \mu_0$ $H_1: \mu > \mu_0$

5%

μ_0 $+t_T$

The t_T values are determined from a t-distribution, such as that in Table 2.5, at the appropriate number of degrees of freedom ($n - 1$, in the examples used here) and for the tail areas indicated in these diagrams ($\alpha/2$ for two-tailed tests and α for one-tailed tests).

For each hypothesis test, a t-value is calculated (t_{calc}) and compared with the critical value from the t-distribution (t_T). If the calculated value is further into the tail of the distribution than the table value, we have an observation that is extreme, given the assumption inherent in H_0, and so H_0 is rejected. That is, we have sufficient evidence to reject the null hypothesis (H_0) when the *absolute value* of t_{calc} is greater than t_T. Otherwise we fail to reject the premise in H_0.

The calculated t-statistic is found as follows:

$$t_{calc} = \frac{\overline{X} - \mu_0}{s/\sqrt{n}}$$

where $\overline{X}$ is our sample mean and our best point estimate of μ. The value we are testing against is μ_0. The sample standard deviation is s and the sample size is n.

Let us now apply these concepts to our three situations. Starting with case I, let us assume that a sample of 49 people resulted in a mean of $200 per month with a standard deviation of $84. The national average is $220 per month. The hypotheses are:

$$H_0: \mu = 220$$
$$H_1: \mu \neq 220$$

The calculated value is:

$$t_{calc} = \frac{200 - 220}{84/\sqrt{49}} = \frac{-20}{12} = -1.67$$

If we want a 95 percent confidence level ($\alpha = 0.05$), the critical or table value of t is ± 1.96. Notice that the $t_{.025}$ column of Table 2.5 was used. This is because we have a two-tailed test, and the α of 0.05 is split equally between the two tails. Since our calculated t-value (t_{calc}) has an absolute value that is less than the critical value from the t-table (t_T), we fail to reject the null hypothesis. Thus, we conclude that the evidence from this sample is not sufficient to say that entertainment expenditures by people in this city are any different from the national average.

This result is summarized in the following diagram:

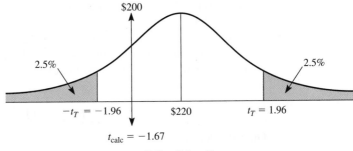

We see here that the observed mean of $200 or its corresponding t-value (-1.67) is not extreme. That is, it does not fall into either of the shaded areas. These shaded areas taken together are often called the *rejection region*, because t_{calc} values in the shaded areas would call for rejection of H_0.

Let us now look at case II. Assume that for a sample of 25 retired people the mean was 1.2 six-packs per week with a standard deviation of 0.6. The national average (μ_0) is 1.5. The hypotheses are:

$$H_0: \mu \geq 1.5$$
$$H_1: \mu < 1.5$$

The calculated t-value is:

$$t_{calc} = \frac{1.2 - 1.5}{0.6/\sqrt{25}} = \frac{-0.3}{0.12} = -2.50$$

The critical value from the t-distribution in Table 2.5, assuming a 95 percent confidence level ($\alpha = 0.05$), is $t_T = -1.711$. Note that there are 24 degrees of freedom. Since the absolute value of t_{calc} is greater than the table value of t, we reject H_0. Thus, we conclude that there is sufficient evidence to support the notion that retired people consume fewer soft drinks than the national average.

This result is shown in graphic form as follows:

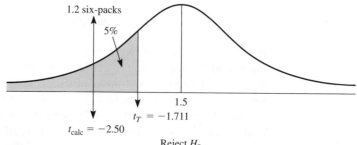

Here we see that the sample mean of 1.2 is extreme, given $\alpha = 0.05$ and $df = 24$, and so we reject H_0. The calculated value of t falls in the rejection region.

Finally, let us consider case III. We will assume that we have a sample of 144 professional women and that the mean number of hours per week worked for that sample is 45 with a sample standard deviation of 29. The national norm is the 40-hour work week. The hypotheses are:

$$H_0: \mu \leq 40$$
$$H_1: \mu > 40$$

Our calculated t-value is:

$$t_{calc} = \frac{45 - 40}{29/\sqrt{144}} = \frac{5}{2.42} = 2.07$$

The relevant table value is 1.645 ($\alpha = 0.05$ and $df = 143$). Since $T_{calc} > t_T$, we reject the null hypothesis and conclude that the mean for professional women is greater than 40 hours per week.

This result is shown graphically as follows:

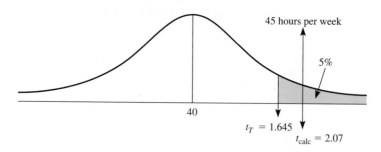

The calculated t-value lies in the shaded (or rejection) region, and so H_0 is rejected.

The t-tests illustrated in this section involved making judgments about a population mean based on information from a sample. In each t-test, the calculated value of t was determined by dividing some difference $(\overline{X} - \mu_0)$ by a standard error $(s/\sqrt{n})$. All t-statistics are calculated in this general way:

$$t = \frac{\text{the difference being evaluated}}{\text{the corresponding standard error}}$$

We will use this general form later in this chapter as well as in subsequent chapters of the text when t-tests are appropriate.

There are other statistical tests and other distributions that are applicable to forecasting. These include F-tests, Durbin-Watson tests, and chi-square tests, which will be discussed later in the text as they are applied. If you have a basic understanding of the use of t-tests, these other statistical tests will not be difficult to use.

Correlation

It is often useful to have a measure of the degree of association between two variables. For example, if you believe that sales may be affected by expenditures on advertising, you might want to measure the degree of association between sales and advertising. One measure of association that is often used is the Pearson product-moment correlation coefficient, which is designated ρ (rho) for a population and r for a sample. There are other measures of correlation, but Pearson's is the most common and the most useful for the type of data encountered in forecasting situations. Thus, when we refer to correlation or a correlation coefficient, we mean the Pearson product-moment correlation.

There are several alternative ways to write the algebraic expression for the correlation coefficient. For our purposes the following is the most instructive:

$$r = \frac{\Sigma(X - \overline{X})(Y - \overline{Y})}{\sqrt{[\Sigma(X - \overline{X})^2][\Sigma(Y - \overline{Y})^2]}}$$

where X and Y represent the two variables of interest (e.g., advertising and sales). This is the sample correlation coefficient. The calculation of the population correlation coefficient (ρ) is strictly analogous except that the population means for X and Y would be used rather than the sample means. It is important to note that the correlation coefficient defined here measures the degree of linear association between X and Y.

The correlation coefficient can have any value in the range from -1 to $+1$. A perfect positive correlation would be $r = +1$, while a perfect negative correlation would be $r = -1$. These cases are shown in scatterplots A and B of Figure 2.6. You can see that when there is a perfect correlation (positive or negative) all of the data points fall along a straight line.

In scatterplot C it appears that in general when X increases, Y_C increases as well. That is, there appears to be a positive (or direct) association between X and Y_C. However, all five points do not fall along a single straight line, and so there is not a perfect linear association. In this case the correlation coefficient is $+0.79$. Scatterplot D shows a negative (or inverse) association between X and Y_D, but one that is not perfectly linear. For scatterplot D, $r = -0.89$.

FIGURE 2.6   **Representative Scatterplots with the Corresponding Correlation Coefficients**
These scatterplots show correlation coefficients that range from a perfect positive correlation (*A*) and a perfect negative correlation (*B*) to zero correlations (*E* and *F*).

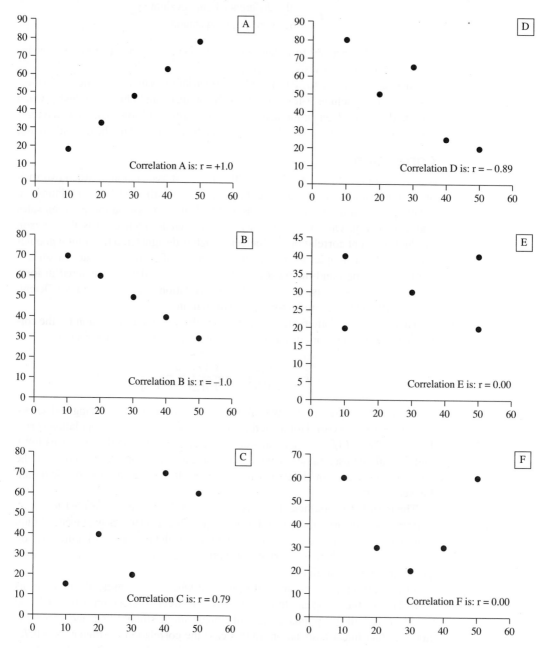

The remaining two scatterplots in Figure 2.6 illustrate cases for which the correlation coefficient is zero. In both cases there is no linear association between the variables. However, note that in panel F there is a clear nonlinear association between X and Y_F.

We could perform a hypothesis test to determine whether the value of a sample correlation coefficient (r) gives us reason to believe that the true population correlation coefficient (ρ) is significantly different from zero. If it is not, then there would be no linear association between the two measures. The hypothesis test would be:

$$H_0: \rho = 0$$
$$H_1: \rho \neq 0$$

and t would be calculated as:

$$t = \frac{r - 0}{\sqrt{(1 - r^2)/(n - 2)}}$$

where $\sqrt{(1 - r^2)/(n - 2)}$ is the standard error of r.

Let us apply this to the data in scatterplots C and D of Figure 2.6. In both of these cases, for a two-tailed test, with $\alpha = 0.05$ and $n = 5$, the table value of t_T is 3.182 (there are $n - 2$, or 3 degrees of freedom for this test). For panel C the calculated value of t is:

$$t_{\text{calc}} = \frac{0.79 - 0}{\sqrt{[1 - (0.79)^2]/(5 - 2)}}$$

$$= \frac{0.79}{\sqrt{0.3759/3}} = \frac{0.79}{\sqrt{0.1253}} = -2.2318$$

Since t_{calc} is in the interval between $\pm t_T$ (i.e., ± 3.182), we would fail to reject the null hypothesis on the basis of a sample of five observations at a 95 percent confidence level ($\alpha = 0.05$). Thus, we conclude that there is not enough evidence to say that ρ is different from zero. While the $r = 0.79$ is a fairly strong correlation, we are not able to say it is significantly different from zero in this case, largely because we have such a small sample. If $n = 50$ and $r = 0.79$, the calculated value for t would be 26.06, and the table value would be 1.96, so that the null hypothesis would be rejected.

For the data in panel D, the calculated value of t is:

$$t_{\text{calc}} = \frac{-0.89 - 0}{\sqrt{(1 - 0.89^2)/(5 - 2)}} = -3.3808$$

Since this t_{calc} is not in the interval between $\pm t_T$, we would reject H_0 and would conclude that we do have enough evidence to suggest that ρ is different from zero (at a 95 percent confidence level, or $\alpha = 0.05$, and on the basis of a sample of five observations).

CORRELOGRAMS: ANOTHER METHOD
OF DATA EXPLORATION

In evaluating a time series of data, it is useful to look at the correlation between successive observations over time. This measure of correlation is called an *autocorrelation*.

In evaluating a time series of data, it is useful to look at the correlation between successive observations over time. This measure of correlation is called an *autocorrelation* and may be calculated as follows:

$$r_k = \frac{\sum_{t=1}^{n-k}(Y_{t-k} - \bar{Y})(Y_t - \bar{Y})}{\sum_{t-1}^{n}(Y_t - \bar{Y})^2}$$

where:

r_k = Autocorrelation for a k-period lag
Y_t = Value of the time series at period t
Y_{t-k} = Value of time series k periods before period t
$\bar{Y}$ = Mean of the time series

If the time series is stationary, the value of r_k should diminish rapidly toward zero as k increases. If, on the other hand, there is a trend, r_k will decline toward zero slowly. If a seasonal pattern exists, the value of r_k may be significantly different from zero at $k = 4$ for quarterly data, or $k = 12$ for monthly data. (For quarterly data, r_k for $k = 8, k = 12, k = 16, \ldots$ may also be large. For monthly data, a large r_k may also be found for $k = 24, k = 36$, etc.)

A k-period plot of autocorrelations is called an *autocorrelation function* (ACF), or a *correlogram*. We will look at a number of such graphics as we further analyze disposable personal income, total houses sold, and The Gap data.

To determine whether the autocorrelation at lag k is significantly different from zero, the following hypothesis test and rule of thumb may be used:

$$H_0: \rho_k = 0$$
$$H_1: \rho_k \neq 0$$

For any k, reject H_0 if $|r_k| > 2/\sqrt{n}$, where n is the number of observations. This rule of thumb is for a 95 percent confidence level.[5]

The use of autocorrelations and correlograms can be illustrated by looking at some of the data used earlier in this chapter. Let us begin with the disposable personal income (DPI) data graphed in Figure 2.7. From that plot it is clear that DPI has a fairly strong positive trend, so that we might expect high autocorrelation coefficients. The month-to-month change in DPI (ΔDPI) is shown along with DPI

[5] The complete t-test would be to reject H_0 if $|t_{calc}| > t_T$, where:

$$t_{calc} = \frac{(r_k - 0)}{1/\sqrt{(n-k)}}$$

and t_T is from the t-table for $\alpha/2$ and $n - k$ degrees of freedom (n = number of observations, k = period of the lag).

FIGURE 2.7
DPI and Change in DPI
We see that there is a strong positive trend in DPI, but the month-to-month change has little trend. (c2f7)

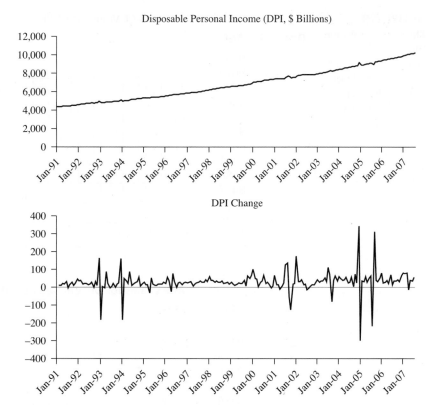

in Figure 2.7. While there is a great deal of fluctuation in ΔDPI, the series is much more flat than are the data for DPI.

The autocorrelation structures of DPI and ΔDPI are shown in Figure 2.8. For DPI 199 observations were used. Thus, $2/\sqrt{n} = 2/\sqrt{199} = 0.142$. Since all of the autocorrelation coefficients in Figure 2.8 are greater than 0.142, we can conclude, by our rule of thumb, that they are all significantly different from zero. Therefore, we have additional evidence of a trend in the GDP data.[6] The

[6] The more formal hypothesis test is:

$$H_0: \rho_k = 0$$
$$H_1: \rho_k \neq 0$$

and the calculated *t*-ratio is:

$$t_{calc} = \frac{r_k - 0}{1/\sqrt{n-k}}$$

For example, for $k = 12$ where $r_k = 0.8124$,

$$t_{calc} = \frac{0.8124 - 0}{1/\sqrt{199-12}} = 11.109$$

which is greater than the table value of 1.96 at $\alpha/2 = 0.025$ (a 95 percent confidence level).

FIGURE 2.8

The ACF Graphs for DPI and ΔDPI
From the upper graph we see evidence that DPI does have a positive trend. The lower graph suggests that DPI is stationary. (c2f8)

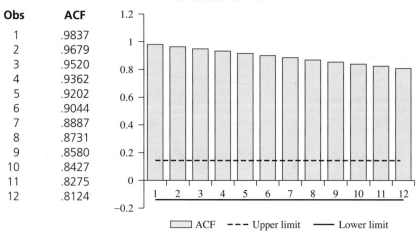

ACF Values for DPI

Obs	ACF
1	.9837
2	.9679
3	.9520
4	.9362
5	.9202
6	.9044
7	.8887
8	.8731
9	.8580
10	.8427
11	.8275
12	.8124

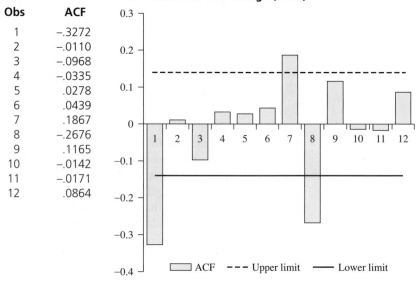

ACF Values for DPI Change (ΔDPI)

Obs	ACF
1	−.3272
2	−.0110
3	−.0968
4	−.0335
5	.0278
6	.0439
7	.1867
8	−.2676
9	.1165
10	−.0142
11	−.0171
12	.0864

actual 95 percent confidence interval is shown by the two horizontal lines labeled "Upper limit" and "Lower limit."

If we want to try a forecasting method for DPI that requires stationary data, we must first transform the DPI data to a stationary series. Often this can be done by using first differences. For DPI, the first differences can be calculated as:

$$\Delta DPI_t = DPI_t - DPI_{t-1}$$

where ΔDPI_t is the first difference (or change) in DPI. We can check for stationarity in ΔDPI by examining the autocorrelation structure for ΔDPI as shown in Figure 2.8. For ΔDPI the autocorrelations are nearly all within the upper and lower bounds, so this series is stationary.

TOTAL HOUSES SOLD: EXPLORATORY DATA ANALYSIS AND MODEL SELECTION

Let us apply exploratory data analysis techniques to the total houses sold data that were introduced in Chapter 1 and that will be used as a running example throughout the text. Figure 2.9 shows the raw data for total houses sold (THS) and a trend line. In this plot we see several things of interest. First, there appear to be fairly regular, sharp up-and-down movements that may be a reflection of seasonality in THS. Second, the long-term trend appears positive. The autocorrelation structure of THS is shown in Figure 2.10.

We see that the autocorrelations for THS do not fall quickly to zero. The autocorrelation coefficients are all significantly different from zero. Thus, we have evidence of a significant trend in THS. We also show the ACF for the month-to-month change of THS in Figure 2.10.

From this exploratory analysis of the total houses sold, we can conclude that there is trend and seasonality. From Table 2.1 we can, therefore, suggest the following as potential forecasting methods for total houses sold:

Winters' exponential smoothing

Regression trend with seasonality

FIGURE 2.9

Total Houses Sold

This graph shows total houses sold (in thousands) by month from January 1991 through July 2007, along with the long-term upward trend.   (c2f9)

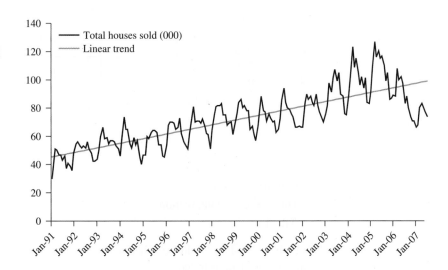

FIGURE 2.10

ACF Values for Total Houses Sold and Changes in Total Houses Sold

All coefficients are outside the 95 percent confidence band indicating the positive trend in THS.

For the change in THS the coefficients fall quickly and are mainly within the 95 percent confidence band indicating no trend in the month-to-month changes in THS. (c2f10)

Obs	ACF
1	0.9134
2	0.8286
3	0.7395
4	0.6718
5	0.6526
6	0.6211
7	0.6321
8	0.6330
9	0.6659
10	0.7208
11	0.7646
12	0.7905

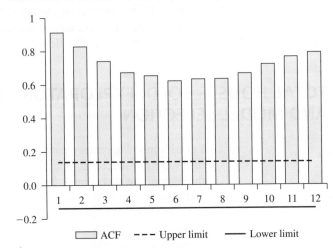

ACF Values for Total Houses Sold (000)

Obs	ACF
1	.0256
2	.0686
3	−.1476
4	−.3378
5	.0844
6	−.3006
7	.0780
8	−.2498
9	−.1337
10	.0650
11	.1061
12	.6161

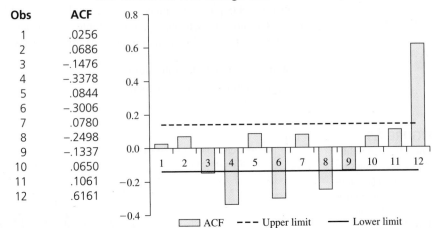

ACF Values for THS Change (First Differences)

Causal regression

Time-series decomposition

ARIMA

Note that ARIMA is included, since the data could be transformed to a stationary state, as was demonstrated.

Charles W. Chase, Jr.

Current literature and experience dictate that the best forecasting system provides easy access, review, and modification of forecast results across all corporate disciplines; provides alternative modeling capabilities (multidimensional); includes the ability to create a knowledge base by which future forecasts can be refined; and provides timely and accurate automated link/feed interfaces with other systems such as I.R.I.

(Information Resources Inc.)/Nielsen syndicated databases and the mainframe shipment database. The present industry trend has been redirected away from mainframe systems toward PC-based software applications due to the lack of flexibility associated with mainframe access and reporting. Mainframes are being utilized primarily as storage bins for PC-based systems to extract and store information.

Source: *Journal of Business Forecasting* 11, no. 3 (Fall 1992), pp. 12–13. Reprinted by permission.

Integrative Case

The Gap

PART 2: DATA ANALYSIS OF THE GAP SALES DATA

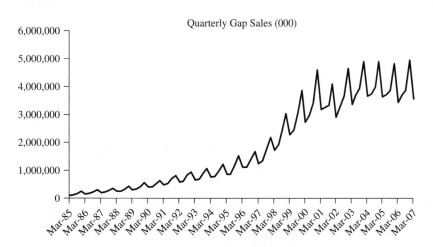

Quarterly Gap Sales (000)

From this graph it is clear that The Gap sales are seasonal and increased until about 2001. There does not appear to be a cycle. (c2Gap)

Case
Questions

1. In 2006, The Gap sales by quarter were as given below:

Quarter	Gap Sales ($000)
2006Q1	3,441,000
2006Q2	3,716,000
2006Q3	3,856,000
2006Q4	4,930,000

Based on these data, calculate a 95 percent confidence interval for quarterly sales of The Gap.

2. The Gap sales on an annual basis are shown in the following table.

Date	Annual Gap Sales ($000)
Dec-85	701,598
Dec-86	899,089
Dec-87	1,092,309
Dec-88	1,320,674
Dec-89	1,679,039
Dec-90	2,021,712
Dec-91	2,617,457
Dec-92	3,015,125
Dec-93	3,403,769
Dec-94	3,819,955
Dec-95	4,659,714
Dec-96	5,402,426
Dec-97	6,996,351
Dec-98	9,612,504
Dec-99	12,089,654
Dec-00	14,121,126
Dec-01	13,559,057
Dec-02	14,916,640
Dec-03	16,168,584
Dec-04	16,224,939
Dec-05	15,838,000
Dec-06	16,060,000

Plot these data in a time-series plot. Based on this graph, what pattern do you see in The Gap's annual sales?

3. Using data for 1985Q1 through 2007Q1, calculate the autocorrelation coefficients for The Gap's quarterly sales (the quarterly data are in Table 1.6 and in the C2Gap.xls data file) using twelve lags, and construct the corresponding correlogram (plot of the autocorrelations) for lags of 1 through 12. What do the autocorrelation coefficients and the correlogram tell you about the series?

4. Based on the plot of The Gap sales, on what you learned from question 3, as well as the information in Table 2.1, what forecasting methods might you suggest if you were to forecast The Gap's quarterly sales?

Solutions to Case Questions

1. The 95 percent confidence interval is calculated as:

Mean of The Gap Sales $\pm t$(Standard Deviation of The Gap Sales $\div \sqrt{n}$)

In this case, $n = 4$ and $df = n - 1$, so $df = 3$ and the corresponding value of t is 3.182 (see Table 2.5).

$$3,985,750 \pm 3.182(652,676.73 \div \sqrt{4})$$
$$3,985,750 \pm 1,038,408.68$$
$$2,947,341.32 \text{ to } 5,024,158.68$$

2. The plot of annual The Gap sales shown below indicates that there is a positive trend to its sales over time.

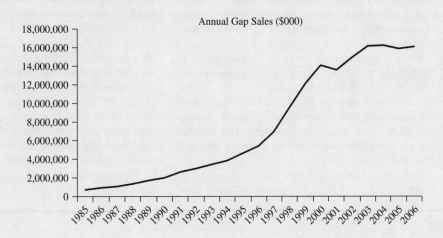

Annual Gap Sales ($000)

3. As you see from the autocorrelations and correlogram below, the autocorrelations decline gradually. Thus, we have further evidence of a trend in The Gap data.

ACF for Quarterly Gap Sales ($000)

(c2Gap)

Obs	ACF
1	.9247
2	.8838
3	.8721
4	.9069
5	.8327
6	.7874
7	.7711
8	.7967
9	.7214
10	.6710
11	.6489
12	.6665

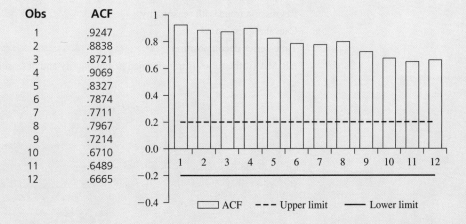

ANCHORAGE ECONOMIC DEVELOPMENT CENTER SECURES TIME-SAVING FORECASTING ACCURACY

AEDC (Anchorage Economic Development Center) is a private, nonprofit corporation that has been in operation since 1987, and is seeking to improve the economic conditions in Anchorage by expanding value-added industries, increasing business services, and developing tourism. The AEDC needed to accurately forecast the economic outlook for such industries as mining, government, finance, insurance, real estate, manufacturing, construction, transportation, communications, utilities, trade, and services.

Using historical data from the Alaska Department of Labor, the AEDC had used ratio-to-moving averages classical decomposition formulas in Microsoft Excel to forecast the economic outlook. But this long and fairly complicated process usually took about one month to complete. The results, though complete, were not as accurate as they should be.

The AEDC determined that John Galt Solutions could provide software (ForecastX Wizard) that would more accurately—and efficiently—define and forecast the economic conditions in Anchorage. AEDC wanted a solution that would minimize its time formatting and forecasting data and allow more time for analyzing and marketing the results of the forecasts.

The AEDC found ForecastX to be an easy-to-integrate tool that required no data preparation. AEDC was also happy to continue using Microsoft Excel and still have the ability to use the advanced forecasting methods. Flawlessly integrated, ForecastX Wizard provided the AEDC with Procast (expert selection); the ability to handle unlimited amounts of data; and the ability to forecast data on a monthly, quarterly, or yearly basis.

With the advanced features and functionality of ForecastX and its ease of use, AEDC was able to cut its forecasting prep time down to one week. More time, therefore, could be spent focusing on evaluating the results of forecasts and bringing more businesses to Anchorage. ForecastX Wizard provided AEDC with the tool it needed to more efficiently and accurately complete its forecasts.

4. Based on the plot of The Gap's quarterly sales, as well as the data analysis from question 3, the following forecasting methods might be suggested from the information in Table 2.1:

    Winters' exponential smoothing

    Regression trend with seasonality

    Causal regression

    Time-series decomposition

    ARIMA (if the series is transformed to stationarity and deseasonalized)

USING FORECASTX™ TO FIND AUTOCORRELATION FUNCTIONS

The most difficult calculations in this chapter were the autocorrelation coefficients. These can be calculated easily in the ForecastX™ software that accompanies your text. What follows is a brief discussion of how to use ForecastX™ for this purpose. This also serves as a good introduction to the ease of use of ForecastX™.

First, put your data into an Excel spreadsheet in column format such as the sample of The Gap data shown in Table 2.7. Once you have your data in this format, while in Excel highlight the data you want to use and then start ForecastX™. The following dialog box appears:

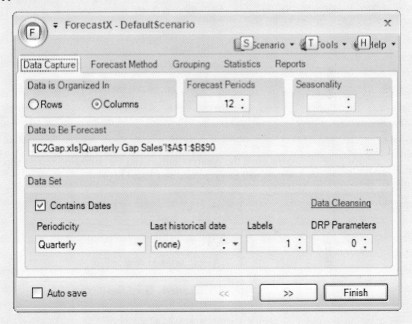

TABLE 2.7
A Sample of The Gap Data in Column Format

Date	Quarterly Gap Sales ($000)
Mar-05	3,626,000
Jun-05	3,716,000
Sep-05	3,860,000
Dec-05	4,821,000
Mar-06	3,441,000
Jun-06	3,716,000
Sep-06	3,856,000
Dec-06	4,930,000
Mar-07	3,558,000

Dates are the middle months of The Gap sales quarters.
The full data set is in c2Gap.

Set the Periodicity box to the periodicity of your data (**Quarterly** for this example), then click the **Forecast Method** tab at the top and the following screen appears:

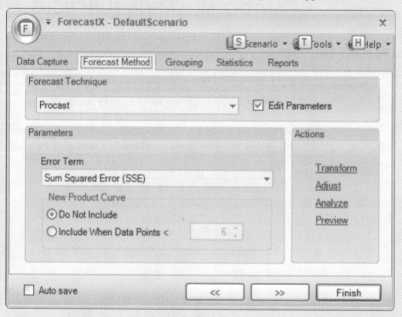

Now click the **Analyze** button and the following screen appears. Click **Export**, and the results will be saved to a new Excel book.

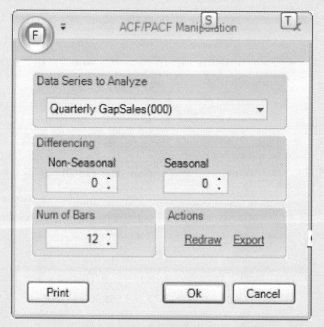

You will have the results shown at the top of the next page (along with some other results) in that new Excel book.

ACF for Quarterly Gap Sales ($000)

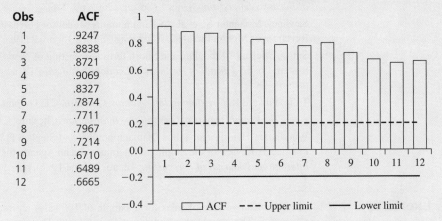

Obs	ACF
1	.9247
2	.8838
3	.8721
4	.9069
5	.8327
6	.7874
7	.7711
8	.7967
9	.7214
10	.6710
11	.6489
12	.6665

Note: **Throughout the text you may find some situations in which the standard calculations that we show do not match exactly with the ForecastX results. This is because they, at times, invoke proprietary alterations from the standard calculations. The results are always very close but sometimes do not match perfectly with "hand" calculations.**

Suggested Readings

Aghazadeh, Seyed-Mahmoud; and Jane B. Romal. "A Directory of 66 Packages for Forecasting and Statistical Analyses." *Journal of Business Forecasting* 11, no. 2 (Summer 1992), pp. 14–20.

"Beyond the Business Cycle?" *The Economist* 353, no. 8142 (October 1999), p. 90.

Bowerman, Bruce L.; and Richard T. O'Connell. *Applied Statistics: Improving Business Processes.* Chicago: Richard D. Irwin, 1997. (Especially chapters 5 and 7.)

Chatterjee, Satyajit. "From Cycles to Shocks: Progress in Business-Cycle Theory." *Business Review*, Federal Reserve Bank of Philadelphia (March/April 2000), pp. 27–37.

Chen, Rong, et al. "Forecasting with Stable Seasonal Pattern Models with an Application to Hawaiian Tourism Data." *Journal of Business & Economic Statistics* 17, no. 4 (October 1999), pp. 497–504.

Drumm, William J. "Living with Forecast Error." *Journal of Business Forecasting* 11, no. 2 (Summer 1992), p. 23.

Ermer, Charles M. "Cost of Error Affects the Forecasting Model Selection." *Journal of Business Forecasting* 10, no. 1 (Spring 1991), pp. 10–11.

Huff, Darrell. *How to Lie with Statistics.* New York: W. W. Norton, 1954.

Makridakis, Spyros. "Forecasting: Its Role and Value for Planning and Strategy." *International Journal of Forecasting* 12, no. 4 (December 1996), pp. 513–37.

Mentzer, John T.; and Carol C. Bienstock. *Sales Forecasting Management.* Thousand Oaks, CA: Sage Publications, 1998.

Mentzer, John T.; and Kenneth B. Kahn. "Forecasting Technique Familiarity, Satisfaction, Usage, and Application." *Journal of Forecasting* 14, no. 5 (September 1995), pp. 465–76.

———. "State of Sales Forecasting Systems in Corporate America." *Journal of Business Forecasting* 16, no. 1 (Spring 1997), pp. 6–13.

O'Clock, George; and Priscilla M. O'Clock. "Political Realities of Forecasting." *Journal of Business Forecasting* 8, no. 1 (Spring 1989), pp. 2–6.

Sawhney, Mohanbir S., et al. "A Parsimonious Model for Forecasting Gross Box-Office Revenues of Motion Pictures." *Marketing Science* 15, no. 2 (1996), pp. 113–31.

Smith, Michael. "Modeling and Short-Term Forecasting of New South Wales Electricity System Load." *Journal of Business & Economic Statistics* 18, no. 4 (October 2000), pp. 465–78.

Tufte, Edward R. *Envisioning Information.* Cheshire, CT: Graphics Press, 1990.

———. *The Visual Display of Quantitative Information.* Cheshire, CT: Graphics Press, 1983.

Winklhofer, Heidi; Adamantios Diamantopoulos; and Stephen F. Witt. "Forecasting Practice: A Review of the Empirical Literature and an Agenda for Future Research." *International Journal of Forecasting* 12, no. 2 (June 1996), pp. 193–221.

Exercises

1. The mean volume of sales for a sample of 100 sales representatives is $25,350 per month. The sample standard deviation is $7,490. The vice president for sales would like to know whether this result is significantly different from $24,000 at a 95 percent confidence level. Set up the appropriate null and alternative hypotheses, and perform the appropriate statistical test.

2. Larry Bomser has been asked to evaluate sizes of tire inventories for retail outlets of a major tire manufacturer. From a sample of 120 stores he has found a mean of 310 tires. The industry average is 325. If the standard deviation for the sample was 72, would you say that the inventory level maintained by this manufacturer is significantly different from the industry norm? Explain why. (Use a 95 percent confidence level.)

3. Twenty graduate students in business were asked how many credit hours they were taking in the current quarter. Their responses are shown as follows:

(c2p3)	Student Number	Credit Hours	Student Number	Credit Hours	Student Number	Credit Hours
	1	2	8	8	15	10
	2	7	9	12	16	6
	3	9	10	11	17	9
	4	9	11	6	18	6
	5	8	12	5	19	9
	6	11	13	9	20	10
	7	6	14	13		

   a. Determine the mean, median, and mode for this sample of data. Write a sentence explaining what each means.

   b. It has been suggested that graduate students in business take fewer credits per quarter than the typical graduate student at this university. The mean for all graduate students is 9.1 credit hours per quarter, and the data are normally distributed. Set up the appropriate null and alternative hypotheses, and determine whether the null hypothesis can be rejected at a 95 percent confidence level.

4. Arbon Computer Corporation (ACC) produces a popular PC clone. The sales manager for ACC has recently read a report that indicated that sales per sales representative for

other producers are normally distributed with a mean of $255,000. She is interested in knowing whether her sales staff is comparable. She picked a random sample of 16 salespeople and obtained the following results:

(c2p4)	Person	Sales		Person	Sales
	1	$177,406		9	$110,027
	2	339,753		10	182,577
	3	310,170		11	177,707
	4	175,520		12	154,096
	5	293,332		13	236,083
	6	323,175		14	301,051
	7	144,031		15	158,792
	8	279,670		16	140,891

At a 5 percent significance level, can you reject the null hypothesis that ACC's mean sales per salesperson was $255,000? Draw a diagram that illustrates your answer.

5. Assume that the weights of college football players are normally distributed with a mean of 205 pounds and a standard deviation of 30.

   a. What percentage of players would have weights greater than 205 pounds?

   b. What percentage of players would weigh less than 250 pounds?

   c. Ninety percentage of players would weigh more than what number of pounds?

   d. What percentage of players would weigh between 180 and 230 pounds?

6. Mutual Savings Bank of Appleton has done a market research survey in which people were asked to rate their image of the bank on a scale of 1 to 10, with 10 being the most favorable. The mean response for the sample of 400 people was 7.25, with a standard deviation of 2.51. On this same question a state association of mutual savings banks has found a mean of 7.01.

   a. Clara Wharton, marketing director for the bank, would like to test to see whether the rating for her bank is significantly greater than the norm of 7.01. Perform the appropriate hypothesis test for a 95 percent confidence level.

   b. Draw a diagram to illustrate your result.

   c. How would your result be affected if the sample size had been 100 rather than 400, with everything else being the same?

7. In a sample of 25 classes, the following numbers of students were observed:

(c2p7)				
40	50	42	20	29
39	49	46	52	45
51	64	43	37	35
44	10	40	36	20
20	29	58	51	54

   a. Calculate the mean, median, standard deviation, variance, and range for this sample.

   b. What is the standard error of the mean based on this information?

   c. What would be the best point estimate for the population class size?

   d. What is the 95 percent confidence interval for class size? What is the 90 percent confidence interval? Does the difference between these two make sense?

8. CoastCo Insurance, Inc., is interested in forecasting annual larceny thefts in the United States using the following data:

(c2p8)

Year	Larceny Thefts*	Year	Larceny Thefts*
1972	4,151	1984	6,592
1973	4,348	1985	6,926
1974	5,263	1986	7,257
1975	5,978	1987	7,500
1976	6,271	1988	7,706
1977	5,906	1989	7,872
1978	5,983	1990	7,946
1979	6,578	1991	8,142
1980	7,137	1992	7,915
1981	7,194	1993	7,821
1982	7,143	1994	7,876
1983	6,713		

* Data are in thousands.

SOURCE: U.S. Bureau of the Census, at http://www.census.gov.

a. Prepare a time-series plot of these data. On the basis of this graph, do you think there is a trend in the data? Explain.

b. Look at the autocorrelation structure of larceny thefts for lags of 1, 2, 3, 4, and 5. Do the autocorrelation coefficients fall quickly toward zero? Demonstrate that the critical value for r_k is 0.417. Explain what these results tell you about a trend in the data.

c. On the basis of what is found in parts a and b, suggest a forecasting method from Table 2.1 that you think might be appropriate for this series.

9. Use exploratory data analysis to determine whether there is a trend and/or seasonality in mobile home shipments (MHS). The data by quarter are shown in the following table:

(c2p9)

Year	Q1	Q2	Q3	Q4
1981	54.9	70.1	65.8	50.2
1982	53.3	67.9	63.1	55.3
1983	63.3	81.5	81.7	69.2
1984	67.8	82.7	79.0	66.2
1985	62.3	79.3	76.5	65.5
1986	58.1	66.8	63.4	56.1
1987	51.9	62.8	64.7	53.5
1988	47.0	60.5	59.2	51.6
1989	48.1	55.1	50.3	44.5
1990	43.3	51.7	50.5	42.6
1991	35.4	47.4	47.2	40.9
1992	43.0	52.8	57.0	57.6
1993	56.4	64.3	67.1	66.4
1994	69.1	78.7	78.7	77.5
1995	79.2	86.8	87.6	86.4

*Data are in thousands.

On the basis of your analysis, do you think there is a significant trend in MHS? Is there seasonality? What forecasting methods might be appropriate for MHS according to the guidelines in Table 2.1?

10. Home sales are often considered an important determinant of the future health of the economy. Thus, there is widespread interest in being able to forecast total houses sold (THS). Quarterly data for THS are shown in the following table in thousands of units:

(c2p10)

Date	Total Houses Sold (000) per Quarter	Date	Total Houses Sold (000) per Quarter
Mar-89	161	Mar-98	220
Jun-89	179	Jun-98	247
Sep-89	172	Sep-98	218
Dec-89	138	Dec-98	200
Mar-90	153	Mar-99	227
Jun-90	152	Jun-99	248
Sep-90	130	Sep-99	221
Dec-90	100	Dec-99	185
Mar-91	121	Mar-00	233
Jun-91	144	Jun-00	226
Sep-91	126	Sep-00	219
Dec-91	116	Dec-00	199
Mar-92	159	Mar-01	251
Jun-92	158	Jun-01	243
Sep-92	159	Sep-01	216
Dec-92	132	Dec-01	199
Mar-93	154	Mar-02	240
Jun-93	183	Jun-02	258
Sep-93	169	Sep-02	254
Dec-93	160	Dec-02	220
Mar-94	178	Mar-03	256
Jun-94	185	Jun-03	299
Sep-94	165	Sep-03	294
Dec-94	142	Dec-03	239
Mar-95	154	Mar-04	314
Jun-95	185	Jun-04	329
Sep-95	181	Sep-04	292
Dec-95	145	Dec-04	268
Mar-96	192	Mar-05	328
Jun-96	204	Jun-05	351
Sep-96	201	Sep-05	326
Dec-96	161	Dec-05	278
Mar-97	211	Mar-06	285
Jun-97	212	Jun-06	300
Sep-97	208	Sep-06	251
Dec-97	174	Dec-06	216
		Mar-07	214
		Jun-07	240

a. Prepare a time-series plot of THS. Describe what you see in this plot in terms of trend and seasonality.

b. Calculate and plot the first twelve autocorrelation coefficients for PHS. What does this autocorrelation structure suggest about the trend?

c. De-trend the data by calculating first differences:

$$\text{DTHS}_t = \text{THS}_t - \text{THS}_{t-1}$$

Calculate and plot the first eight autocorrelation coefficients for DTHS. Is there a trend in DTHS?

11. Exercise 8 of Chapter 1 includes data on the Japanese exchange rate (EXRJ) by month. On the basis of a time-series plot of these data and the autocorrelation structure of EXRJ, would you say the data are stationary? Explain your answer. (c2p11)

Moving Averages and Exponential Smoothing

Consider the situation facing a manager who must periodically forecast the inventories for hundreds of products. Each day, or week, or month, updated forecasts for the many inventories are required within a short time period. While it might well be possible to develop sophisticated forecasting models for each of the items, in many cases some very simple short-term forecasting tools are adequate for the job.

A manager facing such a task is likely to use some form of time-series *smoothing*. All the time-series smoothing methods use a form of weighted average of past observations to smooth up-and-down movements, that is, some statistical method of suppressing short-term fluctuations. The assumption underlying these methods is that the fluctuations in past values represent random departures from some smooth curve that, once identified, can plausibly be extrapolated into the future to produce a forecast or series of forecasts.

We will examine five basic smoothing techniques in this chapter. All five of these have the common characteristic that only a past history of the time series to be forecast is necessary to produce the forecast. Further, all are based on the concept that there is some underlying pattern to the data; that is, all time-series data to be forecast are assumed to have some cycles or fluctuations that tend to recur. The five methods, to be examined in turn, are:

1. Moving averages
2. Simple exponential smoothing
3. Holt's exponential smoothing
4. Winters' exponential smoothing
5. Adaptive–response-rate single exponential smoothing

MOVING AVERAGES

The simple statistical method of moving averages may mimic some data better than a complicated mathematical function. Figure 3.1 shows the exchange rate between the Japanese yen and the U.S. dollar from 1985Q1 through 2007Q1. Figure 3.1 does not exhibit a simple linear, exponential, or quadratic trend similar

FIGURE 3.1

Exchange Rate of Japanese Yen per U.S. Dollar

(c3t1)

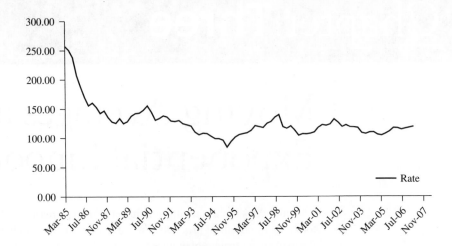

The simple statistical method of moving averages may mimic some data better than a complicated mathematical function.

to those we will examine in Chapters 4 and 5. Instead, the series appears to show substantial randomness, which we may be able to eliminate with a technique that averages the most recent values.

To illustrate how a moving average is used, consider Table 3.1, which displays the exchange rate between the Japanese yen and one U.S. dollar, shown in Figure 3.1. To calculate the three-quarter moving average first requires that we sum the first three observations (257.53, 250.81, and 238.38). This three-quarter total is then divided by 3 to obtain 248.90 (with rounding), which is the first number in the "Three-Quarter Moving Average" column. This "smoothed" number, 248.90, becomes the forecast for 1985Q4.

The final value in the "Three-Quarter Moving Average" column (117.82) is the forecast for 2007Q2; it was arrived at by summing the final three values in the "Actual" column and then dividing by 3 (353.45/3 = 117.82).

The five-quarter moving averages displayed in the same table are calculated in like manner: the first moving average of 228.34 is calculated by summing the first five actual values and dividing by 5:

$$\frac{257.53 + 250.81 + 238.38 + 207.18 + 187.81}{5} = \frac{1{,}141.71}{5} = 228.34$$

Thus, 228.34 becomes the forecast for the next period (1986Q2). The five entries from Mar-06 through Mar-07 in the "Actual" column are averaged to give the final five-quarter moving average:

$$\frac{116.87 + 114.48 + 116.30 + 117.75 + 119.40}{5} = \frac{584.8}{5} = 116.96$$

This final moving average serves as the forecast for 2007Q2.

TABLE 3.1 Exchange Rate with Japan and Two Moving-Average Forecasts (c3t1)

Date	Rate	Three-Quarter Moving Average	Three-Quarter Forecast	Five-Quarter Moving Average	Five-Quarter Forecast
Mar-85	257.53	missing	missing	missing	missing
Jun-85	250.81	missing	missing	missing	missing
Sep-85	238.38	248.90	missing	missing	missing
Dec-85	207.18	232.12	248.90	missing	missing
Mar-86	187.81	211.12	232.12	228.34	missing
Jun-86	169.89	188.29	211.12	210.81	228.34
Sep-86	155.84	171.18	188.29	191.82	210.81
Dec-86	160.46	162.06	171.18	176.23	191.82
Mar-87	153.22	156.51	162.06	165.44	176.23
Jun-87	142.64	152.11	156.51	156.41	165.44
Sep-87	146.97	147.61	152.11	151.83	156.41
Dec-87	135.65	141.76	147.61	147.79	151.83
Mar-88	127.99	136.87	141.76	141.30	147.79
Jun-88	125.72	129.79	136.87	135.80	141.30
Sep-88	133.70	129.14	129.79	134.01	135.80
Dec-88	125.16	128.20	129.14	129.65	134.01
Mar-89	128.55	129.14	128.20	128.23	129.65
Jun-89	137.96	130.56	129.14	130.22	128.23
Sep-89	142.33	136.28	130.56	133.54	130.22
Dec-89	143.14	141.14	136.28	135.43	133.54
Mar-90	147.99	144.49	141.14	139.99	135.43
Jun-90	155.40	148.85	144.49	145.36	139.99
Sep-90	144.98	149.46	148.85	146.77	145.36
Dec-90	130.90	143.76	149.46	144.48	146.77
Mar-91	133.88	136.59	143.76	142.63	144.48
Jun-91	138.36	134.38	136.59	140.70	142.63
Sep-91	136.32	136.18	134.38	136.89	140.70
Dec-91	129.48	134.72	136.18	133.79	136.89
Mar-92	128.67	131.49	134.72	133.34	133.79
Jun-92	130.38	129.51	131.49	132.64	133.34
Sep-92	124.90	127.99	129.51	129.95	132.64
Dec-92	123.03	126.11	127.99	127.29	129.95
Mar-93	120.92	122.95	126.11	125.58	127.29
Jun-93	110.05	118.00	122.95	121.86	125.58
Sep-93	105.68	112.22	118.00	116.92	121.86
Dec-93	108.27	108.00	112.22	113.59	116.92
Mar-94	107.61	107.19	108.00	110.51	113.59
Jun-94	103.25	106.38	107.19	106.97	110.51
Sep-94	99.05	103.31	106.38	104.77	106.97
Dec-94	98.86	100.39	103.31	103.41	104.77
Mar-95	96.18	98.03	100.39	100.99	103.41
Jun-95	84.48	93.17	98.03	96.36	100.99

(continued on next page)

TABLE 3.1   (continued)

Date	Rate	Three-Quarter Moving Average	Three-Quarter Forecast	Five-Quarter Moving Average	Five-Quarter Forecast
Sep-95	94.23	91.63	93.17	94.56	96.36
Dec-95	101.54	93.42	91.63	95.06	94.56
Mar-96	105.83	100.53	93.42	96.45	95.06
Jun-96	107.50	104.96	100.53	98.72	96.45
Sep-96	109.00	107.44	104.96	103.62	98.72
Dec-96	112.90	109.80	107.44	107.35	103.62
Mar-97	121.21	114.37	109.80	111.29	107.35
Jun-97	119.71	117.94	114.37	114.06	111.29
Sep-97	118.07	119.66	117.94	116.18	114.06
Dec-97	125.39	121.05	119.66	119.45	116.18
Mar-98	128.16	123.87	121.05	122.51	119.45
Jun-98	135.66	129.74	123.87	125.40	122.51
Sep-98	139.98	134.60	129.74	129.45	125.40
Dec-98	119.47	131.70	134.60	129.73	129.45
Mar-99	116.48	125.31	131.70	127.95	129.73
Jun-99	120.83	118.93	125.31	126.48	127.95
Sep-99	113.15	116.82	118.93	121.98	126.48
Dec-99	104.40	112.79	116.82	114.86	121.98
Mar-00	107.00	108.18	112.79	112.37	114.86
Jun-00	106.69	106.03	108.18	110.41	112.37
Sep-00	107.71	107.13	106.03	107.79	110.41
Dec-00	109.89	108.10	107.13	107.14	107.79
Mar-01	118.14	111.91	108.10	109.89	107.14
Jun-01	122.63	116.88	111.91	113.01	109.89
Sep-01	121.49	120.75	116.88	115.97	113.01
Dec-01	123.82	122.65	120.75	119.19	115.97
Mar-02	132.46	125.92	122.65	123.71	119.19
Jun-02	126.81	127.70	125.92	125.44	123.71
Sep-02	119.32	126.20	127.70	124.78	125.44
Dec-02	122.47	122.87	126.20	124.98	124.78
Mar-03	118.95	120.25	122.87	124.00	124.98
Jun-03	118.53	119.98	120.25	121.22	124.00
Sep-03	117.39	118.29	119.98	119.33	121.22
Dec-03	108.81	114.91	118.29	117.23	119.33
Mar-04	107.17	111.12	114.91	114.17	117.23
Jun-04	109.76	108.58	111.12	112.33	114.17
Sep-04	109.94	108.96	108.58	110.61	112.33
Dec-04	105.76	108.49	108.96	108.29	110.61
Mar-05	104.51	106.74	108.49	107.43	108.29
Jun-05	107.51	105.93	106.74	107.50	107.43
Sep-05	111.27	107.76	105.93	107.80	107.50
Dec-05	117.26	112.01	107.76	109.26	107.80
Mar-06	116.87	115.13	112.01	111.48	109.26
Jun-06	114.48	116.20	115.13	113.48	111.48

TABLE 3.1 (continued)

Date	Rate	Three-Quarter Moving Average	Three-Quarter Forecast	Five-Quarter Moving Average	Five-Quarter Forecast
Sep-06	116.30	115.88	116.20	115.24	113.48
Dec-06	117.75	116.18	115.88	116.53	115.24
Mar-07	119.40	117.82	116.18	116.96	116.53
Jun-07	120.80*	missing	117.82	missing	116.96

* Value assumed not to be known in developing moving-average forecasts.

RMSE for March 1985–March 2007

Three-Quarter Moving-Average Model	13.0
Five-Quarter Moving-Average Model	15.28

The choice of the interval for the moving average depends on the length of the underlying cycle or pattern in the original data.

Obviously, three- and five-quarter moving averages are not the only kinds of moving averages. We could calculate seven- or nine-quarter moving averages if we wished, or eight- or ten-quarter averages, and so on. The choice of the interval for the moving average depends on the length of the underlying cycle or pattern in the original data. If we believe the actual data to be exhibiting a cycle that recurs every four periods, we would choose a four-period moving average in order to best dampen the short-run fluctuation. The simplest naive model of Chapter 1 used each period's actual value as the forecast for the next period; you could correctly think of this model as a one-period moving average, that is, a special case of the model we are examining here.

In order to compute whether the three-quarter or five-quarter moving average is the better forecasting model, it is useful to compute the root-mean-squared error (RMSE) as we calculated it in Chapter 1. Table 3.1 shows the RMSE for both forecasts at the bottom of the table. The RMSE of 13.0 for the three-quarter moving average is less than the 15.28 calculated for the five-quarter case, and so we might conclude that the better forecast in this particular case is generated by the three-quarter model.

In preparing the forecasts for 2007Q2, it was assumed that the actual value for that quarter was unknown. However, the actual value for that quarter is known in this situation and is shown in Table 3.1. Thus, we can see which of the two moving-average forecasts developed above was really the best for 2007Q2. The forecast for the single quarter (2007Q2) shows that the three-quarter moving average was slightly more accurate in this instance.

The three- and five-quarter moving averages are shown graphically in Figures 3.2 and 3.3, respectively. Notice in Figures 3.2 and 3.3 that the peaks and troughs of the actual series are different from those for either moving average. This failure of the moving averages to predict peaks and troughs is one of the shortcomings of moving-average models.

The moving-average forecasting method has fooled more than one forecaster by appearing to identify a cycle.

One final and important observation: The moving-average forecasting method has fooled more than one forecaster by appearing to identify a cycle when, in fact, no cycle was present in the actual data. Such an occurrence can be understood if

FIGURE 3.2

Three-Quarter Moving-Average Forecast of the U.S. Exchange Rate with Japan (c3t1)

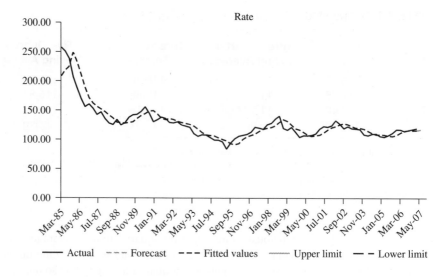

Rate

── Actual   --- Forecast   --- Fitted values   ── Upper limit   ── Lower limit

FIGURE 3.3

Five-Quarter Moving-Average Forecast of the U.S. Exchange Rate with Japan (c3t1)

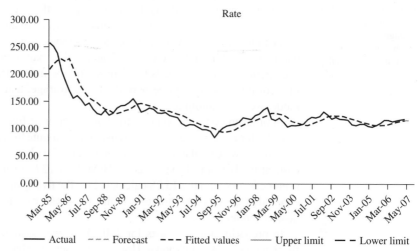

Rate

── Actual   --- Forecast   --- Fitted values   ── Upper limit   ── Lower limit

you think of an actual data series as being simply a series of random numbers. Since any moving average is serially correlated, because a number of contiguous periods have been averaged, *any* sequence of random numbers could appear to exhibit cyclical fluctuation.[1]

[1] This incorrect conclusion is sometimes called the *Slutsky-Yule* effect, named after Eugen Slutsky and G. Udny Yule, who first pointed out the possibility of making a mistake in this manner. See Eugen E. Slutsky, "The Summation of Random Causes as the Source of Cyclic Processes," *Econometrica* 5 (1937), pp. 105–46; and G. Udny Yule, "On a Method of Investigating Periodicities in Disturbed Series, with Special Reference to Wolfer's Sunspot Numbers," Royal Society of London, *Philosophical Transactions* (1927), pp. 267–98.

SIMPLE EXPONENTIAL SMOOTHING

With exponential smoothing, the forecast value at any time is a weighted average of all the available previous values.

Simple exponential smoothing, like moving averages, uses only past values of a time series to forecast future values of the same series and is properly employed when there is no trend or seasonality present in the data. With exponential smoothing, the forecast value at any time is a weighted average of all the available previous values; the weights decline geometrically as you go back in time. Moving-average forecasting gives equal weights to the past values included in each average; exponential smoothing gives more weight to the recent observations and less to the older observations. The weights are made to decline geometrically with the age of the observation to conform to the argument that the most recent observations contain the most relevant information, so that they should be accorded proportionately more influence than older observations.

The number we choose for α is called the *level smoothing constant*.

Exponential smoothing proceeds as do moving averages by smoothing past values of the series; the calculations for producing exponentially smoothed forecasts can be expressed as an equation. The weight of the most recent observation is assigned by multiplying the observed value by α, the next most recent observation by $(1 - \alpha)\alpha$, the next observation by $(1 - \alpha)^2\alpha$, and so on. The number we choose for α is called the *level smoothing constant.*[2]

The simple exponential smoothing model can be written in the following manner:

$$F_{t+1} = \alpha X_t + (1 - \alpha)F_t \qquad (3.1)$$

where[2]:

F_{t+1} = Forecast value for period $t + 1$
α = Smoothing constant ($0 < \alpha < 1$)
X_t = Actual value now (in period t)
F_t = Forecast (i.e., smoothed) value for period t

In using this equation the forecaster does not need to deal with every actual past value at every step; only the exponentially smoothed value for the last period and the actual value for this period are necessary. An alternative way of writing Equation 3.1 results from rearranging the terms as follows:

$$
\begin{aligned}
F_{t+1} &= \alpha X_t + (1 - \alpha)F_t \qquad (3.2)\\
&= \alpha X_t + F_t - \alpha F_t \\
&= F_t + \alpha(X_t - F_t)
\end{aligned}
$$

[2] Our notation throughout the chapter for exponential smoothing follows approximately the notation found in Everette S. Gardner, "Exponential Smoothing: The State of the Art," *Journal of Forecasting* 4, no. 1 (1985), pp. 1–28. This article contains a very complete description of different forms of smoothing that are in common use and explains (with advanced mathematics) that there may be theoretical advantages for employing smoothing in situations where it can be shown that certain assumptions concerning the probability distribution of the series are met.

If α close to 1 recent values
obtain series are more
heavily weighted.

From this form we can see that the exponential smoothing model "learns" from past errors. The forecast value at period $t + 1$ is increased if the actual value for period t is greater than it was forecast to be, and it is decreased if X_t is less than F_t. Forecasting the value for the next period (F_{t+1}) requires us to know only the actual value for this period (X_t) and the forecast value for this period (F_t). However, all historical observations are included, as follows:

$$F_{t+1} = \alpha X_t + (1 - \alpha)F_t \qquad\qquad (3.3)$$

and $\qquad F_t = \alpha X_{t-1} + (1 - \alpha)F_{t-1}$

therefore, $\quad F_{t+1} = \alpha X_t + (1 - \alpha)\alpha X_{t-1} + (1 - \alpha)^2 F_{t-1}$

and $\qquad F_{t-1} = \alpha X_{t-2} + (1 - \alpha)F_{t-2}$

thus, $\qquad F_{t+1} = \alpha X_t + (1 - \alpha)\alpha X_{t-1} + (1 - \alpha)^2 \alpha X_{t-2} + (1 - \alpha)^3 F_{t-2}$

We could continue this expansion to include X terms as far back as we have data, but this is probably far enough to help you see how the weights for previous time periods become smaller and smaller at a rate that depends on the value of α, as will be shown in the following tables for two alternative values of α.

The value of the level smoothing constant α is commonly constrained to be in the range of zero to one. If a value close to 1 is chosen, recent values of the time series are weighted heavily relative to those of the distant past when the smoothed values are calculated. Likewise, if the value of α is chosen close to 0, then the values of the time series in the distant past are given weights comparable to those given the recent values. The rate at which the weights decrease can be seen from their values for an α of 0.1:

Time	$\alpha = 0.1$ Calculation	Weight
t		0.1
$t - 1$	0.9×0.1	0.090
$t - 2$	$0.9 \times 0.9 \times 0.1$	0.081
$t - 3$	$0.9 \times 0.9 \times 0.9 \times 0.1$	0.073
$\vdots$		$\vdots$
Total		1.000

Regardless of the smoothing constant chosen, the weights will eventually sum to 1. Whether the sum of the weights converges on 1 quickly or slowly depends on the smoothing constant chosen. If, for example, we choose a smoothing constant of 0.9, the sum of the weights will approach 1 much more rapidly than when the level smoothing constant is 0.1:

Time	$\alpha = 0.9$ Calculation	Weight
t		0.9
$t - 1$	0.1×0.9	0.09
$t - 2$	$0.1 \times 0.1 \times 0.9$	0.009
$t - 3$	$0.1 \times 0.1 \times 0.1 \times 0.9$	0.0009
$\vdots$		$\vdots$
Total		1.000

As a guide in choosing α, select values close to 0 if the series has a great deal of random variation; select values close to 1 if you wish the forecast values to depend strongly on recent changes in the actual values. The root-mean-squared error (RMSE) is often used as the criterion for assigning an appropriate smoothing constant; the smoothing constant giving the smallest RMSE would be selected as the model likely to produce the smallest error in generating additional forecasts. In practice, relatively small values of alpha (α) generally work best when simple exponential smoothing is the most appropriate model.

In practice, relatively small values of alpha (α) generally work best when simple exponential smoothing is the most appropriate model.

The following example will demonstrate the technique. Suppose we wish to forecast the University of Michigan Index of Consumer Sentiment for September 2007 based on data from January 1998 through August 2007. These values are shown in the "Actual" column of Table 3.2 for January 1998 through August 2007. Since no previous forecast is available for the first period (January 1998), we have arbitrarily chosen to use 107; thus 107 becomes the first entry in the "Forecast" column. This process of choosing an initial value for the smoothed series is called *initializing* the model, or *warming up* the model.[3] All the other values in the "Forecast" column were calculated by using Equation 3.1 with a level smoothing constant (α) of 0.88, which was selected by ForecastX™ to minimize the RMSE. The actual and forecast values are shown in Figure 3.4.

[3] The choice of a starting value in exponential smoothing models has been a matter of some discussion, with little empirical evidence favoring any particular approach. R. G. Brown first suggested using the mean of the data for the starting value, and this suggestion has been quite popular in actual practice. A linear regression (like that described in Chapter 4) is sometimes used when selecting starting values for seasonal factors, and time-series decomposition (as discussed in Chapter 6) has also been used. If the data include a trend, backcasting is sometimes used to select a starting value; but if the trend is erratic, this sometimes leads to negative starting values, which make little sense. A discussion of the various alternatives (including using the first value in the series or using the mean of the series, which are both popular in practice) appears in the Gardner article (footnote 2).

TABLE 3.2 Simple Exponential Smoothing Forecast of the University of Michigan Index of Consumer Sentiment (c3t2)

Date	Actual	Forecast	Error	Date	Actual	Forecast	Error
Jan-98	106.6	107.00	−0.40	Sep-01	81.8	91.61	−9.81
Feb-98	110.4	106.65	3.75	Oct-01	82.7	82.96	−0.26
Mar-98	106.5	109.96	−3.46	Nov-01	83.9	82.73	1.17
Apr-98	108.7	106.91	1.79	Dec-01	88.8	83.76	5.04
May-98	106.5	108.49	−1.99	Jan-02	93	88.21	4.79
Jun-98	105.6	106.73	−1.13	Feb-02	90.7	92.43	−1.73
Jul-98	105.2	105.73	−0.53	Mar-02	95.7	90.90	4.80
Aug-98	104.4	105.26	−0.86	Apr-02	93	95.13	−2.13
Sep-98	100.9	104.50	−3.60	May-02	96.9	93.25	3.65
Oct-98	97.4	101.33	−3.93	Jun-02	92.4	96.47	−4.07
Nov-98	102.7	97.86	4.84	Jul-02	88.1	92.88	−4.78
Dec-98	100.5	102.13	−1.63	Aug-02	87.6	88.66	−1.06
Jan-99	103.9	100.69	3.21	Sep-02	86.1	87.73	−1.63
Feb-99	108.1	103.52	4.58	Oct-02	80.6	86.29	−5.69
Mar-99	105.7	107.56	−1.86	Nov-02	84.2	81.27	2.93
Apr-99	104.6	105.92	−1.32	Dec-02	86.7	83.85	2.85
May-99	106.8	104.76	2.04	Jan-03	82.4	86.36	−3.96
Jun-99	107.3	106.56	0.74	Feb-03	79.9	82.87	−2.97
Jul-99	106	107.21	−1.21	Mar-03	77.6	80.25	−2.65
Aug-99	104.5	106.14	−1.64	Apr-03	86	77.91	8.09
Sep-99	107.2	104.69	2.51	May-03	92.1	85.05	7.05
Oct-99	103.2	106.90	−3.70	Jun-03	89.7	91.27	−1.57
Nov-99	107.2	103.64	3.56	Jul-03	90.9	89.88	1.02
Dec-99	105.4	106.78	−1.38	Aug-03	89.3	90.78	−1.48
Jan-00	112	105.56	6.44	Sep-03	87.7	89.47	−1.77
Feb-00	111.3	111.24	0.06	Oct-03	89.6	87.91	1.69
Mar-00	107.1	111.29	−4.19	Nov-03	93.7	89.40	4.30
Apr-00	109.2	107.59	1.61	Dec-03	92.6	93.19	−0.59
May-00	110.7	109.01	1.69	Jan-04	103.8	92.67	11.13
Jun-00	106.4	110.50	−4.10	Feb-04	94.4	102.49	−8.09
Jul-00	108.3	106.88	1.42	Mar-04	95.8	95.35	0.45
Aug-00	107.3	108.13	−0.83	Apr-04	94.2	95.75	−1.55
Sep-00	106.8	107.40	−0.60	May-04	90.2	94.38	−4.18
Oct-00	105.8	106.87	−1.07	Jun-04	95.6	90.69	4.91
Nov-00	107.6	105.93	1.67	Jul-04	96.7	95.02	1.68
Dec-00	98.4	107.40	−9.00	Aug-04	95.9	96.50	−0.60
Jan-01	94.7	99.46	−4.76	Sep-04	94.2	95.97	−1.77
Feb-01	90.6	95.26	−4.66	Oct-04	91.7	94.41	−2.71
Mar-01	91.5	91.15	0.35	Nov-04	92.8	92.02	0.78
Apr-01	88.4	91.46	−3.06	Dec-04	97.1	92.71	4.39
May-01	92	88.76	3.24	Jan-05	95.5	96.58	−1.08
Jun-01	92.6	91.62	0.98	Feb-05	94.1	95.63	−1.53
Jul-01	92.4	92.48	−0.08	Mar-05	92.6	94.28	−1.68
Aug-01	91.5	92.41	−0.91	Apr-05	87.7	92.80	−5.10

TABLE 3.2 (continued)

Date	Actual	Forecast	Error	Date	Actual	Forecast	Error
May-05	86.9	88.30	−1.40	Aug-06	82	84.66	−2.66
Jun-05	96	87.07	8.93	Sep-06	85.4	82.31	3.09
Jul-05	96.5	94.95	1.55	Oct-06	93.6	85.04	8.56
Aug-05	89.1	96.32	−7.22	Nov-06	92.1	92.59	−0.49
Sep-05	76.9	89.95	−13.05	Dec-06	91.7	92.16	−0.46
Oct-05	74.2	78.44	−4.24	Jan-07	96.9	91.75	5.15
Nov-05	81.6	74.70	6.90	Feb-07	91.3	96.29	−4.99
Dec-05	91.5	80.79	10.71	Mar-07	88.4	91.89	−3.49
Jan-06	91.2	90.24	0.96	Apr-07	87.1	88.81	−1.71
Feb-06	86.7	91.09	−4.39	May-07	88.3	87.30	1.00
Mar-06	88.9	87.22	1.68	Jun-07	85.3	88.18	−2.88
Apr-06	87.4	88.70	−1.30	Jul-07	90.4	85.64	4.76
May-06	79.1	87.55	−8.45	Aug-07	83.4	89.84	−6.44
Jun-06	84.9	80.10	4.80				
Jul-06	84.7	84.33	0.37	**Sep-07**		**84.16**	

Level = 0.88
Root-mean-squared error (RMSE) = 4.15

Let us illustrate the calculation of the forecast value for March 1998 by using Equation 3.1 as follows:

$$F_{t+1} = \alpha X_t + (1 - \alpha)F_t$$

$$F_{2+1} = \alpha X_2 + (1 - \alpha)F_2$$

$$F_3 = 0.88(110.4) + (1 - 0.88)(106.65) = 109.96$$

FIGURE 3.4

A Simple Exponential Smoothing Forecast of the University of Michigan Index of Consumer Sentiment (c3t2)

In this forecast an alpha of 0.88 was selected to minimize the root-mean-squared error (RMSE).

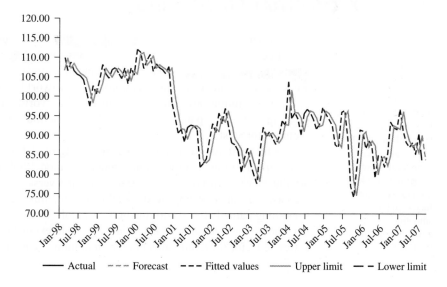

This smoothed value of 109.96 is the forecast for March ($t = 3$). Once actual data for March become available, the model is used to forecast April, and so on.

Taking this one step further, assume now that the actual sales figure for March 1998 has become available. In Table 3.2 we see that this figure is 106.50. We now wish to forecast the sales figure for $t = 4$ (April 1998). The technique applied before is repeated:

$$F_{t+1} = \alpha X_t + (1 - \alpha)F_t$$

$$F_{3+1} = \alpha X_3 + (1 - \alpha)F_3$$

$$F_4 = 0.88(106.50) + (1 - 0.88)(109.96) = 106.91$$

The error for the March 1998 forecast (rounded) is calculated as:

$$e_3 = X_3 - F_3 = 106.50 - 109.96 = -3.46$$

The error for the April 1998 forecast (rounded) is calculated as:

$$e_4 = X_4 - F_4 = 108.70 - 106.91 = 1.79$$

The predominant reason for using simple smoothing is that it requires a limited quantity of data and it is simpler than most other forecasting methods. Its limitations, however, are that its forecasts lag behind the actual data and it has no ability to adjust for any trend or seasonality in the data.

adds a growth factor!

HOLT'S EXPONENTIAL SMOOTHING

Holt's two-parameter exponential smoothing method (called Double Exponential Smoothing Holt in ForecastX™) is an extension of simple exponential smoothing; it adds a growth factor (or trend factor) to the smoothing equation as a way of adjusting for the trend.

Two further extensions of the smoothing model can be used in order to bring the forecast values closer to the values observed if the data series exhibits a trend and/or seasonality (the first extension is discussed in this section, and the second in the following section). In real-world situations one or both of these techniques are often used because real-world data are not very often so simple in their patterns that simple exponential smoothing provides an accurate forecast.

The first extension is to adjust the smoothing model for any trend in the data; with a trend in the data the simple smoothing model will have large errors that usually move from positive to negative or vice versa. When a trend exists, the forecast may then be improved by adjusting for this trend by using a form of smoothing named after its originator, C. C. Holt. Holt's two-parameter exponential smoothing method is an extension of simple exponential smoothing; it adds a growth factor (or trend factor) to the smoothing equation as a way of adjusting for the trend. Three equations and two smoothing constants are used in the model.

$$F_{t+1} = \alpha X_t + (1 - \alpha)(F_t + T_t) \qquad (3.4)$$

$$T_{t+1} = \gamma(F_{t+1} - F_t) + (1 - \gamma)T_t \qquad (3.5)$$

$$H_{t+m} = F_{t+1} + mT_{t+1} \qquad (3.6)$$

where:

F_{t+1} = Smoothed value for period $t + 1$

α = Smoothing constant for the level $(0 < \alpha < 1)$

X_t = Actual value now (in period t)

F_t = Forecast (i.e., smoothed) value for time period t

T_{t+1} = Trend estimate

γ = Smoothing constant for the trend estimate $(0 < \gamma < 1)$

m = Number of periods ahead to be forecast

H_{t+m} = Holt's forecast value for period $t + m$

Equation 3.4 adjusts F_{t+1} for the growth of the previous period, T_t, by adding T_t to the smoothed value of the previous period, F_t. The trend estimate is calculated in Equation 3.5, where the difference of the last two smoothed values is calculated. Because these two values have already been smoothed, the difference between them is assumed to be an estimate of trend in the data. The second smoothing constant, γ in Equation 3.5, is arrived at by using the same principle employed in simple exponential smoothing. The most recent trend $(F_{t+1} - F_t)$, is weighted by γ, and the last previous smoothed trend, T_t, is weighted by $(1 - \gamma)$. The sum of the weighted values is the new smoothed trend value T_{t+1}.

Equation 3.6 is used to forecast m periods into the future by adding the product of the trend component, T_{t+1}, and the number of periods to forecast, m, to the current value of the smoothed data F_{t+1}.

This method accurately accounts for any linear trend in the data.[4] Table 3.3 illustrates the application of Holt's model to consumer credit outstanding. The two smoothing constants are $\alpha = 0.77$ and $\gamma = 0.39$. Two starting values are needed: one for the first smoothed value and another for the first trend value. The initial smoothed value is often a recent actual value available; the initial trend value is often 0.00 if no past data are available (see footnote 3). The following naming

---

[4] All trends, of course, do not have to be linear, and there are smoothing models that can account for nonlinear trends. In this chapter we are examining only a subset of the number of possible smoothing models. For a listing of smoothing models, see Carl C. Pegels, "Exponential Forecasting: Some New Variations," *Management Science* 15, no. 12 (1969), pp. 311–15, or the Gardner article (1985). Both of these articles cover many smoothing models, including some that are very rarely used in actual practice.

TABLE 3.3
Personal
Consumption
Expenditures in
Billions of Dollars
(SA) (c3t3)

Dates	Original Data	Fitted Data	Error
Jan-1990	4,757.10	4,766.41	−9.31
Apr-1990	4,773.00	4,761.70	11.30
Jul-1990	4,792.60	4,776.21	16.39
Oct-1990	4,758.30	4,799.52	−41.22
Jan-1991	4,738.10	4,766.22	−28.12
Apr-1991	4,779.40	4,734.64	44.76
Jul-1991	4,800.10	4,772.47	27.63
Oct-1991	4,795.90	4,805.34	−9.44
Jan-1992	4,875.00	4,806.87	68.13
Apr-1992	4,903.00	4,888.37	14.63
Jul-1992	4,951.80	4,933.05	18.75
Oct-1992	5,009.40	4,986.48	22.92
Jan-1993	5,027.30	5,049.94	−22.64
Apr-1993	5,071.90	5,071.60	0.30
Jul-1993	5,127.30	5,111.00	16.30
Oct-1993	5,172.90	5,167.57	5.33
Jan-1994	5,230.30	5,217.28	13.02
Apr-1994	5,268.00	5,276.78	−8.78
Jul-1994	5,305.70	5,316.89	−11.19
Oct-1994	5,358.70	5,351.82	6.88
Jan-1995	5,367.20	5,402.70	−35.50
Apr-1995	5,411.70	5,410.40	1.30
Jul-1995	5,458.80	5,446.81	11.99
Oct-1995	5,496.10	5,495.02	1.08
Jan-1996	5,544.60	5,535.15	9.45
Apr-1996	5,604.90	5,584.54	20.36
Jul-1996	5,640.70	5,648.38	−7.68
Oct-1996	5,687.60	5,688.36	−0.76
Jan-1997	5,749.10	5,733.44	15.66
Apr-1997	5,775.80	5,795.81	−20.01
Jul-1997	5,870.70	5,824.78	45.92
Oct-1997	5,931.40	5,918.15	13.25
Jan-1998	5,996.80	5,990.32	6.48
Apr-1998	6,092.10	6,059.21	32.89
Jul-1998	6,165.70	6,158.21	7.49
Oct-1998	6,248.80	6,239.89	8.91
Jan-1999	6,311.30	6,325.32	−14.02
Apr-1999	6,409.70	6,388.92	20.78
Jul-1999	6,476.70	6,485.49	−8.79
Oct-1999	6,556.80	6,556.69	0.11
Jan-2000	6,661.30	6,634.77	26.53
Apr-2000	6,703.30	6,741.08	−37.78
Jul-2000	6,768.00	6,786.65	−18.65
Oct-2000	6,825.00	6,841.39	−16.39
Jan-2001	6,853.10	6,893.00	−39.90
Apr-2001	6,870.30	6,914.64	−44.34

TABLE 3.3
(continued)

Dates	Original Data	Fitted Data	Error
Jul-2001	6,900.50	6,919.67	−19.17
Oct-2001	7,017.60	6,938.37	79.23
Jan-2002	7,042.20	7,056.38	−14.18
Apr-2002	7,083.50	7,098.28	−14.78
Jul-2002	7,123.20	7,135.32	−12.12
Oct-2002	7,148.20	7,170.80	−22.60
Jan-2003	7,184.90	7,191.49	−6.59
Apr-2003	7,249.30	7,222.54	26.76
Jul-2003	7,352.90	7,287.22	65.68
Oct-2003	7,394.30	7,401.40	−7.10
Jan-2004	7,475.10	7,457.45	17.65
Apr-2004	7,520.50	7,537.80	−17.30
Jul-2004	7,585.50	7,586.10	−0.60
Oct-2004	7,664.30	7,647.08	17.22
Jan-2005	7,709.40	7,726.90	−17.50
Apr-2005	7,775.20	7,774.79	0.41
Jul-2005	7,852.80	7,836.58	16.22
Oct-2005	7,876.90	7,915.37	−38.47
Jan-2006	7,961.90	7,940.62	21.28
Apr-2006	8,009.30	8,018.19	−8.89
Jul-2006	8,063.80	8,069.89	−6.09
Oct-2006	8,141.20	8,121.94	19.26
Jan-2007	8,215.70	8,199.23	16.47
Apr-2007	8,244.30	8,279.27	−34.97
Jul-2007	8,302.20	8,309.31	−7.11
Oct-2007	8,341.30	8,358.68	−17.38

Accuracy Measures	Value
AIC	671.12
BIC	675.67
Mean Absolute Percentage Error (MAPE)	0.31%
R-Square	99.95%
Adjusted R-Square	99.95%
Root-Mean-Square-Error	24.87
Theil	0.46

Method Statistics	Value
Method Selected	Double Holt
Level	0.77
Trend	0.39

conventions are used by ForecastX™ for all smoothing models (simple, Holt's, and Winters'):

ForecastX™ Naming Conventions for Smoothing Constants

Alpha (α)   =   the level smoothing constant
Gamma (γ)   =   the trend smoothing constant
Beta (β)   =   the seasonal smoothing constant

Thus 0.39 in the ForecastX™ output in Table 3.3 is the trend smoothing constant.

For the personal consumption data, Equations 3.4 through 3.6 can be used to calculate the Holt's forecast for April 1990. To do so we will arbitrarily select the first actual value as our initial smoothed value ($F_1 = 4757.1$) and 8 as our initial trend ($T_1 = 8$). The smoothed value for period 2 (April 1990) is calculated by:

$$F_{t+1} = \alpha X_t + (1 - \alpha)(F_t + T_1)$$
$$F_2 = 0.77(4757.10) + (1 - 0.77)(4757.1 + 8)$$
$$= 3662.967 + 1095.973$$
$$= 4758.94$$

The trend estimate for period 2 is calculated as:

$$T_{t+1} = \gamma(F_{t+1} - F_t) + (1 - \gamma)T_t$$
$$T_2 = 0.39(4758.94 - 4757.10) + (1 - 0.39)(8)$$
$$= 0.39(1.84) + (0.61)(8)$$
$$= 0.7176 + 4.88$$
$$= 5.5976$$

The forecast for period 2 is calculated as:

$$H_{t+m} = F_{t+1} + mT_{t+1}$$
$$H_2 = F_2 + 1T_2$$
$$= 4758.94 + (1)(5.5976)$$
$$= 4764.54$$

Our calculated forecast for April 1990 differs from what you see in Table 3.3. This is because our arbitrary selection of seed values differs from those selected by ForecastX™. Over the course of many quarters the effect of differing seed values would diminish to almost nothing, and if we continued the hand calculations our final forecasts would be virtually identical to those in Table 3.3.

Figure 3.5 shows a plot of both the actual values and the forecast values generated by this model. Some commercially available forecasting packages allow the forecaster to minimize the value of RMSE (or some similar summary statistic) by automatically adjusting the smoothing constants (ForecastX™ automatically adjusts). This, of course, is preferable to making numerous adjustments by hand. We picked the smoothing constants here using ForecastX™.

FIGURE 3.5
Personal
Consumption
Expenditures and
Holt's Forecast
(Level = 0.77;
Trend = 0.39)
(c3t3)

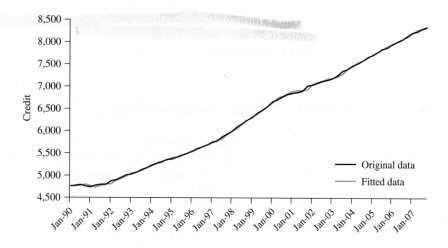

Dates	Original Data	Fitted Data	Dates	Original Data	Fitted Data
Jan-1990	4,757.10	4,766.41	Jan-1999	6,311.30	6,325.32
Apr-1990	4,773.00	4,761.70	Apr-1999	6,409.70	6,388.92
Jul-1990	4,792.60	4,776.21	Jul-1999	6,476.70	6,485.49
Oct-1990	4,758.30	4,799.52	Oct-1999	6,556.80	6,556.69
Jan-1991	4,738.10	4,766.22	Jan-2000	6,661.30	6,634.77
Apr-1991	4,779.40	4,734.64	Apr-2000	6,703.30	6,741.08
Jul-1991	4,800.10	4,772.47	Jul-2000	6,768.00	6,786.65
Oct-1991	4,795.90	4,805.34	Oct-2000	6,825.00	6,841.39
Jan-1992	4,875.00	4,806.87	Jan-2001	6,853.10	6,893.00
Apr-1992	4,903.00	4,888.37	Apr-2001	6,870.30	6,914.64
Jul-1992	4,951.80	4,933.05	Jul-2001	6,900.50	6,919.67
Oct-1992	5,009.40	4,986.48	Oct-2001	7,017.60	6,938.37
Jan-1993	5,027.30	5,049.94	Jan-2002	7,042.20	7,056.38
Apr-1993	5,071.90	5,071.60	Apr-2002	7,083.50	7,098.28
Jul-1993	5,127.30	5,111.00	Jul-2002	7,123.20	7,135.32
Oct-1993	5,172.90	5,167.57	Oct-2002	7,148.20	7,170.80
Jan-1994	5,230.30	5,217.28	Jan-2003	7,184.90	7,191.49
Apr-1994	5,268.00	5,276.78	Apr-2003	7,249.30	7,222.54
Jul-1994	5,305.70	5,316.89	Jul-2003	7,352.90	7,287.22
Oct-1994	5,358.70	5,351.82	Oct-2003	7,394.30	7,401.40
Jan-1995	5,367.20	5,402.70	Jan-2004	7,475.10	7,457.45
Apr-1995	5,411.70	5,410.40	Apr-2004	7,520.50	7,537.80
Jul-1995	5,458.80	5,446.81	Jul-2004	7,585.50	7,586.10
Oct-1995	5,496.10	5,495.02	Oct-2004	7,664.30	7,647.08
Jan-1996	5,544.60	5,535.15	Jan-2005	7,709.40	7,726.90
Apr-1996	5,604.90	5,584.54	Apr-2005	7,775.20	7,774.79
Jul-1996	5,640.70	5,648.38	Jul-2005	7,852.80	7,836.58
Oct-1996	5,687.60	5,688.36	Oct-2005	7,876.90	7,915.37
Jan-1997	5,749.10	5,733.44	Jan-2006	7,961.90	7,940.62
Apr-1997	5,775.80	5,795.81	Apr-2006	8,009.30	8,018.19
Jul-1997	5,870.70	5,824.78	Jul-2006	8,063.80	8,069.89
Oct-1997	5,931.40	5,918.15	Oct-2006	8,141.20	8,121.94
Jan-1998	5,996.80	5,990.32	Jan-2007	8,215.70	8,199.23
Apr-1998	6,092.10	6,059.21	Apr-2007	8,244.30	8,279.27
Jul-1998	6,165.70	6,158.21	Jul-2007	8,302.20	8,309.31
Oct-1998	6,248.80	6,239.89	Oct-2007	8,341.30	8,358.68

Holt's form of exponential smoothing is then best used when the data show some linear trend but little or no seasonality. A descriptive name for Holt's smoothing might be *linear-trend smoothing.*

WINTERS' EXPONENTIAL SMOOTHING

Winters' exponential smoothing model is the second extension of the basic smoothing model; it is used for data that exhibit both trend and seasonality.

Winters' exponential smoothing model is the second extension of the basic smoothing model; it is used for data that exhibit both trend and seasonality. It is a three-parameter model that is an extension of Holt's model. An additional equation adjusts the model for the seasonal component. The four equations necessary for Winters' model are:

$$F_t = \alpha X_t/S_{t-p} + (1-\alpha)(F_{t-1} + T_{t-1}) \qquad (3.7)$$
$$S_t = \beta X_t/F_t + (1-\beta)S_{t-p} \qquad (3.8)$$
$$T_t = \gamma(F_t - F_{t-1}) + (1-\gamma)T_{t-1} \qquad (3.9)$$
$$W_{t+m} = (F_t + mT_t)\,S_{t+m-p} \qquad (3.10)$$

where:

F_t = Smoothed value for period t
α = Smoothing constant for the level $(0 < \alpha < 1)$
X_t = Actual value now (in period t)
F_{t-1} = Average experience of series smoothed to period $t-1$
T_{t+1} = Trend estimate
S_t = Seasonality estimate
β = Smoothing constant for seasonality estimate $(0 < \beta < 1)$
γ = Smoothing constant for trend estimate $(0 < \gamma < 1)$
m = Number of periods in the forecast lead period
p = Number of periods in the seasonal cycle
W_{t+m} = Winters' forecast for m periods into the future

Equation 3.7 updates the smoothed series for both trend and seasonality; note that the equation is only slightly different from Equation 3.4 in Holt's model. In Equation 3.7, X_t is divided by S_{t-p} to adjust for seasonality; this operation deseasonalizes the data or removes any seasonal effects left in the data. It is easy to see how this deseasonalizes the data if you consider what happens when S_{t-p} is greater than 1, as it would be when the value in period $t-p$ is greater than the average in its seasonality. Dividing X_t by S_{t-p} reduces the original value by a percentage equal to the percentage that the seasonality of the period was above the average. An opposite adjustment would take place if the period were below the average in terms of seasonality.

FIGURE 3.6
Quarterly Light
Truck Production
in Units (TS) and a
Winters' Exponential
Smoothing Forecast
of Light Truck
Production (Level =
0.41, Seasonal = 0.37,
and Trend = 0.03)
(c3t4)

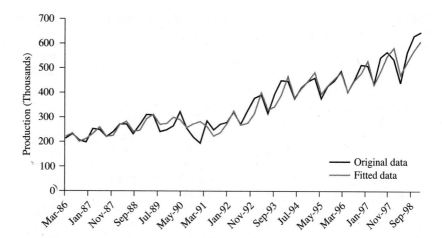

The seasonality estimate itself is smoothed in Equation 3.8, and the trend estimate is smoothed in Equation 3.9; each of these processes is exactly the same as in simple exponential smoothing. The final equation, 3.10, is used to compute the forecast for *m* periods into the future; the procedure is almost identical to that in Holt's model (Equation 3.6).

To illustrate Winters' exponential smoothing we will use data for the production of light trucks in the United States by quarter. Light truck production is quite seasonal, with quarter 2 typically being the strongest production quarter (this includes the months of April, May, and June). As you can see in Figure 3.6, there has been an overall upward trend in the data since our 1986Q1 starting point. You have seen already how to apply the equations to do a few of the calculations for simple and Holt's exponential smoothing. We will not repeat that process for the Winters' model.

Having ForecastX™ determine the parameters that would minimize the RMSE results in a level of 0.41, a seasonal of 0.37, and a trend of 0.03. The last period for this model is 1999Q2.

As with simple and Holt's exponential smoothing, initial values must be selected to *initialize* or *warm up* the model. Over a long time period, such as in this example, the particular values selected have little effect on the forecast of light truck production for 2000. These initial values are also determined within the software.

The results of the Winters' exponential smoothing forecast of light truck production are shown in Table 3.4 and in Figure 3.6. You can see, especially in the graph, that the model works quite well. The root-mean-squared error (RMSE) of 16.33 for the forecast period is only about 2.6 percent of the average quarterly production for the last two quarters of 1999 and the first two quarters of 2000. (The average quarterly sales for these four quarters was 615.78.)

TABLE 3.4 Winters' Three-Parameter Linear and Seasonal Exponential Smoothing for Light Truck Production   (c3t4)

Date	Original Data	Fitted Data	Error	Date	Original Data	Fitted Data	Error
Mar-1986	213.83	220.59	−6.76	Sep-1993	315.82	330.88	−15.07
Jun-1986	231.68	234.30	−2.62	Dec-1993	394.48	343.51	50.97
Sep-1986	205.90	200.72	5.19	Mar-1994	449.78	389.52	60.26
Dec-1986	197.82	211.83	−14.02	Jun-1994	447.02	465.95	−18.93
Mar-1987	252.45	232.49	19.95	Sep-1994	376.37	380.11	−3.73
Jun-1987	249.02	259.55	−10.53	Dec-1994	421.07	417.25	3.81
Sep-1987	220.37	220.94	−0.57	Mar-1995	446.75	448.00	−1.25
Dec-1987	239.85	225.35	14.49	Jun-1995	460.55	482.79	−22.24
Mar-1988	271.03	269.32	1.71	Sep-1995	377.20	395.11	−17.92
Jun-1988	271.92	282.98	−11.05	Dec-1995	427.25	428.41	−1.17
Sep-1988	231.70	242.69	−10.99	Mar-1996	448.99	455.79	−6.80
Dec-1988	269.23	246.17	23.06	Jun-1996	488.18	483.21	4.98
Mar-1989	311.13	293.63	17.50	Sep-1996	403.40	404.38	−0.98
Jun-1989	309.74	311.78	−2.04	Dec-1996	452.82	450.24	2.57
Sep-1989	240.94	270.41	−29.47	Mar-1997	513.58	479.05	34.54
Dec-1989	248.50	274.57	−26.07	Jun-1997	509.55	529.09	−19.54
Mar-1990	264.41	300.17	−35.76	Sep-1997	437.25	432.84	4.41
Jun-1990	322.82	290.63	32.19	Dec-1997	543.44	485.16	58.27
Sep-1990	254.99	257.40	−2.41	Mar-1998	566.82	548.40	18.42
Dec-1990	218.56	272.98	−54.42	Jun-1998	535.83	582.86	−47.03
Mar-1991	194.56	282.58	−88.02	Sep-1998	440.15	472.96	−32.82
Jun-1991	285.71	262.43	23.27	Dec-1998	565.61	524.00	41.60
Sep-1991	248.66	223.70	24.96	Mar-1999	632.32	572.19	60.12
Dec-1991	271.55	237.01	34.54	Jun-1999	646.66	609.86	36.79
Mar-1992	279.71	274.17	5.53	Sep-1999	547.793	*526.45*	
Jun-1992	322.26	326.10	−3.84	Dec-1999	601.651	*620.95*	
Sep-1992	271.39	268.52	2.87	Mar-2000	660.525	*660.37*	
Dec-1992	326.65	275.18	51.47	Jun-2000	653.024	*668.50*	
Mar-1993	378.13	315.74	62.39				
Jun-1993	391.59	400.91	−9.32				

Level = 0.41; Seasonal = 0.37; Trend = 0.03
Historical root-mean-squared error (RMSE) = 30.05; holdout 🔊 period RMSE = 16.33
Mean absolute percentage error (MAPE) = 6.64%
Please note carefully that some software packages assign the names *Alpha* to the simple smoothing factor, *Gamma* to the smoothing factor for the trend estimate, and *Beta* to the smoothing factor for the seasonality estimate.

The Seasonal Indices

Winters' exponential smoothing provides forecasters with one additional piece of information that can often be of value. As part of the calculation with an adjustment for seasonality, seasonal indices are calculated and displayed in most forecasting software. ForecastX™ produces seasonal indices with each Winters' model. For the quarterly light truck production model we estimated, the seasonal indices were calculated as:

Seasonal Indices	Value
Index 1	1.04
Index 2	1.10
Index 3	0.92
Index 4	0.94

Since our data set began with the first quarter of the year 1986 (i.e., January, February, and March), index 1 above refers to this first quarter of the year as well. The remaining three quarters also match the calendar quarters. These indices may be easily interpreted as percentages. Index 1 is interpreted as indicating that quarter 1 truck production is usually about 4 percent above an "average quarter." An average quarter is the result of adding all four quarters together and dividing by four.

With this interpretation in mind it becomes easy to see that the "big" quarter for truck production is quarter 2; quarters 3 and 4 are below-average quarters. Some products and services will exhibit very strong seasonality, while others may be affected only to a minor degree. When working with business and economic data, it is usually a good assumption to expect the data to be seasonal. Computing a Winters' model for the data will help the researcher determine the magnitude of the seasonality and identify precisely when above-average and below-average occurrences take place.

ADAPTIVE–RESPONSE-RATE SINGLE EXPONENTIAL SMOOTHING

An interesting variant on simple smoothing called *adaptive–response-rate single exponential smoothing (ADRES)* has an important advantage over normal smoothing models because of the manner in which the smoothing constant is chosen. In ADRES smoothing there is no requirement to actually choose an α value! This is an attractive feature if what you need is a very low cost method of forecasting requiring no sophisticated knowledge of the technique. Real-world situations requiring the frequent forecasting of many items (perhaps thousands) would be ideal candidates for ADRES smoothing forecasts.

Adaptive-response smoothing does not use one single α value like the simple exponential smoothing model does. The word *adaptive* in its name gives a clue to how the model works. The α value in the ADRES model is not just a single number, but rather *adapts* to the data. When there is a change in the basic pattern of the data, the α value adapts.

For instance, suppose that some data to be forecast fluctuate around a mean value of m. The best estimate of the next observation of the data might then be that mean value (m). But suppose further that after some time an outside force

Adaptive-response smoothing does not use one single α value like the simple exponential smoothing model does.

changes the mean value of m and the new value is now m'. The data then fluctuate around the new mean value of m'. If we had a way of adapting to the new mean of m', we could then use that adapted estimate as the forecast for future values of the data. In fact, we would like to be able to adapt each time the mean value of the data changed; sometimes we would adapt very often, if the mean changed frequently, and at other times we would adapt very rarely, if the data changed only infrequently.

Because of the simplicity of the ADRES smoothing model and its ability to adapt to changing circumstances, it is quite often used in actual practice. Keep in mind, however, that it is a variant of the simple smoothing model and so assumes that the data to be forecast have little trend or seasonality (or that the trend or seasonality in the data has been removed).

The ADRES model looks very much like the simple smoothing model presented earlier:

$$F_{t+1} = \alpha_t X_t + (1 - \alpha_t)F_t \qquad \text{(ADRES equation)} \qquad \textbf{(3.11)}$$

where:

$$\alpha_t = \left| \frac{S_t}{A_t} \right| \qquad \textbf{(3.12)}$$

$$S_t = \beta e_t + (1 - \beta)S_{t-1} \qquad \text{(Smoothed error)} \qquad \textbf{(3.13)}$$

$$A_t = \beta|e_t| + (1 - \beta)A_{t-1} \quad \text{(Absolute smoothed error)} \qquad \textbf{(3.14)}$$

$$e_t = X_t - F_t \qquad\qquad\qquad \text{(Error)} \qquad \textbf{(3.15)}$$

Note carefully the subscripts on the α term! There may now be a different α value for each period.

The ADRES equation is the same as the one for simple exponential smoothing with the exception of the manner in which the α value is chosen. In the simple exponential smoothing model we chose the α value by selecting the value that minimized the root-mean-squared error associated with the model. But in simple smoothing we were allowed to choose only a single value for α. In the ADRES smoothing model we may allow the α value to adapt as the data change.

The smoothing value (α) is now given as the absolute value of the smoothed error divided by the absolute smoothed error. The smoothed error is itself a smoothed value, with a smoothing factor of β. The absolute smoothed error is also a smoothed value, again using the smoothing constant β. In most cases, β is assigned a value of either 0.1 or 0.2. Thus, the first term of both the smoothed error and absolute smoothed error equations has a lighter weight than the second term.

To explain ADRES smoothing, consider Table 3.5, which lists 12 values of an observed data series. We would like to model the series using an adaptive–response-rate smoothing model. Note that the first six values of the series average

TABLE 3.5
Adaptive-Response
Example   (c3t5)

Period	Observed	Forecast	Error	Smoothed Error	Absolute Smoothed Error	α
1	100					
2	96	100.000	−4.00	−0.800	0.800	1.000
3	107	96.000	11.00	1.560	2.840	0.549
4	98	102.042	−4.04	0.440	3.080	0.143
5	103	101.464	1.53	0.659	2.771	0.238
6	99	101.830	−2.83	−0.039	2.783	0.014
7	126	101.790	24.21	4.811	7.068	0.681
8	128	118.267	9.73	5.795	7.601	0.762
9	122	125.687	−3.69	3.899	6.818	0.572
10	130	123.579	6.42	4.403	6.739	0.653
11	125	127.774	−2.77	2.968	5.946	0.499
12	124	126.390	−2.39	1.896	5.235	0.362

about 100; the last six values in the series average about 125. This is a situation similar to that described in the preceding paragraphs and one conducive to the use of this technique. An adaptive–response-rate model should do quite well in modeling these data.

For period 5 the computations are as follows (with some rounding difference in the third decimal place):

$$F_5 = \alpha_4 X_4 + (1 - \alpha_4)F_4$$
$$= (0.143)(98) + (1 - 0.143)(102.042)$$
$$= 14.014 + 87.450$$
$$= 101.464$$

Once the observed value of 103 becomes available for period 5, it is possible to make the following computations (assuming $\beta = .2$):

$$e_5 = 103 - 101.464 = 1.536$$
$$S_5 = (0.2)(1.536) + (1 - 0.2)(0.440) = 0.659$$
$$A_5 = (0.2)(|1.536|) + (1 - 0.2)(3.080) = 2.771$$

and finally

$$\alpha_5 = \left| \frac{0.659}{2.771} \right| = 0.238$$

The process continues iteratively for all the remaining values in the example. In ForecastX™ you will get somewhat different results due to its use of a somewhat different algorithm.

Perhaps the most important consideration in adaptive–response-rate single exponential smoothing is the selection of the appropriate β factor. The β factor is usually set near 0.1 or 0.2 because these values reduce the effects of previous errors (i.e., they allow adaptation) but the values are small enough that the adaptation takes place gradually.

The ADRES model has no explicit way to handle seasonality. There are ways of using the ADRES model, however, with seasonal data. In fact, simple smoothing, Holt's smoothing, and the ADRES smoothing model may all be used with seasonal data. An example follows in the next section.

USING SINGLE, HOLT'S, OR ADRES SMOOTHING TO FORECAST A SEASONAL DATA SERIES

When data have a seasonal pattern, the Winters' model provides an easy way to incorporate the seasonality *explicitly* into the model. An alternative method, however, is widely practiced. This alternative consists of first "deseasonalizing" the data. Deseasonalizing is a process that removes the effects of seasonality from the raw data before the forecasting model is employed.[5] The forecasting model is then applied to the deseasonalized data, and finally, the results are "reseasonalized" to provide accurate forecasts. In sum, the process consists of these steps:

1. Calculate seasonal indices for the series. This can be done in different ways, one of which is to use the **Holt Winters** command routine in ForecastX™.

2. Deseasonalize the original data by dividing each value by its corresponding seasonal index.

---

[5] A complete description of deseasonalizing and reseasonalizing data appears in Chapter 6. The results that follow here are computed with ForecastX™ using the **Holt Winters** command routine.

3. Apply a forecasting method (such as simple, Holt's, or adaptive-response exponential smoothing) to the deseasonalized series to produce an intermediate forecast of the deseasonalized data.

4. Reseasonalize the series by multiplying each deseasonalized forecast by its corresponding seasonal index.

Many forecasters have found this method more accurate than using Winters' smoothing to incorporate seasonality.

Many forecasters have found this method more accurate than using Winters' smoothing to incorporate seasonality. This method is more flexible than the Winters' method alone because it allows for the use of simple smoothing in situations without any trend whatsoever while allowing Holt's smoothing to be used if a trend is present. (Recall that Winters' model assumes that a trend is present.) Further, the ADRES model could be used in situations where some adaptation of the α factor is desirable.

To illustrate this approach to forecasting a seasonal series, let us return to the light truck production data used in our example of the application of Winters' exponential smoothing. Table 3.6 shows seasonally adjusted light truck production data (TPSA), a Holt's exponential smoothing forecast of the deseasonalized light truck production (TPSA_FCST), the seasonal indices (SI) obtained from the **Holt Winters** command routine in ForecastX™, and the reseasonalized forecast of light truck production (TPF). In this table TPSA = TP ÷ SI, and TPF = TPSA_FCST × SI. You may want to check a couple of these calculations to verify the process for yourself (you will get slightly different answers due to rounding effects).

The results of this forecast of light truck production are shown in Figure 3.7. The RMSE for the historical period is higher than that from the Winters' forecast (see Table 3.4). For this approach the forecast period RMSE is about 5.9 percent of the average quarterly production for the forecast period compared to 2.6 percent for the Winters' forecast.

NEW-PRODUCT FORECASTING (GROWTH CURVE FITTING)

For new products, because they typically lack historical data, most forecasting techniques cannot produce satisfying results. For example, it is typically impossible for Holt's exponential smoothing to determine the trend since the data set is too small. Alternatively, it may only predict a strong trend despite the fact that the new product has a growth limitation. To overcome this difficulty, forecasters use a number of models that generally fall in the category called *diffusion models* (probably because they described the manner in which technological innovations and new products "diffused" through an industry). These models are alternatively called S-curves, growth models, saturation models, or substitution curves. We have already seen one of these diffusion models in Chapter 1: the Bass model. An understanding of how to correctly use these models in the forecasting process can make them important tools for managerial decisions. These models as a group

TABLE 3.6 Seasonally Adjusted Light Truck Production (TPSA), Holt's Exponential Smoothing Forecast of Seasonally Adjusted Light Truck Production (TPSA_FCST), the Seasonal Indices (SI), and the Reseasonalized Forecast of Light Truck Production (TPF)   (c3t6)

Date	TPSA	TPSA_FCST	SI	TPF	Date	TPSA	TPSA_FCST	SI	TPF
Mar-1986	204.88	211.66	1.04	220.902	Sep-1994	408.68	418.79	0.92	385.689
Jun-1986	211.44	213.28	1.10	233.702	Dec-1994	448.13	420.30	0.94	394.913
Sep-1986	223.58	217.18	0.92	200.012	Mar-1995	428.05	439.88	1.04	459.101
Dec-1986	210.53	225.01	0.94	211.423	Jun-1995	420.31	440.80	1.10	483.012
Mar-1987	241.88	222.91	1.04	232.644	Sep-1995	409.57	437.40	0.92	402.826
Jun-1987	227.25	236.66	1.10	259.325	Dec-1995	454.71	430.19	0.94	404.214
Sep-1987	239.29	237.06	0.92	218.317	Mar-1996	430.19	447.74	1.04	467.299
Dec-1987	255.26	242.91	0.94	228.238	Jun-1996	445.52	445.42	1.10	488.074
Mar-1988	259.68	253.65	1.04	264.733	Sep-1996	438.03	451.34	0.92	415.662
Jun-1988	248.16	261.53	1.10	286.572	Dec-1996	481.92	450.82	0.94	423.590
Sep-1988	251.58	260.17	0.92	239.608	Mar-1997	492.08	471.44	1.04	492.035
Dec-1988	286.54	260.93	0.94	245.171	Jun-1997	465.02	487.47	1.10	534.146
Mar-1989	298.11	277.99	1.04	290.133	Sep-1997	474.78	483.09	0.92	444.903
Jun-1989	282.68	292.77	1.10	320.800	Dec-1997	578.37	485.19	0.94	455.889
Sep-1989	261.62	293.32	0.92	270.129	Mar-1998	543.09	535.91	1.04	559.328
Dec-1989	264.47	283.35	0.94	266.236	Jun-1998	489.01	546.63	1.10	598.969
Mar-1990	253.34	279.10	1.04	291.291	Sep-1998	477.93	526.32	0.92	484.718
Jun-1990	294.61	271.28	1.10	297.257	Dec-1998	601.96	509.65	0.94	478.870
Sep-1990	276.88	286.68	0.92	264.020	Mar-1999	605.85	559.88	1.04	584.341
Dec-1990	232.61	286.49	0.94	269.191	Jun-1999	590.15	589.14	1.10	645.546
Mar-1991	186.42	265.00	1.04	276.576	Sep-99	594.81214	633.28	0.92	583.223
Jun-1991	260.74	230.90	1.10	253.004	Dec-99	640.32096	629.27	0.94	591.270
Sep-1991	270.01	247.78	0.92	228.190	Mar-00	632.87576	639.27	1.04	667.203
Dec-1991	289.01	261.41	0.94	245.627	Jun-00	595.95967	652.76	1.10	715.263
Mar-1992	268.00	277.94	1.04	290.078					
Jun-1992	294.10	276.81	1.10	303.320	**Holdout-Period Forecast RMSE**				
Sep-1992	294.69	288.63	0.92	265.812					
Dec-1992	347.64	295.29	0.94	277.458	**Forecast**	**Actual**	$(A_t - F_t)$	$(A_t - F_t)^2$	
Mar-1993	362.30	324.27	1.04	338.439	583.223	547.793	−35.43	1255.27	
Jun-1993	357.37	347.10	1.10	380.334	591.270	601.651	10.38	107.77	
Sep-1993	342.92	357.12	0.92	328.895	667.203	660.525	−6.68	44.59	
Dec-1993	419.84	355.54	0.94	334.067	715.263	653.024	−62.24	3873.75	
Mar-1994	430.95	391.46	1.04	408.558					
Jun-1994	407.95	416.35	1.10	456.218	Holdout RMSE = 36.34				

Historic RMSE = 32.56 ←

Holdout period ←

allow the forecaster to model the characteristic patterns that economists have identified for a number of processes (most importantly including the introduction of new products).

In this section we present two new product models. The two diffusion models are the Gompertz curve and the logistic curve. There are two main differences between these models. The first difference is in the shapes of the product curve

FIGURE 3.7 **Light Truck Production and Light Truck Production Forecast Based on a Holt's Exponential Smoothing Forecast of Deseasonalized Light Truck Production** (c3t6)

TP = Actual light truck production

TPF = Forecast of light truck production

Historical period: RMSE = 32.56

Forecast period: RMSE = 36.34

Light truck production was first deseasonalized, then a Holt's forecast was done, and the results were reseasonalized.

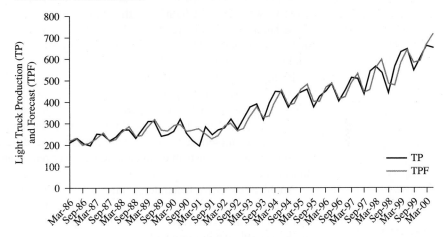

(i.e., amount of time that lapses before a product's growth curve stabilizes). The second difference lies in the fact that these new-product models may use different lower and upper limits for the same forecast data.

These models are most commonly used to forecast the sales of new products and technology life cycles. Just as new products have life cycles, technologies also have life cycles that follow a common pattern:

1. A period of slow growth just after introduction during an embryonic stage.

2. A period of rapid growth.

3. Slowing growth in a mature phase.

4. Decline.

The forecaster's task is to identify and estimate the parameters of such a pattern of growth using the same set of diagnostic statistics we have already learned to use with smoothing models in general.

Each new-product model has its own lower and upper limit. Expert opinion is needed to determine the correct upper and lower limits on the growth curves. In most instances, the lower limitation is 0 (e.g., sales cannot be below zero). Determining the upper limit is a more complicated undertaking. Regardless of the complication, diffusion models provide an important technique to use for forecasting when new products or technologies will replace existing products or technologies.

A significant benefit of using diffusion models in new-product forecasting is to identify and predict the timing of the four phases of the life cycle. In the late 1990s the U.S. government decided to adopt a national standard for high-definition television (HDTV) and set a timetable for the changeover from analog to HDTV. The original plan called for broadcasters to begin broadcasting digital signals by 2002 and to turn off their analog transmitters altogether in 2006. This was a very ambitious plan and assumed that the adoption of HDTV by consumers would take place very quickly. Realizing that the elimination of analog transmissions would cause hardship if it occurred too early, another provision set forth by the FCC was that a market needed 85 percent penetration by HDTV before the analog signal could be eliminated.

Being able to forecast the growth and maturity of HDTV technology would allow broadcasters the opportunity to see if the 2006 "drop dead" date for analog television was reasonable. If 85 percent penetration was not reasonably achieved by this date, then broadcasters would be in the unenviable position of having to keep two transmitters functioning with, perhaps, two different and costly sets of programming. The costs in extra electricity, tower rental, and insurance would be substantial.

Analyses of many technology introductions (like HDTV) have shown that technology develops initially at a very slow growth rate. But it is also the case that these same technologies soon begin to grow in predictable patterns such as the S-curve shown in Figure 3.8.

The usual reason for the transition from very slow initial growth to rapid growth is often the result of solutions to technical difficulties and the market's acceptance of the new technology. But such growth curves also have their limits; the rapid growth cannot be sustained indefinitely. There are upper limits on the

FIGURE 3.8
Characteristic
S-Curve

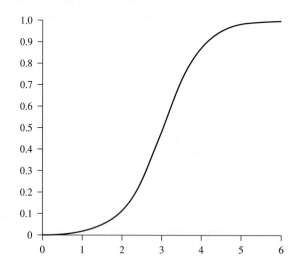

FIGURE 3.9
Shipments and
Cumulative
Shipments of HDTV
Units   (c3t7)

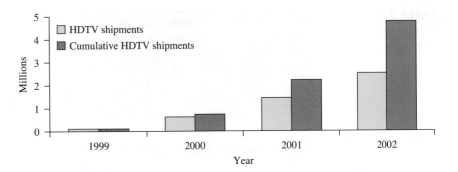

adoptions of new technology or the sales of new products. As the upper limit is reached, a maturity phase occurs in which growth slows and finally ceases. The economic law of diminishing marginal returns is usually at work in these processes.

Figure 3.9 contains information on the early years of HDTV shipments in the United States. During the entire time represented in the graph, there were very few broadcast stations operating in HDTV mode, but in each year the number of HDTV broadcasters increased and the hours of HDTV programming available also increased. This entire four years of data represent the period of experimentation and slow growth characteristic of all new products and technologies.

When a new technology like HDTV enters the marketplace, we can expect an S-curve to accurately predict future shipments or sales. There is, however, more than one technique that could be used to model this S-curve.

Fortunately, ForecastX™ provides flexible settings for a multitude of situations. If you do not know what the upper limit should be, you can use ForecastX™ to determine the best upper limit to fit your data. Of course, if you know the exact upper limit, ForecastX™ can use it to determine an optimal model.

The two most common forms of S-curves used in forecasting are the Gompertz curve and the logistics curve (also called the Pearl curve). A third useful model called the Bass model was discussed in Chapter 1; we will again cover that model and provide an example of its use.

Gompertz Curve

The Gompertz curve is named after its developer, Benjamin Gompertz, an English actuary. Gompertz applied calculus to actuarial questions and is most well known for *Gompertz's Law of Mortality*. Gompertz's law showed that the mortality rate increases in a geometric progression. Thus, when death rates are plotted on a logarithmic scale, a straight line known as the *Gompertz function* is obtained. The Gompertz curve is the most used actuarial function for investigating the process of aging. The slope of this function is known as the rate of actuarial aging, and differences in the longevity between species are the result in large part of differences in this rate of aging.

TABLE 3.7

Data on HDTV Shipments (c3t7)

Date	Cumulative HDTV Shipments (millions)
12/31/1999	0.12
12/31/2000	0.77
12/31/2001	2.23
12/31/2002	4.76

The Gompertz function is given as

$$Y_t = Le^{-ae^{-bt}}$$

where:

L = Upper limit of Y

e = Natural number 2.718282 . . .

a and b = coefficients describing the curve (estimated by ForecastX™)

The Gompertz curve will range in value from zero to L as t varies from $-\infty$ to ∞. The curve is widely used in the fields of biology and demography to model (i.e., forecast) the level of populations at a given point in time for plants and animals as well as many organisms. The Gompertz curve is an elegant way to summarize the growth of a population with just a few parameters.

Consider the HDTV shipments charted above; the actual figures are given earlier in Table 3.7.

The Gompertz curve estimated from this data (with the assumption that 248 million televisions is the upper limit) is shown in Figure 3.10. The assumption of 248 million television sets is used as the upper limit because in the year 2002 this was the total number of televisions of all types in use. This rather generous assumption reflects the opportunity for every existing television to be converted to an HDTV. An actual forecaster might choose a different upper limit if another rationale seemed more plausible.

Note the characteristic S-shape to the curve. In fitting the curve we have used the first few data points and the known maximum value for television shipments to estimate a forecast of how HDTV shipments will progress through time. We have

FIGURE 3.10

An Estimate of HDTV Shipments Using 4 Years of Data (c3t7)

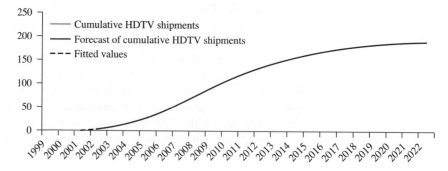

FIGURE 3.11
ForecastX™ Method
Selection Dialog Box
for a Gompertz
Model

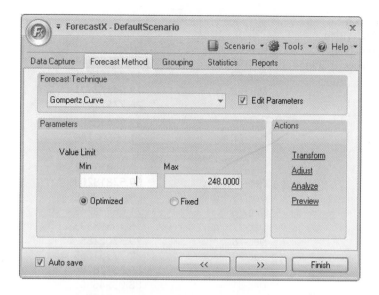

ample evidence that this Gompertz function will model the situation well; when color televisions were introduced in the 1960s, their adoption followed a very similar pattern. This form of curve fitting is often used, as it is here, to make forecasts far into the future. Unlike the moving-average and exponential smoothing models, growth curves are routinely used to make mid- to long-range forecasts.

In order to use ForecastX™ to make the estimate shown in Figure 3.10, the Method Selection dialog box would be filled out as shown in Figure 3.11.

The Edit Parameters box is checked in Figure 3.11 and the maximum value of 248 is entered; this, along with the information on the first four years of actual shipments, allows the estimation of the best-fit Gompertz curve shown in Figure 3.10.

The Gompertz curve is best used in situations where it becomes more difficult to achieve an increase in the growth rate as the maximum value is approached. We will see that this is the exact opposite of the recommendation for the best situation in which to use the logistics function. Consider the adoption of color televisions shown in Table 3.8.

Using only the first five years of data on color television adoptions (and the assumption of a maximum of 100 percent), it is possible to very closely approximate the future growth pattern with a Gompertz function. Figure 3.12 shows the actual and predicted shipments obtained using only the first five data points from Table 3.8.

Had you been asked in late 1969 to forecast color television adoptions with only the first five years of annual data, you would have produced very accurate forecasts if you had used a Gompertz model. The assumption regarding the increased difficulty of obtaining the maximum value as it is approached probably describes color television adoptions quite well. The same assumption might also apply to HDTV adoptions and sales since the situation is similar.

TABLE 3.8
Color Television
Adoption in
Percentages (c3t8)

Year	Percent Adoptions
Dec-65	*0*
Dec-66	*6.145835684*
Dec-67	*12.72965645*
Dec-68	*19.64872441*
Dec-69	*26.77512032*
Dec-70	33.96440431
Dec-71	41.06698245
Dec-72	47.94034951
Dec-73	54.46013052
Dec-74	60.52818203
Dec-75	66.07679819
Dec-76	71.06899248
Dec-77	75.49558333
Dec-78	79.37021852
Dec-79	82.72351665
Dec-80	85.59728784
Dec-81	88.03946805
Dec-82	90.10007711
Dec-83	91.82826105
Dec-84	93.27031978
Dec-85	94.46854445
Dec-86	95.46066873
Dec-87	96.27975333
Dec-88	96.95435387
Dec-89	97.50885698
Dec-90	97.96390133

FIGURE 3.12
Actual and Predicted
Adoptions of Color
Televisions Obtained
by Using the First
Five Years of Adop-
tions and a Gompertz
Estimate (c3t8)

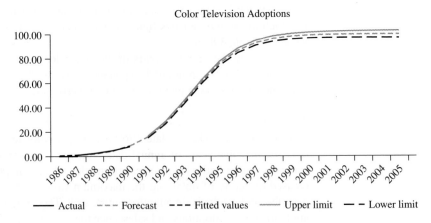

Logistics Curve

The logistics curve is a second way of forecasting with sparse data and is also used frequently to forecast new-product sales. The logistics curve has the following form:

$$Y_t = \frac{L}{1 + ae^{-bt}}$$

where:

L = Upper limit of Y

e = Natural number 2.718282 . . .

a and b = coefficients describing the curve (estimated by ForecastX™)

Just as in the Gompertz function there is an upper limit to Y called L, and e is the base of natural logarithms. The logistics curve is symmetric about its point of inflection (the upper half of the curve is a reflection of the lower half); the Gompertz curve is not necessarily symmetric about its points of inflection. Why would you use the logistics curve rather than the Gompertz curve?

The answer lies in whether, in a particular situation, it is easier to achieve the maximum value the closer you get to it, or whether it becomes more difficult to attain the maximum value the closer you get to it. The question of which function to use in a particular estimate comes down to whether there are factors assisting the attainment of the maximum value once you get close to it, or whether there are factors preventing the attainment of the maximum value once it is nearly attained. If there is an offsetting factor such that growth is more difficult to maintain as the maximum is approached, then the Gompertz curve will be the best choice. If there are no such offsetting factors hindering the attainment of the maximum value, the logistics curve will be the best choice.

A clear case of the appropriate use of a logistics function might be the prediction of U.S. households with telephones. There is a "network effect" at work here such that, as more people have a telephone, telephones become more useful to everyone (since you are now able to call a larger number of people). The larger the network, the greater the advantage to being a member of the network. The more recent case of the adoption of cellular telephones would likely progress in much the same manner as the original telephone adoption. The adoption data for cellular telephones in the United States is presented in Table 3.9.

By fitting a logistics curve to the first five years of cellular telephone data, the results in Figure 3.13 are calculated.

It is not surprising that a logistics estimate of cellular telephone adoption works so well; as individuals have cellular telephones, it becomes more advantageous to have one yourself. Thus there is a factor assisting the attainment of the maximum value the closer you get to the maximum value (i.e., the network effect).

Note that there should be some theoretical reason for choosing a logistics function for your forecast estimate before estimating the model. In the case of cellular

TABLE 3.9
Percentage of
Cellular Telephone
Adoption in the
United States   (c3t9)

Year	Cellular Telephone Adoption
12/31/1986	*0*
12/31/1987	*0.989132021*
12/31/1988	*2.47063319*
12/31/1989	*4.661420125*
12/31/1990	*7.840611381*
12/31/1991	12.33023714
12/31/1992	18.43261935
12/31/1993	26.3098137
12/31/1994	35.82721276
12/31/1995	46.4488152
12/31/1996	57.30203601
12/31/1997	67.43707273
12/31/1998	76.13611792
12/31/1999	83.07839603
12/31/2000	88.3037847
12/31/2001	92.06622305
12/31/2002	94.68961176
12/31/2003	96.47806155
12/31/2004	97.6786669

FIGURE 3.13   Actual and Predicted Adoptions of Cellular Telephones in the United States   (c3t9)

Year	Cellular Telephone Adoption	Logistics
12/31/1986	0	0.54
12/31/1987	0.989132021	1.09
12/31/1988	2.47063319	2.20
12/31/1989	4.661420125	4.37
12/31/1990	7.840611381	8.48
12/31/1991		15.84
12/31/1992		27.65
12/31/1993		43.70
12/31/1994		61.18
12/31/1995		78.19
12/31/1996		86.66
12/31/1997		92.96
12/31/1998		96.40
12/31/1999		98.20
12/31/2000		99.10
12/31/2001		99.56
12/31/2002		99.78
12/31/2003		99.89
12/31/2004		99.95
12/31/2005		99.97

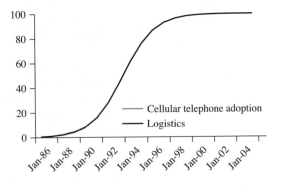

FIGURE 3.14
ForecastX™ Method
Selection Dialog Box
for a Logistics Model

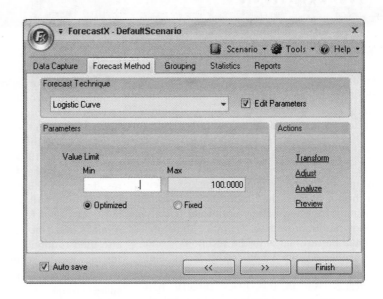

phones the hypothesized existence of a network effect would lead a researcher to choose a logistics model. The ForecastX™ Method Selection dialog box used to select the cellular telephone model appears in Figure 3.14.

Let's generalize our suggestions for employing the Gompertz and logistics models. Use a Gompertz model when you expect it to be more difficult to attain constant improvement as the maximum value is approached. On the other hand, select a logistics model when there are factors that help maintain improvements as the maximum value is approached. At times it will not be easy to predict which of the two models may work best; in those instances ForecastX™ allows the choice of "New Product Forecasting" as a selection in the Method Selection dialog box. Choosing New Product Forecasting allows ForecastX™ to choose the optimal model from among three contenders: the logistics model, the Gompertz model, and a Probit curve.

Bass Model

Named after Professor Frank M. Bass, this model has been used for over 30 years to forecast the diffusion of innovations, to forecast the penetration of new products in a market, and in a variety of biological, medical, and scientific forecasts. This is a relatively simple model in which only three parameters are chosen by the researcher.

As they are used in ForecastX™, the three parameters are p, r, and qbar, where:

p = The innovation rate

r = The imitation rate (called q in the forecasting literature)

qbar = The cumulative value of all the historical values

Christophe Van den Bulte

The United States Department of Energy in 1980 used the Bass model to forecast the adoption of solar batteries. The DOE used a survey of home builders to aid in its initial choices for *p* and *q* values. Using these empirically suggested values, the DOE concluded that solar battery technology was not sufficiently robust to encourage word-of-mouth propagation. Because of their finding they postponed their proposed wide-scale introduction of the technology until solar battery technology had improved to the point that new users would be satisfied with the technology and thus the higher *q* value would predict faster sales growth.

A decade later in the 1990s DirecTV had planned a launch of its subscription satellite television delivery service. Prudently, it attempted to obtain a prelaunch forecast for five years into the future. DirecTV's forecast was again based on the Bass model and the *p* and *q* values were also obtained from a survey of prospective users; this information was combined with histories of similar services. The forecasts produced in 1992 were quite good from the company's point of view and, after the fact, the estimates compared favorably with the actual 1994 to 1999 experience.

Numerous other firms have reported productive results using the Bass model. RCA in the mid-1980s used a modified Bass model to forecast the sales of music CDs as a function of CD player sales. The model proved quite accurate. The Bass model is also used routinely to predict box office revenues for movies and to make decisions on how many screens to use for a particular movie.

Source: Excerpted from "Want to Know How Diffusion Speed Varies across Countries and Products? Try Using a Bass Model," *PDMA Visions* 26, no. 4 (2002), pp. 12–15.

The Bass model could be called a model of social contagion where the *p* (the innovation rate) refers to the probability of initial purchase of a new good independent of the influence of previous buyers (i.e., with no network effect considered). The *r* (the imitation rate) refers to the pressure of imitation on previous purchasers. The Bass model would appear most often in a graph like the S-curves we have been examining. As we indicated in Chapter 1, getting the estimates of the three parameters of the model is the difficult part. We can be helped significantly here by using past studies to suggest parameters that may place us in the ballpark for our own estimates.

Christopher Van den Bulte of the Wharton School has constructed a database of 1,586 sets of *p* and *q* parameters from 113 separate recent articles.[6] Some suggestions from Van den Bulte's work appear in Table 3.10.

An interesting set of patterns emerges from this large number of *p* and *q* estimations. Recall that the parameter Van den Bulte refers to as *q* is the *r* parameter (the imitation rate) in ForecastX™. What estimates for *p* and *q* would be best for your product? Van den Bulte took as a baseline durable goods launched in the United States in 1976. The *p* factor measures the intrinsic tendency for an individual to adopt a new product, while the *q* measures the "word of mouth" or "social contagion" effect on purchases. Van den Bulte recommends that when a

q = "social contagion"

p = new product expansion

[6] Christophe Van den Bulte, "Want to Know How Diffusion Speed Varies across Countries and Products? Try Using a Bass Model," *PDMA Visions* 26, no. 4 (2002), pp. 12–15.

TABLE 3.10
Van den Bulte's *p* and *q* Estimates from Selected Articles

p Estimates	Best Guess	90% Confidence Interval		
Baseline case: U.S. consumer, durable, launch in 1976	0.409	0.355	(t_0)	0.471
For other cases, multiply by the following factors:				
Cellular telephone	0.635	0.465		0.868
Nondurable product	0.931	0.713		1.216
Industrial	1.149	0.909		1.451
Noncommercial innovation	2.406	1.488		3.891
Western Europe	0.949	0.748		1.203
Asia	0.743	0.571		0.966
Other regions	0.699	0.429		1.137
For each year after 1976, multiply by	1.028	1.018		1.039
***q* Estimates (labeled *r* in ForecastX)**				
Baseline case: U.S. consumer, durable, launch in 1976	0.016	0.012		0.021
For other cases, multiply by the following factors:				
Cellular telephone	0.226	0.125		0.409
Nondurable product	0.689	0.415		1.143
Industrial	1.058	0.679		1.650
Noncommercial innovation	0.365	0.146		0.910
Western Europe	0.464	0.296		0.729
Asia	0.595	0.360		0.981
Other regions	0.796	0.315		2.008
For each year after 1976, multiply by	1.021	1.002		1.041

forecaster tries to set the values of *p* and *q* in a Bass model, you should use a range of values within his estimated confidence interval (given in Table 3.10). For countries with a collectivist mentality (like Japan) as opposed to an individualistic mentality (like the United States), a higher *q* value is better. People in collectivist cultures care more about what others think of them, according to Van den Bulte's study. In countries with higher purchasing power, the *p* tends to be higher. More disposable income makes it easier to adopt innovations. Finally, products that exhibit significant network effects or require heavy investment in complementary infrastructure (like television and the cellular telephone) will have higher values for *q*. Van den Bulte has summarized these results in a set of conclusions presented in Table 3.11.

Table 3.12 presents data for the adoption of telephone-answering devices in the United States.

Using only the first five observations in Table 3.12, it is possible to accurately represent the entire adoption cycle for telephone-answering devices. After some

TABLE 3.11

Van den Bulte's Conclusions Regarding p and q Values

- There are systematic regional differences in diffusion patterns.
- The average coefficient of innovation p (speed of takeoff) in Europe and Asia is roughly half of that in the United States.
- The average coefficient of imitation q (speed of late growth) in Asia is roughly a quarter less than that in the United States and Europe.
- Also, economic differences explain national variations in speed better than cultural differences do.
- There are systematic product differences in diffusion patterns. For instance, takeoff is slower for nondurables and products with competing standards that require heavy investments in infrastructure, while late growth is faster for industrial products and products with competing standards, which require heavy investments in infrastructure.

TABLE 3.12

Adoption of Telephone-Answering Devices in the United States (c3t12)

Year	Adoption
Dec-84	*0*
Dec-85	*3.030551*
Dec-86	*7.351138*
Dec-87	*13.29582*
Dec-88	*21.08724*
Dec-89	30.67365
Dec-90	41.59211
Dec-91	52.98598
Dec-92	63.84035
Dec-93	73.31923
Dec-94	80.98819
Dec-95	86.81843
Dec-96	91.04448
Dec-97	94.00304
Dec-98	96.02418
Dec-99	97.38195
Dec-00	98.28381
Dec-01	98.87837
Dec-02	99.26839
Dec-03	99.52341
Dec-04	99.6898

trial and error the researcher has selected a p value of 0.035 and an r value of 0.406. Note that the r value in ForecastX™ is the same as the q value used for explaining the imitation rate in the Bass model, as shown in Figure 3.15. The qbar value is 100 because we are working with percentages.

The resulting plot of actual and predicted values in Figure 3.16 shows a model that closely approximates the actual occurrence in the United States for answering-machine adoptions.

FIGURE 3.15
ForecastX™ Method
Selection Dialog for
the Bass Model

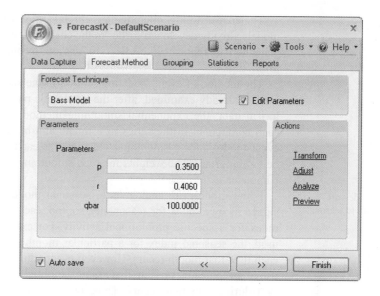

FIGURE 3.16
Bass Model of
Telephone-Answering
Machine Adoptions
in the United States
(c3t12)

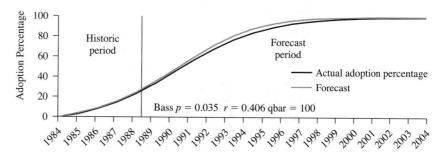

EVENT MODELING

When forecasting sales or demand in a highly promoted market, using the smoothing technique of event modeling will significantly improve forecast accuracy.

Event modeling is a feature of some exponential smoothing programs such as ForecastX™. This feature allows the user to specify the time of one or more special events, such as irregular promotions and natural disasters, in the calibration data. For each type of special event, the effect is estimated and the data adjusted so that the events do not distort the trend and seasonal patterns of the time series.

When forecasting sales or demand in a highly promoted market, using this smoothing technique will significantly improve forecast accuracy. Consider the case of a manufacturer of a popular condiment (e.g., ketchup, mustard, steak sauce, and so on). This type of product tends to be highly seasonal and also tends to be aggressively promoted by marketers. Is there a method for modeling the effect of future promotions on the sales or demand for such a product?

The answer to this dilemma is *event modeling.* By using the basic smoothing models already developed earlier in the chapter as a base, an event model may be generated to replicate the effects of various promotions and combinations of promotions.

The method of event modeling follows in the same pattern for the smoothing models already examined: after the systematic patterns are identified in the historical data, the exponential smoothing method uses smoothing equations for each component in the series to estimate and build up structural patterns. The event model adds a smoothing equation for each of the "events" identified as being important. The weights for each smoothing equation are represented by a parameter.

Event models are analogous to seasonal models.

Event models are analogous to seasonal models: just as each month is assigned its own index for seasonality, so, too, each event type is assigned its own index for a specific promotional activity. For example, when monthly data are used, the seasonal index for a particular month is updated at regular intervals, each time that month recurs. However, event adjustments are created through the use of an indicator variable that assigns an integer for each event type to the period during which it recurs. Thus, one example of integer value assignment would be that 0 indicates a period where no event has occurred, 1 indicates a period where a free-standing insert (FSI) was circulated, 8 indicates a period where thematic advertising was used, and so on. The event indicator variable must be defined for each historic period *and* future period in the forecast horizon. In this way, the event smoothing equation is used to calculate the historical lift in sales above baseline that occurred as a result of a particular type of promotion, and applies that lift to the baseline forecast in the future period where the same promotion is planned.

To illustrate how this method is used in actual practice, we examine some actual demand data. The product, mustard, is a condiment commonly used in American households and found at every picnic. The company that produces and sells mustard uses a number of marketing promotions to enhance sales and maintain market share. Free-standing inserts are perhaps the most common of the promotions for this type of product; these are the familiar coupons found in Sunday newspapers and redeemable when the item is purchased. These FSIs are often used in conjunction with themed advertising campaigns, especially during particular seasons of the year. Our condiment manufacturer uses a separate event value, 7, to stand for the combination of FSIs and an advertising campaign. On-pack coupons are a separate type of coupon usually attached to the product packaging itself and redeemed at the cash register at checkout.

In addition to adjusting the price to the consumer through coupons, the mustard manufacturer also adjusts the price to the jobber by reducing case prices for a short period of time. When this takes place it is common for jobbers to stock up on the reduced price item and delay future purchase. Because of this, the manufacturer uses two event values called *load* and *deload* to signify periods of reduced prices and the periods immediately following such a promotion; these are actually two separate events.

The event values for this particular condiment manufacturer are listed in the following table.

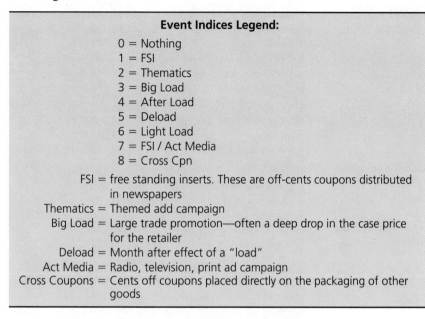

Event Indices Legend:
0 = Nothing
1 = FSI
2 = Thematics
3 = Big Load
4 = After Load
5 = Deload
6 = Light Load
7 = FSI / Act Media
8 = Cross Cpn

FSI = free standing inserts. These are off-cents coupons distributed in newspapers

Thematics = Themed add campaign

Big Load = Large trade promotion—often a deep drop in the case price for the retailer

Deload = Month after effect of a "load"

Act Media = Radio, television, print ad campaign

Cross Coupons = Cents off coupons placed directly on the packaging of other goods

Figure 3.17 shows monthly historical demand of mustard over time. Table 3.13 shows the events related to each of these historical months and the company's planned promotions for the next six months.

Using a Winters' smoothing model on these data picks up the implied seasonality and trend quite well; the calculated level, seasonal, and trend are 0.05, 0.88, and 0.26, respectively. This indicates that there is very little trend in the data but a high degree of seasonality. Actually, some of the apparent seasonality is not seasonality at all; instead, it is "induced seasonality" caused by the company's various promotions. Using the Winters' smoothing model again, but with eight event

FIGURE 3.17
Mustard
Consumption
(c3t13)

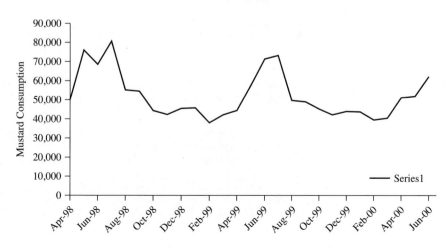

TABLE 3.13
**An Event Model
Example** (c3t13)

Date	Mustard	Event Index
Apr-98	50,137	7
May-98	76,030	7
Jun-98	68,590	3
Jul-98	80,681	4
Aug-05	55,228	5
Sep-05	54,577	0
Oct-05	44,384	8
Nov-05	42,337	0
Dec-05	45,512	6
Jan-06	45,798	4
Feb-06	38,045	5
Mar-06	42,127	0
Apr-06	44,422	2
May-06	57,662	1
Jun-06	71,427	6
Jul-06	73,269	5
Aug-06	49,695	8
Sep-06	49,021	1
Oct-06	45,263	0
Nov-06	42,210	1
Dec-06	43,968	6
Jan-07	43,778	4
Feb-07	39,524	0
Mar-07	40,476	0
Apr-07	51,167	2
May-07	51,916	1
Jun-07	62,274	6
Jul-07		4
Aug-07		5
Sep-07		0
Oct-07		2
Nov-07		1
Dec-07		6

Legend:

0 = Nothing
1 = FSI
2 = Thematics
3 = Big Load
4 = After Load
5 = Deload
6 = Light Load
7 = FSI / Act Media
8 = Cross Cpn

FSI = free-standing inserts. These are off-cents coupons distributed in newspapers
Thematics = Themed ad campaign
Big Load = Large trade promotion—often a deep drop in the case price for the retailer
Deload = Month after effect of a "load"
Act Media = Radio, television, print ad campaign
On-Pack Coupons = Cents off coupons placed directly on the packaging

smoothing factors added in as well, the level, seasonal, and trend factors are 0.2, 0.92, and 0.26. By examining these factors we see that there is definitely little trend, but now the seasonality has also apparently changed.

The seasonality has not disappeared; it is changed by the eight event indices.

	Winters' Model	Winters' Model with Event Indices
Historical RMSE	4,059	2,526.85
Level Smoothing Factor (alpha)	0.05	0.20
Seasonal Smoothing Factor (beta)	0.88	0.92
Trend Smoothing Factor (gamma)	0.26	0.26
Event Index 1	NA	0.94
Event Index 2	NA	1.16
Event Index 3	NA	0.99
Event Index 4	NA	1.03
Event Index 5	NA	1.00
Event Index 6	NA	0.94
Event Index 7	NA	1.03
Event Index 8	NA	0.99

Note that the RMSE for the event model is much lower than the RMSE for the Winters' model (2,526 compared to 4,059). The addition of the events to the historical period caused a tighter fit between the actual mustard demand and predicted mustard demand. Using the knowledge of the planned company promotions for the next six months allows the forecaster to calculate a much better picture of predicted demand than the Winters' model alone.

In this particular case we used the Winters' model as a base because we believed the original data had both trend and seasonality. If the data had lacked trend or seasonality, we could have used simple smoothing as the base model. ForecastX™ allows any number of models to be used as the underlying basis for event forecasting.

Ignoring events (usually promotions) that a company has scheduled in advance will likely lead to poorer forecasts when those events have significant impacts.

However, an event may be any occurrence that has taken place in the historical period that you believe will either be replicated in the forecast period (such as advertising promotions) or require adjustment to the parameters because of its large effect (such as a natural disaster).

FORECASTING JEWELRY SALES AND HOUSES SOLD WITH EXPONENTIAL SMOOTHING

Jewelry Sales

Let us now look at monthly data on jewelry sales in the United States (in millions of dollars), which show a great deal of seasonality, some cycle, and a trend, shown in Figure 3.18.

FIGURE 3.18
Jewelry Sales
(c3f18)

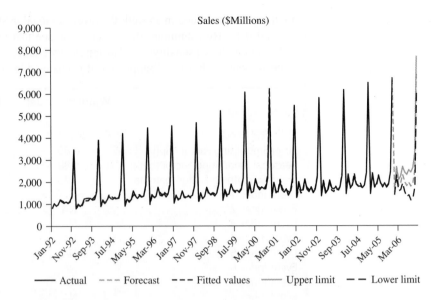

In this chapter Winters' exponential smoothing is the only method we have used so far in which seasonality was explicitly taken into account. Thus, a Winters' model would appear to be an excellent candidate as a forecasting technique for jewelry sales. You might want to go back to Table 2.1, which provided a guide to model selection, to see how this handy table would help you select Winters' model for this series. The Holt's exponential smoothing model might also be a good candidate *if we first deseasonalized the jewelry sales data*. You will note that we do not apply simple or Holt's exponential smoothing to the jewelry sales data because neither of those methods would be an appropriate model given the guidelines in Table 2.1.

Applying the Winters' model, ForecastX™ finds the optimum values for the weights to be level, 0.31; seasonal, 0.86; trend, 0.16. The historic RMSE for this Winters' model is 87.02. The seasonal value shows that we indeed do have a rather high degree of seasonality, and the trend value indicates trend is also present.

The seasonal indices for this model are quite revealing:

Seasonal Indices	Value
Index 1	0.61
Index 2	0.77
Index 3	0.70
Index 4	0.75
Index 5	0.92
Index 6	0.89
Index 7	0.86
Index 8	0.90
Index 9	0.85
Index 10	0.91
Index 11	1.11
Index 12	2.72

The dramatic seasonal index of 2.72 for the month of December is likely due to the gift giving that takes place during the holiday season; even the relatively high index of 1.11 for the month of November is affected by the holiday season. This degree of seasonality shows up clearly in the plot of actual and predicted values in Figure 3.18.

Houses Sold

In Chapter 1 we presented data on total houses sold in the United States; this time series also exhibits trend, seasonality, and some cycle. The data suggest that a Winters' exponential smoothing model might closely approximate the pattern displayed in the historical data.

Figure 3.19 displays the results of running a Winters' model on the houses sold data from 1990 through 1994. Applying the Winters' model, ForecastX™ finds the optimum values for the weights to be level, 0.50; seasonal, 0.30; and trend, 0.00. The historic RMSE for this Winters' model is 4.63. The seasonal value shows that again we have a high degree of seasonality. Note in Figure 3.19 that the housing data actually has two distinctly different trends; until the middle of 2005 the trend is clearly upward, while the trend decreases after this point. What we have in this data is called an inconsistent trend. When this occurs, trend extrapolation (which is what the Winters' model uses) is risky. For short-term forecasts it might be better for the researcher to use only the most recent data exhibiting the downward trend. For longer-term estimates some adjustment taking into account the longer-term trend may be useful.[7]

FIGURE 3.19
Houses Sold (c3f19)

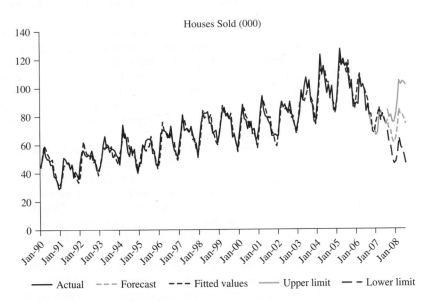

Houses Sold (000)

— Actual   - - - Forecast   - - - Fitted values   —— Upper limit   — - Lower limit

[7] For a more detailed description of this difficulty (and some methods for handling it) see J. S. Armstrong, M. Adya, and F. Collopy, "Rule-Based Forecasting: Using Judgment in Time-Series Extrapolation," in J. S. Armstrong (ed.) *Principles of Forecasting* (Norwell, MA: Kluwer Academic Press, 2001).

The seasonal indices for the houses sold data provide useful information:

Seasonal Indices	Value
Index 1	0.84
Index 2	0.97
Index 3	1.15
Index 4	1.12
Index 5	1.11
Index 6	1.10
Index 7	1.06
Index 8	1.11
Index 9	0.97
Index 10	0.95
Index 11	0.85
Index 12	0.77

Note that the period March through August is above average in seasonality, while the winter months tend to be below average in houses sold.

Summary

If the time series you are forecasting is a stationary one, the moving-average method of forecasting may accurately predict future values. The moving-average method calculates the average of the past observations, and this average becomes the forecast for the next period.

When recent-past observations are thought to contain more information than distant-past observations, some form of exponential smoothing may be appropriate. Exponential smoothing provides self-correcting forecasts that adjust so as to regulate the forecast values by changing them in the opposite direction from recent errors. It is a characteristic of smoothing models in general, however, that their forecasts lag behind movements in the original time-series data. Exponential smoothing requires the specification of a smoothing constant, which determines the relative weights accorded to recent as opposed to more distant historical observations.

A suggested method for choosing an optimal smoothing constant is to minimize the root-mean-squared error (RMSE) or the mean absolute percentage error (MAPE).

When some trend is observed in the original time series, simple exponential smoothing becomes less able to perform accurate prediction; adding a procedure to adjust for the trend results in Holt's two-parameter exponential smoothing. Holt's smoothing adds a growth factor to the smoothing model to account for trend; in a sense, the growth or trend factor itself is smoothed in the same manner as the original data.

When seasonality is also present in the original data, Winters' three-parameter exponential smoothing adds a correction factor to Holt's smoothing model to correct for the seasonality. The correction factor is provided by an additional equation.

Adaptive–response-rate single exponential smoothing provides another technique that can be useful when the "level" of the forecasted variable changes infrequently. Adaptive-response models adjust the smoothing factor for changing conditions rather than choosing a constant smoothing factor.

In addition to trying Winters' exponential smoothing for seasonal data, you might also deseasonalize the data and then use another forecasting tool to forecast the deseasonalized series. The deseasonalized forecast can then be reseasonalized by multiplying the deseasonalized forecast by the corresponding seasonal indices.

INTEGRATIVE CASE

THE GAP

PART 3: FORECASTING THE GAP SALES DATA WITH EXPONENTIAL SMOOTHING

The sales of The Gap stores for the 76 quarters covering 1985Q1 through 2004Q4 are once again shown below. From this graph it is clear that The Gap sales are quite seasonal and are increasing over time. Recall that the 2004 data are used as a holdout period.

(c3Gap)

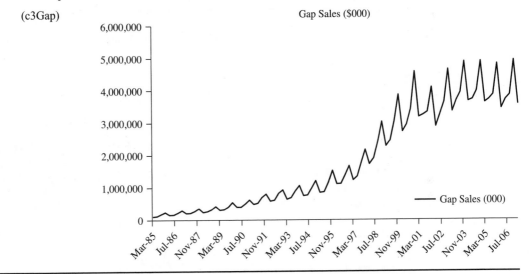

Gap Sales ($000)

| | Gap Sales (000) |

Case Questions

1. Using The Gap data, which are not adjusted to remove the seasonality, what exponential smoothing model do you think would be the most appropriate if you want to develop a quarterly forecast for 2004 sales? Explain why. Make a forecast for The Gap sales using the method you selected, and use the RMSE to evaluate your historic fit and your forecast accuracy for the four quarters of 2004. For the entire year of 2004, what percentage error is there in your forecast?

2. What are the seasonal indices for the The Gap sales, and what do they tell you about this company's sales pattern?

Solutions
to Case
Questions

1. Of the exponential smoothing models discussed in the text, the one that is most appropriate for the nonseasonally adjusted data is Winters' exponential smoothing. This model takes both trend and seasonality into account. Allowing ForecastX™ to determine the optimal smoothing weights we obtain level = 0.68, seasonal = 1, and trend = 0.25. The RMSE using the historic period is 114,748, while for the four holdout quarters the RMSE is 229,426 (remember that our data are in thousands of dollars). If we compare the RMSE for these last holdout quarters to the mean level of sales for those quarters (4,015,000), we find that the RMSE is about 5.7 percent of the mean actual quarterly sales.

   The original The Gap sales and the Winters' forecast (fitted) of The Gap sales (in thousands of dollars) are shown below for the four holdout quarters.

	The Gap Sales	Forecast
Jun-06	3,716,000	3,519,701.32
Sep-06	3,856,000	3,696,441.80
Dec-06	4,930,000	4,616,218.34
Mar-07	3,558,000	3,338,697.05

   The graph below shows actual The Gap sales and the Winters' forecast of The Gap sales for both the historical and forecast periods.

(c3Gap)

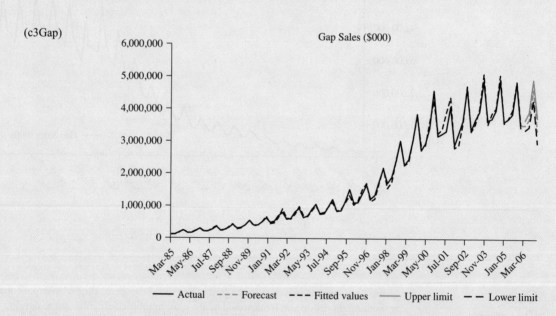

Gap Sales ($000)

—— Actual   - - - Forecast   - - - Fitted values   —— Upper limit   - - Lower limit

2. The seasonal factors for The Gap sales in quarters one through four are 0.84, 0.80, 1.03, and 1.33. This indicates strong sales during the fall back-to-school buying season (for The Gap, the third quarter includes the months of August, September, and October) followed by even stronger sales in their fourth quarter due to the Christmas season (the fourth quarter includes November, December, and January).

USING FORECASTX™ TO MAKE EXPONENTIAL SMOOTHING FORECASTS

What follows is a brief discussion of how to use ForecastX™ for preparing an exponential smoothing forecast. This also serves as a further introduction to the ease of use of ForecastX™. The illustration used here is for a forecast of The Gap data that has trend and seasonality.

First, put your data into an Excel spreadsheet in column format, such as the sample of The Gap data shown in the table below. Once you have your data in this format, while in Excel highlight the data you want to use, then start ForecastX™. The dialog box to the right of the data table appears.

A Sample of the Gap Data in Column Format

Date	Gap Sales (000)
Mar-85	105,715
Jun-85	120,136
Sep-85	181,669
Dec-85	239,813
Mar-86	159,980
Jun-86	164,760
Sep-86	224,800
Dec-86	298,469
Mar-87	211,060
Jun-87	217,753
Sep-87	273,616
Dec-87	359,592
Mar-88	241,348
Jun-88	264,328
Sep-88	322,752
Dec-88	423,669
Mar-89	309,925
Jun-89	325,939
Sep-89	405,601
Dec-89	545,131
Mar-90	402,368
Jun-90	404,996
Sep-90	501,690
Dec-90	624,726

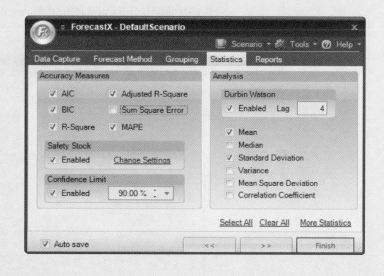

Set the **Dates** window to the periodicity of your data (**Quarterly** for this example), then click the **Forecast Method** tab at the top. The following screen appears.

Click the down arrow in the **Forecasting Technique** window and select **Holt Winters,** which is what ForecastX™ calls what we have referred to as simply Winters' in this chapter. This would be an appropriate method for data such as The Gap series. You can enter desired weights or you can leave those spaces blank and let ForecastX™ select the best set of values.

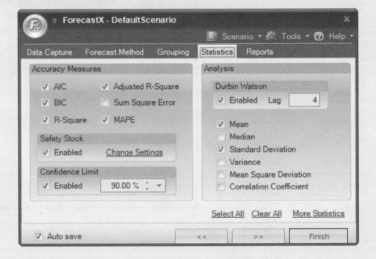

Next, click the **Statistics** tab and the following dialog box will appear.

Here you select the statistics you want to have reported. You will want to experiment with various selections.

Next click the **Reports** tab and the **Report Options** dialog box will appear.

As you place a check next to each of the five boxes for various reports, the options available in that report will appear below. For example, in the **Audit** report box you will normally check **Fitted Values Table.**

Again you will want to experiment with the various reports to get a feel for the ones that will give you the output you want for your specific application. After you click **Finish!** in the lower right corner, reports will be put in new Excel workbooks—Book 2, Book 3, and so forth. The book numbers will vary depending on how many books have previously been opened.

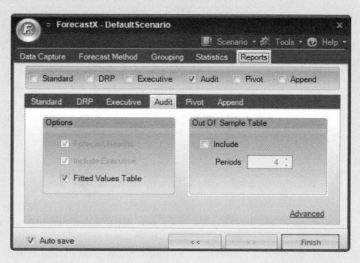

Suggested Readings

Armstrong, J. Scott, ed. *Principles of Forecasting: A Handbook for Researchers and Practitioners.* Boston: Kluwer Academic Publishers, 2001. [See also Professor Armstrong's Web, site: http://www-marketing.wharton.upenn.edu/forecast.]

Bass, Frank M. "A New Product Growth Model for Consumer Durables." *Management Science* 15 (January 1969), pp. 215–27. [Web site: http://www.basseconomics.com.]

Gardner, Everette S. "Exponential Smoothing: The State of the Art." *Journal of Forecasting* 4, no. 1 (1985), pp. 1–28.

Holt, C. C. "Forecasting Seasonal and Trends by Exponentially Weighted Moving Averages." Office of Naval Research, Memorandum No. 52, 1957.

Lilien, Gary L.; and Arvind Rangaswamy. *Marketing Engineering: Computer-Assisted Marketing Analysis and Planning.* 2nd ed. Upper Saddle River, NJ: Prentice-Hall, 2003. [Web site: http://www.mktgeng.com.]

Lilien, Gary L.; Arvind Rangaswamy; and Christophe Van den Bulte, "Diffusion Models: Managerial Applications and Software." In *New-Product Diffusion Models,* edited by Vijay Mahajan, Eitan Muller, and Jerry Wind. Boston, MA: Kluwer Academic Publishers, 2000, pp. 295–336.

Makridakis, Spyros; and Steven C. Wheelwright. *Forecasting Methods for Management.* 5th ed. New York: John Wiley & Sons, 1989.

Makridakis, Spyros, et al. "The M2-Competition: A Real-Time Judgmentally Based Forecasting Study." *International Journal of Forecasting* 9, no. 1 (April 1993), pp. 5–22.

Makridakis, Spyros; Steven C. Wheelwright; and Victor E. McGee. *Forecasting: Methods and Applications.* 2nd ed. New York: John Wiley & Sons, 1983.

Pegels, Carl C. "Exponential Forecasting: Some New Variations." *Management Science* 15, no. 12 (January 1969), pp. 311–15.

West, Douglas C. "Number of Sales Forecast Methods and Marketing Management." *Journal of Forecasting* 13, no. 4 (August 1994), pp. 395–407.

Winters, P. R. "Forecasting Sales by Exponentially Weighted Moving Averages." *Management Science* 6 (1960), pp. 324–42.

Exercises

1. Assume you were to use α values of 0.1, 0.5, and 0.9 in a simple exponential smoothing model. How would these different α values weight past observations of the variable to be forecast? How would you know which of these α values provided the best forecasting model? If the $\alpha = 0.9$ value provided the best forecast for your data, would this imply that you should do anything else? Does exponential smoothing place more or less weight on the most recent data when compared with the moving-average method? What weight is applied to each observation in a moving-average model? Why is smoothing (simple, Holt's, and Winters') also called *exponential* smoothing?

2. Under what conditions would you choose to use simple exponential smoothing, Holt's exponential smoothing, and Winters' exponential smoothing? Are these the only smoothing models possible to construct? If there are other possible models, suggest one that might be useful.

3. Exponential smoothing is meant to be used with time-series data when the data are made up of some or all of the basic components of average, trend, seasonality, and error. If the data series only fluctuates about an average with no trend and no seasonality, which form of smoothing would you employ? If the data include all of these components, which form of smoothing would you employ? How should the correct smoothing factors be chosen?

4. The smoothing factor chosen in simple exponential smoothing determines the weight to be placed on different terms of time-series data. If the smoothing factor is high rather than low, is more or less weight placed on recent observations? If α is .3, what weight is applied to the observation four periods ago?

5. Consider the following rates offered on certificates of deposit at a large metropolitan bank during a recent year:

Month	Rate (%)	Month	Rate (%)
January	7.025	July	7.575
February	9.047	August	8.612
March	8.280	September	8.985
April	8.650	October	9.298
May	9.714	November	7.454
June	8.963	December	8.461

Use a three-month average to forecast the rate for the following January.

6. The following inventory pattern has been observed in the Zahm Corporation over 12 months:

Month	Inventory	Month	Inventory
January	1,544	July	1,208
February	1,913	August	2,467
March	2,028	September	2,101
April	1,178	October	1,662
May	1,554	November	2,432
June	1,910	December	2,443

Use both three-month and five-month moving-average models to forecast the inventory for the next January. Use root-mean-squared error (RMSE) to evaluate these two forecasts.

7. Consider the following data on full-service restaurant sales. Calculate both the three-month and five-month moving averages for these data, and compare the forecasts by calculating the root-mean-squared errors and MAPEs. The data are in millions of dollars.

U.S. Retail Sales at Full-Service Restaurants (in Millions of Dollars, NSA)

Date	Sales (000,000)	Date	Sales (000,000)
Jan-92	6,910	Apr-95	8,269
Feb-92	6,959	May-95	8,615
Mar-92	7,268	Jun-95	8,549
Apr-92	7,023	Jul-95	8,902
May-92	7,555	Aug-95	9,035
Jun-92	7,021	Sep-95	8,271
Jul-92	7,297	Oct-95	8,328
Aug-92	7,558	Nov-95	7,987
Sep-92	6,945	Dec-95	8,383
Oct-92	7,464	Jan-96	7,532
Nov-92	7,138	Feb-96	7,943
Dec-92	7,355	Mar-96	8,685
Jan-93	6,854	Apr-96	8,502
Feb-93	6,699	May-96	8,977
Mar-93	7,324	Jun-96	8,716
Apr-93	7,514	Jul-96	8,978
May-93	7,898	Aug-96	9,548
Jun-93	7,814	Sep-96	8,675
Jul-93	8,049	Oct-96	9,032
Aug-93	8,322	Nov-96	9,005
Sep-93	7,730	Dec-96	8,921
Oct-93	8,049	Jan-97	8,688
Nov-93	7,449	Feb-97	8,640
Dec-93	7,774	Mar-97	9,592
Jan-94	6,998	Apr-97	9,332
Feb-94	7,275	May-97	9,976
Mar-94	8,177	Jun-97	9,460
Apr-94	8,143	Jul-97	10,071
May-94	8,364	Aug-97	10,517
Jun-94	8,292	Sep-97	9,539
Jul-94	8,689	Oct-97	9,850
Aug-94	8,661	Nov-97	9,227
Sep-94	8,080	Dec-97	9,699
Oct-94	8,264	Jan-98	9,147
Nov-94	7,822	Feb-98	9,114
Dec-94	8,352	Mar-98	9,972
Jan-95	7,507	Apr-98	9,825
Feb-95	7,341	May-98	10,423
Mar-95	8,243	Jun-98	10,203

(continued on next page)

Restaurants Sales (continued)

Date	Sales (000,000)	Date	Sales (000,000)
Jul-98	10,458	Apr-02	12,140
Aug-98	10,541	May-02	12,857
Sep-98	9,844	Jun-02	12,685
Oct-98	10,455	Jul-02	12,873
Nov-98	9,715	Aug-02	13,357
Dec-98	10,338	Sep-02	11,743
Jan-99	9,583	Oct-02	12,129
Feb-99	9,515	Nov-02	12,003
Mar-99	10,385	Dec-02	12,794
Apr-99	10,571	Jan-03	11,811
May-99	10,792	Feb-03	11,523
Jun-99	10,553	Mar-03	12,957
Jul-99	11,083	Apr-03	12,423
Aug-99	10,939	May-03	13,741
Sep-99	10,297	Jun-03	13,250
Oct-99	11,056	Jul-03	13,673
Nov-99	10,229	Aug-03	14,329
Dec-99	10,703	Sep-03	12,465
Jan-00	10,092	Oct-03	13,026
Feb-00	10,532	Nov-03	12,606
Mar-00	11,464	Dec-03	13,281
Apr-00	11,240	Jan-04	12,953
May-00	11,393	Feb-04	12,926
Jun-00	11,332	Mar-04	13,709
Jul-00	11,752	Apr-04	13,324
Aug-00	11,581	May-04	14,042
Sep-00	11,257	Jun-04	13,669
Oct-00	11,447	Jul-04	14,572
Nov-00	10,742	Aug-04	14,149
Dec-00	11,372	Sep-04	13,268
Jan-01	10,726	Oct-04	13,918
Feb-01	10,691	Nov-04	12,992
Mar-01	11,919	Dec-04	14,312
Apr-01	11,312	Jan-05	13,202
May-01	12,002	Feb-05	13,260
Jun-01	12,191	Mar-05	14,359
Jul-01	12,374	Apr-05	14,368
Aug-01	12,797	May-05	14,687
Sep-01	11,292	Jun-05	14,445
Oct-01	11,523	Jul-05	15,142
Nov-01	11,259	Aug-05	14,905
Dec-01	12,596	Sep-05	13,982
Jan-02	11,520	Oct-05	14,575
Feb-02	11,414	Nov-05	13,838
Mar-02	12,696	Dec-05	15,478

8. Forecasters at Siegfried Corporation are using simple exponential smoothing to forecast the sales of its major product. They are trying to decide what smoothing constant will give the best results. They have tried a number of smoothing constants with the following results:

Smoothing Constant	RMSE
0.10	125
0.15	97
0.20	136
0.25	141

Which smoothing constant appears best from these results? Why? Could you perhaps get even better results given these outcomes? How would you go about improving the RMSE?

9. The number of tons of brake assemblies received at an auto parts distribution center last month was 670. The forecast tonnage was 720. The company uses a simple exponential smoothing model with a smoothing constant of 0.6 to develop its forecasts. What will be the company's forecast for the next month?

10. The number of service calls received at LaFortune Electric during four months is shown in the following table:

Month	Number of Service Calls
April	19
May	31
June	27
July	29

Forecast the number of service calls in August by using a simple exponential smoothing model with a smoothing constant of 0.1. (Assume the forecast for April was 21.)

11. *a.* Plot the data presented in Exercise 7 to examine the possible existence of trend and seasonality in the data.

b. Prepare four separate smoothing models to examine the full-service restaurant sales data using the monthly data.

1. A simple smoothing model
2. Holt's model
3. Winters' model

c. Examine the accuracy of each model by calculating the root-mean-squared error for each during the historical period. Explain carefully what characteristics of the original data led one of these models to minimize the root-mean-squared error.

12. The data in the table below represent warehouse club and superstore sales in the United States on a monthly basis.

U.S. Retail Sales at Warehouse Clubs and Superstores (in Millions of Dollars, NSA)

Date	Sales	Date	Sales
Jan-92	2,580	Oct-95	5,460
Feb-92	2,616	Nov-95	6,288
Mar-92	2,838	Dec-95	8,403
Apr-92	2,985	Jan-96	4,758
May-92	3,258	Feb-96	4,914
Jun-92	3,107	Mar-96	5,431
Jul-92	3,097	Apr-96	5,474
Aug-92	3,288	May-96	6,124
Sep-92	3,077	Jun-96	6,027
Oct-92	3,429	Jul-96	5,914
Nov-92	4,011	Aug-96	6,244
Dec-92	5,739	Sep-96	5,808
Jan-93	2,877	Oct-96	6,373
Feb-93	2,885	Nov-96	6,994
Mar-93	3,259	Dec-96	9,018
Apr-93	3,454	Jan-97	5,694
May-93	3,771	Feb-97	5,431
Jun-93	3,667	Mar-97	6,240
Jul-93	3,743	Apr-97	6,101
Aug-93	3,792	May-97	6,849
Sep-93	3,699	Jun-97	6,694
Oct-93	4,082	Jul-97	6,815
Nov-93	4,727	Aug-97	6,948
Dec-93	6,672	Sep-97	6,450
Jan-94	3,560	Oct-97	7,190
Feb-94	3,575	Nov-97	7,738
Mar-94	4,220	Dec-97	9,769
Apr-94	4,282	Jan-98	6,665
May-94	4,594	Feb-98	6,400
Jun-94	4,691	Mar-98	7,277
Jul-94	4,629	Apr-98	7,584
Aug-94	4,795	May-98	8,169
Sep-94	4,632	Jun-98	8,179
Oct-94	5,067	Jul-98	8,118
Nov-94	5,746	Aug-98	8,284
Dec-94	7,965	Sep-98	7,962
Jan-95	4,317	Oct-98	8,636
Feb-95	4,118	Nov-98	9,433
Mar-95	4,855	Dec-98	11,786
Apr-95	4,999	Jan-99	8,082
May-95	5,343	Feb-99	7,761
Jun-95	5,392	Mar-99	8,994
Jul-95	5,274	Apr-99	8,803
Aug-95	5,435	May-99	9,712
Sep-95	5,217	Jun-99	9,843

Date	Sales		Date	Sales
Jul-99	9,769		Aug-03	18,907
Aug-99	9,944		Sep-03	16,735
Sep-99	9,582		Oct-03	18,146
Oct-99	10,209		Nov-03	20,336
Nov-99	11,115		Dec-03	24,665
Dec-99	14,995		Jan-04	17,686
Jan-00	9,183		Feb-04	17,908
Feb-00	9,478		Mar-04	18,691
Mar-00	10,751		Apr-04	19,030
Apr-00	10,518		May-04	20,623
May-00	11,349		Jun-04	19,596
Jun-00	11,728		Jul-04	20,122
Jul-00	11,590		Aug-04	20,029
Aug-00	11,871		Sep-04	18,669
Sep-00	11,336		Oct-04	20,518
Oct-00	11,986		Nov-04	21,967
Nov-00	13,130		Dec-04	27,584
Dec-00	16,694		Jan-05	19,315
Jan-01	11,195		Feb-05	19,186
Feb-01	10,919		Mar-05	21,211
Mar-01	12,389		Apr-05	20,985
Apr-01	12,619		May-05	22,385
May-01	13,489		Jun-05	22,223
Jun-01	13,620		Jul-05	22,602
Jul-01	13,438		Aug-05	22,456
Aug-01	14,084		Sep-05	21,418
Sep-01	13,172		Oct-05	23,092
Oct-01	14,040		Nov-05	24,598
Nov-01	15,759		Dec-05	30,706
Dec-01	19,992		Jan-06	21,692
Jan-02	13,162		Feb-06	21,699
Feb-02	13,394		Mar-06	23,402
Mar-02	15,285		Apr-06	24,046
Apr-02	14,467		May-06	24,881
May-02	16,086		Jun-06	24,602
Jun-02	16,027		Jul-06	24,631
Jul-02	15,622		Aug-06	24,831
Aug-02	16,360		Sep-06	23,603
Sep-02	14,714		Oct-06	24,608
Oct-02	15,894		Nov-06	26,705
Nov-02	18,152		Dec-06	34,023
Dec-02	22,089		Jan-07	23,837
Jan-03	15,161		Feb-07	23,438
Feb-03	15,342		Mar-07	26,305
Mar-03	16,997		Apr-07	25,429
Apr-03	16,623		May-07	27,152
May-03	18,064		Jun-07	27,218
Jun-03	17,605		Jul-07	26,722
Jul-03	17,746			

a. Prepare a time-series plot of the data, and visually inspect that plot to determine the characteristics you see in this series.

b. Use a smoothing model to develop a forecast of sales for the next 12 months, and explain why you selected that model. Plot the actual and forecast values. Determine the RMSE for your model during the historical period.

13. The data in the table below are for retail sales in book stores by quarter.

U.S. Retail Sales in Book Stores (in Millions of Dollars, NSA)

Date	Sales	Date	Sales
Mar-92	1,866	Mar-99	3,480
Jun-92	1,666	Jun-99	2,943
Sep-92	2,351	Sep-99	3,654
Dec-92	2,455	Dec-99	4,108
Mar-93	2,169	Mar-00	3,628
Jun-93	1,815	Jun-00	3,203
Sep-93	2,498	Sep-00	4,051
Dec-93	2,637	Dec-00	4,010
Mar-94	2,326	Mar-01	3,719
Jun-94	2,020	Jun-01	3,084
Sep-94	2,858	Sep-01	4,234
Dec-94	2,915	Dec-01	4,073
Mar-95	2,725	Mar-02	3,983
Jun-95	2,283	Jun-02	3,132
Sep-95	3,134	Sep-02	4,328
Dec-95	3,066	Dec-02	4,007
Mar-96	2,876	Mar-03	3,969
Jun-96	2,445	Jun-03	3,257
Sep-96	3,190	Sep-03	4,824
Dec-96	3,407	Dec-03	4,129
Mar-97	3,197	Mar-04	4,298
Jun-97	2,575	Jun-04	3,312
Sep-97	3,290	Sep-04	4,811
Dec-97	3,693	Dec-04	4,336
Mar-98	3,273	Mar-05	4,261
Jun-98	2,713	Jun-05	3,278
Sep-98	3,514	Sep-05	4,991
Dec-98	3,794	Dec-05	4,447

a. Plot these data and examine the plot. Does this view of the data suggest a particular smoothing model? Do the data appear to be seasonal? Explain.

b. Use a smoothing method to forecast the next four quarters. Plot the actual and forecast values.

14. The United States Department of Agriculture's Child and Adult Care Food Program (CACPF) plays a vital role in improving the quality of day care and making it more affordable for many low-income families. Each day, 2.9 million children receive nutritious meals and snacks through CACFP. The program also provides meals and snacks to 86,000 adults who receive care in nonresidential adult day care centers. CACFP reaches even further to provide meals to children residing in emergency shelters, and

snacks and suppers to youths participating in eligible afterschool care programs.[8] Many will know of the School Lunch Program that is a part of the CACFP.

We will use data from the Child Care Center program of CACFP. "Eligible public or private nonprofit child care centers, outside-school-hours care centers, Head Start programs, and other institutions which are licensed or approved to provide day care services may participate in CACFP, independently or as sponsored centers. For profit centers must receive Title XX funds for at least 25 percent of enrolled children or licensed capacity (whichever is less) or at least 25 percent of the children in care must be eligible for free and reduced price meals. Meals served to children are reimbursed at rates based upon a child's eligibility for free, reduced price, or paid meals."[9]

Monthly data from March 2004 through September 2007 is provided below. You are charged with making a 12-month forecast of the meals to be served. Begin by plotting the data and examining it for the patterns of trend and seasonality. Choose an appropriate model for the data and forecast for the next 12 months.

Meals Served In:

Month Year	Child Care Center	Month Year	Child Care Center
Mar-04	108,371,749	Jan-06	98,887,496
Apr-04	99,199,094	Feb-06	96,477,065
May-04	92,195,689	Mar-06	114,094,756
Jun-04	81,447,374	Apr-06	96,093,092
Jul-04	72,792,981	May-06	107,527,897
Aug-04	78,931,911	Jun-06	87,135,336
Sep-04	89,982,843	Jul-06	72,397,374
Oct-04	96,761,533	Aug-06	88,657,480
Nov-04	92,772,827	Sep-06	94,566,627
Dec-04	83,103,478	Oct-06	106,889,806
Jan-05	93,109,115	Nov-06	97,638,605
Feb-05	93,267,674	Dec-06	83,280,944
Mar-05	105,290,897	Jan-07	102,522,133
Apr-05	103,625,467	Feb-07	95,537,211
May-05	100,549,323	Mar-07	111,462,237
Jun-05	85,155,854	Apr-07	103,542,365
Jul-05	71,406,448	May-07	111,242,080
Aug-05	85,623,392	Jun-07	85,765,747
Sep-05	94,828,432	Jul-07	78,943,762
Oct-05	97,917,922	Aug-07	89,965,185
Nov-05	95,753,418	Sep-07	92,934,809
Dec-05	83,145,194		

---

[8] http://www.fns.usda.gov/cnd/Care/CACFP/aboutcacfp.htm.
[9] Ibid.

Introduction to Forecasting with Regression Methods

In this chapter the fundamentals of bivariate regression analysis are presented in the context of forecasting applications. Regression models are developed for jewelry sales (JS) and disposable personal income (DPI), based on quarterly data. These regression models are then used to make forecasts of each series. At the end of the chapter, we return to our continuing examples of forecasting total houses sold and to the continuing The Gap case study.

THE BIVARIATE REGRESSION MODEL

Bivariate regression analysis (also called *simple linear least-squares regression*) is a statistical tool that gives us the ability to estimate the mathematical relationship between a dependent variable (usually called Y) and a single independent variable (usually called X).[1] The dependent variable is the variable for which we want to develop a forecast. While various nonlinear forms may be used, simple linear regression models are the most common. Nonlinear models will be discussed in Chapter 5.

In using regression analyses we begin by supposing that Y is a function of X. That is:

$$Y = f(X)$$

Since we most often begin by using linear functions, we may write the population regression model as:

$$Y = \beta_0 + \beta_1 X + \varepsilon$$

where β_0 represents the intercept of the regression line on the vertical (or Y) axis and β_1 is the slope of the regression line. Thus, β_1 tells us the rate of change in Y per unit change in X. The intercept (β_0) is the value that the dependent variable

[1] For a more detailed discussion of the regression model, including underlying assumptions, see Bruce Bowerman and Richard T. O'Connell, *Business Statistics in Practice,* 4th ed. (Burr Ridge, IL: McGraw-Hill/Irwin, 2007).

would have if $X = 0$. While this is a correct interpretation from an algebraic perspective, such an interpretation is often not valid in applications, since a value of $X = 0$ is frequently not in the relevant range of observations on X. The ε in this model represents an error term. That is, every Y is not likely to be predicted exactly from the values of β_0 and $\beta_1 X$. The resulting error is ε.

We would like to estimate values of β_0 and β_1 such that the resulting equation best fits the data. To do so we need to decide on a criterion against which the fit of the estimated model can be evaluated. The most common such rule is called the *ordinary least-squares* (OLS) criterion. This rule says that the best model is the one that minimizes the sum of the squared error terms.

The unobserved model that describes the whole population of data is expressed as

$$Y = \beta_0 + \beta_1 X + \varepsilon$$

These values of the intercept (β_0) and slope (β_1) are population parameters that are typically estimated using sample data. The corresponding sample statistics are b_0 and b_1. The estimated regression model is expressed as

$$\hat{Y} = b_0 + b_1 X$$

Deviations of predicted values ($\hat{Y}$) from the actual values of Y are called *residuals* or *errors* and are denoted by e, where

$$e = Y - \hat{Y}$$

or,

$$e = Y - b_0 - b_1 X$$

The ordinary least-squares method seeks to find estimates of the slope and intercept parameters that minimize the sum of squared residuals:

$$\textit{Minimize } \sum e^2 = \sum (Y - b_0 - b_1 X)^2$$

By taking partial derivatives of the sum of squared residuals with respect to b_0 and b_1, setting the partial derivatives equal to zero, and solving the two equations simultaneously, we obtain estimating formulas:

$$b_1 = \left(\sum XY - n\overline{X}\overline{Y} \right) \Big/ \left(\sum X^2 - n\overline{X}^2 \right)$$
$$b_0 = \overline{Y} - b_1 \overline{X}$$

These formulas could be used to calculate b_0 and b_1 by hand. However, even for simple regression, a computer program is normally used for such calculations.

VISUALIZATION OF DATA: AN IMPORTANT STEP IN REGRESSION ANALYSIS

There was a time when regression lines were estimated in a rather ad hoc manner, based solely on an analyst's visual interpretation of the data. The analyst would plot the data by hand and would "eyeball" the resulting scatter of points to determine the position of a straight line that was believed to "best" represent the

TABLE 4.1
Four Dissimilar Data Sets with Similar Regression Results
(c4t1)

Source: F. J. Anscombe,
"Graphs in Statistical Analysis,"
American Statistician 27
(February 1973), pp. 17–21, as
reported in Edward R. Tufte,
*The Visual Display of
Quantitative Information,*
(Cheshire, CT: Graphics Press,
1983), p. 13.

Set A		Set B		Set C		Set D	
X	Y	X	Y	X	Y	X	Y
10	8.04	10	9.14	10	7.46	8	6.58
8	6.95	8	8.14	8	6.77	8	5.76
13	7.58	13	8.74	13	12.74	8	7.71
9	8.81	9	8.77	9	7.11	8	8.84
11	8.33	11	9.26	11	7.81	8	8.47
14	9.96	14	8.10	14	8.84	8	7.04
6	7.24	6	6.13	6	6.08	8	5.25
4	4.26	4	3.10	4	5.39	19	12.50
12	10.84	12	9.13	12	8.15	8	5.56
7	4.82	7	7.26	7	6.42	8	7.91
5	5.68	5	4.74	5	5.73	8	6.89

general relationship between Y and X. Such a straight line was then drawn through the scatterplot and, by selecting two points from the line, its algebraic equation was calculated (i.e., values for b_0 and b_1 were estimated). One obvious problem with such a procedure is that different analysts would almost surely come up with differing estimates of b_0 and b_1.

Today it is doubtful that anyone would take this approach to estimating a regression equation. Modern computer technology makes it very easy to obtain the OLS equation without ever looking at the data. This equation is best, according to the ordinary least-squares criterion, and numerous evaluative statistics can be simultaneously determined. Every analyst obtains precisely the same results, and those results are easily replicated. Thus it may appear that computer-based regression analysis is a clearly superior method. However, something is lost. Analysts may just enter data, issue appropriate commands, get the corresponding statistical results, and run off to apply the model in some decision-based context such as forecasting. In the process, they would never have *looked* at the data. Such blind attention to statistical estimates can be dangerous.

To illustrate this point, consider the four data sets in Table 4.1. For all four of the data sets in Table 4.1, the calculated regression results show an OLS equation of:

$$\hat{Y} = 3 + 0.5X$$

It might also be noted that the mean of the X's is 9.0 and the mean of the Y's is 7.5 in all four cases. The standard deviation is 3.32 for all of the X variables and 2.03 for all of the Y variables. Similarly, the correlation for each pair of X and Y variables is 0.82.[2]

---

[2] Many statistical diagnostics on the regression equations, which we will cover later in this chapter, are also equal. These include standard errors of the regression, t-ratios for the coefficients, R-squared, and the regression sum of squares. Statistics related to the evaluation of residuals, such as the Durbin-Watson statistic, show some differences.

FIGURE 4.1

Scatterplots of Four *XY* Data Sets That Have Very Similar Statistical Properties but Are Visually Quite Different

(c4f1)

For each of the data sets, the OLS regression equation is

$$Y = 3 + 0.5X$$

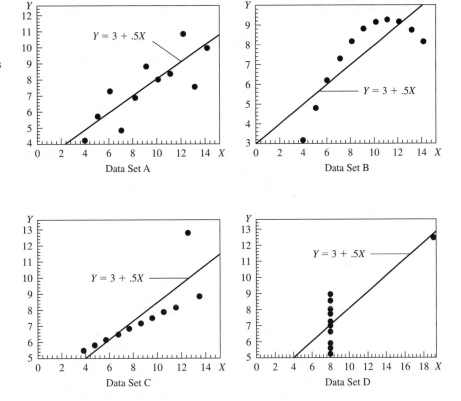

From these results, an analyst who looks only at these summary statistics would likely conclude that the four data sets are identical or, at the very least, quite similar. But, oh, how wrong this conclusion would be. If you take the time to prepare a scattergram of each of the four data sets, dramatic differences become apparent. In Figure 4.1 we have plotted each *XY* pair in a separate plot, along with the corresponding OLS regression lines (all four of the regression lines have the same equation: $\hat{Y} = 3 + 0.5X$).

It is important to *look* at the data before plunging into data analysis and the selection of an appropriate set of forecasting techniques.

Visualization of these data allows us to see stark differences that would not be apparent from the descriptive statistics we have reviewed. The regression line is most clearly inappropriate for the data in the lower right plot. The lower left plot has, with the exception of one outlier, a perfectly linear relationship between *Y* and *X*, which is not so clear without visual inspection of the data. The upper right plot of data suggests that a nonlinear model would fit the data better than a linear function. Only the upper left plot suggests a data set that is a good candidate for a linear regression model. Visually, these data sets are quite dissimilar even though they have some very similar statistical properties.

Forecasters can benefit from this example.

A PROCESS FOR REGRESSION FORECASTING

It is useful to have a plan at hand when approaching any task. And so it is with developing a regression-based forecast. In this section we suggest one such plan, or process, that helps to organize the task of preparing a regression forecast. What we say here is not separate from the forecast process discussed in Chapter 2. Rather, it complements that process, especially data considerations, model selection, model evaluation, and forecast preparation.

We begin with data considerations, which become somewhat more complex for regression models. Not only do we need to pay attention to the dependent variable, the series to be forecast, but we must also consider the independent variable(s) that will drive the regression forecast. We should utilize graphic techniques to inspect the data, looking especially for trend, seasonal, and cyclical components, as well as for outliers. This will help in determining what type of regression model may be most appropriate (e.g., linear versus nonlinear, or trend versus causal).

The forecaster should utilize graphic techniques to inspect the data, looking especially for trend, seasonal, and cyclical components, as well as for outliers.

Next we must make a forecast of the independent variable(s). This becomes a separate, yet related, forecasting effort. Each potential independent variable should be forecast using a method that is appropriate to that particular series, taking into account the model-selection guidelines discussed in Chapter 2 and summarized in Table 2.1.

Once the data have been thoroughly reviewed and the type of regression model has been selected, it is time to specify the model. By model specification, we mean the statistical process of estimating the regression coefficients (b_0 and b_1, in simple bivariate regression models). In doing so we recommend using a holdout period for evaluation. Thus, if you have 10 years of quarterly data ($n = 40$), you might use 9 years of data ($n = 36$) to estimate the regression coefficients. Initial evaluation of regression models (based on diagnostic statistics we will discuss shortly) can be done on this subsample of the historical data. However, the real test of a forecasting model is in the actual forecast. Thus, if you have set aside a holdout period of data, you can then test the model in this period to get a truer feel for how well the model meets your needs.

This relates to our discussion of fit versus accuracy in Chapter 2. When the model is evaluated in comparison with the data used in specifying the model, we are determining how well the model "fits" the data. This is a retrospective approach, often called an *in-sample* evaluation. By using a holdout period, we have an opportunity to evaluate the model "out of sample." That is, we can determine how "accurate" the model is for an actual forecast horizon. After an evaluation of fit and accuracy, a forecaster should respecify the best of the models using the entire span of data that are available. The newly specified model is then used to forecast beyond the frontier of what is known at the time of the forecast.

FORECASTING WITH A SIMPLE LINEAR TREND[3]

It is sometimes possible to make reasonably good forecasts on the basis of a simple linear time trend. To do so we set up a time index (T) to use as the independent or X variable in the basic regression model, where T is usually set equal to 1 for the first observation and increased by 1 for each subsequent observation. The regression model is then:

$$\hat{Y} = b_0 + b_1(T)$$

where Y is the series we wish to forecast.

To illustrate this process, consider the data in Table 4.2. DPI is disposable personal income in billions of dollars and is given from January 1993 through July 2007. Only data though December 2006 will be used to develop a forecast so

TABLE 4.2 **Disposable Personal Income in Billions of Dollars, January 1993 through July 2007** (c4t2&f2)

Date	DPI	Time Index	Date	DPI	Time Index	Date	DPI	Time Index
Jan-93	4,800.90	1	Oct-94	5,281.40	22	Jul-96	5,702.60	43
Feb-93	4,803.90	2	Nov-94	5,288.10	23	Aug-96	5,725.70	44
Mar-93	4,800.10	3	Dec-94	5,309.80	24	Sep-96	5,754.20	45
Apr-93	4,887.40	4	Jan-95	5,337.30	25	Oct-96	5,768.60	46
May-93	4,909.90	5	Feb-95	5,350.00	26	Nov-96	5,794.70	47
Jun-93	4,906.10	6	Mar-95	5,365.50	27	Dec-96	5,822.50	48
Jul-93	4,909.30	7	Apr-95	5,335.10	28	Jan-97	5,847.40	49
Aug-93	4,931.40	8	May-95	5,389.00	29	Feb-97	5,876.60	50
Sep-93	4,932.10	9	Jun-95	5,404.90	30	Mar-97	5,908.30	51
Oct-93	4,951.00	10	Jul-95	5,415.10	31	Apr-97	5,915.50	52
Nov-93	4,974.30	11	Aug-95	5,424.00	32	May-97	5,934.40	53
Dec-93	5,137.00	12	Sep-95	5,442.30	33	Jun-97	5,960.10	54
Jan-94	4,955.90	13	Oct-95	5,458.20	34	Jul-97	5,986.60	55
Feb-94	5,003.30	14	Nov-95	5,475.40	35	Aug-97	6,023.40	56
Mar-94	5,037.00	15	Dec-95	5,502.20	36	Sep-97	6,052.30	57
Apr-94	5,057.20	16	Jan-96	5,524.50	37	Oct-97	6,081.50	58
May-94	5,143.50	17	Feb-96	5,580.90	38	Nov-97	6,123.30	59
Jun-94	5,153.50	18	Mar-96	5,618.00	39	Dec-97	6,156.60	60
Jul-94	5,172.10	19	Apr-96	5,594.30	40	Jan-98	6,216.30	61
Aug-94	5,195.00	20	May-96	5,671.30	41	Feb-98	6,256.60	62
Sep-94	5,225.30	21	Jun-96	5,704.30	42	Mar-98	6,294.90	63

(continued on next page)

[3] Throughout this chapter you may find some situations in which the standard calculations that we show do not match exactly with the ForecastX results. This is because, at times, they invoke proprietary alterations from the standard calculations. The results are usually very close but may not match perfectly with "hand" calculations.

TABLE 4.2 (continued)

Date	DPI	Time Index	Date	DPI	Time Index	Date	DPI	Time Index
Apr-98	6,323.30	64	Jun-01	7,425.7	102	Aug-04	8,727.4	140
May-98	6,360.10	65	Jul-01	7,550.9	103	Sep-04	8,729.4	141
Jun-98	6,389.60	66	Aug-01	7,686.3	104	Oct-04	8,804.1	142
Jul-98	6,418.60	67	Sep-01	7,631.3	105	Nov-04	8,828.6	143
Aug-98	6,452.90	68	Oct-01	7,506.3	106	Dec-04	9,171.9	144
Sep-98	6,472.70	69	Nov-01	7,523.5	107	Jan-05	8,873.5	145
Oct-98	6,497.70	70	Dec-01	7,544.7	108	Feb-05	8,908.3	146
Nov-98	6,526.30	71	Jan-02	7,718.9	109	Mar-05	8,941.3	147
Dec-98	6,542.20	72	Feb-02	7,751.7	110	Apr-05	9,001.4	148
Jan-99	6,571.20	73	Mar-02	7,784.0	111	May-05	9,030.8	149
Feb-99	6,588.50	74	Apr-02	7,827.3	112	Jun-05	9,083.6	150
Mar-99	6,600.50	75	May-02	7,840.3	113	Jul-05	9,147.4	151
Apr-99	6,616.40	76	Jun-02	7,857.4	114	Aug-05	8,928.3	152
May-99	6,639.70	77	Jul-02	7,845.1	115	Sep-05	9,239.7	153
Jun-99	6,659.80	78	Aug-02	7,842.3	116	Oct-05	9,277.3	154
Jul-99	6,679.70	79	Sep-02	7,848.9	117	Nov-05	9,309.0	155
Aug-99	6,718.50	80	Oct-02	7,864.2	118	Dec-05	9,362.9	156
Sep-99	6,726.50	81	Nov-02	7,877.1	119	Jan-06	9,442.9	157
Oct-99	6,790.80	82	Dec-02	7,903.7	120	Feb-06	9,467.3	158
Nov-99	6,840.30	83	Jan-03	7,945.8	121	Mar-06	9,495.5	159
Dec-99	6,907.60	84	Feb-03	7,972.4	122	Apr-06	9,535.7	160
Jan-00	7,009.70	85	Mar-03	8,008.3	123	May-06	9,555.9	161
Feb-00	7,060.40	86	Apr-03	8,041.7	124	Jun-06	9,627.1	162
Mar-00	7,107.50	87	May-03	8,094.3	125	Jul-06	9,639.8	163
Apr-00	7,110.80	88	Jun-03	8,126.9	126	Aug-06	9,675.3	164
May-00	7,138.70	89	Jul-03	8,240.4	127	Sep-06	9,712.1	165
Jun-00	7,174.20	90	Aug-03	8,311.0	128	Oct-06	9,755.7	166
Jul-00	7,242.40	91	Sep-03	8,231.6	129	Nov-06	9,787.5	167
Aug-00	7,265.00	92	Oct-03	8,271.2	130	Dec-06	9,854.4	168
Sep-00	7,291.80	93	Nov-03	8,335.8	131	Jan-07	9,934.7	169
Oct-00	7,309.20	94	Dec-03	8,370.9	132	Feb-07	10,013.3	170
Nov-00	7,306.60	95	Jan-04	8,428.8	133	Mar-07	10,095.5	171
Dec-00	7,312.10	96	Feb-04	8,478.1	134	Apr-07	10,082.9	172
Jan-01	7,377.8	97	Mar-04	8,517.1	135	May-07	10,123.1	173
Feb-01	7,392.0	98	Apr-04	8,559.3	136	Jun-07	10,159.6	174
Mar-01	7,406.6	99	May-04	8,615.5	137	Jul-07	**10,216.9**	175
Apr-01	7,394.7	100	Jun-04	8,640.6	138			
May-01	7,402.3	101	Jul-04	8,669.8	139			

that we can evaluate it against actual data for the first seven months of 2007. This is an important economic series, since income is an important determinant for many kinds of sales. The linear time-trend model for DPI is:

$$\widehat{DPI} = b_0 + b_1(T)$$

FIGURE 4.2

Graph of Disposable Personal Income (DPI) over Time
While DPI does not follow a perfectly linear path, it does follow a trend that is very close to linear. (c4t2&f2)

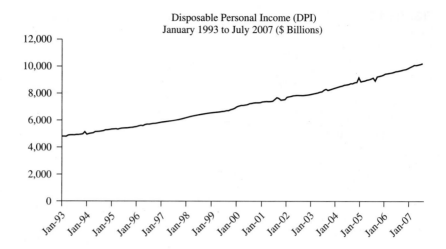

Disposable Personal Income (DPI)
January 1993 to July 2007 ($ Billions)

You see in Table 4.2 that T (time) equals 1 for January 1993 and 168 for December 2006.

It is usually a good idea to look at data such as those given in Table 4.2 in graphic form before beginning to do any regression analysis. A visual inspection of the data can be helpful in deciding whether a linear or nonlinear model would be most appropriate. A graph of DPI versus T is shown in Figure 4.2. From this graph you can get a good feel for how this important measure of income has increased over the period presented. All observations do not fall on a single straight line. However, it does appear that a linear trend line would fit the data well. The positive trend to DPI is more easily seen in the graphic form of Figure 4.2 than in the tabular form of Table 4.2.

Suppose that you are asked to forecast DPI for the first seven months of 2007, using a simple linear trend, based only on data through 2006. The first thing you would do is to use the linear regression part of your regression software to provide the estimates of b_0 and b_1 for the following model:

$$\text{DPI} = b_0 + b_1(T)$$

The regression results from Forecast X and from Excel are shown at the bottom of Figure 4.3. From those results we see that the intercept (b_0) is 4,478.265 and that the coefficient on T (b_1, or the slope) is 30.11. Thus, the regression forecast model may be written as:

$$\widehat{\text{DPI}} = 4{,}478.265 + 30.11(T)$$

The slope term in this model tells us that, on average, disposable personal income increased by 30.11 billion dollars per month. The other statistical results shown at the bottom of Figure 4.3 are helpful in evaluating the usefulness of the model. Most of these will be discussed in detail in the section "Statistical Evaluation of Regression Models," later in this chapter. Our discussion of others will be held in abeyance until Chapter 5. For now we will just comment that statistical evaluation suggests that this linear equation provides a very good fit to the data.

FIGURE 4.3

Disposable Personal Income (DPI) with a Linear Trend Line Forecast

The linear trend follows the actual DPI quite well and provides a forecast for 2004 that looks very reasonable. The trend equation is:

DPI = 4,478.265
      + 30.11(*T*)

(c4t3&f3)

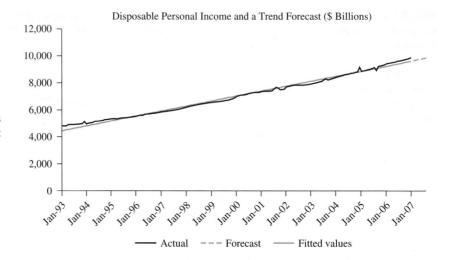

Disposable Personal Income and a Trend Forecast ($ Billions)

— Actual --- Forecast — Fitted values

These results are from the ForecastX Audit Trail Report (F value added) when Trend (Linear) Regression is selected as the forecast method.

Audit Trail--ANOVA Table (Trend (Linear) Regression Selected)

Source of Variation	SS	df	MS	F	SEE
Regression	358,218,615.21	1	358,218,615.21	18796.156	
Error	3,163,640.99	166	19,058.08		**138.05**
Total	361,382,256.20	167			

Audit Trail--Statistics

Accuracy Measures	Value	Forecast Statistics	Value
Mean Absolute Percentage Error (MAPE)	1.68%	Durbin Watson (1)	0.18
R-Square	99.12%		
Root Mean Square Error	137.23		

Method Statistics	Value
Method Selected	Trend (Linear) Regression

These results are from Excel. The actual regression equation comes from the Coefficients column and is: DPI = 4478.265 + 30.110*(Time Index).

Regression Statistics	
Multiple R	0.9956
R Square	0.9912
Adjusted R Square	0.9912
Standard Error	138.05
Observations	168

ANOVA					
	df	SS	MS	F	Significance F
Regression	1	358,218,615.210	358,218,615.210	18,796.156	0.000
Residual	166	3,163,640.988	19,058.078		
Total	167	361382256.2			

	Coefficients	Standard Error	t Stat	P-value
Intercept	4,478.265	21.397	209.292	0.000
Time Index	30.110	0.220	137.099	0.000

To use this equation to make a forecast for the first seven months of 2007, we need only substitute the appropriate values for time (T). These are 169 through 175 as seen in Table 4.2. The trend estimates of DPI for three representative months follow:

January 2007: DPI = 4,478.265 + 30.11(169) = 9,566.9

April ~~June~~ 2007: DPI = 4,478.265 + 30.11(172) = 9,657.2

July ~~December~~ 2007: DPI = 4,478.265 + 30.11(175) = 9,747.5

You can see in Figure 4.3 that the simple linear trend line does fit the actual data quite well and provides a reasonable forecast for the first seven months of 2007.

The actual values of DPI are shown in Table 4.3 along with the trend values in order to determine the root-mean-squared error (RMSE) for the historic and forecast periods. The calculation of the RMSE is done by subtracting the forecast values from the actual values and then squaring the difference. The average of the squared differences is called the mean-squared error (MSE). The square root of the MSE is the root-mean-squared error (RMSE).

We see that the long-term linear trend forecasts of DPI are quite accurate overall. The RMSE is about 4.3 percent of the mean for DPI during the forecast period. The RMSE for this method could be compared with that of other techniques to determine the most appropriate method to use.[4]

Trend models such as this can sometimes be very helpful in forecasting, and, as you see, they are easy to develop and to implement. In such models we simply track the past time trend and project it forward for the forecast horizon of interest.

---

[4] For example, based on 1993 through 2006 data, the optimal Holt's exponential smoothing model for DPI (alpha = 0.50, gamma = 0.03) produces a forecast that has an RMSE for the forecast period of 103.6 (i.e., the smoothing model would be a better model because of the lower RMSE).

TABLE 4.3 **Disposable Personal Income with Linear Trend Forecast**

The squared errors, mean-squared errors, and root-mean-squared errors are shown for both historic and forecast periods. The RMSE is only about 4.3 percent of the mean DPI for the first seven months of 2007. (c4t3&f3)

Date	DPI	ForecastX Results	Error	Error Squared		
Jan-93	4,800.9	4,508.4	292.5	85,571.1		
Feb-93	4,803.9	4,538.5	265.4	70,445.4	Historic Period	
Mar-93	4,800.1	4,568.6	231.5	53,594.9	Mean Squared Error	
Apr-93	4,887.4	4,598.7	288.7	83,345.3	(MSE)	18,831.20
May-93	4,909.9	4,628.8	281.1	79,009.3		
Jun-93	4,906.1	4,658.9	247.2	61,096.0	Root Mean Sq. Error	
Jul-93	4,909.3	4,689.0	220.3	48,517.2	(RMSE)	137.23
Aug-93	4,931.4	4,719.1	212.3	45,052.8		
Sep-93	4,932.1	4,749.3	182.8	33,432.9		
Oct-93	4,951	4,779.4	171.6	29,459.2		
Nov-93	4,974.3	4,809.5	164.8	27,167.9		
Dec-93	5,137	4,839.6	297.4	88,456.9		
⋮	⋮	⋮	⋮	⋮		
Jan-06	9,442.9	9,205.5	237.4	56,354.0		
Feb-06	9,467.3	9,235.6	231.7	53,675.7		
Mar-06	9,495.5	9,265.7	229.8	52,794.4		
Apr-06	9,535.7	9,295.8	239.9	57,533.1		
May-06	9,555.9	9,325.9	230.0	52,877.3		
Jun-06	9,627.1	9,356.1	271.0	73,463.1		
Jul-06	9,639.8	9,386.2	253.6	64,328.7		
Aug-06	9,675.3	9,416.3	259.0	67,092.0		
Sep-06	9,712.1	9,446.4	265.7	70,602.5		
Oct-06	9,755.7	9,476.5	279.2	77,953.5		
Nov-06	9,787.5	9,506.6	280.9	78,900.1		
Dec-06	9,854.4	9,536.7	317.7	100,921.7		
⋮	⋮	⋮	⋮	⋮		
Jan-07	9,934.7	9,566.9	367.9	135,329.8		
Feb-07	10,013.3	9,596.9	416.4	173,357.4	Forecast Period (Holdout Period)	
Mar-07	10,095.5	9,627.0	468.5	219,447.5		
Apr-07	10,082.9	9,657.2	425.7	181,256.6	Mean Squared Error	
May-07	10,123.1	9,687.3	435.8	189,950.1	(MSE)	187,892.98
Jun-07	10,159.6	9,717.4	442.2	195,561.0	Root Mean Sq. Error	
Jul-07	10,216.9	9,747.5	469.4	220,348.5	(RMSE)	433.47
Mean 2007	10,089.43					
2007 RMSE as % of Mean		4.30				

Note that we do not imply any sense of causality in such a model. Time does not cause income to rise. Income has increased over time at a reasonably steady rate for reasons not explained by our model.

USING A CAUSAL REGRESSION MODEL TO FORECAST

Trend models, such as the one we looked at in the previous section for disposable personal income, use the power of regression analysis to determine the best linear trend line. However, such uses do not exploit the full potential of this powerful statistical tool. Regression analysis is especially useful for developing causal models.

In a causal model, expressed as $Y = f(X)$, a change in the independent variable (X) is assumed to cause a change in the dependent variable (Y). The selection of an appropriate causal variable (X) should be based on some insight that suggests that a causal relationship is reasonable. A forecaster does not arbitrarily select an X variable, but rather looks to past experience and understanding to identify potential causal factors. For example, suppose that you were attempting to develop a bivariate regression model that might be helpful in explaining and predicting the level of jewelry sales in the United States. What factors do you think might have an impact on jewelry sales? Some potential causal variables that might come to mind could include income, some measure of the level of interest rates, and the unemployment rate, among others.

Discussions with knowledgeable people in the jewelry industry would help you determine other variables and would be helpful in prioritizing those that are identified. Library research in areas related to jewelry sales and to consumer behavior may turn up yet other potential X variables. One thing you would learn quickly is that there is a substantial seasonal aspect to jewelry sales.

It is important that the independent variable be selected on the basis of a logical construct that relates it to the dependent variable. Otherwise you might find a variable through an arbitrary search process that works well enough in a given historical period, more or less by accident, but then breaks down severely out of sample. Consider, for example, William Stanley Jevons' sunspot theory of business cycles. For a certain historical period a reasonably strong correlation appeared to support such a notion. Outside that period, however, the relationship was quite weak. In this case it is difficult to develop a strong conceptual theory tying business cycles to sunspot activity.

To illustrate the use of a causal model, we will consider how well jewelry sales (JS) can be forecast on the basis of disposable personal income, as a measure of overall purchasing power.

Before we start to develop a forecast of jewelry sales, we should take a look at a time-series plot of the series. In this example we will use monthly data for jewelry sales from January 1994 through December 2004 and we want to forecast JS for each of the 12 months of 2005. A time-series plot of JS is found in Figure 4.4, and the raw data are in Table 4.4.

TABLE 4.4   Jewelry Sales in Millions of Dollars

The 2005 values are held out in developing forecasts so that we can evaluate our results out of sample.   (c4t4&f4)

Date	Jewelry Sales ($ Millions)	Date	Jewelry Sales ($ Millions)	Date	Jewelry Sales ($ Millions)
Jan-94	904	Jan-98	1,119	Jan-02	1,304
Feb-94	1,191	Feb-98	1,513	Feb-02	2,004
Mar-94	1,058	Mar-98	1,238	Mar-02	1,612
Apr-94	1,171	Apr-98	1,362	Apr-02	1,626
May-94	1,367	May-98	1,756	May-02	2,120
Jun-94	1,257	Jun-98	1,527	Jun-02	1,667
Jul-94	1,224	Jul-98	1,415	Jul-02	1,554
Aug-94	1,320	Aug-98	1,466	Aug-02	1,746
Sep-94	1,246	Sep-98	1,372	Sep-02	1,503
Oct-94	1,323	Oct-98	1,506	Oct-02	1,662
Nov-94	1,731	Nov-98	1,923	Nov-02	2,208
Dec-94	4,204	Dec-98	5,233	Dec-02	5,810
Jan-95	914	Jan-99	1,163	Jan-03	1,361
Feb-95	1,223	Feb-99	1,662	Feb-03	2,019
Mar-95	1,138	Mar-99	1,402	Mar-03	1,477
Apr-95	1,204	Apr-99	1,468	Apr-03	1,616
May-95	1,603	May-99	1,877	May-03	2,071
Jun-95	1,388	Jun-99	1,635	Jun-03	1,711
Jul-95	1,259	Jul-99	1,596	Jul-03	1,677
Aug-95	1,393	Aug-99	1,617	Aug-03	1,761
Sep-95	1,325	Sep-99	1,530	Sep-03	1,629
Oct-95	1,371	Oct-99	1,653	Oct-03	1,759
Nov-95	1,867	Nov-99	2,179	Nov-03	2,291
Dec-95	4,467	Dec-99	6,075	Dec-03	6,171
Jan-96	1,043	Jan-00	1,253	Jan-04	1,461
Feb-96	1,439	Feb-00	1,991	Feb-04	2,344
Mar-96	1,316	Mar-00	1,510	Mar-04	1,764
Apr-96	1,359	Apr-00	1,570	Apr-04	1,826
May-96	1,768	May-00	2,139	May-04	2,226
Jun-96	1,408	Jun-00	1,783	Jun-04	1,882
Jul-96	1,375	Jul-00	1,643	Jul-04	1,787
Aug-96	1,477	Aug-00	1,770	Aug-04	1,794
Sep-96	1,332	Sep-00	1,705	Sep-04	1,726
Oct-96	1,462	Oct-00	1,681	Oct-04	1,845
Nov-96	1,843	Nov-00	2,174	Nov-04	2,399
Dec-96	4,495	Dec-00	5,769	Dec-04	6,489
Jan-97	1,041	Jan-01	1,331	Jan-05	1,458
Feb-97	1,411	Feb-01	1,973	Feb-05	2,394
Mar-97	1,183	Mar-01	1,580	Mar-05	1,773
Apr-97	1,267	Apr-01	1,545	Apr-05	1,909
May-97	1,597	May-01	1,992	May-05	2,243
Jun-97	1,341	Jun-01	1,629	Jun-05	1,953
Jul-97	1,322	Jul-01	1,530	Jul-05	1,754
Aug-97	1,359	Aug-01	1,679	Aug-05	1,940
Sep-97	1,344	Sep-01	1,394	Sep-05	1,743
Oct-97	1,406	Oct-01	1,586	Oct-05	1,878
Nov-97	1,813	Nov-01	2,152	Nov-05	2,454
Dec-97	4,694	Dec-01	5,337	Dec-05	6,717

FIGURE 4.4

Jewelry Sales in Millions of Dollars

Here we see clearly the seasonality of jewelry sales in the raw data (dashed line). The deseasonalized data (solid line) helps us see the upward trend more clearly. (c4t4&f4)

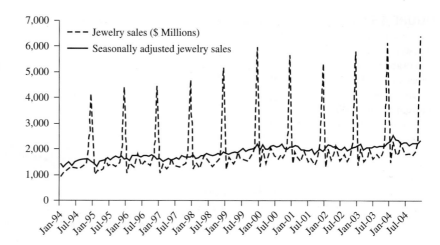

A JEWELRY SALES FORECAST BASED ON DISPOSABLE PERSONAL INCOME

If we hypothesize that disposable personal income (DPI) is influential in determining JS, we might initially want to look at a scattergram of these two variables. This is shown in Figure 4.5, where JS is plotted on the vertical axis and DPI is on the horizontal axis. You can see that higher values of JS appear to be associated with higher incomes. All observations do not fall on a single straight line. In the top graph you can see the effect of seasonality in a dramatic way. The 12 highest points are all December data points due to high holiday season sales.

In the lower graph the JS data are shown after the seasonality has been removed. In Chapter 6 you will learn how to deseasonalize data and how to find seasonal indices. In the bottom graph you can see that a straight line through those points could provide a reasonably good fit to the data. You also can see that all of these observations are well away from the origin. The importance of this observation will be apparent as we discuss the regression results below.

The bivariate regression model for JS as a function of DPI may be written as:

$$JS = b_0 + b_1(DPI)$$

The JS data used to estimate values for b_0 and b_1 are given in Table 4.4 and the data for DPI are in Table 4.2. The basic regression results are shown in Figure 4.6, along with a graph of the actual and predicted values based on this model. To use this model to forecast for 2005, a Holt's exponential smoothing forecast of DPI was used. On the basis of these results the forecast model (equation) for jewelry sales as a function of disposable personal income per capita is:

$$JS = 125.57 + 0.26(DPI)$$

FIGURE 4.5

**Scatter Graphs
of Jewelry Sales
(top graph) and
Deseasonalized
Jewelry Sales
(bottom graph) with
Disposable Personal
Income** (c4f5)

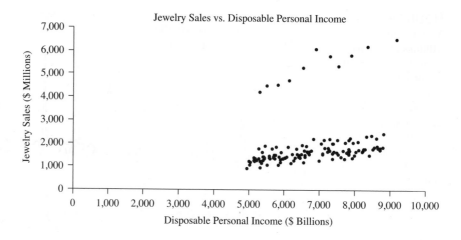

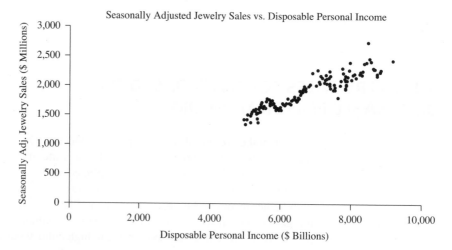

Data for 1994–2004 were used to estimate this model. The positive slope (0.26) indicates that, on average, JS increases by 0.26 million dollars for each additional 1 billion dollar increase in disposable personal income. A major problem with this model is apparent in Figure 4.6. It is clear from the graph of actual and predicted retail sales that this model fails to deal with the seasonality in JS.

The failure of this model to deal well with the seasonal nature of jewelry sales suggests that either we should use a model that can account for seasonality directly or we should deseasonalize the data before developing the regression forecasting model. In Chapter 3 you learned how to forecast a seasonal series with Winters' exponential smoothing. In the next chapter you will see how regression methods can also incorporate seasonality, and in Chapter 6 you will see how a seasonal pattern can be modeled using time-series decomposition. We will now develop a model based on seasonally adjusted jewelry sales data (SAJS) and then reintroduce the seasonality as we develop forecasts.

FIGURE 4.6
Jewelry Sales Forecast as a Function of DPI
We see that the upward trend in jewelry sales is accounted for by the regression model but the seasonality is not taken into account. Thus, for any given month in 2005 the forecast is likely to be substantially incorrect. The December 2005 forecast is surely much too low.   (c4f6)

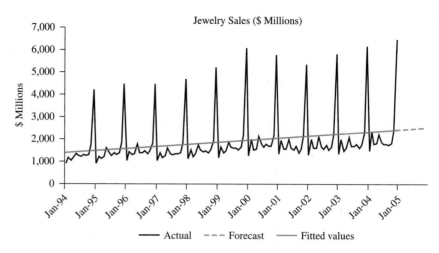

Multiple Regression--Result Formula

Jewelry Sales ($Millions) = 125.57 + ((DPI) * 0.259512)

Forecast--Multiple Regression Selected

Date	Monthly	Forecast Quarterly	Annual
Jan-2005	2,516.26		
Feb-2005	2,526.73		
Mar-2005	2,537.20	7,580.20	
Apr-2005	2,547.68		
May-2005	2,558.15		
Jun-2005	2,568.62	7,674.44	
Jul-2005	2,579.09		
Aug-2005	2,589.56		
Sep-2005	2,600.03	7,768.69	
Oct-2005	2,610.51		
Nov-2005	2,620.98		
Dec-2005	2,631.45	7,862.93	30,886.27

Audit Trail--ANOVA Table (Multiple Regression Selected)

Source of Variation	SS	df	MS	Overall F-test	SEE
Regression	11,261,517.30	1	11,261,517.30	9.78	
Error	149,658,345.67	130	1,151,218.04		1,072.95
Total	160,919,862.97	131			

```
Audit Trail--Coefficient Table (Multiple Regression Selected)

    Series           Included                    Standard
  Description        in model   Coefficient        error     T-test   P-value
---------------------------------------------------------------------------------
Jewelry Sales        Dependent    125.57          571.02       0.22     0.83
DPI                  Yes            0.26             0.08       3.13     0.00


Audit Trail--Statistics

Accuracy Measures                Value    Forecast Statistics          Value
-----------------------------------------  -------------------------------------
Mean Absolute Percentage                   Durbin Watson (1)             1.99
  Error (MAPE)                   26.99%    Root Mean Square
R-Square                          7.00%      Error                    1,064.79
```

When jewelry sales are seasonally adjusted, the following seasonal indices are found (arithmetically normalized to average 1):

January	0.63
February	0.92
March	0.75
April	0.78
May	1.01
June	0.83
July	0.79
August	0.84
September	0.77
October	0.83
November	1.08
December	2.77

Note that the seasonal index is highest during the holiday shopping months of November and December. The index of 2.77 for December indicates that December sales are typically 2.77 times the monthly average for the year. There are several ways to calculate seasonal indices. The method used here is described in Chapter 6 using time-series decomposition.[5] In Chapter 3 you saw similar indices based on Winters' exponential smoothing.

When we regress the seasonally adjusted values of jewelry sales (SAJS) as a function of disposable personal income using data for 1994–2004, we get the results shown at the bottom of Figure 4.7 and summarized by the following equation:

$$SAJS = 313.84 + 0.23(DPI)$$

[5] In ForecastX use the "Decomposition" forecast method. Then for "Type" select "Multiplicative" and for "Decomposed Data" select "Trend (Linear) Regression."

FIGURE 4.7

Seasonally Adjusted Jewelry Sales as a Function of DPI

The upward trend in SAJS is seen clearly in this graph. The forecast values for 2005, however, now need to be readjusted to put the seasonality back into the forecast. This is done for 2005 in Figure 4.8. (c4f7)

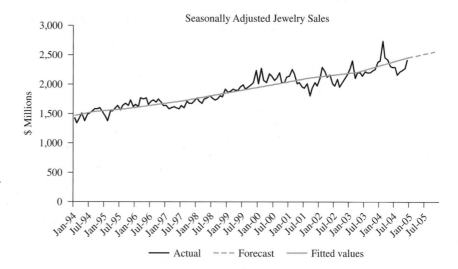

Multiple Regression--Result Formula

Seasonally Adjusted Jewelry Sales = 313.84 + ((DPI) * 0.234484)

Forecast--Multiple Regression Selected

Date	Monthly	Forecast Quarterly	Annual
Jan-2005	2,473.96		
Feb-2005	2,483.42		
Mar-2005	2,492.89	7,450.27	
Apr-2005	2,502.35		
May-2005	2,511.81		
Jun-2005	2,521.27	7,535.43	
Jul-2005	2,530.73		
Aug-2005	2,540.19		
Sep-2005	2,549.66	7,620.58	
Oct-2005	2,559.12		
Nov-2005	2,568.58		
Dec-2005	2,578.04	7,705.74	30,312.02

Audit Trail--ANOVA Table (Multiple Regression Selected)

Source of Variation	SS	df	MS	Overall F-test	SEE
Regression	9,194,067.24	1	9,194,067.24	787.42	
Error	1,517,899.59	130	11,676.15		108.06
Total	10,711,966.83	131			

```
Audit Trail--Coefficient Table (Multiple Regression Selected)
SAJS=Seasonally Adjusted Jewelry Sales


   Series           Included                        Standard
   Description      in model       Coefficient       error     T-test    P-value
   -----------------------------------------------------------------------------
   SAJS             Dependent         313.84          57.51      5.46      0.00
   DPI              Yes                 0.23            0.01     28.06      0.00


Audit Trail--Statistics


Accuracy Measures              Value     Forecast Statistics          Value
----------------------------------     ----------------------------------
Mean Absolute Percentage                 Durbin Watson (1)             0.78
   Error (MAPE)                4.28%     Root Mean Square Error
R-Square                      85.83%                                  107.23
---------------------------------------------------------------------------
```

We can substitute values of DPI into this equation to get predictions for seasonally adjusted jewelry sales (SAJS).

These values, as well as the values the model predicts for the historical period, are plotted in Figure 4.7, along with the actual data for 1994 through 2004. During the historical period, actual values of DPI were used to calculate SAJS, while in the forecast period (2005) forecast values of DPI using Holt's exponential smoothing were used.

Then, multiplying SAJS by the seasonal index for each quarter, we obtain a prediction of the unadjusted jewelry sales for each quarter. This process is illustrated in Figure 4.8 along with a graph of the actual and forecast values for jewelry sales for 2005. The RMSE for 2005 for the final forecast is 227.61, which is 9.7 percent of the actual sales for that 12-month period. The comparison between actual and forecast values for 2005 is shown in the graph at the bottom of Figure 4.8.

STATISTICAL EVALUATION OF REGRESSION MODELS

Now that you have a basic understanding of how simple bivariate regression models can be applied to forecasting, let us look more closely at some things that should be considered in evaluating regression models. The three regression models developed above will be used as the basis for our initial discussion. These are reproduced in Table 4.5. After evaluating these models in more detail, we will turn our attention to the use of bivariate regression models to forecast total houses sold and the sales of The Gap.

Basic Diagnostic Checks for Evaluating Regression Results

First, ask yourself whether the sign on the slope term makes sense.

There are several things you should consider when you look at regression results. First, ask yourself whether the sign on the slope term makes sense. There is almost always an economic or business logic that indicates whether the relationship between the dependent variable (Y) and the independent variable (X) should be positive or negative.

FIGURE 4.8
Jewelry Sales Final Forecast for 2005
The final forecast was found by first forecasting the trend for seasonally adjusted jewelry sales (SAJS). These values were then multiplied by the seasonal indices to get the final forecast. Actual and forecast values are shown in the graph for each month of 2005.   (c4f8)

Date	Actual SAJS	SAJS Trend Forecast	Error Squared
Jan-05	2,301.31	2,473.96	29,808.31
Feb-05	2,601.46	2,483.42	13,931.98
Mar-05	2,368.89	2,492.89	15,374.44
Apr-05	2,445.54	2,502.35	3,227.12
May-05	2,231.30	2,511.81	78,683.88
Jun-05	2,342.79	2,521.27	31,855.04
Jul-05	2,220.57	2,530.73	96,202.60
Aug-05	2,308.28	2,540.19	53,784.93
Sep-05	2,252.70	2,549.66	88,183.83
Oct-05	2,272.84	2,559.12	81,955.47
Nov-05	2,276.38	2,568.58	85,380.47
Dec-05	2,425.01	2,578.04	23,419.05

MSE = 50,150.59
RMSE = 223.94

Date	SAJS Trend Forecast	Seasonal Indices	Re-seasonalized Forecast	Actual JS	Error Squared
Jan-05	2,473.96	0.63	1,567.38	1458	11,964.70
Feb-05	2,483.42	0.92	2,285.38	2394	11,798.53
Mar-05	2,492.89	0.75	1,865.80	1773	8,612.45
Apr-05	2,502.35	0.78	1,953.34	1909	1,966.43
May-05	2,511.81	1.01	2,524.98	2243	79,511.05
Jun-05	2,521.27	0.83	2,101.78	1953	22,136.84
Jul-05	2,530.73	0.79	1,999.00	1754	60,023.08
Aug-05	2,540.19	0.84	2,134.91	1940	37,991.62
Sep-05	2,549.66	0.77	1,972.77	1743	52,793.17
Oct-05	2,559.12	0.83	2,114.55	1878	55,954.08
Nov-05	2,568.58	1.08	2,769.00	2454	99,224.32
Dec-05	2,578.04	2.77	7,140.88	6717	179,677.45

MSE = 51,804.47
RMSE = 227.61

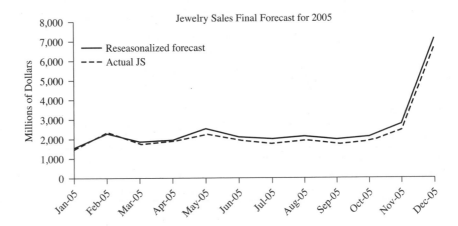

TABLE 4.5 Basic Results for Three Bivariate Regression Models (c4t5)

Model 1. DPI = 4,478.26 + 30.11 (Time Index)

Audit Trail--Coefficient Table (Multiple Regression Selected)

Series Description	Coefficient	Standard error	T-test	P-value
DPI	4,478.26	21.40	209.29	0.00
Time Index	30.11	0.22	137.10	0.00

Audit Trail--Statistics

Accuracy Measures	Value	Forecast Statistics	Value
Mean Absolute Percentage Error (MAPE)	1.68%	Durbin Watson (1)	0.18
R-Square	99.12%	Root Mean Square Error	137.23
		SEE	138.05

Model 2. Jewelry Sales ($ Millions) = 125.57 + 0.259512(DPI)

Audit Trail--Coefficient Table (Multiple Regression Selected)

Series Description	Coefficient	Standard error	T-test	P-value
Jewelry Sales	125.57	571.02	0.22	0.83
DPI	0.26	0.08	3.13	0.00

Audit Trail--Statistics

Accuracy Measures	Value	Forecast Statistics	Value
Mean Absolute Percentage Error (MAPE)	26.99%	Durbin Watson (1)	1.99
R-Square	7.00%	Root Mean Square Error	1,064.79
		SEE	1,072.95

Models 3. Seasonally Adjusted Jewelry Sales (SAJS) = 313.84 + 0.234484(DPI)

Audit Trail--Coefficient Table (Multiple Regression Selected)

Series Description	Coefficient	Standard error	T-test	P-value
SAJS	313.84	57.51	5.46	0.00
DPI	0.23	0.01	28.06	0.00

Audit Trail--Statistics

Accuracy Measures	Value	Forecast Statistics	Value
Mean Absolute Percentage Error (MAPE)	4.28%	Durbin Watson (1)	0.78
R-Square	85.83%	Root Mean Square Error	107.23
		SEE	108.06

In the examples considered in this chapter, a positive sign makes sense. In the first model we know that disposable personal income in the United States has generally increased over time. There have been some short periods of decline but such periods have been exceptions. Thus, we would expect the positive sign on the coefficient for the time index in the trend model for DPI. In the other examples, where jewelry sales (JS) and seasonally adjusted jewelry sales (SAJS) are modeled as a function of disposable personal income (DPI), a positive sign is also logical. For most goods and services, sales can be expected to increase as income increases.

What if the signs do not make sense? This is a clear indication that something is wrong with the regression model. It may be that the model is incomplete and that more than one independent variable is needed. In such a case the model is said to be *underspecified*. If so, a multiple-regression model may be appropriate. (Such models will be discussed in Chapter 5.) It would not be wise to use regression models that have coefficients with signs that are not logical.

The second thing that should be considered in an initial evaluation of a regression model is whether or not the slope term is significantly positive or negative. If not, then there is probably no statistical relationship between the dependent and independent variables. If the slope is zero, the regression line is perfectly horizontal, indicating that the value of Y is independent of the value of X (i.e., there is probably no relationship between X and Y).

But how far from zero need the slope term be? In the first example in Table 4.5 the slope is 30.11, in the second it is 0.26, and in the third model the slope is 0.23. The first is a relatively large number in terms of how much above zero it is, but we must be cautious about evaluating just the size of the slope term. To determine if the slope is significantly greater or less than zero, we must test a hypothesis concerning the true slope. Remember that our basic regression model is:

$$Y = \beta_0 + \beta_1 X + \varepsilon$$

If $\beta_1 = 0$, then $Y = \beta_0$ regardless of the value of X.

When we have a predisposition about whether the coefficient should be positive or negative based on our knowledge of the relationship, a one-tailed hypothesis test is appropriate. If our belief suggests a positive coefficient, the hypothesis would be set up as follows:

$$H_0: \beta_1 \leq 0$$
$$H_1: \beta_1 > 0$$

This form would be correct for the three cases in Table 4.5, since in all these cases a direct (positive) relationship is expected.

When our belief suggests a negative coefficient, the hypothesis would be set up as follows:

$$H_0: \beta_1 \geq 0$$
$$H_1: \beta_1 < 0$$

This form would be correct when an inverse (negative) relationship is expected.

It would not be wise to use regression models that have coefficients with signs that are not logical.

The second thing that should be considered in an initial evaluation of a regression model is whether or not the slope term is significantly positive or negative.

In some situations we may not have a specific expectation about the direction of causality, in which case a two-tailed hypothesis test is used. The hypothesis would be set up as follows:

$$H_0: \beta = 0$$
$$H_1: \beta = 0$$

The appropriate statistical test is a t-test, where the calculated value of t (t_{calc}) is equal to the slope term minus zero, divided by the standard error of the slope.[6] That is:

$$t_{calc} = (b_1 - 0)/(\text{s.e. of } b_1)$$

It is typical to use a 95 percent confidence level (an α, or significance level, of 5 percent) in testing this type of hypothesis. The appropriate number of degrees of freedom in bivariate regression is always $n - 2$, where n is the number of observations used in estimating the model. As described above, when we have a greater-than or less-than sign in the alternative hypothesis, a one-tailed test is appropriate.

For our present examples there are 130 degrees of freedom ($132 - 2$). From the t-table on page 73 we find the critical value of t (such that 0.05 is in one tail) to be 1.645 (using the infinity row). The calculated values of t are:

For the DPI Trend Model	For the JS = f(DPI) Causal Model	For the SAJS = f(DPI) Causal Model
$t_{calc} = (30.11 - 0)/0.22$ $= 137.1$	$t_{calc} = (0.26 - 0)/0.08$ $= 3.13$	$t_{calc} = (0.23 - 0)/0.01$ $= 28.06$

The t-values shown here are from Table 4.5. If you do these calculations by hand, results will differ from the values shown here and in Table 4.5 due to rounding.

For all three cases the calculated values are larger (more positive) than the critical, or table, value so we can reject H_0 in all cases and conclude that the regression coefficients are significantly greater than zero. If this statistical evaluation of the coefficients in a regression analysis results in failure to reject the null hypothesis, then it is probably not wise to use the model as a forecasting tool.[7] However, it is not uncommon to relax the criterion for evaluation of the hypothesis test to a 90 percent confidence level (a 10 percent significance level).

In determining whether or not to reject H_0, an alternative to comparing t-values is to consider the significance level (often called the P-value) given in most computer output. Let us assume that we desire a 95 percent confidence level. This is the equivalent of saying that we desire a 5 percent significance level.[8]

---

[6] The standard error of the estimated regression coefficient measures the sampling variability of b_1 about its expected value β_1, the true population parameter.

[7] A phenomenon known as *serial correlation* (which we will discuss shortly) may cause coefficients to appear significantly different from zero (as measured by the t-test) when in fact they are not.

[8] Remember that the confidence level and the significance level add to one. Thus, if we know one of these, we can easily determine the other.

For a two-tailed hypothesis test (H_1: $\beta_1 \neq 0$), we can then reject H_0 if the reported two-tailed significance level[9] in the output is less than 0.05. For a one-tailed hypothesis test (H_1: $\beta_1 < 0$ or H_1: $\beta_1 > 0$), we can reject H_0 if one-half of the reported two-tailed significance level is less than 0.05.

In all three of the examples in Table 4.5 the two-tailed significance levels associated with the calculated *t*-ratios are 0.00. Clearly, one-half of 0.00 is less than 0.05, so it is appropriate to reject H_0 in all three cases. Note that we reach the same conclusion whether we evaluate the hypotheses by comparing the calculated and table *t*-ratios or by looking at the significance levels.

The third check of regression results is to evaluate what percent of the variation (i.e., up-and-down movement) in the dependent variable is explained by variation in the independent variable.

The third check of regression results is to evaluate what percent of the variation (i.e., up-and-down movement) in the dependent variable is explained by variation in the independent variable. This is evaluated by interpreting the *R*-squared value that is reported in regression output. *R*-squared is the coefficient of determination, which tells us the fraction of the variation in the dependent variable that is explained by variation in the independent variable. Thus, *R*-squared can range between zero and one. Zero would indicate no explanatory power, while one would indicate that all of the variation in *Y* is explained by the variation in *X*. (A related statistic, adjusted *R*-squared, will be discussed in Chapter 5.)

Our trend model for disposable personal income (DPI) has an *R*-squared of .9912. Thus, 99.12 percent of the variation in disposable personal income is accounted for by this simple linear trend model. The causal model for jewelry sales as a function of DPI has an *R*-squared of .07, which suggests that 7.0 percent of the variation in jewelry sales is explained by variations in disposable personal income. The model for seasonally adjusted jewelry sales as a function of DPI has an *R*-squared of .8583. Thus, variations in the DPI explain only 85.83 percent of the variation in seasonally adjusted jewelry sales.

It is possible to perform a statistical test to determine whether the the coefficient of determination (R^2) is significantly different from zero. The hypothesis test may be stated as:

$$H_0: R^2 = 0$$

$$H_1: R^2 \neq 0$$

The appropriate statistical test is an *F*-test, which will be presented in Chapter 5. With bivariate regression it turns out that the *t*-test for the slope term in the regression equation is equivalent to the *F*-test for *R*-squared. Thus, we will wait until we explore multiple-regression models to discuss the application of the *F*-test.

Before considering other statistical diagnostics, let us summarize these three initial evaluative steps for bivariate regression models:

1. Ask whether the sign for the slope term makes sense.
2. Check to see whether the slope term is statistically positive or negative at the desired significance level by using a *t*-test.

[9] In ForecastX™, as well as most other statistical packages, two-tailed significance levels are reported. These are frequently referred to as *P-values,* as is the case in ForecastX™.

3. Evaluate how much of the variation in the dependent variable is explained by the regression model using the R-squared (R^2) value.

These three items can be evaluated from the results presented in standard computer output, such as those shown in Table 4.5.

USING THE STANDARD ERROR OF THE ESTIMATE

The forecasts we made in the preceding pages—using a simple linear trend model and the two causal regression models—were point estimates. In each case we substituted a value for the independent variable into the regression equation to obtain a single number representing our best estimate (forecast) of the dependent variable. It is sometimes useful to provide an interval estimate rather than a point estimate.

The standard error of the estimate (SEE) can be used to generate *approximate* confidence intervals with relative ease. The SEE is often also called the *standard error of the regression*. The confidence intervals we present here are approximate because the true confidence band is not parallel to the regression line but rather bows away from the regression line at values of Y and X far from the means. This is illustrated in Figure 4.9. The approximate 95 percent confidence interval can be calculated as follows:[10]

$$\text{Point estimate} \pm 2 \text{ (standard error of the estimate)}$$

FIGURE 4.9
Confidence Bands around a Regression Line
The true confidence band bows away from the regression line. An approximate 95 percent confidence band can be calculated by taking the point estimate for each X, plus or minus 2 times the standard error of the estimate.

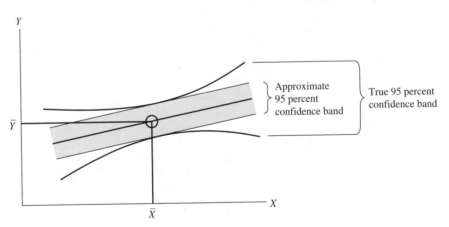

[10] The true 95 percent confidence band for predicting Y for a given value of X (X_0) can be found as follows:

$$\hat{Y} \pm t(\text{SEE})\sqrt{1 + (1/n) + [(X_0 + \bar{X})^2/\Sigma(X - \bar{X})^2]}$$

where t is the appropriate value from the t-distribution at $n - 2$ degrees of freedom and the desired significance level, SEE is the standard error of the estimate, and $\hat{Y}$ is the point estimate determined from the estimated regression equation.

TABLE 4.6
Representative
Calculations of
Approximate
95 Percent ~~Confidence~~
Intervals: Point
Estimate ±2 ×
Standard Error of
the Estimate (SEE)*

prediction

For DPI: 2 × SEE = 2 × 138.05 = 276.1		
Period	**95 Percent Confidence Interval**	**Actual DPI**
January 2007	9,934.7 ± 276.1 = 9,658.6 to 10,210.8	9,934.7
For SAJS: 2 × SEE = 2 × 108.06 = 216.12		
Period	**95 Percent Confidence Interval**	**Actual SAJS†**
December 2005	2,578.04 ± 216.12 = 2,361.92 to 2,794.16	2,424.9

* Point estimates have been rounded to integers.
† Note that this is for jewelry sales seasonally adjusted.

The value of 2 is used as an easy approximation for the correct *t*-value. Recall that if there are a large number of degrees of freedom, $t = 1.96$.

Representative calculations of approximate 95 percent confidence bands for the regression forecasts developed for DPI and SAJS are shown in Table 4.6. The standard errors of the regressions are taken from Table 4.5, while the point estimates for each model and each quarter are those that were found in the previous sections "Forecasting with a Simple Linear Trend" and "Using a Causal Regression Model to Forecast."

SERIAL CORRELATION

Business and economic data used in forecasting are most often time-series data. The retail sales data and the real disposable personal income data used in this chapter are typical of such time series. In using regression analysis with time-series data, the problem known as *serial correlation* (also called autocorrelation) can cause some difficulty.

One of the assumptions of the ordinary least-squares regression model is that the error terms are independent and normally distributed, with a mean of zero and a constant variance. If this is true for a particular case, we would not expect to find any regular pattern in the error terms. When a significant time pattern that violates the independence assumption is found in the error terms, serial correlation is indicated.

Figure 4.10 illustrates the two possible cases of serial correlation. In the left-hand graph, the case of negative serial correlation is apparent. Negative serial correlation exists when a negative error is followed by a positive error, then another negative error, and so on. The error terms alternate in sign. Positive serial correlation is shown in the right-hand graph in Figure 4.10. In positive serial correlation, positive errors tend to be followed by other positive errors, while negative errors are followed by other negative errors.

When serial correlation exists, problems can develop in using and interpreting the OLS regression function. The existence of serial correlation does not bias the

FIGURE 4.10 **Negative and Positive Serial Correlation**
The left-hand graph shows an example of negative serial correlation; the right-hand graph illustrates positive serial correlation. The latter is common when dealing with business data.

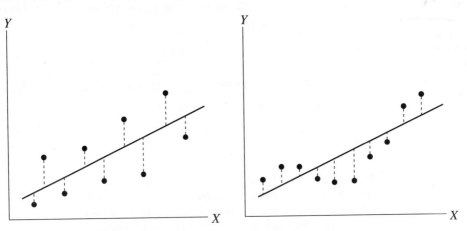

coefficients that are estimated, but it does make the estimates of the standard errors smaller than the true standard errors. This means that the t-ratios calculated for each coefficient will be overstated, which in turn may lead to the rejection of null hypotheses that should not have been rejected. That is, regression coefficients may be deemed statistically significant when indeed they are not. In addition, the existence of serial correlation causes the R-squared and F-statistics to be unreliable in evaluating the overall significance of the regression function (the F-statistic will be discussed in Chapter 5).

There are a number of ways to test statistically for the existence of serial correlation. The method most frequently used is the evaluation of the Durbin-Watson statistic (DW). This statistic is calculated as follows:

$$DW = \frac{\Sigma(e_t - e_{t-1})^2}{\Sigma e_t^2}$$

where e_t is the residual for the time period t, and e_{t-1} is the residual for the preceding time period $(t - 1)$. Almost all computer programs for regression analysis include the Durbin-Watson statistic, so you are not likely to have to calculate it directly.

The DW statistic will always be in the range of 0 to 4. As a rule of thumb, a value close to 2 (e.g., between 1.50 and 2.50) indicates that there is no serial correlation. As the degree of negative serial correlation increases, the value of the DW statistic approaches 4. If positive serial correlation exists, the value of DW approaches 0.

To be more precise in evaluating the significance and meaning of the calculated DW statistic, we must refer to a Durbin-Watson table, such as Table 4.7. Note that

TABLE 4.7
The Durbin-Watson Statistic

Source: J. Durbin and G. S. Watson, "Testing for Serial Correlation in Least Squares Regression," *Biometrika* 38 (June 1951), p. 173.

N	k = 1		k = 2		k = 3		k = 4		k = 5	
	d_l	d_u	d_l	d_u	d_l	d_u	d_l	d_u	d_l	d_u
15	1.08	1.36	0.95	1.54	0.82	1.75	0.69	1.97	0.56	2.21
16	1.10	1.37	0.98	1.54	0.86	1.73	0.74	1.93	0.62	2.15
17	1.13	1.38	1.02	1.54	0.90	1.71	0.78	1.90	0.67	2.10
18	1.16	1.39	1.05	1.53	0.93	1.69	0.82	1.87	0.71	2.06
19	1.18	1.40	1.08	1.53	0.97	1.68	0.86	1.85	0.75	2.02
20	1.20	1.41	1.10	1.54	1.00	1.68	0.90	1.83	0.79	1.99
21	1.22	1.42	1.13	1.54	1.03	1.67	0.93	1.81	0.83	1.96
22	1.24	1.43	1.15	1.54	1.05	1.66	0.96	1.80	0.86	1.94
23	1.26	1.44	1.17	1.54	1.08	1.66	0.99	1.79	0.90	1.92
24	1.27	1.45	1.19	1.55	1.10	1.66	1.01	1.78	0.93	1.90
25	1.29	1.45	1.21	1.55	1.12	1.66	1.04	1.77	0.95	1.89
26	1.30	1.46	1.22	1.55	1.14	1.65	1.06	1.76	0.98	1.88
27	1.32	1.47	1.24	1.56	1.16	1.65	1.08	1.76	1.01	1.86
28	1.33	1.48	1.26	1.56	1.18	1.65	1.10	1.75	1.03	1.85
29	1.34	1.48	1.27	1.56	1.20	1.65	1.12	1.74	1.05	1.84
30	1.35	1.49	1.28	1.57	1.21	1.65	1.14	1.74	1.07	1.83
31	1.36	1.50	1.30	1.57	1.23	1.65	1.16	1.74	1.09	1.83
32	1.37	1.50	1.31	1.57	1.24	1.65	1.18	1.73	1.11	1.82
33	1.38	1.51	1.32	1.58	1.26	1.65	1.19	1.73	1.13	1.81
34	1.39	1.51	1.33	1.58	1.27	1.65	1.21	1.73	1.15	1.81
35	1.40	1.52	1.34	1.53	1.28	1.65	1.22	1.73	1.16	1.80
36	1.41	1.52	1.35	1.59	1.29	1.65	1.24	1.73	1.18	1.80
37	1.42	1.53	1.36	1.59	1.31	1.66	1.25	1.72	1.19	1.80
38	1.43	1.54	1.37	1.59	1.32	1.66	1.26	1.72	1.21	1.79
39	1.43	1.54	1.38	1.60	1.33	1.66	1.27	1.72	1.22	1.79
40	1.44	1.54	1.39	1.60	1.34	1.66	1.29	1.72	1.23	1.79
45	1.48	1.57	1.43	1.62	1.38	1.67	1.34	1.72	1.29	1.78
50	1.50	1.59	1.46	1.63	1.42	1.67	1.38	1.72	1.34	1.77
55	1.53	1.60	1.49	1.64	1.45	1.68	1.41	1.72	1.38	1.77
60	1.55	1.62	1.51	1.65	1.48	1.69	1.44	1.73	1.41	1.77
65	1.57	1.63	1.54	1.66	1.50	1.70	1.47	1.73	1.44	1.77
70	1.58	1.64	1.55	1.67	1.52	1.70	1.49	1.74	1.46	1.77
75	1.60	1.65	1.57	1.68	1.54	1.71	1.51	1.74	1.49	1.77
80	1.61	1.66	1.59	1.69	1.56	1.72	1.53	1.74	1.51	1.77
85	1.62	1.67	1.60	1.70	1.57	1.72	1.55	1.75	1.52	1.77
90	1.63	1.68	1.61	1.70	1.59	1.73	1.57	1.75	1.54	1.78
95	1.64	1.69	1.62	1.71	1.60	1.73	1.58	1.75	1.56	1.78
100	1.65	1.69	1.63	1.72	1.61	1.74	1.59	1.76	1.57	1.78

k = the number of independent variables; N = the number of observations used in the regression.

for each number of independent variables (k), two columns of values labeled d_l and d_u are given. The values in these columns for the appropriate number of observations (N) are used in evaluating the calculated value of DW according to the criteria shown in Figure 4.11.

FIGURE 4.11

A Schematic for Evaluating Serial Correlation Using the Durbin-Watson Statistic

d_u = Upper value of Durbin-Watson from Table 4.7

d_l = Lower value of Durbin-Watson from Table 4.7

H_0: $\rho = 0$ (i.e., no serial correlation)

H_1: $\rho \neq 0$ (i.e., serial correlation exists)

Value of Calculated Durbin-Watson	Result	Region Designator
4		
	Negative serial correlation (reject H_0)	A
$4 - d_l$		
	Indeterminate	B
$4 - d_u$		
2	No serial correlation (do not reject H_0)	C
d_u		
	Indeterminate	D
d_l		
	Positive serial correlation (reject H_0)	E
0		

To illustrate, let us consider the simple trend regression for disposable personal income (DPI). From Table 4.5 (see page 180) you see that the calculated Durbin-Watson statistic is 0.18. Using Table 4.7, we find for $k = 1$ and $N = 168$ that:

$$d_l = 1.65$$
$$d_u = 1.69$$

For a sample size not in this table, use the closest value. For example, in the above case in which $N = 168$ we use the row for $N = 100$.

Using these values and our calculated value, we can evaluate the criteria in Figure 4.11:

Region	Comparison	Result
A	$4 > 0.18 > (4 - 1.65)$	False
B	$(4 - 1.65) > 0.18 > (4 - 1.69)$	False
C	$(4 - 1.69) > 0.18 > 1.69$	False
D	$1.69 > 0.18 > 1.65$	False
E	$1.65 > 0.18 > 0$	True

Since our result is in region E, we can conclude that positive serial correlation exists in this case.[11] You can see evidence of this positive serial correlation if you look in Figure 4.3 (page 168) at how the regression line (fitted) is at first below, then above, and then below the actual data in a recurring pattern.

You might well ask: What causes serial correlation and what can be done about it? A primary cause of serial correlation is the existence of long-term cycles and trends in economic and business data. Such trends and cycles are particularly

A primary cause of serial correlation is the existence of long-term cycles and trends in economic and business data.

---

[11] Check for serial correlation in the regression of SAJS as a function of DPI. You should find that with a calculated Durbin-Watson statistic of 0.78, with $k = 1$, and using $N = 100$, the criterion in region E is satisfied, indicating positive serial correlation.

likely to produce positive serial correlation. Serial correlation can also be caused by a misspecification of the model. Either leaving out one or more important variables or failing to include a nonlinear term when one is called for can be a cause.

We can try several relatively simple things to reduce serial correlation. One is to use first differences of the variables rather than the actual values when performing the regression analysis. That is, use the change in each variable from period to period in the regression. For example, we could try the following:

$$\Delta Y = b_0 + b_1(\Delta X)$$

where Δ means "change in" and is calculated as follows:

$$\Delta Y_t = Y_t - Y_{t-1}$$
$$\Delta X_t = X_t - X_{t-1}$$

This process of "first-differencing" will be seen again in Chapter 7, when we discuss ARIMA forecasting models.

Other approaches to solving the serial correlation problem often involve moving into the realm of multiple regression, where there is more than one independent variable in the regression model. For example, it may be that other causal factors account for the differences between the actual and predicted values. For example, in the jewelry sales regression, we might add the interest rate and the unemployment rate as additional independent variables.

A third, and somewhat related, approach to dealing with serial correlation is to introduce the square of an existing causal variable as another independent variable. Also, we might introduce a lag of the dependent variable as an independent variable. Such a model might look as follows:

$$Y_t = b_0 + b_1 X_t + b_2 Y_{t-1}$$

where t represents the current time period and $t - 1$ represents the previous time period.

There are other procedures, based on more sophisticated statistical models, that are helpful in dealing with the problems created by serial correlation. These are typically based on an extension of the use of first differences in that they involve the use of generalized differencing to alter the basic linear regression model into one for which the error terms are independent of one another (i.e., $\rho = 0$, where ρ [rho] is the correlation between successive error terms).

The basic regression model is:

$$Y_t = \beta_0 + \beta_1 X_t + \varepsilon_t$$

and since this is true for all time periods, it follows that:

$$Y_{t-1} = \beta_0 + \beta_1 X_{t-1} + \varepsilon_{t-1}$$

Multiplying the second of these equations by ρ and subtracting the result from the first yields the following generalized-differencing transformed equation:

$$Y_t^* = (1 - \rho)\beta_0 + \beta_1 X_t^* + v_t$$

where:

$$Y_t^* = Y_t - \rho Y_{t-1}$$
$$X_t^* = X_t - \rho X_{t-1}$$
$$v_t = \varepsilon_t - \rho \varepsilon_{t-1}$$

It can be shown that the resulting error term, v_t, is independently distributed with a mean of zero and a constant variance.[12] The problem with this generalized-differencing model is that we do not know the correct value for ρ. Two common methods for estimating ρ and the corresponding regression model are the Cochrane-Orcutt procedure and the Hildreth-Lu procedure.[13]

The Cochrane-Orcutt procedure uses an iterative approach to estimate the value for ρ, starting with the standard OLS regression model, from which the residuals (e_t) are used to estimate the equation $e_t = \rho e_{t-1} + v_t$. The estimated value of ρ is then used to perform the generalized-differencing transformation, and a new regression is run. New error terms result and are used to make another estimate of ρ. This process continues until the newest estimate of ρ differs from the previous one by a prescribed amount (such as 0.01).

HETEROSCEDASTICITY

One of the assumptions of regression analysis is that the error terms in the population regression (ε_i) have a constant variance across all values of the independent variable (X). When this is true, the model is said to be *homoscedastic,* and if this assumption is violated, the model is termed *heteroscedastic.* With heteroscedasticity, the standard errors of the regression coefficients may be underestimated, causing the calculated t-ratios to be larger than they should be, which may lead us to conclude incorrectly that a variable is statistically significant. Heteroscedasticity is more common with cross-sectional data than with time-series data.

We can evaluate a regression model for heteroscedasticity by looking at a scatterplot of the residuals (on the vertical axis) versus the independent variable (on the horizontal axis). In an ideal model, the plot of the residuals would fall within a horizontal band, as shown in the top graph of Figure 4.12. This graph illustrates a residual pattern representative of homoscedasticity. A typical heteroscedastic situation is shown by the funnel-shaped pattern of residuals in the lower graph of Figure 4.12.

One common way to reduce or eliminate a problem of heteroscedasticity is to use the logarithm of the dependent variable in the estimation of the regression model. This often works because the logarithms will have less overall variability

logs reduce heteroscedasticity

[12] Most econometrics books describe the underlying statistical theory as well as the two correction procedures we include herein. For example, see Pindyck and Rubinfeld, *Econometric Models and Economic Forecasts,* 3rd ed., 1991, pp. 137–47.

[13] While these methods help solve the serial-correlation problem, they are not often used in practice for forecasting, largely due to their added complexity and inability to produce forecasts beyond a very short time frame.

FIGURE 4.12
Residual Patterns
Indicative of
Homoscedasticity
(Top Graph) and
Heteroscedasticity
(Bottom Graph)

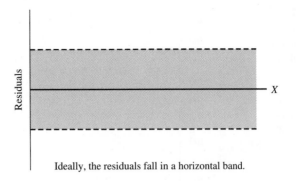

Ideally, the residuals fall in a horizontal band.

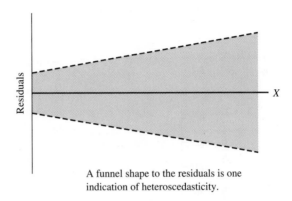

A funnel shape to the residuals is one
indication of heteroscedasticity.

than the raw data. A second possible solution would be to use a form of regression analysis other than the ordinary least-squares method. Discussion of such methods is beyond the scope of this text but can be found in many econometric texts.

To illustrate the evaluation of a specific model for heteroscedasticity, let us look at the model of seasonally adjusted jewelry sales (SAJS) as a function of disposable personal income (DPI). The top graph in Figure 4.13 shows a scattergram of the residuals from that model. There does appear to be a systematic pattern to the residuals that would lead us to suspect heteroscedasticity in this case. However, when the natural logarithm of SAJS is used as the dependent variable, the pattern of residuals is much better.

CROSS-SECTIONAL FORECASTING

While most forecasting is based on time-series data, there are situations in which cross-sectional analysis is useful. In cross-sectional analysis the data all pertain to one time period rather than a sequence of periods. Suppose, for example, that you are the sales manager for a firm that sells small specialty sandwiches through convenience stores. You currently operate in eight cities and are

FIGURE 4.13

Scatterplot of the Residuals from the Regression of SAJS with DPI

The top scatterplot shows a pattern that would suggest het-eroscedasticity. The lower graph, in which logarithms are used, has a more desirable pattern. (c4f13)

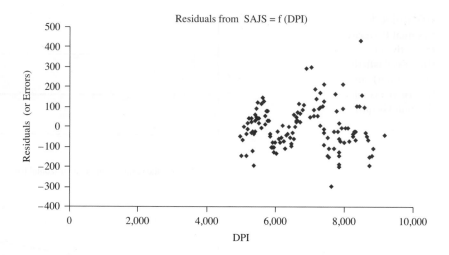

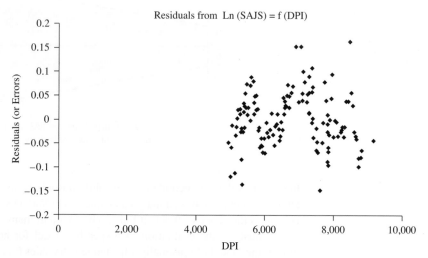

considering expanding into another. You have the data shown at the top of Table 4.8 for the most recent year's sales and the population of each city. You may try to predict sales based on population by using a bivariate regression model. The model may be written as:

$$\text{Sales} = b_0 + b_1(\text{POP})$$

While most forecasting is based on time-series data, there are situations in which cross-sectional analysis is useful. In cross-sectional analysis the data all pertain to one time period rather than a sequence of periods.

Regression results for this model, given the eight data points just shown, are presented in Table 4.8.

These results show the expected positive sign for the coefficient of population. The critical value of t from the t-table at six degrees of freedom ($n - 2 = 6$) and a 5 percent significance level (one-tailed test) is 1.943. Since the calculated value for population is greater ($8.00 > 1.943$), we conclude that there is a statistically significant positive relationship between sales and population. The coefficient of

TABLE 4.8
Regression Results for Sales as a Function of Population

Population (000)	Sales (000)
505	372
351	275
186	214
175	135
132	81
115	144
108	90
79	97

Regression Statistic	
Multiple R	0.956
R-Square	0.914
Standard error	32.72
Observations	8

	Coefficient	Standard Error	T-test	P-value
Intercept	37.02	20.86	1.77	0.126
Population (000)	0.67	0.08	8.00	0.000

The Durbin-Watson statistic is not shown because it is not relevant for cross-sectional data. Indeed, the order in which the data are placed will change the Durbin-Watson statistics.

determination (*R*-squared) is 0.914, which tells us that 91.4 percent of the variation in sales is explained by the variation in population.

Now suppose that the city that you are considering expanding into has a population of 155,000. You can use the regression results to forecast sales as follows:

$$Sales = 37.02 + 0.67(POP)$$
$$= 37.02 + 0.67(155)$$
$$= 140.87$$

Remember that sales are in thousands, so this is a point estimate of 140,870 sandwiches. An approximate 95 percent confidence band could be constructed as follows:

$$Point\ estimate \pm 2(standard\ error\ of\ regression) = 140.870 \pm 2(32.72)$$
$$= 140.870 \pm 65.44$$
$$= 75.43\ to\ 206.31$$

That is, about 75,430 to 206,310 sandwiches.

FORECASTING TOTAL HOUSES SOLD WITH TWO BIVARIATE REGRESSION MODELS

You may recall that the total houses sold (THS) series that we forecast in Chapters 1 and 3 showed quite a bit of variability, including a substantial seasonal component. Therefore, you might expect that it would be difficult to forecast such a series based on a simple regression equation with one causal variable. One thing that would make the process more workable would be to deseasonalize the THS data prior to attempting to build a regression model. The original THS data and the seasonal indices are shown in Table 4.9.

TABLE 4.9

Data and Seasonal Indices for Forecasting Total Houses Sold (THS) Data for 1993 through 2006 are used to make a forecast for the first 7 months of 2007. The trend regression results for seasonally adjusted THS are shown in Figure 4.14. The forecast for the first 7 months of 2007 are shown in Figure 4.15.   (c4t9)

Date	Total Houses Sold (000)	Date	Total Houses Sold (000)	Date	Total Houses Sold (000)	Date	Total Houses Sold (000)
Jan-93	44	Jan-97	61	Jan-01	72	Jan-05	92
Feb-93	50	Feb-97	69	Feb-01	85	Feb-05	109
Mar-93	60	Mar-97	81	Mar-01	94	Mar-05	127
Apr-93	66	Apr-97	70	Apr-01	84	Apr-05	116
May-93	58	May-97	71	May-01	80	May-05	120
Jun-93	59	Jun-97	71	Jun-01	79	Jun-05	115
Jul-93	55	Jul-97	69	Jul-01	76	Jul-05	117
Aug-93	57	Aug-97	72	Aug-01	74	Aug-05	110
Sep-93	57	Sep-97	67	Sep-01	66	Sep-05	99
Oct-93	56	Oct-97	62	Oct-01	66	Oct-05	105
Nov-93	53	Nov-97	61	Nov-01	67	Nov-05	86
Dec-93	51	Dec-97	51	Dec-01	66	Dec-05	87
Jan-94	46	Jan-98	64	Jan-02	66	Jan-06	89
Feb-94	58	Feb-98	75	Feb-02	84	Feb-06	88
Mar-94	74	Mar-98	81	Mar-02	90	Mar-06	108
Apr-94	65	Apr-98	82	Apr-02	86	Apr-06	100
May-94	65	May-98	82	May-02	88	May-06	102
Jun-94	55	Jun-98	83	Jun-02	84	Jun-06	98
Jul-94	52	Jul-98	75	Jul-02	82	Jul-06	83
Aug-94	59	Aug-98	75	Aug-02	90	Aug-06	88
Sep-94	54	Sep-98	68	Sep-02	82	Sep-06	80
Oct-94	57	Oct-98	69	Oct-02	77	Oct-06	74
Nov-94	45	Nov-98	70	Nov-02	73	Nov-06	71
Dec-94	40	Dec-98	61	Dec-02	70	Dec-06	71
Jan-95	47	Jan-99	67	Jan-03	76		
Feb-95	47	Feb-99	76	Feb-03	82	Jan-07	66
Mar-95	60	Mar-99	84	Mar-03	98	Feb-07	68
Apr-95	58	Apr-99	86	Apr-03	91	Mar-07	80
May-95	63	May-99	80	May-03	101	Apr-07	83
Jun-95	64	Jun-99	82	Jun-03	107	May-07	80
Jul-95	64	Jul-99	78	Jul-03	99	Jun-07	77
Aug-95	63	Aug-99	78	Aug-03	105	Jul-07	74
Sep-95	54	Sep-99	65	Sep-03	90		
Oct-95	54	Oct-99	67	Oct-03	88		
Nov-95	46	Nov-99	61	Nov-03	76	**Seasonal Indices**	
Dec-95	45	Dec-99	57	Dec-03	75		
Jan-96	54	Jan-00	67	Jan-04	89		1.02
Feb-96	68	Feb-00	78	Feb-04	102		1.05
Mar-96	70	Mar-00	88	Mar-04	123		0.95
Apr-96	70	Apr-00	78	Apr-04	109		0.94
May-96	69	May-00	77	May-04	115		0.85
Jun-96	65	Jun-00	71	Jun-04	105		0.81
Jul-96	66	Jul-00	76	Jul-04	96		0.89
Aug-96	73	Aug-00	73	Aug-04	102		1.02
Sep-96	62	Sep-00	70	Sep-04	94		1.18
Oct-96	56	Oct-00	71	Oct-04	101		1.09
Nov-96	54	Nov-00	63	Nov-04	84		1.11
Dec-96	51	Dec-00	65	Dec-04	83		1.07

What are the causal factors that you think would influence the sales of houses? You might come up with a fairly long list. Some of the variables that might be on such a list are:

Income

Unemployment rate

Interest or mortgage rates

Consumer attitudes[14]

Housing prices

In this section we will first prepare a forecast of THS based solely on a simple linear trend; then we will do a second forecast using disposable personal income as a causal variable.

When seasonally adjusted monthly data for total houses sold (SATHS) are regressed as a function of a time index, where $t = 1$ for January 1993, the results are as shown in Figure 4.14. Data used to develop the model and forecast were from January 1991 through December 2006. The forecast was made through the first seven months of 2007. The equation for seasonally adjusted total houses sold is:

$$SATHS = 50.25 + 0.30(\text{Time})$$

The positive slope for time of 0.30 is logical, and from the t-ratio (27.13) we see that the slope is quite statistically significant in this model (the significance level, or p-value, is .000—even at a two-tailed level). The R-squared (R^2) tells us that 81.60 percent of the variation in seasonally adjusted total houses sold is explained by this model. We see that the Durbin-Watson test for serial correlation indicates positive serial correlation (D-W = 0.45).

---

[14] Consumer attitudes are often measured by the University of Michigan's Index of Consumer Sentiment. This is an index that is released each month by the University of Michigan Survey Research Center. Each month 500 respondents in a national survey are interviewed about a variety of topics. There are five specific questions in the survey that go into the calculation of the Index of Consumer Sentiment, which has been adjusted to a base of 100 for 1966. Those five questions are:

1. We are interested in how people are getting along financially these days. Would you say that you (and your family living there) are better off or worse off financially than you were a year ago?

2. Now looking ahead—do you think that a year from now you (and your family living there) will be better off financially, or worse off, or about the same as now?

3. Now turning to business conditions in the country as a whole—do you think that during the next 12 months we'll have good times financially, or bad times, or what?

4. Looking ahead, which would you say is more likely—that in the country as a whole we'll have continuous good times during the next five years or so, or that we will have periods of widespread unemployment or depression, or what?

5. About the big things people buy for their homes—such as furniture, a refrigerator, stove, television, and things like that. Generally speaking, do you think now is a good or bad time for people to buy major household items?

The way in which the index is computed makes it higher when people's responses to these questions are more positive.

FIGURE 4.14

Trend Forecast for Seasonally Adjusted Total Houses Sold (000)

The straight line in this graph represents the forecast values. It is solid in the 2007 forecast horizon. Data from 1993 through 2006 were used to develop the forecast. (c4f14)

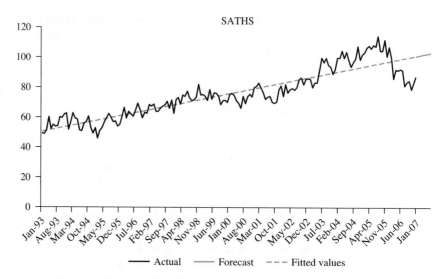

Multiple Regression--Result Formula

SATHS = 50.25 + ((Time) * 0.301306)

Forecast--Multiple Regression Selected

	Forecast	
Date	Monthly	Quarterly
Jan-2007	101.17	
Feb-2007	101.47	
Mar-2007	101.77	304.40
Apr-2007	102.07	
May-2007	102.37	
Jun-2007	102.67	307.11
Jul-2007	102.97	

Audit Trail--Coefficient Table (Multiple Regression Selected)

Description	Coefficient	error	T-test	P-value
SATHS	50.25	1.08	46.44	0.00
Time	0.30	0.01	27.13	0.00

Audit Trail--Statistics

Accuracy Measures	Value	Forecast Statistics	Value
Mean Absolute Percentage Error (MAPE)	6.93%	Durbin Watson (1)	0.45
R-Square	81.60%	SEE	6.98
Root Mean Square Error	6.94		

FIGURE 4.15 **The Trend Forecast for Total Houses Sold**

The reseasonalized forecast is calculated by multiplying each seasonal index by the trend forecast of seasonally adjusted total houses sold for the corresponding month. The error is Actual minus Forecast. (c4f15)

Date	THS (Actual)*	Seasonal Indices	Trend Forecast of SATHS	Reseasonalized Forecast	Error Squared $(A - F)^2$
Jan-07	66	0.89	101.17	90.08	579.86
Feb-07	68	1.02	101.47	103.92	1290.03
Mar-07	80	1.18	101.77	119.84	1587.09
Apr-07	83	1.09	102.07	111.74	825.79
May-07	80	1.11	102.37	113.47	1120.00
Jun-07	77	1.07	102.67	110.06	1092.95
Jul-07	74	1.02	102.97	105.48	990.89

* 2007 data not used in developing the 2007 forecast.

MSE = 1069.52
RMSE = 32.70
RMSE as % of Actual = 43.4%

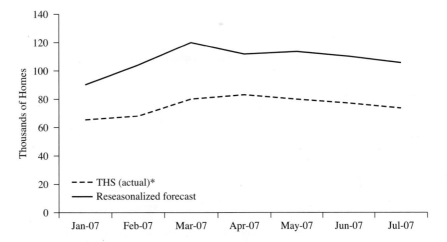

To make a forecast of SATHS for 2004 with this model, we use time index values of 169 for January 2007 through 175 for July 2007. Doing so gives us the the solid portion of the straight line in Figure 4.14. These are values for the seasonally adjusted total houses sold in the first 7 months of 2007.

To get the forecast of nonseasonally adjusted values we multiply the seasonally adjusted values by the corresponding seasonal index for each month.[15] This is shown in Figure 4.15 along with the calculation of the root-mean-squared error (RMSE) for the seven 2007 monthly forecasts.

---

[15] The seasonal indices used are from a time-series decomposition of the data using ForecastX™. This will be discussed in Chapter 6.

FIGURE 4.16
**Forecast of Season-
ally Adjusted Total
Houses Sold as a
Function of Dispos-
able Personal Income
(DPI)**
Data for 1993 through
2006 were used to de-
velop the forecast. For
2007 Holti's exponen-
tial smoothing was
used to forecast DPI.
(c4f16)

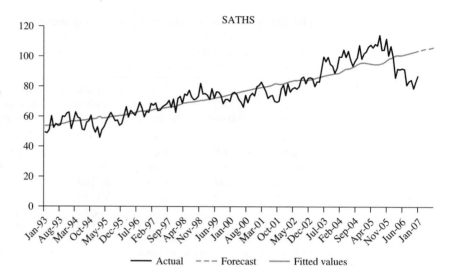

```
Multiple Regression--Result Formula

SATHS = 6.29 + ((DPI) * 0.009885


Forecast--Multiple Regression Selected

                      Forecast
                 --------------------
      Date       Monthly    Quarterly
------------------------------------------
Jan-2007         103.92
Feb-2007         104.29
Mar-2007         104.66      312.88
Apr-2007         105.03
May-2007         105.39
Jun-2007         105.76      316.18
Jul-2007         106.13
```

```
Audit Trail--Coefficient Table (Multiple Regression Selected)

Series Description   Coefficient   Standard error   T-test   P-value
---------------------------------------------------------------------
SATHS                   6.29           2.72           2.31     0.02
dpi                     0.01           0.00          26.04     0.00
```

```
Audit Trail--Statistics

Accuracy Measures                        Value   Forecast Statistics   Value
-----------------------------------------------------------------------------
Mean Absolute Percentage Error (MAPE)    7.09%   Durbin Watson(1)       0.41
R-Square                                80.33%   Mean                  75.71
Root Mean Square Error                   7.17    SEE                    7.22
```

To develop a forecast of THS as a function of disposable personal income
(DPI), the THS data were again deseasonalized; then those values were regressed
as a function of DPI. These results are shown in Figure 4.16. The slope of 0.01 is
logical since you would expect that more new houses would be sold as income
increases. The *t*-value of 26.04 is very significant, as indicated by the two-tailed

FIGURE 4.17 **A Forecast of Total Houses Sold (THS) as a Function of Disposable Personal Income**

For each month the seasonal index is multiplied by the forecast values for the seasonally adjusted total home sales to get the final forecast for THS. Error is Actual minus Forecast. (c4f17)

Date	THS (Actual)*	Seasonal Indices	DPI Forecast of SATHS	Reseasonalized Forecast	Error Squared $(A-F)^2$
Jan-07	74.1	0.89	103.92	92.54	339.08
Feb-07	66.4	1.02	104.29	106.81	1,633.22
Mar-07	67.9	1.18	104.66	123.24	3,058.75
Apr-07	75.8	1.09	105.03	114.97	1,533.15
May-07	72.2	1.11	105.39	116.82	1,992.87
Jun-07	71.8	1.07	105.76	113.37	1,725.73
Jul-07	72.2	1.02	106.13	108.71	1,330.08

*2007 data not used in developing the 2007 forecast.

MSE = 1,658.98
RMSE = 40.73
RMSE as % of Actual = 57.0%

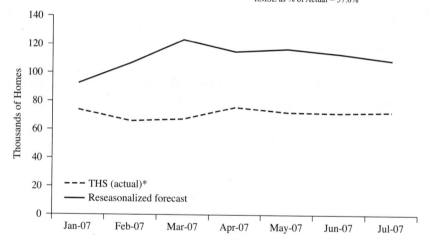

P-value of 0.00. The R^2 indicates that 80.33 percent of the variation in new houses sold is explained by this model. The equation for SATHS is:

$$\text{Seasonally adjusted total houses sold (000)} = 6.29 + 0.01(\text{DPI})$$

as shown in Figure 4.16.

The seasonally adjusted forecast for the first seven months of 2007 was then multiplied by each month's seasonal index to get nonseasonally adjusted forecasts. This is shown in Figure 4.17. The dotted line in this graph represents the forecast for THS, while the solid lines are the values that were actually observed in the first seven months of 2007 (these 2007 values were not used in developing the forecast).

While working for Dow Plastics, a business group of the Dow Chemical Company, Jan Neuenfeldt received on-the-job training while assisting others in developing forecasts. This led her to enroll in an MBA forecasting class in which she obtained formal training in quantitative forecasting methods.

The methodology that Jan uses most is regression analysis. On occasion she also uses exponential smoothing models, such as Winters'. However, the marketing and product managers who use the forecasts usually are interested in *why* as well as in the forecast values. Most of the forecasts Jan prepares are on a quarterly basis. It is fairly typical for annual forecasts one year out to be within a 5 percent margin of error. For large-volume items in mature market segments the annual margin for error is frequently only about 2 percent.

Each quarter, Jan reports forecast results to management, using a newsletter format. She begins with an exposition of the results, followed by the supporting statistical information and a graphic presentation of the forecast. She finds that graphics are extremely useful as she prepares forecasts, as well as when she communicates results to end users.

Source: This comment is based on an interview with Jan Neuenfeldt.

Integrative Case

The Gap

PART 4: FORECASTING THE GAP SALES DATA WITH A SIMPLE REGRESSION MODEL

The sales of The Gap stores for the period covering 1985Q1 through 2005Q4 are shown in the graph below. From this graph it is clear that The Gap sales are quite seasonal and have generally increased over time. The dashed line represents actual sales, while the solid line shows the deseasonalized sales for each quarter. March is the middle month of The Gap's first quarter of its fiscal year.

(c4Gap)

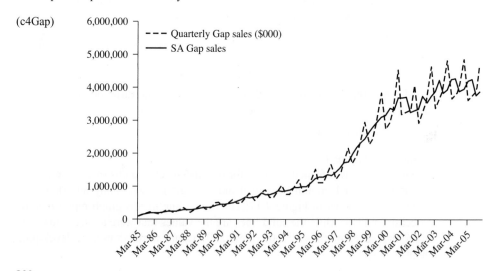

Case Questions

1. Do you think that the general growth path of The Gap sales has followed a linear path over the period shown? As part of your answer, show a graph of the deseasonalized The Gap sales along with a linear trend line. What does this graph suggest to you about the results you might expect from using a linear trend as the basis of a forecast of The Gap sales for 2006?

2. Use a regression of deseasonalized The Gap sales as a function of disposable personal income as the basis for a forecast of The Gap sales for 2006. Be sure to reseasonalize your forecast; then graph the actual The Gap sales along with your forecast. What do you think would happen to the accuracy of your forecast if you extended it out through 2010? Why?

3. Calculate the root-mean-squared errors for both the historical period and for the 2006Q1 through 2006Q4 forecast horizon.

Solutions to Case Questions

1. When The Gap sales data are deseasonalized and a linear trend is plotted through the deseasonalized series, it becomes clear that the trend in sales was increasing at an increasing rate during much of the 1985 through 2001 period. This can be seen in the graph below, in which actual sales (seasonally adjusted) are at first above the trend line, then fall below the linear trend, then are again greater than the trend, and most recently are below the trend. The trend would fall below zero for the four quarters of 1985, but we know negative sales do not make sense. It might be expected based on this graph that a forecast based on a linear trend would overestimate sales for the coming quarters because sales have become more flat. This graph also suggests that a regression trend model would have positive serial correlation.

(c4Gap)

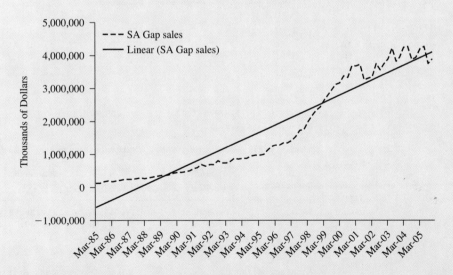

2. The Gap sales data were deseasonalized using the following seasonal indices: Q1 = 0.86, Q2 = 0.87, Q3 = 1.03, and Q4 = 1.24. The deseasonalized sales data for 1985Q1 through 2005Q4 were then regressed against disposable personal income (DPI). The regression results are shown in the following graph.

(c4Gap)

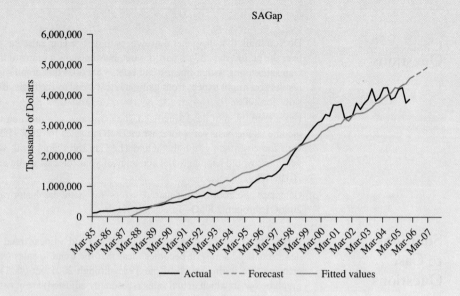

SAGap

Multiple Regression--Result Formula

SAGap = -2,712,019.94 + ((DPI)*781.02)

Forecast--Multiple Regression Selected

	Forecast	
Date	Quarterly	Annual
Mar-2006	4,624,470.78	
Jun-2006	4,709,103.16	
Sep-2006	4,793,735.54	
Dec-2006	4,878,367.92	19,005,677.40
Mar-2007	4,963,000.30	

Audit Trail--Coefficient Table (Multiple Regression Selected)

Series Description	Included in model	Coefficient	Standard Error	T-test	P-value
SAGap	Dependent	-2,712,019.94	123,826.68	-21.90	0.00
dpi	Yes	781.02	20.70	37.73	0.00

Audit Trail--Statistics

Accuracy Measures	Value	Forecast Statistics	Value
Mean Absolute Percentage Error (MAPE)	31.85%	Durbin Watson(1)	0.24
		Mean	1,743,941.12
R-Square	95.17%	SEE	321,062.09
Root Mean Square Error	317,216.89		

The equation is: SAGap = –2,712,019.94 + 781.02(DPI). All of the diagnostic statistics for this model look good (*t*-ratio = 37.73 and *R*-squared = 95.17 percent) except for the Durbin-Watson statistic (DW = 0.24). From the DW tests it is determined that this model does exhibit positive serial correlation. In this situation the positive serial correlation looks to be caused by the nonlinearity in the data. (In Chapter 5 you will learn how to account for such a nonlinearity using more advanced regression methods.)

The predicted values of SAGap were multiplied by the seasonal indices to get the forecast values graphed below.

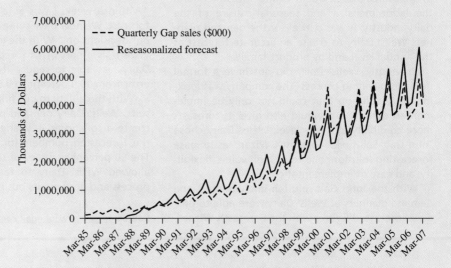

The actual and forecast The Gap sales (in thousands of dollars) are shown below for the four quarters of 2006 and the first quarter of 2007.

Date	Forecast	Actual
Mar-06	3,989,182.9	3,441,000
Jun-06	4,104,738.6	3,716,000
Sep-06	4,916,380.8	3,856,000
Dec-06	6,049,812.4	4,930,000
Mar-07	4,281,206.8	3,558,000

If this model were used to forecast through 2010, it is likely that low forecasts would result if The Gap sales resume their historic rate of growth.

3. The RMSEs for the historical period and the forecast horizon are:

Sep 1987–Dec 2005   Root-mean-squared error = 337,449.3

Note that for the historic period only results from September 1987 forward are used because prior to that forecasts would have been negative.

Mar 2006–Mar 2007   Root-mean-squared error = 818,906.3

If we compare the RMSE for these last five quarters to the mean level of sales for those quarters (3,900,200), we find that the RMSE is about 21 percent of the mean actual quarterly sales.

WELLS' DAIRY MAKERS OF BLUE BUNNY DAIRY PRODUCTS

Wells' Dairy manufactures Blue Bunny® branded dairy products, including ice cream and frozen novelties. Wells' Dairy was founded in 1913 and is the largest family-owned and managed dairy processor in the United States. Due to capital investment and the labor-intensive and seasonal nature of the dairy industry, it was critical for the demand planners Wells' Dairy to create an accurate forecast at the annual level and by product family.

Previously, Wells' Dairy did not have a formal demand planning process. The company was looking for a solution that could not only be implemented quickly, but would also give its forecasts more credibility at every level. Wells' Dairy chose John Galt Solutions' ForecastX Wizard as its base forecasting solution, due to its high value, flexibility, and ease of implementation.

With the John Galt solution implemented, the demand planners at Wells' Dairy were able to produce forecasted figures with the ForecastX Wizard, meet with the sales staff to review projections, and then reconcile the numbers. The Wizard has also given Wells' Dairy the ability to forecast at hierarchical levels, allowing for an increase in both visibility and accountability.

"It's a great product and it has worked," said a demand planner for Wells' Dairy. He added, "Within a week, I was able to complete my first forecast. We now have some solid numbers to base our decisions on." With the implementation of the Wizard as a part of its forecasting process, Wells' Dairy was able to reduce its forecast percentage error from 13.9 percent to 9.5 percent.

With the ability to put full confidence in the results, Wells' Dairy demand planners were able to create a collaborative yearly forecast based upon the forecasted numbers for each product family. The 90 percent accuracy of the yearly forecast has allowed Wells' Dairy to focus on enhancing its process and growing its business.

Source: http://www.johngalt.com.

USING FORECASTX™ TO MAKE REGRESSION FORECASTS

What follows is a brief discussion of how to use ForecastX™ for making a forecast based on a regression model. This will increase your familiarity with the of use of ForecastX™. The illustration used here is for a trend forecast.

First, put your data into an Excel spreadsheet in column format, such as the sample of The Gap data shown in the table below. Once you have your data in this format, while in Excel highlight the data you want to use, then start ForecastX™. The following dialog box appears.

A Sample of The Gap Data in Column Format

Date	The Gap Sales ($000)
Mar-1994	751,670
Jun-1994	773,131
Sep-1994	988,346
Dec-1994	1,209,790
Mar-1995	848,688
Jun-1995	868,514
Sep-1995	1,155,930
Dec-1995	1,522,120
Mar-1996	1,113,150
Jun-1996	1,120,340
Sep-1996	1,383,000
Dec-1996	1,667,900
Mar-1997	1,231,186
Jun-1997	1,345,221
Sep-1997	1,765,939
Dec-1997	2,165,479
Mar-1998	1,719,712
Jun-1998	1,904,970
Sep-1998	2,399,900
Dec-1998	3,029,90

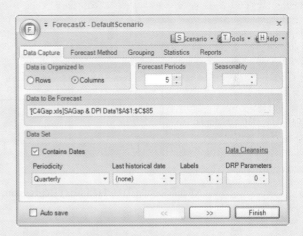

Verify the periodicity of your data (**Quarterly** for this example); then click the **Forecast Method** tab at the top and the following screen appears.

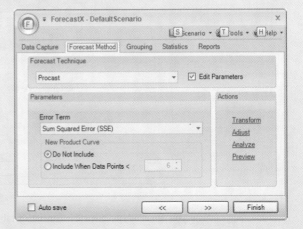

Click the down arrow in the **Forecasting Technique** window, and select **Trend (Linear) Regression.** The following window will result. In the terminology used by ForecastX™, *linear regression* refers to a method that makes a regression trend forecast. If you want to develop a causal regression model, select **Multiple Regression.** (See "Further Comments on Regression Models" on page 210.)

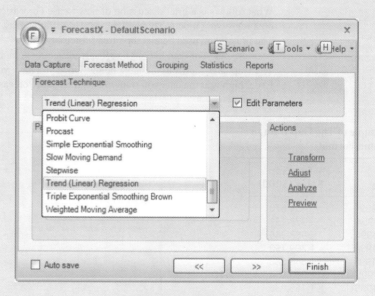

After selecting **Trend (Linear) Regression,** the dialog box will then look like the one below.

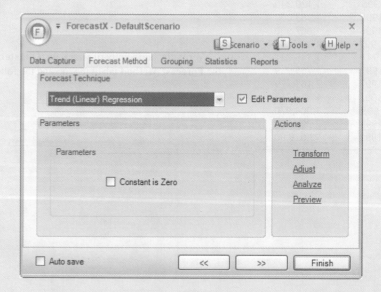

Now you are ready to click the **Statistics** tab, which will take you to the next dialog box.

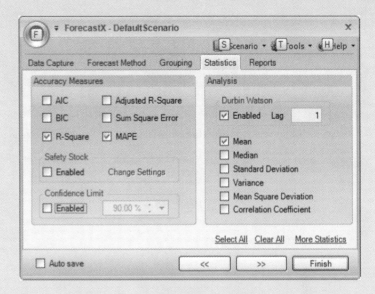

Here you want to select the desired statistics. Often the ones selected in this example would be what you would want for simple regression models.

In addition, you will want to click the **More Statistics** button at the bottom and check the box for **P-value** (in **Coeff table**) under the **Regression** tab. Look at the other tabs in this box and select desired statistics such as the RMSE in the Accuracy tab. Then click **OK** and you return to the **Statistics** box. These are shown in the following:

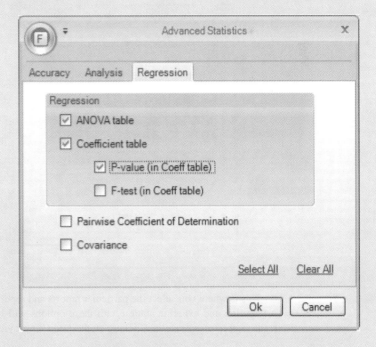

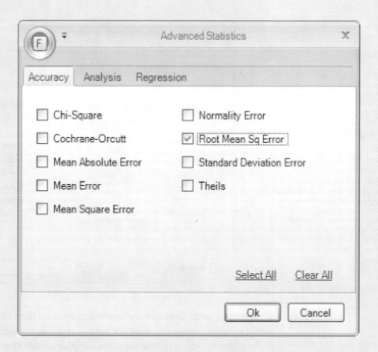

Next click the **Reports** tab to get the **Reports** dialog box. The default looks as follows:

This is where you select the particular reports and report contents that you want. Some exploration and experimentation with these options will help you see what each option leads to in terms of results. Clicking on the Audit report yields the following:

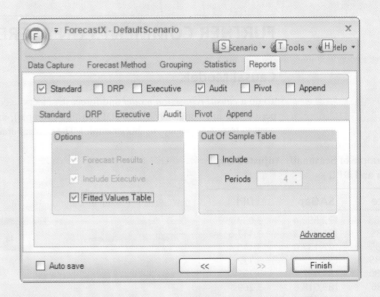

After you click **Finish!** in the lower right corner, reports will be put in new Excel workbooks—Book 2, Book 3, and so forth. The book numbers will vary depending on what you have been doing in Excel up to that point.

FURTHER COMMENTS ON REGRESSION MODELS

Causal Models

To do a *causal regression model* and forecast, select the columns in the data file with the period, the independent variable (DPI in this example), and the dependent variable you want to forecast (SAGap, in this example). Then open ForecastX™.

A Sample of Seasonally Adjusted Gap Data and DPI.

Date	SAGap	DPI
Mar-85	122,550.4	3,032.2
Jun-85	137,824.3	3,117.5
Sep-85	177,137.0	3,115.4
Dec-85	193,377.2	3,172.2
Mar-86	185,457.2	3,233.4
Jun-86	189,018.6	3,269.1
Sep-86	219,192.1	3,307.2
Dec-86	240,675.5	3,330.7
Mar-87	244,671.9	3,397.1
Jun-87	249,814.0	3,389.4
Sep-87	266,790.3	3,484.5
Dec-87	289,963.1	3,562.1
Mar-88	279,783.3	3,638.5
Jun-88	303,246.5	3,711.3
Sep-88	314,700.6	3,786.9
Dec-88	341,632.6	3,858.2

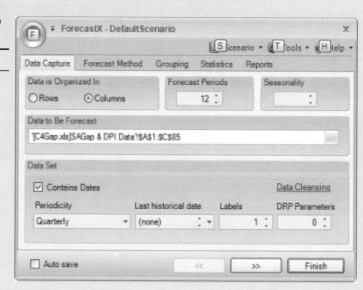

In the **Data Capture** tab of the **Data Capture** window look at the default selection. If it is not the columns you want, click inside the **Data To Be Forecast** window on the _ button to the right of the **Data to Be Forecast** box. In the following window, highlight the data columns you want, then click **OK**.

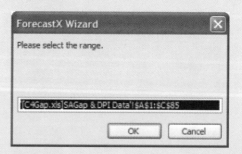

Next click the **Forecast Method** tab and select **Multiple Regression** in the **Forecasting Technique** window. In the **Dependent Series** window select the variable you want to forecast (**SAGap** in this example).

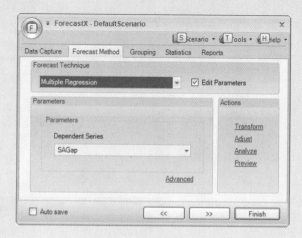

From this point on you follow the same selections as described above for regression trend forecasts.

You are probably wondering how you forecast the independent variable into the future and unknown forecast horizon. You can use any acceptable method to do this, but ForecastX™ makes it easy by doing an automated forecast using a procedure called ProCast™.

Deseasonalizing Data

The following is a review of what was covered in Chapter 3. To deseasonalize data in ForecastX™ we use a method called *decomposition* (this method of forecasting will be discussed in detail in Chapter 6). For now we will simply look at the portion of the method and results that we need to take the seasonality out of a data series.

Begin by opening your data file in Excel, then start the ForecastX™ software and capture the desired data. In the **Method Selection** dialog box select **Decomposition** as the **Forecasting Technique,** check **Multiplicative,** and select **Trend (Linear) Regression,** as the **Forecast Method for Decomposed Data.**

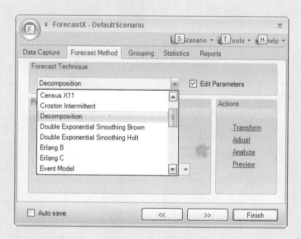

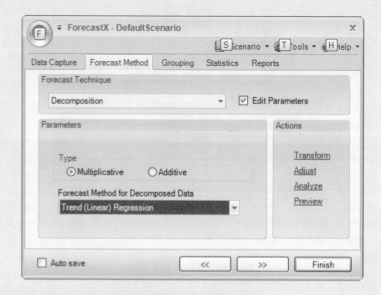

Then click the **Reports** tab, and select only the **Audit** report.

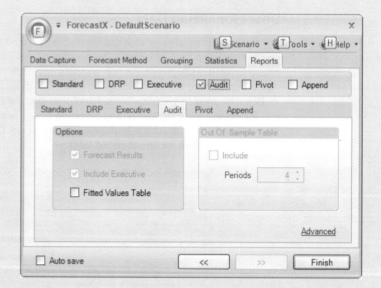

Now click **Finish!** and you will get results that will include the following:

Components of Decomposition

Date	Original Data	Forecasted Data	Centered Moving Average	CMA Trend	Seasonal Indices
Mar-1985	105,715.00	−527,508.23		−611,515.31	**0.86**
Jun-1985	120,136.00	−483,559.98		−554,757.32	**0.87**
Sep-1985	181,669.00	−510,740.39	168,616.38	−497,999.33	**1.03**
Dec-1985	239,813.00	−547,196.81	180,977.50	−441,241.35	**1.24**
Mar-1986	159,980.00	−331,664.86	191,946.88	−384,483.36	**0.86**
Jun-1986	164,760.00	−285,665.22	204,670.25	−327,725.37	**0.87**
Sep-1986	224,800.00	−277,899.95	218,387.25	−270,967.39	**1.03**
Dec-1986	298,469.00	−265,647.59	231,396.38	−214,209.40	**1.24**
Mar-1987	211,060.00	−135,821.49	244,122.50	−157,451.42	**0.86**
Jun-1987	217,753.00	−87,770.47	257,864.88	−100,693.43	**0.87**
Sep-1987	273,616.00	−45,059.51	269,291.25	−43,935.44	**1.03**
Dec-1987	359,592.00	15,901.62	278,899.13	12,822.54	**1.24**
Mar-1988	241,348.00	60,021.88	290,863.00	69,580.53	**0.86**
Jun-1988	264,328.00	110,124.28	305,014.63	126,338.51	**0.87**
Sep-1988	322,752.00	187,780.93	321,596.38	183,096.50	**1.03**
Dec-1988	423,669.00	297,450.84	337,869.88	239,854.49	**1.24**
Mar-1989	309,925.00	255,865.26	355,927.38	296,612.47	**0.86**
Jun-1989	325,939.00	308,019.03	381,466.25	353,370.46	**0.87**
Sep-1989	405,601.00	420,621.37	408,204.38	410,128.44	**1.03**
Dec-1989	545,131.00	579,000.06	429,641.88	466,886.43	**1.24**

The "Seasonal Indices" column is in bold here but will not be in bold in your output. These are the indices that you will use to deseasonalize the original data and to reseasonalize results. You should copy this column of seasonal indices and paste it into your Excel workbook along with your original data.

You can now calculate a deseasonalized series by dividing the original data by the seasonal indices.

Deseasonalized series = Original series ÷ Seasonal indices

To reseasonalize results, reverse the process.

Reseasonalized results = Deseasonalized results × Seasonal indices

Suggested Readings

Bassin, William M. "How to Anticipate the Accuracy of a Regression Based Model." *Journal of Business Forecasting* 6, no. 4 (Winter 1987–88), pp. 26–28.

Bowerman, Bruce L.; and Richard T. O' Connell. *Applied Statistics: Improving Business Processes.* Chicago: Irwin, 1997.

Bowerman, Bruce L.; Richard T. O' Connell; and J. B. Orris. *Essentials of Business Statistics.* Boston: Irwin/McGraw-Hill, 2004.

Dalrymple, Douglas J.; William M. Strahle; and Douglas B. Bock. "How Many Observations Should Be Used in Trend Regression Forecasts?" *Journal of Business Forecasting* 8, no. 1 (Spring 1989), pp. 7–9.

Harris, John L.; and Lon-Mu Liu. "GNP as a Predictor of Electricity Consumption." *Journal of Business Forecasting,* Winter 1990–91, pp. 24–27.

Lapide, Larry. "Do You Need to Use Causal Forecasting?" *Journal of Business Forecasting,* Summer 1999, pp. 13–14.

Lind, Douglas A.; Robert D. Mason; and William G. Marchal. *Basic Statistics for Business and Economics,* 3rd ed. New York: Irwin/McGraw-Hill, 2000.

Meade, Nigel; and Towhidul Islam. "Forecasting with Growth Curves: An Empirical Comparison." *International Journal of Forecasting* 11, no. 2 (June 1995), pp. 199–215.

Monaco, Ralph M. "MEXVAL: A Simple Regression Diagnostic Tool." *Journal of Business Forecasting,* Winter 1989–90, pp. 23–27.

Morrison, Jeffrey S. "Target Marketing with Logit Regression." *Journal of Business Forecasting* 14, no. 4 (Winter 1995–96), pp. 10–12.

Pindyck, Robert S.; and Daniel L. Rubinfeld. *Econometric Models and Economic Forecasts.* 3rd ed. New York: McGraw-Hill, 1991.

Wang, George C. S.; and Charles K. Akabay. "Heteroscedasticity: How to Handle in Regression Modeling." *Journal of Business Forecasting* 13, no. 2 (Summer 1992), pp. 11–17.

West, Kenneth D.; et al. "Regression-Based Tests of Predictive Ability." *International Economic Review* 39, no. 4 (November 1998), pp. 817–40.

Wooldridge, Jeffrey M. *Introductory Econometrics.* 2nd ed. Mason, OH: Thompson/South-Western, 2003.

Exercises

1. What are the steps that should be used in evaluating regression models? Write each step in the order it should be evaluated, and following each one write a sentence or two in your own words to explain its importance.

2. In this chapter a number of graphic displays have been presented. What advantage(s) do you see in showing data in graphic form rather than, or in addition to, tabular form?

3. In evaluating regression models, we have tested a hypothesis to determine whether the slope term is significantly different from zero. Why do we test this hypothesis? Why do we not test the comparable hypothesis for the intercept?

4. The following regression results relate to a study of the salaries of public school teachers in a midwestern city:

Variable	Coefficient	Standard Error	t-ratio
Constant	20,720	6,820	3.04
EXP	805	258	

R-squared $= 0.684$; $n = 105$.
Standard error of the estimate $= 2,000$.
EXP is the experience of teachers in years of full-time teaching.

a. What is the *t*-ratio for EXP? Does it indicate that experience is a statistically significant determinant of salary if a 95 percent confidence level is desired?

b. What percentage of the variation in salary is explained by this model?

    c. Determine the point estimate of salary for a teacher with 20 years of experience.

    d. What is the approximate 95 percent confidence interval for your point estimate from part (*c*)?

5. Nelson Industries manufactures a part for a type of aircraft engine that is becoming obsolete. The sales history for the last 10 years is as follows:

(c4p5) **Year**	**Sales**	**Year**	**Sales**
1998	945	2003	420
1999	875	2004	305
2000	760	2005	285
2001	690	2006	250
2002	545	2007	210

    a. Plot sales versus time.

    b. Estimate the regression model for a linear time trend of sales.

    c. What is the root-mean-squared error of the linear regression estimates for these 10 years?

    d. Using this model, estimate sales for year 11.

6. Mid-Valley Travel Agency (MVTA) has offices in 12 cities. The company believes that its monthly airline bookings are related to the mean income in those cities and has collected the following data:

(c4p6)	**Location**	**Bookings**	**Income**
	1	1,098	$43,299
	2	1,131	45,021
	3	1,120	40,290
	4	1,142	41,893
	5	971	30,620
	6	1,403	48,105
	7	855	27,482
	8	1,054	33,025
	9	1,081	34,687
	10	982	28,725
	11	1,098	37,892
	12	1,387	46,198

    a. Develop a linear regression model of monthly airline bookings as a function of income.

    b. Use the process described in the chapter to evaluate your results.

    c. Make the point and approximate 95 percent confidence interval estimates of monthly airline bookings for another city in which MVTA is considering opening a branch, given that income in that city is $39,020.

7. Barbara Lynch is the product manager for a line of skiwear produced by HeathCo Industries and privately branded for sale under several different names, including Northern Slopes and Jacque Monri. A new part of Ms. Lynch's job is to provide a

quarterly forecast of sales for the northern United States, a region composed of 27 states stretching from Maine to Washington. A 10-year sales history is shown:

(c4p7)

	Sales ($000)			
Year	1st Quarter	2nd Quarter	3rd Quarter	4th Quarter
1998	$ 72,962	$ 81,921	$ 97,729	$ 142,161
1999	145,592	117,129	114,159	151,402
2000	153,907	100,144	123,242	128,497
2001	176,076	180,440	162,665	220,818
2002	202,415	211,780	163,710	200,135
2003	174,200	182,556	198,990	243,700
2004	253,142	218,755	225,422	253,653
2005	257,156	202,568	224,482	229,879
2006	289,321	266,095	262,938	322,052
2007	313,769	315,011	264,939	301,479

a. Because Ms. Lynch has so many other job responsibilities, she has hired you to help with the forecasting effort. First, she would like you to prepare a time-series plot of the data and to write her a memo indicating what the plot appears to show and whether it seems likely that a simple linear trend would be useful in preparing forecasts.

b. In addition to plotting the data over time, you should estimate the least-squares trend line in the form:

$$SALES = a + b(TIME)$$

Set TIME = 1 for 1994Q1 through TIME = 40 for 2003Q4. Write the trend equation:

$$SALES = \underline{\hspace{2cm}} +/- \underline{\hspace{2cm}}(TIME)$$

(Circle + or − as appropriate)

c. Do your regression results indicate to you that there is a significant trend to the data? Explain why or why not.

d. On the basis of your results, prepare a forecast for the four quarters of 2008.

Period	TIME	Sales Forecast (F1)
2008Q1	41	_____
2008Q2	42	_____
2008Q3	43	_____
2008Q4	44	_____

e. A year later, Barbara gives you a call and tells you that the actual sales for the four quarters of 2008 were: Q1 = 334,271, Q2 = 328,982, Q3 = 317,921, and Q4 = 350,118. How accurate was your model? What was the root-mean-squared error?

8. Dick Staples, another product manager with HeathCo (see Exercise 7), has mentioned to Barbara Lynch that he has found both the unemployment rate and the level of income to be useful predictors for some of the products under his responsibility.

   a. Suppose that Ms. Lynch provides you with the following unemployment data for the northern region she is concerned with:

(c4p8)

	Unemployment Rate (%)			
Year	1st Quarter	2nd Quarter	3rd Quarter	4th Quarter
1998	8.4%	8.2%	8.4%	8.4%
1999	8.1	7.7	7.5	7.2
2000	6.9	6.5	6.5	6.4
2001	6.3	6.2	6.3	6.5
2002	6.8	7.9	8.3	8.0
2003	8.0	8.0	8.0	8.9
2004	9.6	10.2	10.7	11.5
2005	11.2	11.0	10.1	9.2
2006	8.5	8.0	8.0	7.9
2007	7.9	7.9	7.8	7.6

   b. Plot a scattergram of SALES versus northern-region unemployment rate (NRUR). Does there appear to be a relationship? Explain.

   c. Prepare a bivariate regression model of sales as a function of NRUR in the following form:

   $$\text{SALES} = a + b(\text{NRUR})$$

   Write your answer in the following equation:

   SALES = _____ +/− _____(NRUR)

   (Circle + or − as appropriate)

   d. Write a memo to Ms. Lynch in which you evaluate these results and indicate how well you think this model would work in forecasting her sales series.

   e. Use the model to make a forecast of sales for each quarter of 2008, given the forecast for unemployment (FNRUR) that HeathCo has purchased from a macroeconomic consulting firm (MacroCast):

Period	FNRUR	Sales Forecast (F2)
2008Q1	7.6%	_____
2008Q2	7.7	_____
2008Q3	7.5	_____
2008Q4	7.4	_____

   f. For the actual sales given in Exercise 7(*e*), calculate the root-mean-squared error for this model. How does it compare with what you found in Exercise 7(*e*)?

g. Barbara Lynch also has data on income (INC), in billions of dollars, for the region as follows:

(c4p8)

	Income ($ Billions)			
Year	1st Quarter	2nd Quarter	3rd Quarter	4th Quarter
1998	$ 218	$ 237	$ 263	$ 293
1999	318	359	404	436
2000	475	534	574	622
2001	667	702	753	796
2002	858	870	934	1,010
2003	1,066	1,096	1,162	1,187
2004	1,207	1,242	1,279	1,318
2005	1,346	1,395	1,443	1,528
2006	1,613	1,646	1,694	1,730
2007	1,755	1,842	1,832	1,882

Plot a scattergram of SALES with INC. Does there appear to be a relationship? Explain.

h. Prepare a bivariate regression model of SALES as a function of income (INC) and write your results in the equation:

$$SALES = a + b(INC)$$

SALES = _____ +/− _____(INC)

(Circle + or − as appropriate)

i. Write a memo to Ms. Lynch in which you explain and evaluate this model, indicating how well you think it would work in forecasting sales.

j. HeathCo has also purchased a forecast of income from MacroCast. Use the following income forecast (INCF) to make your own forecast of SALES for 2008:

Period	INCF	Sales Forecast (F3)
2008Q1	$1,928	_____
2008Q2	1,972	_____
2008Q3	2,017	_____
2008Q4	2,062	_____

k. On the basis of the actual sales given in Exercise 7(e), calculate the root-mean-squared error for this model. How does it compare with the other two models you have used to forecast sales?

l. Prepare a time-series plot with actual sales for 1998Q1 through 2007Q4 along with the sales forecast you found in part (j) of this exercise. To accompany this plot, write a brief memo to Ms. Lynch in which you comment on the strengths and weaknesses of the forecasting model.

9. Carolina Wood Products, Inc., a major manufacturer of household furniture, is interested in predicting expenditures on furniture (FURN) for the entire United States. It has the following data by quarter for 1998 through 2007:

(c4p9)

	FURN (in $ Billions)			
Year	1st Quarter	2nd Quarter	3rd Quarter	4th Quarter
1998	$ 98.1	$ 96.8	$ 96.0	$ 95.0
1999	93.2	95.1	96.2	98.4
2000	100.7	104.4	108.1	111.1
2001	114.3	117.2	119.4	122.7
2002	125.9	129.3	132.2	136.6
2003	137.4	141.4	145.3	147.7
2004	148.8	150.2	153.4	154.2
2005	159.8	164.4	166.2	169.7
2006	173.7	175.5	175.0	175.7
2007	181.4	180.0	179.7	176.3

a. Prepare a naive forecast for 2008Q1 based on the following model (see Chapter 1):

$$NFURN_t = FURN_{t-1}$$

Period	Naive Forecast
2008Q1	_____

b. Estimate the bivariate linear trend model for the data where TIME = 1 for 1998Q1 through TIME = 40 for 2007Q4.

$$FURN = a + b(TIME)$$
$$FURN = \underline{\hspace{1cm}} +/- \underline{\hspace{1cm}}(TIME)$$
(Circle + or − as appropriate)

c. Write a paragraph in which you evaluate this model, with particular emphasis on its usefulness in forecasting.

d. Prepare a time-trend forecast of furniture and household equipment expenditures for 2008 based on the model in part (b).

Period	TIME	Trend Forecast
2008Q1	41	_____
2008Q2	42	_____
2008Q3	43	_____
2008Q4	44	_____

e. Suppose that the actual values of FURN for 2008 were as shown in the following table. Calculate the RMSE for both of your forecasts and interpret the results. (For the naive forecast, there will be only one observation, for 2008Q1.)

Period	Actual FURN ($ Billions)
2008Q1	177.6
2008Q2	180.5
2008Q3	182.8
2008Q4	178.7

10. Fifteen midwestern and mountain states have united in an effort to promote and fore-cast tourism. One aspect of their work has been related to the dollar amount spent per year on domestic travel (DTE) in each state. They have the following estimates for dis-posable personal income per capita (DPI) and DTE:

(c4p10)

State	DPI	DTE ($ Millions)
Minnesota	$17,907	$4,933
Iowa	15,782	1,766
Missouri	17,158	4,692
North Dakota	15,688	628
South Dakota	15,981	551
Nebraska	17,416	1,250
Kansas	17,635	1,729
Montana	15,128	725
Idaho	15,974	934
Wyoming	17,504	778
Colorado	18,628	4,628
New Mexico	14,587	1,724
Arizona	15,921	3,836
Utah	14,066	1,757
Nevada	19,781	6,455

a. From these data estimate a bivariate linear regression equation for domestic travel expenditures (DTE) as a function of disposable income per capita (DPI):

$$DTE = a + b(DPI)$$

DTE = _____ +/− _____(DPI)

(Circle + or − as appropriate)

Evaluate the statistical significance of this model.

b. Illinois, a bordering state, has asked that this model be used to forecast DTE for Illi-nois under the assumption that DPI will be $19,648. Make the appropriate point and approximate 95 percent interval estimates.

c. Given that actual DTE turned out to be $7,754 (million), calculate the percentage error in your forecast.

11. Collect data on population for your state (http://www.economagic.com may be a good source for these data) over the past 20 years and use a bivariate regression trend line to forecast population for the next five years. Prepare a time-series plot that shows both actual and forecast values. Do you think the model looks as though it will provide rea-sonably accurate forecasts for the five-year horizon? (c4p11)

12. AmerPlas, Inc., produces 20-ounce plastic drinking cups that are embossed with the names of prominent beers and soft drinks. It has been observed that sales of the cups match closely the seasonal pattern associated with beer production, but that, unlike beer production, there has been a positive trend over time. The sales data, by month, for 2004 through 2007 are as follows:

(c4p12)

Period	T	Sales	Period	T	Sales
2004M01	1	857	2006M01	25	1,604
2004M02	2	921	2006M02	26	1,643
2004M03	3	1,071	2006M03	27	1,795
2004M04	4	1,133	2006M04	28	1,868
2004M05	5	1,209	2006M05	29	1,920
2004M06	6	1,234	2006M06	30	1,953
2004M07	7	1,262	2006M07	31	1,980
2004M08	8	1,258	2006M08	32	1,989
2004M09	9	1,175	2006M09	33	1,897
2004M10	10	1,174	2006M10	34	1,910
2004M11	11	1,123	2006M11	35	1,854
2004M12	12	1,159	2006M12	36	1,957
2005M01	13	1,250	2007M01	37	1,955
2005M02	14	1,289	2007M02	38	2,008
2005M03	15	1,448	2007M03	39	2,171
2005M04	16	1,497	2007M04	40	2,202
2005M05	17	1,560	2007M05	41	2,288
2005M06	18	1,586	2007M06	42	2,314
2005M07	19	1,597	2007M07	43	2,343
2005M08	20	1,615	2007M08	44	2,339
2005M09	21	1,535	2007M09	45	2,239
2005M10	22	1,543	2007M10	46	2,267
2005M11	23	1,493	2007M11	47	2,206
2005M12	24	1,510	2007M12	48	2,226

a. Use these data to estimate a linear time trend as follows:
$$SALES = a + b(T)$$
$$SALES = \text{_____} +/- \text{_____}(T)$$
(Circle + or − as appropriate)

Do your regression results support the notion that there has been a positive time trend in the SALES data? Explain.

b. Use your equation to forecast SALES for the 12 months of 2008:

Period	SALES Forecast	Period	SALES Forecast
2008M01	_____	2008M07	_____
M02	_____	M08	_____
M03	_____	M09	_____
M04	_____	M10	_____
M05	_____	M11	_____
M06	_____	M12	_____

c. Actual SALES for 2008 are:

Period	Actual SALES	Period	Actual SALES
2008M01	2,318	2008M07	2,697
M02	2,367	M08	2,702
M03	2,523	M09	2,613
M04	2,577	M10	2,626
M05	2,646	M11	2,570
M06	2,674	M12	2,590

On the basis of your results in part (b) in comparison with these actual sales, how well do you think your model works? What is the RMSE for 2008?

d. Prepare a time-series plot of the actual sales and the forecast of sales for 2004M01 through 2008M12. Do the same for just the last two years (2007M01 to 2008M12). Do your plots show any evidence of seasonality in the data? If so, how might you account for it in preparing a forecast?

13. Alexander Enterprises manufactures plastic parts for the automotive industry. Its sales (in thousands of dollars) for 2003Q1 through 2007Q4 are as follows:

(c4p13)

Period	Sales	Period	Sales
2003Q1	3,816.5	2006Q1	4,406.4
Q2	3916.7 ~~3,816.7~~	Q2	4,394.6
Q3	3,978.8	Q3	4,422.3
Q4	4,046.6	Q4	4,430.8
2004Q1	4,119.1	2007Q1	4,463.9
Q2	4,169.4	Q2	4,517.8
Q3	4,193.0	Q3	4,563.6
Q4	4,216.4	Q4	4,633.0
2005Q1	4,238.1	2008Q1	NA
Q2	4,270.5	Q2	NA
Q3	4,321.8	Q3	NA
Q4	4,349.5	Q4	NA

You are asked to forecast sales for 2008Q1 through 2008Q4.

a. Begin by preparing a time-series plot of sales. Does it appear from this plot that a linear trend model might be appropriate? Explain.

b. Use a bivariate linear regression trend model to estimate the following trend equation:

$$SALES = a + b(TIME)$$

Is the sign for b what you would expect? Is b significantly different from zero? What is the coefficient of determination for this model? Is there a potential problem with serial correlation? Explain.

c. Based on this model, make a trend forecast of sales (SALESFT) for the four quarters of 2008.

d. Given that actual sales (SALESA) for the four quarters of 2008 are:

2008Q1	4,667.1
2008Q2	4,710.3
2008Q3	4,738.7
2008Q4	4,789.0

calculate the root-mean-squared error for this forecast model in the historical period (2003Q1–2007Q4) as well as for the forecast horizon (2008Q1–2008Q4). Which of these measures accuracy and which measures fit?

14. The following data are for shoe store sales in the United States in millions of dollars after being seasonally adjusted (SASSS).

(c4p14)

Date	SASSS	Date	SASSS	Date	SASSS	Date	SASSS
Jan-92	1,627	Jan-96	1,745	Jan-00	1,885	Jan-04	1,969
Feb-92	1,588	Feb-96	1,728	Feb-00	1,885	Feb-04	1,989
Mar-92	1,567	Mar-96	1,776	Mar-00	1,925	Mar-04	2,040
Apr-92	1,578	Apr-96	1,807	Apr-00	1,891	Apr-04	1,976
May-92	1,515	May-96	1,800	May-00	1,900	May-04	1,964
Jun-92	1,520	Jun-96	1,758	Jun-00	1,888	Jun-04	1,947
Jul-92	1,498	Jul-96	1,784	Jul-00	1,865	Jul-04	1,961
Aug-92	1,522	Aug-96	1,791	Aug-00	1,921	Aug-04	1,931
Sep-92	1,560	Sep-96	1,743	Sep-00	1,949	Sep-04	1,960
Oct-92	1,569	Oct-96	1,785	Oct-00	1,923	Oct-04	1,980
Nov-92	1,528	Nov-96	1,765	Nov-00	1,922	Nov-04	1,944
Dec-92	1,556	Dec-96	1,753	Dec-00	1,894	Dec-04	2,014
Jan-93	1,593	Jan-97	1,753	Jan-01	1,908	Jan-05	2,013
Feb-93	1,527	Feb-97	1,790	Feb-01	1,855	Feb-05	2,143
Mar-93	1,524	Mar-97	1,830	Mar-01	1,858	Mar-05	2,002
Apr-93	1,560	Apr-97	1,702	Apr-01	1,941	Apr-05	2,090
May-93	1,575	May-97	1,769	May-01	1,938	May-05	2,104
Jun-93	1,588	Jun-97	1,793	Jun-01	1,901	Jun-05	2,114
Jul-93	1,567	Jul-97	1,801	Jul-01	1,964	Jul-05	2,124
Aug-93	1,602	Aug-97	1,789	Aug-01	1,963	Aug-05	2,098
Sep-93	1,624	Sep-97	1,791	Sep-01	1,838	Sep-05	2,105
Oct-93	1,597	Oct-97	1,799	Oct-01	1,877	Oct-05	2,206
Nov-93	1,614	Nov-97	1,811	Nov-01	1,927	Nov-05	2,232
Dec-93	1,644	Dec-97	1,849	Dec-01	1,911	Dec-05	2,194
Jan-94	1,637	Jan-98	1,824	Jan-02	1,962	Jan-06	2,218
Feb-94	1,617	Feb-98	1,882	Feb-02	1,980	Feb-06	2,271
Mar-94	1,679	Mar-98	1,859	Mar-02	1,955	Mar-06	2,165
Apr-94	1,607	Apr-98	1,831	Apr-02	1,967	Apr-06	2,253
May-94	1,623	May-98	1,832	May-02	1,940	May-06	2,232
Jun-94	1,619	Jun-98	1,842	Jun-02	1,963	Jun-06	2,237
Jul-94	1,667	Jul-98	1,874	Jul-02	1,920	Jul-06	2,231
Aug-94	1,660	Aug-98	1,845	Aug-02	1,937	Aug-06	2,278
Sep-94	1,681	Sep-98	1,811	Sep-02	1,867	Sep-06	2,259
Oct-94	1,696	Oct-98	1,898	Oct-02	1,918	Oct-06	2,231
Nov-94	1,710	Nov-98	1,878	Nov-02	1,914	Nov-06	2,217
Dec-94	1,694	Dec-98	1,901	Dec-02	1,931	Dec-06	2,197
Jan-95	1,663	Jan-99	1,916	Jan-03	1,867		
Feb-95	1,531	Feb-99	1,894	Feb-03	1,887		
Mar-95	1,707	Mar-99	1,883	Mar-03	1,939		
Apr-95	1,707	Apr-99	1,871	Apr-03	1,860		
May-95	1,715	May-99	1,918	May-03	1,898		
Jun-95	1,735	Jun-99	1,943	Jun-03	1,924		
Jul-95	1,692	Jul-99	1,905	Jul-03	1,967		
Aug-95	1,695	Aug-99	1,892	Aug-03	1,994		
Sep-95	1,721	Sep-99	1,893	Sep-03	1,966		
Oct-95	1,698	Oct-99	1,869	Oct-03	1,943		
Nov-95	1,770	Nov-99	1,867	Nov-03	1,973		
Dec-95	1,703	Dec-99	1,887	Dec-03	1,976		

a. Make a linear trend forecast for SASSS though the first seven months of 2007. Given that the actual seasonally adjusted values for 2007 were the following, calculate the RMSE for 2007.

Date	SASSS
Jan-07	2,317
Feb-07	2,224
Mar-07	2,279
Apr-07	2,223
May-07	2,250
Jun-07	2,260
Jul-07	2,305

b. Reseasonalize the 2007 forecast and the 2007 actual sales using the following seasonal indices:

Month	SI
Jan	0.74
Feb	0.81
Mar	1.00
Apr	1.03
May	1.04
Jun	0.98
Jul	0.98
Aug	1.23
Sep	0.96
Oct	0.94
Nov	0.98
Dec	1.31

c. Plot the final forecast along with the actual sales data. Does the forecast appear reasonable? Explain.

d. Why do you think the April, May, August, and December seasonal indices are greater than 1?

Chapter **Five**

Forecasting with Multiple Regression

In this chapter we will build on the introduction to the use of regression in forecasting developed in Chapter 4. We will model new houses sold (NHS) with multiple independent variables. We will also forecast total houses sold (THS). We will examine the mortgage rate as a causal factor. In addition we will add variables to account for seasonality in the data and also consider the effect that consumer sentiment has on our ability to forecast THS. We will continue with our ongoing example of forecasting The Gap sales at the end of this chapter. These extensions of the bivariate regression model take us into the realm of multiple regression, so let us begin by looking at the general multiple-regression model.

THE MULTIPLE-REGRESSION MODEL

Multiple regression is a statistical procedure in which a dependent variable (Y) is modeled as a function of more than one independent variable ($X_1, X_2, X_3, \ldots, X_n$).[1] The population multiple-regression model may be written as:

$$Y = f(X_1, X_2, X_3, \ldots, X_n)$$
$$= \beta_0 + \beta_1 X_1 + \beta_2 X_2 + \beta_3 X_3 + \cdots + \beta_k X_k + \varepsilon$$

where β_0 is the intercept and the other β_i's are the slope terms associated with the respective independent variables (i.e., the X_i's). In this model ε represents the population error term, which is the difference between the actual Y and that predicted by the regression model ($\hat{Y}$).

The ordinary least-squares (OLS) criterion for the best multiple-regression model is that the sum of the squares of all the error terms be minimized. That is, we want to minimize Σe^2, where

$$\Sigma e^2 = \Sigma (Y - \hat{Y})^2$$

[1] For more detailed discussions of the multiple-regression model, see the following: John Neter, William Wasserman, and Michael H. Kutner, *Applied Linear Regression Models* (New York: McGraw-Hill, 1996), and Damodar N. Gujarati, *Basic Econometrics* (New York: McGraw-Hill, 2003). The latter is particularly recommended.

Thus, the ordinary least-squares criterion for multiple regression is to minimize:

$$\sum(Y - \beta_0 - \beta_1X_1 - \beta_2X_2 - \beta_3X_3 - \cdots - \beta_kX_k)^2$$

The process of achieving this is more complicated than in the bivariate regression case and involves the use of matrix algebra.

Values of the true regression parameters (β_i) are typically estimated from sample data. The resulting sample regression model is:

$$\hat{Y} = b_0 + b_1X_1 + b_2X_2 + b_3X_3 + \cdots + b_kX_k$$

where b_0, b_1, b_2, b_3, and so on, are sample statistics that are estimates of the corresponding population parameters β_0, β_1, β_2, β_3, and so on. Deviations between the predicted values based on the sample regression $(\hat{Y})$ and the actual values (Y) of the dependent variable for each observation are called *residuals* and are equal to $(Y - \hat{Y})$. The values of the sample statistics b_0, b_1, b_2, b_3, and so on, are almost always determined for us by a computer software package. Standard errors, t-ratios, the multiple coefficient of determination, the Durbin-Watson statistic, and other evaluative statistics, as well as a table of residuals, are also found in most regression output.

SELECTING INDEPENDENT VARIABLES

As with bivariate regression, the process of building a multiple-regression model begins by identifying the dependent variable.

As with bivariate regression, the process of building a multiple-regression model begins by identifying the dependent variable. In our context, that is the variable that we are most interested in forecasting. It may be some "prime mover" such as disposable personal income or another macroeconomic variable, or it may be total company sales, or sales of a particular product line, or the number of patient-days for a hospital, or state tax revenues.

Once the dependent variable is determined, we begin to think about what factors contribute to its changes. In our bivariate example of new houses sold (NHS) we will use disposable personal income per capita (DPIPC) as an explanatory variable. In this chapter, as we think of other potential independent variables that might improve that model, we want to think of other things that influence NHS but that do not measure the same basic relationship that is being measured by DPIPC. Think, for example, of the possibility of adding GDP to the model. Both GDP and DPIPC are measures of aggregate income in the economy, so there would be a lot of overlap in the part of the variation in NHS they explain. In fact, the correlation between GDP and DPIPC is $+0.99$. A similar overlap would result if population and DPIPC were used in the same model. There is a high correlation between population size and real disposable personal income per capita (approximately $+0.95$), and so they would have a lot of overlap in their ability to explain variations in NHS. Such overlaps can cause a problem known as *multicollinearity*, which we will discuss later in this chapter.[2]

---

[2] Note that multicollinearity in regression analysis is really just strong correlation between two or more independent variables. Correlation here is measured just as we did in Chapter 2 with the Pearson product-moment correlation coefficient.

In considering the set of independent variables to use, we should find ones that are not highly correlated with one another.

Thus, in considering the set of independent variables to use, we should find ones that are not highly correlated with one another. For example, suppose that we hypothesize that at least some portion of NHS may be influenced by the mortgage interest rate, since many purchases are financed. It seems less likely that there would be a stronger correlation between personal income and the mortgage interest rate than between personal income and either GDP or population size. The correlation between the mortgage interest rate and disposable personal income turns out to be just -0.65, so there is less overlap between those two variables.

Sometimes it is difficult, or even impossible, to find a variable that measures exactly what we want to have in our model. For example, in the NHS model we might like to have as a measure of the interest rate a national average of the rate charged on installment loans. However, a more readily available series, the mortgage interest rate (IR), may be a reasonable proxy for what we want to measure, since all interest rates tend to be closely related.

Later in this chapter in our model of total houses sold (THS), we will also begin looking at the relationship between THS and the mortgage rate. However, in plotting the data you will see that there is a regular seasonal pattern in THS that is not accounted for by the mortgage rate. You will want to consider adding another variable (or set of variables) to account for the seasonality in THS. But how do we measure spring, or fall, or summer, or winter? The seasons are qualitative attributes that have no direct quantitative counterpart. We will see (in the section "Accounting for Seasonality in a Multiple-Regression Model") that a special kind of variable, known as a *dummy variable,* can be used to measure such a qualitative attribute as spring.

FORECASTING WITH A MULTIPLE-REGRESSION MODEL

Our first example of a multiple-regression model in forecasting will involve new houses sold (NHS) using data from which seasonality has been removed.

The quarterly data for NHS from 1992Q1 through 2004Q4 are shown in Figure 5.1. Our beginning bivariate regression forecasting model is:

$$\text{NHSF} = b_0 + b_1(\text{IR})$$
$$= 5,543.74 - 415.90(\text{IR})$$

where NHSF stands for the forecast of new houses sold (NHS) and IR is the mortgage interest rate.

Now we will expand this model to include disposable personal income per capita (DPIPC) as a second independent variable. We will let NHSF2 represent the second forecasting model for NHS.

$$\text{NHSF2} = b_0 + b_1(\text{DPIPC}) + b_2(\text{IR})$$

Before running the regression, think about what signs should be expected for b_1 and b_2. Business and economic logic would suggest that b_1 should be positive

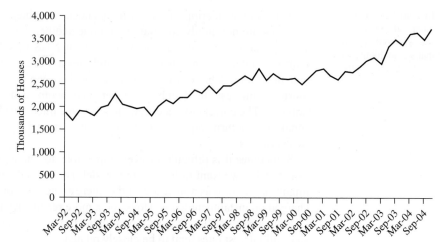

FIGURE 5.1

New Houses Sold (NHS) in Thousands of Units Seasonally Adjusted (c5t1)

Source: The Bureau of the Census (http://www.census.gov)

($b_1 > 0$) and that b_2 should be negative ($b_2 < 0$). As shown in Table 5.1, the regression results support this notion. The model estimate is:

$$NHSF2 = -324.33 + 0.17(DPIPC) - 168.13(IR)$$

The raw data for this model, along with the complete regression results, are shown in Table 5.1. Statistical evaluation of this model, based on the information provided in Table 5.1, will be considered in the next section. For now, we can see that at least the signs for the coefficients are consistent with our expectations.

To use this model to forecast retail sales for 2004, we must first forecast the independent variables: real disposable personal income (DPIPC) and the mortgage interest rate (IR). Forecasts for the four quarters of 2004 for these two independent variables, based on Holt's exponential smoothing models, are:

Period	IR	DPIPC
2004Q1	5.89	26,984.00
2004Q2	5.85	27,106.17
2004Q3	5.82	27,228.35
2004Q4	5.79	27,350.53

Our multiple-regression forecasts of new houses sold (NHSF2) can be found as follows (using our Holt's model estimates of DPIPC and IR):

$$NHSF2 = -324.33 + 0.17 \, (DPIPC) - 168.13 \, (IR)$$

2004Q1

$$NHSF2 = -324.33 + 0.17 \, (26,984.00) - 168.13 \, (5.89) = 3,255.31$$

TABLE 5.1
Data and Regression Results for New Houses Sold (NHS) as a Function of Disposable Income per Capita (DPIPC) and the Mortgage Interest Rate (IR)
(c5t1)

Date	NHS	IR	DPIPC
Mar-92	1,869	8.71	21,417
Jun-92	1,696	8.676667	21,505
Sep-92	1,913	8.01	21,514
Dec-92	1,885	8.206667	21,757
Mar-93	1,802	7.733333	21,279
Jun-93	1,980	7.453333	21,515
Sep-93	2,026	7.08	21,469
Dec-93	2,285	7.053333	21,706
Mar-94	2,052	7.296667	21,468
Jun-94	2,004	8.44	21,797
Sep-94	1,961	8.586667	21,870
Dec-94	1,990	9.1	22,106
Mar-95	1,801	8.813333	22,180
Jun-95	2,020	7.95	22,100
Sep-95	2,144	7.703333	22,143
Dec-95	2,069	7.353333	22,191
Mar-96	2,204	7.243333	22,385
Jun-96	2,203	8.106667	22,506
Sep-96	2,366	8.16	22,624
Dec-96	2,296	7.713333	22,667
Mar-97	2,462	7.79	22,823
Jun-97	2,297	7.923333	22,944
Sep-97	2,460	7.47	23,129
Dec-97	2,457	7.2	23,361
Mar-98	2,574	7.053333	23,798
Jun-98	2,676	7.093333	24,079
Sep-98	2,586	6.863333	24,265
Dec-98	2,837	6.766667	24,380
Mar-99	2,586	6.88	24,498
Jun-99	2,729	7.206667	24,464
Sep-99	2,619	7.796667	24,507
Dec-99	2,608	7.833333	24,789
Mar-00	2,629	8.26	25,274
Jun-00	2,491	8.32	25,380
Sep-00	2,647	8.03	25,633
Dec-00	2,796	7.643333	25,599
Mar-01	2,838	7.01	25,620
Jun-01	2,676	7.13	25,450
Sep-01	2,599	6.966667	26,081
Dec-01	2,774	6.783333	25,640
Mar-02	2,751	6.966667	26,249
Jun-02	2,871	6.816667	26,366
Sep-02	3,014	6.29	26,181
Dec-02	3,078	6.076667	26,123
Mar-03	2,939	5.836667	26,179
Jun-03	3,314	5.506667	26,392
Sep-03	3,472	6.013333	26,842
Dec-03	3,347	5.92	26,862
Mar-04	**3,590**	**5.61**	**26,964**
Jun-04	**3,618**	**6.13**	**27,088**
Sep-04	**3,464**	**5.893333**	**27,214** <- Holdout
Dec-04	**3,703**	**5.733333**	**27,691**

(continued on next page)

TABLE 5.1   (continued)

Audit Trail--Coefficient Table (Multiple Regression Selected)

Series Description	Included in Model	Coefficient	Standard Error	T-test	P-value	F-test	Elasticity	Overall F-test
NHS	Dependent	−324.33	483.01	−0.67	0.51	0.45		259.83
IR	Yes	−168.13	29.29	−5.74	0.00	32.95	−0.51	
DPIPC	Yes	0.17	0.01	12.93	0.00	167.28	1.64	

Audit Trail--Correlation Coefficient Table

Series Description	Included in Model	NHS	IR	DPIPC
NHS	Dependent	1.00	−0.79	0.93
IR	Yes	−0.79	1.00	−0.65
DPIPC	Yes	0.93	−0.65	1.00

Audit Trail--Statistics

Accuracy Measures	Value	Forecast Statistics	Value
AIC	599.11	Durbin Watson(4)	1.50
BIC	600.99	Mean	2,451.94
Mean Absolute Percentage Error (MAPE)	4.17%	Max	3,472.00
R-Square	92.03%	Min	1,696.00
Adjusted R-Square	91.68%	Sum Squared Deviation	8,910,888.81
Root Mean Square Error	121.63	Range	1,776.00
Theil	0.80	Ljung-Box	20.06

2004Q2

$$NHSF2 = -324.33 + 0.17\,(27,106.17) - 168.13\,(5.85) = 3,282.73$$

2004Q3

$$NHSF2 = -324.33 + 0.17\,(27,228.35) - 168.13\,(5.82) = 3,308.47$$

2004Q4

$$NHSF2 = -324.33 + 0.17\,(27,350.53) - 168.13\,(5.79) = 3,334.2$$

The precision of the regression coefficients may cause a small difference between the results above and those calculated with truncated coefficients.

FIGURE 5.2

New Houses Sold and Forecast of New Houses Sold (NHSF2) in Thousands of Units (c5t1)

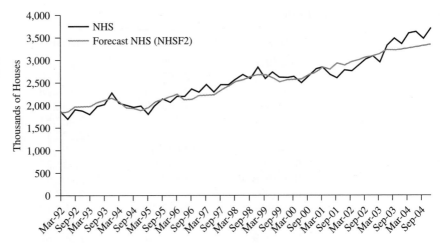

These values are plotted in Figure 5.2 along with the values predicted by the equation for the historical period. The forecasts here were produced in ForecastX™ and the calculations involve more significant digits than shown here.

Date	NHS	NHSF2
Mar-1992	1,869.00	1,838.41
Jun-1992	1,696.00	1,858.92
Sep-1992	1,913.00	1,972.53
Dec-1992	1,885.00	1,980.62
Mar-1993	1,802.00	1,979.24
Jun-1993	1,980.00	2,066.29
Sep-1993	2,026.00	2,121.26
Dec-1993	2,285.00	2,165.88
Mar-1994	2,052.00	2,084.67
Jun-1994	2,004.00	1,948.16
Sep-1994	1,961.00	1,935.87
Dec-1994	1,990.00	1,889.53
Mar-1995	1,801.00	1,950.26
Jun-1995	2,020.00	2,081.86
Sep-1995	2,144.00	2,130.61
Dec-1995	2,069.00	2,197.58
Mar-1996	2,204.00	2,248.93
Jun-1996	2,203.00	2,124.28
Sep-1996	2,366.00	2,135.29

(continued on next page)

(continued)

Date	NHS	NHSF2	
Dec-1996	2,296.00	2,217.67	
Mar-1997	2,462.00	2,231.20	
Jun-1997	2,297.00	2,229.28	
Sep-1997	2,460.00	2,336.83	
Dec-1997	2,457.00	2,421.51	
Mar-1998	2,574.00	2,520.18	
Jun-1998	2,676.00	2,561.04	
Sep-1998	2,586.00	2,631.21	
Dec-1998	2,837.00	2,666.94	
Mar-1999	2,586.00	2,667.87	
Jun-1999	2,729.00	2,607.19	
Sep-1999	2,619.00	2,515.28	
Dec-1999	2,608.00	2,556.87	
Mar-2000	2,629.00	2,567.28	
Jun-2000	2,491.00	2,575.14	
Sep-2000	2,647.00	2,666.74	
Dec-2000	2,796.00	2,725.99	
Mar-2001	2,838.00	2,836.03	
Jun-2001	2,676.00	2,787.06	
Sep-2001	2,599.00	2,921.39	
Dec-2001	2,774.00	2,877.53	
Mar-2002	2,751.00	2,949.84	
Jun-2002	2,871.00	2,994.87	
Sep-2002	3,014.00	3,052.09	
Dec-2002	3,078.00	3,078.13	
Mar-2003	2,939.00	3,127.97	
Jun-2003	3,314.00	3,219.52	
Sep-2003	3,472.00	3,210.55	
Dec-2003	3,347.00	3,229.63	
Mar-2004	**3,590.00**	**3,255.31**	
Jun-2004	**3,618.00**	**3,282.73**	
Sep-2004	**3,464.00**	**3,308.47**	**<- Holdout period**
Dec-2004	**3,703.00**	**3,334.20**	

In Figure 5.2 the dark line shows actual values of new houses sold (NHS) for 1992Q1 through 2004Q4. The light line shows the values predicted by this model for 1992Q1 through 2004Q4 (NHSF2). For the historical period, actual values for the independent variables were used in determining NHSF2. In the holdout period, forecast values (from smoothing models) for DPIPC and IR, as shown on page 228, were used to calculate NHSF2.

Actual and forecast values of retail sales for the four quarters of 2004 are shown, along with the calculation of the root-mean-squared error (RMSE) for the forecast period:

Holdout Period (2004) Forecast RMSE

Forecast	Actual	$(A_t - F_t)$	$(A_t - F_t)^2$
3,255.31	3,590.00	334.69	112,014.9944
3,282.73	3,618.00	335.27	112,406.5545
3,308.47	3,464.00	155.53	24,191.11415
3,334.20	3,703.00	368.80	136,012.6956
RMSE = 310			

This RMSE is about 9 percent of the mean for NHS during these four quarters. The total for NHS in 2004 was 14,375, and the total of the four quarterly forecasts was 13,181, so the error for the year was −1,194, or about 8.3 percent.

The Regression Plane

In our three-variable case (with NHS as the dependent variable and with IR and DPIPC as independent variables), three measured values are made for each sample point (i.e., for each quarter). Table 5.1 shows these three measured values for every quarter. In the period 1992Q1, for instance, the three values are 1,869 for NHS, 8.71 for IR, and 21,417 for DPIPC. These observations can be depicted in a scatter diagram like those in Chapter 2, but the scatter diagram must be three-dimensional. Figure 5.3 shows the new houses sold (NHS) of any observation as measured vertically from the DPIPC/IR plane. The value of IR is measured along

FIGURE 5.3
New Houses Sold (NHS) in Thousands of Units Viewed in Three Dimensions

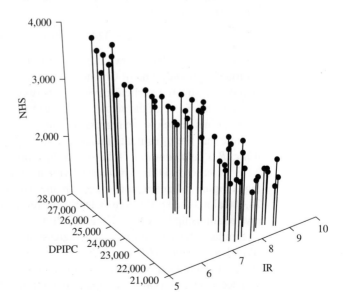

FIGURE 5.4

New Homes Sold (NHS) in Thousands Viewed in Three Dimensions with the Regression Plane Superimposed

Regression plane has the equation:
NHS = −1,422,517
− 9,945(IR)
+ 110.77(DPIPC).
See Table 5.2 for the estimation of this equation.

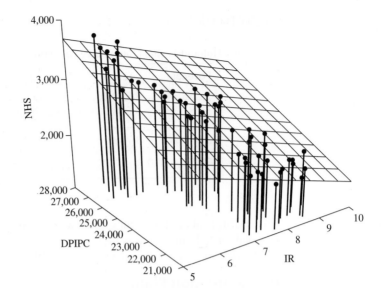

the "IR" axis and the value of DPIPC is measured along the "DPIPC" axis. All 52 observations are represented as points in the diagram.

In multiple-regression analysis, our task is to suspend a linear three-dimensional plane (called the *regression plane*) among the observations in such a way that the plane best represents the observations. Multiple-regression analysis estimates an equation ($Y = a + b_1X + b_2Z$) in such a manner that all the estimates of Y made with the equation fall on the surface of the linear plane. The exact equation we estimated for retail sales,

$$\text{NHS} = -324.33 + 0.17(\text{DPIPC}) - 168.13(\text{IR})$$

is graphed as the plane shown in Figure 5.4. This regression plane, like the simple bivariate regression line of Chapter 4, is drawn in such a way as to minimize the sum of the squared vertical deviations between the sample points and the estimated plane. Some of the actual points lie above the regression plane, while other actual points lie below the regression plane.

Note that the b_1 estimate indicates how NHS changes with respect to DPIPC *while IR is held constant*. If the sign of b_1 is positive, as it is in this example, then NHS increases as DPIPC increases (with all other variables held constant). Looking at Figure 5.4 again, note that the plane "tilts up" as you move from 23,000 to 28,000 along the DPIPC axis. Clearly, the regression plane is reacting to the positive relationship between NHS and DPIPC.

Similarly, the sign for b_2 in this regression represents the relationship between IR and NHS *while DPIPC is held constant*. Since the estimated sign of b_2 is negative, we should expect that as IR increases in value, all else being equal, NHS will decrease. This is also easily seen by examining the regression plane. Note that the plane is tilted in such a way that higher interest rates (IR) are associated with lower new homes sold (NHS) values.

Finally, if all the actual data points were to lie very close to the regression plane, the adjusted *R*-squared of the equation would be very high. If, on the other hand, most of the actual points were far above and below the regression plane, the adjusted *R*-squared would be lower than it otherwise would be. Normally, regression packages do not have a provision for the graphing of output in three-dimensional form. This is because relatively few of the problems faced in the real world involve exactly three variables. Sometimes you are working with only two variables, while at other times you will be working with more than three. Thus, while the three-dimensional diagram will be useful only in a few cases, it is instructive to see it once in order to understand that a regression package is simply estimating the equation of a plane in three-dimensional space when multiple regression is used. The plane is a normal plane when there are two independent variables, and it is called a *hyperplane* (more than three-dimensional) when there are more than two independent variables.

If all the actual data points were to lie very close to the regression plane, the adjusted R-squared of the equation would be very high.

STATISTICAL EVALUATION OF MULTIPLE-REGRESSION MODELS

The statistical evaluation of multiple-regression models is similar to that discussed in Chapter 4 for simple bivariate regression models. However, some important differences will be brought out in this section. In addition to evaluating the multiple-regression model, we will be comparing these results with a corresponding bivariate model. Thus, in Table 5.2 you see the regression results for both models. The multiple-regression results appear at the bottom of the table.

Three Quick Checks in Evaluating Multiple-Regression Models

The first thing you should do in reviewing regression results is to see whether the signs on the coefficients make sense.

As suggested in Chapter 4, the first thing you should do in reviewing regression results is to see whether the signs on the coefficients make sense. For our current model, that is:

$$\text{NHS} = b_0 + b_1(\text{DPIPC}) + b_2(\text{IR})$$

we have said that we expect a negative relationship between NHS and the interest rate, and a positive relationship between disposable personal income and NHS. Our expectations are confirmed, since:

$$b_1 = +0.17 > 0$$
$$b_2 = -168.17 < 0$$

The second thing to consider is whether these results are statistically significant at our desired level of confidence.

The second thing to consider is whether these results are statistically significant at our desired level of confidence. We will follow the convention of using

TABLE 5.2   Regression Results for Multiple- and Bivariate-Regression Models of New Homes Sold (NHS) (c5t1)

Bivariate Regression

Audit Trail--ANOVA Table (Multiple Regression Selected)

Source of Variation	SS	df	MS	SEE
Regression	5,560,860.59	1	5,560,860.59	
Error	3,350,028.22	46	72,826.70	269.86
Total	8,910,888.81	47		

Audit Trail--Coefficient Table (Multiple Regression Selected)

Series Description	Included in Model	Coefficient	Standard Error	T-test	P-value	F-test	Elasticity	Overall F-test
NHS	Dependent	5,543.74	355.96	15.57	0.00	242.55		76.36
IR	Yes	−415.90	47.59	−8.74	0.00	76.36	−1.26	

Audit Trail--Correlation Coefficient Table

Series Description	Included in Model	NHS	IR
NHS	Dependent	1.00	−0.79
IR	Yes	−0.79	1.00

Audit Trail--Statistics

Accuracy Measures	Value	Forecast Statistics	Value
AIC	673.58	Durbin Watson(4)	1.24
BIC	675.45	Mean	2,451.94
Mean Absolute Percentage Error (MAPE)	9.04%	Max	3,472.00
R-Square	62.41%	Min	1,696.00
Adjusted R-Square	61.59%	Sum Squared Deviation	8,910,888.81
Root Mean Square Error	264.18	Range	1,776.00
Theil	1.88	Ljung-Box	81.83

Multiple Regression

Audit Trail--Coefficient Table (Multiple Regression Selected)

Series Description	Included in Model	Coefficient	Standard Error	T-test	P-value	F-test	Elasticity	Overall F-test
NHS	Dependent	−324.33	483.01	−0.67	0.51	0.45		259.83
IR	Yes	−168.13	29.29	−5.74	0.00	32.95	−0.51	
DPIPC	Yes	0.17	0.01	12.93	0.00	167.28	1.64	

Audit Trail--Correlation Coefficient Table

Series Description	Included in Model	NHS	IR	DPIPC
NHS	Dependent	1.00	−0.79	0.93
IR	Yes	−0.79	1.00	−0.65
DPIPC	Yes	0.93	−0.65	1.00

TABLE 5.2   (continued)

Accuracy Measures	Value	Forecast Statistics	Value
AIC	599.11	Durbin Watson(4)	1.50
BIC	600.99	Mean	2,451.94
Mean Absolute Percentage Error (MAPE)	4.17%	Max	3,472.00
R-Square	92.03%	Min	1,696.00
Adjusted R-Square	91.68%	Sum Squared Deviation	8,910,888.81
Root Mean Square Error	121.63	Range	1,776.00
Theil	0.80	Ljung-Box	20.06

Audit Trail--Statistics

a 95 percent confidence level, and thus a 0.05 significance level. The hypotheses to be tested are summarized as follows:

For DPIPC	For IR
$H_0: \beta_1 \leq 0$	$H_0: \beta_2 \geq 0$
$H_1: \beta_1 > 0$	$H_1: \beta_2 < 0$

These hypotheses are evaluated using a *t*-test where, as with bivariate regression, the calculated *t*-ratio is found by dividing the estimated regression coefficient by its standard error (i.e., $t_{calc} = b_i/$s.e. of b_i). The table value of $t(t_T)$ can be found from Table 2.5 (page 71) at $n - (K + 1)$ degrees of freedom, where n = the number of observations and K = the number of independent variables. For our current problem $n = 48$ (recall the holdout period) and $K = 2$, so df $= 48 - (2 + 1) = 45$. We will follow the rule that if df ≥ 30 the infinity row of the *t*-table will be used. Thus, the table value is 1.645. Note that we have used the 0.05 column, since we have one-tailed tests, and in such cases the entire significance level (0.05) goes in one tail.

Remember that since the *t*-distribution is symmetrical, we compare the absolute value of t_{calc} with the table value. For our hypothesis tests, the results can be summarized as follows:

For DPIPC	For IR
$t_{calc} = 12.93$	$t_{calc} = -5.74$
$\lvert t_{calc} \rvert > t_T$	$\lvert t_{calc} \rvert > t_T$
$12.93 > 1.645$	$\lvert -5.74 \rvert > 1.645$
$\therefore$Reject H_0	$\therefore$Reject H_0

In both cases, the absolute value of t_{calc} is greater than the table value at $\alpha = 0.05$ and df $= 33$. Thus we reject the null hypothesis at the 0.05 level for the DPIPC coefficient, and we are also able to reject the null hypothesis for the IR coefficient.

By setting the 95 percent confidence level as our criterion, we are at the same time saying that we are willing to accept a 5 percent chance of error or, alternatively, that we set a 5 percent desired significance level.

The third part of our quick check of regression results involves an evaluation of the coefficient of determination.

The third part of our quick check of regression results involves an evaluation of the multiple coefficient of determination, which, you may recall, measures the percentage of the variation in the dependent variable that is explained by the regression model. In Chapter 4 we designated the coefficient of determination as R-squared. If you look at the second ForecastX™ output in Table 5.2, you will see that in addition to R-squared there is another measure called the *adjusted R-squared*. (See "Adjusted R-Square = 91.68%.") In evaluating multiple-regression equations, you should always consider the adjusted R-squared value. The reason for the adjustment is that adding another independent variable will always increase R-squared even if the variable has no meaningful relation to the dependent variable. Indeed, if we added enough independent variables, we could get very close to an R-squared of 1.00—a perfect fit for the historical period. However, the model would probably work very poorly for values of the independent variables other than those used in estimation. To get around this and to show only meaningful changes in R-squared, an adjustment is made to account for a decrease in the number of degrees of freedom.[3] The adjusted R-squared is often denoted R^{-2} (called R-bar-squared or the multiple coefficient of determination).

For our multiple-regression model of new homes sold (NHS), we see, in Table 5.2, that the adjusted R-squared is 91.68 percent. Thus, this model explains 91.68 percent of the variation in new homes sold. This compares with an adjusted R-squared of 61.59 percent for the bivariate model (using only IR as an independent variable).

In looking at regression output, you often see an F-statistic. This statistic can be used to test the following joint hypothesis:

$$H_0: \beta_1 = \beta_2 = \beta_3 = \cdots = \beta_k = 0 \quad \text{or } H_0 : R^2 = 0$$

(i.e., all slope terms are simultaneously equal to zero);

H_1: All slope terms are not simultaneously equal to zero or $H_1 : R^2 \neq 0$

If the null hypothesis is true, it follows that none of the variation in the dependent variable would be explained by the regression model. It follows that, if H_0 is true, the true coefficient of determination would be zero.

The F-statistic is calculated as follows:

$$F = \frac{\text{Explained variation}/K}{\text{Unexplained variation}/[n - (K + 1)]}$$

The F-test is a test of the overall significance of the estimated multiple regression. To test the hypothesis, this calculated F-statistic is compared with the F-value from Table 5.3 at K degrees of freedom for the numerator and $n - (K + 1)$ degrees of freedom for the denominator.[4] For our current regression, $K = 2$ and

---

[3] These concepts are expanded in J. Scott Armstrong, *Long-Range Forecasting* (New York: John Wiley & Sons, 1978), pp. 323–25, 466.

[4] This F-table corresponds to a 95 percent confidence level ($\alpha = 0.05$). You could use any α value and the corresponding F-distribution.

TABLE 5.3   Critical Values of the *F*-Distribution at a 95 Percent Confidence Level ($\alpha = .05$)

	1*	2	3	4	5	6	7	8	9
1†	161.40	199.50	215.70	224.60	230.20	234.00	236.80	238.90	240.50
2	18.51	19.00	19.16	19.25	19.30	19.33	19.35	19.37	19.38
3	10.13	9.55	9.28	9.12	9.01	8.94	8.89	8.85	8.81
4	7.71	6.94	6.59	6.39	6.26	6.16	6.09	6.04	6.00
5	6.61	5.79	5.41	5.19	5.05	4.95	4.88	4.82	4.77
6	5.99	5.14	4.76	4.53	4.39	4.28	4.21	4.15	4.10
7	5.59	4.74	4.35	4.12	3.97	3.87	3.79	3.73	3.68
8	5.32	4.46	4.07	3.84	3.69	3.58	3.50	3.44	3.39
9	5.12	4.26	3.86	3.63	3.48	3.37	3.29	3.23	3.18
10	4.96	4.10	3.71	3.48	3.33	3.22	3.14	3.07	3.02
11	4.84	3.98	3.59	3.36	3.20	3.09	3.01	2.95	2.90
12	4.75	3.89	3.49	3.26	3.11	3.00	2.91	2.85	2.80
13	4.67	3.81	3.41	3.18	3.03	2.92	2.83	2.77	2.71
14	4.60	3.74	3.34	3.11	2.96	2.85	2.76	2.70	2.65
15	4.54	3.68	3.29	3.06	2.90	2.79	2.71	2.64	2.59
16	4.49	3.63	3.24	3.01	2.85	2.74	2.66	2.59	2.54
17	4.45	3.59	3.20	2.96	2.81	2.70	2.61	2.55	2.49
18	4.41	3.55	3.16	2.93	2.77	2.66	2.58	2.51	2.46
19	4.38	3.52	3.13	2.90	2.74	2.63	2.54	2.48	2.42
20	4.35	3.49	3.10	2.87	2.71	2.60	2.51	2.45	2.39
21	4.32	3.47	3.07	2.84	2.68	2.57	2.49	2.42	2.37
22	4.30	3.44	3.05	2.82	2.66	2.55	2.46	2.40	2.34
23	4.28	3.42	3.03	2.80	2.64	2.53	2.44	2.37	2.32
24	4.26	3.40	3.01	2.78	2.62	2.51	2.42	2.36	2.30
25	4.24	3.39	2.99	2.76	2.60	2.49	2.40	2.34	2.28
26	4.23	3.37	2.98	2.74	2.59	2.47	2.39	2.32	2.27
27	4.21	3.35	2.96	2.73	2.57	2.46	2.37	2.31	2.25
28	4.20	3.34	2.95	2.71	2.56	2.45	2.36	2.29	2.24
29	4.18	3.33	2.93	2.70	2.55	2.43	2.35	2.28	2.22
30	4.17	3.32	2.92	2.69	2.53	2.42	2.33	2.27	2.21
40	4.08	3.23	2.84	2.61	2.45	2.34	2.25	2.18	2.12
60	4.00	3.15	2.76	2.53	2.37	2.25	2.17	2.10	2.04
120	3.92	3.07	2.68	2.45	2.29	2.17	2.09	2.02	1.96
∞	3.84	3.00	2.60	2.37	2.21	2.10	2.01	1.94	1.88

* Degrees of freedom for the numerator $= K$
† Degrees of freedom for the denominator $= n - (K + 1)$

$[n - (K + 1)] = 45$, so the table value of *F* is 3.23 (taking the closest value). In using an *F*-test, the criterion for rejection of the null hypothesis is that $F_{calc} > F_T$ (the calculated *F* must be greater than the table value). In this case the calculated value is 259.83, so we would reject H_0 (i.e., our equation passes the *F*-test).

In multiple-regression
analysis, one of the
assumptions that is
made is that the
independent variables
are not highly linearly
correlated with each
other or with linear
combinations of other
independent variables.
If this assumption is
violated, a problem
known as
multicollinearity
results.

Multicollinearity

In multiple-regression analysis, one of the assumptions that is made is that the independent variables are not highly linearly correlated with each other or with linear combinations of other independent variables. If this assumption is violated, a problem known as *multicollinearity* results. If your regression results show that one or more independent variables appear not to be statistically significant when theory suggests that they should be, and/or if the signs on coefficients are not logical, multicollinearity may be indicated. Sometimes it is possible to spot the cause of the multicollinearity by looking at a correlation matrix for the independent variables.

To illustrate the multicollinearity problem, suppose that we model new homes sold (NHS) as a function of disposable personal income (DPIPC), the mortgage interest rate (IR), and the gross domestic product (GDP). The model would be:

$$NHS = b_0 + b_1(DPIPC) + b_2(GDP) + b_3(IR)$$

Business and economic logic would tell us to expect a positive sign for b_1, a positive sign for b_2, and a negative sign for b_3. The actual regression results are:

(c5t1)

	Coefficient	*t*-Ratio
Constant	1,884	2.09
DPIPC	**−0.01**	−0.21
GDP	0.23	2.83
IR	−147.82	−5.25

We see that the coefficient for DPIPC is negative, which does not make sense. It would be difficult to argue persuasively that NHS would fall as DPIPC rises.

If we look at the correlations between these variables, we can see the source of the problem. The correlations are:

	DPIPC	GDP	IR
DPIPC	1		
GDP	**0.99**	1	
IR	−0.65	−0.67	1

Clearly there is a very strong linear association between GDP and DPIPC. In this case both of these variables are measuring essentially the same thing. There are no firm rules in deciding how strong a correlation is too great. Two rules of thumb, however, provide some guidance. First, we might avoid correlations between independent variables that are close to 1 in absolute value. Second, we might try to avoid situations in which the correlation between independent variables is greater

In early 2002 hospitals in New Jersey were beginning to experience difficulty in budgeting for registered nurses (RNs) because of uncertainty about the number of RNs needed in future years. Dr. Geri Dickson, RN, authored a demand study for nurses in New Jersey using multiple regression as its primary statistical tool.

The New Jersey model is a multiple regression that forecasts the demand for RNs at the state and county level; demand is used in the study to mean the number of nurses that employers would hire given their availability. An important feature of the study was that it was based upon a longitudinal (sometimes called panel) set of data that held constant many economic variables that might have been thought to change over the time period.

There was a need to use some independent variables that themselves had to be forecast in order to produce the final RN forecast. For instance, the total number of HIV/AIDs patients was found to be a significant predictor of nursing demand; the growth rate in HIV/AIDs was predicted to be 7 percent over the forecast horizon using time-series forecasting methods applied to past HIV/AIDs data. Likewise, the rate of HMO penetration into the New Jersey market was also found to be a predic-

tor of nursing demand. Once again time-series methods were used to make forecasts of this independent variable; since this variable was growing at a nonlinear rate, a nonlinear model was used to forecast future penetration.

Some variables the researchers considered as independent variables in the forecasting model turned out to be insignificant. For example, the mortality rate and per capita income in New Jersey seemed to have little effect on nursing demand. The model estimated for predicting hospital employment of registered nurses (in full-time equivalents, or FTEs) is shown below.

It is easy to see that some of the variables seem to make economic sense. The "population over 65 rate" increases as those over age 65 increase relative to the general population; since this is the group that most often requires extensive hospital stays, we would expect a positive sign on the variable. Likewise, if the "birthrate" increases, we could expect the demand for RNs' services to increase, and so we would expect this variable also to have a positive sign. In the equation above both these variables have the expected sign and both variables are significant at the 99 percent confidence level (as shown by the P-value).

Dependent Variable—Hospital Employment of Registered Nurses (FTEs)

Variable	Coefficient	Std. Dev.	T-statistic	P-value
Constant	−0.947	0.415	−2.278	0.023*
HIV/AIDS rate	0.001	0.000	4.180	0.000*
Employment/population Ratio	−0.543	0.732	−0.742	0.458
HMO penetration rate	0.024	0.006	4.304	0.000*
Population over 65 Rate	0.064	0.017	3.743	0.000*
Birthrate	0.093	0.018	5.103	0.000*
Surgery rate	0.010	0.003	3.753	0.000*
Inpatient days rate	0.853	0.162	5.278	0.000*

R-squared = 0.861
Adjusted R-squared = 0.848
* Significant at the 99 percent confidence level

(continued on next page)

The author points out that the most useful characteristic of using multiple regression as the forecasting technique is the ability to conduct what-if exercises with the prediction model. For instance, in the forecast period the ratio of employment to population in the state of New Jersey is expected to increase. But what if this prediction proves unfounded and the ratio actually falls by 1 percent? Multiple-regression models allow the researcher to use the coefficient on this ratio (here it is -0.543 in the forecasting model) to predict that as the ratio falls there will be increased demand for registered nurses; the researcher is even able to place a magnitude on the increased demand if the change in the ratio is known.

Sources: Geri Dickson, "Forecasting The Demand for Nurses in New Jersey" (March 2002), New Jersey Collaborating Center for Nursing (http://www.njccn.org); and M. Biviano, T. M. Dall, M. S. Fritz, and W. Spencer, "What Is Behind HRS's Projected Supply, Demand, and Shortage of Registered Nurses" (September 2004), National Center for Workforce Analysis, Bureau of Health Professions, Health Resources and Services Administration.

than the correlation of those variables with the dependent variable. One thing to do when multicollinearity exists is to drop all but one of the highly correlated variables. The use of first differences can also help when there is a common trend in the two highly correlated independent variables.

Serial Correlation: A Second Look

Serial correlation results when there is a significant time pattern in the error terms of a regression analysis.

The problem known as *serial correlation* (or autocorrelation) was introduced in Chapter 4, where we indicated that serial correlation results when there is a significant time pattern in the error terms of a regression analysis that violates the assumption that the errors are independent over time. Positive serial correlation, as shown in the right-hand graph of Figure 4.10 (page 186), is common in business and economic data.

A test involving six comparisons between table values of the Durbin-Watson statistic and the calculated Durbin-Watson statistic is commonly used to detect serial correlation. These six comparisons are repeated here, where d_l and d_u represent the lower and upper bounds of the Durbin-Watson statistic from Table 4.7 (page 187) and DW is the calculated value:

Test	Value of Calculated DW	Conclusion
1	$d_l < DW < d_u$	Result is indeterminate.
2	$0 < DW < d_l$	Positive serial correlation exists.
3	$2 < DW < (4 - d_u)$	No serial correlation exists.
4	$d_u < DW < 2$	No serial correlation exists.
5	$(4 - d_l) < DW < 4$	Negative serial correlation exists.
6	$(4 - d_u) < DW < (4 - d_l)$	Result is indeterminate.

In Table 5.2 you see that for the bivariate regression of NHS with IR, the DW is 1.24, indicating positive serial correlation.

For the multiple regression of NHS with DPIPC and IR, the calculated Durbin-Watson statistic is approximately 1.5. (See Table 5.2, which has DW for both the bivariate and the multiple regressions.) This satisfies the region "1" test:

$$d_l < \text{DW} < d_u$$
$$1.46 < 1.5 < 1.63$$

where d_u and d_l were found from Table 4.7 for $k = 2$ and $N = 50$ (approximately). Thus, we conclude that the result is indeterminate. This illustrates one possible solution to the serial-correlation problem. Our bivariate model was underspecified: An important independent variable was missing. In this case it was disposable personal income (DPIPC). While the addition of this variable did not definitively solve the problem in this case, the DW statistic did move in the correct direction.

The careful reader will have noted that the Durbin-Watson statistic reported in Table 5.2 for the NHS regressions is labeled as Durbin Watson (4). This is a fourth-order Durbin-Watson statistic. In practice it is often assumed that a first-order check for autocorrelation of the residuals will suffice. Remember that the normal Durbin-Watson statistic checks the error terms for autocorrelation by comparing errors that are lagged a single period. When a regression fails the Durbin-Watson test, the usual interpretation is that this represents the effect of an omitted or unobservable variable (or variables) on the dependent variable. The easiest correction is to collect data on the omitted variable and include it in a new formulation of the model; if the correct variable is added, the serial correlation problem will disappear.

When quarterly data are employed, however, the presence of nonsystematic seasonal variation, or an incomplete accounting for seasonality by the included variables, will produce seasonal effects in the error terms, with the consequence that the fourth-order autocorrelation will be significant. The same argument can be made when monthly data are employed for twelfth-order autocorrelation.

The Durbin-Watson statistic has then been generalized to test for such upper-order instances of autocorrelation in the error terms. The fourth-order test statistic has a distribution that differs from that of the normal Durbin-Watson statistic and tables of its critical values as presented in Table 4.7. However, the differences are small, and the user may wish to simply use Table 4.7 to interpret the upper-order Durbin-Watson statistics.[5]

When a regression with quarterly data fails the DW(4) test for fourth-order correlation among the error terms, the usual culprit is that the seasonality in the data has not been fully accounted for by the variables included.

---

[5] For a table showing the exact critical values of the Durbin-Watson statistic for quarterly data (both with and without seasonal dummy variables), see the K. F. Wallis article in the Suggested Readings list at the end of this chapter.

SERIAL CORRELATION AND THE OMITTED-VARIABLE PROBLEM

The most common reason for serial correlation is that an important explanatory variable has been omitted.

Table 5.4 presents quarterly data for a firm's sales, the price the firm charges for its product, and the income of potential purchasers. The most common reason for serial correlation is that an important explanatory variable has been omitted. To address this situation, it will be necessary at times to add an additional explanatory variable to the equation to correct for serial correlation.

In the first regression displayed in Table 5.4, price is used as the single independent variable to explain the firm's sales. The results are somewhat less than satisfactory on a number of accounts. First, the R-squared is quite low, explaining only about 39 percent of the variation in sales. More importantly, the sign on the price coefficient is positive, indicating that as price increases, sales also increase. This does not seem to follow economic theory.

The problem may be that an important variable that could account for the large errors and the incorrect sign of the price coefficient has been omitted from the regression. The second regression in Table 5.4 adds income as a second explanatory variable. The results are dramatic. The adjusted R-squared shows that the model now accounts for about 96 percent of the variation in sales. The signs of both the explanatory variable coefficients are as expected. The price coefficient is negative, indicating that sales decrease as price increases, while the income coefficient is positive, indicating that sales of the good rise as incomes increase (which would be reasonable for a "normal" economic good).

The Durbin-Watson statistic is within the rule-of-thumb 1.5 to 2.5 range. There does not seem to be serial correlation (and so the R-squared and t-statistics are probably accurate). The formal test for serial correlation requires us to look for the upper and lower values in the Durbin-Watson table (Table 4.7). Note carefully that the appropriate values are 0.95 and 1.54 (i.e., $N = 15$ and column $k = 2$).

Using these values and our calculated value, we can evaluate each of the six tests explained earlier.

Test	Value	Conclusion
1	.95 < 1.67 < 1.54	False
2	0 < 1.67 < 0.95	False
3	2 < 1.67 < 2.46	False
4	1.54 < 1.67 < 2	True
5	3.05 < 1.67 < 4	False
6	2.46 < 1.67 < 3.05	False

Since our result is true for test number 4, we conclude that no serial correlation is present. Apparently, the addition of the second explanatory variable explained the pattern in the residuals that the Durbin-Watson statistic identified.

TABLE 5.4 **Data for a Firm's Sales, the Price the Firm Charges for Its Product, and the Income of Potential Purchasers**   (c5t4)

Period	Sales	Price	Income
Mar-02	80	5	2,620
Jun-02	86	4.87	2,733
Sep-02	93	4.86	2,898
Dec-02	99	4.79	3,056
Mar-03	106	4.79	3,271
Jun-03	107	4.87	3,479
Sep-03	109	5.01	3,736
Dec-03	110	5.31	3,868
Mar-04	111	5.55	4,016
Jun-04	113	5.72	4,152
Sep-04	110	5.74	4,336
Dec-04	112	5.59	4,477
Mar-05	131	5.5	4,619
Jun-05	136	5.48	4,764
Sep-05	137	5.47	4,802
Dec-05	139	5.49	4,916

Bivariate Regression

```
Audit Trail--Coefficient Table (Multiple Regression Selected)

  Series    Included              Standard                                          Overall
Description in Model  Coefficient   Error   T-test  P-value  F-test  Elasticity     F-test
-----------------------------------------------------------------------------------------
Sales       Dependent   -51.24     54.32    -0.94    0.36     0.89                    8.98
Price       Yes          30.92     10.32     3.00    0.01     8.98      1.46
```

```
Audit Trail--Statistics

Accuracy Measures                       Value    Forecast Statistics        Value
--------------------------------------------     ---------------------------------
AIC                                     130.02   Durbin Watson (1)           0.34
BIC                                     130.80   Standard Deviation         17.49
Mean Absolute Percentage Error (MAPE)   10.67%   Ljung-Box                  16.57
R-Square                                39.07%
Adjusted R-Square                       39.07%
Root Mean Square Error                  13.22
Theil                                    1.78
```

Multiple Regression

```
Audit Trail--Coefficient Table (Multiple Regression Selected)

  Series    Included              Standard                                          Overall
Description in Model  Coefficient   Error   T-test  P-value  F-test  Elasticity     F-test
-----------------------------------------------------------------------------------------
Sales       Dependent   123.47     19.40     6.36    0.00    40.51                  154.86
Price       Yes         -24.84      4.95    -5.02    0.00    25.17     -1.17
Income      Yes           0.03      0.00    13.55    0.00   183.62      1.06
```

(continued on next page)

TABLE 5.4　(continued)

Audit Trail--Statistics				
Accuracy Measures	Value		Forecast Statistics	Value
AIC	86.56		Durbin Watson (1)	1.67
BIC	87.34		Standard Deviation	17.49
Mean Absolute Percentage Error (MAPE)	2.22%		Ljung-Box	9.27
R-Square	95.97%			
Adjusted R-Square	95.97%			
Root Mean Square Error	3.40			
Theil	0.53			

Alternative-Variable Selection Criteria

There is a strong tendency for forecasters to use a single criterion for deciding which of several variables ought to be used as independent variables in a regression. The criterion many people use appears to be the coefficient of determination, or R-squared. Recall that R-squared is a measure of the proportion of total variance accounted for by the linear influence of the explanatory variables (only *linear* influence is accounted for, since we are using linear least-squares regression). The R-squared measure has at least one obvious fault when used in this manner: it can be increased by simply increasing the number of independent variables. Because of this, we proposed the corrected or adjusted R-squared, which uses unbiased estimators of the respective variances. Most forecasters use the adjusted R-squared to lead them to the correct model by selecting the model that maximizes adjusted R-squared. The adjusted R-squared measure is based on selecting the correct model by using a quadratic form of the residuals or squared errors in which the true model minimizes those squared errors. But the adjusted R-squared measure may not be the most powerful of the measures involving the squared errors.

> There are two other model-specification statistics reported by ForecastX™ and other statistical packages that can be of use in selecting the "correct" independent variables.

There are two other model-specification statistics reported by ForecastX™ and other statistical packages that can be of use in selecting the "correct" independent variables. These are the Akaike information criterion (AIC) and the Bayesian information criterion (BIC).[6]

The Akaike information criterion selects the best model by considering the accuracy of the estimation and the "best" approximation to reality. The statistic (which is minimized by the best model) involves both the use of a measure of the accuracy of the estimate *and* a measure of the principle of parsimony (i.e., the concept that fewer independent variables are better than more, all other things

---

[6] The Bayesian information criterion is also called the Schwarz information criterion, after its creator.

In actual practice, a decrease in the AIC as a variable is added indicates that accuracy has increased after adjustment for the rule of parsimony.

being equal). The calculation of the AIC is detailed in Judge et al.[7] We can say that the statistic is constructed so that, as the number of independent variables increases, the AIC has a tendency to increase as well; this means that there is a penalty for "extra" independent variables that must be sufficiently offset by an increase in estimation accuracy to keep the AIC from increasing. In actual practice, a decrease in the AIC as a variable is added indicates that accuracy has increased after adjustment for the rule of parsimony.

The Bayesian criterion is quite similar to the AIC. The BIC uses Bayesian arguments about the prior probability of the true model to suggest the correct model. While the calculation routine for the BIC is quite different from that for the AIC, the results are usually quite consistent.[8] The BIC is also to be minimized, so that, if the BIC decreases after the addition of a new independent variable, the resulting model specification is seen as superior to the prior model specification. Often, AIC and BIC lead to the same model choice.

In a study of the model-selection process, Judge and coauthors created five independent variables that were to be used to estimate a dependent variable. Two of the five independent variables were actually related to the dependent variable, while the remaining three were extraneous variables. Various combinations of the five independent variables were used to estimate the dependent variable, and three measures were used to select the "best" model. The three measures used were the adjusted *R*-squared, the AIC, and the BIC.

The correct model containing only the two variables actually related to the dependent variable was chosen 27 percent of the time in repeated experiments by the adjusted *R*-squared criterion. The AIC chose the correct model in 45 percent of the cases, and the BIC chose the correct model in 46 percent of the cases. The results should make the forecaster wary of accepting only the statistical results of what constitutes the best model without some economic interpretation of why a variable is included. It should be clear, however, that the adjusted *R*-squared criterion is actually quite a poor judge to use in model selection; either the AIC or the BIC is far superior. The same study also showed that in 9 percent of the repeated trials the adjusted *R*-squared criterion chose the model with all five variables (i.e., the two "correct" ones and the three extraneous ones). The AIC and the BIC made the same incorrect choice in only 3 percent of the cases.

Examine the ForecastX™ output in Table 5.2, which includes the calculated AIC and BIC criteria. In the upper half of Table 5.2, the new homes sold (NHS) regression includes only the mortgage interest rate (IR) as an independent variable. For this specification of the model, the AIC is 673.58, while the BIC is 675.45. When the disposable personal income (DPIPC) variable is added to the regression, the AIC decreases to 599.11 and the BIC decreases to 600.99. These

[7] For a complete description of the calculation routine, see George G. Judge, R. Carter Hill, William E. Griffiths, Helmut Lutkepohl, and Tsoung-Chao Lee, *Introduction to the Theory and Practice of Econometrics,* 2nd ed., (New York: John Wiley & Sons, 1988), Chapter 20.

[8] Again see Judge et al. for a complete description of the calculation routine.

changes in the AIC and BIC indicate that the addition of DPIPC to the model was probably a correct choice.

In Table 5.4 we added a second variable to a regression. When both price and income were included, the AIC decreased to 86.56 from 130.02 and the BIC decreased to 87.34 from 130.80. Apparently, the inclusion of income as a variable was also likely a correct choice.

How much of a decrease in the Akaike information criterion (AIC) constitutes a "better" model? According to Hirotugu Akaike, there is a clear indication of a better identified model if the two competing models differ by more than 10 in their AIC score. If the difference is between 4 and 7, there is much less certainty that a clear winner has emerged. If the difference in AIC scores is 2 or less, then both candidate models have strong support. In both instances above, the differences in the Akaike scores between the candidate models exceeded 10, and therefore one model was clearly chosen as the best identified model.

> There is a clear indication of a better identified model if the two competing models differ by more than 10 in their AIC score.

The researcher should not compare the AIC or BIC of one series with the AIC or BIC of another series; the assumption is that models with identical dependent variables are being compared. There is no easy interpretation of the magnitude of the AIC and BIC, nor is one necessary. Only the relative size of the statistics is important.

ACCOUNTING FOR SEASONALITY IN A MULTIPLE-REGRESSION MODEL

Many business and economic data series display pronounced seasonal patterns that recur with some regularity year after year. The pattern may be associated with weather conditions typical of the four seasons of the year. For example, sales of ski equipment would be expected to be greater during the fall and winter (the fourth and first quarters of the calendar year, respectively) than during the spring and summer (the second and third quarters).

Other regular patterns that would be referred to as seasonal patterns may have nothing to do with weather conditions. For example, jewelry sales in the United States tend to be high in November and December because of Christmas shopping and gift giving, and turkey sales are also highest in these months because of traditional Thanksgiving and Christmas dinners.

Patterns such as these are not easily accounted for by the typical causal variables that we use in regression analysis. However, a special type of variable known as a dummy variable can be used effectively to account for seasonality or any other qualitative attribute. The dependent variable in a regression is often influenced not only by continuous variables like income, price, and advertising expenditures, but also by variables that may be qualitative or nominally scaled (such as the season of the year). A dummy variable typically takes on a value of either 0 or 1. It is 0 if the condition does not exist for an observation, and it is 1 if the condition does exist.

Suppose that we were studying monthly data on turkey sales at grocery stores and we would like to include the November and December seasonality in our model. We could define a dummy variable called M11, for the eleventh month, to be equal to 1 for November observations and 0 otherwise. Another dummy variable, M12, could be defined similarly for December. Thus, for every year these variables would be as follows:

Month	M11	M12	Month	M11	M12
January	0	0	July	0	0
February	0	0	August	0	0
March	0	0	September	0	0
April	0	0	October	0	0
May	0	0	November	1	0
June	0	0	December	0	1

In the regression results, the coefficients for M11 and M12 would reveal the degree of difference in sales for November and December, respectively, compared to other months of the year. In both of these cases we would expect the coefficients to be positive (indicating that sales in these two months were higher, on average, than in the remaining months of the year).

To illustrate very specifically the use of dummy variables to account for and measure seasonality, let us use new cars sold (NCS) in the United States measured in millions of dollars (not seasonally adjusted). These data are plotted for Jan-97 through Dec-07 in Figure 5.5. To help you see the seasonality,

FIGURE 5.5
Total New Cars Sold (NCS)
(c5t5)

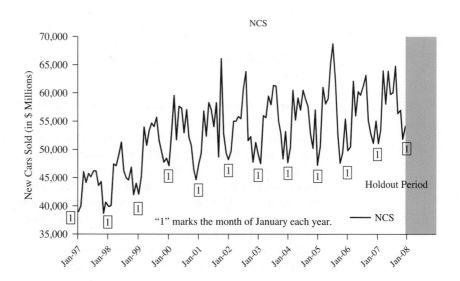

each January is marked with the number 1. You see in this figure that through the 11 years, there are typically fewer new cars sold during January than in the other months of the year; in most years there is a peak in sales sometime during the summer months. This pattern is reasonably consistent, although there is variability in the degree of seasonality and some deviation from the overall pattern.

To account for and measure this seasonality in a regression model, we will use 11 dummy variables: These will be coded as follows:

feb = 1 for February and zero otherwise
mar = 1 for March and zero otherwise
apr = 1 for April and zero otherwise
may = 1 for May and zero otherwise
jun = 1 for June and zero otherwise
jul = 1 for July and zero otherwise
aug = 1 for August and zero otherwise
sep = 1 for September and zero otherwise
oct = 1 for October and zero otherwise
nov = 1 for November and zero otherwise
dec = 1 for December and zero otherwise

Data for new cars sold (NCS), a time index, the University of Michigan Index of Consumer Sentiment (ICS), the bank prime loan rate (Prime), and these seasonal dummy variables are shown in Table 5.5. Examine the data carefully to verify your understanding of the coding of the dummy variables.

Since we have assigned dummy variables for each month except January, the first month (January) is the base month for our regression model. Any month could be used as the base month, with dummy variables to adjust for differences attributed to the other months. The number of seasonal dummy variables to use depends upon the data. There is one important rule (the Iron Rule of Dummy Variables):

If we have P states of nature, we cannot use more than $P - 1$ dummy variables.

In our current example $P = 12$, since we have monthly data, and so we would use only 11 seasonal dummy variables at a maximum. There are 12 states of nature: the 12 months in the year. We could use fewer than 11 if we found that all 11 were unnecessary by evaluating their statistical significance by t-tests. But, if we violate the rule and use 12 dummy variables to represent all the months, we create a situation of perfect multicollinearity (because there is more than one exact relationship among the variables).

Let us now add these dummy variables to the regression model for new cars sold (NCS). Our regression model will include the index of time variable (Time),

TABLE 5.5 Data for New Car Sales (NCS), the Time Index (Time), the Index of Consumer Sentiment (ICS), the Prime Rate (Prime), and Seasonal Dummy Variables (c5t5)

Date	NCS	Time	ICS	Prime	feb	mar	apr	may	jun	jul	aug	sep	oct	nov	dec
Jan-97	38,922	1	97.4	8.25	0	0	0	0	0	0	0	0	0	0	0
Feb-97	40,002	2	99.7	8.25	1	0	0	0	0	0	0	0	0	0	0
Mar-97	45,926	3	100.0	8.3	0	1	0	0	0	0	0	0	0	0	0
Apr-97	44,068	4	101.4	8.5	0	0	1	0	0	0	0	0	0	0	0
May-97	45,638	5	103.2	8.5	0	0	0	1	0	0	0	0	0	0	0
Jun-97	45,170	6	104.5	8.5	0	0	0	0	1	0	0	0	0	0	0
Jul-97	46,076	7	107.1	8.5	0	0	0	0	0	1	0	0	0	0	0
Aug-97	46,084	8	104.4	8.5	0	0	0	0	0	0	1	0	0	0	0
Sep-97	43,646	9	106.0	8.5	0	0	0	0	0	0	0	1	0	0	0
Oct-97	44,164	10	105.6	8.5	0	0	0	0	0	0	0	0	1	0	0
Nov-97	38,715	11	107.2	8.5	0	0	0	0	0	0	0	0	0	1	0
Dec-97	40,561	12	102.1	8.5	0	0	0	0	0	0	0	0	0	0	1
Jan-98	39,755	13	106.6	8.5	0	0	0	0	0	0	0	0	0	0	0
Feb-98	39,981	14	110.4	8.5	1	0	0	0	0	0	0	0	0	0	0
Mar-98	47,285	15	106.5	8.5	0	1	0	0	0	0	0	0	0	0	0
Apr-98	47,102	16	108.7	8.5	0	0	1	0	0	0	0	0	0	0	0
May-98	48,975	17	106.5	8.5	0	0	0	1	0	0	0	0	0	0	0
Jun-98	51,208	18	105.6	8.5	0	0	0	0	1	0	0	0	0	0	0
Jul-98	46,200	19	105.2	8.5	0	0	0	0	0	1	0	0	0	0	0
Aug-98	44,939	20	104.4	8.5	0	0	0	0	0	0	1	0	0	0	0
Sep-98	44,531	21	100.9	8.49	0	0	0	0	0	0	0	1	0	0	0
Oct-98	46,710	22	97.4	8.12	0	0	0	0	0	0	0	0	1	0	0
Nov-98	41,922	23	102.7	7.89	0	0	0	0	0	0	0	0	0	1	0
Dec-98	43,951	24	100.5	7.75	0	0	0	0	0	0	0	0	0	0	1
Jan-99	42,026	25	103.9	7.75	0	0	0	0	0	0	0	0	0	0	0
Feb-99	45,217	26	108.1	7.75	1	0	0	0	0	0	0	0	0	0	0
Mar-99	53,829	27	105.7	7.75	0	1	0	0	0	0	0	0	0	0	0
Apr-99	50,675	28	104.6	7.75	0	0	1	0	0	0	0	0	0	0	0
May-99	53,276	29	106.8	7.75	0	0	0	1	0	0	0	0	0	0	0
Jun-99	54,568	30	107.3	7.75	0	0	0	0	1	0	0	0	0	0	0
Jul-99	54,028	31	106.0	8	0	0	0	0	0	1	0	0	0	0	0
Aug-99	55,562	32	104.5	8.06	0	0	0	0	0	0	1	0	0	0	0
Sep-99	51,577	33	107.2	8.25	0	0	0	0	0	0	0	1	0	0	0
Oct-99	49,387	34	103.2	8.25	0	0	0	0	0	0	0	0	1	0	0
Nov-99	47,703	35	107.2	8.37	0	0	0	0	0	0	0	0	0	1	0
Dec-99	48,319	36	105.4	8.5	0	0	0	0	0	0	0	0	0	0	1
Jan-00	47,038	37	112.0	8.5	0	0	0	0	0	0	0	0	0	0	0
Feb-00	53,507	38	111.3	8.73	1	0	0	0	0	0	0	0	0	0	0
Mar-00	59,385	39	107.1	8.83	0	1	0	0	0	0	0	0	0	0	0

(continued on next page)

TABLE 5.5   (continued)

Date	NCS	Time	ICS	Prime	feb	mar	apr	may	jun	jul	aug	sep	oct	nov	dec
Apr-00	51,686	40	109.2	9	0	0	1	0	0	0	0	0	0	0	0
May-00	57,483	41	110.7	9.24	0	0	0	1	0	0	0	0	0	0	0
Jun-00	57,237	42	106.4	9.5	0	0	0	0	1	0	0	0	0	0	0
Jul-00	52,953	43	108.3	9.5	0	0	0	0	0	1	0	0	0	0	0
Aug-00	56,929	44	107.3	9.5	0	0	0	0	0	0	1	0	0	0	0
Sep-00	52,109	45	106.8	9.5	0	0	0	0	0	0	0	1	0	0	0
Oct-00	50,740	46	105.8	9.5	0	0	0	0	0	0	0	0	1	0	0
Nov-00	46,452	47	107.6	9.5	0	0	0	0	0	0	0	0	0	1	0
Dec-00	44,604	48	98.4	9.5	0	0	0	0	0	0	0	0	0	0	1
Jan-01	47,298	49	94.7	9.05	0	0	0	0	0	0	0	0	0	0	0
Feb-01	49,242	50	90.6	8.5	1	0	0	0	0	0	0	0	0	0	0
Mar-01	56,665	51	91.5	8.32	0	1	0	0	0	0	0	0	0	0	0
Apr-01	52,329	52	88.4	7.8	0	0	1	0	0	0	0	0	0	0	0
May-01	58,137	53	92.0	7.24	0	0	0	1	0	0	0	0	0	0	0
Jun-01	57,020	54	92.6	6.98	0	0	0	0	1	0	0	0	0	0	0
Jul-01	54,087	55	92.4	6.75	0	0	0	0	0	1	0	0	0	0	0
Aug-01	58,126	56	91.5	6.67	0	0	0	0	0	0	1	0	0	0	0
Sep-01	48,656	57	81.8	6.28	0	0	0	0	0	0	0	1	0	0	0
Oct-01	65,956	58	82.7	5.53	0	0	0	0	0	0	0	0	1	0	0
Nov-01	52,701	59	83.9	5.1	0	0	0	0	0	0	0	0	0	1	0
Dec-01	49,196	60	88.8	4.84	0	0	0	0	0	0	0	0	0	0	1
Jan-02	48,169	61	93.0	4.75	0	0	0	0	0	0	0	0	0	0	0
Feb-02	49,618	62	90.7	4.75	1	0	0	0	0	0	0	0	0	0	0
Mar-02	54,935	63	95.7	4.75	0	1	0	0	0	0	0	0	0	0	0
Apr-02	55,013	64	93.0	4.75	0	0	1	0	0	0	0	0	0	0	0
May-02	55,706	65	96.9	4.75	0	0	0	1	0	0	0	0	0	0	0
Jun-02	55,398	66	92.4	4.75	0	0	0	0	1	0	0	0	0	0	0
Jul-02	60,611	67	88.1	4.75	0	0	0	0	0	1	0	0	0	0	0
Aug-02	63,691	68	87.6	4.75	0	0	0	0	0	0	1	0	0	0	0
Sep-02	51,564	69	86.1	4.75	0	0	0	0	0	0	0	1	0	0	0
Oct-02	52,236	70	80.6	4.75	0	0	0	0	0	0	0	0	1	0	0
Nov-02	47,693	71	84.2	4.35	0	0	0	0	0	0	0	0	0	1	0
Dec-02	51,125	72	86.7	4.25	0	0	0	0	0	0	0	0	0	0	1
Jan-03	49,072	73	82.4	4.25	0	0	0	0	0	0	0	0	0	0	0
Feb-03	47,557	74	79.9	4.25	1	0	0	0	0	0	0	0	0	0	0
Mar-03	55,849	75	77.6	4.25	0	1	0	0	0	0	0	0	0	0	0
Apr-03	55,593	76	86.0	4.25	0	0	1	0	0	0	0	0	0	0	0
May-03	59,308	77	92.1	4.25	0	0	0	1	0	0	0	0	0	0	0
Jun-03	57,881	78	89.7	4.22	0	0	0	0	1	0	0	0	0	0	0
Jul-03	61,200	79	90.9	4	0	0	0	0	0	1	0	0	0	0	0
Aug-03	61,111	80	89.3	4	0	0	0	0	0	0	1	0	0	0	0

Date	NCS	Time	ICS	Prime	feb	mar	apr	may	jun	jul	aug	sep	oct	nov	dec
Sep-03	55,067	81	87.7	4	0	0	0	0	0	0	0	1	0	0	0
Oct-03	52,839	82	89.6	4	0	0	0	0	0	0	0	0	1	0	0
Nov-03	48,326	83	93.7	4	0	0	0	0	0	0	0	0	0	1	0
Dec-03	53,082	84	92.6	4	0	0	0	0	0	0	0	0	0	0	1
Jan-04	47,627	85	103.8	4	0	0	0	0	0	0	0	0	0	0	0
Feb-04	50,313	86	94.4	4	1	0	0	0	0	0	0	0	0	0	0
Mar-04	60,297	87	95.8	4	0	1	0	0	0	0	0	0	0	0	0
Apr-04	55,239	88	94.2	4	0	0	1	0	0	0	0	0	0	0	0
May-04	58,950	89	90.2	4	0	0	0	1	0	0	0	0	0	0	0
Jun-04	56,874	90	95.6	4.01	0	0	0	0	1	0	0	0	0	0	0
Jul-04	60,424	91	96.7	4.25	0	0	0	0	0	1	0	0	0	0	0
Aug-04	58,803	92	95.9	4.43	0	0	0	0	0	0	1	0	0	0	0
Sep-04	57,519	93	94.2	4.58	0	0	0	0	0	0	0	1	0	0	0
Oct-04	52,694	94	91.7	4.75	0	0	0	0	0	0	0	0	1	0	0
Nov-04	50,286	95	92.8	4.93	0	0	0	0	0	0	0	0	0	1	0
Dec-04	56,868	96	97.1	5.15	0	0	0	0	0	0	0	0	0	0	1
Jan-05	47,268	97	95.5	5.25	0	0	0	0	0	0	0	0	0	0	0
Feb-05	50,452	98	94.1	5.49	1	0	0	0	0	0	0	0	0	0	0
Mar-05	60,854	99	92.6	5.58	0	1	0	0	0	0	0	0	0	0	0
Apr-05	57,975	100	87.7	5.75	0	0	1	0	0	0	0	0	0	0	0
May-05	58,902	101	86.9	5.98	0	0	0	1	0	0	0	0	0	0	0
Jun-05	64,957	102	96.0	6.01	0	0	0	0	1	0	0	0	0	0	0
Jul-05	68,573	103	96.5	6.25	0	0	0	0	0	1	0	0	0	0	0
Aug-05	61,927	104	89.1	6.44	0	0	0	0	0	0	1	0	0	0	0
Sep-05	52,666	105	76.9	6.59	0	0	0	0	0	0	0	1	0	0	0
Oct-05	47,549	106	74.2	6.75	0	0	0	0	0	0	0	0	1	0	0
Nov-05	49,323	107	81.6	7	0	0	0	0	0	0	0	0	0	1	0
Dec-05	55,280	108	91.5	7.15	0	0	0	0	0	0	0	0	0	0	1
Jan-06	49,726	109	91.2	7.26	0	0	0	0	0	0	0	0	0	0	0
Feb-06	50,426	110	86.7	7.5	1	0	0	0	0	0	0	0	0	0	0
Mar-06	61,857	111	88.9	7.53	0	1	0	0	0	0	0	0	0	0	0
Apr-06	55,942	112	87.4	7.75	0	0	1	0	0	0	0	0	0	0	0
May-06	60,066	113	79.1	7.93	0	0	0	1	0	0	0	0	0	0	0
Jun-06	59,569	114	84.9	8.02	0	0	0	0	1	0	0	0	0	0	0
Jul-06	61,067	115	84.7	8.25	0	0	0	0	0	1	0	0	0	0	0
Aug-06	62,997	116	82.0	8.25	0	0	0	0	0	0	1	0	0	0	0
Sep-06	55,016	117	85.4	8.25	0	0	0	0	0	0	0	1	0	0	0
Oct-06	52,740	118	93.6	8.25	0	0	0	0	0	0	0	0	1	0	0
Nov-06	51,072	119	92.1	8.25	0	0	0	0	0	0	0	0	0	1	0
Dec-06	54,991	120	91.7	8.25	0	0	0	0	0	0	0	0	0	0	1

(continued on next page)

TABLE 5.5 (continued)

Date	NCS	Time	ICS	Prime	feb	mar	apr	may	jun	jul	aug	sep	oct	nov	dec
Jan-07	51,064	121	96.9	8.25	0	0	0	0	0	0	0	0	0	0	0
Feb-07	53,428	122	91.3	8.25	1	0	0	0	0	0	0	0	0	0	0
Mar-07	63,804	123	88.4	8.25	0	1	0	0	0	0	0	0	0	0	0
Apr-07	57,967	124	87.1	8.25	0	0	1	0	0	0	0	0	0	0	0
May-07	63,714	125	88.3	8.25	0	0	0	1	0	0	0	0	0	0	0
Jun-07	59,607	126	85.3	8.25	0	0	0	0	1	0	0	0	0	0	0
Jul-07	59,933	127	90.4	8.25	0	0	0	0	0	1	0	0	0	0	0
Aug-07	64,575	128	83.4	8.25	0	0	0	0	0	0	1	0	0	0	0
Sep-07	56,349	129	83.4	8.03	0	0	0	0	0	0	0	1	0	0	0
Oct-07	56,855	130	80.9	7.74	0	0	0	0	0	0	0	0	1	0	0
Nov-07	51,856	131	76.1	7.5	0	0	0	0	0	0	0	0	0	1	0
Dec-07	54,106	132	75.5	7.33	0	0	0	0	0	0	0	0	0	0	1

the Index of Consumer Sentiment (ICS), the prime rate (Prime), and the 11 dummy variables for seasonality as independent variables. The model is:

$$NCS = b_0 + 1b_1(\text{Time}) + b_2(\text{ICS}) + b_3(\text{Prime}) + b_4(\text{feb}) + b_5(\text{mar})$$
$$+ b_6(\text{apr}) + b_7(\text{may}) + b_8(\text{jun}) + b_9(\text{jul}) + b_{10}(\text{aug})$$
$$+ b_{11}(\text{sep}) + b_{12}(\text{oct}) + b_{13}(\text{nov}) + b_{14}(\text{dec})$$

In this model we would expect b_1 to have a positive sign (because sales are generally rising over time), and we would expect b_2 (the Index of Consumer Sentiment) to have a positive sign. We should expect b_3 to have a negative sign (as the prime rate rises, cars essentially become more expensive). We would expect b_4 through b_{14} (the seasonal dummy variables) to have signs representing their relationship to the omitted, or base, month (i.e., January). Since January is, on average, the worst month of the year for sales, we would expect all the seasonal dummy variables to exhibit positive coefficients.

Regression results for this model are shown in Table 5.6 along with the results for NCS $= f$ (Prime), where the prime rate (Prime) is the only independent variable; this model is labeled NCSF1. Also shown is the result for NCS $= f$ (Time, ICS, Prime), where Time is the index of time and ICS is the Index of Consumer Sentiment. Both models hold out the 2007 year data for these estimations. This second model is labeled NCSF2. The final model (NCSF3) displayed in Table 5.6 includes all 11 dummy variables for all the months except January.

The two models that exclude the seasonal dummy variables (NCSF1 and NCSF2) are shown here to facilitate comparison. Looking at the output at the top of Table 5.6, you see that the signs for the coefficients are all consistent with our expectations.

TABLE 5.6 **Regression Results for New Car Sales (NCS)** (c5t5)

Single Independent Variable Regression NCSF1

Audit Trail--ANOVA Table (Multiple Regression Selected)

Source of Variation	SS	df	MS	SEE
Regression	672,100,235.96	1	672,100,235.96	
Error	4,062,420,183.96	118	34,427,289.69	5,867.48
Total	4,734,520,419.93	119		

Audit Trail--Coefficient Table (Multiple Regression Selected)

Series Description	Included in model	Coefficient	Standard error	T-test	Elasticity	Overall F-test
NCS	Dependent	60,915.30	2,038.53	29.88		19.52
Prime	Yes	−1,273.75	288.28	−4.42	−0.17	

Audit Trail--Statistics

Accuracy Measures	Value	Forecast Statistics	Value
AIC	2,423.05	Durbin Watson (12)	0.48
BIC	2,425.84	Mean	52,224.73
Mean Absolute Percentage Error (MAPE)	9.41%	Standard Deviation	6,307.61
R-Square	14.20%	Ljung-Box	364.24
Adjusted R-Square	14.20%		
Root Mean Square Error	5,818.38		
Theil	1.24		

Two-Independent Variable Regression NCSF2

Audit Trail--ANOVA Table (Multiple Regression Selected)

Source of variation	SS	df	MS	SEE
Regression	1,918,975,688.04	3	639,658,562.68	
Error	2,815,544,731.88	116	24,271,937.34	4,926.66
Total	4,734,520,419.93	119		

Audit Trail--Coefficient Table (Multiple Regression Selected)

Series Description	Included in model	Coefficient	Standard error	T-test	P-value	F-test	Elasticity	Overall F-test
NCS	Dependent	37,947.63	7,653.65	4.96	0.00	24.58		26.35
Time	Yes	121.52	18.85	6.45	0.00	41.56	0.14	
ICS	Yes	99.95	75.69	1.32	0.19	1.74	0.18	
Prime	Yes	−389.44	301.70	−1.29	0.20	1.67	−0.05	

(continued on next page)

TABLE 5.6   (continued)

Audit Trail--Statistics

Accuracy Measures	Value	Forecast Statistics	Value
AIC	2,379.06	Durbin Watson (12)	0.52
BIC	2,381.84	Standard Deviation	6,307.61
Mean Absolute Percentage Error (MAPE)	7.61%	Ljung-Box	47.26
R-Square	40.53%		
Adjusted R-Square	40.53%		
Root Mean Square Error	4,843.85		
Theil	1.03		

Regression with Seasonal Dummy Variables NCSF3

Audit Trail--ANOVA Table (Multiple Regression Selected)

Source of variation	SS	df	MS	SEE
Regression	3,653,230,823.64	14	260,945,058.83	
Error	1,081,289,596.28	105	10,297,996.16	3,209.05
Total	4,734,520,419.93	119		

Audit Trail--Coefficient Table (Multiple Regression Selected)

Series Description	Included in model	Coefficient	Standard error	T-test	P-value	F-test	Elasticity	Overall F-test
NCS	Dependent	33,384.54	5,236.70	6.38	0.00	40.64		25.34
Time	Yes	119.10	12.39	9.61	0.00	92.43	0.14	
ICS	Yes	86.53	50.64	1.71	0.09	2.92	0.16	
Prime	Yes	-403.93	198.28	-2.04	0.04	4.15	-0.05	
feb	Yes	1,955.09	1,436.77	1.36	0.18	1.85	0.00	
mar	Yes	9,935.26	1,437.75	6.91	0.00	47.75	0.02	
apr	Yes	6,706.77	1,437.92	4.66	0.00	21.76	0.01	
may	Yes	9,640.32	1,436.97	6.71	0.00	45.01	0.02	
jun	Yes	9,777.64	1,436.28	6.81	0.00	46.34	0.02	
jul	Yes	10,205.05	1,437.06	7.10	0.00	50.43	0.02	
aug	Yes	10,767.27	1,440.24	7.48	0.00	55.89	0.02	
sep	Yes	5,069.01	1,451.44	3.49	0.00	12.20	0.01	
oct	Yes	5,258.81	1,455.79	3.61	0.00	13.05	0.01	
nov	Yes	789.44	1,440.40	0.55	0.58	0.30	0.00	
dec	Yes	3,033.16	1,440.46	2.11	0.04	4.43	0.00	

Audit Trail--Statistics

Accuracy Measures	Value	Forecast Statistics	Value
AIC	2,264.22	Durbin-Watson (12)	1.34
BIC	2,267.00	Standard Deviation	6,307.61
Mean Absolute Percentage Error (MAPE)	4.23%	Ljung-Box	46.26
R-Square	77.16%		
Adjusted R-Square	77.16%		
Root Mean Square Error	3,001.79		
Theil	0.65		

A comparison of the three regression results shown in Table 5.6 shows that important improvements result from adding the seasonal dummy variables. Note that the model with the seasonal dummy variables explains about 77.16 percent of the variation in new cars sold (see the adjusted *R*-squared), which is a considerable improvement over the two other models' adjusted *R*-squareds of 14.20 percent and 40.53 percent. The AIC and BIC for NCSF3 both fall by more than 10 when compared to NCSF2, reflecting substantial improvement from the addition of the seasonal dummy variables. Also, the standard error of the regression (labeled SEE in ForecastX™) has fallen from 4,926.66 to 2,309.05. The Durbin-Watson twelfth-order DW (12) statistic shows improvement as the seasonal dummy variables are added. Apparently, some of the serial correlation present in the simpler models was as a result of not accounting for the rather heavy seasonal variation in the dependent variable. In the next section, we will work further with this NCS model and see further improvement in the Durbin-Watson statistic.

Let us now use these models to make forecasts for each of the 12 months of 2007. The independent variables in the forecast period are automatically estimated using exponential smoothing by ForecastX™.

Date	NCS	NCSF1	NCSF2	NCSF3
Jan-07	51064	50,400.88	58,605.53	52,399.32
Feb-07	53428	50,394.89	58,725.01	54,471.41
Mar-07	63804	50,388.89	58,844.49	62,568.58
Apr-07	57967	50,382.90	58,963.97	59,457.09
May-07	63714	50,376.91	59,083.45	62,507.65
Jun-07	59607	50,370.92	59,202.94	62,761.97
Jul-07	59933	50,364.92	59,322.42	63,306.38
Aug-07	64575	50,358.93	59,441.90	63,985.60
Sep-07	56349	50,352.94	59,561.38	58,404.34
Oct-07	56855	50,346.94	59,680.86	58,711.14
Nov-07	51856	50,340.95	59,800.34	54,358.77
Dec-07	54106	50,334.96	59,919.82	56,719.50

where:

NCS = Actual new cars sold
NCSF1 = Forecasts of NCS using only the prime rate as an independent variable
NCSF2 = Forecasts of NCS using the prime rate, a time index, and the Index of Consumer Sentiment as independent variables
NCSF3 = Forecasts of NCS with the seasonal dummies included

Note that ForecastX™ produced these estimates by first forecasting the independent variables and then using these estimates with the estimated regression model to produce the forecasts of NCS. The forecasts of all three models for the historical period (i.e., 1997 through 2006) are plotted in Figure 5.6 along with the actual and fitted values. If you examine Figure 5.6, you will see how much better the multiple-regression model with the seasonal dummies appears to be in comparison with the other two models of new cars sold. To see whether the model with the seasonal dummies (NCSF3) actually did provide better forecasts for the 12 months of 2007, let us look at the root-mean-squared error (RMSE) for these models:

Holdout Period (2007) Forecast RMSE for NCSF1

	Forecast	Actual	$(A_t - F_t)$	$(A_t - F_t)^2$
Jan-07	50,400.88	51,064	663.12	439,727.68
Feb-07	50,394.89	53,428	3,033.11	9,199,772.22
Mar-07	50,388.89	63,804	13,415.11	179,965,058.25
Apr-07	50,382.90	57,967	7,584.10	57,518,551.12
May-07	50,376.91	63,714	13,337.09	177,878,010.77
Jun-07	50,370.92	59,607	9,236.08	85,305,257.10
Jul-07	50,364.92	59,933	9,568.08	91,548,106.70
Aug-07	50,358.93	64,575	14,216.07	202,096,659.10
Sep-07	50,352.94	56,349	5,996.06	35,952,776.57
Oct-07	50,346.94	56,855	6,508.06	42,354,798.02
Nov-07	50,340.95	51,856	1,515.05	2,295,374.57
Dec-07	50,334.96	54,106	3,771.04	14,220,760.29

RMSE = 8,654

Holdout Period (2007) Forecast RMSE for NCSF2

	Forecast	Actual	$(A_t - F_t)$	$(A_t - F_t)^2$
Jan-07	58,605.53	51,064	−7,541.53	56,874,687.68
Feb-07	58,725.01	53,428	−5,297.01	28,058,333.17
Mar-07	58,844.49	63,804	4,959.51	24,596,713.81
Apr-07	58,963.97	57,967	−996.97	993,956.06
May-07	59,083.45	63,714	4,630.55	21,441,953.38
Jun-07	59,202.94	59,607	404.06	163,268.38
Jul-07	59,322.42	59,933	610.58	372,812.77
Aug-07	59,441.90	64,575	5,133.10	26,348,747.42
Sep-07	59,561.38	56,349	−3,212.38	10,319,370.90
Oct-07	59,680.86	56,855	−2,825.86	7,985,476.99
Nov-07	59,800.34	51,856	−7,944.34	63,112,529.96
Dec-07	59,919.82	54,106	−5,813.82	33,800,507.12

RMSE = 4,779

Holdout Period (2007) Forecast RMSE for NCSF3

	Forecast	Actual	$(A_t - F_t)$	$(A_t - F_t)^2$
Jan-07	52,399.32	51,064	−1,335.32	1,783,078.88
Feb-07	54,471.41	53,428	−1,043.41	1,088,699.48
Mar-07	62,568.58	63,804	1,235.42	1,526,269.17
Apr-07	59,457.09	57,967	−1,490.09	2,220,372.89
May-07	62,507.65	63,714	1,206.35	1,455,291.94
Jun-07	62,761.97	59,607	−3,154.97	9,953,807.01
Jul-07	63,306.38	59,933	−3,373.38	11,379,668.74
Aug-07	63,985.60	64,575	589.40	347,395.37
Sep-07	58,404.34	56,349	−2,055.34	4,224,418.99
Oct-07	58,711.14	56,855	−1,856.14	3,445,250.10
Nov-07	54,358.77	51,856	−2,502.77	6,263,874.44
Dec-07	56,719.50	54,106	−2,613.50	6,830,364.91

RMSE = 2,052

FIGURE 5.6
New Cars Sold (NCS) with Three Forecasting Models: NCSF1, NCSF2, and NCSF3 (c5t5)

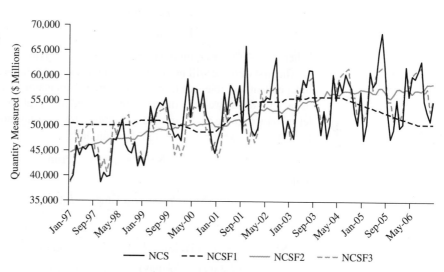

The RMSE of 2,052 for NCSF3 (the model with seasonal dummies) compares favorably with an RMSE of 8,654 for NCSF1 (the model using only the prime rate as an independent variable) and an RMSE of 4,779 for NCSF2 (the model using the time index, the prime rate, and the Index of Consumer Sentiment as independent variables). The conclusion is that adding the seasonal dummy variables significantly increased both the accuracy and the fit of the model.

EXTENSIONS OF THE MULTIPLE-REGRESSION MODEL

In some situations nonlinear terms may be called for as independent variables in a regression analysis. Why? Business or economic logic may suggest that some nonlinearity is expected. A graphic display of the data may be helpful in determining whether the nonlinearity occurs over time. One common cause for nonlinearity is diminishing returns. For example, the effect of advertising on sales may diminish on a dollar-spent basis as increased advertising is used. Another common cause is referred to an Engel's law: As an individual's income doubles, the amount spent on food usually less than doubles (i.e., the proportion spent on food decreases). Both these situations are properly modeled as nonlinearities. In this section we will add the square of the time index as an independent variable to the multiple-regression model that includes seasonal dummy variables and investigate if the growth rate in new car sales is diminishing over time (i.e., if new car sales is growing at a slower rate over the time period of our data).

Some common forms of nonlinear functions are the following:

$$Y = b_0 + b_1(X) + b_2(X^2)$$
$$Y = b_0 + b_1(X) + b_2(X^2) + (X^3)$$
$$Y = b_0 + b_1(1/X)$$
$$Y = B_0 X^{b_1}$$

Where $B_0 = e^{b_0}$, based on the regression of $\ln Y = f(\ln X) = b_0 + b_1(\ln X)$.

The first of these will be shown later in this section. In these examples only one independent variable (X) is shown but other explanatory variables could be used in each model as well. To illustrate the use and interpretation of a nonlinear term, let us return to the problem of developing a forecasting model for new car sales (NCS). So far we have estimated three models:

$$\text{NSC} = b_0 + 1b_1(\text{Prime})$$

and

$$\text{NSC} = b_0 + 1b_1(\text{Time}) + b_2(\text{ICS}) + b_3(\text{Prime})$$

and

$$\text{NSC} = b_0 + 1b_1(\text{Time}) + b_2(\text{ICS}) + b_3(\text{Prime}) + b_4(\text{feb}) + b_5(\text{mar})$$
$$+ b_6(\text{apr}) + b_7(\text{may}) + b_8(\text{jun}) + b_9(\text{jul}) + b_{10}(\text{aug})$$
$$+ b_{11}(\text{sep}) + b_{12}(\text{oct}) + b_{13}(\text{nov}) + b_{14}(\text{dec})$$

Where Time = the index of time, Prime = the bank prime loan rate, ICS = the Index of Consumer Sentiment, and feb, mar, and so on are dummy variables for the months of the year. Our results have been encouraging, the best of these—in terms of adjusted R-squared and RMSE (NCSF3)—explaining about 77 percent of the variation in NCS during the historical period but with some twelfth-order serial correlation. Results for an additional regression model for NCS labeled NCSF4 are summarized in Table 5.7.

TABLE 5.7   **Estimated Regression with Nonlinear Independent Variable**

Audit Trail--ANOVA Table (Multiple Regression Selected)

Source of Variation	SS	df	MS	SEE
Regression	3,928,895,790.97	14	280,635,413.64	
Error	805,624,628.95	105	7,672,615.51	2,769.95
Total	4,734,520,419.93	119		

Audit Trail--Coefficient Table (Multiple Regression Selected)

Series Description	Included in Model	Coefficient	Standard Error	T-test	P-value	F-test	Elasticity	Overall F-test
NCS	Dependent	27,092.58	4,639.49	5.84	0.00	34.10		36.58
Time	Yes	313.96	31.41	10.00	0.00	99.94	0.36	
ICS	Yes	79.23	40.96	1.93	0.06	3.74	0.15	
T Sq	Yes	-1.53	0.24	-6.44	0.00	41.50	-0.14	
feb	Yes	1,912.75	1,239.87	1.54	0.13	2.38	0.00	
mar	Yes	9,863.83	1,240.43	7.95	0.00	63.23	0.02	
apr	Yes	6,605.96	1,240.32	5.33	0.00	28.37	0.01	
may	Yes	9,522.60	1,239.61	7.68	0.00	59.01	0.02	
jun	Yes	9,650.62	1,239.43	7.79	0.00	60.63	0.02	
jul	Yes	10,048.15	1,239.87	8.10	0.00	65.68	0.02	
aug	Yes	10,574.82	1,240.70	8.52	0.00	72.65	0.02	
sep	Yes	4,852.32	1,247.27	3.89	0.00	15.13	0.01	
oct	Yes	5,066.98	1,250.89	4.05	0.00	16.41	0.01	
nov	Yes	641.37	1,241.46	0.52	0.61	0.27	0.00	
dec	Yes	2,891.75	1,241.57	2.33	0.02	5.42	0.00	

Audit Trail--Statistics

Accuracy Measures	Value	Forecast Statistics	Value
AIC	2,228.90	Durbin Watson (12)	1.72
BIC	2,231.69	Standard Deviation	6,307.61
Mean Absolute Percentage Error (MAPE)	3.40%	Ljung-Box	6.25
R-Square	82.98%		
Adjusted R-Square	82.98%		
Root Mean Square Error	2,591.05		
Theil	0.54		

It is in this fourth model (NCSF4) that we introduce a nonlinear term into the regression. The square of the time index variable (T Sq) is included in the regression model and the prime rate variable is removed. The *t*-statistic for the time squared variable (T Sq) is −6.44. This fourth model increases the adjusted *R*-squared to 82.98 percent. The standard error of the estimate falls to 2,769.95 and the DW(12) increases to 1.72.

The values for actual new car sales and the forecast for this model are plotted in Figure 5.7. The forecast values (NCSF4) are seen to follow the actual data quite well throughout the historical period. If you compare the forecast

FIGURE 5.7
New Car Sales (NCS)
with Fitted Values
(NCSF4) (c5t5)

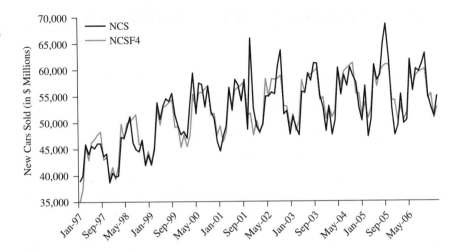

values in Figures 5.6 and 5.7, you can see the improvement between NCSF3 and NCSF4 visually. This graphic comparison should reinforce the statistical findings for the two models presented in Table 5.7. Note also that the AIC has decreased to 2,228.90 in NCSF4 from 2,264.22 in NCSF3. Data that were used in all of the regression models for new car sales (NCS) are shown in Table 5.8.

ADVICE ON USING MULTIPLE REGRESSION IN FORECASTING

Multiple-regression models are a very important part of the set of tools available to anyone interested in forecasting. Apart from their use in generating forecasts, they have considerable value in helping us to uncover structural relationships between the dependent variable and some set of independent variables. Knowing such relationships helps the forecaster understand the sensitivity of the variable to be forecast to other factors. This enhancement of our understanding of the business environment can only serve to improve our ability to make judgments about the future course of events. It is important not to downplay the role of judgments in forecasting. No one should ever rely solely on some quantitative procedure in developing a forecast. Expert judgments are crucial, and multiple-regression analyses can be helpful in improving your level of expertise.

In developing forecasts with regression models, perhaps the best advice is to follow the "KIS" principle: keep it simple.[9] The more complex the model becomes, the more difficult it is to use. As more causal variables are used, the cost of maintaining the needed database increases in terms of both time and money. Further, complex models are more difficult to communicate to others who may be the

---

[9] This is also called the *principle of parsimony* by Box and Jenkins. G. E. P. Box and G. M. Jenkins, *Time Series Analysis: Forecasting and Control,* 2nd ed. (San Francisco: Holden Day, 1976).

TABLE 5.8 Data for Regression Models of New Car Sales (NCS)　(c5t5)

Date	NCS	Time	Prime	ICS	T Sq	feb	mar	apr	may	jun	jul	aug	sep	oct	nov	dec
Jan-97	38,922	1	8.25	97.4	1	0	0	0	0	0	0	0	0	0	0	0
Feb-97	40,002	2	8.25	99.7	4	1	0	0	0	0	0	0	0	0	0	0
Mar-97	45,926	3	8.3	100.0	9	0	1	0	0	0	0	0	0	0	0	0
Apr-97	44,068	4	8.5	101.4	16	0	0	1	0	0	0	0	0	0	0	0
May-97	45,638	5	8.5	103.2	25	0	0	0	1	0	0	0	0	0	0	0
Jun-97	45,170	6	8.5	104.5	36	0	0	0	0	1	0	0	0	0	0	0
Jul-97	46,076	7	8.5	107.1	49	0	0	0	0	0	1	0	0	0	0	0
Aug-97	46,084	8	8.5	104.4	64	0	0	0	0	0	0	1	0	0	0	0
Sep-97	43,646	9	8.5	106.0	81	0	0	0	0	0	0	0	1	0	0	0
Oct-97	44,164	10	8.5	105.6	100	0	0	0	0	0	0	0	0	1	0	0
Nov-97	38,715	11	8.5	107.2	121	0	0	0	0	0	0	0	0	0	1	0
Dec-97	40,561	12	8.5	102.1	144	0	0	0	0	0	0	0	0	0	0	1
Jan-98	39,755	13	8.5	106.6	169	0	0	0	0	0	0	0	0	0	0	0
Feb-98	39,981	14	8.5	110.4	196	1	0	0	0	0	0	0	0	0	0	0
Mar-98	47,285	15	8.5	106.5	225	0	1	0	0	0	0	0	0	0	0	0
Apr-98	47,102	16	8.5	108.7	256	0	0	1	0	0	0	0	0	0	0	0
May-98	48,975	17	8.5	106.5	289	0	0	0	1	0	0	0	0	0	0	0
Jun-98	51,208	18	8.5	105.6	324	0	0	0	0	1	0	0	0	0	0	0
Jul-98	46,200	19	8.5	105.2	361	0	0	0	0	0	1	0	0	0	0	0
Aug-98	44,939	20	8.5	104.4	400	0	0	0	0	0	0	1	0	0	0	0
Sep-98	44,531	21	8.49	100.9	441	0	0	0	0	0	0	0	1	0	0	0
Oct-98	46,710	22	8.12	97.4	484	0	0	0	0	0	0	0	0	1	0	0
Nov-98	41,922	23	7.89	102.7	529	0	0	0	0	0	0	0	0	0	1	0
Dec-98	43,951	24	7.75	100.5	576	0	0	0	0	0	0	0	0	0	0	1
Jan-99	42,026	25	7.75	103.9	625	0	0	0	0	0	0	0	0	0	0	0
Feb-99	45,217	26	7.75	108.1	676	1	0	0	0	0	0	0	0	0	0	0
Mar-99	53,829	27	7.75	105.7	729	0	1	0	0	0	0	0	0	0	0	0
Apr-99	50,675	28	7.75	104.6	784	0	0	1	0	0	0	0	0	0	0	0
May-99	53,276	29	7.75	106.8	841	0	0	0	1	0	0	0	0	0	0	0
Jun-99	54,568	30	7.75	107.3	900	0	0	0	0	1	0	0	0	0	0	0
Jul-99	54,028	31	8	106.0	961	0	0	0	0	0	1	0	0	0	0	0
Aug-99	55,562	32	8.06	104.5	1024	0	0	0	0	0	0	1	0	0	0	0
Sep-99	51,577	33	8.25	107.2	1089	0	0	0	0	0	0	0	1	0	0	0

(continued on next page)

TABLE 5.8 (continued)

Date	NCS	Time	Prime	ICS	T Sq	feb	mar	apr	may	jun	jul	aug	sep	oct	nov	dec
Oct-99	49,387	34	8.25	103.2	1156	0	0	0	0	0	0	0	0	1	0	0
Nov-99	47,703	35	8.37	107.2	1225	0	0	0	0	0	0	0	0	0	1	0
Dec-99	48,319	36	8.5	105.4	1296	0	0	0	0	0	0	0	0	0	0	1
Jan-00	47,038	37	8.5	112.0	1369	0	0	0	0	0	0	0	0	0	0	0
Feb-00	53,507	38	8.73	111.3	1444	1	0	0	0	0	0	0	0	0	0	0
Mar-00	59,385	39	8.83	107.1	1521	0	1	0	0	0	0	0	0	0	0	0
Apr-00	51,686	40	9	109.2	1600	0	0	1	0	0	0	0	0	0	0	0
May-00	57,483	41	9.24	110.7	1681	0	0	0	1	0	0	0	0	0	0	0
Jun-00	57,237	42	9.5	106.4	1764	0	0	0	0	1	0	0	0	0	0	0
Jul-00	52,953	43	9.5	108.3	1849	0	0	0	0	0	1	0	0	0	0	0
Aug-00	56,929	44	9.5	107.3	1936	0	0	0	0	0	0	1	0	0	0	0
Sep-00	52,109	45	9.5	106.8	2025	0	0	0	0	0	0	0	1	0	0	0
Oct-00	50,740	46	9.5	105.8	2116	0	0	0	0	0	0	0	0	1	0	0
Nov-00	46,452	47	9.5	107.6	2209	0	0	0	0	0	0	0	0	0	1	0
Dec-00	44,604	48	9.5	98.4	2304	0	0	0	0	0	0	0	0	0	0	1
Jan-01	47,298	49	9.05	94.7	2401	0	0	0	0	0	0	0	0	0	0	0
Feb-01	49,242	50	8.5	90.6	2500	1	0	0	0	0	0	0	0	0	0	0
Mar-01	56,665	51	8.32	91.5	2601	0	1	0	0	0	0	0	0	0	0	0
Apr-01	52,329	52	7.8	88.4	2704	0	0	1	0	0	0	0	0	0	0	0
May-01	58,137	53	7.24	92.0	2809	0	0	0	1	0	0	0	0	0	0	0
Jun-01	57,020	54	6.98	92.6	2916	0	0	0	0	1	0	0	0	0	0	0
Jul-01	54,087	55	6.75	92.4	3025	0	0	0	0	0	1	0	0	0	0	0
Aug-01	58,126	56	6.67	91.5	3136	0	0	0	0	0	0	1	0	0	0	0
Sep-01	48,656	57	6.28	81.8	3249	0	0	0	0	0	0	0	1	0	0	0
Oct-01	65,956	58	5.53	82.7	3364	0	0	0	0	0	0	0	0	1	0	0
Nov-01	52,701	59	5.1	83.9	3481	0	0	0	0	0	0	0	0	0	1	0
Dec-01	49,196	60	4.84	88.8	3600	0	0	0	0	0	0	0	0	0	0	1
Jan-02	48,169	61	4.75	93.0	3721	0	0	0	0	0	0	0	0	0	0	0
Feb-02	49,618	62	4.75	90.7	3844	1	0	0	0	0	0	0	0	0	0	0
Mar-02	54,935	63	4.75	95.7	3969	0	1	0	0	0	0	0	0	0	0	0
Apr-02	55,013	64	4.75	93.0	4096	0	0	1	0	0	0	0	0	0	0	0
May-02	55,706	65	4.75	96.9	4225	0	0	0	1	0	0	0	0	0	0	0
Jun-02	55,398	66	4.75	92.4	4356	0	0	0	0	1	0	0	0	0	0	0
Jul-02	60,611	67	4.75	88.1	4489	0	0	0	0	0	1	0	0	0	0	0

Date	NCS	Time	Prime	ICS	T Sq	feb	mar	apr	may	jun	jul	aug	sep	oct	nov	dec
Aug-02	63,691	68	4.75	87.6	4624	0	0	0	0	0	0	1	0	0	0	0
Sep-02	51,564	69	4.75	86.1	4761	0	0	0	0	0	0	0	1	0	0	0
Oct-02	52,236	70	4.75	80.6	4900	0	0	0	0	0	0	0	0	1	0	0
Nov-02	47,693	71	4.35	84.2	5041	0	0	0	0	0	0	0	0	0	1	0
Dec-02	51,125	72	4.25	86.7	5184	0	0	0	0	0	0	0	0	0	0	1
Jan-03	49,072	73	4.25	82.4	5329	0	0	0	0	0	0	0	0	0	0	0
Feb-03	47,557	74	4.25	79.9	5476	1	0	0	0	0	0	0	0	0	0	0
Mar-03	55,849	75	4.25	77.6	5625	0	1	0	0	0	0	0	0	0	0	0
Apr-03	55,593	76	4.25	86.0	5776	0	0	1	0	0	0	0	0	0	0	0
May-03	59,308	77	4.25	92.1	5929	0	0	0	1	0	0	0	0	0	0	0
Jun-03	57,881	78	4.22	89.7	6084	0	0	0	0	1	0	0	0	0	0	0
Jul-03	61,200	79	4	90.9	6241	0	0	0	0	0	1	0	0	0	0	0
Aug-03	61,111	80	4	89.3	6400	0	0	0	0	0	0	1	0	0	0	0
Sep-03	55,067	81	4	87.7	6561	0	0	0	0	0	0	0	1	0	0	0
Oct-03	52,839	82	4	89.6	6724	0	0	0	0	0	0	0	0	1	0	0
Nov-03	48,326	83	4	93.7	6889	0	0	0	0	0	0	0	0	0	1	0
Dec-03	53,082	84	4	92.6	7056	0	0	0	0	0	0	0	0	0	0	1
Jan-04	47,627	85	4	103.8	7225	0	0	0	0	0	0	0	0	0	0	0
Feb-04	50,313	86	4	94.4	7396	1	0	0	0	0	0	0	0	0	0	0
Mar-04	60,297	87	4	95.8	7569	0	1	0	0	0	0	0	0	0	0	0
Apr-04	55,239	88	4	94.2	7744	0	0	1	0	0	0	0	0	0	0	0
May-04	58,950	89	4	90.2	7921	0	0	0	1	0	0	0	0	0	0	0
Jun-04	56,874	90	4.01	95.6	8100	0	0	0	0	1	0	0	0	0	0	0
Jul-04	60,424	91	4.25	96.7	8281	0	0	0	0	0	1	0	0	0	0	0
Aug-04	58,803	92	4.43	95.9	8464	0	0	0	0	0	0	1	0	0	0	0
Sep-04	57,519	93	4.58	94.2	8649	0	0	0	0	0	0	0	1	0	0	0
Oct-04	52,694	94	4.75	91.7	8836	0	0	0	0	0	0	0	0	1	0	0
Nov-04	50,286	95	4.93	92.8	9025	0	0	0	0	0	0	0	0	0	1	0
Dec-04	56,868	96	5.15	97.1	9216	0	0	0	0	0	0	0	0	0	0	1
Jan-05	47,268	97	5.25	95.5	9409	0	0	0	0	0	0	0	0	0	0	0
Feb-05	50,452	98	5.49	94.1	9604	1	0	0	0	0	0	0	0	0	0	0
Mar-05	60,854	99	5.58	92.6	9801	0	1	0	0	0	0	0	0	0	0	0
Apr-05	57,975	100	5.75	87.7	10000	0	0	1	0	0	0	0	0	0	0	0
May-05	58,902	101	5.98	86.9	10201	0	0	0	1	0	0	0	0	0	0	0
Jun-05	64,957	102	6.01	96.0	10404	0	0	0	0	1	0	0	0	0	0	0

(continued on next page)

TABLE 5.8 (continued)

Date	NCS	Time	Prime	ICS	T Sq	feb	mar	apr	may	jun	jul	aug	sep	oct	nov	dec
Jul-05	68,573	103	6.25	96.5	10609	0	0	0	0	0	1	0	0	0	0	0
Aug-05	61,927	104	6.44	89.1	10816	0	0	0	0	0	0	1	0	0	0	0
Sep-05	52,666	105	6.59	76.9	11025	0	0	0	0	0	0	0	1	0	0	0
Oct-05	47,549	106	6.75	74.2	11236	0	0	0	0	0	0	0	0	1	0	0
Nov-05	49,323	107	7	81.6	11449	0	0	0	0	0	0	0	0	0	1	0
Dec-05	55,280	108	7.15	91.5	11664	0	0	0	0	0	0	0	0	0	0	1
Jan-06	49,726	109	7.26	91.2	11881	0	0	0	0	0	0	0	0	0	0	0
Feb-06	50,426	110	7.5	86.7	12100	1	0	0	0	0	0	0	0	0	0	0
Mar-06	61,857	111	7.53	88.9	12321	0	1	0	0	0	0	0	0	0	0	0
Apr-06	55,942	112	7.75	87.4	12544	0	0	1	0	0	0	0	0	0	0	0
May-06	60,066	113	7.93	79.1	12769	0	0	0	1	0	0	0	0	0	0	0
Jun-06	59,569	114	8.02	84.9	12996	0	0	0	0	1	0	0	0	0	0	0
Jul-06	61,067	115	8.25	84.7	13225	0	0	0	0	0	1	0	0	0	0	0
Aug-06	62,997	116	8.25	82.0	13456	0	0	0	0	0	0	1	0	0	0	0
Sep-06	55,016	117	8.25	85.4	13689	0	0	0	0	0	0	0	1	0	0	0
Oct-06	52,740	118	8.25	93.6	13924	0	0	0	0	0	0	0	0	1	0	0
Nov-06	51,072	119	8.25	92.1	14161	0	0	0	0	0	0	0	0	0	1	0
Dec-06	54,991	120	8.25	91.7	14400	0	0	0	0	0	0	0	0	0	0	1
Jan-07	51,064	121	8.25	96.9	14641	0	0	0	0	0	0	0	0	0	0	0
Feb-07	53,428	122	8.25	91.3	14884	1	0	0	0	0	0	0	0	0	0	0
Mar-07	63,804	123	8.25	88.4	15129	0	1	0	0	0	0	0	0	0	0	0
Apr-07	57,967	124	8.25	87.1	15376	0	0	1	0	0	0	0	0	0	0	0
May-07	63,714	125	8.25	88.3	15625	0	0	0	1	0	0	0	0	0	0	0
Jun-07	59,607	126	8.25	85.3	15876	0	0	0	0	1	0	0	0	0	0	0
Jul-07	59,933	127	8.25	90.4	16129	0	0	0	0	0	1	0	0	0	0	0
Aug-07	64,575	128	8.25	83.4	16384	0	0	0	0	0	0	1	0	0	0	0
Sep-07	56,349	129	8.03	83.4	16641	0	0	0	0	0	0	0	1	0	0	0
Oct-07	56,855	130	7.74	80.9	16900	0	0	0	0	0	0	0	0	1	0	0
Nov-07	51,856	131	7.5	76.1	17161	0	0	0	0	0	0	0	0	0	1	0
Dec-07	54,106	132	7.33	75.5	17424	0	0	0	0	0	0	0	0	0	0	1

actual users of the forecast. They are less likely to trust a model that they do not understand than a simpler model that they do understand.

In evaluating alternative multiple-regression models, is it better to compare adjusted R-squared values, or root-mean-squared errors? Remember that R-squared relates to the in-sample period, that is, to the past. A model may work well for the in-sample period but not work nearly so well in forecasting. Thus, it is usually best to focus on RMSE or MAPE for actual forecasts (note that we say "focus on" and not "use exclusively"). You might track the RMSE or MAPE for several alternative models for some period to see whether any one model consistently outperforms others in the forecast horizon. Use the AIC and BIC measures to help select appropriate independent variables. It is also desirable periodically to update the regression models to reflect possible changes in the parameter estimates.

FORECASTING JEWELRY SALES
WITH MULTIPLE REGRESSION

In this section we apply the concepts covered in this chapter to the problem of forecasting jewelry sales by using a multiple-regression model. The explanatory variables selected are based on business logic and are ones for which data are readily available, should you want to look up the most recent data to update the results shown here. Explanatory variables used in the multiple regression are:

DPI = Disposable personal income in constant 1996 dollars (expected sign of coefficient is positive)

UR = The unemployment rate (expected sign negative)

911 = Dummy variable equal to 1 for September and October 2001 (expected sign negative)

feb through dec = Dummy variable equal to 1 for that month and zero otherwise (expected sign thought positive in all months because January is the excluded month)

Two regressions for jewelry sales (JS) are presented in Table 5.9. The data used to generate both regressions appear in Table 5.10.

At the top of Table 5.9 is the regression JS with only disposable personal income (DPI) and the unemployment rate (UR) used as independent variables (2005 data is held out). The overall regression has an adjusted R-squared of only 10.57 percent. The Durbin-Watson(12) statistic is at 0.02.[10] The signs of the coefficient are, however, as expected. JS decreases as DPI falls and as UR increases. The UR variable is, however, insignificant. We show this regression because it is again possible to examine a figure showing the data points with the regression plane superimposed.

---

[10] While the DW(1) calculated value of 2.01 indicates no first-order serial correlation, note that calculating the DW(12) produces a result of 0.02. This would seem to indicate that seasonality is not accounted for by the model.

TABLE 5.9   Regression Results for Jewelry Sales   (c5t10)

Regression with Two Independent Variables

Audit Trail--ANOVA Table (Multiple Regression Selected)

Source of Variation	SS	df	MS	SEE
Regression	19,030,298.69	2	9,515,149.34	
Error	160,943,032.31	153	1,051,915.24	1,025.63
Total	179,973,330.99	155		

Audit Trail--Coefficient Table (Multiple Regression Selected)

Series Description	Included in model	Coefficient	Standard error	T-test	Elasticity	Overall F-test
JS	Dependent	537.90	820.49	0.66		9.05
dpi	Yes	0.25	0.07	3.46	0.90	
UR	Yes	−66.97	90.41	−0.74	−0.20	

Audit Trail--Statistics

Accuracy Measures	Value	Forecast Statistics	Value
AIC	2,604.79	Durbin Watson (12)	0.02
BIC	2,607.84	Mean	1,800.66
Mean Absolute Percentage Error (MAPE)	26.51%	Standard Deviation	1,077.55
R-Square	10.57%	Ljung-Box	439.06
Adjusted R-Square	10.57%		
Root Mean Square Error	1,015.72		
Theil	0.96		

Regression with Additional Variables

Audit Trail--ANOVA Table (Multiple Regression Selected)

Source of Variation	SS	df	MS	SEE
Regression	173,202,541.94	14	12,371,610.14	
Error	6,770,789.06	141	48,019.78	219.13
Total	179,973,330.99	155		

Audit Trail--Coefficient Table (Multiple Regression Selected)

Series Description	Included in model	Coefficient	Standard error	T-test	Elasticity	Overall F-test
JS	Dependent	66.70	184.21	0.36		257.64
dpi	Yes	0.22	0.02	13.95	0.78	
UR	Yes	−59.46	19.33	−3.08	−0.18	
911	Yes	−222.41	162.02	−1.37	0.00	
feb	Yes	476.46	85.95	5.54	0.02	

TABLE 5.9 (continued)

Series Description	Included in model	Coefficient	Standard error	T-test	Elasticity	Overall F-test
mar	Yes	185.51	85.96	2.16	0.01	
apr	Yes	250.96	85.96	2.92	0.01	
may	Yes	621.25	85.97	7.23	0.03	
jun	Yes	361.80	85.98	4.21	0.02	
jul	Yes	284.94	85.99	3.31	0.01	
aug	Yes	353.42	86.00	4.11	0.02	
sep	Yes	260.87	86.86	3.00	0.01	
oct	Yes	350.36	86.88	4.03	0.02	
nov	Yes	783.11	86.03	9.10	0.04	
dec	Yes	3,884.49	86.08	45.13	0.18	

```
Audit Trail--Statistics
```

Accuracy Measures	Value	Forecast Statistics	Value
AIC	2,110.52	Durbin Watson (1)	1.88
BIC	2,113.57	Mean	1,800.66
Mean Absolute Percentage Error (MAPE)	6.78%	Standard Deviation	1,077.55
R-Square	96.24%	Ljung-Box	141.10
Adjusted R-Square	96.24%		
Root Mean Square Error	208.33		
Theil	0.23		

TABLE 5.10 Jewelry Sales Data Used for Regressions In Table 5.9 (c5t10)

Date	JS	DPI ($000)	UR	911	feb	mar	apr	may	jun	jul	aug	sep	oct	nov	dec
Jan-92	803	0.0	7.3	0	0	0	0	0	0	0	0	0	0	0	0
Feb-92	1,030	4,658.4	7.4	0	1	0	0	0	0	0	0	0	0	0	0
Mar-92	922	4,676.5	7.4	0	0	1	0	0	0	0	0	0	0	0	0
Apr-92	977	4,696.2	7.4	0	0	0	1	0	0	0	0	0	0	0	0
May-92	1,182	4,718.6	7.6	0	0	0	0	1	0	0	0	0	0	0	0
Jun-92	1,104	4,733.5	7.8	0	0	0	0	0	1	0	0	0	0	0	0
Jul-92	1,046	4,750.8	7.7	0	0	0	0	0	0	1	0	0	0	0	0
Aug-92	1,100	4,777.9	7.6	0	0	0	0	0	0	0	1	0	0	0	0
Sep-92	1,043	4,777.2	7.6	0	0	0	0	0	0	0	0	1	0	0	0
Oct-92	1,132	4,807.4	7.3	0	0	0	0	0	0	0	0	0	1	0	0
Nov-92	1,376	4,818.3	7.4	0	0	0	0	0	0	0	0	0	0	1	0
Dec-92	3,469	4,983.1	7.4	0	0	0	0	0	0	0	0	0	0	0	1
Jan-93	802	4,800.9	7.3	0	0	0	0	0	0	0	0	0	0	0	0
Feb-93	1,002	4,803.9	7.1	0	1	0	0	0	0	0	0	0	0	0	0
Mar-93	902	4,800.1	7	0	0	1	0	0	0	0	0	0	0	0	0
Apr-93	1,007	4,887.4	7.1	0	0	0	1	0	0	0	0	0	0	0	0
May-93	1,246	4,909.9	7.1	0	0	0	0	1	0	0	0	0	0	0	0
Jun-93	1,270	4,906.1	7	0	0	0	0	0	1	0	0	0	0	0	0
Jul-93	1,278	4,909.3	6.9	0	0	0	0	0	0	1	0	0	0	0	0
Aug-93	1,270	4,931.4	6.8	0	0	0	0	0	0	0	1	0	0	0	0

(continued on next page)

TABLE 5.10   (continued)

Date	JS	DPI ($000)	UR	911	feb	mar	apr	may	jun	jul	aug	sep	oct	nov	dec
Sep-93	1,191	4,932.1	6.7	0	0	0	0	0	0	0	0	1	0	0	0
Oct-93	1,213	4,951.0	6.8	0	0	0	0	0	0	0	0	0	1	0	0
Nov-93	1,561	4,974.3	6.6	0	0	0	0	0	0	0	0	0	0	1	0
Dec-93	3,829	5,137.0	6.5	0	0	0	0	0	0	0	0	0	0	0	1
Jan-94	904	4,955.9	6.6	0	0	0	0	0	0	0	0	0	0	0	0
Feb-94	1,191	5,003.3	6.6	0	1	0	0	0	0	0	0	0	0	0	0
Mar-94	1,058	5,037.0	6.5	0	0	1	0	0	0	0	0	0	0	0	0
Apr-94	1,171	5,057.2	6.4	0	0	0	1	0	0	0	0	0	0	0	0
May-94	1,367	5,143.5	6.1	0	0	0	0	1	0	0	0	0	0	0	0
Jun-94	1,257	5,153.5	6.1	0	0	0	0	0	1	0	0	0	0	0	0
Jul-94	1,224	5,172.1	6.1	0	0	0	0	0	0	1	0	0	0	0	0
Aug-94	1,320	5,195.0	6	0	0	0	0	0	0	0	1	0	0	0	0
Sep-94	1,246	5,225.3	5.9	0	0	0	0	0	0	0	0	1	0	0	0
Oct-94	1,323	5,281.4	5.8	0	0	0	0	0	0	0	0	0	1	0	0
Nov-94	1,731	5,288.1	5.6	0	0	0	0	0	0	0	0	0	0	1	0
Dec-94	4,204	5,309.8	5.5	0	0	0	0	0	0	0	0	0	0	0	1
Jan-95	914	5,337.3	5.6	0	0	0	0	0	0	0	0	0	0	0	0
Feb-95	1,223	5,350.0	5.4	0	1	0	0	0	0	0	0	0	0	0	0
Mar-95	1,138	5,365.5	5.4	0	0	1	0	0	0	0	0	0	0	0	0
Apr-95	1,204	5,335.1	5.8	0	0	0	1	0	0	0	0	0	0	0	0
May-95	1,603	5,389.0	5.6	0	0	0	0	1	0	0	0	0	0	0	0
Jun-95	1,388	5,404.9	5.6	0	0	0	0	0	1	0	0	0	0	0	0
Jul-95	1,259	5,415.1	5.7	0	0	0	0	0	0	1	0	0	0	0	0
Aug-95	1,393	5,424.0	5.7	0	0	0	0	0	0	0	1	0	0	0	0
Sep-95	1,325	5,442.3	5.6	0	0	0	0	0	0	0	0	1	0	0	0
Oct-95	1,371	5,458.2	5.5	0	0	0	0	0	0	0	0	0	1	0	0
Nov-95	1,867	5,475.4	5.6	0	0	0	0	0	0	0	0	0	0	1	0
Dec-95	4,467	5,502.2	5.6	0	0	0	0	0	0	0	0	0	0	0	1
Jan-96	1,043	5,524.5	5.6	0	0	0	0	0	0	0	0	0	0	0	0
Feb-96	1,439	5,580.9	5.5	0	1	0	0	0	0	0	0	0	0	0	0
Mar-96	1,316	5,618.0	5.5	0	0	1	0	0	0	0	0	0	0	0	0
Apr-96	1,359	5,594.3	5.6	0	0	0	1	0	0	0	0	0	0	0	0
May-96	1,768	5,671.3	5.6	0	0	0	0	1	0	0	0	0	0	0	0
Jun-96	1,408	5,704.3	5.3	0	0	0	0	0	1	0	0	0	0	0	0
Jul-96	1,375	5,702.6	5.5	0	0	0	0	0	0	1	0	0	0	0	0
Aug-96	1,477	5,725.7	5.1	0	0	0	0	0	0	0	1	0	0	0	0
Sep-96	1,332	5,754.2	5.2	0	0	0	0	0	0	0	0	1	0	0	0
Oct-96	1,462	5,768.6	5.2	0	0	0	0	0	0	0	0	0	1	0	0
Nov-96	1,843	5,794.7	5.4	0	0	0	0	0	0	0	0	0	0	1	0
Dec-96	4,495	5,822.5	5.4	0	0	0	0	0	0	0	0	0	0	0	1
Jan-97	1,041	5,847.4	5.3	0	0	0	0	0	0	0	0	0	0	0	0
Feb-97	1,411	5,876.6	5.2	0	1	0	0	0	0	0	0	0	0	0	0
Mar-97	1,183	5,908.3	5.2	0	0	1	0	0	0	0	0	0	0	0	0
Apr-97	1,267	5,915.5	5.1	0	0	0	1	0	0	0	0	0	0	0	0
May-97	1,597	5,934.4	4.9	0	0	0	0	1	0	0	0	0	0	0	0

Date	JS	DPI ($000)	UR	911	feb	mar	apr	may	jun	jul	aug	sep	oct	nov	dec
Jun-97	1,341	5,960.1	5	0	0	0	0	0	1	0	0	0	0	0	0
Jul-97	1,322	5,986.6	4.9	0	0	0	0	0	0	1	0	0	0	0	0
Aug-97	1,359	6,023.4	4.8	0	0	0	0	0	0	0	1	0	0	0	0
Sep-97	1,344	6,052.3	4.9	0	0	0	0	0	0	0	0	1	0	0	0
Oct-97	1,406	6,081.5	4.7	0	0	0	0	0	0	0	0	0	1	0	0
Nov-97	1,813	6,123.3	4.6	0	0	0	0	0	0	0	0	0	0	1	0
Dec-97	4,694	6,156.6	4.7	0	0	0	0	0	0	0	0	0	0	0	1
Jan-98	1,119	6,216.3	4.6	0	0	0	0	0	0	0	0	0	0	0	0
Feb-98	1,513	6,256.6	4.6	0	1	0	0	0	0	0	0	0	0	0	0
Mar-98	1,238	6,294.9	4.7	0	0	1	0	0	0	0	0	0	0	0	0
Apr-98	1,362	6,323.3	4.3	0	0	0	1	0	0	0	0	0	0	0	0
May-98	1,756	6,360.1	4.4	0	0	0	0	1	0	0	0	0	0	0	0
Jun-98	1,527	6,389.6	4.5	0	0	0	0	0	1	0	0	0	0	0	0
Jul-98	1,415	6,418.6	4.5	0	0	0	0	0	0	1	0	0	0	0	0
Aug-98	1,466	6,452.9	4.5	0	0	0	0	0	0	0	1	0	0	0	0
Sep-98	1,372	6,472.7	4.6	0	0	0	0	0	0	0	0	1	0	0	0
Oct-98	1,506	6,497.7	4.5	0	0	0	0	0	0	0	0	0	1	0	0
Nov-98	1,923	6,526.3	4.4	0	0	0	0	0	0	0	0	0	0	1	0
Dec-98	5,233	6,542.2	4.4	0	0	0	0	0	0	0	0	0	0	0	1
Jan-99	1,163	6,571.2	4.3	0	0	0	0	0	0	0	0	0	0	0	0
Feb-99	1,662	6,588.5	4.4	0	1	0	0	0	0	0	0	0	0	0	0
Mar-99	1,402	6,600.5	4.2	0	0	1	0	0	0	0	0	0	0	0	0
Apr-99	1,468	6,616.4	4.3	0	0	0	1	0	0	0	0	0	0	0	0
May-99	1,877	6,639.7	4.2	0	0	0	0	1	0	0	0	0	0	0	0
Jun-99	1,635	6,659.8	4.3	0	0	0	0	0	1	0	0	0	0	0	0
Jul-99	1,596	6,679.7	4.3	0	0	0	0	0	0	1	0	0	0	0	0
Aug-99	1,617	6,718.5	4.2	0	0	0	0	0	0	0	1	0	0	0	0
Sep-99	1,530	6,726.5	4.2	0	0	0	0	0	0	0	0	1	0	0	0
Oct-99	1,653	6,790.8	4.1	0	0	0	0	0	0	0	0	0	1	0	0
Nov-99	2,179	6,840.3	4.1	0	0	0	0	0	0	0	0	0	0	1	0
Dec-99	6,075	6,907.6	4	0	0	0	0	0	0	0	0	0	0	0	1
Jan-00	1,253	7,009.7	4	0	0	0	0	0	0	0	0	0	0	0	0
Feb-00	1,991	7,060.4	4.1	0	1	0	0	0	0	0	0	0	0	0	0
Mar-00	1,510	7,107.5	4	0	0	1	0	0	0	0	0	0	0	0	0
Apr-00	1,570	7,110.8	3.8	0	0	0	1	0	0	0	0	0	0	0	0
May-00	2,139	7,138.7	4	0	0	0	0	1	0	0	0	0	0	0	0
Jun-00	1,783	7,174.2	4	0	0	0	0	0	1	0	0	0	0	0	0
Jul-00	1,643	7,242.4	4	0	0	0	0	0	0	1	0	0	0	0	0
Aug-00	1,770	7,265.0	4.1	0	0	0	0	0	0	0	1	0	0	0	0
Sep-00	1,705	7,291.8	3.9	0	0	0	0	0	0	0	0	1	0	0	0
Oct-00	1,681	7,309.2	3.9	0	0	0	0	0	0	0	0	0	1	0	0
Nov-00	2,174	7,306.6	3.9	0	0	0	0	0	0	0	0	0	0	1	0
Dec-00	5,769	7,312.1	3.9	0	0	0	0	0	0	0	0	0	0	0	1
Jan-01	1,331	7,377.8	4.2	0	0	0	0	0	0	0	0	0	0	0	0
Feb-01	1,973	7,392.0	4.2	0	1	0	0	0	0	0	0	0	0	0	0

(continued on next page)

TABLE 5.10 (continued)

Date	JS	DPI ($000)	UR	911	feb	mar	apr	may	jun	jul	aug	sep	oct	nov	dec
Mar-01	1,580	7,406.6	4.3	0	0	1	0	0	0	0	0	0	0	0	0
Apr-01	1,545	7,394.7	4.4	0	0	0	1	0	0	0	0	0	0	0	0
May-01	1,992	7,402.3	4.3	0	0	0	0	1	0	0	0	0	0	0	0
Jun-01	1,629	7,425.7	4.5	0	0	0	0	0	1	0	0	0	0	0	0
Jul-01	1,530	7,550.9	4.6	0	0	0	0	0	0	1	0	0	0	0	0
Aug-01	1,679	7,686.3	4.9	0	0	0	0	0	0	0	1	0	0	0	0
Sep-01	1,394	7,631.3	5	1	0	0	0	0	0	0	0	1	0	0	0
Oct-01	1,586	7,506.3	5.3	1	0	0	0	0	0	0	0	0	1	0	0
Nov-01	2,152	7,523.5	5.5	0	0	0	0	0	0	0	0	0	0	1	0
Dec-01	5,337	7,544.7	5.7	0	0	0	0	0	0	0	0	0	0	0	1
Jan-02	1,304	7,718.9	5.7	0	0	0	0	0	0	0	0	0	0	0	0
Feb-02	2,004	7,751.7	5.7	0	1	0	0	0	0	0	0	0	0	0	0
Mar-02	1,612	7,784.0	5.7	0	0	1	0	0	0	0	0	0	0	0	0
Apr-02	1,626	7,827.3	5.9	0	0	0	1	0	0	0	0	0	0	0	0
May-02	2,120	7,840.3	5.8	0	0	0	0	1	0	0	0	0	0	0	0
Jun-02	1,667	7,857.4	5.8	0	0	0	0	0	1	0	0	0	0	0	0
Jul-02	1,554	7,845.1	5.8	0	0	0	0	0	0	1	0	0	0	0	0
Aug-02	1,746	7,842.3	5.7	0	0	0	0	0	0	0	1	0	0	0	0
Sep-02	1,503	7,848.9	5.7	0	0	0	0	0	0	0	0	1	0	0	0
Oct-02	1,662	7,864.2	5.7	0	0	0	0	0	0	0	0	0	1	0	0
Nov-02	2,208	7,877.1	5.9	0	0	0	0	0	0	0	0	0	0	1	0
Dec-02	5,810	7,903.7	6	0	0	0	0	0	0	0	0	0	0	0	1
Jan-03	1,361	7,945.8	5.8	0	0	0	0	0	0	0	0	0	0	0	0
Feb-03	2,019	7,972.4	5.9	0	1	0	0	0	0	0	0	0	0	0	0
Mar-03	1,477	8,008.3	5.9	0	0	1	0	0	0	0	0	0	0	0	0
Apr-03	1,616	8,041.7	6	0	0	0	1	0	0	0	0	0	0	0	0
May-03	2,071	8,094.3	6.1	0	0	0	0	1	0	0	0	0	0	0	0
Jun-03	1,711	8,126.9	6.3	0	0	0	0	0	1	0	0	0	0	0	0
Jul-03	1,677	8,240.4	6.2	0	0	0	0	0	0	1	0	0	0	0	0
Aug-03	1,761	8,311.0	6.1	0	0	0	0	0	0	0	1	0	0	0	0
Sep-03	1,629	8,231.6	6.1	0	0	0	0	0	0	0	0	1	0	0	0
Oct-03	1,759	8,271.2	6	0	0	0	0	0	0	0	0	0	1	0	0
Nov-03	2,291	8,335.8	5.8	0	0	0	0	0	0	0	0	0	0	1	0
Dec-03	6,171	8,370.9	5.7	0	0	0	0	0	0	0	0	0	0	0	1
Jan-04	1,461	8,428.8	5.7	0	0	0	0	0	0	0	0	0	0	0	0
Feb-04	2,344	8,478.1	5.6	0	1	0	0	0	0	0	0	0	0	0	0
Mar-04	1,764	8,517.1	5.8	0	0	1	0	0	0	0	0	0	0	0	0
Apr-04	1,826	8,559.3	5.6	0	0	0	1	0	0	0	0	0	0	0	0
May-04	2,226	8,615.5	5.6	0	0	0	0	1	0	0	0	0	0	0	0
Jun-04	1,882	8,640.6	5.6	0	0	0	0	0	1	0	0	0	0	0	0
Jul-04	1,787	8,669.8	5.5	0	0	0	0	0	0	1	0	0	0	0	0
Aug-04	1,794	8,727.4	5.4	0	0	0	0	0	0	0	1	0	0	0	0
Sep-04	1,726	8,729.4	5.4	0	0	0	0	0	0	0	0	1	0	0	0

Date	JS	DPI ($000)	UR	911	feb	mar	apr	may	jun	jul	aug	sep	oct	nov	dec
Oct-04	1,845	8,804.1	5.4	0	0	0	0	0	0	0	0	0	1	0	0
Nov-04	2,399	8,828.6	5.4	0	0	0	0	0	0	0	0	0	0	1	0
Dec-04	6,489	9,171.9	5.4	0	0	0	0	0	0	0	0	0	0	0	1
Jan-05	1,458	8,873.5	5.2	0	0	0	0	0	0	0	0	0	0	0	0
Feb-05	2,394	8,908.3	5.4	0	1	0	0	0	0	0	0	0	0	0	0
Mar-05	1,773	8,941.3	5.2	0	0	1	0	0	0	0	0	0	0	0	0
Apr-05	1,909	9,001.4	5.1	0	0	0	1	0	0	0	0	0	0	0	0
May-05	2,243	9,030.8	5.1	0	0	0	0	1	0	0	0	0	0	0	0
Jun-05	1,953	9,083.6	5	0	0	0	0	0	1	0	0	0	0	0	0
Jul-05	1,754	9,147.4	5	0	0	0	0	0	0	1	0	0	0	0	0
Aug-05	1,940	8,928.3	4.9	0	0	0	0	0	0	0	1	0	0	0	0
Sep-05	1,743	9,239.7	5.1	0	0	0	0	0	0	0	0	1	0	0	0
Oct-05	1,878	9,277.3	5	0	0	0	0	0	0	0	0	0	1	0	0
Nov-05	2,454	9,309.0	5	0	0	0	0	0	0	0	0	0	0	1	0
Dec-05	6,717	9,362.9	4.9	0	0	0	0	0	0	0	0	0	0	0	1

Figure 5.8 depicts the data points for the 156 observations and the estimated regression plane. It is easy to see in the figure that, as the unemployment rate increases, jewelry sales decrease. This can clearly be seen by looking at the edge of the regression plane along which DPI equals 4,000; as UR increases from 3 to 8, the regression plane slopes downward. Remember that the "height" of the regression plane is the measure of jewelry sales, so that as the plane slopes downward, JS is decreasing. Thus, as UR increases (while DPI is held constant), JS decreases.

FIGURE 5.8

Regression Plane for JS = *f*(DPI, UR)

(c5t10)

This figure shows the data points and the estimated regression plane for the two-independent-variable model estimated in the upper half of Table 5.9. The regression plane has the equation:

$$JS = 537.90 + 0.25(DPI) - 66.97(UR)$$

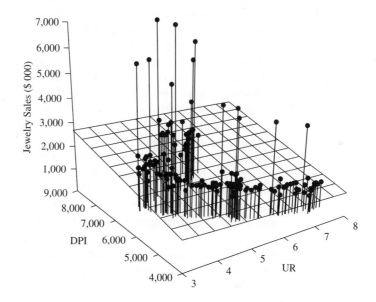

FIGURE 5.9
Jewelry Sales and
Multivariate Forecast
of Jewelry Sales
(c5t10)

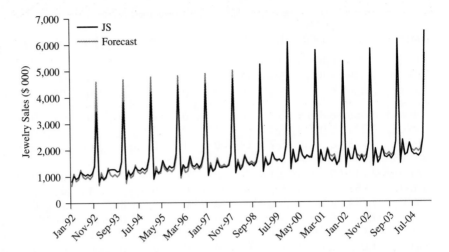

It is also possible to see the effect of disposable personal income (DPI) on JS. Look at the edge of the plane along which UR equals 3; as DPI increases from 4,000 to 9,000, the regression plane tilts upward. Thus, as DPI increases (while UR is held constant), JS increases.

It is obvious why the adjusted R-squared for the regression is quite low: Many of the data points are quite a distance above or below the estimated regression plane. Because the adjusted R-squared is quite low, the improved regression presented in the lower half of Table 5.9 was estimated.

This equation (in the lower half of Table 5.9) adds dummy variables for the 11 months of each year February through December, and a dummy variable for the "911 effect" that equals one in September and October 2001. Recall that the JS time series is quite seasonal (which would suggest the use of seasonal dummies) with some trend. The forecasting equation is improved in a number of ways by the addition of these independent variables. Note that the adjusted R-squared has increased from 10.57 to 96.24 percent. The standard error of regression (labeled SEE) has fallen, both the BIC and Akaike criteria show substantial improvement, the F-statistic has increased, and the Durbin-Watson(1) statistic indicates that no first-order serial correlation is present.[11] Note that it is impossible to graph the data points and the regression plane for this estimate (which has 14 independent variables) because it would require a drawing in 15 dimensions. In fact, the regression plane would now be referred to as a *hyperplane*. The actual and predicted jewelry sales, however, are shown in Figure 5.9.

A forecaster could expect that estimates made with the second regression using seasonal dummy variables and the 911 dummy would be much more accurate than with the two-variable regression presented first.

---

[11] The DW(12) for this model improves to 0.45, but this value suggests that even adding the seasonal dummy variables may not have completely accounted for the seasonality in the jewelry sales data.

Charles W. Chase, Jr., Reckitt & Colman

The job of a practicing forecaster is very different from that of the academic one. He has to prepare forecasts for thousands of different items on a monthly, quarterly, or annual basis, versus one or two products, as is usually the case with an academic forecaster. Unlike an academic forecaster, he has deadlines to meet. If forecasts are not prepared at a set time, the entire planning process comes to a halt. His concern for bringing the error down to the last decimal point is not as great as that of an academic forecaster. He constantly weighs the costs and benefits of reducing the error further. In some cases, any further reduction in the error may not have any effect on the decision. Plus, each time a practicing forecaster prepares forecasts, his job is at stake. If the forecasts go awry, so does his future. The stake of an academic forecaster, on the other hand, is whether or not his article on forecasting is accepted for publication. The objective of this article is to explain how forecasts of consumer products are prepared in a business situation where thousands of items are involved, and deadlines are for real.

PROCEDURE
Here is a step-by-step procedure for forecasting the sales demand for consumer products:

Step 1
Establish an objective, which in this case is to forecast the sales of consumer products. For the purposes of simplicity we will refer to these products as Brand X. Aggregate forecasts are generally more accurate than individual forecasts. "Aggregate forecasts" in this case refer to the forecasts of all the products of Brand X. Individual forecasts, then, will be the forecasts of each item (product code) of this brand.

Step 2
Decide on the method to be used for forecasting the sales of Brand X. There are several considerations that have to be made in the selection of a method. How much error is the company willing to

tolerate? In this case, 10 percent error at the brand level was the chosen target. The industry average is much higher, according to several recent studies. Next, consider the time horizon (how far ahead we want to forecast—one month, one quarter, or one year). This certainly has a bearing on the selection of a method, because some methods are good for short-term forecasting and others for long-term forecasting. In the consumer products industry the time horizon is generally 3 to 12 months out into the future. This is necessary to accommodate the long lead times of several of the components used in producing various consumer products. Components include such things as plastic bottles, labels, and cartons.

Forecasting is 80 percent mathematics and 20 percent judgment. Within mathematical methods, there are two categories: (1) time-series and (2) cause-and-effect. In time-series methods, forecasts are made simply by extrapolating the past data. They assume that the sales are related to time and nothing else. Time-series methods include simple moving averages, exponential smoothing, decomposition, and Box-Jenkins. Cause-and-effect methods use causal relationships. For example, sales are a function of advertising expenditures, price, trade and consumer promotions, and inventory levels. Sales, in this case, are a dependent variable, and advertising expenditures, price, and so forth, are independent variables. These methods assume that there exists a constant relationship between dependent and independent variables. Such methods are simple and multiple regressions, and econometrics.

The consumer products industry in recent years has encountered a shift in power from manufacturers to the trade. Today, the dominant players in the markets are not manufacturers but big chains such as Wal-Mart, Kmart, Kroger, CVS, and Walgreens. As a result, manufacturers have reduced their expenditures on national advertising and increased them on consumer and trade promotions. This shift has played havoc with forecasting, as it has made time-series methods obsolete. Constant changes in amount and period of promotions have

(continued on next page)

disrupted the seasonality and trend of the historical data. Thus, forecasting with time-series methods is like driving down a highway in your car with the windshield blacked out. It's all well and good if you are driving in a desert with no bends in the road. However, if you are driving on a normal highway, sooner or later you will hit a turn. When you do, you won't see it until it's in your rearview mirror. At that point, it would be too late to react.

Taking this information into consideration, multiple regression was chosen as the forecasting method. There are several reasons for this. First, multiple regression has the ability to incorporate all the variables that impact the demand for a brand. Second, it produces extremely accurate forecasts for periods anywhere from three months to one year out into the future. Finally, multiple regression has the ability to measure the relationships of each independent variable with the demand for a brand. (The latter attribute has important implications for making managerial decisions. It helps management to determine how much to spend on national advertising, what should be the appropriate pricing strategy, and what are the most effective promotional programs.)

Step 3

Choose proper independent variables and gather proper data. This is an important step in the forecasting process for two reasons: (1) judgmental influence comes into play; (2) it involves the users in the process. We found that the best way to make the users accept our forecasts is to use the variables they believe have strong impact on their products, and to use the source of data that they are most comfortable with. In the consumer products industry, the marketing department, in most cases, is the primary user of sales forecasts. In fact, those same forecasts ultimately become the marketing plan. Since they are the main users, we chose from their variables—the variables they believe had a strong impact on their products. We used Nielsen syndicated data (Scantrack and Audit), as well as the data furnished by the marketing department. The Nielsen syndicated data was used because the marketing people were most comfortable with it.

When Step 3 is completed, the best possible match has been made between the situation and the method.

In the consumer products industry, trade shipments are forecasted—shipments to the brokers, food and drug chains, and mass merchandisers who sell the products to the consumer. The relationship between the trade and retail consumption plays a significant role in predicting trade shipments. Most users (brand managers) agree that retail consumption has some impact on trade shipments. For Brand X, 10 variables were selected to predict retail consumption (see Table 5.11). Several dummy variables were used to capture the impact of consumer promotions along with average retail price, national advertising expenditures, and Nielsen shipment data of the category for Brand X. Dummy variables are used where the variable is defined in terms of yes (when a certain element exists) and no (when it doesn't exist). It is used in the form of "1" for yes and "0" for no. For example, for FSI (free-standing insert) coupon 1, we used "1" in the equation when this coupon was used, and "0" when it was not.

TABLE 5.11 Variables and Statistics of Consumption Model

R-squared = 0.96 F-stat = 24.55
Adj. R-squared = 0.92   DW = 2.26

Variable	t-Stat
1. Time	−0.72
2. Average retail price	−2.70
3. National advertising expenditures	2.52
4. Nielsen shipment data in units	6.48
5. FSI 1	4.38
6. FSI 2	2.31
7. Direct mail coupon	1.93
8. FSI 3	1.25
9. FSI 4	2.15
10. FSI 5	2.81

Notes: (1) Dummy variables are used to capture the effects of variables that have no quantitative data.
(2) FSI stands for "free-standing insert."

Step 4

Compute the predictive regression equation for retail consumption of Brand X. The equation gives an excellent fit with an R-squared of 0.96. (See Table 5.11 for this and other statistics.) The ex post forecasts had an MAPE (mean absolute percentage error) of less than 1 percent (see Table 5.12). (Ex post forecasts are those for which actuals are known.)

Step 5

Forecast the retail consumption by plugging the values of independent variables into the predictive equation computed above. To do so, we need the values of the independent variables for the periods we want to forecast. For example, if we want to develop a forecast for Brand X for 2000, we need the values of average retail price, Nielsen shipment data of that category, national advertising expenditures, and so forth, for those periods. As for the dummy variables, we have no problem because we control them. However, for Nielsen shipment data we have to forecast the value, which we do by extrapolating the historical data.

Step 6

Compute the predictive regression equation for trade shipments. The equation included retail consumption as the primary variable along with Nielsen inventory, trade price, and several dummy variables to capture trade promotions (see Table 5.13). Again, the fit was excellent with an R-squared of 0.96. The ex post forecasts had an MAPE of 3 percent, which is significantly lower than the original target of 10 percent (see Table 5.14). Those familiar with the rule of thumb for the t-statistic (variables are not significant if their value is less than 2) may feel that several of the variables should have been excluded from the model. I found through experience that if the

TABLE 5.13 Variables and Statistics of Trade Shipment Model

R-squared = 0.96	F-stat = 36.93
Adj. R-squared = 0.93	DW = 2.41

Variable	t-Stat
1. Time	2.40
2. Retail consumption	3.59
3. Trade inventory	1.87
4. Trade price	−1.55
5. Trade promotion 1 early shipment	5.82
6. Trade promotion 1 sell in	16.01
7. Trade promotion 1 post shipment	4.19
8. Trade promotion 2 early shipment	9.57
9. Trade promotion 2 sell in	1.18
10. Trade promotion 3 early shipment	2.62
11. Trade promotion 3 sell in	7.29
12. Trade promotion 3 post shipment	13.55

Note: Dummy variables are used to capture the effects of variables that have no quantitative data.

TABLE 5.12 Forecasts versus Actuals: Consumption Model
Brand X

Month	Actuals	Forecasts	Absolute Error
January	2,578	2,563	1%
February	2,788	2,783	0%
March	2,957	2,957	0%
April	2,670	2,758	3%
May	2,447	2,466	1%
June	3,016	3,016	0%

Note: Mean absolute percentage error (MAPE) = 0.81%

TABLE 5.14 Forecasts versus Actuals: Trade Shipment Model
Brand X

Month	Actuals	Forecasts	Absolute Error
January	69,158	69,190	0%
February	45,927	47,216	3%
March	40,183	40,183	0%
April	56,427	54,841	3%
May	81,854	72,788	12%
June	50,505	52,726	4%
July	37,064	36,992	0%
August	58,212	57,347	2%
September	96,566	95,112	2%

Note: Mean absolute percentage error (MAPE) = 3.0%

forecasts are more accurate with the variables whose *t*-statistics are less than 2, then they should be left in the model. As you know, as practitioners, our primary objective is to produce good forecasts.

Step 7

Forecast trade shipments by plugging the values of the independent variables (retail consumption, Nielsen inventory, and so forth) into the predictive equation computed above. Here again, we need the values of independent variables for the period we want to forecast. The only independent variable over which we have no control is the Nielsen inventory, which we estimate by extrapolating its historical data.

Step 8

Prepare item-by-item forecasts for all the products of Brand X. This is achieved by using the past-six-month rolling average ratio of each item. If item 1 represents 5 percent of the total, then the forecast of item 1 will be 5 percent of the trade total of Brand X; if item 2 represents 10 percent of the total, then 10 percent of the total will be the forecast of item 2; and so on.

Clearly, the main challenge to a business forecaster is to improve the quality of forecasts and consequently the decisions. This can best be achieved by sharing our forecasting experience with others.

Source: *Journal of Business Forecasting* 10, no. 1 (Spring 1991), pp. 2–6. Reprinted by permission.

Integrative Case

The Gap

PART 5: FORECASTING THE GAP SALES DATA WITH A MULTIPLE-REGRESSION MODEL

The sales of The Gap stores in thousands of dollars for the 80 quarters covering 1985Q1 through 2006Q4 are again shown in the graph below. Recall that The Gap sales data are quite seasonal and are increasing over time. Data for 2006 is used as a holdout period.

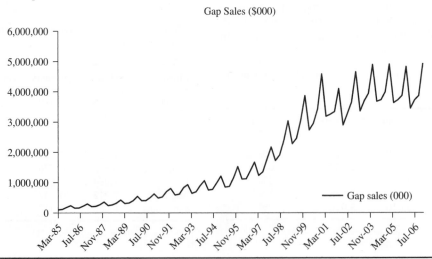

Case Questions

1. Have The Gap sales generally followed a linear path over time? Does the graph suggest to you that some accommodation for seasonality should be used in any forecast? Does the graph suggest that some nonlinear term should be used in any forecast model?
2. Use a multiple regression of raw (i.e., nonseasonally adjusted) The Gap sales as the basis to forecast sales for 2006.
3. Calculate the root-mean-squared errors both for the historical period and for the 2006Q1 through 2006Q4 forecast horizon.

Solutions to Case Questions

1. The Gap sales appear to have followed a highly seasonal pattern over time; in addition, the sales pattern appears to show an increase in the rate of sales over time. In other words, the pattern over time appears to be nonlinear and may require some accommodation in a forecasting model.
2. The raw (or nonseasonally adjusted) The Gap sales were used as a dependent variable in a multiple regression that includes the following explanatory (or independent) variables:

$$T = \text{The index of time}$$
$$T^2 = \text{The index of time squared (to account for the nonlinearity)}$$
$$Q2 = \text{A seasonal dummy variable for quarter 2}$$
$$Q3 = \text{A seasonal dummy variable for quarter 3}$$
$$Q4 = \text{A seasonal dummy variable for quarter 4}$$
$$ICS = \text{Index of Consumer Sentiment}$$

The regression results follow:

```
Audit Trail--ANOVA Table (Multiple Regression Selected)

    Source
of Variation          SS            df          MS               SEE
-----------------------------------------------------------------------
Regression   175,455,195,145,618.00   6    29,242,532,524,269.60
Error          8,836,934,593,396.99  77       114,765,384,329.83   338,770.40
-----------------------------------------------------------------------
  Total      184,292,129,739,015.00  83
```

```
Audit Trail--Coefficient Table (Multiple Regression Selected)

  Series      Included                   Standard                        Overall
Description   in model    Coefficient     error     T-test  Elasticity   F-test
-----------------------------------------------------------------------------------
GapSales(000) Dependent  -1,085,796.81   400,944.00  -2.71                254.80
T             Yes             2,561.10     6,189.35   0.41      0.06
T2            Yes               626.22        70.33   8.90      0.86
Q2            Yes            28,811.97   104,564.77   0.28      0.00
Q3            Yes           216,828.74   104,666.12   2.07      0.03
Q4            Yes           631,743.47   105,492.74   5.99      0.09
ICS           Yes            10,926.90     4,264.03   2.56      0.58
```

(continued on next page)

```
Audit Trail--Statistics

Accuracy Measures                        Value    Forecast Statistics              Value
-----------------------------------------------  -------------------------------------------
AIC                                    2,372.23   Durbin Watson (4)                 0.50
BIC                                    2,374.66   Mean                      1,747,909.96
Mean Absolute Percentage Error (MAPE)    29.00%   Standard Deviation        1,490,096.34
R-Square                                 95.20%   Ljung-Box                       290.58
Adjusted R-Square                        95.20%
Root Mean Square Error               324,347.96
Theil                                      1.86
```

Since the T^2 variable is significant at the 95 percent level, it appears that The Gap sales have indeed been increasing *at an increasing rate* over time. Our impressions are confirmed by the regression equation. Two of the seasonal dummy variables are statistically significant; this confirms our impression of the seasonality of the data. The ICS variable was included to account for the general level of economic activity in the economy over time; it is also significant.

Overall, the regression appears to be a reasonable fit, as seen in the graph of actual and predicted values on the following page.

The equation for The Gap sales here takes seasonality into account in a very different manner than the one in Chapter 4 (which seasonally adjusted the data before running the model). The results, however, are quite similar.

In this model we have also added T^2 as a variable to take into account that sales seem to be increasing at an increasing rate over time. The ICS adds some further explanatory power. The results do not seem much different from the simple regression results of Chapter 4, but the difference lies in the explanatory power of this model in the forecast horizon.

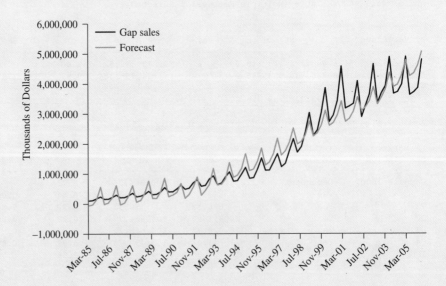

3. The RMSEs for the historical period and the 2006 forecast horizon are:

$$1985Q1\text{--}2003Q4 \text{ root-mean-squared error} = 324,347$$

$$2004Q1\text{--}2004Q4 \text{ root-mean-squared error} = 973,944$$

If we compare these results with the results presented at the end of Chapter 4, we find that the historical period forecast has much the same RMSE, but the forecast horizon RMSE is much lower with the multiple regression. This is due in part to the explanatory power of the nonlinear T^2 variable.

Holdout Period (2006) Forecast RMSE for Gap Sales				
Date	Forecast	Actual	$(A_t - F_t)$	$(A_t - F_t)^2$
Mar-2006	4,553,914.17	3,441,000	−1,112,914	1.23858E+12
Jun-2006	4,689,792.96	3,716,000	−973,793	9.48273E+11
Sep-2006	4,984,939.98	3,856,000	−1,128,940	1.27451E+12
Dec-2006	5,506,987.13	4,930,000	−576,987	3.32914E+11

RMSE = **973,944**

USING FORECASTX™ TO MAKE MULTIPLE-REGRESSION FORECASTS

As usual, begin by opening your data file in Excel and start ForecastX™. In the **Data Capture** dialog box identify the data you want to use, as shown below. Then click the **Forecast Method** tab.

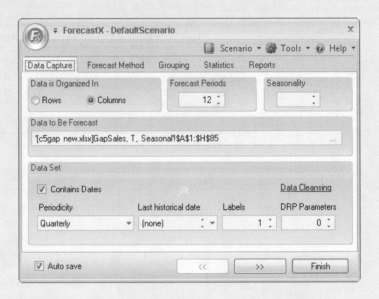

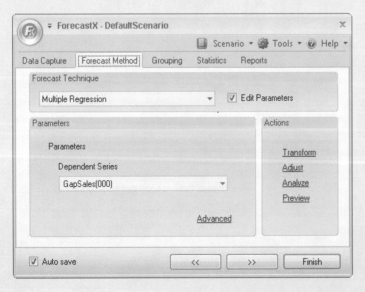

In the **Forecast Method** dialog box, click the down arrow in the **Forecasting Technique** box and select **Multiple Regression.** Make sure the desired variable is selected as the **Dependent Series**, which is **GapSales(000)** in this example. Then click the **Statistics** tab.

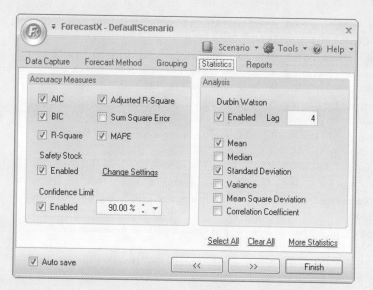

In this dialog box, select the statistics that you desire. Do not forget that there are more choices if you click the **More . . .** button at the bottom.

After selecting the statistics you want to see, click the **Reports** tab.

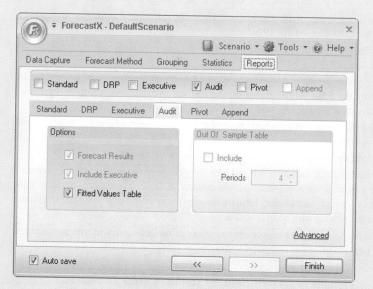

In the **Report Options** dialog box, select those you want. Typical selections might be those shown here. If you click the Standard tab you will want to be sure to select the **Chart** box. In the **Audit Trail** tab (the active tab shown here) click the **Fitted Values Table.**

Then click the **Finish!** button.

ForecastX™ will automatically apply a time-series method to forecast the independent variables. The methods used to forecast the independent variables are given in the Standard Report.

Suggested Readings

Akaike, Hirotugu. "A New Look at Statistical Model Identification." IEEE Transactions on Automatic Control, AC-19, 6 (1974).

Aykac, Ahmed; and Antonio Borges. "Econometric Methods for Managerial Applications." In *The Handbook of Forecasting: A Managers Guide.* Eds. Spyros Makridakis and Steven C. Wheelwright. New York: John Wiley & Sons, 1982, pp. 185–203.

Doran, Howard; and Jan Kmenta. "Multiple Minima in the Estimation of Models with Auto-regressive Disturbances." *Review of Economics and Statistics* 24 (May 1992), pp. 354–57.

Griffiths, William E.; R. Carter Hill; and George G. Judge. *Learning and Practicing Econometrics.* New York: John Wiley & Sons, 1992.

Gujarati, Damodar N. *Essentials of Econometrics.* New York: McGraw-Hill, 2006.

Jarrell, Stephen B. *Basic Business Statistics.* Boston: Allyn & Bacon, 1988. Especially Chapter 23, "Regression," and Chapter 24, "Evaluating and Forecasting: Two Variable Regression Models."

Johnson, Aaron C., Jr.; Marvin B. Johnson; and Reuben C. Buse. *Econometrics: Basic and Applied.* New York: Macmillan, 1987.

Lewis-Beck, Michael S. *Applied Regression: An Introduction.* Beverly Hills, CA: Sage Publications, 1980.

Mendenhall, William; Robert J. Beaver; and Barbara M. Beaver. *Introduction to Probability and Statistics.* 13th ed. Belmont, CA: Brooks/Cole Cenage Learning, 2009.

Neter, John; William Wasserman; and Michael H. Kutner. *Applied Linear Regression Models.* New York: McGraw-Hill, 1996.

Wallis, K. F. "Testing for Fourth Order Correlation in Quarterly Regression Equations." *Econometrica* 40 (1972), pp. 617–36.

Exercises

1. Explain why the adjusted R-squared should be used in evaluating multiple-regression models rather than the unadjusted value.

2. Review the three quick checks that should be used in evaluating a multiple-regression model. Apply these to the model for jewelry sales discussed in this chapter, using your own words to describe each step and the conclusions you reach.

3. Explain what dummy variables are and how they can be used to account for seasonality. Give an example of how you might use dummy variables to measure seasonality for a good or service of your choice. Explain the signs you would expect on each. Assume that you are working with quarterly data.

4. The following regression results relate to a study of fuel efficiency of cars as measured by miles per gallon of gas (adjusted R-squared = 0.569; $n = 120$).

Variable*	Coefficient	Standard Error	t-Ratio
Intercept	6.51	1.28	
CID	0.031	0.012	
D	9.46	2.67	
M4	14.64	2.09	
M5	14.86	2.42	
US	4.64	2.48	

*CID = Cubic-inch displacement (engine size)
   D = 1 for diesel cars and 0 otherwise
   M4 = 1 for cars with a four-speed manual transmission and 0 otherwise
   M5 = 1 for cars with a five-speed manual transmission and 0 otherwise
   US = 1 for cars made in the United States and 0 otherwise

a. Calculate the *t*-ratios for each explanatory variable.

b. Use the three quick-check regression-evaluation procedures to evaluate this model.

5. Develop a multiple-regression model for auto sales as a function of population and household income from the following data for 10 metropolitan areas:

(c5p5)

Area	Auto Sales (AS) ($000)	Household Income (INC) ($000)	Population (POP) (000)
1	$185,792	$23,409	133.17
2	85,643	19,215	110.86
3	97,101	20,374	68.04
4	100,249	16,107	99.59
5	527,817	23,432	289.52
6	403,916	19,426	339.98
7	78,283	18,742	89.53
8	188,756	18,553	155.78
9	329,531	21,953	248.95
10	91,944	16,358	102.13

a. Estimate values for b_0, b_1, and b_2 for the following model:

$$AS = b_0 + b_1(INC) + b_2(POP)$$

b. Are the signs you find for the coefficients consistent with your expectations? Explain.

c. Are the coefficients for the two explanatory variables significantly different from zero? Explain.

d. What percentage of the variation in AS is explained by this model?

e. What point estimate of AS would you make for a city where INC = $23,175 and POP = 128.07? What would the approximate 95 percent confidence interval be?

6. In Exercises 7 and 8 of Chapter 4 you worked with data on sales for a line of skiwear that is produced by HeathCo Industries. Barbara Lynch, product manager for the skiwear, has the responsibility of providing forecasts to top management of sales by quarter one year ahead. One of Ms. Lynch's colleagues, Dick Staples, suggested that unemployment and income in the regions in which the clothes are marketed might be causally connected to sales. If you worked the exercises in Chapter 4, you have developed three bivariate regression models of sales as a function of time (TIME), unemployment (NRUR), and income (INC). Data for these variables and for sales are as follows:

(c5p6)

Period	SALES ($000)	INC ($ Billions)	NRUR (%)	TIME
Mar-98	72,962	218	8.4	1
Jun-98	81,921	237	8.2	2
Sep-98	97,729	263	8.4	3
Dec-98	142,161	293	8.4	4
Mar-99	145,592	318	8.1	5
Jun-99	117,129	359	7.7	6
Sep-99	114,159	404	7.5	7

(continued on next page)

Period	SALES ($000)	INC ($ Billions)	NRUR (%)	TIME
Dec-99	151,402	436	7.2	8
Mar-00	153,907	475	6.9	9
Jun-00	100,144	534	6.5	10
Sep-00	123,242	574	6.5	11
Dec-00	128,497	622	6.4	12
Mar-01	176,076	667	6.3	13
Jun-01	180,440	702	6.2	14
Sep-01	162,665	753	6.3	15
Dec-01	220,818	796	6.5	16
Mar-02	202,415	858	6.8	17
Jun-02	211,780	870	7.9	18
Sep-02	163,710	934	8.3	19
Dec-02	200,135	1,010	8	20
Mar-03	174,200	1,066	8	21
Jun-03	182,556	1,096	8	22
Sep-03	198,990	1,162	8	23
Dec-03	243,700	1,187	8.9	24
Mar-04	253,142	1,207	9.6	25
Jun-04	218,755	1,242	10.2	26
Sep-04	225,422	1,279	10.7	27
Dec-04	253,653	1,318	11.5	28
Mar-05	257,156	1,346	11.2	29
Jun-05	202,568	1,395	11	30
Sep-05	224,482	1,443	10.1	31
Dec-05	229,879	1,528	9.2	32
Mar-06	289,321	1,613	8.5	33
Jun-06	266,095	1,646	8	34
Sep-06	262,938	1,694	8	35
Dec-06	322,052	1,730	7.9	36
Mar-07	313,769	1,755	7.9	37
Jun-07	315,011	1,842	7.9	38
Sep-07	264,939	1,832	7.8	39
Dec-07	301,479	1,882	7.6	40

a. Now you can expand your analysis to see whether a multiple-regression model would work well. Estimate the following model:

$$\text{SALES} = b_0 + b_1(\text{INC}) + b_2(\text{NRUR})$$

$$\text{SALES} = \underline{} +/- \underline{}(\text{INC}) +/- \underline{}(\text{NRUR})$$

(Circle + or − as appropriate for each variable)

Do the signs on the coefficients make sense? Explain why.

b. Test to see whether the coefficients you have estimated are statistically different from zero, using a 95 percent confidence level and a one-tailed test.

c. What percentage of the variation in sales is explained by this model?

d. Use this model to make a sales forecast (SF1) for 2008Q1 through 2008Q4, given the previously forecast values for unemployment (NRURF) and income (INCF) as follows:

Period	NRURF (%)	INCF ($ Billions)	SF1 ($000)
2008Q1	7.6	1,928	—
2008Q2	7.7	1,972	—
2008Q3	7.5	2,017	—
2008Q4	7.4	2,062	—

e. Actual sales for 2008 were: Q1 = 334,271; Q2 = 328,982; Q3 = 317,921; Q4 = 350,118. On the basis of this information, how well would you say the model worked? What is the root-mean-squared error (RMSE)?

f. Plot the actual data for 2008Q1 through 2008Q4 along with the values predicted for each quarter based on this model, for 2008Q1 through 2008Q4.

7. a. If you have not looked at a time-series graph of the sales data for HeathCo's line of skiwear (see data in Exercise 6), do so now. On this plot write a 1 next to the data point for each first quarter, a 2 next to each second quarter, and so forth for all four quarters. Does there appear to be a seasonal pattern in the sales data? Explain why you think the results are as you have found. (c5p6)

b. It seems logical that skiwear would sell better from October through March than from April through September. To test this hypothesis, begin by adding two dummy variables to the data: dummy variable Q2 = 1 for each second quarter (April, May, June) and Q2 = 0 otherwise; dummy variable Q3 = 1 for each third quarter (July, August, September) and Q3 = 0 otherwise. Once the dummy variables have been entered into your data set, estimate the following trend model:

$$SALES = b_0 + b_1(TIME) + b_2Q2 + b_3Q3$$
$$SALES = \underline{\quad} +/- \underline{\quad} TIME$$
$$+/- \underline{\quad} Q2 +/- \underline{\quad} Q3$$

(Circle + or − as appropriate for each variable)

Evaluate these results by answering the following:
- Do the signs make sense?
- Are the coefficients statistically different from zero at a 95 percent confidence level (one-tailed test)?
- What percentage of the variation in SALES is explained by this model?

c. Use this model to make a forecast of SALES (SF2) for the four quarters of 2008 and calculate the RMSE for the forecast period.

Period	SALES ($000)	SF2 ($000)
2008Q1	334,271	—
2008Q2	328,982	—
2008Q3	317,921	—
2008Q4	350,118	—

d. Prepare a time-series plot of SALES (for 1998Q1 through 2007Q4) and SF2 (for 1998Q1 through 2007Q4) to illustrate how SALES and SF2 compare.

8. Consider now that you have been asked to prepare a forecast of wholesale furniture sales for the entire United States. You have been given the monthly time-series data in the accompanying table:

(c5p8)

Data for Exercise 8

	WFS	UR	PHS		WFS	UR	PHS
1990M1	1,226.00	8.60000	843.00	1994M1	1,866.00	6.70000	1,938.00
1990M2	1,287.00	8.90000	866.00	1994M2	1,843.00	7.20000	1,869.00
1990M3	1,473.00	9.00000	931.00	1994M3	2,001.00	7.10000	1,873.00
1990M4	1,383.00	9.30000	917.00	1994M4	2,165.00	7.20000	1,947.00
1990M5	1,208.00	9.40000	1,025.00	1994M5	2,211.00	7.20000	1,847.00
1990M6	1,344.00	9.60000	902.00	1994M6	2,321.00	7.20000	1,845.00
1990M7	1,161.00	9.80000	1,166.00	1994M7	2,210.00	7.00000	1,789.00
1990M8	1,221.00	9.80000	1,046.00	1994M8	2,253.00	6.90000	1,804.00
1990M9	1,367.00	10.1000	1,144.00	1994M9	2,561.00	7.00000	1,685.00
1990M10	1,380.00	10.4000	1,173.00	1994M10	2,619.00	7.00000	1,683.00
1990M11	1,310.00	10.8000	1,372.00	1994M11	2,118.00	6.90000	1,630.00
1990M12	1,302.00	10.8000	1,303.00	1994M12	2,169.00	6.70000	1,837.00
1991M1	1,344.00	10.4000	1,586.00	1995M1	2,063.00	6.60000	1,804.00
1991M2	1,362.00	10.4000	1,699.00	1995M2	2,032.00	6.60000	1,809.00
1991M3	1,694.00	10.3000	1,606.00	1995M3	2,349.00	6.50000	1,723.00
1991M4	1,611.00	10.2000	1,472.00	1995M4	2,218.00	6.40000	1,635.00
1991M5	1,648.00	10.1000	1,776.00	1995M5	2,159.00	6.30000	1,599.00
1991M6	1,722.00	10.1000	1,733.00	1995M6	2,240.00	6.20000	1,583.00
1991M7	1,488.00	9.40000	1,785.00	1995M7	2,335.00	6.10000	1,594.00
1991M8	1,776.00	9.50000	1,910.00	1995M8	2,388.00	6.00000	1,583.00
1991M9	1,839.00	9.20000	1,710.00	1995M9	2,865.00	5.90000	1,679.00
1991M10	2,017.00	8.80000	1,715.00	1995M10	2,829.00	6.00000	1,538.00
1991M11	1,920.00	8.50000	1,785.00	1995M11	2,432.00	5.90000	1,661.00
1991M12	1,778.00	8.30000	1,688.00	1995M12	2,395.00	5.80000	1,399.00
1992M1	1,683.00	8.00000	1,897.00	1996M1	1,995.00	5.70000	1,382.00
1992M2	1,829.00	7.80000	2,260.00	1996M2	2,232.00	5.70000	1,519.00
1992M3	2,012.00	7.80000	1,663.00	1996M3	2,355.00	5.70000	1,529.00
1992M4	2,033.00	7.70000	1,851.00	1996M4	2,188.00	5.50000	1,584.00
1992M5	2,305.00	7.40000	1,774.00	1996M5	2,177.00	5.60000	1,393.00
1992M6	2,007.00	7.20000	1,843.00	1996M6	2,333.00	5.40000	1,465.00
1992M7	1,941.00	7.50000	1,732.00	1996M7	2,124.00	5.50000	1,477.00
1992M8	2,027.00	7.50000	1,586.00	1996M8	2,463.00	5.60000	1,461.00
1992M9	1,922.00	7.30000	1,698.00	1996M9	2,435.00	5.40000	1,467.00
1992M10	2,173.00	7.40000	1,590.00	1996M10	2,688.00	5.30000	1,533.00
1992M11	2,097.00	7.20000	1,689.00	1996M11	2,604.00	5.30000	1,558.00
1992M12	1,687.00	7.30000	1,612.00	1996M12	2,393.00	5.30000	1,524.00
1993M1	1,679.00	7.40000	1,711.00	1997M1	2,171.00	5.40000	1,678.00
1993M2	1,696.00	7.20000	1,632.00	1997M2	2,136.00	5.20000	1,465.00
1993M3	1,826.00	7.20000	1,800.00	1997M3	2,428.00	5.00000	1,409.00
1993M4	1,985.00	7.30000	1,821.00	1997M4	2,264.00	5.30000	1,343.00
1993M5	2,051.00	7.20000	1,680.00	1997M5	2,402.00	5.20000	1,308.00
1993M6	2,027.00	7.30000	1,676.00	1997M6	2,320.00	5.30000	1,406.00
1993M7	2,107.00	7.40000	1,684.00	1997M7	2,258.00	5.30000	1,420.00
1993M8	2,138.00	7.10000	1,743.00	1997M8	2,675.00	5.30000	1,329.00
1993M9	2,089.00	7.10000	1,676.00	1997M9	2,676.00	5.30000	1,264.00
1993M10	2,399.00	7.20000	1,834.00	1997M10	2,629.00	5.30000	1,428.00
1993M11	2,143.00	7.00000	1,698.00	1997M11	2,610.00	5.30000	1,361.00
1993M12	2,070.00	7.00000	1,942.00				

WFS is wholesale furniture sales in millions of dollars. It is not seasonally adjusted. PHS measures new private housing starts in thousands. UR is the unemployment rate as a percent. You believe that furniture sales are quite probably related to the general state of the economy and decide to test whether the unemployment rate affects furniture sales. You expect that as the unemployment rate rises (and the economy thus shows some sign of difficulty), furniture sales will decline.

a. Summarize the results of your bivariate regression by completing the following table:

Independent Variable	Intercept	Slope	t-Ratio	R-squared
UR				
		R-squared =		
		Durbin-Watson =		

b. After discussing the results at a staff meeting, someone suggests that you fit a multiple-regression model of the following form:

$$WFS = b_0 + b_1(UR) + b_2(M1) + b_3(M2)$$
$$+ b_4(M4) + b_5(M9) + b_6(M10)$$

where:

M1 = A dummy variable for January

M2 = A dummy variable for February

M4 = A dummy variable for April

M9 = A dummy variable for September

M10 = A dummy variable for October

Summarize the results in the following table:

Independent Variable	Intercept	Slope	t-Ratio
UR			
M1			
M2			
M4			
M9			
M10			
	Adjusted R-squared =		
	Durbin-Watson =		

- Do the signs of the coefficients make sense?
- Are the coefficients statistically significant at a 95 percent confidence level (one-tailed test)?
- What percentage of the variation in WFS is explained by the model?

c. After a staff meeting where these results were presented, another analyst suggested that serial correlation can cause problems in such regression models. Interpret the Durbin-Watson statistic in part (*b*) and suggest what problems could result if serial correlation is a problem.

Add PHS lagged three months and time-squared (T^2) to the model and again examine the results for serial correlation. Summarize the results:

Independent Variable	Intercept	Slope	*t*-Ratio	*R*-squared
UR				
M1				
M2				
M4				
M9				
M10				
T^2				
PHS(-3)				

Adjusted *R*-squared =
Durbin-Watson =

Have the additional two variables affected the existence of serial correlation?

9. AmeriPlas, Inc., produces 20-ounce plastic drinking cups that are embossed with the names of prominent beers and soft drinks.

(c5p9)

Period	Sales	Time	M2	M3	M4	M5	M6	M7	M8	M9	M10	M11	M12
Jan-04	857	1	0	0	0	0	0	0	0	0	0	0	0
Feb-04	921	2	1	0	0	0	0	0	0	0	0	0	0
Mar-04	1,071	3	0	1	0	0	0	0	0	0	0	0	0
Apr-04	1,133	4	0	0	1	0	0	0	0	0	0	0	0
May-04	1,209	5	0	0	0	1	0	0	0	0	0	0	0
Jun-04	1,234	6	0	0	0	0	1	0	0	0	0	0	0
Jul-04	1,262	7	0	0	0	0	0	1	0	0	0	0	0
Aug-04	1,258	8	0	0	0	0	0	0	1	0	0	0	0
Sep-04	1,175	9	0	0	0	0	0	0	0	1	0	0	0
Oct-04	1,174	10	0	0	0	0	0	0	0	0	1	0	0
Nov-04	1,123	11	0	0	0	0	0	0	0	0	0	1	0
Dec-04	1,159	12	0	0	0	0	0	0	0	0	0	0	1
Jan-05	1,250	13	0	0	0	0	0	0	0	0	0	0	0
Feb-05	1,289	14	1	0	0	0	0	0	0	0	0	0	0
Mar-05	1,448	15	0	1	0	0	0	0	0	0	0	0	0
Apr-05	1,497	16	0	0	1	0	0	0	0	0	0	0	0
May-05	1,560	17	0	0	0	1	0	0	0	0	0	0	0
Jun-05	1,586	18	0	0	0	0	1	0	0	0	0	0	0
Jul-05	1,597	19	0	0	0	0	0	1	0	0	0	0	0

(continued on next page)

Period	Sales	Time	M2	M3	M4	M5	M6	M7	M8	M9	M10	M11	M12
Aug-05	1,615	20	0	0	0	0	0	0	1	0	0	0	0
Sep-05	1,535	21	0	0	0	0	0	0	0	1	0	0	0
Oct-05	1,543	22	0	0	0	0	0	0	0	0	1	0	0
Nov-05	1,493	23	0	0	0	0	0	0	0	0	0	1	0
Dec-05	1,510	24	0	0	0	0	0	0	0	0	0	0	1
Jan-06	1,604	25	0	0	0	0	0	0	0	0	0	0	0
Feb-06	1,643	26	1	0	0	0	0	0	0	0	0	0	0
Mar-06	1,795	27	0	1	0	0	0	0	0	0	0	0	0
Apr-06	1,868	28	0	0	1	0	0	0	0	0	0	0	0
May-06	1,920	29	0	0	0	1	0	0	0	0	0	0	0
Jun-06	1,953	30	0	0	0	0	1	0	0	0	0	0	0
Jul-06	1,980	31	0	0	0	0	0	1	0	0	0	0	0
Aug-06	1,989	32	0	0	0	0	0	0	1	0	0	0	0
Sep-06	1,897	33	0	0	0	0	0	0	0	1	0	0	0
Oct-06	1,910	34	0	0	0	0	0	0	0	0	1	0	0
Nov-06	1,854	35	0	0	0	0	0	0	0	0	0	1	0
Dec-06	1,957	36	0	0	0	0	0	0	0	0	0	0	1
Jan-07	1,955	37	0	0	0	0	0	0	0	0	0	0	0
Feb-07	2,008	38	1	0	0	0	0	0	0	0	0	0	0
Mar-07	2,171	39	0	1	0	0	0	0	0	0	0	0	0
Apr-07	2,202	40	0	0	1	0	0	0	0	0	0	0	0
May-07	2,288	41	0	0	0	1	0	0	0	0	0	0	0
Jun-07	2,314	42	0	0	0	0	1	0	0	0	0	0	0
Jul-07	2,343	43	0	0	0	0	0	1	0	0	0	0	0
Aug-07	2,339	44	0	0	0	0	0	0	1	0	0	0	0
Sep-07	2,239	45	0	0	0	0	0	0	0	1	0	0	0
Oct-07	2,267	46	0	0	0	0	0	0	0	0	1	0	0
Nov-07	2,206	47	0	0	0	0	0	0	0	0	0	1	0
Dec-07	2,226	48	0	0	0	0	0	0	0	0	0	0	1

a. Prepare a time-series plot of the sales data. Does there appear to be a regular pattern of movement in the data that may be seasonal? Ronnie Newton, the product manager for this product line, believes that her brief review of sales data for the four-year period indicates that sales are slower in the colder months of November through February than in other months. Do you agree?

b. Since production is closely related to orders for current shipment, Ronnie would like to have a monthly sales forecast that incorporates monthly fluctuations. She has asked you to develop a trend model that includes dummy variables, with January as the base period (i.e., 11 dummy variables for February through December). Use M2 for the February dummy variable, which will equal 1 for each February and zero otherwise; M3 for the March dummy variable, which will equal 1 for each March and zero otherwise; and so forth to M12 for the December dummy variable, which will equal 1 for each December and zero otherwise. Summarize your results:

Variable	Coefficient	*t*-Ratio
Intercept		
T		
M2		
M3		
M4		
M5		
M6		
M7		
M8		
M9		
M10		
M11		
M12		
	Adjusted *R*-squared =	
	Durbin-Watson =	

Do these results support Ronnie Newton's observations? Explain.

c. While sales of this new product have experienced considerable growth in the first four years, Ronnie believes that there has been some decrease in the rate of growth. To test this and to include such a possibility in the forecasting effort, she has asked that you add the square of the time index (T) to your model (call this new term $T2$). Summarize the new results:

Variable	Coefficient	*t*-Ratio
Intercept		
T		
M2		
M3		
M4		
M5		
M6		
M7		
M8		
M9		
M10		
M11		
M12		
	Adjusted *R*-squared =	
	Durbin-Watson =	

Is there any evidence of a slowing of sales growth? Compare the results of this model with those found in part (b).

d. Use the model in part (c) to forecast sales for 2008 and calculate the RMSE for the forecast period. Actual sales are as follows:

Month	Actual Sales	Forecast Sales	Squared Error
Jan	2,318		
Feb	2,367		
Mar	2,523		
Apr	2,577		
May	2,646		
Jun	2,674		
Jul	2,697		
Aug	2,702		
Sep	2,613		
Oct	2,626		
Nov	2,570		
Dec	2,590		

Sum of squared errors = _____
RMSE = _____

10. Norm Marks has recently been assigned the responsibility of forecasting the demand for P2CL, a coating produced by ChemCo that is used to line beer cans. He has decided to begin by trying to forecast beer, wine, and liquor sales and has hired you as an outside consultant for this purpose.

   a. Go to the http://www.economagic.com and/or *Business Statistics* and gather data on retail monthly beer, wine, and liquor store sales for a recent four-year period. Prepare a time-series plot of the data. Use data that is not seasonally adjusted (usually noted by "NSA").

   b. Develop a multiple-regression trend model with monthly dummy variables for February (M2) through December (M12) for beer, wine, and liquor sales (i.e., use January as the base period). Summarize your findings:

(c5p10) Variable	Coefficient	*t*-Ratio
Intercept		
T		
M2		
M3		
M4		
M5		
M6		
M7		
M8		
M9		
M10		
M11		
M12		

Adjusted *R*-squared =
Durbin-Watson =

Write a paragraph in which you communicate your findings to Norm Marks.

   c. Prepare a forecast for the year following the four years for which you collected data.

11. The data presented below are for retail sales in the United States quarterly from the period 1992Q1 through 2003Q4. Also included is disposable personal income per capita (DPIPC) (to use as a measure of the well-being of the economy).

Date	RS	DPIPC	Q2	Q3	Q4	T	T^2	DPIPC^2
Mar-96	534,392	20,763	0	0	0	1	1	431,102,169
Jun-96	595,893	21,009	1	0	0	2	4	441,378,081
Sep-96	592,083	21,203	0	1	0	3	9	449,567,209
Dec-96	644,297	21,385	0	0	1	4	16	457,318,225
Mar-97	564,164	21,631	0	0	0	5	25	467,900,161
Jun-97	617,252	21,787	1	0	0	6	36	474,673,369
Sep-97	623,555	22,023	0	1	0	7	49	485,012,529
Dec-97	669,032	22,317	0	0	1	8	64	498,048,489
Mar-98	580,778	22,753	0	0	0	9	81	517,699,009
Jun-98	655,691	23,060	1	0	0	10	100	531,763,600
Sep-98	644,369	23,315	0	1	0	11	121	543,589,225
Dec-98	706,267	23,511	0	0	1	12	144	552,767,121
Mar-99	627,589	23,684	0	0	0	13	169	560,931,856
Jun-99	702,714	23,806	1	0	0	14	196	566,725,636
Sep-99	709,527	23,979	0	1	0	15	225	574,992,441
Dec-99	768,726	24,399	0	0	1	16	256	595,311,201
Mar-00	696,048	25,094	0	0	0	17	289	629,708,836
Jun-00	753,211	25,321	1	0	0	18	324	641,153,041
Sep-00	746,875	25,690	0	1	0	19	361	659,976,100
Dec-00	792,622	25,768	0	0	1	20	400	663,989,824
Mar-01	704,757	25,996	0	0	0	21	441	675,792,016
Jun-01	779,011	25,985	1	0	0	22	484	675,220,225
Sep-01	756,128	26,665	0	1	0	23	529	711,022,225
Dec-01	827,829	26,250	0	0	1	24	576	689,062,500
Mar-02	717,302	26,976	0	0	0	25	625	727,704,576
Jun-02	790,486	27,224	1	0	0	26	676	741,146,176
Sep-02	792,657	27,163	0	1	0	27	729	737,828,569
Dec-02	833,877	27,217	0	0	1	28	784	740,765,089
Mar-03	741,060	27,480	0	0	0	29	841	755,150,400
Jun-03	819,232	27,800	1	0	0	30	900	772,840,000
Sep-03	830,692	28,322	0	1	0	31	961	802,135,684
Dec-03	874,493	28,473	0	0	1	32	1024	810,711,729
Mar-04	794,720	28,922	0	0	0	33	1089	836,482,084
Jun-04	870,834	29,300	1	0	0	34	1156	858,490,000
Sep-04	872,340	29,576	0	1	0	35	1225	874,739,776
Dec-04	936,446	30,265	0	0	1	36	1296	915,970,225
Mar-05	835,280	30,106	0	0	0	37	1369	906,371,236
Jun-05	931,513	30,477	1	0	0	38	1444	928,847,529
Sep-05	939,788	30,622	0	1	0	39	1521	937,706,884
Dec-05	986,849	31,252	0	0	1	40	1600	976,687,504
Mar-06	906,635	31,693	0	0	0	41	1681	1,004,446,249
Jun-06	1,002,064	31,970	1	0	0	42	1764	1,022,080,900
Sep-06	993,749	32,231	0	1	0	43	1849	1,038,837,361
Dec-06	1,034,094	32,561	0	0	1	44	1936	1,060,218,721
Mar-07	934,619	33,206	0	0	0	45	2025	1,102,638,436
Jun-07	1,030,508	33,525	1	0	0	46	2116	1,123,925,625
Sep-07	1,017,608	33,940	0	1	0	47	2209	1,151,923,600

a. Develop a regression model of retail sales as a function of the S&P 500. Comment on the relevant summary statistics.

b. Estimate a new multiple-regression model using seasonal dummy variables for quarters 2, 3, and 4. Additionally, add a time index to account for trend. Comment on the relevant statistics of this model. Is this model an improvement on the model above? What evidence is there that this second model provides an improvement (no improvement)?

c. Square the time index variable and add it to the multiple-regression model above. Does the resulting model perform better than either previous model? Explain your reasoning.

12. An interesting experiment took place beginning in April 1979 in Albuquerque, New Mexico. The local police department tried a procedure they thought might have the effect of reducing driving-while-intoxicated (DWI) related accidents. The procedure was quite simple. A squad of police officers used a special van that housed a blood alcohol testing (BAT) device; the van became known as the "Batmobile."

In the quarterly data set below is information on the following variables:

ACC = Injuries and fatalities from Wednesday through Saturday nighttime accidents

FUEL = Fuel consumption (millions of gallons) in Albuquerque

QTR	ACC	FUEL	QTR	ACC	FUEL
1	192	32.592	27	354	54.646
2	238	37.25	28	331	53.398
3	232	40.032	29	291	50.584
4	246	35.852	30	377	51.32
5	185	38.226	31	327	50.81
6	274	38.711	32	301	46.272
7	266	43.139	33	269	48.664
8	196	40.434	34	314	48.122
9	170	35.898	35	318	47.483
10	234	37.111	36	288	44.732
11	272	38.944	37	242	46.143
12	234	37.717	38	268	44.129
13	210	37.861	39	327	46.258
14	280	42.524	40	253	48.23
15	246	43.965	41	215	46.459
16	248	41.976	42	263	50.686
17	269	42.918	43	319	49.681
18	326	49.789	44	263	51.029
19	342	48.454	45	206	47.236
20	257	45.056	46	286	51.717
21	280	49.385	47	323	51.824
22	290	42.524	48	306	49.38
23	356	51.224	49	230	47.961
24	295	48.562	50	304	46.039
25	279	48.167	51	311	55.683
26	330	51.362	52	292	52.263

The first 29 observations in the data set are a control period before the implementation of the Batmobile program. The following 23 quarterly observations are for the experimental period.

Your job is to explain statistically using standard forecasting procedures whether the Batmobile program was effective.

a. Using the "fuel" variable as a proxy for the amount of driving in any given period, calculate the average injuries per gallon of fuel for both the pre-Batmobile period and for the treatment period. Do the results lead to the inference that the Batmobile was effective?

b. The data appear to have some seasonality. Construct a multiple-regression model using the fuel variable, seasonal dummy variables, and a separate dummy variable for the Batmobile program to explain the injuries and fatalities variable. Explain the diagnostic statistics and present your reasoned opinion on the efficacy of the Batmobile program.

c. There is some evidence that programs like the Batmobile program take some time to "catch on." If this is actually the case, the dummy variable representing the existence of the Batmobile program can be modified to examine whether there is a "cascading" effect to the program. The data set also contains a "ramped" version of the Batmobile dummy in which the variable is zero in the pretreatment period but takes on a value of one in the first treatment period and increases in value by one for each subsequent treatment period. In a sense, this treatment mimics a ramping up of the effectiveness of the Batmobile effort. Run such a model and examine the relevant summary statistics. Is there evidence of a ramping effect? What degree of confidence do you have in your answer?

13. This is a problem in model selection. A "big box" home improvement store has collected data on its sales and demographic variables relating to its various stores. The cross-sectional data set for these variables is below:

Sales	X1	X2	X3	X4	X5
281	878	6,575	175	7.94	2,387
269	887	6,236	134	7.59	3,003
267	1,174	5,665	88	8.88	3,079
231	957	5,255	72	7.78	3,030
265	987	5,956	151	7.92	3,466
260	871	5,976	82	8.19	2,563
310	1,042	7,028	82	7.77	2,888
324	1,165	7,162	27	8.15	3,457
222	745	5,201	99	9.01	3,004
283	801	6,563	185	7.88	3,559
241	946	5,540	82	9.79	2,592
333	1,375	6,936	129	7.93	3,379
231	842	5,446	154	8.28	3,374
239	1,006	5,333	172	7.77	3,743
281	1,294	5,824	94	9.06	3,249
276	1,002	6,332	70	9.86	3,155
299	1,208	6,716	96	7.74	2,287
272	943	6,348	152	9.66	2,803

(continued on next page)

Sales	X1	X2	X3	X4	X5
273	581	6,500	133	6.85	3,212
246	1,044	5,545	117	8.47	2,796
239	1,005	5,432	144	7.95	2,232
273	963	6,215	138	10.49	2,926
301	1,104	6,861	86	10.35	2,888
267	967	6,127	194	8.87	2,627
282	1,095	6,335	55	9.35	2,956
274	701	6,633	100	9.11	2,885
244	839	5,616	82	8.86	3,442
279	1,200	5,921	92	8.69	3,252
241	803	5,625	156	9.08	2,477
276	1,085	6,160	90	8.4	3,233
235	874	5,258	137	10.24	3,775
288	1,317	6,312	156	9.95	2,210
223	1,109	4,774	103	9.36	2,905
232	865	5,202	68	10.41	3,134
273	922	6,364	137	9.03	2,567
325	1,142	7,356	94	8.07	2,476
235	1,009	5,099	144	8.09	3,493
278	1,178	6,058	63	10.6	3,462
293	1,126	6,559	153	9.37	3,317
237	222	5,872	115	5.84	2,377

where:

Sales = average monthly store sales (in thousands of dollars)

X1 = Households in a 5-mile ring that are do-it-youselfers (in thousands)

X2 = Average monthly advertising expenditures (in dollars)

X3 = Square footage of competitor stores in a 5-mile ring (in thousands)

X4 = Households in a 5-mile ring that are below the poverty level (in hundreds)

X5 = Weighted average daily traffic count at store intersection

a. Begin by estimating a model with independent variables X1, X2, and X3. Comment on the appropriateness of this model and its accuracy.

b. Now add X4 to the model above and again comment on the appropriateness of the model. Has the accuracy improved?

c. Finally, add X5 to the model and again comment on the accuracy of the model. Use the appropriate summary statistics of the three models to suggest which of the five independent variables should be in the model. Advise the "big box" retailer on which characteristics are important when choosing new store locations.

Time-Series Decomposition

Many business and economic time series contain underlying components that, when examined individually, can help the forecaster better understand data movements and therefore make better forecasts. As discussed in Chapter 2, these components include the long-term trend, seasonal fluctuations, cyclical movements, and irregular or random fluctuations. Time-series decomposition models can be used to identify such underlying components by breaking the series into its component parts and then reassembling the parts to construct a forecast.

> The information provided by time-series decomposition is consistent with the way managers tend to look at data and often helps them to get a better handle on data movements by providing concrete measurements for factors that are otherwise not quantified.

These models are among the oldest of the forecasting techniques available and yet remain popular today. Their popularity is due primarily to three factors. First, in many situations, time-series decomposition models provide excellent forecasts. Second, these models are relatively easy to understand and to explain to forecast users. This enhances the likelihood that the forecasts will be correctly interpreted and properly used. Third, the information provided by time-series decomposition is consistent with the way managers tend to look at data, and often helps them to get a better handle on data movements by providing concrete measurements for factors that are otherwise not quantified.

There are a number of different methods for decomposing a time series. The one we will use is usually referred to as *classical time-series decomposition* and involves the ratio-to-moving-average technique. The classical time-series decomposition model uses the concepts of moving averages presented in Chapter 3 and trend projections discussed in Chapter 4. It also accounts for seasonality in a multiplicative way that is similar to what you have seen in Winters' exponential smoothing and the way we used seasonal indices in earlier chapters.[1]

THE BASIC TIME-SERIES DECOMPOSITION MODEL

Look at the data on private housing starts (PHS) that are shown in Table 6.1 and Figure 6.1. While the series appears quite volatile, there is also some pattern to the movement in the data. The sharp increases and decreases in housing starts appear

---

[1] Remember that you have also accounted for seasonality using dummy variables in regression models. That method uses additive factors rather than multiplicative ones to account for seasonal patterns.

TABLE 6.1 Private Housing Starts (PHS) in Thousands of Units (c6t1&f1)

Date	Private Housing Starts (000)	Date	Private Housing Starts (000)	Date	Private Housing Starts (000)	Date	Private Housing Starts (000)	Date	Private Housing Starts (000)
Aug-75	117.3	Jan-79	88.2	Jun-82	91.1	Nov-85	124.1	Apr-89	129.4
Sep-75	111.9	Feb-79	84.2	Jul-82	106.8	Dec-85	120.5	May-89	131.7
Oct-75	123.6	Mar-79	152.9	Aug-82	96	Jan-86	115.6	Jun-89	143.2
Nov-75	96.9	Apr-79	161	Sep-82	106.4	Feb-86	107.2	Jul-89	134.7
Dec-75	76.1	May-79	189.1	Oct-82	110.5	Mar-86	151	Aug-89	122.4
Jan-76	72.5	Jun-79	191.8	Nov-82	108.9	Apr-86	188.2	Sep-89	109.3
Feb-76	89.9	Jul-79	164.2	Dec-82	82.9	May-86	186.6	Oct-89	130.1
Mar-76	118.4	Aug-79	170.3	Jan-83	91.3	Jun-86	183.6	Nov-89	96.6
Apr-76	137.2	Sep-79	163.7	Feb-83	96.3	Jul-86	172	Dec-89	75
May-76	147.9	Oct-79	169	Mar-83	134.6	Aug-86	163.8	Jan-90	99.2
Jun-76	154.2	Nov-79	118.7	Apr-83	135.8	Sep-86	154	Feb-90	86.9
Jul-76	136.6	Dec-79	91.6	May-83	174.9	Oct-86	154.8	Mar-90	108.5
Aug-76	145.9	Jan-80	73.1	Jun-83	173.2	Nov-86	115.6	Apr-90	119
Sep-76	151.8	Feb-80	79.9	Jul-83	161.6	Dec-86	113	May-90	121.1
Oct-76	148.4	Mar-80	85.1	Aug-83	176.8	Jan-87	105.1	Jun-90	117.8
Nov-76	127.1	Apr-80	96.2	Sep-83	154.9	Feb-87	102.8	Jul-90	111.2
Dec-76	107.4	May-80	91.7	Oct-83	159.3	Mar-87	141.2	Aug-90	102.8
Jan-77	81.3	Jun-80	116.4	Nov-83	136	Apr-87	159.3	Sep-90	93.1
Feb-77	112.5	Jul-80	120.1	Dec-83	108.3	May-87	158	Oct-90	94.2
Mar-77	173.6	Aug-80	129.9	Jan-84	109.1	Jun-87	162.9	Nov-90	81.4
Apr-77	182.2	Sep-80	138.3	Feb-84	130	Jul-87	152.4	Dec-90	57.4
May-77	201.3	Oct-80	152.7	Mar-84	137.5	Aug-87	143.6	Jan-91	52.5
Jun-77	197.6	Nov-80	112.9	Apr-84	172.7	Sep-87	152	Feb-91	59.1
Jul-77	189.8	Dec-80	95.9	May-84	180.7	Oct-87	139.1	Mar-91	73.8
Aug-77	194	Jan-81	84.5	Jun-84	184	Nov-87	118.8	Apr-91	99.7
Sep-77	177.7	Feb-81	71.9	Jul-84	162.1	Dec-87	85.4	May-91	97.7
Oct-77	193.1	Mar-81	107.8	Aug-84	147.4	Jan-88	78.2	Jun-91	103.4
Nov-77	154.8	Apr-81	123	Sep-84	148.5	Feb-88	90.2	Jul-91	103.5
Dec-77	129.2	May-81	109.9	Oct-84	152.3	Mar-88	128.8	Aug-91	94.7
Jan-78	88.6	Jun-81	105.8	Nov-84	126.2	Apr-88	153.2	Sep-91	86.6
Feb-78	101.3	Jul-81	99.9	Dec-84	98.9	May-88	140.2	Oct-91	101.8
Mar-78	172.1	Aug-81	86.3	Jan-85	105.4	Jun-88	150.2	Nov-91	75.6
Apr-78	197.5	Sep-81	84.1	Feb-85	95.4	Jul-88	137	Dec-91	65.6
May-78	211	Oct-81	87.2	Mar-85	145	Aug-88	136.8	Jan-92	71.6
Jun-78	216	Nov-81	64.6	Apr-85	175.8	Sep-88	131.1	Feb-92	78.8
Jul-78	192.2	Dec-81	59.1	May-85	170.2	Oct-88	135.1	Mar-92	111.6
Aug-78	190.9	Jan-82	47.2	Jun-85	163.2	Nov-88	113	Apr-92	107.6
Sep-78	180.5	Feb-82	51.3	Jul-85	160.7	Dec-88	94.2	May-92	115.2
Oct-78	192.1	Mar-82	78.2	Aug-85	160.7	Jan-89	100.1	Jun-92	117.8
Nov-78	158.6	Apr-82	84.1	Sep-85	147.7	Feb-89	85.8	Jul-92	106.2
Dec-78	119.5	May-82	98.8	Oct-85	173	Mar-89	117.8	Aug-92	109.9

(continued on next page)

10

TABLE 6.1 (continued)

Date	Private Housing Starts (000)	Date	Private Housing Starts (000)	Date	Private Housing Starts (000)	Date	Private Housing Starts (000)	Date	Private Housing Starts (000)
Sep-92	106	Sep-95	122.4	Sep-98	141.5	Sep-01	133.1	Sep-04	164
Oct-92	111.8	Oct-95	126.2	Oct-98	155.5	Oct-01	139.8	Oct-04	181.3
Nov-92	84.5	Nov-95	107.2	Nov-98	124.2	Nov-01	121	Nov-04	138.1
Dec-92	78.6	Dec-95	92.8	Dec-98	119.6	Dec-01	104.6	Dec-04	140.2
Jan-93	70.5	Jan-96	90.7	Jan-99	106.8	Jan-02	110.4	Jan-05	142.9
Feb-93	74.6	Feb-96	95.9	Feb-99	110.2	Feb-02	120.4	Feb-05	149.1
Mar-93	95.5	Mar-96	116	Mar-99	147.3	Mar-02	138.2	Mar-05	156.2
Apr-93	117.8	Apr-96	146.6	Apr-99	144.6	Apr-02	148.8	Apr-05	184.6
May-93	120.9	May-96	143.9	May-99	153.2	May-02	165.5	May-05	197.9
Jun-93	128.5	Jun-96	138	Jun-99	149.4	Jun-02	160.3	Jun-05	192.8
Jul-93	115.3	Jul-96	137.5	Jul-99	152.6	Jul-02	155.9	Jul-05	187.6
Aug-93	121.8	Aug-96	144.2	Aug-99	152.9	Aug-02	147	Aug-05	192
Sep-93	118.5	Sep-96	128.7	Sep-99	140.3	Sep-02	155.6	Sep-05	187.9
Oct-93	123.3	Oct-96	130.8	Oct-99	142.9	Oct-02	146.8	Oct-05	180.4
Nov-93	102.3	Nov-96	111.5	Nov-99	127.4	Nov-02	133	Nov-05	160.7
Dec-93	98.7	Dec-96	93.1	Dec-99	113.6	Dec-02	123.1	Dec-05	136
Jan-94	76.2	Jan-97	82.2	Jan-00	104	Jan-03	117.8	Jan-06	153
Feb-94	83.5	Feb-97	94.7	Feb-00	119.7	Feb-03	109.7	Feb-06	145.1
Mar-94	134.3	Mar-97	120.4	Mar-00	133.4	Mar-03	147.2	Mar-06	165.9
Apr-94	137.6	Apr-97	142.3	Apr-00	149.5	Apr-03	151.2	Apr-06	160.5
May-94	148.8	May-97	136.3	May-00	152.9	May-03	165	May-06	190.2
Jun-94	136.4	Jun-97	140.4	Jun-00	146.3	Jun-03	174.5	Jun-06	170.2
Jul-94	127.8	Jul-97	134.6	Jul-00	135	Jul-03	175.8	Jul-06	160.9
Aug-94	139.8	Aug-97	126.5	Aug-00	141.4	Aug-03	163.8	Aug-06	146.8
Sep-94	130.1	Sep-97	139.2	Sep-00	128.9	Sep-03	171.3	Sep-06	150.1
Oct-94	130.6	Oct-97	139	Oct-00	139.7	Oct-03	173.5	Oct-06	130.6
Nov-94	113.4	Nov-97	112.4	Nov-00	117.1	Nov-03	153.7	Nov-06	115.2
Dec-94	98.5	Dec-97	106	Dec-00	100.7	Dec-03	144.2	Dec-06	112.4
Jan-95	84.5	Jan-98	91.2	Jan-01	106.4	Jan-04	124.5	Jan-07	95
Feb-95	81.6	Feb-98	101.1	Feb-01	108.2	Feb-04	126.4	Feb-07	103.1
Mar-95	103.8	Mar-98	132.6	Mar-01	133.2	Mar-04	173.8	Mar-07	123.8
Apr-95	116.9	Apr-98	144.9	Apr-01	151.3	Apr-04	179.5	Apr-07	135.6
May-95	130.5	May-98	143.3	May-01	154	May-04	187.6	May-07	136.5
Jun-95	123.4	Jun-98	159.6	Jun-01	155.2	Jun-04	172.3	Jun-07	137.8
Jul-95	129.1	Jul-98	156	Jul-01	154.6	Jul-04	182	Jul-07	127
Aug-95	135.8	Aug-98	147.5	Aug-01	141.5	Aug-04	185.9	Aug-07	119.2

to follow one another in a reasonably regular manner, which may reflect a seasonal component. There also appears to be some long-term wavelike movement to the data as well as a slight negative trend. Patterns such as these are relatively common and can best be understood if they can each be isolated and examined individually. The classical time-series decomposition forecasting technique is a well-established procedure for accomplishing this end.

FIGURE 6.1 **Private Housing Starts in Thousands of Units by Month** (c6t1&f1)
This plot of private housing starts shows the volatility in the data. There are repeated
sharp upward and downward movements that appear regular and may be of a seasonal
nature. There also appears to be some wavelike cyclical pattern and perhaps a very slight
positive trend.

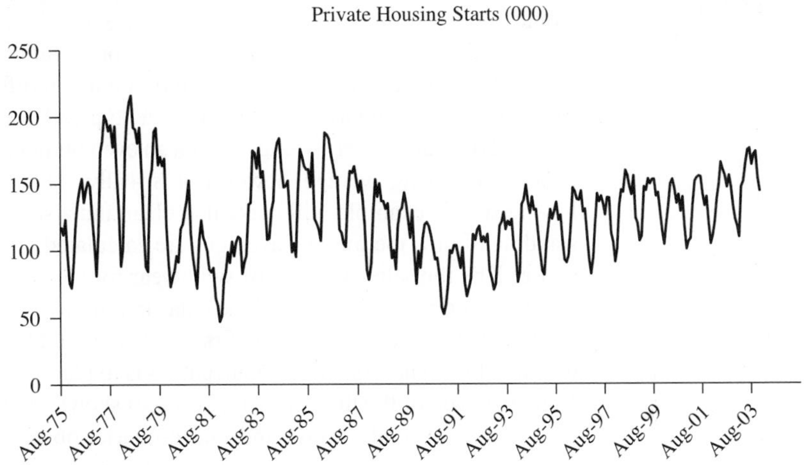

Private Housing Starts (000)

The model can be represented by a simple algebraic statement, as follows:

$$Y = T \times S \times C \times I$$

where Y is the variable that is to be forecast, T is the long-term (or secular) trend
in the data, S is a seasonal adjustment factor, C is the cyclical adjustment factor,
and I represents irregular or random variations in the series. Our objective will be
to find a way to decompose this series into the individual components.

DESEASONALIZING THE DATA AND FINDING SEASONAL INDICES

The first step in working
with this model is to
remove the short-term
fluctuations from the
data so that the longer-
term trend and cycle
components can be
more clearly identified.

The first step in working with this model is to remove the short-term fluctuations
from the data so that the longer-term trend and cycle components can be more
clearly identified. These short-term fluctuations include both seasonal patterns
and irregular variations. They can be removed by calculating an appropriate moving average (MA) for the series. The moving average should contain the same
number of periods as there are in the seasonality that you want to identify. Thus, if
you have quarterly data and suspect seasonality on a quarterly basis, a four-period
moving average is appropriate. If you have monthly data and want to identify the
monthly pattern in the data, a 12-period moving average should be used. The moving average for time period t (MA_t) is calculated as follows:

For quarterly data:

$$MA_t = (Y_{t-2} + Y_{t-1} + Y_t + Y_{t+1})/4$$

For monthly data:

$$MA_t = (Y_{t-6} + Y_{t-5} + \cdots + Y_t + Y_{t+1} + \cdots + Y_{t+5})/12$$

The moving average represents a "typical" level of Y for the year that is centered on that moving average.

The moving average for each time period contains one element from each of the seasons. For example, in the case of quarterly data, each moving average would contain a first-quarter observation, a second-quarter observation, a third-quarter observation, and a fourth-quarter observation (not necessarily in that order). The average of these four quarters should therefore not have any seasonality. Thus, the moving average represents a "typical" level of Y for the year that is centered on that moving average. When an even number of periods are used in calculating a moving average, however, it is really not centered in the year. The following simple example will make that clear and also help you verify your understanding of how the moving averages are calculated.

Let Y be the sales of a line of swimwear for which we have quarterly data (we will look at only six quarters of the data stream). MA_3 is the average of quarters 1 through 4. To be centered in the first year, it should be halfway between the second and third quarters, but the convention is to place it at the third quarter ($t = 3$). Note that each of the three moving averages shown in the following example contains a first-, second-, third-, and fourth-quarter observation. Thus, seasonality in the data is removed. Irregular fluctuations are also largely removed, since such variations are random events that are likely to offset one another over time.

	Time Index	Y	Moving Average	Centered Moving Average
Year 1:				
First quarter	1	10	MISSING	MISSING
Second quarter	2	18	MISSING	MISSING
Third quarter	3	20	15.0(MA$_3$)	15.25(CMA$_3$)
Fourth quarter	4	12	15.5(MA$_4$)	15.75(CMA$_4$)
Year 2:				
First quarter	5	12	16.0(MA$_5$)	MISSING
Second quarter	6	20	MISSING	MISSING

$$MA_3 = (10 + 18 + 20 + 12)/4 = 15.0$$
$$MA_4 = (18 + 20 + 12 + 12)/4 = 15.5$$
$$MA_5 = (20 + 12 + 12 + 20)/4 = 16.0$$

As noted, when an even number of periods are used, the moving averages are not really centered in the middle of the year. To center the moving averages, a two-period moving average of the moving averages is calculated.[2] This is called a

---

[2] If the number of periods used is odd, the moving averages will automatically be centered, and no further adjustment is usually made.

centered moving average. The centered moving average for time period t (CMA_t) is found as follows:

$$CMA_t = (MA_t + MA_{t+1})/2$$

For the swimwear data used in our example we have:

$$CMA_3 = (15.0 + 15.5)/2 = 15.25$$
$$CMA_4 = (15.5 + 16.0)/2 = 15.75$$

This second moving average further helps to smooth out irregular or random fluctuations in the data.

Note the "MISSING" that appears under the moving average and centered moving average columns in the data table. With just six data points, we could not calculate four-period moving averages for the first, second, or sixth time period. We then lose one more time period in calculating the centered moving average. Thus, the smoothing process has a cost in terms of the loss of some data points. If an n-period moving average is used, $n/2$ points will be lost at each end of the data series by the time the centered moving averages have been calculated. This cost is not without benefit, however, since the process will eventually provide clarification of the patterns in the data.

By comparing the actual value of the series in any time period (Y_t) with the deseasonalized value (CMA_t), you can get a measure of the degree of seasonality.

The centered moving averages represent the deseasonalized data (i.e., seasonal variations have been removed through an averaging process). By comparing the actual value of the series in any time period (Y_t) with the deseasonalized value (CMA_t), you can get a measure of the degree of seasonality. In classical time-series decomposition this is done by finding the ratio of the actual value to the deseasonalized value. The result is called a *seasonal factor* (SF_t). That is:

$$SF_t = Y_t/CMA_t$$

A seasonal factor greater than 1 indicates a period in which Y is greater than the yearly average, while the reverse is true if SF is less than 1. For our brief swimwear sales example, we can calculate seasonal factors for the third and fourth time periods as follows:

$$SF_3 = Y_3/CMA_3 = 20/15.25 = 1.31$$
$$SF_4 = Y_4/CMA_4 = 12/15.75 = 0.76$$

We see that the third period (third quarter of year 1) is a high-sales quarter while the fourth period is a low-sales quarter. This makes sense, since swimwear would be expected to sell well in July, August, and September, but not in October, November, and December.

When we look at all of the seasonal factors for an extended time period, we generally see reasonable consistency in the values for each season. We would not expect all first-quarter seasonal factors to be exactly the same, but they are likely to be similar. To establish a seasonal index (SI), we average the seasonal factors for each season. This will now be illustrated for the private housing starts data shown initially in Table 6.1 and Figure 6.1.

The data for private housing starts are reproduced in part in Table 6.2. Only the beginning and near the end of the series are shown, but that is sufficient to illustrate

TABLE 6.2 Time-Series Decomposition of Private Housing Starts (c6t2)

1	2	3	4	5	6	7	8	9
Date	Time Index	PHS (000)	PHSMA	PHSCMA	PHSCMAT	CF	SF	SI
Aug-75	1	117.3						1.10
Sep-75	2	111.9						1.06
Oct-75	3	123.6						1.11
Nov-75	4	96.9						0.90
Dec-75	5	76.1						0.78
Jan-76	6	72.5						0.73
Feb-76	7	89.9	115.21	116.40	123.16	0.95	0.77	0.75
Mar-76	8	118.4	117.59	119.25	123.20	0.97	0.99	1.00
Apr-76	9	137.2	120.92	121.95	123.24	0.99	1.13	1.12
May-76	10	147.9	122.98	124.24	123.28	1.01	1.19	1.16
Jun-76	11	154.2	125.50	126.80	123.32	1.03	1.22	1.17
Jul-76	12	136.6	128.11	128.48	123.35	1.04	1.06	1.12
Aug-76	13	145.9	128.84	129.78	123.39	1.05	1.12	1.10
Sep-76	14	151.8	130.73	133.03	123.43	1.08	1.14	1.06
Oct-76	15	148.4	135.33	137.20	123.47	1.11	1.08	1.11
Nov-76	16	127.1	139.08	141.30	123.51	1.14	0.90	0.90
Dec-76	17	107.4	143.53	145.33	123.55	1.18	0.74	0.78
.	.	.	.	.	.	.	.	.
.	.	.	.	.	.	.	.	.
.	.	.	.	.	.	.	.	.
Aug-05	361	192	173.18	173.02	136.80	1.26	1.11	1.10
Sep-05	362	187.9	172.85	173.25	136.83	1.27	1.08	1.06
Oct-05	363	180.4	173.66	172.65	136.87	1.26	1.04	1.11
Nov-05	364	160.7	171.65	171.33	136.91	1.25	0.94	0.90
Dec-05	365	136	171.01	170.07	136.95	1.24	0.80	0.78
Jan-06	366	153	169.13	168.01	136.99	1.23	0.91	0.73
Feb-06	367	145.1	166.90	165.02	137.03	1.20	0.88	0.75
Mar-06	368	165.9	163.13	161.56	137.06	1.18	1.03	1.00
Apr-06	369	160.5	159.98	157.91	137.10	1.15	1.02	1.12
May-06	370	190.2	155.83	153.94	137.14	1.12	1.24	1.16
Jun-06	371	170.2	152.04	151.06	137.18	1.10	1.13	1.17
Jul-06	372	160.9	150.08	147.66	137.22	1.08	1.09	1.12
Aug-06	373	146.8	145.24	143.49	137.26	1.05	1.02	1.10
Sep-06	374	150.1	141.74	139.99	137.30	1.02	1.07	1.06
Oct-06	375	130.6	138.23	137.20	137.33	1.00	0.95	1.11
Nov-06	376	115.2	136.16	133.92	137.37	0.97	0.86	0.90
Dec-06	377	112.4	131.68	130.33	137.41	0.95	0.86	0.78

PHS = Private housing starts (in thousands)
PHSMA = Private housing starts moving average
PHSCMA = Private housing starts centered moving average
PHSCMAT = Private housing starts centered moving-average trend (trend component)
CF = Cycle factor (PHSCMA/PHSCMAT)
SF = Seasonal factor (PHS/PHSCMA)
SI = Seasonal indices (normalized mean of seasonal factors)

all of the necessary calculations. The moving average for private housing starts is denoted as PHSMA (private housing starts moving average) and is shown in the fourth column of Table 6.2. The elements included in two values of PHSMA are shown by the brackets in the table and are calculated by adding the corresponding 12 months and then dividing by 12.

The centered moving average (PHSCMA) is shown in the next column. The calculation of PHSCMA for Feb-76 is:

$$PHSCMA = (115.21 + 117.59)/2 = 116.40$$

Notice that for PHSCMA there is no value for each of the first six and last six months. This loss of 12 months of data over 385 months is not too severe. The six lost months that are most critical are the last six, since they are the closest to the period to be forecast.

Figure 6.2 shows a plot of the original private housing starts (PHS) data (lighter line) along with the deseasonalized data (darker line) represented by the centered moving averages (PHSCMAs). Notice how much smoother the data appear once seasonal variations and random fluctuations have been removed.

The process of deseasonalizing the data has two useful results:

The deseasonalized data allow us to see better the underlying pattern in the data.

1. The deseasonalized data allow us to see better the underlying pattern in the data, as illustrated in Figure 6.2.
2. It provides us with measures of the extent of seasonality in the form of seasonal indices.

FIGURE 6.2   **Private Housing Starts (PHS) with the Centered Moving Average of Private Housing Starts (PHSCMA) in Thousands of Units**   (c6f2)

The centered moving-average series, shown by the darker line, is much smoother than the original series of private housing starts data (lighter line) because the seasonal pattern and the irregular or random fluctuations in the data are removed by the process of calculating the centered moving averages.

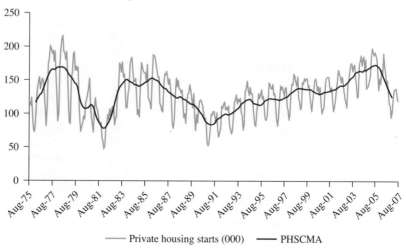

Private housing starts (000)   PHSCMA

The seasonal factors for each quarter are shown in the eighth column of Table 6.2. Recall that the seasonal factors measure the extent to which the observed value for each quarter is above or below the deseasonalized value (SF $>$ 1 and SF $<$ 1, respectively). For this example:

$$SF_t = PHS_t/PHSCMA_t$$

For the first six and the last six months, seasonal factors cannot be calculated, since there are no centered moving averages for those months. The calculations of the seasonal factor for Feb-76 is:

$$SF = 89.9/116.4 = 0.77$$

It makes sense that winter months would have a low SF (less than 1), since these are often not good months in which to start building. The reverse is true in the spring and summer.

In Table 6.3 the seasonal factors and seasonal indices for the months of April through August are all at or above 1 and indicate that these months are generally high for private housing starts. Since the seasonal factors for each period are bound to have some variability, we calculate a seasonal index (SI) for each period, which is a standardized average of all of that period's seasonal factors.

TABLE 6.3
Seasonal Factors and Seasonal Indices for Private Housing Starts (Selected Years) (c6t3)

Date	SF	SI	Date	SF	SI
Aug-75	na	1.10	Jan-05	0.85	0.73
Sep-75	na	1.06	Feb-05	0.88	0.75
Oct-75	na	1.11	Mar-05	0.92	1.00
Nov-75	na	0.90	Apr-05	1.08	1.12
Dec-75	na	0.78	May-05	1.15	1.16
Jan-76	na	0.73	Jun-05	1.12	1.17
Feb-76	0.77	0.75	Jul-05	1.09	1.12
Mar-76	0.99	1.00	Aug-05	1.11	1.10
Apr-76	1.13	1.12	Sep-05	1.08	1.06
May-76	1.19	1.16	Oct-05	1.04	1.11
Jun-76	1.22	1.17	Nov-05	0.94	0.90
Jul-76	1.06	1.12	Dec-05	0.80	0.78
Aug-76	1.12	1.10	Jan-06	0.91	0.73
Sep-76	1.14	1.06	Feb-06	0.88	0.75
Oct-76	1.08	1.11	Mar-06	1.03	1.00
Nov-76	0.90	0.90	Apr-06	1.02	1.12
Dec-76	0.74	0.78	May-06	1.24	1.16
			Jun-06	1.13	1.17

This table is abbreviated to save space. All of the SFs are in the data file c6t2.

The determination of the seasonal indices are calculated as follows. The seasonal factors for each of the 12 months are summed and divided by the number of observations to arrive at the average, or mean, seasonal factor for each quarter.[3] The sum of the average seasonal factors should equal the number of periods (4 for quarters, 12 for months). If it does not, the average seasonal factors should be normalized by multiplying each by the ratio of the number of periods (12 for monthly data) to the sum of the average seasonal factors.

Doing this we find that seasonal indices for private housing starts are as follows (rounded to two decimal places):

January:	0.73	May:	1.17	September:	1.06
February:	0.76	June:	1.17	October:	1.10
March:	1.00	July:	1.12	November:	0.90
April:	1.12	August:	1.10	December:	0.78

These add to 12.00 as expected. The warmer spring and summer months are the strongest seasons for housing starts.

As shown above, the private housing starts' seasonal index for January is 0.73. This means that the typical January PHS is only 73 percent of the average monthly value for the year. Thus, if the housing starts for a year totaled 400, we would expect 24.3 to occur in January. The 24.3 is found by dividing the yearly total (400) by 12, and then multiplying the result by the seasonal index [(400/12) $\times$ 0.73 = 24.3].

Another useful application of seasonal indices is in projecting what one month's observation may portend for the entire year. For example, assume that you were working for a manufacturer of major household appliances in April 2007 and heard that housing starts for January 2007 were 95. Since your sales depend heavily on new construction, you want to project this forward for the year. Let's see how you would do this, taking seasonality into account. Once the seasonal indices are known you can deseasonalize data by dividing by the appropriate index. That is:

$$\text{Deseasonalized data} = \text{Raw data}/\text{Seasonal index}$$

For January 2007 we have:

$$\text{Deseasonalized data} = 95.0/0.73 = 130.1$$

Multiplying this deseasonalized value by 12 would give a projection for the year of 1,561.2.

[3] A medial average is sometimes used to reduce the effect of outliers. The medial average is the average that is calculated after the highest and lowest values are removed from the data.

FINDING THE LONG-TERM TREND

The long-term trend is estimated from the deseasonalized data for the variable to be forecast. Remember that the centered moving average (CMA) is the series that remains after the seasonality and irregular components have been smoothed out by using moving averages. Thus, to find the long-term trend, we estimate a simple linear equation as:[4]

$$CMA = f(TIME)$$
$$= a + b(TIME)$$

where TIME = 1 for the first period in the data set and increases by 1 each quarter thereafter. The values of a and b are normally estimated by using a computer regression program, but they can also be found quickly on most hand-held business calculators.

Once the trend equation has been determined, it is used to generate an estimate of the trend value of the centered moving average for the historical and forecast periods. This new series is the centered moving-average trend (CMAT).

For our example involving private housing starts, the linear trend of the deseasonalized data (PHSCMA) has been found to be slightly negative. The centered moving-average trend for this example is denoted PHSCMAT, for "private housing starts centered moving-average trend." The equation is:

$$PHSCMAT = 122.94 + 0.04(TIME)$$

where TIME = 1 for August 1975. This line is shown in Figure 6.3, along with the graph of private housing starts (PHS) and the deseasonalized data (PHSCMA).

MEASURING THE CYCLICAL COMPONENT

The cyclical component of a time series is the extended wavelike movement about the long-term trend. It is measured by a cycle factor (CF), which is the ratio of the centered moving average (CMA) to the centered moving-average trend (CMAT). That is:

$$CF = CMA/CMAT$$

A cycle factor greater than 1 indicates that the deseasonalized value for that period is above the long-term trend of the data. If CF is less than 1, the reverse is true.

---

[4] A linear trend is most often used, but a nonlinear trend may also be used. Looking at a graph such as the one shown in Figure 6.2 is helpful in determining which form would be most appropriate for the trend line.

FIGURE 6.3 **Private Housing Starts (PHS) with Centered Moving Average (PHSCMA) and Centered Moving-Average Trend (PHSCMAT) in Thousands of Units** (c6f3)

The long-term trend in private housing starts is shown by the straight dotted line (PHSCMAT). The lighter line is the raw data (PHS), while the wavelike dark line is the deseasonalized data (PHSCMA). The long-term trend is seen to be slightly negative. The equation for the trend line is: PHSCMAT = 122.94 + .04(TIME).

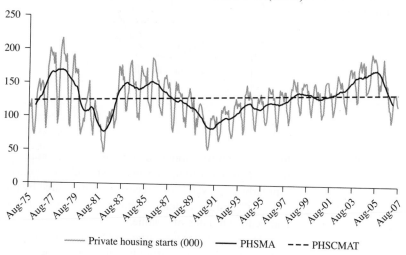

Private housing starts (000) ——— PHSMA --- PHSCMAT

> Looking at the length and amplitude of previous cycles may enable us to anticipate the next turning point in the current cycle.

The cycle factor is the most difficult component of a time series to analyze and to project into the forecast period. If analyzed carefully, however, it may also be the component that has the most to offer in terms of understanding where the industry may be headed. Looking at the length and amplitude of previous cycles may enable us to anticipate the next turning point in the current cycle. This is a major advantage of the time-series decomposition technique. An individual familiar with an industry can often explain cyclic movements around the trend line in terms of variables or events that, in retrospect, can be seen to have had some import. By looking at those variables or events in the present, we can sometimes get some hint of the likely future direction of the cycle component.

Overview of Business Cycles

Business cycles are long-term wavelike fluctuations in the general level of economic activity. They are often described by a diagram such as the one shown in Figure 6.4. The period of time between the beginning trough (*A*) and the peak (*B*) is called the *expansion phase,* while the period from peak (*B*) to the ending trough (*C*) is termed the *recession,* or *contraction, phase.*

The vertical distance between *A* and *B'* provides a measure of the degree of the expansion. The start of the expansion beginning at point *A* is determined by

FIGURE 6.4
The General Business Cycle
A business cycle goes through successive periods of expansion, contraction, expansion, contraction, and so on.

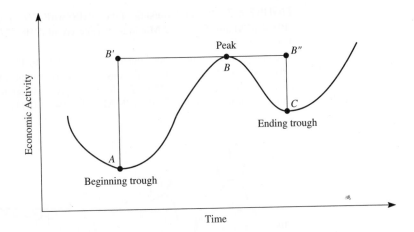

three consecutive months of increase in economic activity. Thus, the preceding recession is only officially over three months after the economy has turned around. Similarly, the severity of a recession is measured by the vertical distance between B'' and C, and the official beginning of the recession is dated as the first of three consecutive months of decline.

If business cycles were true cycles, they would have a constant amplitude. That is, the vertical distance from trough to peak and peak to trough would always be the same. In addition, a true cycle would also have a constant periodicity. That would mean that the length of time between successive peaks (or troughs) would always be the same. However, with economic and business activity this degree of regularity is unlikely. As you will see when we look at the cyclical component for private housing starts, the vertical distances from trough to peak (or peak to trough) have some variability, as does the distance between successive peaks and successive troughs.

Business Cycle Indicators

There are a number of possible business cycle indicators, but three are particularly noteworthy:

1. The index of leading economic indicators
2. The index of coincident economic indicators
3. The index of lagging economic indicators

The individual series that make up each index are shown in Table 6.4.

It is possible that one of these indices, or one of the series that make up an index, may be useful in predicting the cycle factor in a time-series decomposition. This could be done in a regression analysis with the cycle factor (CF) as the

TABLE 6.4
U.S. Business Cycle Indicators

Source: The Conference Board (http://www.conference-board.org/economics/bci/component.cfm). Data in this table are from The Conference Board, which produces the U.S. Business Cycle Indicators.

Components of the Composite Indices*

Leading Index

Average weekly hours, manufacturing
Average weekly initial claims for unemployment insurance
Manufacturers' new orders, consumer goods and materials
Vendor performance, slower deliveries diffusion index
Manufacturers' new orders, nondefense capital goods
Building permits, new private housing units
Stock prices, 500 common stocks
Money supply, M2
Interest rate spread, 10-year Treasury bonds less federal funds
Index of consumer expectations

Coincident Index

Employees on nonagricultural payrolls
Personal income less transfer payments
Industrial production index
Manufacturing and trade sales

Lagging Index

Average duration of unemployment
Inventories-to-sales ratio, manufacturing and trade
Labor cost per unit of output, manufacturing
Average prime rate
Commercial and industrial loans
Consumer installment credit–to–personal income ratio
Consumer price index for services

*A short description of each of the indicators is found in the appendix to this chapter.

dependent variable. These indices, or their components, may also be quite useful as independent variables in other regression models, such as those discussed in Chapters 4 and 5.

Figure 6.5 shows what are considered the official business cycles for the U.S. economy in recent years. The shaded vertical bars identify the officially designated periods of recession.

The Cycle Factor for Private Housing Starts

Let us return to our example involving private housing starts to examine how to calculate the cycle factor and how it might be projected into the forecast period. In Table 6.2 the cycle factors (CF) are shown in column seven. As indicated previously,

FIGURE 6.5

Official Business Cycles in the United States

For each graph the top line (right hand axis) represents the corresponding index, while the bottom line (left hand axis) is the six-month growth rate.

Source: *Business Cycle Indicators* 10, no. 1 (January 2005). The Conference Board (accessed from http://www.conference-board.org/economics).

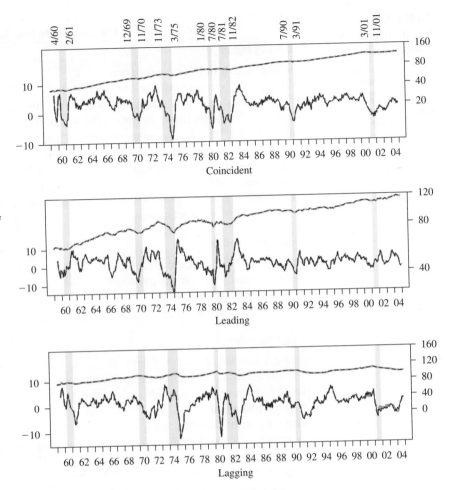

each cycle factor is the ratio of the deseasonalized data (CMA) to the trend value (CMAT). For the private housing starts data, we have:

$$CF = PHSCMA/PHSCMAT$$

The actual calculation for Jun-06 is:

$$CF = 151.06/137.18 = 1.10$$

You can see in Figure 6.3 that in Jun-06 the centered moving average was above the trend line.

The cycle factor is plotted in Figure 6.6. You can see that the cycle factor (CF) moves above and below the line at 1.00 in Figure 6.6 exactly as the centered moving average moves above and below the trend line in Figure 6.3. By isolating the cycle factor in Figure 6.6, we can better analyze its movements over time.

FIGURE 6.6

Cycle Factor (CF) for Private Housing Starts (c6f6)
The cycle factor is the ratio of the centered moving average to the long-term trend in the data. As this plot shows, the cycle factor moves slowly around the base line (1.00) with little regularity. Dates and values of cycle factors at peaks and troughs are shown.

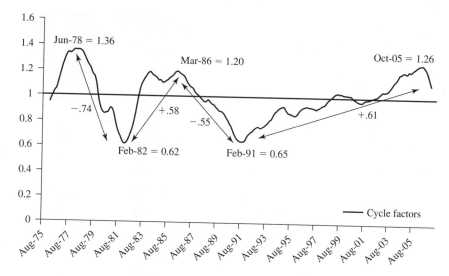

You see that the cyclical component for private housing starts does not have a constant amplitude or periodicity. The dates for peaks and troughs are shown in Figure 6.6, along with the values of the cycle factor at those points. Identification of these dates and values is often helpful in considering when the cycle factor may next turn around (i.e., when the next trough or peak may occur). For example, for the PHS cycle factor the average of the three peaks shown in Figure 6.6 was 1.27. The most recent peak in Oct-05 was at 1.26. We also see that the peak-to-trough distance between Jun-78 and Feb-82 was −.74 and that the distance from peak to trough between Mar-86 and Feb-91 was −.55. You can see the trough-to-peak changes in Figure 6.6 are 0.58 and 0.61. The latter covered an unusually long period from Feb-91 through Oct-05.[5]

The determination of where the cycle factor will be in the forecast horizon is a difficult task. One approach would be to examine the past pattern visually, focusing on prior peaks and troughs, with particular attention to their amplitude and periodicity, and then making a subjective projection into the forecast horizon. Another approach would be to use another forecasting method to forecast values because CF. Holt's exponential smoothing may sometimes be a good candidate for this task, but we must remember that such a model will not pick up a turning point until after it has occurred. Thus, the forecaster would never predict that the current rise or fall in the cycle would end. If we have recently observed a turning point and have several quarters of data since the turning point, and *if* we believe another turning point is unlikely during the forecast horizon, then Holt's exponential smoothing may be useful. In this example ForecastX produced a forecast of the cycle factor for private housing starts with the following results:

---

[5] As of the date of this edition of the text, a new trough had not yet been identified.

Month	CF Forecast
Jul-06	1.21
Aug-06	1.21
Sep-06	1.20
Oct-06	1.20
Nov-06	1.19
Dec-06	1.19
Jan-07	1.18
Feb-07	1.18
Mar-07	1.18
Apr-07	1.18
May-07	1.18
Jun-07	1.18
Jul-07	1.19
Aug-07	1.19
Sep-07	1.19
Oct-07	1.18
Nov-07	1.18
Dec-07	1.18

We see that this forecast projects a flattening of the cycle factor. Note that we have to forecast the cycle factor for the last six months of 2006, even though we had original PHS data for all of 2006. This is because we lost the last six observations in developing the centered moving averages. A graph of the actual and forecast cycle factors is shown in Figure 6.7.

FIGURE 6.7

Cycle Factor Forecast Here we see that the ForecastX forecast for the PHS cycle goes up to 1.21, then flattens out through the end of the forecast horizon (December 2007).

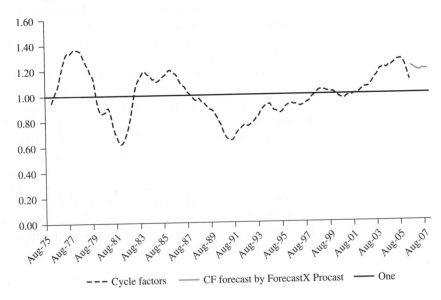

- - - Cycle factors   —— CF forecast by ForecastX Procast   —— One

It is important to recognize that there is no way to know exactly where the cycle factor will be in the forecast horizon, and there is no a priori way to determine the best technique for projecting the cycle factor. A thorough review of the past behavior of the cycle factor, along with alternative forecasts, should be evaluated for consistency and congruity before selecting values of the cycle factor for the forecast horizon.

Perhaps most frequently the cycle factor forecast is made on a largely judgmental basis by looking carefully at the historical values, especially historical turning points and the rates of descent or rise in the historical series. You might look at the peak-to-peak, trough-to-trough, peak-to-trough, and trough-to-peak distances by dating each turning point, such as we show in Figure 6.6. Then, you could calculate the average distance between troughs (or peaks) to get a feeling for when another such point is likely. You can also analyze the rates of increase and/or decrease in the cycle factor as a basis on which to judge the expected slope of the forecast of the cycle factor.

It is important to recognize that there is no way to know exactly where the cycle factor will be in the forecast horizon, and there is no a priori way to determine the best technique for projecting the cycle factor. A thorough review of the past behavior of the cycle factor, along with alternative forecasts, should be evaluated for consistency and congruity before selecting values of the cycle factor for the forecast horizon.

THE TIME-SERIES DECOMPOSITION FORECAST

You have seen that a time series of data can be decomposed into the product of four components:

$$Y = T \cdot S \cdot C \cdot I$$

where Y is the series to be forecast. The four components are:

T = The long-term trend based on the deseasonalized data. It is often called the *centered moving-average trend* (CMAT), since the deseasonalized data are centered moving averages (CMA) of the original Y values.

S = Seasonal indices (SI). These are normalized averages of seasonal factors that are determined as the ratio of each period's actual value (Y) to the deseasonalized value (CMA) for that period.

C = The cycle component. The cycle factor (CF) is the ratio of CMA to CMAT and represents the gradual wavelike movements in the series around the trend line.

I = The irregular component. This is assumed equal to 1 unless the forecaster has reason to believe a shock may take place, in which case I could be different from 1 for all or part of the forecast period.

Previous sections of this chapter have illustrated how these components can be isolated and measured.

To prepare a forecast based on the time-series decomposition model, we simply reassemble the components. In general terms, the forecast for Y (FY) is:

$$FY = (CMAT)(SI)(CF)(I)$$

FIGURE 6.8

Private Housing Starts (PHS) and a Time-Series Decomposition Forecast (PHSFTSD) for 1994 through 2007
(c6f8)
The actual values for private housing starts are shown by the lighter line, and the time-series decomposition forecast values are shown by the darker line.

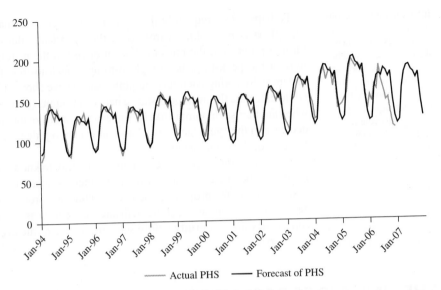

For our private housing starts example we will denote the forecast value based on the model as PHSFTSD. Thus,

$$\text{PHSFTSD} = (\text{PHSCMAT})(\text{SI})(\text{CF})(I)$$

where PHSCMAT is the private housing starts centered moving-average trend. The irregular factor (I) is assumed equal to 1, since we have no reason to expect it to be greater or less than 1 because of its random nature. The actual and forecast values for private housing starts are shown for 1994 through 2007 in Figure 6.8. The actual values (PHS) are shown by the lighter line; forecast values based on the time-series decomposition model are shown by the darker line. The forecast calculations are shown in Table 6.5 for the first and last parts of the series. You will note that this method takes the trend (PHSCMAT) and makes two adjustments to it: the first adjusts it for seasonality (with SI), and the second adjusts it for cycle variations (with CF).

Because time-series decomposition models do not involve a lot of mathematics or statistics, they are relatively easy to explain to the end user. This is a major advantage, because if the end user has an appreciation of how the forecast was developed, he or she may have more confidence in its use for decision making.

Forecasting Shoe Store Sales by Using Time-Series Decomposition

Let us now apply the classic time-series decomposition method to the problem of forecasting shoe store sales. Figure 6.9 shows the data for 1992 through 2003 that will be used to make a forecast for 2004. The original sales series (SSS) is the lighter solid line that fluctuates widely. The deseasonalized series (the centered moving averages, or CMAs) is shown by the heavy dashed line, and the long-term trend (CMAT) is shown by the thinner straight line.

TABLE 6.5
PHS Time-Series Decomposition Forecast   (c6t5)

Date	PHS (000)	Forecasted Data	PHSCMA	PHSCMAT	SI	CF
Aug-1975	117.30				1.10	
Sep-1975	111.90				1.06	
Oct-1975	123.60				1.11	
Nov-1975	96.90				0.90	
Dec-1975	76.10				0.78	
Jan-1976	72.50				0.73	
Feb-1976	89.90	87.71	116.40	123.21	0.75	0.94
Mar-1976	118.40	119.09	119.25	123.25	1.00	0.97
Apr-1976	137.20	136.00	121.95	123.28	1.12	0.99
May-1976	147.90	144.70	124.24	123.32	1.16	1.01
Jun-1976	154.20	148.04	126.80	123.36	1.17	1.03
Jul-1976	136.60	143.89	128.48	123.40	1.12	1.04
Aug-1976	145.90	143.31	129.78	123.44	1.10	1.05
Sep-1976	151.80	141.27	133.03	123.47	1.06	1.08
Oct-1976	148.40	151.68	137.20	123.51	1.11	1.11
Nov-1976	127.10	127.80	141.30	123.55	0.90	1.14
Dec-1976	107.40	112.98	145.33	123.59	0.78	1.18
.	.	.	.	.	.	.
.	.	.	.	.	.	.
.	.	.	.	.	.	.
Jan-2006	153.00	122.13	168.01	136.90	0.73	1.23
Feb-2006	145.10	124.34	165.02	136.93	0.75	1.21
Mar-2006	165.90	161.33	161.56	136.97	1.00	1.18
Apr-2006	160.50	176.11	157.91	137.01	1.12	1.15
May-2006	190.20	179.29	153.94	137.05	1.16	1.12
Jun-2006	170.20	176.36	151.06	137.09	1.17	1.10
Jul-2006	160.90	186.13		137.13	1.12	1.21
Aug-2006	146.80	182.91		137.16	1.10	1.21
Sep-2006	150.10	175.24		137.20	1.06	1.20
Oct-2006	130.60	181.67		137.24	1.11	1.20
Nov-2006	115.20	148.01		137.28	0.90	1.19
Dec-2006	112.40	126.71		137.32	0.78	1.19
Jan-2007	**95**	118.05		137.35	0.73	1.18
Feb-2007	**103.1**	122.01		137.39	0.75	1.18
Mar-2007	**123.8**	161.45		137.43	1.00	1.18
Apr-2007	**135.6**	180.32		137.47	1.12	1.18
May-2007	**136.5**	188.68		137.51	1.16	1.18
Jun-2007	**137.8**	189.92		137.54	1.17	1.18
Jul-2007	**127**	183.28		137.58	1.12	1.19
Aug-2007	**119.2**	180.47		137.62	1.10	1.19
Sep-2007	**na**	173.36		137.66	1.06	1.19
Oct-2007	**na**	180.31		137.70	1.11	1.18

(continued on next page)

TABLE 6.5
(continued)

Date	PHS (000)	Forecasted Data	PHSCMA	PHSCMAT	SI	CF
Nov-2007	na	147.43		137.74	0.90	1.18
Dec-2007	na	126.67		137.77	0.78	1.18

MSE Jan 07 to Aug 07 = 2,083.18
RMSE Jan 07 to Aug 07 = 45.64
RMSE as % of Mean = 37.3

Feb76 to Dec06
RMSE = 9.9
RMSE as % Mean = 7.6

Notes:
1. The cycle factors starting in July 2006 are estimated values rather than actual ratios of PHSCMA to PHSCMAT.
2. Forecast values for private housing starts (PHSFTSD) are determined as follows: PHSFTSD = (PHSCMAT)(SI)(CF)
3. The results that you get for PHS Forecast may vary slightly from those shown due to rounding.

FIGURE 6.9
**Time-Series
Decomposition
of Shoe Store
Sales Data ($000)**

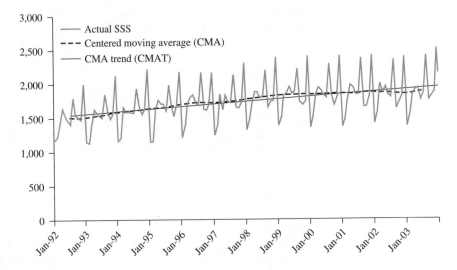

Note how the original series moves above and below the deseasonalized series and the trend in a fairly regular seasonal pattern. The seasonal indices, based on the normalized mean of the seasonal factors for shoe store sales, are:

January:	0.737	May:	1.043	September:	0.963
February:	0.800	June:	0.989	October:	0.935
March:	1.003	July:	0.982	November:	0.985
April:	1.031	August:	1.225	December:	1.308

In the spring months people may be buying shoes for summer activities, in August there are back-to-school sales, and in December sales increase related to the holiday season. These are indicated by the seasonal indices that are above 1.

The final time-series decomposition forecast (using ForecastX™) is shown by the thin solid line in Figure 6.10. The actual shoe store sales (including actual sales

FIGURE 6.10
Time-Series Decomposition Forecast of Shoe Store Sales Data ($000)

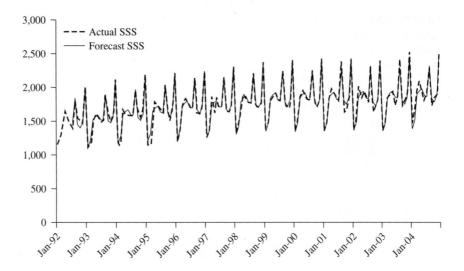

for 2004) are shown by the dashed line in Figure 6.10. For the period from July 1992 through December 2003 the RMSE for this monthly forecast was 56.3, which is about 3.2 percent of the mean actual sales for that period. For the 12 months of 2004 (which were not used in developing the forecast) the RMSE was 95.9 or about 5 percent of actual sales for that year based on monthly forecasts. For all of 2004 actual sales totaled 23,187, while the total forecast for the year was 22,849. Thus, for the entire year the forecast would have been low by just under 1.5 percent.

Forecasting Total Houses Sold by Using Time-Series Decomposition

Now we will apply the classic time-series decomposition method, as described in this chapter, to the problem of forecasting total houses sold (THS). Figure 6.11 shows the original series (THS) as the lighter line from January 1978 through December 2006. The centered moving averages (THSCMAs) are shown by the darker line, and the long-term trend values (THSCMAT) are shown by the dashed line.

Note how the original series moves above and below the deseasonalized series in a regular seasonal pattern. The seasonal indices, based on the normalized mean of the seasonal factors for total houses sold, are:

January:	0.89	May:	1.11	September:	0.96
February:	1.00	June:	1.08	October:	0.95
March:	1.18	July:	1.03	November:	0.84
April:	1.12	August:	1.05	December:	0.79

These seasonal indices provide evidence of generally slow sales during the fall and winter months. The positive slope for the trend (THSCMAT), as shown in Figure 6.11, indicates long-term growth in total houses sold.

The actual and forecast values for January 2000 through July 2007 are shown in Figure 6.12. The RMSE for the period 1978 (starting with July) through 2006 (June)

FIGURE 6.11

Total Houses Sold (000) Time-Series Decomposition

Actual total houses sold (THS) are shown by the lighter line (Jan78–Dec06). The centered moving averages (THSCMA) are shown by the darker line. The long-term trend is shown by the dashed line and extends to July 2007.

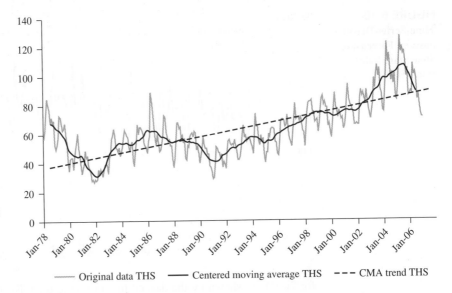

is 4.43 (000), which is about 7.0 percent of the mean for that period. For the first seven months of 2007 which were not used in developing the forecast the RMSE is 27.3 (000), which is about 36.2 percent of the mean for that 7-month period.

FIGURE 6.12 **Time Series Decomposition Forecast for Total Houses Sold (THS) in Thousands**

This graph shows the most recent years of the time-series decomposition forecast of total houses sold. Actual sales for 1978 through 2006 were used to develop the forecast through July 2007. These results were obtained using the decomposition method in ForecastX. We see that this model did not foresee the continuing downturn in the housing market.

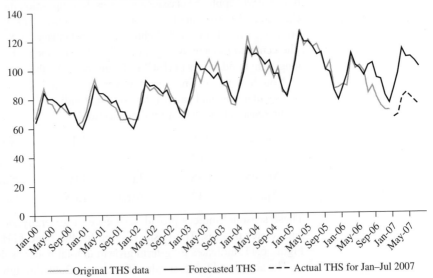

Mike Flock, Distribution Engineer, Vermont Gas Systems, Inc.

Vermont Gas Systems is a natural gas utility with approximately 26,000 residential, business, and industrial customers in 13 towns and cities in northwestern Vermont. Vermont Gas Systems' Gas Control Department forecasts the gas demand, and arranges the gas supply and transportation from suppliers in western Canada and storage facilities along the Trans-Canada Pipeline that deliver the gas to our pipeline. The quantities of gas must be specified to the suppliers at least 24 hours in advance. The Gas Control Department must request enough natural gas to meet the needs of the customers but must not over-request gas that will needlessly and expensively tax Trans-Canada Pipelines' facilities. Because Vermont Gas Systems has the storage capacity for only one hour's use of gas as a buffer between supply and demand, an accurate forecast of daily natural gas demand is critical.

Source: *Journal of Business Forecasting* 13, no. 1 (Spring 1994), p. 23.

Integrative Case

The Gap

PART 6: FORECASTING THE GAP SALES DATA WITH TIME-SERIES DECOMPOSITION

The sales of The Gap stores for the 76 quarters covering 1985Q1 (Mar-85) through 2005Q4 (Dec-05) are shown below.

(c6Gap)

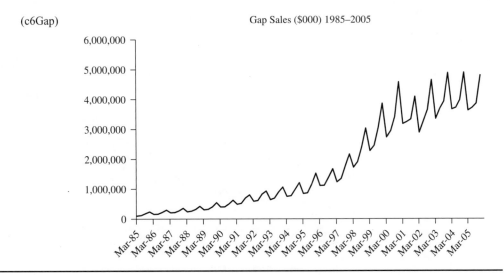

Gap Sales ($000) 1985–2005

Case Questions

1. Describe what you see in the 1985–2005 The Gap sales in the terms used in time-series decomposition: *trend, seasonality,* and *cycle.*

2. Using The Gap sales data for 1985Q1 through 2005Q4, calculate the four-period centered moving average of The Gap sales (call it GAPCMA). Then, using a time index that goes from 1 for 1985Q1 through 84 for 2005Q4, estimate the trend of GAPCMA (call this trend GAPCMAT and extend it through the entire 1985Q1–2007Q1 period). Plot The Gap sales, GAPCMA, and GAPCMAT on the same graph for the period from 1985Q1 through 2005Q4.

3. Calculate the seasonal indices (SI) based on the 1985–2005 data. Are they consistent with your expectations? Explain.

4. Calculate the cycle factors (CF) for this situation and plot CF along with a horizontal line at one. Your calculated cycle factors end at 2005Q2. Why do they not extend farther? Make a forecast of CF for 2005Q3 through 2007Q1, explaining why you forecast as you do.

5. Prepare a forecast of The Gap sales for the five quarters of 2006Q1–2007Q1 using the trend (GAPCMAT), cycle factors (CF), and the seasonal indices (SI) determined above. Plot the actual and forecast sales.

6. Use the historical period (1985Q1–2005Q4) and holdout period (2006Q1–2007Q1) RMSEs to evaluate your results.

Solutions to Case Questions

1. The Gap sales exhibit an increasing positive trend over the time frame being evaluated and a very clear seasonal pattern that repeats itself year to year. It appears that the seasonality may be more pronounced in the more recent years than it was in the early years. From this graph it is not clear that there are the long-term swings that are normally associated with a cyclical pattern. However, because of the long-term nature of cycles, it may be that these data are insufficient to make an identification of a cyclical pattern.

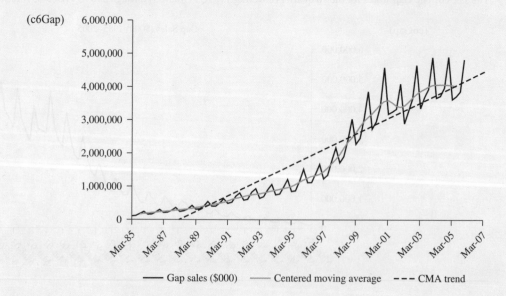

(c6Gap)

— Gap sales ($000) —— Centered moving average --- CMA trend

2. Actual The Gap sales are shown by the dark solid line in the graph on the previous page. The centered moving average is the lighter solid line, and the centered moving-average trend is the dashed line. The early part of the trend is stopped where it would become negative.

3. The normalized seasonal indices (SI) are shown below.

Date	Seasonal Indices
Mar (Q1)	0.86
Jun (Q2)	0.87
Sep (Q3)	1.03
Dec (Q4)	1.24

The seasonal indices for The Gap sales in quarters three and four indicate strong sales during the fall back-to-school buying season, followed by even stronger sales in the fourth quarter due to holiday sales.

4. The cycle factors are calculated as: CF = GAPCMA/GAPCMAT. The cycle factors are shown only starting in 1989 because earlier values were overly influenced by the fact that the trend became artificially small and then negative in 1985 through 1988. The dashed line in the graph of the cycle factors represents the actual values (CF), and the solid line shows the forecast values (CFF).

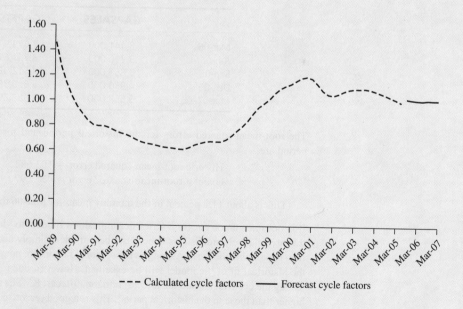

--- Calculated cycle factors   —— Forecast cycle factors

5. The forecast of The Gap sales based on the time-series decomposition method is calculated as: GAPFTSD = GAPCMAT · SI · CF. A time-series plot of these results follows.

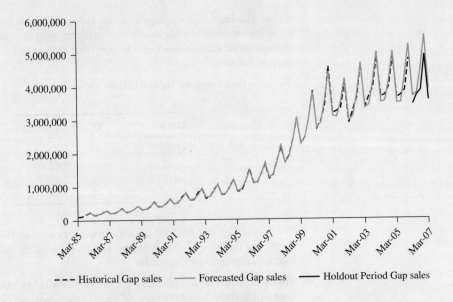

--- Historical Gap sales   —— Forecasted Gap sales   —— Holdout Period Gap sales

6. The actual (GAPSALES) and time-series decomposition forecast (GAPFTSD) of The
   Gap sales are shown below for the five quarters that were forecast (in thousands).

	GAPSALES	GAPFTSD
Mar-06	3,441,000	3,679,979
Jun-06	3,716,000	3,767,610
Sep-06	3,856,000	4,512,937
Dec-06	4,930,000	5,520,357
Mar-07–06	3,558,000	3,888,599

The root-mean-squared errors for the historical period and for the holdout forecast
period are:

Historic root-mean-squared error = 103,682

Forecast root-mean-squared error = 435,697

(This is about 11.2 percent of the monthly mean for Mar-06 through Mar-07)

It is not uncommon for time-series decomposition models to yield historical RMSEs
that are relatively small. This is because these models simply decompose the data and
then reassemble the parts. As long as the seasonal factors are not dramatically different,
the historical fit of the model will be excellent. However, due to the difficulty of projecting the cycle factor into the forecast horizon, forecast RMSEs are often considerably
higher than those in the historical period. This is a good reason to test models in a holdout forecast horizon so that you get a realistic measure of forecast accuracy.

USING FORECASTX™ TO MAKE TIME-SERIES DECOMPOSITION FORECASTS

As usual, begin by opening your data file in Excel and select any cell in the data you want to forecast. Then start ForecastX™. In the **Data Capture** dialog box identify the data you want to use if the correct cells are not automatically selected (they almost always will be). Then click the **Forecast Method** tab.

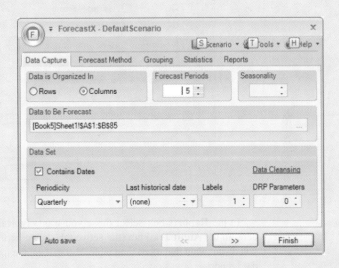

In the **Forecast Method** dialog box, click the down arrow in the **Forecasting Technique** box and select **Decomposition.** Click **Multiplicative** and select **Trend (Linear) Regression** as the **Forecast Method for Decomposited Data.** Then click the **Statistics tab.**

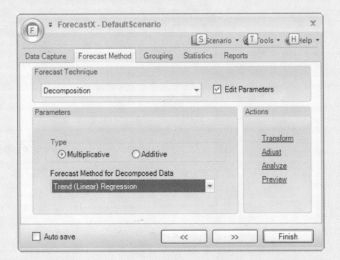

In the following dialog box select the statistics that you desire. Remember that there are more choices if you click the **More** button at the bottom.

After selecting the statistics you want to see, click the **Reports** tab.

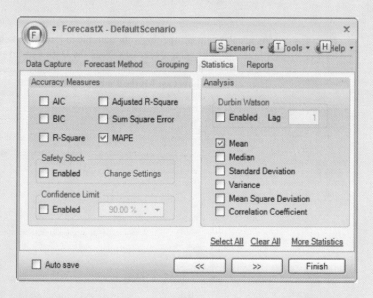

In the **Reports** box select those you want. Typical selections might be those shown here. In the **Audit Trail** tab (the active tab shown here) click **Fitted Values Table,** unless you do not want that often long table. You will get the forecast and actual values in the standard report.

Then click the **Finish!** button.

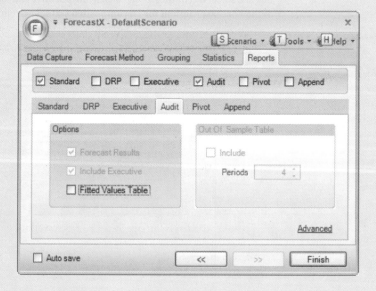

Suggested Readings

Aczel, Amir D.; and Jayavel Sounderpandian. "Time Series, Forecasting and Index Numbers." In *Complete Business Statistics.* 6th ed. Boston: McGraw-Hill/Irwin, 2006, pp. 582–602.

Austin, John S. "How to Use and Interpret Seasonal Factors." *Business Economics* 16, no. 4 (September 1981), pp. 40–42.

Campbell, Jeffrey R. "Entry, Exit, Embodied Technology, and Business Cycles." *Review of Economic Dynamics* 1 (1998), pp. 371–408.

Chatterjee, Satyajit. "From Cycles to Shocks: Progress in Business-Cycle Theory." *Business Review,* Federal Reserve Bank of Philadelphia (March/April 2000), pp. 27–37.

Chatterjee, Satyajit. "Productivity Growth and the American Business Cycle." *Business Review,* Federal Reserve Bank of Philadelphia, September/October 1995.

Espasa, Antoni; and Daniel Pena. "The Decomposition of Forecast in Seasonal ARIMA Models." *Journal of Forecasting* 14, no. 7 (December 1995), pp. 565–83.

Layton, Allan P. "Dating and Predicting Phase Changes in the U.S. Business Cycle." *International Journal of Forecasting* 12, no. 3 (September 1996), pp. 417–28.

Majani, Bernard E. "Decomposition Methods for Medium-Term Planning and Budgeting." In *The Handbook of Forecasting.* Eds. Spyros Makridakis and Steven C. Wheelwright. New York: John Wiley & Sons, 1982, pp. 153–72.

Makridakis, Spyros; Steven C. Wheelwright; and Victor E. McGee. *Forecasting Methods and Applications.* 2nd ed. New York: John Wiley & Sons, 1983, pp. 130–78.

Sommers, Albert T. *The U.S. Economy Demystified.* Rev. ed. Lexington, MA: Lexington Books, 1988.

Temin, Peter. "The Causes of American Business Cycles: An Essay in Economic Historiography." In *Beyond Shocks: What Causes Business Cycles?* Eds. Jeffrey Fuhrer and Scott Schuh. Federal Reserve Bank of Boston, 1998.

Veloce, William. "An Evaluation of the Leading Indicators for the Canadian Economy Using Time Series Analysis." *International Journal of Forecasting* 12, no. 3 (September 1996), pp. 403–16.

Zellner, Arnold, ed. *Seasonal Analysis of Economic Time Series.* U.S. Department of Commerce, Bureau of the Census, 1978.

Exercises

1. Using your own words, write a description of each of the four components of the classic time-series decomposition technique. Avoid using mathematical relationships and technical jargon as much as possible so that your explanations can be understood by almost anyone.

2. Define each of the components of the classic time-series decomposition method. Explain how the trend, seasonal, and cyclical components are determined.

3. Suppose that sales of a household appliance are reported to be 13,000 units during the first quarter of the year. The seasonal index for the first quarter is 1.24. Use this information to make a forecast of sales for the entire year. Actual sales for the year were 42,000 units. Calculate your percentage error for the year. What percentage error would result if you forecast sales for the year by simply multiplying the 13,000 units for the first quarter by 4?

4. In a time-series decomposition of sales (in millions of units), the following trend has been estimated:

$$CMAT = 4.7 + 0.37(T)$$

The seasonal indices have been found to be:

Quarter	Seasonal Index
1	1.24
2	1.01
3	0.76
4	0.99

For the coming year the time index and cycle factors are:

Quarter	T	CF
1	21	1.01
2	22	1.04
3	23	1.06
4	24	1.04

a. From this information prepare a forecast for each quarter of the coming year.

b. Actual sales for the year you forecast in part (*a*) were 17.2, 13.2, 10.8, and 14.2 for quarters 1, 2, 3, and 4, respectively. Use these actual sales figures along with your forecasts to calculate the root-mean-squared error for the forecast period.

5. A tanning parlor located in a major shopping center near a large New England city has the following history of customers over the last four years (data are in hundreds of customers):

(c6p5)

	Mid-Month of Quarter				
Year	Feb	May	Aug	Nov	Yearly Totals
2004	3.5	2.9	2.0	3.2	11.6
2005	4.1	3.4	2.9	3.6	14.0
2006	5.2	4.5	3.1	4.5	17.3
2007	6.1	5.0	4.4	6.0	21.5

a. Construct a table in which you show the actual data (given in the table), the centered moving average, the centered moving-average trend, the seasonal factors, and the cycle factors for every quarter for which they can be calculated in years 1 through 4.

b. Determine the seasonal index for each quarter.

c. Do the best you can to project the cycle factor through 2008.

d. Make a forecast for each quarter of 2008.

e. The actual numbers of customers served per quarter in 2008 were 6.8, 5.1, 4.7, and 6.5 for quarters 1 through 4, respectively (numbers are in hundreds). Calculate the RMSE for 2008.

f. Prepare a time-series plot of the actual data, the centered moving averages, the long-term trend, and the values predicted by your model for 2004 through 2008 (where data are available).

6. Barbara Lynch, the product manager for a line of skiwear produced by HeathCo Industries, has been working on developing sales forecasts for the skiwear that is sold under the Northern Slopes and Jacque Monri brands. She has had various regression-based forecasting models developed (see Exercises 7 and 8 in Chapter 4 and Exercises 6 and 7 in Chapter 5). Quarterly sales for 1998 through 2007 are as follows:

(c6p6)

	Quarterly Sales ($000) at End-Month of Quarter			
Year	March	June	September	December
1998	72,962	81,921	97,729	142,161
1999	145,592	117,129	114,159	151,402
2000	153,907	100,144	123,242	128,497
2001	176,076	180,440	162,665	220,818
2002	202,415	211,780	163,710	200,135
2003	174,200	182,556	198,990	243,700
2004	253,142	218,755	225,422	253,653
2005	257,156	202,568	224,482	229,879
2006	289,321	266,095	262,938	322,052
2007	313,769	315,011	264,939	301,479

a. Prepare a time-series plot of the data, and on the basis of what you see in the plot, write a brief paragraph in which you explain what patterns you think are present in the sales series.

b. Smooth out seasonal influences and irregular movements by calculating the centered moving averages. Add the centered moving averages to the original data you plotted in part (*a*). Has the process of calculating centered moving averages been effective in smoothing out the seasonal and irregular fluctuations in the data? Explain.

c. Determine the degree of seasonality by calculating seasonal indices for each quarter of the year. Do this by finding the normalized average of the seasonal factors for each quarter, where the seasonal factors are actual sales divided by the centered moving average for each period. If you have done Exercise 7 in Chapter 5, explain how these seasonal indices compare with the seasonality identified by the regression model.

d. Determine the long-term trend in the sales data by regressing the centered moving average on time, where $T = 1$ for Mar-98. That is, estimate the values for b_0 and b_1 for the following model:

$$\text{CMAT} = b_0 + b_1(T)$$

Plot this equation, called the *centered moving-average trend* (CMAT), along with the raw data and the CMA on the same plot developed in part (*a*).

e. Find the cycle factor (CF) for each quarter by dividing the CMA by the CMAT. Plot the cycle factors on a new graph and project (CF) forward through Dec-08.

f. Develop a forecast for Ms. Lynch for the four quarters of 2008 by calculating the product of the trend, the seasonal index, and the cycle factor. Given that actual sales (in thousands of dollars) were 334,271, 328,982, 317,921, and 350,118 for quarters 1 through 4, respectively, calculate the RMSE for this model based only on the 2008 forecast period.

g. If you have done Exercises 7 and 8 in Chapter 4 and Exercises 6 and 7 in Chapter 5, write a comparison of your findings.

7. Mr. Carl Lipke is the marketing VP for a propane gas distributor. He would like to have a forecast of sales on a quarterly basis, and he has asked you to prepare a time-series decomposition model. The data for 1996 through 2007 follow:

(c6p7)   **Propane Gas Sales in Millions of Pounds (total at end-month of each quarter)**

Year	March	June	September	December
1996	6.44	4.85	4.67	5.77
1997	6.22	4.25	4.14	5.34
1998	6.07	4.36	4.07	5.84
1999	6.06	4.24	4.20	5.43
2000	6.56	4.25	3.92	5.26
2001	6.65	4.42	4.09	5.51
2002	6.61	4.25	3.98	5.55
2003	6.24	4.34	4.00	5.36
2004	6.40	3.84	3.53	4.74
2005	5.37	3.57	3.32	5.09
2006	6.03	3.98	3.57	4.92
2007	6.16	3.79	3.39	4.51

a. To help Mr. Lipke see how propane gas sales have varied over the 12-year period, prepare a time-series plot of the raw data and the deseasonalized data (i.e., the centered moving averages).

b. Prepare seasonal indices for quarters 1 through 4 based on the normalized averages of the seasonal factors (the seasonal factors equal actual values divided by the corresponding centered moving averages). Write a short paragraph in which you explain to Carl Lipke exactly what these indices mean.

c. Estimate the long-term trend for the sales series by using a bivariate linear regression of the centered moving average as a function of time, where TIME = 1 for 1996Q1.

d. Develop cycle factors for the sales data, and plot them on a graph that extends from 1996Q1 through 2007Q4. Analyze the plot of the cycle factor and project it through the four quarters of 2008. Write a brief explanation of why you forecast the cycle factor as you did.

e. Plot the values of sales that would be estimated by this model along with the original data. Does the model appear to work well for this data series?

f. Prepare a forecast for 2008Q1 through 2008Q4 from your time-series decomposition model. Write your forecast values in the accompanying table. Given the actual values shown in the table, calculate the root-mean-squared error (RMSE) for 2008.

	Sales		
Period	Forecast	Actual	Squared Error
2008Q1		5.39	
2008Q2		3.56	
2008Q3		3.03	
2008Q4		4.03	

Sum of squared errors =
Mean-squared error =
Root-mean-squared error =

8. Kim Brite and Larry Short have developed a series of exclusive mobile-home parks in which each unit occupies a site at least 100×150 feet. Each site is well landscaped to provide privacy and a pleasant living environment. Kim and Larry are considering opening more such facilities, but to help manage their cash flow they need better forecasts of mobile-home shipments (MHS), since MHS appears to influence their vacancy rates and the rate at which they can fill newly opened parks. They have 16 years of data on mobile-home shipments, beginning with 1988Q1 and ending with 2003Q4, as shown:

(c6p8)

Mobile Home Shipments (MHS) (000s)

Year	Q1	Q2	Q3	Q4
1988	56.6	49.1	58.5	57.5
1989	54.9	70.1	65.8	50.2
1990	53.3	67.9	63.1	55.3
1991	63.3	81.5	81.7	69.2
1992	67.8	82.7	79.0	66.2
1993	62.3	79.3	76.5	65.5
1994	58.1	66.8	63.4	56.1
1995	51.9	62.8	64.7	53.5
1996	47.0	60.5	59.2	51.6
1997	48.1	55.1	50.3	44.5
1998	43.3	51.7	50.5	42.6
1999	35.4	47.4	47.2	40.9
2000	43.0	52.8	57.0	57.6
2001	56.4	64.3	67.1	66.4
2002	69.1	78.7	78.7	77.5
2003	79.2	86.8	87.6	86.4

Assuming that Kim Brite and Larry Short have hired you as a forecasting consultant:

a. Provide a time-series plot of the actual MHS data along with the deseasonalized data. Write a brief memo in which you report the nature and extent of the seasonality in the data. Include seasonal indices in your report.

b. Develop a long-term linear trend for the data, based on the centered moving averages. Let time equal 1 for 1988Q1 in your trend equation. On the basis of this trend, does the future look promising for Brite and Short?

c. One of the things Ms. Brite and Mr. Short are concerned about is the degree to which MHS is subject to cyclical fluctuations. Calculate cycle factors and plot them in a time-series graph, including projections of the cycle factor through 2004. In evaluating the cycle factor, see whether interest rates appear to have any effect on the cyclical pattern. The rate for 1988Q1 through 2003Q4 is provided in the following table, should you wish to use this measure of interest rates.

(c6p8)

Interest Rate

Year	Q1	Q2	Q3	Q4
1988	16.4	16.3	11.6	16.7
1989	19.2	18.9	20.3	17.0
1990	16.3	16.5	14.7	12.0
1991	10.9	10.5	10.8	11.0
1992	11.1	12.3	13.0	11.8
1993	10.5	10.2	9.5	9.5
1994	9.4	8.6	7.9	7.5
1995	7.5	8.0	8.4	8.9
1996	8.6	8.8	9.7	10.2
1997	11.0	11.4	10.7	10.5
1998	10.0	10.0	10.0	10.0
1999	9.2	8.7	8.4	7.6
2000	6.5	6.5	6.0	6.0
2001	6.0	6.0	6.0	6.0
2002	6.0	6.9	7.5	8.1
2003	8.8	9.0	8.8	8.7

d. Demonstrate for Ms. Brite and Mr. Short how well your time-series decomposition model follows the historical pattern in the data by plotting the actual values of MHS and those estimated by the model in a single time-series plot.

e. Prepare a forecast for 2004 and calculate the root-mean-squared error (RMSE), given the actual values of MHS for 2004 shown:

Period	MHS Forecast	Actual	Squared Error
2004Q1		35.4	
2004Q2		47.3	
2004Q3		47.2	
2004Q4		40.9	

Sum of squared errors =
Mean-squared error =
Root-mean-squared error =

9. The Bechtal Tire Company (BTC) is a supplier of automotive tires for U.S. car companies. BTC has hired you to analyze its sales. Data from 1976Q1 through 2007Q4 are given in the following table (in thousands of units):

(c6p9)

BTC Sales of Tires

Year	Q1	Q2	Q3	Q4
1986	2,029	2,347	1,926	2,162
1987	1,783	2,190	1,656	1,491
1988	1,974	2,276	1,987	2,425
1989	2,064	2,517	2,147	2,524
1990	2,451	2,718	2,229	2,190
1991	1,752	2,138	1,927	1,546
1992	1,506	1,709	1,734	2,002
1993	2,025	2,376	1,970	2,122
1994	2,128	2,538	2,081	2,223
1995	2,027	2,727	2,140	2,270
1996	2,155	2,231	1,971	1,875
1997	1,850	1,551	1,515	1,666
1998	1,733	1,576	1,618	1,282
1999	1,401	1,535	1,327	1,494
2000	1,456	1,876	1,646	1,813
2001	1,994	2,251	1,855	1,852
2002	2,042	2,273	2,218	1,672
2003	1,898	2,242	2,247	1,827
2004	1,669	1,973	1,878	1,561
2005	1,914	2,076	1,787	1,763
2006	1,707	2,019	1,898	1,454
2007	1,706	1,878	1,752	1,560

a. Write a report to Bechtal Tire Company in which you explain what a time-series decomposition analysis shows about its tire sales. Include in your discussion seasonal, cyclical, and trend components. Show the raw data, the deseasonalized data, and the long-term trend on one time-series plot. Also provide a plot of the cycle factor with a projection through 2008.

b. In the last section of your report, show a time-series graph with the actual data and the values that the time-series decomposition model would predict for each quarter from 1986Q3 through 2007Q4, along with a forecast for 2008. If actual sales for 2008 were Q1 = 1,445.1, Q2 = 1,683.8, Q3 = 1,586.6, and Q4 = 1,421.3, what RMSE would result from your 2008 forecast?

10. A national supplier of jet fuel is interested in forecasting its sales. These sales data are shown for the period from 1992Q1 to 2007Q4 (data in billions of gallons):

(c6p10)

Jet Fuel Sales (Billions of Gallons)

Year	Q1	Q2	Q3	Q4
1992	23.86	23.97	29.23	24.32
1993	23.89	26.84	29.36	26.30
1994	27.09	29.42	32.43	29.17
1995	28.86	32.10	34.82	30.48
1996	30.87	33.75	35.11	30.00

(continued on next page)

Year	Q1	Q2	Q3	Q4
1997	29.95	32.63	36.78	32.34
1998	33.63	36.97	39.71	34.96
1999	35.78	38.59	42.96	39.27
2000	40.77	45.31	51.45	45.13
2001	48.13	50.35	56.73	48.83
2002	49.02	50.73	53.74	46.38
2003	46.32	51.65	52.73	47.45
2004	49.01	53.99	55.63	50.04
2005	54.77	56.89	57.82	53.30
2006	54.69	60.88	63.59	59.46
2007	61.59	68.75	71.33	64.88

a. Convert these data to a time-series plot. What, if any, seasonal pattern do you see in the plot? Explain.

b. Deseasonalize the data by calculating the centered moving average, and plot the deseasonalized data on the same graph used in part (a). Calculate the seasonal index for each quarter, and write a short explanation of why the results make sense.

c. Develop a trend for the data based on the centered moving averages, and plot that trend line on the graph developed in part (a). Compare the deseasonalized data (CMA) and the trend line. Does there appear to be a cyclical pattern to the data? Explain.

d. Calculate the cycle factors and plot them on a separate time-series graph. Project the cycle factor ahead one year.

e. For the historical period, plot the values estimated by the time-series decomposition model along with the original data.

f. Make a forecast of sales for the four quarters of 2008, and given the following actual data for that year, calculate the root-mean-squared error:

	Jet Fuel Sales		
Quarter	Forecast	Actual	Squared Error
1		64.81	
2		75.52	
3		81.93	
4		72.89	

Sum of squared errors =
Mean-squared error =
Root-mean-squared error =

g. Develop two other forecasts of jet fuel sales with:

1. An exponential smoothing method; and

2. A regression model using just time and quarterly dummy variables.

Compare the RMSE for the three models you have developed, and comment on what you like or dislike about each of the three models for this application.

11. The following table contains quarterly data on upper midwest car sales (CS) in the United States for 1987Q1 through 2007Q4:

(c6p11)

Upper Midwest Car Sales (CS)

Year	Q1	Q2	Q3	Q4
1987	407.6	431.5	441.6	306.2
1988	328.7	381.3	422.6	369.4
1989	456.3	624.3	557.5	436.7
1990	485.0	564.3	538.3	412.5
1991	555.0	682.7	581.3	509.7
1992	662.7	591.1	616.9	529.7
1993	641.2	632.7	576.6	475.0
1994	542.8	558.9	581.7	537.8
1995	588.1	626.5	590.9	580.1
1996	589.2	643.2	593.9	612.2
1997	586.1	699.4	734.4	753.8
1998	691.6	793.4	864.9	840.8
1999	653.9	754.8	883.6	797.7
2000	722.2	788.6	769.9	725.5
2001	629.3	738.6	732.0	598.8
2002	603.9	653.6	606.1	539.7
2003	461.3	548.0	548.4	480.4
2004	476.6	528.2	480.4	452.6
2005	407.2	498.5	474.3	403.7
2006	418.6	470.2	470.7	375.7
2007	371.1	425.5	397.3	313.5

a. Prepare a time-series plot of upper midwest car sales from 1987Q1 through 2007Q4.

b. On the basis of these data, calculate the centered moving average (CSCMA) and the centered moving-average trend (CSCMAT). Plot CS, CSCMA, and CSCMAT on a single time-series plot.

c. Calculate a seasonal factor (SF = CS/CSCMA) for each quarter from 1987Q3 through 2007Q2. Calculate the seasonal indices (SI) for this series.

d. Determine the cycle factors CF = CSCMA/CSCMAT for the period from 1987Q3 through 2007Q2 and plot them along with a horizontal line at 1.

e. Evaluate the cycle factor (CF) and project it forward from 2007Q3 through 2008Q4.

f. Prepare a time-series decomposition forecast of CS (CSFTSD = CSCMAT × SI × CF).

g. Calculate the historic RMSE as a measure of fit; then calculate the RMSE for the 2008Q1–2008Q4 forecast horizon as a measure of accuracy, given that the actual values of CS for 2008 were:

2008Q1	301.1
2008Q2	336.7
2008Q3	341.8
2008Q4	293.5

h. Prepare a Winters' exponential smoothing forecast of CS using data from 1987Q1 through 2007Q4 as the basis for a forecast of 2008Q1–2008Q4. Compare these results in terms of fit and accuracy with the results from the time-series decomposition forecast.

12. *a.* Use the following data on retail truck sales in the southern United States (TS), in thousands of dollars, to prepare a time-series decomposition forecast of TS for 2008Q1–2008Q4:

(c6p12)

Truck Sales

Year	Q1	Q2	Q3	Q4
1987	4,78,124	6,12,719	6,13,902	6,46,312
1988	7,12,170	8,21,845	7,84,493	7,25,615
1989	8,48,323	9,34,438	8,17,396	8,85,389
1990	8,94,359	11,26,400	9,46,504	9,47,141
1991	9,21,967	8,38,559	7,64,035	7,11,234
1992	6,34,427	5,68,758	5,32,143	4,96,188
1993	4,99,968	5,59,593	4,95,349	4,17,391
1994	5,97,296	6,05,965	5,16,173	5,28,238
1995	5,82,202	7,22,965	6,63,528	7,40,694
1996	8,52,774	9,79,159	8,28,721	8,77,681
1997	9,93,431	10,47,300	9,82,917	9,59,867
1998	9,01,757	10,95,580	10,98,730	9,32,177
1999	9,35,125	11,45,360	10,71,020	10,22,050
2000	11,39,130	12,52,900	11,16,670	10,99,110
2001	10,80,950	12,22,890	11,95,190	9,83,803
2002	10,85,270	11,72,960	10,81,380	9,21,370
2003	8,45,992	10,44,490	10,28,720	9,22,831
2004	9,57,733	12,40,610	11,71,230	11,43,440
2005	11,45,370	14,93,980	13,28,300	13,50,470
2006	14,30,080	16,36,760	14,56,740	15,02,440
2007	14,38,960	16,61,130	14,90,620	15,00,120

b. Evaluate your model in terms of fit and accuracy using RMSE.

c. Plot your forecast values of TS along with the actual values.

d. Compare the results from your time-series decomposition model with those obtained using a Winters' exponential smoothing model in terms of both fit and accuracy.

13. *a.* Use the following data on millions of dollars of jewelry sales (JS) to prepare a time-series decomposition forecast of JS for the four quarters of 2005:

(c6p13)

Date	Jewelry Sales ($Millions)	Date	Jewelry Sales ($Millions)	Date	Jewelry Sales ($Millions)
Jan-94	904	May-94	1,367	Sep-94	1,246
Feb-94	1,191	Jun-94	1,257	Oct-94	1,323
Mar-94	1,058	Jul-94	1,224	Nov-94	1,731
Apr-94	1,171	Aug-94	1,320	Dec-94	4,204

(continued on next page)

Date	Jewelry Sales ($Millions)	Date	Jewelry Sales ($Millions)	Date	Jewelry Sales ($Millions)
Jan-95	914	Sep-98	1,372	May-02	2,120
Feb-95	1,223	Oct-98	1,506	Jun-02	1,667
Mar-95	1,138	Nov-98	1,923	Jul-02	1,554
Apr-95	1,204	Dec-98	5,233	Aug-02	1,746
May-95	1,603	Jan-99	1,163	Sep-02	1,503
Jun-95	1,388	Feb-99	1,662	Oct-02	1,662
Jul-95	1,259	Mar-99	1,402	Nov-02	2,208
Aug-95	1,393	Apr-99	1,468	Dec-02	5,810
Sep-95	1,325	May-99	1,877	Jan-03	1,361
Oct-95	1,371	Jun-99	1,635	Feb-03	2,019
Nov-95	1,867	Jul-99	1,596	Mar-03	1,477
Dec-95	4,467	Aug-99	1,617	Apr-03	1,616
Jan-96	1,043	Sep-99	1,530	May-03	2,071
Feb-96	1,439	Oct-99	1,653	Jun-03	1,711
Mar-96	1,316	Nov-99	2,179	Jul-03	1,677
Apr-96	1,359	Dec-99	6,075	Aug-03	1,761
May-96	1,768	Jan-00	1,253	Sep-03	1,629
Jun-96	1,408	Feb-00	1,991	Oct-03	1,759
Jul-96	1,375	Mar-00	1,510	Nov-03	2,291
Aug-96	1,477	Apr-00	1,570	Dec-03	6,171
Sep-96	1,332	May-00	2,139	Jan-04	1,461
Oct-96	1,462	Jun-00	1,783	Feb-04	2,344
Nov-96	1,843	Jul-00	1,643	Mar-04	1,764
Dec-96	4,495	Aug-00	1,770	Apr-04	1,826
Jan-97	1,041	Sep-00	1,705	May-04	2,226
Feb-97	1,411	Oct-00	1,681	Jun-04	1,882
Mar-97	1,183	Nov-00	2,174	Jul-04	1,787
Apr-97	1,267	Dec-00	5,769	Aug-04	1,794
May-97	1,597	Jan-01	1,331	Sep-04	1,726
Jun-97	1,341	Feb-01	1,973	Oct-04	1,845
Jul-97	1,322	Mar-01	1,580	Nov-04	2,399
Aug-97	1,359	Apr-01	1,545	Dec-04	6,489
Sep-97	1,344	May-01	1,992	Jan-05	?
Oct-97	1,406	Jun-01	1,629	Feb-05	?
Nov-97	1,813	Jul-01	1,530	Mar-05	?
Dec-97	4,694	Aug-01	1,679	Apr-05	?
Jan-98	1,119	Sep-01	1,394	May-05	?
Feb-98	1,513	Oct-01	1,586	Jun-05	?
Mar-98	1,238	Nov-01	2,152	Jul-05	?
Apr-98	1,362	Dec-01	5,337	Aug-05	?
May-98	1,756	Jan-02	1,304	Sep-05	?
Jun-98	1,527	Feb-02	2,004	Oct-05	?
Jul-98	1,415	Mar-02	1,612	Nov-05	?
Aug-98	1,466	Apr-02	1,626	Dec-05	?

The actual data for 2005 are:

Date	Jewelry Sales ($ Millions)
Jan-05	1,458
Feb-05	2,394
Mar-05	1,773
Apr-05	1,909
May-05	2,243
Jun-05	1,953
Jul-05	1,754
Aug-05	1,940
Sep-05	1,743
Oct-05	1,878
Nov-05	2,454
Dec-05	6,717

b. Evaluate your model in terms of fit and accuracy using RMSE.

c. Plot your forecast values of JS along with the actual values.

d. Look at the seasonal indices, and explain why you think they do or do not make sense.

e. Compare the results from your time-series decomposition model with those obtained using a Winters' exponential smoothing model in terms of both fit and accuracy.

Appendix

Components of the Composite Indices

The composite indices of leading, coincident, and lagging indicators produced by The Conference Board are summary statistics for the U.S. economy. They are constructed by averaging their individual components in order to smooth out a good part of the volatility of the individual series. Historically, the cyclical turning points in the leading index have occurred before those in aggregate economic activity, cyclical turning points in the coincident index have occurred at about the same time as those in aggregate economic activity, and cyclical turning points in the lagging index generally have occurred after those in aggregate economic activity.

LEADING INDEX COMPONENTS

Average weekly hours, manufacturing   The average hours worked per week by production workers in manufacturing industries tend to lead the business cycle because employers usually adjust work hours before increasing or decreasing their work force.

Average weekly initial claims for unemployment insurance   The number of new claims filed for unemployment insurance are typically more sensitive than either total employment or unemployment to overall business conditions, and this series tends to lead the business cycle. It is inverted when included in the leading index; the signs of the month-to-month changes are reversed, because initial claims increase when employment conditions worsen (i.e., layoffs rise and new hirings fall).

Manufacturers' new orders, consumer goods and materials (in 1996 dollars) These goods are primarily used by consumers. The inflation-adjusted value of new orders leads actual production because new orders directly affect the level of both unfilled orders and inventories that firms monitor when making production decisions. The Conference Board deflates the current dollar orders data using price indices constructed from various sources at the industry level and a chain-weighted aggregate price index formula.

Vendor performance, slower deliveries diffusion index   This index measures the relative speed at which industrial companies receive deliveries from their suppliers. Slowdowns in deliveries increase this series and are most often associated with increases in demand for manufacturing supplies (as opposed to a negative shock to supplies) and, therefore, tend to lead the business cycle. Vendor performance is based on a monthly survey conducted by the National Association of Purchasing Management (NAPM) that asks purchasing managers whether their suppliers' deliveries have been faster, slower, or the same as the previous month. The slower-deliveries diffusion index counts the proportion of respondents reporting slower deliveries, plus one-half of the proportion reporting no change in delivery speed.

Manufacturers' new orders, nondefense capital goods (in 1996 dollars)   New orders received by manufacturers in nondefense capital goods industries (in inflation-adjusted dollars) are the producers' counterpart to "Manufacturers' new orders, consumer goods and materials," listed above.

Building permits, new private housing units   The number of residential building permits issued is an indicator of construction activity, which typically leads most other types of economic production.

Stock prices, 500 common stocks   The Standard & Poor's 500 stock index reflects the price movements of a broad selection of common stocks traded on the New York Stock Exchange. Increases (decreases) of the stock index can reflect both the general sentiments of investors and the movements of interest rates, which are usually other good indicators for future economic activity.

Money supply (in 1996 dollars)   In inflation-adjusted dollars, this is the M2 version of the money supply. When the money supply does not keep pace with inflation, bank lending may fall in real terms, making it more difficult for the economy to expand. M2 includes currency, demand deposits, other checkable deposits, travelers checks, savings deposits, small denomination time deposits, and balances in money market mutual funds. The inflation adjustment is based on the implicit deflator for personal consumption expenditures.

Interest rate spread, 10-year Treasury bonds less federal funds   The spread or difference between long and short rates is often called the *yield curve*. This series is constructed using the 10-year Treasury bond rate and the federal funds rate, an overnight interbank borrowing rate. It is felt to be an indicator of the stance of monetary policy and general financial conditions because it rises (falls) when short rates are relatively low (high). When it becomes negative (i.e., short rates are higher than long rates and the yield curve inverts), its record as an indicator of recessions is particularly strong.

Index of consumer expectations   This index reflects changes in consumer attitudes concerning future economic conditions and, therefore, is the only indicator in the leading index that is completely expectations-based. Data are collected in a monthly survey conducted by the University of Michigan's Survey Research Center. Responses to the questions concerning various economic conditions are classified as positive, negative, or unchanged. The expectations series is derived from the responses to three questions relating to: (1) economic prospects for the respondent's family over the next 12 months; (2) the economic prospects for the nation over the next 12 months; and (3) the economic prospects for the nation over the next five years.

COINCIDENT INDEX COMPONENTS

Employees on nonagricultural payrolls   This series from the U.S. Bureau of Labor Statistics is often referred to as *payroll employment*. It includes full-time and part-time workers and does not distinguish between permanent and temporary employees. Because the changes in this series reflect the actual net hiring and firing of all but agricultural establishments and the smallest businesses in the nation, it is one of the most closely watched series for gauging the health of the economy.

Personal income less transfer payments (in 1996 dollars)   The value of the income received from all sources is stated in inflation-adjusted dollars to measure the real salaries and other earnings of all persons. This series excludes government transfers such as Social Security payments and includes an adjustment for wage accruals less disbursements (WALD) that smoothes bonus payments (to more accurately reflect the level of income upon which wage-earners would base their consumption decisions). Income levels are important because they help determine both aggregate spending and the general health of the economy.

Index of industrial production   This index is based on value-added concepts and covers the physical output of all stages of production in the manufacturing, mining, and gas and electric utility industries. It is constructed from numerous sources that measure physical product counts, values of shipments, and employment levels. Although the value-added of the industrial sector is only a fraction of the total economy, this index has historically captured a majority of the fluctuations in total output.

Manufacturing and trade sales (in 1996 dollars)   Sales at the manufacturing, wholesale, and retail levels are invariably procyclical. This series is inflation-adjusted to represent real total spending. The data for this series are collected as part of the National Income and Product Account calculations, and the level of aggregate sales is always larger than GDP when annualized because some products and services are counted more than once (e.g., as intermediate goods or temporary additions to wholesale inventories and as retail sales).

LAGGING INDEX COMPONENTS

Average duration of unemployment   This series measures the average duration (in weeks) that individuals counted as unemployed have been out of work. Because this series tends to be higher during recessions and lower during expansions, it is inverted when it is included in the lagging index (i.e., the signs of the month-to-month changes are reversed). Decreases in the average duration of unemployment invariably occur after an expansion gains strength and the sharpest increases tend to occur after a recession has begun.

Ratio, manufacturing and trade inventories to sales (in 1996 dollars)   The ratio of inventories to sales is a popular gauge of business conditions for individual firms, entire industries, and the whole economy. This series is calculated by the Bureau of Economic Analysis (BEA) using inventory and sales data for manufacturing, wholesale, and retail businesses (in inflation-adjusted and seasonally adjusted form) based on data collected by the U.S. Bureau of the Census. Because inventories tend to increase when the economy slows, and sales fail to meet projections, the ratio typically reaches its cyclical peaks in the middle of a recession. It also tends to decline at the beginning of an expansion as firms meet their sales demand from excess inventories.

Change in labor cost per unit of output, manufacturing   This series measures the rate of change in an index that rises when labor costs for manufacturing firms rise faster than their production (and vice versa). The index is constructed by The Conference Board from various components, including seasonally adjusted data on employee compensation in manufacturing (wages and salaries plus supplements) from the BEA, and seasonally adjusted data on industrial production in manufacturing from the

Board of Governors of the Federal Reserve System. Because monthly percent changes in this series are extremely erratic, percent changes in labor costs are calculated over a six-month span. Cyclical peaks in the six-month annualized rate of change typically occur during recessions, as output declines faster than labor costs despite layoffs of production workers. Troughs in the series are much more difficult to determine and characterize.

Average prime rate charged by banks   Although the prime rate is considered the benchmark that banks use to establish their interest rates for different types of loans, changes tend to lag behind the movements of general economic activities. The monthly data are compiled by the Board of Governors of the Federal Reserve System.

Commercial and industrial loans outstanding (in 1996 dollars)   This series measures the volume of business loans held by banks and commercial paper issued by non-financial companies. The underlying data are compiled by the Board of Governors of the Federal Reserve System. The Conference Board makes price-level adjustments using the same deflator (based on personal consumption expenditures data) used to deflate the money supply series in the leading index. The series tends to peak after an expansion peaks because declining profits usually increase the demand for loans. Troughs are typically seen more than a year after the recession ends. (Users should note that there is a major discontinuity in January 1988, due to a change in the source data; the composite index calculations are adjusted for this fact.)

Ratio, consumer installment credit outstanding to personal income   This series measures the relationship between consumer debt and income. Consumer installment credit outstanding is compiled by the Board of Governors of the Federal Reserve System and personal income data is from the Bureau of Economic Analysis. Because consumers tend to hold off personal borrowing until months after a recession ends, this ratio typically shows a trough after personal income has risen for a year or longer. Lags between peaks in the ratio and peaks in the general economy are much more variable.

Change in Consumer Price Index for services   This series is compiled by the Bureau of Labor Statistics, and it measures the rates of change in the services component of the Consumer Price Index. It is probable that, because of recognition lags and other market rigidities, service sector inflation tends to increase in the initial months of a recession and to decrease in the initial months of an expansion.

Source: The Conference Board (http://www.conference-board.org).

ARIMA (Box-Jenkins)–Type Forecasting Models

INTRODUCTION

A time series of data is a sequence of numerical observations naturally ordered in time. Some examples would be:

- Hourly temperatures at the entrance to Grand Central Station
- Daily closing price of IBM stock
- Weekly automobile production by the Pontiac Division of General Motors
- Data from an individual firm: sales, profits, inventory, back orders
- An electrocardiogram

When a forecaster examines time-series data, two questions are of paramount importance:

1. Do the data exhibit a discernible pattern?
2. Can this pattern be exploited to make meaningful forecasts?

We have already examined some time-series data by using regression analysis to relate sequences of data to explanatory variables. Sales (as the dependent variable), for instance, might be forecast by using the explanatory (or independent) variables of product price, personal income of potential purchasers, and advertising expenditures by the firm. Such a model is a structural or causal forecasting model that requires the forecaster to know in advance at least some of the determinants of sales. But in many real-world situations, we do not know the determinants of the variable to be forecast, or data on these causal variables are not readily available. It is in just these situations that the ARIMA technique has a decided advantage over standard regression models. ARIMA is also used as a benchmark for other forecasting models; we could use an ARIMA model, for example, as a criterion for our best structural regression model. The acronym

ARIMA stands for autoregressive integrated moving average. Exponential smoothing, which we examined in Chapter 3, is actually just a special case of an ARIMA model.

The Box-Jenkins methodology of using ARIMA models is a technically sophisticated way of forecasting a variable by looking *only* at the past pattern of the time series.

The Box-Jenkins methodology of using ARIMA models is a technically sophisticated way of forecasting a variable by looking *only* at the past pattern of the time series. Box-Jenkins thus ignores information that might be contained in a structural regression model; instead, it uses the most recent observation as a starting value and proceeds to analyze recent forecasting errors to select the most appropriate adjustment for future time periods. Since the adjustment usually compensates for only part of the forecast error, the Box-Jenkins process is best suited to longer-range rather than shorter-range forecasting (although it is used for short-, medium-, and long-range forecasts in actual practice).

The Box-Jenkins methodology of using ARIMA models has some advantages over other time-series methods, such as exponential smoothing, time-series decomposition, and simple trend analysis. Box-Jenkins methodology determines a great deal of information from the time series (more so than any other time-series method), and it does so while using a minimum number of parameters. The Box-Jenkins method allows for greater flexibility in the choice of the "correct" model (this, we will see, is called "identification" in Box-Jenkins terminology). Instead of a priori choosing a simple time trend or a specific exponential smoothing method, for example, as the correct model, Box-Jenkins methodology includes a process that allows us to examine a large variety of models in our search for the correct one. This "open-ended" characteristic alone accounts for its appeal to many forecasters.

THE PHILOSOPHY OF BOX-JENKINS

Pretend for a moment that a certain time series is generated by a "black box":

$$\text{Black box} \rightarrow \text{Observed time series}$$

In standard regression analysis we attempt to find the causal variables that explain the observed time series; what we take as a given is that the black box process is actually approximated by a linear regression technique:

$$\begin{array}{ccc} \text{Explanatory} & \text{Black box} & \text{Observed} \\ \text{variables} & \rightarrow \ \ \text{(approximated} \ \rightarrow & \text{time series} \\ & \text{by linear} & \\ & \text{regression)} & \end{array}$$

In the Box-Jenkins methodology, on the other hand, we do not start with any explanatory variables, but rather with the observed time series itself; what we attempt to discern is the "correct" black box that could have produced such a series from white noise:

$$\text{White noise} \rightarrow \text{Black box} \rightarrow \text{Observed time series}$$

The term *white noise* deserves some explanation. Since we are to use no explanatory variables in the ARIMA process, we assume instead that the series we are observing started as white noise and was transformed by the black box process into the series we are trying to forecast.

White noise is essentially a purely random series of numbers. The numbers are normally and independently distributed. Some examples of white noise may serve to make its meaning clearer:

1. The winning numbers in the Illinois lottery's "Pick Four" game (where the four winning digits are drawn daily from four separate urns, each with 10 marked balls inside). Would knowledge of the numbers drawn for the past year help you pick a winner? (No, but there are those who actually believe some numbers are "better" than others.)

2. The last digit in the daily closing Dow Jones Industrial Average (or the last digit in the day-to-day change in the average). Would knowing the digit for the last two weeks help you to pick today's final digit?

White noise, then, has two characteristics:

1. There is no relationship between consecutively observed values.
2. Previous values do not help in predicting future values.

White noise is important in explaining the difference between the standard regression process and the Box-Jenkins methodology. The steps required in each method are shown in Table 7.1. In standard regression analysis we move from

> White noise is essentially a purely random series of numbers.

TABLE 7.1

Comparison of Standard Regression Analysis Box-Jenkins Methodology

For standard regression analysis:
1. Specify the causal variables.
2. Use a linear (or other) regression model.
3. Estimate the constant and slope coefficients.
4. Examine the summary statistics and try other model specifications.
5. Choose the most desirable model specification (perhaps on the basis of RMSE).

Start here:

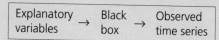

For Box-Jenkins methodology:
1. Start with the observed time series.
2. Pass the observed time series through a black box.
3. Examine the time series that results from passage through the black box.
4. If the black box is correctly specified, only white noise should remain.
5. If the remaining series is not white noise, try another black box.

Start here:

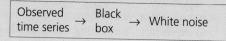

the explanatory variables (which we choose as a result of some knowledge of the real world) to applying the linear regression technique in order to estimate the constant and slope coefficients of the model. We then use the regression equation to actually make up forecasts about future values of the time series. If our regression model does not have good summary statistics (e.g., *t*-statistics, *R*-squared), we may change some or all of the explanatory variables and try again until we are satisfied with the summary statistics (including the root-mean-squared error).

In Box-Jenkins methodology, however, we start instead with the observed time series itself (with no explanatory variables) and examine its characteristics in order to get an idea of what black box we might use to transform the series into white noise. We begin by trying the most likely of many black boxes, and if we get white noise, we assume that this is the "correct" model to use in generating forecasts of the series. If we try a particular black box and do not wind up with white noise, we try other likely black boxes until we finally wind up with white noise. The test to see whether we have succeeded in winding up with only white noise serves the same purpose as the set of summary statistics we generate with standard regression models.

When choosing the correct black box, there are really only three basic types of models for us to examine; there are, however, many variations within each of these three types. The three types of models are: (1) moving-average (MA) models, (2) autoregressive (AR) models, and (3) mixed autoregressive–moving-average models (called ARMA models). We will examine each of these three models in turn in the following sections.

MOVING-AVERAGE MODELS

A moving-average (MA) model is simply one that predicts Y_t as a function of the past forecast errors in predicting Y_t. Consider e_t to be a white noise series; a moving-average model would then take the following form:

$$Y_t = e_t + W_1 e_{t-1} + W_2 e_{t-2} + \cdots + W_q e_{t-q}$$

where:

e_t = The value at time t of the white noise series

Y_t = The generated moving-average time series

$W_{1,2,\ldots,q}$ = The coefficients (or "weights")

$e_{t-1,t-2,\ldots,t-q}$ = Previous values of the white noise series

The name *moving average* is actually not very descriptive of this type of model; we would do better to call it a *weighted-average model,* since it is similar to exponential smoothing. An example of a moving-average model is constructed

TABLE 7.2

Box-Jenkins Example Data Series (c7t2)

	White Noise	MA(1)	AR(1)	AR(2)	ARIMA111
1	0.256454	0.399867	0.240000	0.160000	0.160000
2	0.230240	0.409758	0.350240	0.040000	0.569758
3	0.675186	0.836354	0.850306	0.735186	1.40611
4	0.0475159	0.520146	0.472669	0.570146	1.92626
5	0.716827	0.750089	0.953162	1.26297	2.67635
6	0.854614	1.35639	1.33120	1.85272	4.03274
7	0.557983	1.15621	1.22358	2.10748	5.18895
8	0.0390320	0.429620	0.650822	1.88481	5.61857
9	0.184616	0.211938	0.510027	1.92548	5.83051
10	0.0167999	0.146031	0.271814	1.74160	5.97654
11	0.596069	0.607829	0.731976	2.20029	6.58437
12	0.235672	0.652921	0.601660	2.12419	7.23729
13	0.0724487	0.237419	0.373279	1.99944	7.47471
14	0.858917	0.909631	1.04556	2.68336	8.38434
15	0.830856	1.43210	1.35363	3.10910	9.81644
16	0.215927	0.797527	0.892744	2.92897	10.6140
17	0.223007	0.374156	0.669379	2.89511	10.9881
18	0.254166	0.410271	0.588855	2.86653	11.3984
19	0.764038	0.941954	1.05847	3.34963	12.3403
20	0.286438	0.821265	0.815671	3.20449	13.1616
191	0.323975	0.782538	0.820131	4.36400	150.720
192	0.162109	0.388892	0.572175	4.12794	151.109
193	0.702011	0.815488	0.988099	4.46437	151.924
194	0.854660	1.34607	1.34871	4.80531	153.270
195	0.480850	1.07911	1.15520	4.73744	154.349
196	0.843475	1.18007	1.42108	5.12074	155.530
197	0.408600	0.999033	1.11914	4.94061	156.529
198	0.581711	0.867731	1.14128	5.06429	157.396
199	0.975937	1.38313	1.54658	5.50906	158.779
200	0.683960	1.36712	1.45725	5.55316	160.147

in Table 7.2, which is an abbreviated listing of the entire 200-observation data set. The complete data set is included on the CD accompanying this book.

In the first column of Table 7.2 we show a white noise series generated by randomly selecting numbers between 0 and 1. The moving-average series was constructed from the white noise series by using the following equation:

$$Y_t = e_t + W_1 e_{t-1}$$

where:

Y_t = The series generated, which appears in column 2

e_t = The white noise series appearing in column 1

W_1 = A constant (equal here to 0.7)

e_{t-1} = The white noise value lagged one period

This series—called an MA(1) series because it contains one lag of the white noise term—was constructed with known characteristics. Imagine how we might decide that a time series of unknown origin that we want to forecast could be similar to this known series. How could we go about examining this time series to determine whether it is an MA(1) series like that in column 2 of Table 7.2? We can get an insight into the answer by examining two characteristics of the time series we have purposely constructed to be an MA(1) series in Table 7.2. These characteristics are the autocorrelations and the partial autocorrelations.

First, we examine the autocorrelation (or "serial correlation") among successive values of the time series; this will be the first of two key tools in determining which model (or black box) is the appropriate representation of any given time series. As described in Chapter 2, autocorrelation is the concept that the association between values of the same variable at different time periods is nonrandom—that is, that if autocorrelation does exist in a time series, there is correlation or mutual dependence between the values of the time series at different time periods.

As a simple example of autocorrelation, consider the data in Table 7.3. The first column could represent sales of an item during successive periods; the second column is the first column lagged one period; the third column is the first column lagged two periods. We can now calculate the simple correlation coefficient between the numbers in the first column and the numbers in the second column, treating each column as if it were a separate variable. Remember that the correlation coefficient will always vary between $+1$ and -1. If it is $+1$, it indicates that there is a perfect positive correlation between the two columns—that is, as one increases, so does the other. If the correlation coefficient is -1, it indicates a perfect negative correlation—that is, as one goes up, the other goes down. The closer the number is to $+1$, the more positively correlated the columns; the closer the number is to -1, the more negatively correlated the columns.

First, we examine the autocorrelation (or "serial correlation") among successive values of the time series; this will be the first of two key tools in determining which model (or black box) is the appropriate representation of any given time series.

TABLE 7.3

A Simple Example of Autocorrelation

(c7t3)

Original Variable	One Time Lag	Two Time Lags
121	—	—
123	121	—
134	123	121
133	134	123
151	133	134
141	151	133
176	141	151
187	176	141
183	187	176
214	183	187

Correlation between original variable and one time lag = $+0.867$.
Correlation between original variable and two time lags = $+0.898$.

Here the correlation between the first and second columns is $+0.867$; the correlation between the first and third columns is $+0.898$. These values indicate the extent to which the original series values are correlated with themselves, lagged one and two periods (called *auto*correlation since the second and third columns of our table are not variables separate from column 1, but are actually the same variable at different periods).

Apparently, autocorrelation exists in this variable for both one and two lags, and the autocorrelation coefficients are approximately equal. These autocorrelations provide us with the first important tool for identifying the correct model; if the original data in Table 7.3 had been completely random white noise (ours were not!), the correlation among lagged values (one, two, or more lags) would have been approximately equal to zero, given a large enough data set. We will find that the pattern of the autocorrelations will help us identify a series that behaves as a moving-average model.

The partial autocorrelation coefficient is the second tool we will use to help identify the relationship between the current values and past values of the original time series. Just as the autocorrelation function measures the association of a variable with successive values of the same variable in a time series, partial autocorrelations measure the degree of association between the variable and that same variable in another time period after partialing out (i.e., controlling for) the effects of the other lags. Partial autocorrelation coefficients measure the degree of association between Y_t and Y_{t-k} *when all the other time lags on Y are held constant*. The calculation of the partial autocorrelation terms is beyond the scope of this text, but they are calculated by ForecastX™ and most other statistical packages that deal with time-series analysis. It is possible, however, to indicate how these coefficients are calculated without presenting the rather lengthy derivation.

The partial autocorrelation coefficient is defined in terms of the last autoregressive (AR) term of an AR-type model with m lags. Partial autocorrelations are calculated when we are unsure of the correct order of the autoregressive process to fit the time series. Consider the AR(m) model (which will be explained in more detail in the section "Autoregressive Models") represented in the following equations:

$$Y_t = A_1 Y_{t-1} + e_t$$
$$Y_t = A_1 Y_{t-1} + A_2 Y_{t-2} + e_t$$
$$\vdots$$
$$Y_t = A_1 Y_{t-1} + A_2 Y_{t-2} + \cdots + A_m Y_{t-m} + e_t$$

By solving this system of equations for the $A_1, A_2, \ldots, A_{t-m}$ terms (which are the partial autocorrelation coefficients), we could determine their actual values.

It is most common to view both the autocorrelation coefficients and the partial autocorrelation coefficients in graphic form by constructing a correlogram of the autocorrelation coefficients and a partial correlogram for the partial autocorrelation

The partial autocorrelation coefficient is the second tool we will use to help identify the relationship between the current values and past values of the original time series.

FIGURE 7.1

Examples of Theoretical Autocorrelation and Partial Autocorrelation Plots for MA(1) and MA(2) Models

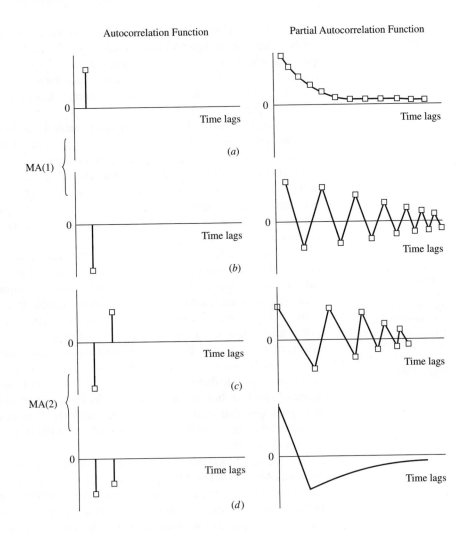

coefficients; both graphics look very much like the residuals output in the ForecastX™ program.

Consider the typical MA(1) correlogram and partial correlogram in Figure 7.1. Two distinctive patterns in the autocorrelation and partial autocorrelation functions are characteristic of an MA(1) model. The *a* frame of Figure 7.1 displays the first of these patterns. Note the gradual falling to zero of the partial autocorrelation function and the single spike in the autocorrelation function. In general, if the autocorrelation function abruptly stops at some point, we know the model is of the MA type; the number of spikes (commonly referred to as *q*) before the abrupt stop tells us the "order" of the MA model. In frame *a* there is only one spike, and so we know the model is likely to be of the MA(1) variety.

Frame *b* represents a variation of this distinctive pattern; here the single spike (now negative) still appears in the autocorrelation function, but the partial autocorrelation function shows alternating positive and negative values, gradually falling to zero. This also would indicate to us an MA(1)-type model.

In any given data there may be more than one significant moving-average term; if there were two significant moving-average terms, for instance, we could find either of the patterns in frames *c* and *d*. Both of these situations are characteristic of an MA(2) model; both frames show two distinct spikes in the autocorrelation function while the partial autocorrelation function gradually slides to zero, either monotonically decreasing or alternating between positive and negative values.

We are now ready to examine the autocorrelation and partial autocorrelation functions for the MA(1) series in column 2 of Table 7.2. The correlograms for each are shown for the first 24 lags in Figure 7.2. If we had not previously known that this was an MA(1) series, we should have been able to deduce this from the characteristic patterns shown in Figure 7.2: note that the autocorrelation function has only one spike that appears to be significantly different from zero. The approximate 95 percent confidence intervals are shown for both the autocorrelation and partial autocorrelation functions in Figure 7.2. A value between the confidence interval is seen to be not significantly different from zero. Also note that the partial autocorrelation function alternates from positive to negative *and* decreases in absolute value as it approaches zero. This pattern is similar to that shown in frame *b* of Figure 7.1 and identifies the time series for us as one of the MA(1) variety. This knowledge of what the autocorrelation and partial autocorrelation functions look like in an MA(1) model will allow us later to use Box-Jenkins methodology to model and forecast any similar time series accurately.

AUTOREGRESSIVE MODELS

The second of the three classes of models we need to examine is the autoregressive (AR) model. The equation for the autoregressive model is similar to the moving-average model, except that the dependent variable Y_t depends on its own previous values rather than the white noise series or residuals. The autoregressive model is produced from a white noise series by using an equation of the form:

$$Y_t = A_1 Y_{t-1} + A_2 Y_{t-2} + \cdots + A_p Y_{t-p} + e_t$$

where:

$$Y_t = \text{The moving-average time series generated}$$
$$A_1, A_2, \ldots, A_p = \text{Coefficients}$$
$$Y_{t-1}, Y_{t-2}, \ldots, Y_{t-p} = \text{Lagged values of the time series (hence the name}$$
$$\textit{autoregressive})$$
$$e_t = \text{White noise series}$$

If the model has only the Y_{t-1} term on the right-hand side, it is referred to as an AR(1) model; if it has Y_{t-1} and Y_{t-2} terms, it is an AR(2); and so on. Column 3 of

FIGURE 7.2
Autocorrelation and Partial Autocorrelation Plots for the MA(1) Series in Table 7.2
(c7t2)

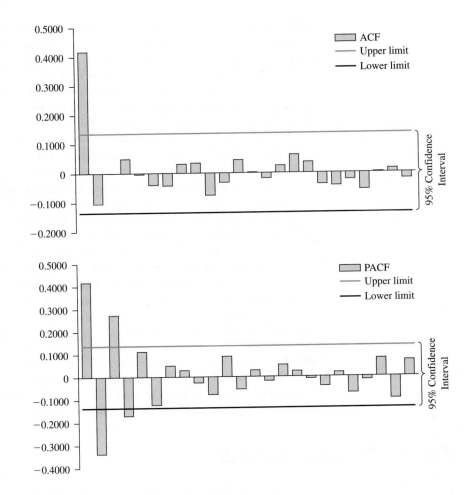

Obs	ACF	PACF	Obs	ACF	PACF
1	.4175	.4175	13	.0019	.0281
2	−.1046	−.3378	14	−.0185	−.0185
3	−.0003	.2724	15	.0246	.0517
4	.0490	−.1709	16	.0614	.0238
5	−.0040	.1112	17	.0363	−.0094
6	−.0405	−.1227	18	−.0392	−.0419
7	−.0429	.0490	19	−.0441	.0181
8	.0309	.0284	20	−.0233	−.0719
9	.0342	−.0262	21	−.0573	−.0146
10	−.0759	−.0779	22	.0020	.0790
11	−.0323	.0897	23	.0134	−.0973
12	.0444	−.0547	24	−.0210	.0703

Table 7.2 is an AR(1) series produced by the following equation:

$$Y_t = A_1 Y_{t-1} + e_t$$

where

Y_t = The series generated, which appears in column 2

e_t = The white noise series appearing in column 1

A_1 = A constant (equal here to 0.5)

Y_{t-1} = The series lagged one period

(Note: The first number in the column [i.e., 0.24] is chosen arbitrarily.)

Once again, as with the MA(1) model presented in the previous section, the AR(1) series in column 3 is constructed from the white noise series with known characteristics; that is, it is an AR(1) series because we constructed it to be one. Again, ask the question: How might we decide that another time series, of unknown origin, that we were given to forecast could be similar to this AR(1) series? In other words, how would we go about examining a series to determine whether it is an AR(1)-type series?

We will answer the question by again examining the characteristics of the known series—the AR(1) series in column 3 of Table 7.2. Once again we first examine the autocorrelation function of the series and then examine the partial autocorrelation function of the series. We are looking for distinctive patterns in each of these functions that will indicate that any time series under examination is an AR(1)-type series.

The typical correlograms and partial correlograms for an AR(1) series are shown in frames *a* and *b* of Figure 7.3. Either of two patterns is distinctive for an AR(1) model. In frame *a* the autocorrelation function falls monotonically to zero while the partial autocorrelation function shows a single spike; note that this is the exact opposite of the pattern exhibited by an MA(1) time series. In general, if the partial autocorrelation function abruptly stops at some point, the model is of the AR type; the number of spikes (*p*) before the abrupt stop is equal to the "order" of the AR model. In frame *a* there is just one spike in the partial autocorrelation function, and so the model is of the AR(1) type.

Frame *b* represents the second of two characteristic patterns for an AR(1) model; here the single spike (now negative) still appears in the partial autocorrelation function, but the autocorrelation function tends to zero by alternating between positive and negative values.

As in MA-type models, there may be more than one significant autoregressive term; if this is the case, patterns like those shown in frames *c* and *d* of Figure 7.3 could result. Patterns like those in either frame *c* or *d* would indicate an AR(2)-type model because of the two significant spikes in the partial autocorrelation function. Note again that the autocorrelation function in both cases falls to zero, either monotonically (as in frame *c*) or alternating between positive and negative values (as in frame *d*).

We should now be able to evaluate the autocorrelation and partial autocorrelation functions for the AR(1) series in column 3 of Table 7.2. Recall that we know

FIGURE 7.3

**Examples of
Theoretical
Autocorrelation
and Partial
Autocorrelation Plots
of AR(1) and AR(2)
Models**

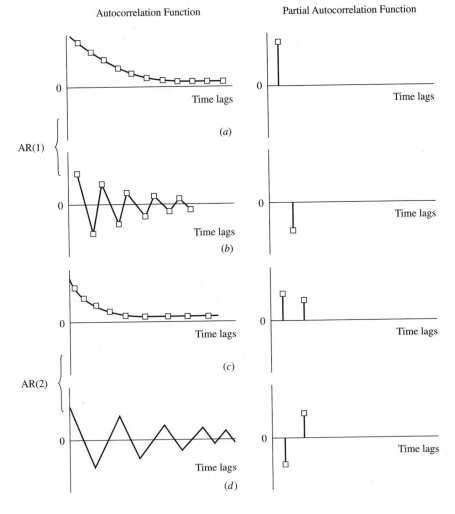

Autocorrelation Function

Partial Autocorrelation Function

AR(1)

(a)

(b)

AR(2)

(c)

(d)

that this particular time series was produced from a white noise series by using the equation:

$$Y_t = A_1 Y_{t-1} + e_t$$

The correlograms for each are shown for the first 24 lags in Figure 7.4. If we had not known that this was an AR(1) series, we should have been able to deduce this from the characteristic patterns in Figure 7.4; note that the partial autocorrelation function has only one significant spike (i.e., it has only one spike that appears significantly different from zero, and so the order is $p = 1$). Also note that the autocorrelation function decreases in value, approaching zero. This pattern is similar to that shown in frame a of Figure 7.3, and this fact identifies the time series as one of the AR(1) variety.

FIGURE 7.4
Autocorrelation and Partial Autocorrelation Plots for the AR(1) Series in Table 7.2
(c7t2)

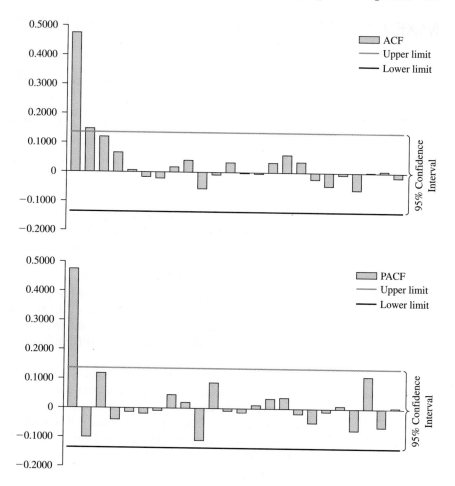

Obs	ACF	PACF	Obs	ACF	PACF
1	.4751	.4751	13	−.0026	−.0143
2	.1478	−.1006	14	−.0042	.0117
3	.1203	.1184	15	.0338	.0341
4	.0659	−.0406	16	.0604	.0376
5	.0064	−.0136	17	.0365	−.0179
6	−.0165	−.0187	18	−.0225	−.0485
7	−.0211	−.0088	19	−.0454	−.0105
8	.0175	.0456	20	−.0073	.0098
9	.0406	.0199	21	−.0587	−.0737
10	−.0562	−.1104	22	.0018	.1101
11	−.0085	.0874	23	.0062	−.0625
12	.0337	−.0084	24	−.0158	.0044

MIXED AUTOREGRESSIVE AND MOVING-AVERAGE MODELS

The third and final of the three classes of models that we need examine is really a combination of an AR and an MA model. This third class of general models is called *ARMA*, which stands for *autoregressive–moving-average model*. This model could be produced from a white noise series by introducing the elements we have already seen in both moving-average and autoregressive models:

$$Y_t = A_1 Y_{t-1} + A_2 Y_{t-2} + \cdots$$
$$+ A_p Y_{t-p} + e_t + W_1 e_{t-1}$$
$$+ W_2 e_{t-2} + \cdots + W_q e_{t-q}$$

This equation defines a mixed autoregressive–moving-average model of order p, q, and is usually written as ARMA(p, q). To identify an ARMA model, we again look for characteristic patterns in the autocorrelation and partial autocorrelation functions.

Figure 7.5 shows the characteristic patterns for an ARMA(1, 1) model; note that *any* of the four frames in Figure 7.5 could be patterns that would identify an ARMA(1, 1) model. In Figure 7.5, in each of the frames, both the autocorrelations and partial autocorrelations gradually fall to zero *rather than abruptly stop*. This observation (both functions falling off gradually) is characteristic of any ARMA(p, q) model.

To identify the order of the AR and MA terms, we need to count the number of AR and MA terms significantly different from zero. In frame *b*, for instance, there is one spike in the partial autocorrelation function (AR process) and one spike in the autocorrelation function (MA process); this would imply an ARMA(1, 1) model. The other patterns exhibited in Figure 7.5 are less easily identified as ARMA(1, 1) processes.

In fact, the particular identification process we have outlined requires some experience to apply in the real world. We have, however, outlined the basic steps to be followed in applying the identification process; skill in actual application requires the consideration of many examples and learning from past mistakes. We have already seen that according to Box-Jenkins methodology, if we are able to identify the type and order of model we are faced with when we are given a time series, then the repetitive pattern in that original time series offers us the method for forecasting it. When we are given a time series in the real world, however, we are not told the type of model that will fit it, and the first task is to figure out which of the infinite variations of the three models (autoregressive, moving average, or mixed) is the "correct" model for our data.

Fortunately, for low-order processes like the ones we have examined so far, the correct specification of the p and q values is rather simple to make. Many real-world processes, once they have been adjusted for seasonality, can be adequately modeled with the low-order models, e.g., MA(1), MA(2), AR(1), AR(2), ARMA(1, 1). If low-order models are not adequate (how to determine whether a model is adequate will be explained in the section "The Box-Jenkins Identification Process"), the selection of the proper p and q becomes more difficult. As a rule of thumb,

Many real-world processes, once they have been adjusted for seasonality, can be adequately modeled with the low-order models.

FIGURE 7.5

Examples of Theoretical Autocorrelation and Partial Autocorrelation Plots of ARMA(1, 1) Models

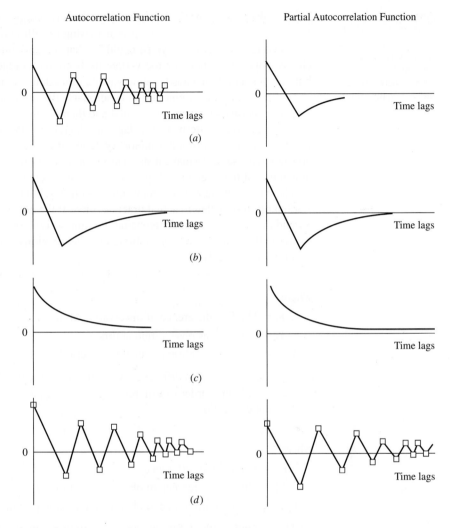

however, spikes in the autocorrelation function indicate moving-average terms, and spikes in the partial autocorrelation function indicate autoregressive terms.

When the correct model is not of a low order, you may be forced to determine an adequate p and q by trial and error; it will be possible, you will see, to check your guesses after the parameters of each model have been determined.

STATIONARITY

In general we have been approaching our data as if they were stationary. A *stationary* time series is one in which two consecutive values in the series depend *only* on the time interval between them and *not* on time itself. For all practical purposes this would be consistent with a series whose mean value did *not* change over time. Real-world time series are most often nonstationary; that is, the mean

A *stationary* time series is one in which two consecutive values in the series depend *only* on the time interval between them and *not* on time itself.

value of the time series changes over time, usually because there is some trend in the series so that the mean value is either rising or falling over time. Nonstationarity can result in other ways (it could be that the variability of the time series changes over time; perhaps the variability becomes exaggerated through time), but the most common cause is simply some trend in the series.

If the series we examine are nonstationary, the autocorrelations are usually significantly different from zero at first and then gradually fall off to zero, or they show a spurious pattern as the lags are increased. Because autocorrelations dominate the pattern of a nonstationary series, it is necessary for us to modify a nonstationary series to make it stationary *before* we try to identify as the "correct" model one of the three models we have so far examined.

There is no single way to remove nonstationarity, but two methods help achieve stationarity most often in actual practice. First, if the nonstationarity is caused by a trend in the series, then differencing the time series may effectively remove the trend. Differencing refers to subtracting the previous observation from each observation in the data set:

$$Y'_t = Y_t - Y_{t-1}$$

where:

Y'_t = The first difference of observation at time t

Y_t = Time-series observation at time t

Y_{t-1} = Time-series observation at time period $t - 1$

In some cases the first difference will not remove the trend and it may be necessary to try a higher order of differencing. For example, second-order differences can be found as follows:

$$Y''_t = Y'_t - Y'_{t-1}$$

where:

Y''_t = The second difference

Y'_t = The first difference of observation at time t

Y'_{t-1} = The first difference of observation at time period $t - 1$

The second method for removing nonstationarity is used when there is a change in the variability of the series (i.e., when there is a trend in the variance). This method involves taking logs of the original time series, which usually transfers the trend in variance to a trend in the mean; this trend can then be handled by differencing. Other, more sophisticated methods of removing nonstationarity are sometimes used but will not be covered here.

Consider the series in column 5 of Table 7.2. Glancing at the numbers down the column, we can easily see that this series has some trend; the numbers are monotonically increasing throughout the time period. Figure 7.6 shows the autocorrelation function for this series. This autocorrelation function is entirely characteristic of series with a trend; that is, it shows dominant autocorrelations for the 24 lags shown, and these autocorrelations only gradually become smaller. Figure 7.7 shows the correlograms for the same series *after* first differences have been taken.

FIGURE 7.6
Autocorrelation
and Partial
Autocorrelation
Plots for the
ARIMA(1, 1, 1)
Series in Table 7.2
(c7t2)

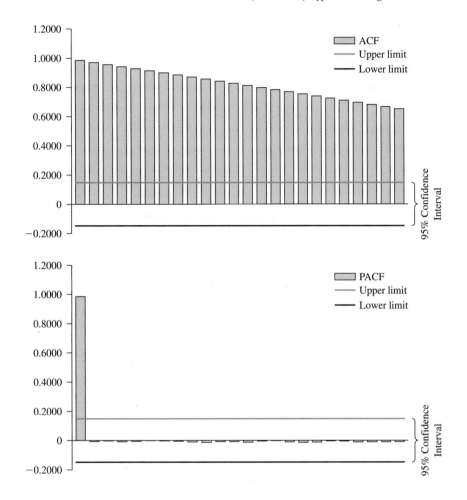

Obs	ACF	PACF	Obs	ACF	PACF
1	.9854	.9854	13	.8124	−.0127
2	.9707	−.0069	14	.7979	−.0045
3	.9562	−.0031	15	.7836	−.0020
4	.9417	−.0085	16	.7693	−.0103
5	.9272	−.0064	17	.7547	−.0139
6	.9129	−.0015	18	.7401	−.0123
7	.8987	−.0031	19	.7255	−.0043
8	.8845	−.0056	20	.7111	−.0052
9	.8703	−.0105	21	.6966	−.0114
10	.8559	−.0138	22	.6820	−.0108
11	.8414	−.0084	23	.6674	−.0102
12	.8270	−.0085	24	.6527	−.0096

FIGURE 7.7
Autocorrelation and
Partial Autocorrela-
tion Plots for the
ARIMA(1, 1, 1)
Series in Table 7.2
after First
Differences Have
Been Taken
(c7t2)

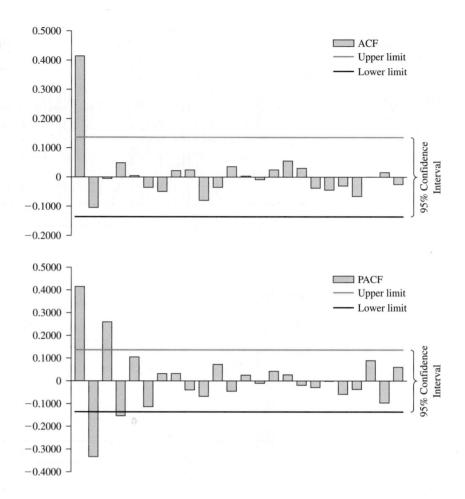

Obs	ACF	PACF	Obs	ACF	PACF
1	.4141	.4141	13	.0035	.0255
2	−.1046	−.3333	14	−.0087	−.0102
3	−.0047	.2594	15	.0246	.0424
4	.0486	−.1538	16	.0550	.0269
5	.0048	.1049	17	.0303	−.0188
6	−.0352	−.1130	18	−.0374	−.0286
7	−.0489	.0320	19	−.0442	−.0013
8	.0221	.0324	20	−.0301	−.0585
9	.0243	−.0396	21	−.0657	−.0367
10	−.0794	−.0677	22	.0003	.0894
11	−.0348	.0724	23	.0157	−.0963
12	.0357	−.0452	24	−.0248	.0603

Apparently, this series contains a trend and could probably easily be modeled with a simple time trend or a low-order ARMA model. Figure 7.7 (which shows the data after taking first differences) could perhaps be best modeled as an ARMA(3, 1), since there appear to be one dominant autocorrelation spike and three dominant partial autocorrelation spikes.

When differencing is used to make a time series stationary, it is common to refer to the resulting model as an ARIMA(p, d, q)-type model. The "I" that has been added to the name of the model refers to the integrated or differencing term in the model; the d inside the parentheses refers to the degree of differencing. An ARIMA(p, d, q) model is then properly referred to as an *autoregressive integrated moving-average model*. For example, a model with one autoregressive term, one degree of differencing, and no moving-average term would be written as an ARIMA(1, 1, 0) model. An ARIMA model is thus classified as an "ARIMA(p, d, q)" model, where:

- p is the number (order) of autoregressive terms,
- d is the number (order) of differences, and
- q is the number (order) of moving-average terms.

THE BOX-JENKINS IDENTIFICATION PROCESS

We are finally in a position to set down the Box-Jenkins methodology in a patterned format. The approach is an iterative one, in which we may loop through the process many times before reaching a model with which we are comfortable. The four steps of the Box-Jenkins process are outlined in Figure 7.8.

As a first step, the raw series is examined to *identify* one of the many available models that we will tentatively select as the best representation of this series. If the raw series is not stationary, it will initially be necessary to modify the original series (perhaps using first differences) to produce a stationary series to model.

The first step in the process is usually accomplished by using an *identify* function, which is a part of every standard Box-Jenkins software package; the identify function simply calculates and displays the autocorrelation and partial autocorrelation functions for the time series in question. Figure 7.2 shows these functions for the series in column 2 of Table 7.2, which you will recall is the MA(1) data we produced from white noise. By examining these correlograms we can observe the distinctive pattern (like that in frame *b* of Figure 7.1) that we earlier identified as representing an MA(1)-type model. It is this pattern produced by the identify function that leads us to the tentative choice of an MA(1) model. The general rules to be followed in this identification stage of the process can be summed up as follows:

1. If the autocorrelation function abruptly stops at some point—say, after q spikes—then the appropriate model is an MA(q) type.
2. If the partial autocorrelation function abruptly stops at some point—say, after p spikes—then the appropriate model is an AR(p) type.
3. If neither function falls off abruptly, but both decline toward zero in some fashion, the appropriate model is an ARMA(p, q) type.

As a first step, the raw series is examined to identify one of the many available models that we will tentatively select as the best representation of this series.

FIGURE 7.8
The Box-Jenkins Methodology

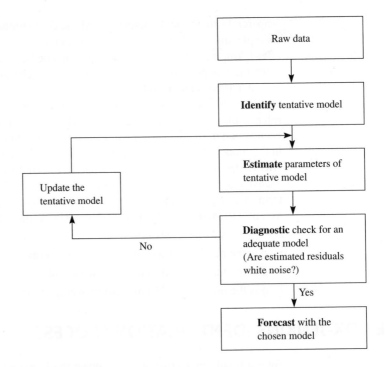

The second step in the process begins after the tentative model has been identified; the actual *estimation* of the parameters of the model is similar to fitting a standard regression to a set of data.

The third step in the Box-Jenkins process is to *diagnose* in order to determine whether the "correct" model has been chosen.

The second step in the process begins after the tentative model has been identified; the actual *estimation* of the parameters of the model is similar to fitting a standard regression to a set of data. If an MA(1) model had been tentatively identified as the "correct" model, we would fit the equation

$$Y_t = e_t + W_1 e_{t-1}$$

The ForecastX™ software package would estimate the value for W_1, using a mean-squared error minimization routine in order to select the optimal value.

Consider again the series in column 2 of Table 7.2; we "identified" these data as being distinctive of an MA(1)-type model when we examined the autocorrelation and partial autocorrelation functions in Figure 7.2. If we now specify an MA(1)-type model—this could also be written as an ARIMA(0, 0, 1) model—in the software package, the output will be as shown in Figure 7.9.

The third step in the Box-Jenkins process is to *diagnose* in order to determine whether the "correct" model has been chosen. In order to do this, again for the example in column 2 of Table 7.2, we will examine the autocorrelation function of the residuals produced by the estimation program; this is also presented in Figure 7.9. Recall that we originally produced the "raw data" series from white noise by specifying a function we knew would behave as an MA(1) model. That is, we passed an MA(1) box over the white noise and turned it into an MA(1) data set. If we now reverse the process and pass an MA(1) box over the contrived data set, we should wind up with white noise. A look at the autocorrelation function

FIGURE 7.9 **The MA(1) Model Estimate from ForecastX™ and Residual Autocorrelation Plot for the MA(1) Model Estimate** (c7t2)

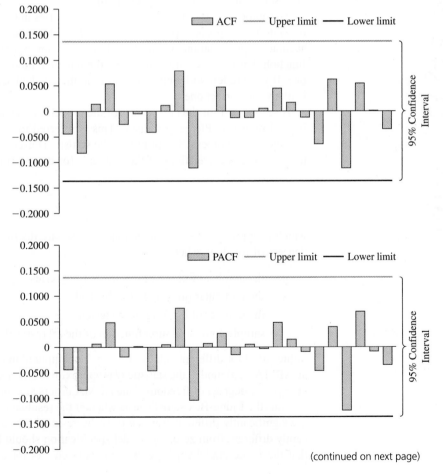

```
Audit Trail--Statistics
```

Accuracy Measure	Value		Forecast Statistic	Value
AIC	75.20		Durbin-Watson	2.08
BIC	81.80		Mean	0.80
Mean Absolute Percentage Error (MAPE)	43.45%		Max	1.64
Sum Squared Error (SSE)	16.72		Min	0.14
R-Square	35.63%		Sum Squared Deviation	25.97
Adjusted R-Square	35.30%		Range	1.50
Root Mean Square Error	0.29		Ljung-Box	7.33

Method Statistic	Value
Method selected	Box-Jenkins
Model selected	ARIMA(0,0,1) * (0,0,0)
T-test for constant	39.07
T-test for nonseasonal MA	−11.13

(continued on next page)

FIGURE 7.9

(continued)

Obs	ACF	PACF	Obs	ACF	PACF
1	−.0440	−.0440	13	−.0128	−.0152
2	−.0820	−.0841	14	−.0125	.0055
3	.0140	.0064	15	.0053	−.0033
4	.0536	.0481	16	.0445	.0481
5	−.0254	−.0191	17	.0168	.0152
6	−.0048	.0013	18	−.0121	−.0093
7	−.0410	−.0463	19	−.0646	−.0466
8	.0113	.0049	20	.0620	.0396
9	.0789	.0761	21	−.1116	−.1239
10	−.1111	−.1040	22	.0542	.0694
11	.0000	.0072	23	.0010	−.0087
12	.0469	.0268	24	−.0350	−.0352

will tell us whether we have been left with just white noise, or whether we will have some unaccounted-for pattern in the series.

The autocorrelation function of the residual series in Figure 7.9 shows virtually no significant spikes. Apparently the MA(1)-type model we estimated was an accurate representation of the data. It is most importantly the autocorrelation function that tells the forecaster when the tentative model is actually the correct one. If you are left with only white noise in the residual series, the model chosen is likely the correct one.

A second test for the correctness of the model (but again, not a definitive test) is the Ljung-Box-Pierce Q statistic. This is referred to simply as the *Ljung-Box* statistic in the ForecastX™ printout. The statistic is used to perform a chi-square test on the autocorrelations of the residuals (or error terms). The test statistic is

$$Q_m = n(n + 2) \sum_{k=1}^{m} \frac{r_k^2}{n - k}$$

which is approximately distributed as a chi-square distribution with $m - p - q$ degrees of freedom, where:

n = the number of observations in the time series
k = the particular time lag to be checked
m = the number of time lags to be tested
r_k = sample autocorrelation function of the kth residual term

Values of Q for different values of k may be computed in a residual analysis. For an ARMA(p, q) model, the statistic Q is approximately chi-square distributed with $m - p - q$ degrees of freedom if the ARMA orders are correctly specified.

Thus the Ljung-Box statistic tests whether the residual autocorrelations as a set are significantly different from zero. If the residual autocorrelations are significantly different from zero, the model specification should be reformulated. Note that the ForecastX™ software automatically checks for a lag length of 12 if a nonseasonal model has been selected; if a seasonal model has been selected, the lag is set equal to four times the seasonal length (e.g., the lag would be set to 16 if the data were quarterly).

The Ljung-Box statistic calculated for the Figure 7.9 model is 7.33 for the first 12 autocorrelations (which result in 11 degrees of freedom). A check with the chi-square table (see the appendix to this chapter) shows the critical value to be *about* 17 at the 0.10 significance level. Since the calculated value is less than the table value, the model is considered appropriate; that is, we believe the residuals to be uncorrelated. If this is the correct model, the residuals should be normally distributed and independent of one another (i.e., the residuals should resemble white noise).

If either the check of the residual series autocorrelations or the Ljung-Box statistic test had shown the model to be inappropriate, the tentative model would have been updated by trying another variation of the possible models. In Box-Jenkins methodology it is possible for two or more models to be very similar in their fit of the data; Occam's razor would suggest that the simpler of the similar models be chosen for actual forecasting. It is important to realize that the selection of an ARIMA model is an art and not a science.

The ForecastX™ software will automatically select a model using Box-Jenkins methodology. The reported model may be examined in the two ways we have shown for checking the adequacy of the model: examine the residual autocorrelations and use the Ljung-Box test. Any model, whether chosen by the forecaster manually or selected automatically by the ForecastX™ algorithm, is not necessarily the optimal model. While the Ljung-Box or Q statistic is a reliable way to check for appropriateness of the ARIMA model chosen, it is not the only diagnostic that should be applied. Don't forget the other measures we have used up to this point to determine if our models would likely make good forecasts.

Simply getting the Ljung-Box to an acceptable value (i.e., lower than the critical value in the chi-square table) while ignoring other, more important, measures such as the MAPE or RMSE begs the question of what is a good ARIMA model?

Just as in assessing other forecasting techniques we have examined earlier in this text, the researcher should pay close attention to whether the model fits the past data well: Does the plot of actual and forecast values show that the forecasts are a good fit? The use of adjusted R^2 (higher is better) is used with ARIMA in the same manner we have used it in the past. Likewise, measures of accuracy such as MAPE (lower is better) and RMSE (lower is also better) are also useful in estimating the degree of fit for an ARIMA model.

The principle of parsimony explained in Chapter 5 holds here as well. The best advice is to "KIS": Keep it simple. The less complex the model, the more useful it is; simple models with few coefficients are best. With this in mind, the Akaike information criterion (and the Bayesian information criterion) can also be used with ARIMA techniques to sort out the best model. An AIC or BIC will be lower for better models, all other things being equal.

Using a holdout period to give the ARIMA model the acid test of forecasting outside the range of the data set used for estimation is again a useful technique for choosing among competing models.

The final step in the Box-Jenkins process is to actually *forecast* using the chosen model.

The final step in the Box-Jenkins process is to actually *forecast* using the chosen model. ForecastX™ performs this function by substituting into the chosen model in much the same manner as a standard regression forecast would be made. It should be remembered that, as forecasts are made more than one period into the future, the size of the forecast error is likely to become larger.

When new observations of the time series become available, the model should be reestimated and checked again by the Box-Jenkins process; it is quite likely that the parameters of the model will have to be recalculated, or perhaps a different model altogether will be chosen as the best representation of the series. Consistent errors observed in estimation as more data become available are an indication that the entire model may require a change.

ARIMA: A SET OF NUMERICAL EXAMPLES

Example 1

Return to the first column of Table 7.2; this is the column containing white noise from which we constructed the other time series in the table. When we run an leases for satellite capacity. These users' inputs describe the technical operating qualities needed for each lease, along with information on anticipated start date, duration, and renewal potential. These requests from all users are aggregated and sorted by geographic region. The aggregated near-term user data can provide, on a systemwide basis, fairly accurate estimates of the potential growth trends to be expected. The 15-year, long-term demand for leases is developed using nonlinear regression analysis, historical trend analysis, and the three- to five-year near-term growth rate projections. Studies indicate that, historically, these projected trends closely correlate to the realized system usages.

Recently, work was begun to look into methodologies to supplement the forecasts as provided by the system users. Two approaches that are currently being investigated are econometric demand models and stochastic time-series models. The development of an econometric model is recognized as a considerable endeavor, and one method that is being considered is to define the model in terms of geographic groups of countries so as to limit the complexity of the demand function.

As a specific example of INTELSAT's forecasting, consider the occasional-use television channel-hours provided to TV broadcasters needing satellites to relay news coverage around the world. Data on such occasional-use television satellite use date back to 1983. A Box-Jenkins second-order autoregressive integrated moving-average model [ARIMA (2, 1, 1)] was applied to the quarterly data of usage statistics from 1983 through 1992Q4. The parameters of the model were estimated by excluding the 1992 data (holdout period), and an "ex-post" forecast was developed and compared with the 1992 period. Having accepted the model performance, an "ex-ante" forecast, for a future time period, was generated.

For the future, work will continue on evaluation and development of forecasting models appropriate to each of INTELSAT's many telecommunications services.

Source: This overview of forecasting at INTELSAT was provided by Martin J. Kelinsky, forecasting manager, INTELSAT, Washington, D.C.

identify test on the white noise (that is, observe the autocorrelation and partial autocorrelation functions), we should be able to see that this column actually contains white noise. Figure 7.10 contains these correlograms; in each case there is no distinctive pattern of spikes, or significant but descending values as we observed with earlier time series.

In this case the appropriate model would be an ARIMA(0, 0, 0); in other words, the best forecast would just be the mean value of the original time series (which is about 0.47).

Example 2

The series in column 3 of Table 7.2 was constructed to be an AR(1) or ARIMA (1, 0, 0) model. When we examined the autocorrelation and partial autocorrelation functions in Figure 7.4, one of the characteristic patterns for an ARIMA(1, 0, 0) model appeared; in addition, no trend is apparent in the series and so it is likely that no differencing is required. We should then be able to specify an ARIMA(1, 0, 0) model and correctly model the time series.

Figure 7.11 presents the results from estimating an AR(1) or ARIMA(1, 0, 0) model. Two tests will determine whether this model is an appropriate model: first,

FIGURE 7.10
Autocorrelation
and Partial
Autocorrelation Plots
for the White Noise
Series in Table 7.2
(Example 1)
(c7t2)

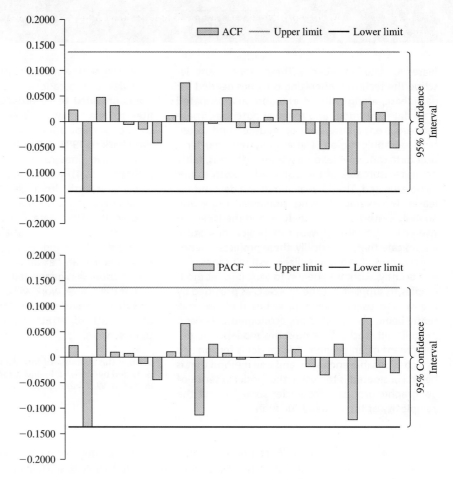

Obs	ACF	PACF	Obs	ACF	PACF
1	.0228	.0228	13	−.0117	−.0036
2	−.1366	−.1371	14	−.0112	−.0005
3	.0475	.0552	15	.0084	.0049
4	.0313	.0098	16	.0414	.0436
5	−.0055	.0074	17	.0235	.0153
6	−.0149	−.0122	18	−.0230	−.0183
7	−.0420	−.0440	19	−.0534	−.0344
8	.0117	.0107	20	.0447	.0257
9	.0757	.0661	21	−.1022	−.1223
10	−.1134	−.1132	22	.0392	.0763
11	−.0031	.0255	23	.0181	−.0193
12	.0465	.0078	24	−.0516	−.0302

FIGURE 7.11 **AR(1) Model Estimate (Example 2) and Residual Autocorrelation Plot for the AR(1) Model Estimate** (c7t2)

```
Audit Trail--Statistics
```

Accuracy Measure	Value
AIC	81.29
BIC	87.88
Mean Absolute Percentage Error (MAPE)	33.12%
Sum Squared Error (SSE)	17.23
R-Square	23.75%
Adjusted R-Square	23.37%
Root Mean Square Error	0.29

Method Statistic	Value
Method selected	Box-Jenkins
Model selected	ARIMA(1,0,0) * (0,0,0)
T-test for nonseasonal AR	8.00
T-test for constant	15.18

Forecast Statistic	Value
Durbin-Watson	1.92
Mean	0.94
Max	1.71
Min	0.24
Sum Squared Deviation	22.60
Range	1.47
Ljung-Box	9.98

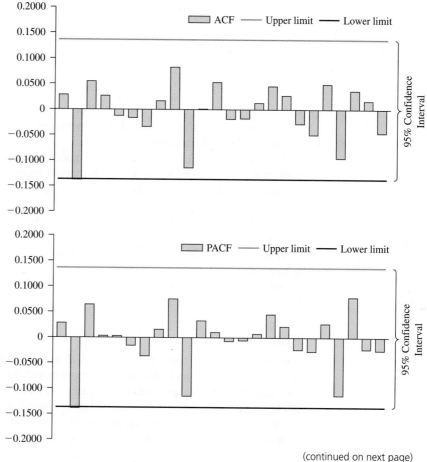

(continued on next page)

FIGURE 7.11

(continued)

Obs	ACF	PACF
1	.0283	.0283
2	−.1375	−.1384
3	.0547	.0643
4	.0266	.0033
5	−.0124	.0030
6	−.0163	−.0156
7	−.0336	−.0365
8	.0166	.0160
9	.0827	.0755
10	−.1140	−.1148
11	.0011	.0330
12	.0531	.0104
13	−.0185	−.0071
14	−.0175	−.0055
15	.0129	.0074
16	.0454	.0456
17	.0272	.0217
18	−.0278	−.0240
19	−.0493	−.0274
20	.0492	.0272
21	−.0952	−.1135
22	.0366	.0787
23	.0167	−.0232
24	−.0457	−.0254

the examination of the autocorrelation coefficients of the residual series, and second, the Ljung-Box statistic.

The autocorrelation function for the residual series shows no distinctive pattern; it appears to be white noise. This would imply that we have chosen the correct model because when the original time series is modified by the model, only white noise remains.

The Ljung-Box statistic offers further evidence that the correct model has been chosen. The calculated Ljung-Box Q is 9.98 for 12 autocorrelations (which give us 11 degrees of freedom). Checking the chi-square table shows the critical value to be *about* 17.275 at the 0.10 significance level. (See the appendix to this chapter for the chi-square table.) Since the calculated Ljung-Box is less than the table value, the model is termed appropriate.

Example 3

The AR(2) series in column 4 of Table 7.2 may be examined in like manner. Assume that we did not know the appropriate model for these data and examine the identification data presented in Figure 7.12. The autocorrelation function gradually falls over almost the entire 24 lags presented; the partial autocorrelation function shows two clear spikes (and possibly a third). The pattern looks like that in frame *c* of Figure 7.3; this identifies the tentative model as an AR(2) or

FIGURE 7.12
Autocorrelation and Partial Autocorrelation Plots for the AR(2) Series in Table 7.2 (Example 3) (c7t2)

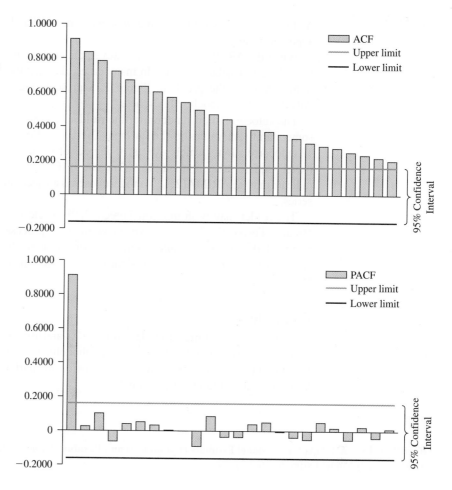

Obs	ACF	PACF	Obs	ACF	PACF
1	.9120	.9120	13	.4063	−.0358
2	.8360	.0252	14	.3834	.0399
3	.7833	.1012	15	.3710	.0511
4	.7222	−.0622	16	.3540	−.0045
5	.6715	.0406	17	.3313	−.0365
6	.6349	.0520	18	.3047	−.0493
7	.6030	.0335	19	.2871	.0514
8	.5716	.0042	20	.2746	.0182
9	.5416	−.0004	21	.2506	−.0508
10	.4979	−.0898	22	.2345	.0242
11	.4720	.0858	23	.2182	−.0394
12	.4435	−.0350	24	.2014	.0124

ARIMA(2, 0, 0). No differencing *appears* to be needed, because there does not appear to be any trend.

When the AR(2) model is run, however, the coefficients fail to damp to zero, indicating a possible problem. In many cases like this, the use of a differencing term eliminates the problem. Figure 7.13 presents the results of applying an ARIMA(2, 1, 0) model to this series.

The autocorrelation function for the residuals shows largely white noise with some significant values in the 24 lags. The Ljung-Box statistic is 4.41 for the 12 autocorrelations (which give us 10 degrees of freedom). The table value from the chi-square table is about 15.987 at the 0.10 significance level; this would indicate that the ARIMA(2, 1, 0) model chosen is an accurate representation of the series.

The reader may wish to allow ForecastX™ to select a model for this series. Because ForecastX™ uses an exhaustive iterative process, the results are often more satisfactory than manual selection. In this case, ForecastX™ selects an ARIMA(0, 1, 1) model that is significantly better than the model presented above.

Example 4

Consider finally the time-series data in Table 7.4 and assume we are given no clues to its origin. Applying the Box-Jenkins methodology, we would first use an identification function to examine the autocorrelation and partial autocorrelation functions; these are presented in Figure 7.14.

FIGURE 7.13 ARIMA(2, 1, 0) Model Estimate (Example 3) and Residual Autocorrelation Plot for ARIMA(2, 1, 0) Model Estimate   (c7t2)

```
Audit Trail--Statistics
```

Accuracy Measure	Value	Forecast Statistic	Value
AIC	228.31	Durbin-Watson	2.29
BIC	234.91	Mean	4.40
Mean Absolute Percentage Error (MAPE)	9.42%	Max	6.36
Sum Squared Error (SSE)	35.94	Min	0.04
R-Square	83.61%	Sum Squared Deviation	219.27
Adjusted R-Square	83.52%	Range	6.32
Root Mean Square Error	0.42	Ljung-Box	4.41
Theil	0.83		

Method Statistic	Value
Method selected	Box-Jenkins
Model selected	ARIMA(2,1,0) * (0,0,0)
T-test for nonseasonal AR	−2.09
T-test for nonseasonal AR	7.04

(continued on next page)

FIGURE 7.13

(continued)

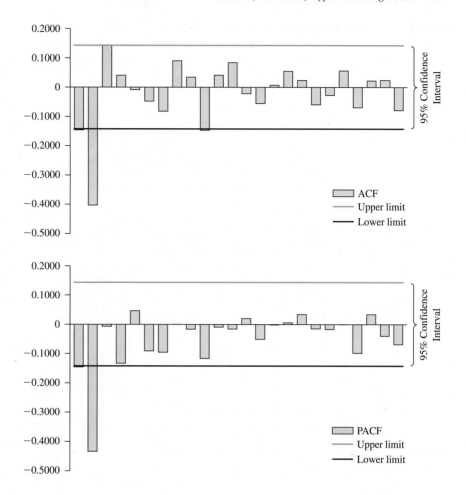

Obs	ACF	PACF	Obs	ACF	PACF
1	−.1460	−.1460	13	−.0218	.0203
2	−.4033	−.4338	14	−.0553	−.0506
3	.1423	−.0069	15	.0070	−.0017
4	.0405	−.1332	16	.0545	.0059
5	−.0088	.0466	17	.0234	.0342
6	−.0477	−.0909	18	−.0596	−.0146
7	−.0819	−.0954	19	−.0275	−.0168
8	.0904	.0004	20	.0560	−.0006
9	.0342	−.0163	21	−.0694	−.0985
10	−.1466	−.1166	22	.0221	.0339
11	.0411	−.0091	23	.0238	−.0396
12	.0845	−.0156	24	−.0787	−.0686

TABLE 7.4 **Example 4 Data Series** (c7t4)

ARIMA				
1 . 0.160000	35 . 22.7092	69 . 45.2098	103 . 74.0750	137 . 99.5781	171 . 126.771
2 . 0.544113	36 . 23.8470	70 . 46.0228	104 . 74.7422	138 . 100.248	172 . 128.169
3 . 1.35744	37 . 24.4950	71 . 46.5587	105 . 75.1037	139 . 101.396	173 . 129.070
4 . 1.81007	38 . 24.7342	72 . 47.2307	106 . 76.1463	140 . 102.778	174 . 130.199
5 . 2.55541	39 . 25.0825	73 . 47.9890	107 . 76.9680	141 . 103.951	175 . 131.363
6 . 3.84012	40 . 25.6879	74 . 49.2088	108 . 77.2119	142 . 105.195	176 . 132.159
7 . 4.91087	41 . 26.9086	75 . 50.5534	109 . 78.1276	143 . 106.493	177 . 132.600
8 . 5.28469	42 . 27.6985	76 . 51.9717	110 . 78.8356	144 . 107.602	178 . 132.974
9 . 5.49273	43 . 27.9592	77 . 52.5793	111 . 79.2148	145 . 108.921	179 . 133.496
10 . 5.62030	44 . 29.0047	78 . 52.7499	112 . 79.4252	146 . 109.953	180 . 134.223
11 . 6.22645	45 . 30.5438	79 . 53.1405	113 . 80.0609	147 . 110.384	181 . 134.735
12 . 6.81976	46 . 31.8912	80 . 53.3826	114 . 81.1088	148 . 111.074	182 . 135.831
13 . 7.03361	47 . 32.7602	81 . 54.3375	115 . 81.5818	149 . 112.112	183 . 136.911
14 . 7.93600	48 . 33.0873	82 . 55.8604	116 . 82.5728	150 . 113.163	184 . 137.315
15 . 9.28220	49 . 33.2974	83 . 57.3969	117 . 83.4074	151 . 113.903	185 . 137.517
16 . 9.99665	50 . 33.7224	84 . 58.2719	118 . 84.0063	152 . 114.280	186 . 137.859
17 . 10.3492	51 . 34.4206	85 . 59.1758	119 . 84.8875	153 . 115.156	187 . 138.897
18 . 10.7372	52 . 35.0356	86 . 60.4877	120 . 86.0977	154 . 116.267	188 . 139.979
19 . 11.6537	53 . 35.6169	87 . 61.6198	121 . 87.1734	155 . 116.826	189 . 140.426
20 . 12.3986	54 . 35.9999	88 . 62.2831	122 . 88.2206	156 . 117.822	190 . 141.150
21 . 12.7508	55 . 36.4831	89 . 62.6991	123 . 88.9342	157 . 118.461	191 . 141.867
22 . 13.0273	56 . 36.8279	90 . 63.5748	124 . 89.6704	158 . 118.806	192 . 142.224
23 . 13.7149	57 . 37.0943	91 . 64.3452	125 . 90.6897	159 . 119.679	193 . 143.023
24 . 14.6099	58 . 37.6164	92 . 65.0968	126 . 91.4675	160 . 120.198	194 . 144.299
25 . 15.1324	59 . 38.7882	93 . 65.4967	127 . 91.7072	161 . 120.534	195 . 145.293
26 . 15.6525	60 . 39.9187	94 . 66.4900	128 . 92.1157	162 . 121.418	196 . 146.425
27 . 16.3994	61 . 40.9344	95 . 67.6714	129 . 92.9512	163 . 121.895	197 . 147.339
28 . 17.3193	62 . 41.5441	96 . 68.1611	130 . 93.4450	164 . 122.030	198 . 148.166
29 . 18.1561	63 . 42.5229	97 . 68.2980	131 . 94.4363	165 . 122.893	199 . 149.491
30 . 19.0496	64 . 43.1073	98 . 68.9562	132 . 95.6413	166 . 123.409	200 . 150.761
31 . 19.8106	65 . 43.4389	99 . 70.3170	133 . 96.2160	167 . 123.898	
32 . 20.7518	66 . 44.2401	100 . 71.5608	134 . 96.6762	168 . 124.924	
33 . 21.2347	67 . 44.6401	101 . 72.3279	135 . 97.2641	169 . 125.618	
34 . 21.5877	68 . 44.7896	102 . 73.2702	136 . 98.4736	170 . 125.903	

The autocorrelation function in Figure 7.14 is entirely characteristic of a series with a trend; that is, it shows dominant autocorrelations for the 24 lags shown. Look at the actual numbers in the original series in Table 7.4 and observe how they gradually creep upward in value. These data apparently have a trend and are therefore nonstationary. Before the Box-Jenkins process can be continued, the series must be transformed to a stationary series. The most common method of achieving stationarity is to take first differences of the original series. Taking these first differences and again applying the identification program to the resulting series gives the autocorrelation and partial autocorrelation functions in Figure 7.15.

FIGURE 7.14
Autocorrelation and Partial Autocorrelation Plots for the Series in Table 7.4 (Example 4)
(c7t4)

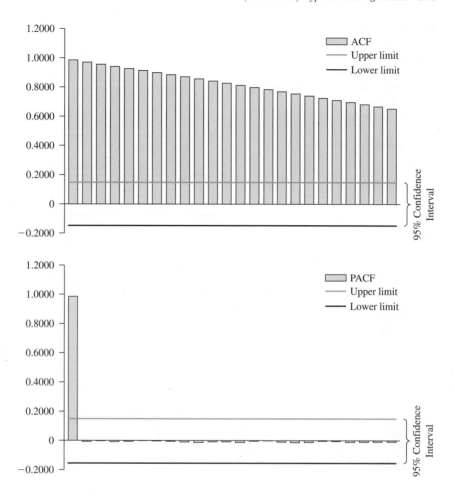

Obs	ACF	PACF	Obs	ACF	PACF
1	.9854	.9854	13	.8124	−.0129
2	.9707	−.0070	14	.7979	−.0043
3	.9562	−.0028	15	.7836	−.0017
4	.9417	−.0087	16	.7692	−.0104
5	.9272	−.0063	17	.7547	−.0138
6	.9129	−.0013	18	.7401	−.0124
7	.8987	−.0033	19	.7255	−.0043
8	.8845	−.0057	20	.7111	−.0051
9	.8703	−.0102	21	.6966	−.0116
10	.8559	−.0139	22	.6820	−.0107
11	.8414	−.0083	23	.6674	−.0100
12	.8270	−.0084	24	.6527	−.0096

FIGURE 7.15
Autocorrelation and Partial Autocorrelation Plots for the Series in Table 7.4 after First Differences Have Been Taken (Example 4)
(c7t4)

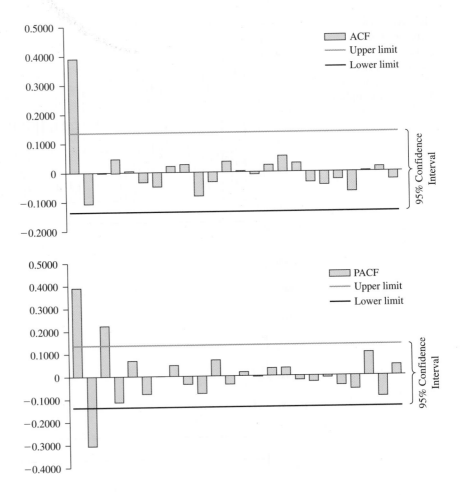

Obs	ACF	PACF	Obs	ACF	PACF
1	.3906	.3906	13	.0032	.0168
2	−.1063	−.3054	14	−.0085	−.0037
3	−.0021	.2231	15	.0233	.0333
4	.0481	−.1128	16	.0537	.0341
5	.0046	.0684	17	.0296	−.0186
6	−.0336	−.0772	18	−.0358	−.0266
7	−.0488	−.0006	19	−.0451	−.0084
8	.0209	.0480	20	−.0260	−.0424
9	.0266	−.0352	21	−.0684	−.0593
10	−.0812	−.0763	22	.0027	.1007
11	−.0333	.0702	23	.0158	−.0923
12	.0359	−.0366	24	−.0269	.0452

The pattern exhibited here (after differencing) is similar to frame *d* of Figure 7.5; perhaps the model is a mixed model, with both AR and MA terms in addition to the differencing required to make the series stationary. Figure 7.16 displays the results of estimating an ARIMA(3, 1, 2) model, that is, a model with three AR terms, one degree of differencing, and two MA terms.

FIGURE 7.16 ARIMA(3, 1, 2) Model Estimate (Example 4) and Residual Autocorrelation Plot for the ARIMA(3, 1, 2) Model Estimate   (c7t4)

```
Audit Trail--Statistics
```

Accuracy Measure	Value
AIC	84.73
BIC	101.22
Mean Absolute Percentage Error (MAPE)	1.12%
Sum Squared Error (SSE)	17.01
R-Square	100.00%
Adjusted R-Square	100.00%
Root Mean Square Error	0.29

Forecast Statistic	Value
Durbin-Watson	1.84
Mean	72.55
Max	150.76
Min	0.16
Sum Squared Deviation	392,388.59
Range	150.60
Ljung-Box	5.14

Method Statistic	Value
Method selected	Box-Jenkins
Model selected	ARIMA(3,1,2) * (0,0,0)
T-test for nonseasonal AR	7.79
T-test for nonseasonal AR	0.02
T-test for nonseasonal AR	1.04
T-test for nonseasonal MA	2.43
T-test for nonseasonal MA	4.46

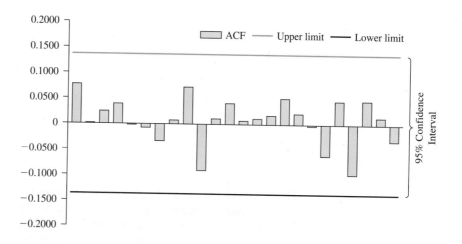

(continued on next page)

FIGURE 7.16
(continued)

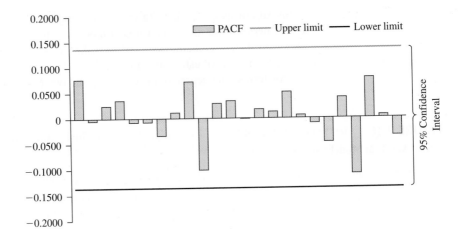

Obs	ACF	PACF
1	.0769	.0769
2	.0013	−.0046
3	.0244	.0248
4	.0390	.0355
5	−.0019	−.0076
6	−.0075	−.0072
7	−.0334	−.0343
8	.0074	.0114
9	.0721	.0718
10	−.0910	−.1013
11	.0108	.0291
12	.0410	.0340
13	.0071	−.0009
14	.0112	.0175
15	.0175	.0125
16	.0510	.0510
17	.0214	.0057
18	−.0027	−.0099
19	−.0614	−.0474
20	.0460	.0399
21	−.0976	−.1097
22	.0469	.0784
23	.0142	.0054
24	−.0317	−.0355

The results in the residual series autocorrelation function indicate that only white noise remains after applying the model. The Ljung-Box statistic is 5.14 for the 12 autocorrelations. The value from the chi-square table is about 12.017 for 7 degrees of freedom at the 0.10 significance level. We would then accept the ARIMA(3, 1, 1) model specification as a "correct" forecasting model for this series.

FORECASTING SEASONAL TIME SERIES

Seasonality can cause some problems in the ARIMA process, since a model fitted to such a series would likely have a very high order.

In many actual business situations the time series to be forecast are quite seasonal. Recall that seasonality refers to a consistent shape in the series that recurs with some periodic regularity (sales of lawn mowers during summer months, for instance, are always higher than in winter months). This seasonality can cause some problems in the ARIMA process, since a model fitted to such a series would likely have a very high order. If monthly data were used and the seasonality occurred in every 12th month, the order of the model might be 12 or more. There is a process for estimating "seasonal MA" and "seasonal AR" terms for the ARIMA process along with seasonal differencing, but the details of estimating such terms are quite complicated. We will use the ability of ForecastX™ to estimate these parameters with a total houses sold series.

TOTAL HOUSES SOLD

The total houses sold figures show trend and appear to exhibit a high degree of seasonality. The mean of the series also shifts significantly from period to period because of a strong seasonal variation. We will allow ForecastX™ to choose seasonal AR and MA terms as appropriate.

The total houses sold data are seen to be very seasonal. Summer months are seen as high sales months while winter months have far fewer sales.

Examining the autocorrelation and partial autocorrelation structure (Figure 7.17A), note the clear pattern of the autocorrelation plot. This pattern is very much like the one in Figure 7.6 and this suggests that the series is nonstationary. Using two degrees of normal differencing and one degree of seasonal differencing on this series eliminates the pattern of nonstationarity. See Figure 7.17B and examine the plot; the nonstationarity characteristic is now absent and the data appear to be stationary. The high degree of seasonality is now clearly evident in the significant spikes in the autocorrelation function every 12 months.

Figure 7.18 is the estimation for an ARIMA(1, 2, 1) (2, 1, 2) model. The second set of P, D, Q values (usually shown as uppercase letters) represents two seasonal AR and MA terms and one degree of seasonal differencing. The residual plot for the first 24 lags of the residuals is also shown in Figure 7.18. Note that we now appear to have only white noise in the residuals, and so the choice of model is probably an accurate one. The Ljung-Box statistic for the first 48 lags is 22.54 and confirms the accuracy of the model.

Calculating the RMSE for the model gives 4.65.

This example introduces the use of *seasonal* AR, MA, and differencing terms. The ability of the ARIMA process to handle the complexity of periodic and recurring events (i.e., seasonality) greatly increases the usability of the ARIMA models. An ARIMA model incorporating seasonal terms, like the total houses sold model represented in Figure 7.18, is usually designated as a model of type ARIMA (p,d,q) $(P,D,Q)^s$. The uppercase P, D, and Q refer to the order of the seasonal terms, and the s refers to the length of the season used.

FIGURE 7.17A **Autocorrelation and Partial Autocorrelation Plots for the Total Houses Sold Series (000)**
Note That the Series Appears to Be Nonstationary. (c7f17)

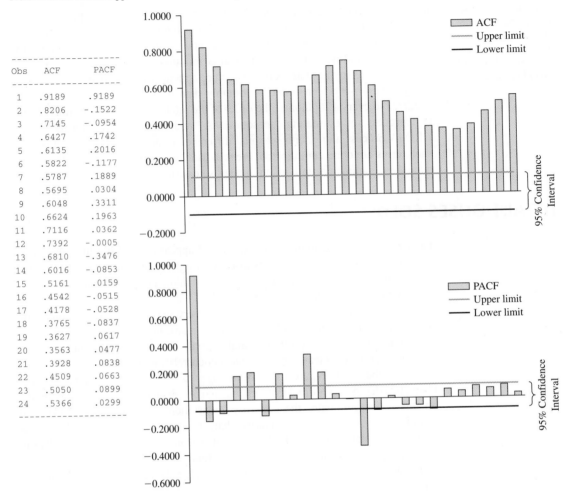

Obs	ACF	PACF
1	.9189	.9189
2	.8206	-.1522
3	.7145	-.0954
4	.6427	.1742
5	.6135	.2016
6	.5822	-.1177
7	.5787	.1889
8	.5695	.0304
9	.6048	.3311
10	.6624	.1963
11	.7116	.0362
12	.7392	-.0005
13	.6810	-.3476
14	.6016	-.0853
15	.5161	.0159
16	.4542	-.0515
17	.4178	-.0528
18	.3765	-.0837
19	.3627	.0617
20	.3563	.0477
21	.3928	.0838
22	.4509	.0663
23	.5050	.0899
24	.5366	.0299

FIGURE 7.17B   **Autocorrelation and Partial Autocorrelation Plots for the Total Houses Sold Series after Two Degrees of Normal Differencing and One Degree of Seasonal Differencing (000)**
Note That the Series Now Appears to Be Stationary. (c7f17)

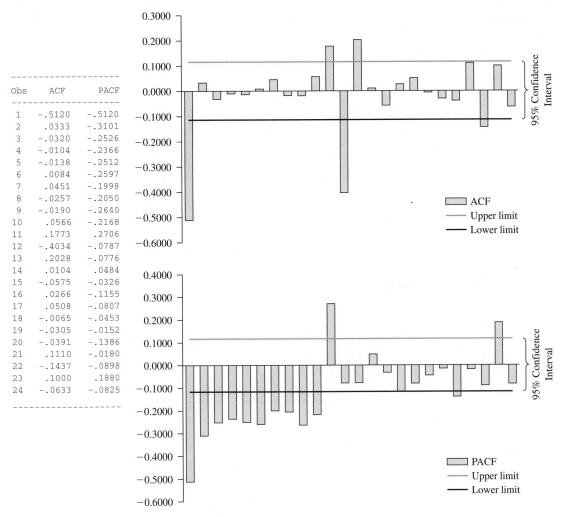

Obs	ACF	PACF
1	-.5120	-.5120
2	.0333	-.3101
3	-.0320	-.2526
4	-.0104	-.2366
5	-.0138	-.2512
6	.0084	-.2597
7	.0451	-.1998
8	-.0257	-.2050
9	-.0190	-.2640
10	.0566	-.2168
11	.1773	.2706
12	-.4034	-.0787
13	.2028	-.0776
14	.0104	.0484
15	-.0575	-.0326
16	.0266	-.1155
17	.0508	-.0807
18	-.0065	-.0453
19	-.0305	-.0152
20	-.0391	-.1386
21	.1110	-.0180
22	-.1437	-.0898
23	.1000	.1880
24	-.0633	-.0825

FIGURE 7.18
Total Houses
Sold Model Estimate
of an ARIMA(1, 2, 1)
(2, 1, 2) Model
(c7f17)

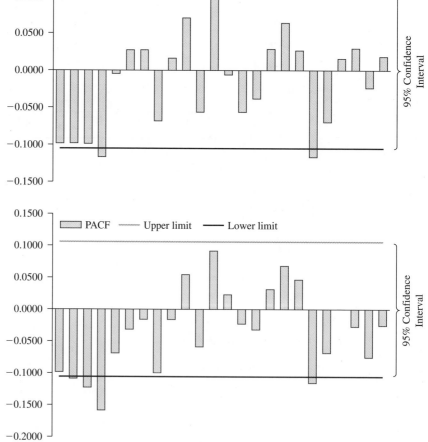

```
Audit Trail--Statistics

Accuracy Measures                        Value    Forecast Statistics        Value
-----------------------------------------------   ------------------------------------
AIC                                   1,926.74    Durbin Watson(1)            2.19
BIC                                   1,949.42    Mean                       60.57
Mean Absolute Percentage Error (MAPE)    6.38%    Max                       123.00
R-Square                                92.70%    Min                        27.00
Adjusted R-Square                       92.59%    Sum Squared Deviation  95,833.37
Root Mean Square Error                    4.65    Range                      96.00
Theil                                     0.69    Ljung-Box                  22.54

Method Statistics                        Value
-----------------------------------------------
Method selected                    Box-Jenkins    Recall that with a seasonal
Model selected      ARIMA(1,2,1) * (2,1,2)        monthly model there are 48
T-Test for nonseasonal AR                -0.82    lags used to calculate the
T-Test for seasonal AR                   -1.69    Ljung-Box.
T-Test for seasonal AR                   -3.39
T-Test for nonseasonal MA                10.64
T-Test for seasonal MA                    1.80
T-Test for seasonal MA                    0.97
```

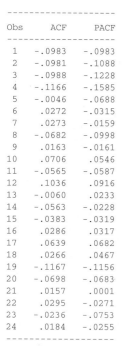

```
--------------------
Obs    ACF     PACF
--------------------
 1   -.0983   -.0983
 2   -.0981   -.1088
 3   -.0988   -.1228
 4   -.1166   -.1585
 5   -.0046   -.0688
 6    .0272   -.0315
 7    .0273   -.0159
 8   -.0682   -.0998
 9    .0163   -.0161
10    .0706    .0546
11   -.0565   -.0587
12    .1036    .0916
13   -.0060    .0233
14   -.0563   -.0228
15   -.0383   -.0319
16    .0286    .0317
17    .0639    .0682
18    .0266    .0467
19   -.1167   -.1156
20   -.0698   -.0683
21    .0157    .0001
22    .0295   -.0271
23   -.0236   -.0753
24    .0184   -.0255
--------------------
```

If you have ever driven around the ring road circling Atlanta or the M25 circling London, you know that congestion can be a problem. In both the United States and the United Kingdom, however, steps have been taken to reduce the costs of congestion not by changing the physical capacity of the existing roadways, but by utilizing them more efficiently. Intelligent transportation systems (ITSs) focus on improving operational efficiency of roadways by effectively using information about dynamic system conditions.

Much of the information about current system conditions is collected by sensors embedded in roads. The information is not only monitored but also collected and archived. Instrumentation on transportation networks became widespread throughout the world in the final years of the 20th century; the effort to collect data continues unabated.

The efficient use of the collected data requires accurate short-term forecasts of roadway conditions. If there are no such forecasts, traveler information and transportation management systems simply react only to currently sensed conditions. The result is that the transportation management systems are essentially using naive forecasts to manage the system; current conditions become the forecast of future conditions. According to professors Billy Williams of North Carolina State University and Lester Hoel of the University of Virginia, this is obviously a poor assumption, especially when traffic conditions are transitioning into or out of congestion.

Williams and Hoel have championed the use of ARIMA forecasting techniques to improve the use of information collected by ITS sensors. They see the need for accurate system forecasts to predict traffic conditions as the key factor in the deployment of smoothly functioning intelligent transportation systems. Their paper in the *Journal of Transportation Engineering* presents their case for a specific type of ARIMA model to predict traffic conditions using fixed in-road sensors. Unlike the data we have been using that tends to be collected quarterly or monthly, Williams and Hoel use data that is collected at intervals ranging from two seconds to two minutes. They selected a discrete time

period to work with that they felt was appropriate to fitting traffic patterns; 15-minute intervals were created by averaging the higher periodicity data. They believed longer intervals would not create the necessary correlations to create stable models of traffic flow.

The problem they tackled was then one of producing short-term (i.e., 15-minute) forecasts of various measures of traffic flow based only upon past observations. Measures of traffic flow included vehicle flow rate per hour, average speed of vehicles, and lane occupancy (the percentage of time a vehicle is present in sensor range).

Not surprisingly, Williams and Hoel first examined the data for stationarity. Their inspection revealed little if any trend week to week, but a high degree of seasonality from week to week. This suggested the use of a "season" of 672 periods. This seemingly strange period was arrived at by using 15-minute intervals and assuming that seasonal patterns would probably occur weekly (i.e., 4 intervals per hour $\times$ 24 hours per day $\times$ 7 days per week $= 672$ periods).

The data used to examine the accuracy of an ARIMA forecast was collected from the Georgia Department of Transportation 10048 sensor located on northbound I-75. The empirical results produced an ARIMA $(1,0,1) (0,1,1)^{672}$ model. The model allowed recursive forecasts for a number of periods into the future. The acid test of this type of forecasting procedure is to examine whether it is superior to those methods now in use in the state of Georgia.

Willams and Hoel used root-mean-squared error, mean absolute percentage error, and mean absolute deviation to compare their ARIMA forecasts with forecasts from models currently in use. With both measures the ARIMA technique proved to be a superior forecast:

I-75 Station 10048 Sensor

Model	RMSE	MAPE	MAD
Seasonal ARIMA	141.73	8.97	75.02
Random walk	180.02	10.10	95.05
Historical average	192.63	12.85	123.56

(continued on next page)

The conclusion was that "the seasonal ARIMA models provided the best forecasts based on all prediction performance statistics." The authors suggested that ITS units begin using ARIMA forecasting with updated parameter estimates as new data are collected. The more accurate forecasts provided by ARIMA would be useful in optimizing traffic flows in many transportation environments.

Source: Billy M. Williams and Lester A. Hoel, "Modeling and Forecasting Vehicular Traffic Flow as a Seasonal ARIMA Process: Theoretical Basis and Empirical Results," *Journal of Transportation Forecasting* 129 (November–December 2003), pp. 664–72.

Since our total houses sold model uses monthly data and the actual seasonality (i.e., recurring pattern) appears to be 12 periods in length, the s in our model is 12. The full model in Figure 7.18 would then be designated as an ARIMA $(1,2,1) (2,1,2)^{12}$.

The complete designation for an ARIMA model would then be:

$$ARIMA(p, d, q) (P, D, Q)^s$$

where:

p = Level of autoregressions

d = Level of normal differencing

q = Level of moving averages

P = Seasonal level of autoregressions

D = Level of seasonal differencing

Q = Seasonal level of moving averages

s = Period of seasonality (usually 4 for quarters, 12 for months, etc.)

When ForecastX™ calculates a seasonal model like this one, the corresponding Ljung-Box statistic is reported with a number of lags equaling 4 times the number of seasons; in this case there would be 4 times 12 (or 48) lags used in the calculation of the reported Ljung-Box statistic. The appropriate degrees of freedom to use in evaluating this statistic would be $m - p - q - P - Q$. Thus, the degrees of freedom for this example would be $48 - 1 - 1 - 2 - 2 = 42$ degrees of freedom. The calculated Ljung-Box of 22.54 is smaller than the table value (imputed, because 42 degrees of freedom is outside the range of the chi-square table in the appendix to this chapter). This means that the model estimated is an appropriate model.

Integrative Case

Forecasting Sales of The Gap

The sales of The Gap stores for the 88 quarters covering 1985Q1 through 2006Q4 are once again shown below. From this graph it is clear that The Gap sales are quite seasonal and are increasing over time. Thus, an optimal ARIMA model will likely require some seasonal terms. Recall that the 2006 data are used as a holdout period.

(c7Gap)

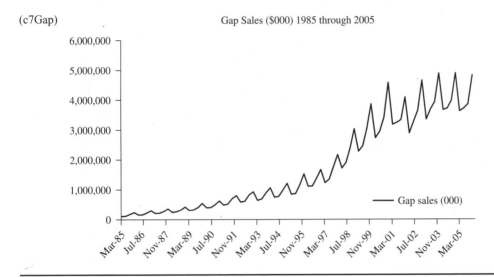

Gap Sales ($000) 1985 through 2005

Case Questions	
	1. From your previous experience plotting The Gap sales over time, what ARIMA techniques should you keep in mind when approaching this data?
	2. Prepare a plot of the autocorrelation and partial autocorrelation coefficients of The Gap sales data. Does this correlogram suggest an ARIMA approach that could be used for forecasting The Gap sales?
	3. Apply a model suggested by the correlogram plot and calculate the RMSE for your forecast of the four quarters of 2006. Recall that the actual 2004 sales (in thousands) were: Quarter 1—3,441,000; Quarter 2—3,716,000; Quarter 3—3,856,000; Quarter 4—4,930,000.

Solutions to Case Questions	
	1. The seasonal pattern and trend should now be familiar. These data will not be stationary, and some adjustment will have to be made to obtain stationarity. The strong seasonal pattern could require some adjustment. It is also the case that the pattern of the data is quite regular and some ARIMA technique should do an excellent job of fitting a model.
	2. The correlogram for the unadjusted The Gap sales shows the possibility of nonstationarity (see Figure 7.19). Since we already know that the data are seasonal, the nonstationarity and the seasonality might be accounted for by using seasonal differencing.

FIGURE 7.19 Autocorrelation and Partial Autocorrelation Plots for The Gap Sales ($000, for the Historical Period of 1985Q1 through 2005Q4) (c7Gap)

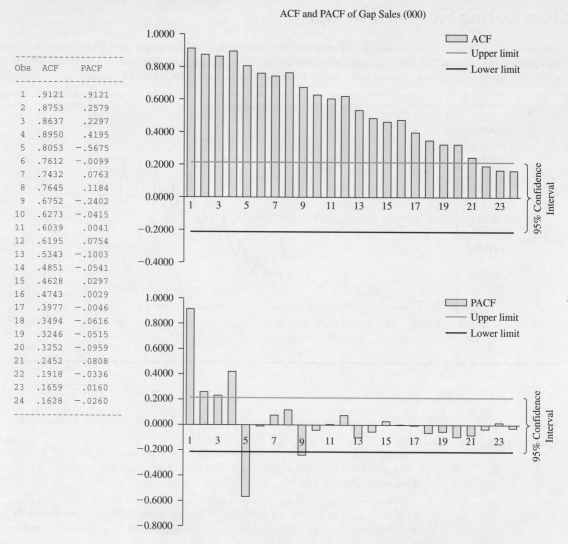

ACF and PACF of Gap Sales (000)

Obs	ACF	PACF
1	.9121	.9121
2	.8753	.2579
3	.8637	.2297
4	.8950	.4195
5	.8053	−.5675
6	.7612	−.0099
7	.7432	.0763
8	.7645	.1184
9	.6752	−.2402
10	.6273	−.0415
11	.6039	.0041
12	.6195	.0754
13	.5343	−.1003
14	.4851	−.0541
15	.4628	.0297
16	.4743	.0029
17	.3977	−.0046
18	.3494	−.0616
19	.3246	−.0515
20	.3252	−.0959
21	.2452	.0808
22	.1918	−.0336
23	.1659	.0160
24	.1628	−.0260

3. While a number of models may perform quite well, the ARIMA(1, 0, 2) (0, 2, 1) model seems to provide a good fit. The model estimation in Figure 7.20 indicates that the Ljung-Box statistic is 29.95 for the 36 autocorrelations, which confirms the accuracy of the model.

The correlogram of the residuals to the model in Figure 7.20 shows only white noise. Also note that the Durbin Watson (4) is just 2.26, showing little residual effects of seasonality.

The actual and predicted values for 2000Q1 through 2006Q4 are shown below. The RMSE for the four holdout quarters is: RMSE = 121,968. This is about a 3.1 percent error based on the average quarterly sales (in thousands of dollars) for the year (3,985,750).

FIGURE 7.20 The Gap Sales Model Audit Trail and Residual Autocorrelation and Partial Autocorrelation Plots for the ARIMA(1, 0, 2) (0, 2, 1) Model Estimate (c7Gap)

Audit Trail--Statistics

Accuracy Measures	Value
AIC	2,202.81
BIC	2,212.53
Mean Absolute Percentage Error (MAPE)	3.89%
R-Square	99.41%
Adjusted R-Square	99.38%
Root Mean Square Error	114,166.24
Theil	0.23

Forecast Statistics	Value
Durbin Watson(4)	2.26
Mean	1,747,909.96
Standard Deviation	1,490,096.34
Ljung-Box	29.95

Method Statistics

	Value
Method Selected	Box Jenkins
Model Selected	ARIMA(1,0,2) * (0,2,1)
T-Test For Non Seasonal AR	7.60
T-Test For Non Seasonal MA	-2.40
T-Test For Non Seasonal MA	-1.18
T-Test For Seasonal MA	5.17

387

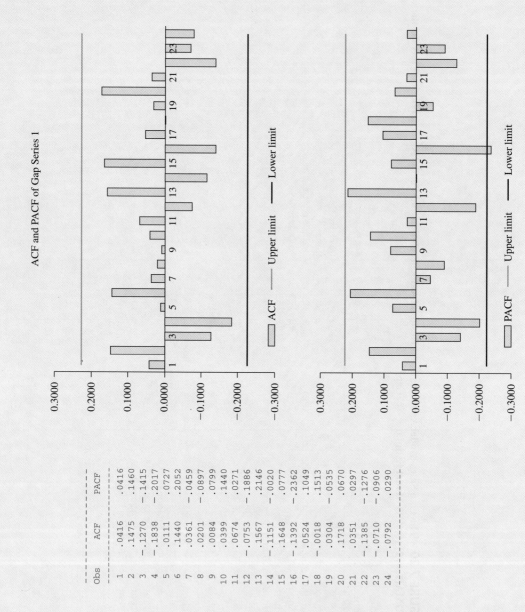

ACF and PACF of Gap Series 1

Obs	ACF	PACF
1	.0416	.0416
2	.1475	.1460
3	-.1270	-.1415
4	-.1838	-.2017
5	.0111	.0727
6	.1440	.2052
7	.0361	-.0459
8	.0201	-.0897
9	.0084	.0799
10	.0399	.1440
11	.0674	.0271
12	-.0753	-.1886
13	.1567	.2146
14	-.1151	-.0020
15	.1648	.0777
16	-.1392	-.2362
17	.0524	.1049
18	-.0018	.1513
19	.0304	-.0535
20	.1718	.0670
21	.0351	.0297
22	-.1385	-.1276
23	-.0710	-.0906
24	-.0792	.0290

Date	The Gap Sales ($000)	Forecast ($000)
Mar-2000	2,731,990.00	2,911,656.70
Jun-2000	2,947,714.00	2,903,175.15
Sep-2000	3,414,668.00	3,638,001.06
Dec-2000	4,579,088.00	4,365,358.66
Mar-2001	3,179,656.00	3,281,453.90
Jun-2001	3,245,219.00	3,478,634.14
Sep-2001	3,333,373.00	3,656,972.77
Dec-2001	4,089,625.00	4,567,978.19
Mar-2002	2,890,840.00	2,864,713.39
Jun-2002	3,268,309.00	3,088,335.18
Sep-2002	3,644,956.00	3,439,302.03
Dec-2002	4,650,604.00	4,658,059.16
Mar-2003	3,352,771.00	3,314,590.28
Jun-2003	3,685,299.00	3,848,073.33
Sep-2003	3,929,456.00	4,008,522.98
Dec-2003	4,886,264.00	5,021,775.91
Mar-2004	3,667,565.00	3,551,078.85
Jun-2004	3,720,789.00	4,130,828.95
Sep-2004	3,980,150.00	3,865,390.50
Dec-2004	4,898,000.00	5,027,058.59
Mar-2005	3,626,000.00	3,802,027.75
Jun-2005	3,716,000.00	3,663,737.38
Sep-2005	3,860,000.00	4,006,558.49
Dec-2005	4,821,000.00	4,818,756.52
Mar-2006	**3,441,000.00**	**3,657,102.22**
Jun-2006	**3,716,000.00**	**3,795,918.50**
Sep-2006	**3,856,000.00**	**3,928,180.50**
Dec-2006	**4,930,000.00**	**4,964,756.45**

← Holdout

The Gap sales ($000)
Forecast ($000)

389

USING FORECASTX™ TO MAKE ARIMA (BOX-JENKINS) FORECASTS

What follows is a brief discussion of how to use ForecastX™ for preparing an ARIMA (Box-Jenkins) forecast. As with other methods, start with your data in an Excel spreadsheet in column format, such as the sample of The Gap data shown in the table below. Once you have your data in this format, while in Excel highlight the data you want to use, then start ForecastX™. The dialog box to the right of the table appears.

A Sample of The Gap Data in Column Format

Date	The Gap Sales ($000)
Mar-1994	751,670
Jun-1994	773,131
Sep-1994	988,346
Dec-1994	1,209,790
Mar-1995	848,688
Jun-1995	868,514
Sep-1995	1,155,930
Dec-1995	1,522,120
Mar-1996	1,113,150
Jun-1996	1,120,340
Sep-1996	1,383,000
Dec-1996	1,667,900
Mar-1997	1,231,186
Jun-1997	1,345,221
Sep-1997	1,765,939
Dec-1997	2,165,479
Mar-1998	1,719,712
Jun-1998	1,904,970
Sep-1998	2,399,900
Dec-1998	3,029,900

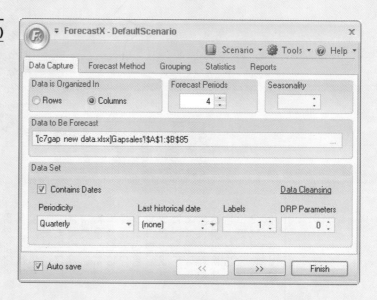

Set the **Dates** window to the periodicity of your data (**Quarterly** for this example); then click the **Forecast Method** tab at the top and the following appears.

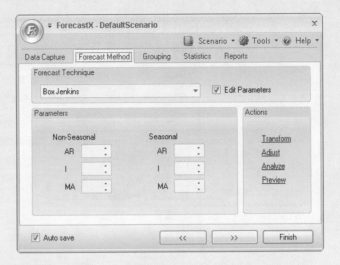

Click the down arrow in the **Forecasting Technique** window and select **Box Jenkins.**
You can enter values for the **AR**, **I**, and **MA** terms, or you can leave those spaces blank and
let ForecastX™ select a suggested set of values.

Next click the **Statistics** tab and the **Statistics** dialog box will appear.

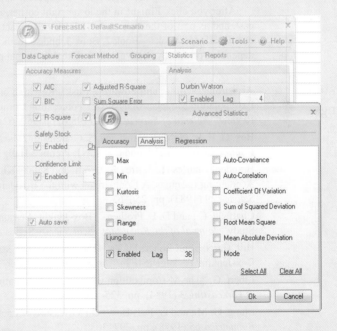

Here you select the statistics you want to have reported. You will want to experiment
with various selections. Use the **More** button to select the **Ljung-Box** statistic. We have
enabled 36 lags in this example.

Next click the **Reports** tab and the **Report Options** dialog box will appear.

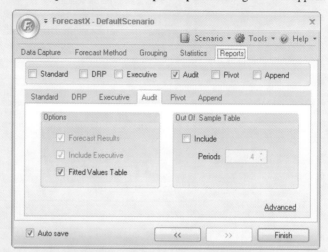

As you place a check next to each of the five boxes for various reports, the options available in that report will appear below. We suggest using the **Audit** report, which provides both graphic and text output that is quite complete.

Again you will want to experiment with the various reports to get a feel for the ones that will give you the output you want for your specific application.

After you click **Finish!** in the lower right corner, ForecastX™ will complete the forecast, and as part of the output, will identify the exact model used. Reports will be put in new Excel workbooks—Book 2, Book 3, and so forth. The numbers of the books will vary depending on what you have done in Excel up to that point.

Suggested Readings

Armstrong, Scott J.; and Edward J. Lusk. "Research on the Accuracy of Alternative Extrapolation Models: Analysis of a Forecasting Competition through Open Peer Review." *Journal of Forecasting* 2 (1983), pp. 259–62.

Box, G. E. P.; G. M. Jenkins; and G. C. Reinsel. *Time Series Analysis: Forecasting and Control.* 3rd ed. Englewood Cliffs, NJ: Prentice-Hall, 1994.

Brandon, Charles H.; Jeffrey E. Jarrett; and Saleha Khumawala. "Revising Forecasts of Accounting Earnings: A Comparison with the Box-Jenkins Method." *Management Science* 29 (1983), pp. 256–63.

Chatfield, C.; and D. L. Prothero. "Box-Jenkins Seasonal Forecasting Problems in a Case Study." *Journal of the Royal Statistical Society* Series A 136 (1973), pp. 295–352.

Hill, Gareth; and Robert Fildes. "The Accuracy of Extrapolation Methods: An Automatic Box-Jenkins Package (SIFT)." *Journal of Forecasting* 3 (1984), pp. 319–23.

Libert, G. "The M-Competition with a Fully Automatic Box-Jenkins Procedure." *Journal of Forecasting* 3 (1984), pp. 325–28.

Ljung, G. M.; and G. E. P. Box. "On a Measure of Lack of Fit in Time Series Models." *Biometrika* 65 (1978), pp. 297–303.

Ludlow, Jorge; and Walter Enders. "Estimating Non-Linear ARMA Models Using Fourier Coefficients." *International Journal of Forecasting* 16, no. 3 (July–September 2000), pp. 333–47.

Lusk, Edward J.; and Joao S. Neves. "A Comparative ARIMA Analysis of the 111 Series of the Makridakis Competition." *Journal of Forecasting* 3 (1984), pp. 329–32.

Nelson, Charles R. *Applied Time Series Analysis for Managerial Forecasting.* San Francisco: Holden-Day, 1973.

Pankratz, Alan. *Forecasting with Univariate Box-Jenkins Models.* New York: John Wiley & Sons, 1983.

Peña, Daniel. "George Box: An Interview with the International Journal of Forecasting." *International Journal of Forecasting* 17, no. 1 (January–March 2001), pp. 1–9.

Pindyck, Robert S.; and Daniel L. Rubinfeld. *Econometric Models and Economic Forecasts.* 3rd ed. New York: McGraw-Hill, 1991.

Exercises

1. A student collects data on the use of the university library on an hourly basis for eight consecutive Mondays. What type of seasonality would you expect to find in these data?

2. When would you use differencing and when would you employ seasonal differencing?

3. Evaluate the following statement: "If an ARIMA model is properly constructed, it has residual autocorrelations that are all equal to zero."

4. Of what use is the chi-square test as applied to residual autocorrelations?

5. *a.* Calculate and display the first 50 autocorrelations for the four data series in the accompanying table, labeled A, B, C, and D; consider each of the four data series to be a quarterly time series. How many of the autocorrelations fall outside the 95 percent confidence interval (positive or negative)?

   b. Is there a pattern to those autocorrelation coefficients falling outside the 95 percent confidence interval?

   c. Calculate and display the first 50 partial autocorrelations for the 100 time-series observations. How many of the partial autocorrelation coefficients fall outside the 95 percent confidence interval?

   d. Is there a pattern to those partial autocorrelation coefficients falling outside the 95 percent confidence interval?

   e. Estimate the appropriate model as determined from your inspections carried out in parts *a* through *d* and forecast for four quarters into the future. Calculate the RMSE for each model.

EXERCISE 5 Four Data Series

A	B	C	D	A	B	C	D
1.62	0.38	0.68	1.11	0.73	0.72	3.15	10.85
1.55	1.02	0.71	2.27	0.44	0.69	3.71	11.99
1.59	0.70	1.22	3.71	0.98	0.41	3.76	12.87
1.55	1.16	1.29	4.52	0.62	1.16	3.73	13.44
1.10	1.11	1.53	5.04	0.44	1.35	3.49	14.26
0.82	0.93	1.52	6.10	0.66	0.98	3.94	14.91
1.06	1.32	1.53	7.61	0.83	1.21	4.01	15.37
0.69	0.78	2.08	8.89	1.25	0.69	3.97	15.90
0.74	0.50	2.57	9.73	0.89	0.35	4.35	17.10

(continued on next page)

EXERCISE 5 **Four Data Series** (continued)

A	B	C	D	A	B	C	D
1.02	0.70	3.84	18.39	1.40	0.33	4.90	49.17
0.72	0.74	3.60	18.98	1.52	0.99	4.80	49.85
0.79	0.52	3.43	19.50	1.20	1.24	4.88	50.55
0.77	0.26	3.43	20.21	1.33	0.77	4.46	51.55
1.18	0.21	3.69	20.85	0.69	0.48	5.09	52.20
1.26	1.06	3.85	21.69	0.30	1.16	4.56	53.06
0.81	1.27	4.20	22.69	0.49	0.62	4.37	54.46
1.05	1.63	4.05	23.56	0.43	0.83	4.20	55.70
0.63	0.98	4.33	24.65	0.95	0.62	4.65	56.51
0.71	0.98	4.76	25.92	1.50	1.11	4.37	57.41
1.02	1.13	4.79	26.87	1.58	0.73	4.67	58.81
0.79	1.30	4.69	28.07	0.92	0.61	5.00	60.10
1.22	1.61	4.65	29.63	0.40	0.90	5.03	61.00
1.01	1.31	4.49	30.41	0.47	1.01	4.78	61.69
0.43	1.20	4.91	31.42	1.03	1.01	5.21	62.63
0.27	1.26	5.01	32.66	1.33	0.61	5.31	63.12
0.41	1.32	4.59	33.49	1.11	1.13	5.14	63.28
0.94	0.85	4.62	34.23	0.60	1.05	5.18	63.52
1.42	1.13	4.83	35.00	0.30	0.89	4.92	64.08
1.22	1.24	4.86	36.27	0.93	1.21	5.24	64.45
1.31	1.08	4.53	37.07	0.92	1.48	4.80	64.62
0.67	0.85	4.44	37.25	0.85	1.62	5.37	64.78
0.22	1.32	4.74	38.10	0.52	1.15	5.19	65.52
0.50	1.53	4.54	39.51	0.07	1.43	4.71	66.18
0.64	1.75	4.13	40.20	0.41	1.33	4.62	67.16
0.41	1.11	4.22	40.27	1.21	1.26	4.42	68.63
0.40	0.80	3.97	40.68	0.96	1.16	5.00	69.67
1.13	0.41	4.29	41.19	0.31	1.04	4.53	70.17
1.06	0.93	4.22	41.58	0.33	1.19	4.44	70.53
0.31	0.66	4.34	42.23	0.52	1.22	4.56	71.32
0.67	1.29	4.85	43.33	0.77	0.70	4.48	71.99
0.68	1.11	4.39	44.27	0.85	0.74	4.88	72.53
0.72	1.16	4.74	44.89	1.27	0.73	4.70	72.89
0.58	1.52	5.09	45.41	1.48	1.00	4.92	73.81
0.74	1.28	4.83	45.69	1.42	1.39	4.74	74.74
1.14	0.76	5.21	46.39	1.29	1.51	4.31	75.15
1.42	0.74	4.74	46.96	0.87	1.11	4.74	75.81
0.94	0.53	4.90	47.34	0.86	1.42	4.64	76.86
0.59	0.44	5.06	47.61	0.76	1.38	4.39	77.83
0.32	0.92	5.29	48.21	0.36	1.68	4.15	78.95
0.68	0.57	4.90	48.77	0.17	1.49	4.35	80.27

6. *a.* Calculate and display the first 50 autocorrelations for the four data series in the table for this exercise, labeled A, B, C, and D; consider each of the four data series to be a quarterly time series. How many of the autocorrelations fall outside the 95 percent confidence interval (positive or negative)?

   b. Is there a pattern to those autocorrelation coefficients falling outside the 95 percent confidence interval?

c. Calculate and display the first 50 partial autocorrelations for the 100 time-series observations. How many of the partial autocorrelation coefficients fall outside the 95 percent confidence interval?

d. Is there a pattern to those partial autocorrelation coefficients falling outside the 95 percent confidence interval?

e. Which frame in Figures 7.1, 7.3, and 7.5 does this pattern of autocorrelation and partial autocorrelation coefficients most closely resemble?

f. Estimate the appropriate model as determined from your inspections carried out in parts *a* through *e,* and forecast for four quarters into the future. Calculate the RMSE for each model.

EXERCISE 6   Four Data Series

A	B	C	D	A	B	C	D
0.77	0.37	0.20	0.93	0.74	0.86	4.87	76.58
0.31	0.32	0.93	1.24	0.28	0.46	4.11	50.73
0.88	0.95	1.62	2.12	0.27	0.49	3.95	50.99
1.48	1.40	1.66	3.60	0.42	0.49	3.72	51.42
0.99	1.04	2.41	4.59	0.30	0.38	3.49	51.72
1.16	1.44	2.63	5.75	0.19	0.29	3.33	51.91
1.26	1.33	2.75	7.01	0.21	0.28	4.01	52.12
0.86	1.10	2.64	7.87	1.08	1.13	3.91	53.21
0.48	0.73	2.66	8.35	1.12	0.99	4.09	54.33
0.39	0.63	2.75	8.74	0.85	1.05	3.94	55.18
0.55	0.68	2.97	9.29	0.68	0.82	4.50	55.86
0.76	0.85	2.84	10.05	1.13	1.33	4.30	56.99
0.56	0.63	3.55	10.62	1.00	1.03	4.03	57.99
1.12	1.29	3.55	11.74	0.38	0.64	4.61	58.37
1.18	1.14	3.30	12.91	1.02	1.25	4.11	59.39
0.45	0.68	3.16	13.37	0.73	0.71	4.11	60.12
0.21	0.48	3.13	13.58	0.36	0.66	4.20	60.48
0.36	0.50	3.71	13.93	0.71	0.83	3.81	61.19
1.06	1.13	3.77	15.00	0.40	0.47	3.56	61.59
1.17	1.12	3.50	16.17	0.09	0.29	3.57	61.69
0.50	0.67	3.86	16.67	0.87	1.14	5.19	24.87
0.74	0.99	3.72	17.41	1.38	1.55	5.26	26.25
0.78	0.82	3.54	18.19	1.37	1.46	5.24	27.62
0.39	0.57	3.92	18.58	1.01	1.26	5.63	28.62
0.82	0.99	4.31	19.39	1.28	1.54	5.77	29.90
1.35	1.35	4.28	20.74	1.42	1.55	5.43	31.32
1.08	1.16	4.70	21.82	0.82	1.04	5.36	32.13
1.18	1.42	4.56	23.00	0.59	0.93	5.15	32.72
1.00	1.12	4.71	24.00	0.60	0.78	5.05	33.32
1.07	0.97	4.68	43.00	0.59	0.75	5.56	33.91
1.00	1.11	4.64	44.01	0.35	0.46	4.05	62.04
0.90	1.05	4.56	65.15	1.06	1.07	4.12	63.09
1.11	1.30	4.57	46.02	1.16	1.10	4.19	64.25
0.71	0.81	4.46	46.73	0.90	1.02	4.97	44.91
0.38	0.68	4.46	47.12	1.15	1.33	4.23	66.30
0.61	0.76	4.71	47.73	0.76	0.86	4.18	67.06
0.99	1.07	4.69	48.72	0.45	0.74	4.59	67.51
0.99	1.04	4.61	49.71	1.03	1.18	5.02	68.54

(continued on next page)

EXERCISE 6 **Four Data Series** (continued)

A	B	C	D	A	B	C	D
1.54	1.56	5.40	70.08	0.76	0.85	4.51	41.93
1.65	1.75	5.44	71.73	1.33	1.53	4.91	73.07
1.25	1.37	5.22	35.16	0.48	0.79	5.33	73.55
1.02	1.01	5.65	36.18	0.82	1.20	5.62	74.37
1.11	1.39	5.85	37.29	1.48	1.51	5.11	75.84
1.47	1.55	5.53	38.76	0.74	0.91	4.18	50.45
0.90	1.08	5.23	39.66	0.25	0.60	4.81	76.83
0.40	0.73	5.14	40.06	0.50	0.68	5.25	77.33
0.50	0.73	4.68	40.56	1.18	1.25	5.45	78.51
0.29	0.40	4.47	40.86	1.45	1.44	5.37	79.95
0.19	0.37	4.07	41.05	1.08	1.23	5.35	81.03
0.12	0.19	4.50	41.17	0.86	1.11	5.02	81.89

7. *a.* An autoregressive model is given by:

$$Y_t = 20.58 + 0.046Y_{t-1} + 0.019Y_{t-2}$$

where Y_t = sales of a product. Explain the meaning of the terms in this autoregressive model.

   b. Write the expressions for the following models:

AR(3)	MA(4)
AR(4)	ARMA(1, 2)
MA(3)	ARIMA(2, 1, 2)

8. A twenty-foot equivalent unit (TEU) is a standard measurement of volume in container shipping. The majority of containers are either 20 or 40 feet in length. A 20-foot container is 1 TEU; a 40-foot container is 2 TEUs. Although the height of containers can also vary, this does not affect the TEU measurement. The following data are the total number of containers shipped from the port of Los Angeles for the years 1995 through 2007.

Date	Total TEUs	Date	Total TEUs	Date	Total TEUs
Jan-95	123,723	Mar-96	96,906	May-97	136,712
Feb-95	99,368	Apr-96	111,204	Jun-97	140,220
Mar-95	118,549	May-96	115,513	Jul-97	143,756
Apr-95	123,411	Jun-96	119,422	Aug-97	143,389
May-95	114,514	Jul-96	129,984	Sep-97	143,700
Jun-95	114,468	Aug-96	134,296	Oct-97	144,425
Jul-95	125,412	Sep-96	134,657	Nov-97	131,877
Aug-95	122,866	Oct-96	144,430	Dec-97	134,315
Sep-95	115,473	Nov-96	128,521	Jan-98	125,930
Oct-95	121,523	Dec-96	122,428	Feb-98	122,976
Nov-95	104,880	Jan-97	127,065	Mar-98	154,947
Dec-95	103,821	Feb-97	112,733	Apr-98	154,522
Jan-96	111,494	Mar-97	113,063	May-98	167,204
Feb-96	99,785	Apr-97	129,797	Jun-98	159,638

(continued on next page)

(continued)

Date	Total TEUs	Date	Total TEUs	Date	Total TEUs
Jul-98	158,948	Sep-01	275,559	Nov-04	340,051
Aug-98	171,152	Oct-01	274,954	Dec-04	283,268
Sep-98	157,267	Nov-01	241,730	Jan-05	305,102
Oct-98	169,364	Dec-01	225,886	Feb-05	294,022
Nov-98	158,255	Jan-02	220,810	Mar-05	262,173
Dec-98	140,165	Feb-02	244,167	Apr-05	336,087
Jan-99	142,116	Mar-02	229,954	May-05	319,472
Feb-99	142,080	Apr-02	276,373	Jun-05	340,582
Mar-99	141,926	May-02	284,385	Jul-05	356,716
Apr-99	153,559	Jun-02	301,447	Aug-05	349,655
May-99	182,975	Jul-02	271,933	Sep-05	356,912
Jun-99	169,682	Aug-02	339,690	Oct-05	375,051
Jul-99	185,017	Sep-02	330,967	Nov-05	332,037
Aug-99	188,281	Oct-02	265,218	Dec-05	328,244
Sep-99	187,081	Nov-02	301,333	Jan-06	327,009
Oct-99	208,163	Dec-02	306,099	Feb-06	251,812
Nov-99	184,662	Jan-03	276,482	Mar-06	345,401
Dec-99	178,493	Feb-03	274,740	Apr-06	370,171
Jan-00	194,180	Mar-03	298,495	May-06	368,864
Feb-00	175,890	Apr-03	326,709	Jun-06	387,957
Mar-00	188,438	May-03	348,276	Jul-06	413,357
Apr-00	220,157	Jun-03	305,892	Aug-06	414,004
May-00	217,749	Jul-03	331,741	Sep-06	431,283
Jun-00	220,071	Aug-03	360,046	Oct-06	421,694
Jul-00	243,695	Sep-03	350,476	Nov-06	390,209
Aug-00	250,551	Oct-03	372,112	Dec-06	365,591
Sep-0	227,848	Nov-03	338,379	Jan-07	367,096
Oct-00	260,469	Dec-03	306,984	Feb-07	358,601
Nov-00	210,209	Jan-04	345,412	Mar-07	323,472
Dec-00	203,021	Feb-04	247,710	Apr-07	375,512
Jan-01	212,323	Mar-04	340,748	May-07	368,874
Feb-01	163,332	Apr-04	345,339	Jun-07	393,187
Mar-01	217,284	May-04	367,128	Jul-07	387,573
Apr-01	221,465	Jun-04	347,056	Aug-07	379,027
May-01	213,860	Jul-04	365,901	Sep-07	407,915
Jun-01	243,053	Aug-04	344,109	Oct-07	393,948
Jul-01	250,344	Sep-04	324,346	Nov-07	383,241
Aug-01	261,705	Oct-04	352,718	Dec-07	346,140

a. Plot the series. What can you learn from examining this plot?

b. Calculate and display the first 24 autocorrelations for the series. What do the ACF and PACF suggest about the series?

c. Suggest and estimate an optimal set of differencing to use with the series.

d. Estimate the ARIMA model that you believe to be a good candidate for forecasting container shipments. It may help to specify the seasonality as "12." Test the Ljung-Box statistic and report your findings. Finally, plot the first 24 autocorrelations of the residuals to your best model.

9. The data below shows the average hourly megawatts of electricity used in New York City for the years 1993 through 2004.

Month	Mean Usage	Month	Mean Usage	Month	Mean Usage
Jan-93	17,074.66	Jan-97	17,860.97	Jan-01	18,439.91
Feb-93	17,822.51	Feb-97	17,030.63	Feb-01	18,069.88
Mar-93	16,900.10	Mar-97	16,586.05	Mar-01	17,608.38
Apr-93	15,417.28	Apr-97	15,712.44	Apr-01	16,140.74
May-93	14,986.03	May-97	15,236.65	May-01	16,556.55
Jun-93	16,929.04	Jun-97	17,608.56	Jun-01	19,185.78
Jul-93	18,694.29	Jul-97	18,964.37	Jul-01	19,157.38
Aug-93	18,332.28	Aug-97	18,145.33	Aug-01	21,327.08
Sep-93	16,468.28	Sep-97	16,788.25	Sep-01	17,540.95
Oct-93	15,474.31	Oct-97	16,103.79	Oct-01	16,663.81
Nov-93	16,028.48	Nov-97	16,499.30	Nov-01	16,624.80
Dec-93	17,155.07	Dec-97	17,389.77	Dec-01	17,267.98
Jan-94	18,404.18	Jan-98	17,056.34	Jan-02	17,808.09
Feb-94	17,884.69	Feb-98	17,036.37	Feb-02	17,404.08
Mar-94	16,754.90	Mar-98	16,833.40	Mar-02	16,809.13
Apr-94	15,277.75	Apr-98	15,739.52	Apr-02	16,561.17
May-94	15,040.02	May-98	16,059.23	May-02	16,168.09
Jun-94	17,836.91	Jun-98	17,779.28	Jun-02	18,691.46
Jul-94	19,349.14	Jul-98	19,460.53	Jul-02	21,372.06
Aug-94	17,734.60	Aug-98	19,705.33	Aug-02	21,300.47
Sep-94	16,015.75	Sep-98	17,751.83	Sep-02	18,505.90
Oct-94	15,382.20	Oct-98	16,035.26	Oct-02	17,157.60
Nov-94	15,941.85	Nov-98	16,490.67	Nov-02	17,201.31
Dec-94	16,833.42	Dec-98	17,349.93	Dec-02	18,362.16
Jan-95	17,056.81	Jan-99	18,014.58	Jan-03	19,065.90
Feb-95	17,695.12	Feb-99	17,472.08	Feb-03	18,741.54
Mar-95	16,351.09	Mar-99	17,188.13	Mar-03	17,400.20
Apr-95	15,495.87	Apr-99	15,811.44	Apr-03	16,358.73
May-95	15,291.26	May-99	15,913.57	May-03	15,929.05
Jun-95	17,252.93	Jun-99	19,271.75	Jun-03	17,999.87
Jul-95	19,154.12	Jul-99	21,652.70	Jul-03	20,717.03
Aug-95	19,166.08	Aug-99	19,652.57	Aug-03	20,730.96
Sep-95	16,178.87	Sep-99	18,180.01	Sep-03	18,038.57
Oct-95	15,619.46	Oct-99	16,478.46	Oct-03	16,531.88
Nov-95	16,434.09	Nov-99	16,739.43	Nov-03	16,758.73
Dec-95	17,627.00	Dec-99	17,742.58	Dec-03	18,137.06
Jan-96	17,932.43	Jan-00	18,485.60	Jan-04	19,333.36
Feb-96	17,669.17	Feb-00	17,955.94	Feb-04	18,313.19
Mar-96	16,816.22	Mar-00	16,834.31	Mar-04	17,351.52
Apr-96	15,702.85	Apr-00	16,218.50	Apr-04	16,384.22
May-96	15,478.36	May-00	16,656.62	May-04	17,001.84
Jun-96	17,209.71	Jun-00	18,980.76	Jun-04	18,798.57
Jul-96	17,770.67	Jul-00	18,745.26	Jul-04	20,040.84
Aug-96	18,314.77	Aug-00	19,480.04	Aug-04	20,222.35
Sep-96	16,906.53	Sep-00	18,018.60	Sep-04	18,643.92
Oct-96	15,745.02	Oct-00	16,607.91	Oct-04	16,775.23
Nov-96	16,486.24	Nov-00	17,231.95	Nov-04	17,308.72
Dec-96	16,880.53	Dec-00	18,737.37	Dec-04	18,617.75

a. Plot the series and explain what can be learned from this plot.

b. Calculate the first 24 autocorrelations for the series, and explain what characteristics of the data are shown in the ACF and PACF.

c. Suggest and estimate an optimal ARIMA model.

d. Estimate the ARIMA model that you believe to be a good candidate for forecasting electricity usage. Test the Ljung-Box statistic and report your findings. Finally, plot the first 24 autocorrelations of the residuals to your best model.

10. The data below show retail sales at hardware stores in the United States monthly between January 1992 and December 2005. The data are in millions of dollars and are not seasonally adjusted.

Date	Sales	Date	Sales	Date	Sales
Jan-92	846	Mar-95	1,061	May-98	1,425
Feb-92	822	Apr-95	1,157	Jun-98	1,427
Mar-92	962	May-95	1,343	Jul-98	1,357
Apr-92	1,077	Jun-95	1,340	Aug-98	1,313
May-92	1,235	Jul-95	1,230	Sep-98	1,297
Jun-92	1,170	Aug-95	1,182	Oct-98	1,302
Jul-92	1,147	Sep-95	1,153	Nov-98	1,227
Aug-92	1,086	Oct-95	1,141	Dec-98	1,363
Sep-92	1,056	Nov-95	1,193	Jan-99	1,104
Oct-92	1,110	Dec-95	1,241	Feb-99	1,007
Nov-92	1,041	Jan-96	977	Mar-99	1,210
Dec-92	1,168	Feb-96	920	Apr-99	1,416
Jan-93	883	Mar-96	1,028	May-99	1,495
Feb-93	808	Apr-96	1,251	Jun-99	1,447
Mar-93	987	May-96	1,369	Jul-99	1,390
Apr-93	1,097	Jun-96	1,306	Aug-99	1,301
May-93	1,289	Jul-96	1,242	Sep-99	1,286
Jun-93	1,210	Aug-96	1,186	Oct-99	1,296
Jul-93	1,186	Sep-96	1,083	Nov-99	1,295
Aug-93	1,101	Oct-96	1,187	Dec-99	1,384
Sep-93	1,077	Nov-96	1,177	Jan-00	1,073
Oct-93	1,111	Dec-96	1,229	Feb-00	1,035
Nov-93	1,098	Jan-97	1,003	Mar-00	1,316
Dec-93	1,204	Feb-97	880	Apr-00	1,429
Jan-94	959	Mar-97	1,027	May-00	1,598
Feb-94	866	Apr-97	1,203	Jun-00	1,551
Mar-94	1,053	May-97	1,339	Jul-00	1,445
Apr-94	1,232	Jun-97	1,303	Aug-00	1,433
May-94	1,296	Jul-97	1,277	Sep-00	1,328
Jun-94	1,271	Aug-97	1,224	Oct-00	1,326
Jul-94	1,217	Sep-97	1,172	Nov-00	1,306
Aug-94	1,193	Oct-97	1,246	Dec-00	1,384
Sep-94	1,138	Nov-97	1,140	Jan-01	1,092
Oct-94	1,198	Dec-97	1,184	Feb-01	1,063
Nov-94	1,165	Jan-98	971	Mar-01	1,290
Dec-94	1,243	Feb-98	900	Apr-01	1,441
Jan-95	875	Mar-98	1,105	May-01	1,657
Feb-95	848	Apr-98	1,323	Jun-01	1,574

(continued on next page)

(continued)

Date	Sales	Date	Sales	Date	Sales
Jul-01	1,460	Jan-03	1,186	Jul-04	1,670
Aug-01	1,437	Feb-03	1,110	Aug-04	1,555
Sep-01	1,328	Mar-03	1,337	Sep-04	1,520
Oct-01	1,386	Apr-03	1,490	Oct-04	1,483
Nov-01	1,399	May-03	1,743	Nov-04	1,478
Dec-01	1,457	Jun-03	1,665	Dec-04	1,581
Jan-02	1,158	Jul-03	1,616	Jan-05	1,241
Feb-02	1,097	Aug-03	1,537	Feb-05	1,170
Mar-02	1,297	Sep-03	1,485	Mar-05	1,442
Apr-02	1,539	Oct-03	1,498	Apr-05	1,688
May-02	1,691	Nov-03	1,432	May-05	1,803
Jun-02	1,605	Dec-03	1,511	Jun-05	1,770
Jul-02	1,560	Jan-04	1,186	Jul-05	1,607
Aug-02	1,471	Feb-04	1,126	Aug-05	1,603
Sep-02	1,325	Mar-04	1,406	Sep-05	1,562
Oct-02	1,406	Apr-04	1,619	Oct-05	1,614
Nov-02	1,400	May-04	1,781	Nov-05	1,582
Dec-02	1,460	Jun-04	1,717	Dec-05	1,673

a. Plot the series. What can you learn from examining this plot?

b. Calculate and display the first 24 autocorrelations for the series. What do the ACF and PACF suggest about the series?

c. Suggest a possible set of differencing to use with the series.

d. Estimate an ARIMA model that you believe to be a good candidate for forecasting future retail sales at hardware stores. Test the Ljung-Box statistic and report your findings. Finally, plot the first 24 autocorrelations of the residuals to your best model.

Appendix

Critical Values of Chi-Square

This table provides values of chi-square that correspond to a given upper-tail area and a specified degrees of freedom. For example, for an upper-tail area of 0.10 and 4 degrees of freedom, the critical value of chi-square equals 7.779. When the number of degrees of freedom exceeds 30, the chi-square can be approximated by the normal distribution.

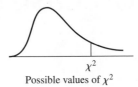

χ^2

Possible values of χ^2

Degrees of Freedom (df)	Right-Tail Area			
	0.10	0.05	0.02	0.01
1	2.706	3.841	5.412	6.635
2	4.605	5.991	7.824	9.210
3	6.251	7.815	9.837	11.345
4	7.779	9.488	11.668	13.277
5	9.236	11.070	13.388	15.086
6	10.645	12.592	15.033	16.812
7	12.017	14.067	16.622	18.475
8	13.362	15.507	18.168	20.090
9	14.684	16.919	19.679	21.666
10	15.987	18.307	21.161	23.209
11	17.275	19.675	22.618	24.725
12	18.549	21.026	24.054	26.217
13	19.812	22.362	25.472	27.688
14	21.064	23.685	26.873	29.141
15	22.307	24.996	28.259	30.578
16	23.542	26.296	29.633	32.000
17	24.769	27.587	30.995	33.409
18	25.989	28.869	32.346	34.805
19	27.204	30.144	33.687	36.191
20	28.412	31.410	35.020	37.566
21	29.615	32.671	36.343	38.932
22	30.813	33.924	37.659	40.289
23	32.007	35.172	38.968	41.638
24	33.196	36.415	40.270	42.980
25	34.382	37.652	41.566	44.314
26	35.563	38.885	42.856	45.642
27	36.741	40.113	44.140	46.963
28	37.916	41.337	45.419	48.278
29	39.087	42.557	46.693	49.588
30	40.256	43.773	47.962	50.892

Source: From Owen P. Hall, Jr., and Harvey M. Adelman, *Computerized Business Statistics* (Homewood, IL: Richard D. Irwin, 1987), p. 95.

Combining
Forecast Results

INTRODUCTION

The use of combinations of forecasts has been the subject of a great deal of research in forecasting. An indication of the importance of this concept is the fact that the prestigious *International Journal of Forecasting* had a special section, composed of seven articles, entitled "Combining Forecasts" in the year-end issue of the volume for 1989. Some of these articles are listed in the "Suggested Readings" section at the end of this chapter. In December 1992 an article in the same journal provided strong evidence on the importance of combining forecasts to improve accuracy. It was found that 83 percent of expert forecasters believe that combining forecasts will produce more accurate forecasts than could be obtained from the individual methods![1]

The idea of combining business forecasting models was originally proposed by Bates and Granger.[2] Since the publication of their article, this strategy has received immense support in almost every empirical test of combined forecasts versus individual uncombined forecasts. The evidence on the usefulness of combining forecasts using different methods and forecasts from different sources has continued to mount over the years. A 2004 article by researchers Fuchun Li and

---

[1] Fred Collopy and J. Scott Armstrong, "Expert Opinions about Extrapolation and the Mystery of the Overlooked Discontinuities," *International Journal of Forecasting* 8, no. 4 (December 1992), pp. 575–82.

[2] Some of the material in this chapter is taken from the original Bates and Granger article; we recommend that readers consult the original article and other articles listed in the bibliography for more detail. J. M. Bates and C. W. J. Granger, "The Combination of Forecasts," *Operational Research Quarterly* 20, no. 4 (1969), pp. 451–68.

We have also drawn from and highly recommend J. Scott Armstrong's book, which is a virtual encyclopedia of forecasting methods. J. Scott Armstrong, *Long-Range Forecasting from Crystal Ball to Computer,* 2nd ed. (New York: John Wiley & Sons, 1985). For a nice overview of the state of the art in combining forecasts, see Robert T. Clemen, "Combining Forecasts: A Review and Annotated Bibliography," *International Journal of Forecasting* 5, no. 4 (1989), pp. 559–83.

Greg Tkacz found that "our results suggest that the practice of combining forecasts, no matter the technique employed in selecting the combination weights, can yield lower forecast errors on average."[3] Robert Winkler and Robert Clemen recently observed that combining forecasts from several experts also leads to improved forecasting accuracy (with diminishing returns as more experts are added).[4] David Hendry and Michael Clements also observe, "Practical experience shows that combining forecasts has value added and can dominate even the best individual device."[5] Even when models are misspecified, Hendry and Clements point out that combining the models provides a degree of "insurance" and usually is more accurate than any single model.

Throughout this book we have emphasized the use of the root-mean-squared error (RMSE), mean absolute percentage error (MAPE), and Theil's U as measures of the effectiveness of a particular forecasting model (*forecast optimality*). The emphasis is very different in this chapter; instead of choosing the best model from among two or more alternatives, we are going to combine the forecasts from these different models to obtain *forecast improvement*. It may actually be unwise to simply determine which of a number of forecasting methods yields the most accurate predictions. A more reasoned approach, according to the empirical evidence, is to combine the forecasts already made in order to obtain a combined forecast that is more accurate than any of the separate predictions.

Any time a particular forecast is ignored because it is not the "best" forecast produced, it is likely that valuable independent information contained in the discarded forecast has been lost. The information lost may be of two types:

1. Some variables included in the discarded forecast may not be included in the "best" forecast.

2. The discarded forecast may make use of a type of relationship ignored by the "best" forecast.

In the first of these cases it is quite possible for several forecasts to be based on different information; thus, ignoring any one of these forecasts would necessarily exclude the explanatory power unique to the information included in the discarded model. In the second situation, it is often the case that different assumptions are made in different models about the form of the relationship between the variables. Each of the different forms of relationship tested, however, may have some explanatory value. Choosing only the "best" of the relationships could exclude functional information.

---

[3] Fuchun Li and Greg Tkacz, "Combining Forecasts with Nonparametric Kernel Regressions," *Studies in Nonlinear Dynamics & Econometrics* 8, no. 4 (2004), article 2, http://www.bepress.com/snde/vol8/iss4/art2.

[4] Robert L. Winkler and Robert T. Clemen, "Multiple Experts vs. Multiple Methods: Combining Correlation Assessments," *Decision Analysis* 1, no. 3 (September 2004), pp. 167–76.

[5] David F. Hendry and Michael P. Clements, "Pooling of Forecasts," *Econometrics Journal* 5 (2002), pp. 1–26.

BIAS

To be useful, forecasts we wish to combine must be unbiased. That is, each of the forecasts cannot consistently overestimate or underestimate the actual value. Note that if we combined an unbiased forecast with one that consistently overestimated the true value, we would always wind up with a biased estimate. Combining forecasts is not a method for eliminating systematic bias in a forecast.

Bias can arise from a number of sources, but perhaps the most common source is the forecaster's preconceived notions. Predictions of forecasters not only reflect what they believe to be the truth, but also what they would *like* the truth to be. This statement is best demonstrated by the results obtained by Hayes in a survey of voters two weeks before the Roosevelt-Hoover election. Hayes found that, of the people who intended to vote for Hoover, 84 percent thought that he would win the election. Of the people who intended to vote for Roosevelt, however, only 6 percent thought that Hoover would win. Apparently those who intended to vote for a particular candidate are biased in the sense that they also believe that their favorite will actually win the election.[6]

A forecaster should spend some time examining multiple forecasting models in the hope of combining some or all of these models into a combined forecast that is superior to any of the individual forecasts.

Professional forecasters may suffer from the same bias as voters—they may look for forecasting models that confirm their own preconceived ideas. To eliminate bias a forecaster will have to examine models that may contradict his or her current beliefs. What this means is that you must do something that runs counter to your intuition in order to examine models you may feel are incorrect; you must examine forecasting models that you may believe to be inferior to your "favorite" model. This prescription is more difficult to implement than it sounds. Much of a forecaster's time is spent in confirming existing beliefs of how the world works. However, we are suggesting that a forecaster should spend some time examining multiple forecasting models in the hope of combining some or all of these models into a combined forecast that is superior to any of the individual forecasts.

AN EXAMPLE

Consider a situation in which two separate forecasts are made of the same event. It is not atypical for a forecaster to attempt in this situation to choose the "best" of the two forecasting models on the basis of some error-minimization criterion such as RMSE. The model not chosen is discarded as being second-best and, therefore, unusable.

If, however, the two forecasting models use different methods, or if the two models use different information, discarding one of the models may cause the loss of some valuable information. To prevent this loss of useful information requires some method for combining the two forecasts into a single "better" forecast.

---

[6] S. P. Hayes, Jr., "The Predictive Ability of Voters," *Journal of Social Psychology* 7 (1936), pp. 183–91.

To illustrate, we will use a classic example taken from an appendix to the original Bates and Granger article. In Table 8.1 we show output indices for the gas, electricity, and water sectors of the economy, drawn from the 1966 edition of *National Income and Expenditure.* The actual index data in column 2 are in 1958 dollars. Our task is to estimate a forecasting model for these data that has a low RMSE.

We will use two separate forecasting techniques that have already been introduced in the text:

1. A linear time-series regression model (see Chapter 4)
2. An exponential or logarithmic model (see Chapter 5)

The regression model for forecasting with a simple linear trend in Chapter 4 was:

$$Y = b_0 + b_1(\text{TIME})$$

where Y is the series we wish to forecast. The linear-trend forecast in column 3 of Table 8.1 is calculated by using the year in column 1 as the independent variable and the actual data in column 2 as the dependent variable. The equation—estimated with simple linear regression—for making the first forecast (the one for 1950) used only the data for 1948 and 1949:

$$Y = -7,734 + 4(\text{YEAR})$$

Substituting the year 1950 gives the linear forecast for 1950, which appears in column 3:

$$Y = -7,734 + 4(1950) = 66$$

The simple linear-trend estimating equation is then estimated again, this time using the data for the first three years (1948–50); this equation is used to forecast for the year 1951, and that value (which is 71.3) is placed in column 3 of Table 8.1. This procedure is repeated for each year, so that the forecast for year t is always made by extrapolating the regression line formed by the least-squares regression of the actual figures for 1948 through the year $t - 1$. The results obtained and displayed in the table would be similar to the results an actual forecaster might record as he or she makes annual forecasts by always using new data as they become available.

For each forecast in column 3, we also calculate the squared deviation from the actual figure as an intermediate step in calculating the RMSE (see Chapter 1 for an explanation of root-mean-squared error). The RMSE for the simple linear-trend approach to forecasting the index is given at the bottom of column 4.

The second model used to forecast the index is the exponential model (it is sometimes called the *logarithmic* or *constant-rate-of-growth* model). The assumption in this model is that the value we are forecasting does not produce a straight-line plot when graphed over time. Instead the data may plot as a curve on arithmetic paper but as a straight line on semilogarithmic paper (graph paper with one arithmetic axis and one logarithmic axis). The equation to estimate is:

$$Y = b_0 m^x$$

TABLE 8.1 Forecast of Output Indices for Gas, Electricity, and Water   (c8t1)

Source: J. M. Bates and C. W. J. Granger, "The Combination of Forecasts," *Operational Research Quarterly* 20, no. 4 (1969), pp. 451–68.

1	2	3	4	5	6	7	8	9	10
Year	Actual Index Data	Linear Forecast	Squared Deviations	Exponential Forecast	Squared Deviations	Combined Forecast (0.16 Weight)*	Squared Deviations	Combined Forecast (0.5 Weight)†	Squared Deviations
1948	58								
1949	62								
1950	67	66.000	1.0	66.276	0.5	66.23	0.59	66.14	0.74
1951	72	71.333	0.4	71.881	0.0	71.79	0.04	71.61	0.15
1952	74	76.500	6.3	77.385	11.5	77.24	10.52	76.94	8.66
1953	77	79.200	4.8	80.289	10.8	80.11	9.70	79.74	7.53
1954	84	81.933	4.3	83.215	0.6	83.01	0.98	82.57	2.03
1955	88	87.000	1.0	88.632	0.4	88.37	0.14	87.82	0.03
1956	92	91.607	0.2	93.656	2.7	93.33	1.76	92.63	0.40
1957	96	95.972	0.0	98.476	6.1	98.08	4.31	97.22	1.50
1958	100	100.200	0.0	103.187	10.2	102.71	7.34	101.69	2.87
1959	103	104.345	1.8	107.843	23.4	107.28	18.34	106.09	9.57
1960	110	108.106	3.6	112.108	4.4	111.47	2.15	110.11	0.01
1961	116	112.846	9.9	117.444	2.1	116.71	0.50	115.15	0.73
1962	125	117.967	49.5	123.241	3.1	122.40	6.77	120.60	19.32
1963	133	124.152	78.3	130.228	7.7	129.02	14.02	127.19	33.76
1964	137	130.850	37.8	137.864	0.7	136.74	0.07	134.36	6.99
1965	145	136.978	64.4	145.034	0.0	143.74	1.58	141.01	15.95
	Sum of squares =		263.3		84.4		78.82		110.25
	RMSE =		4.06		2.30		2.22		2.63

* The 0.16 weight refers to the weight on the linear model. The weight on the exponential model must then be 0.84, since the two weights must sum to 1.
† The 0.5 weight refers to the weight on the linear model. The weight on the exponential model must then be 0.5, since the weights must sum to 1. Note also that the RMSE for the column 9 combined model is not as low (and, therefore, not as good) as the RMSE for the column 7 combined model.

where:

Y = The actual value of the index

b_0 = Value of the trend when $x = 0$

m = The constant rate of growth (which could be negative)

x = The time value (in the present case, 1948 = 1, 1949 = 2, etc.)

The equation can be estimated with a standard regression package by using the log linear equation:

$$\ln Y = \ln b_0 + x \ln m$$

To obtain the equation for the first exponential estimate in Table 8.1, the natural logs of the actual index data for the years 1948 and 1949 were taken and regressed on time (with 1948 = 1 and 1949 = 2). This produced the estimate:

$$\ln Y = 3.994 + (\text{Year})\ 0.067$$

Taking the antilogs of the log values gives the following equation:

$$Y = (54.258)(1.069)^{\text{Year}}$$

Note that the antilog of 3.994 = 54.258 and the antilog of 0.067 = 1.069. The first forecast (the one for 1950) is calculated by making the substitution for year into this equation (recall that the year 1950 = 3):

$$Y = (54.258)(1.069)^3 = 66.276$$

This first exponential forecast is the first number (66.276) in column 5 of Table 8.1. The forecast for the following year (71.9) requires the fitting of another equation of the same form, utilizing the actual index data from all three previous years. Each subsequent forecast then requires the equation to be estimated once again.

For each forecast in column 5 we again calculate the squared deviation from the actual figure as an intermediate step in calculating the RMSE. The results in column 6 are again what could be expected if a forecaster were to use the exponential method over time and keep careful track of the errors made each year as the current year's actual data became available. The RMSE for the exponential model over the 16-year period from 1950 to 1965 is given at the bottom of column 6.

The RMSE for the exponential forecasting model is clearly smaller (and therefore better) than the corresponding figure for the simple linear-trend forecasting model. If we were to choose the "best" model, the exponential model would be the clear choice.

However, since the two forecasts assume different forms of the relationship between the variables, there may be a combination of the two forecasts that will yield considerable improvements from either single model. A combined forecast is a weighted average of the different forecasts, with the weights reflecting in some sense the confidence the researcher has in each of the models. Some forecasters have suggested that the weights should be selected before the forecasts are generated in order to reduce the possibility of bias introduced by the researcher. The use of a mechanical rule to make the selection of weights would also satisfy this objection and will be discussed in what follows.

In our particular situation it appears that we should have more confidence in the exponential model because it has the lower RMSE. This would suggest that in combining the two forecasts we should weight the exponential model more heavily than the simple linear-trend model. In column 7 of Table 8.1 we have arbitrarily weighted the simple linear-trend model by 0.16 and the exponential model by 0.84 (the two weights must sum to 1). The first forecast in column 7 is then calculated as follows:

$$(0.16)(\text{Linear forecast}) + (0.84)(\text{Exponential forecast}) = \text{Combined forecast}$$

$$(0.16)(66.000) + (0.84)(66.276) = 66.23$$

This procedure is repeated for each of the years from 1950 to 1965. Column 8 contains the squared deviations of the combined forecast from the actual index data, and the RMSE for the combined forecast (2.22) is at the bottom of the column.

Note that the RMSE for the combined forecast is better (i.e., lower) than for either individual forecasting model. The combining of forecasts is a practical tool for improving forecast accuracy and has the attraction of being both automatic and conceptually quite simple; apparently even the less accurate simple linear-trend model contained important information that made it possible to obtain a better forecast. Following this approach, it should be clear that most forecast methods contain some information that is independent of the information contained in other forecast methods. If this is the case, combination forecasts will, quite likely, outperform individual forecasts.

Two important observations need to be made about the results in Table 8.1:

1. Considerable improvements in forecast accuracy can be achieved by combining forecast models with an optimal weight. In this case the optimal weight turned out to be 0.16 for the simple linear-trend model (and therefore, 0.84 for the exponential model).

2. While the forecaster cannot assume that combining forecasts will always yield better results, it can be shown that the combined forecasts will have an error variance not greater than the smallest error variance of the individual forecasts.[7]

WHAT KINDS OF FORECASTS CAN BE COMBINED?

The example of combining forecasts we used in the previous section is one of the simpler combinations a researcher could try. In actual practice it would be more common to find a forecaster using very different types of models in order to construct a combination forecast.

---

[7] David A. Bessler and Jon A. Brandt, "Composite Forecasting: An Application with U.S. Hog Prices," *American Journal of Agricultural Economics* 63 (1981), pp. 135–40. See also Li and Tkacz "Combining Forecasts."

FIGURE 8.1
Combining Forecasts from Different Methods

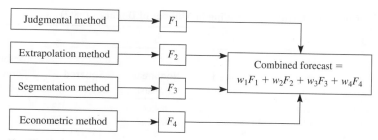

Note: The w's, the relative weights on various forecasts, should sum to 1.0.

Recall that the premise in constructing combined forecasts is:

1. That the different forecasting models *extract different predictive factors* from essentially the same data, or
2. That the different models offer different predictions because they *use different variables.*

We should expect that combinations of forecasts that use very different models are likely to be effective in reducing forecast error.

> We should expect that combinations of forecasts that use very different models are likely to be effective in reducing forecast error.

Consider Figure 8.1, which conceptually presents a 10-year forecast of air travel in the United States. The judgmental method represents a mail survey of experts outside the airline industry. The extrapolation method could be a form of exponential smoothing. The segmentation method surveys airline travelers in different segments of the market and then combines the results to obtain a total picture of the industry. The econometric method refers to a causal regression model. All four methods could be employed and their predictions weighted by the values w_1 to w_4 in order to calculate the combined forecast. Such a diverse combined forecast would benefit from both the use of the different techniques *and* from the use of different sources of data. If each of the methods employed was also constructed and estimated by a different forecaster, another source of possible bias may also have been minimized; this provides a safeguard by making it difficult to cheat.

CONSIDERATIONS IN CHOOSING THE WEIGHTS FOR COMBINED FORECASTS

Combined forecasts are used in place of individual forecasts in order to reduce forecast error, and the results of the combined methods are quite often impressive. Armstrong has reported results from reanalyzing eight separate studies that provided sufficient information to test the combined forecasting method against individual forecast models.[8] In each case Armstrong used equal weights for the individual forecasts, following his belief that weight should be chosen *ex ante.* The combinations of two forecasts reduced error (measured as mean absolute percentage error) by a significant 6.6 percent. In no single case did the accuracy

[8] See Armstrong, *Long-Range Forecasting,* p. 292.

TABLE 8.2   Consumer Credit Outstanding in Millions of Dollars   (c8t2)

1	2	3	4	5	6	7	8
Date	Data	Linear Forecast	Squared Deviations	Nonlinear Forecast	Squared Deviations	Combined Forecast (0.9)	Squared Deviations
1974	180,739	20,333	25,730,080,935	184,069	11,089,833	36,707	20,745,325,061
1975	196,671	74,661	14,886,365,018	199,658	8,923,391	87,161	11,992,440,674
1976	199,384	128,989	4,955,418,029	216,567	295,261,230	137,747	3,799,112,422
1977	214,678	183,317	983,487,311	234,908	409,266,596	188,476	686,518,984
1978	243,672	237,645	36,323,261	254,803	123,886,402	239,361	18,585,995
1979	285,274	291,974	44,884,727	276,382	79,064,974	290,414	26,424,339
1980	330,062	346,302	263,718,529	299,789	916,468,786	341,650	134,285,174
1981	349,771	400,630	2,586,597,789	325,178	604,810,277	393,085	1,876,055,487
1982	363,435	454,958	8,376,445,901	352,718	114,858,139	444,734	6,609,513,434
1983	381,765	509,286	16,261,723,035	382,590	680,729	496,616	13,190,940,855
1984	409,719	563,614	23,683,863,375	414,991	27,802,472	548,752	19,330,270,449
1985	481,656	617,942	18,574,005,439	450,137	993,424,851	601,162	14,281,676,956
1986	564,319	672,270	11,653,601,953	488,260	5,784,981,342	653,869	8,019,338,377
1987	632,345	726,599	8,883,648,403	529,610	10,554,479,492	706,900	5,558,343,309
1988	666,900	780,927	13,002,199,386	574,463	8,544,428,163	760,280	8,719,985,151
1989	713,845	835,255	14,740,314,868	623,115	8,231,951,666	814,041	10,039,181,951
1990	772,998	889,583	13,592,112,303	675,887	9,430,507,271	868,213	9,066,013,035
1991	804,736	943,911	19,369,708,543	733,128	5,127,683,613	922,833	13,946,855,508
1992	803,792	998,239	37,809,581,361	795,217	73,534,642	977,937	30,326,359,321
1993	799,841	1,052,567	63,870,831,068	862,564	3,934,287,021	1,033,567	54,628,077,612
1994	831,385	1,106,896	75,906,141,341	935,615	10,864,032,884	1,089,768	66,761,614,411
1995	930,477	1,161,224	53,243,860,306	1,014,853	7,119,291,169	1,146,587	46,703,216,419
1996	1,074,911	1,215,552	19,779,716,609	1,100,802	670,304,718	1,204,077	16,683,691,970
1997	1,203,964	1,269,880	4,344,870,955	1,194,029	98,708,323	1,262,295	3,402,453,180
1998	1,285,645	1,324,208	1,487,071,984	1,295,152	90,373,584	1,321,302	1,271,419,175
1999	1,370,766	1,378,536	60,368,490	1,404,839	1,160,939,674	1,381,166	108,160,022
2000	1,481,455	1,432,864	2,361,103,012	1,523,815	1,794,372,503	1,441,959	1,559,938,817
2001	1,618,471	1,487,192	17,234,053,163	1,652,868	1,183,169,385	1,503,760	13,158,603,552
2002	1,777,452	1,541,521	55,663,567,575	1,792,850	237,115,769	1,566,654	44,435,920,383
2003	1,893,053	1,595,849	88,330,685,734	1,944,688	2,666,100,287	1,630,733	68,812,243,775
2004	1,978,586	1,650,177	107,852,637,352	2,109,384	17,108,181,960	1,696,098	79,799,754,130
2005	2,064,499	1,704,505	129,595,376,307	2,288,029	49,965,918,037	1,762,857	90,987,391,104
Sum of Squared Deviations =			855,164,364,060		148,225,899,186		666,679,711,032
RMSE =			163,474		68,059		144,339

ever suffer; when more than two forecasts were combined, further improvements were noted (in one case observed by Armstrong, the forecast error was reduced by 17.9 percent).

Even though the use of equal weights for each of the individual forecasts offers the advantage of simplicity and also precludes the forecaster's own bias in the selection of weighting factors, there may be a good reason for weighting one individual forecast more than another, as we have done in the previous example. Equal weights do not take into account the relative accuracy of the individual forecasting models that are combined. Bates and Granger were the first to indicate that, by weighting the more accurate of the methods more heavily, the

9	10	11	12	13	14	15	16
Combined Forecast (0.8)	Squared Deviations	Combined Forecast (0.5)	Squared Deviations	Combined Forecast (0.2)	Squared Deviations	Combined Forecast (0.1)	Squared Deviations
53,080	16,296,759,578	102,201	6,168,205,483	151,322	865,364,917	167,695	170,132,179
99,660	9,411,000,815	137,160	3,541,588,146	174,659	484,535,839	187,158	90,487,373
146,505	2,796,204,577	172,778	707,867,611	199,052	110,498	207,809	70,986,983
193,636	442,783,158	209,113	30,970,687	224,590	98,250,729	229,749	227,142,412
241,077	6,736,190	246,224	6,511,552	251,371	59,274,075	253,087	88,636,508
288,855	12,825,820	284,178	1,201,482	279,500	33,333,968	277,941	53,768,536
336,999	48,120,348	323,045	49,237,045	309,092	439,770,502	304,440	656,485,380
385,540	1,279,371,752	362,904	172,471,947	340,269	90,299,244	332,723	290,625,477
434,510	5,051,641,787	403,838	1,632,391,767	373,166	94,689,129	362,942	243,224
483,947	10,441,198,220	445,938	4,118,207,580	407,929	684,572,837	395,259	182,107,011
533,890	15,418,452,376	489,303	6,333,647,270	444,716	1,224,815,834	429,854	405,421,727
584,381	10,552,519,678	534,040	2,744,075,077	483,698	4,171,325	466,918	217,212,486
635,468	5,062,275,137	580,265	254,287,439	525,062	1,541,102,771	506,661	3,324,441,888
687,201	3,009,124,483	628,105	17,985,607	569,008	4,011,623,137	549,309	6,895,008,181
739,634	5,290,312,497	677,695	116,544,018	615,756	2,615,649,764	595,110	5,153,768,173
792,827	6,238,114,944	729,185	235,309,387	665,543	2,333,097,023	644,329	4,832,491,389
846,844	5,453,233,492	782,735	94,813,218	718,626	2,956,270,473	697,257	5,736,729,009
901,755	9,412,591,483	838,520	1,141,333,462	775,285	867,376,525	754,206	2,553,235,564
957,635	23,667,496,697	896,728	8,637,065,314	835,822	1,025,868,666	815,519	137,521,947
1,014,567	46,107,346,167	957,566	24,877,283,902	900,565	10,145,419,740	881,565	6,678,842,375
1,072,640	58,203,824,389	1,021,255	36,050,875,768	969,871	19,178,559,315	952,743	14,727,927,645
1,131,950	40,591,058,527	1,088,038	24,825,500,813	1,044,127	12,916,317,045	1,029,490	9,803,561,110
1,192,602	13,851,019,209	1,158,177	6,933,112,192	1,123,752	2,385,372,074	1,112,277	1,396,162,457
1,254,710	2,575,102,407	1,231,954	783,452,105	1,209,199	27,404,828	1,201,614	5,523,074
1,318,397	1,072,651,471	1,309,680	577,658,982	1,300,963	234,632,431	1,298,058	154,060,456
1,383,797	169,788,351	1,391,688	437,694,120	1,399,578	830,131,062	1,402,209	988,616,970
1,451,055	924,217,099	1,478,340	9,706,802	1,505,625	584,178,793	1,514,720	1,106,554,410
1,520,328	9,632,123,105	1,570,030	2,346,496,739	1,619,733	1,592,838	1,636,301	317,896,530
1,591,787	34,471,606,970	1,667,185	12,158,669,416	1,742,584	1,215,735,887	1,767,717	94,758,938
1,665,616	51,727,575,908	1,770,268	15,076,216,859	1,874,920	328,824,640	1,909,804	280,575,417
1,742,018	55,964,301,504	1,879,781	9,762,527,203	2,017,543	1,517,628,268	2,063,464	7,204,189,816
1,821,210	59,189,414,652	1,996,267	4,655,537,795	2,171,324	11,411,739,690	2,229,677	27,283,824,489
	504,370,792,791		174,498,446,789		80,207,713,867		101,128,939,133
	125,545		73,845		50,065		56,216

overall forecast could be improved.[9] You have seen in Table 8.1 that the combination using equal weights is not as effective, on the basis of RMSE, as a combination that assigns a smaller weight to the individual forecast having the larger RMSE.

In general, a combined forecast will have a smaller error, as measured by RMSE, *unless individual forecasting models are almost equally good and their forecast errors are highly correlated.*

Consider Table 8.2, which presents data on the consumer credit outstanding in the United States for the years 1974–2005. The actual credit figures appear in

[9] See Bates and Granger, "The Combination of Forecasts," p. 452.

column 2; in columns 3 and 5, respectively, are linear and nonlinear forecasts. The linear forecast here is simply a trend model using the consumer credit outstanding as the dependent variable and the time index as the independent variable. The nonlinear model here uses the natural log of credit as the dependent variable and the time index as the independent variable. The squared deviations of these forecasts from the actual data are given in columns 4 and 6. By calculating the RMSE for each of the forecasting models, it is clear that the nonlinear model is a superior forecasting tool (RMSE of 68,059 for the nonlinear model versus 163,474 for the linear model).

Of interest here is the correlation of the forecast errors (squared) between the two models (see Table 8.3). To do this we calculate the correlation coefficient

TABLE 8.3   **Forecast Errors for Both the Linear and Nonlinear Models of Consumer Credit Outstanding**

Date	Linear Model Errors	Nonlinear Model Errors
1974	160,405.99	−3,330.14
1975	122,009.69	−2,987.20
1976	70,394.73	−17,183.17
1977	31,360.60	−20,230.34
1978	6,026.88	−11,130.43
1979	−6,699.61	8,891.85
1980	−16,239.41	30,273.24
1981	−50,858.61	24,592.89
1982	−91,522.93	10,717.19
1983	−127,521.46	−825.06
1984	−153,895.62	−5,272.80
1985	−136,286.48	31,518.64
1986	−107,951.85	76,059.06
1987	−94,253.11	102,735.00
1988	−114,027.19	92,436.08
1989	−121,409.70	90,730.10
1990	−116,585.21	97,110.80
1991	−139,175.10	71,607.85
1992	−194,446.86	8,575.23
1993	−252,726.79	−62,723.90
1994	−275,510.69	−104,230.67
1995	−230,746.31	−84,375.89
1996	−140,640.38	−25,890.24
1997	−65,915.64	9,935.21
1998	−38,562.57	−9,506.50
1999	−7,769.72	−34,072.56
2000	48,591.18	−42,360.03
2001	131,278.53	−34,397.23
2002	235,931.28	−15,398.56
2003	297,204.79	−51,634.29
2004	328,409.25	−130,798.25
2005	359,993.58	−223,530.58

	Linear Model Errors	Nonlinear Model Errors
Linear model errors	1	
Nonlinear model errors	−0.45	1

between columns 4 and 6 of Table 8.2, which yields 0.69; from this low correlation coefficient it is apparent that these two forecasting models are not highly correlated. This result indicates that possible improvements would result from some combination of the two models.

The simplest combination of the two models is obtained by weighting each equally; this is done in column 11 of Table 8.2. The RMSE for this combined model is 73,845, which is not as low as the nonlinear model alone.

If, however, the forecast model with the lower RMSE is more heavily weighted, the combined forecast should improve even further. In column 15 of Table 8.2, a weight of 0.9 is applied to the linear model and a weight of 0.1 to the nonlinear model. This results in an RMSE of 56,216, which is the best yet. Further experimentation shows that a weighting of 0.8 for the nonlinear model (and 0.2 for the linear model) yields even better results (an RMSE of 50,065).

If, however, you ignore the rule of thumb that the more accurate forecast should receive the larger weight, the accuracy of the combined forecast may deteriorate. Notice that in column 9 of the table we use a weighting of 0.8 for the linear model (and 0.2 for the nonlinear model), which results in an RMSE that is larger than that for the optimal model.

> It is the diversity of information included in the individual models that allows the combined forecast model to assemble the pieces to form a more powerful forecasting model than any one of the parts.

Using an equal-weighting scheme for the two models yields a combined forecast with an RMSE of 73,845, which is better than the linear model but worse than the nonlinear model. By using heavier weights for the "better" forecasting model (in this case the nonlinear model), we are able to improve the forecast. A weight of 0.8 for the nonlinear model (and correspondingly 0.2 for the linear model) resulted in an RMSE of 50,065 for the combined model. This result emphasizes that it is the diversity of information included in the individual models that allows the combined forecast model to assemble the pieces to form a more powerful forecasting model than any one of the parts.

THREE TECHNIQUES FOR SELECTING WEIGHTS WHEN COMBINING FORECASTS

Is there any way to choose the weights to use in combining the individual forecasts other than by trying all possible combinations? Yes, several researchers have suggested techniques for choosing weights that take advantage of the facts we have just demonstrated. We will present three of these techniques here.

First, Bates and Granger have suggested a method that assumes the individual forecasts are consistent over time and that minimizes the variance of the forecast errors over the time period covered. The weight assigned to the first forecast model, k, is calculated in the following manner (note that the second forecast model would receive a weight of $1 - k$):

$$k = \frac{(\sigma_2)^2 - \rho\sigma_1\sigma_2}{(\sigma_1)^2 - (\sigma_2)^2 - 2\rho\sigma_1\sigma_2}$$

where:

k = The weight assigned to the first forecast model

$(\sigma_1)^2$ = The variance of errors for the first model

$(\sigma_2)^2$ = The variance of errors for the second model

ρ = The coefficient of correlation between the errors in the first set of forecast and those in the second set

A second, and quite different, approach to selecting the best weighting scheme involves allowing the weights to adapt or change from period to period. The power of this method rests on the assumption that forecasting models may not have a constant performance over time. An adaptive set of weights may be calculated in the following manner:

$$\alpha_{1,T+1} = \sum_{t=T-v}^{T} \frac{e_{2t}^2}{e_{1t}^2 + e_{2t}^2}$$

where:

$\alpha_{1,T+1}$ = The weight assigned to forecast model 1 in period $T + 1$

e_{it} = The error made by forecast model i in period t

v = The choice variable, which represents the number of periods included in the adaptive weighting procedure

T = The total number of periods for which there is a history of forecast errors

What is not clear is the superiority of these two methods for choosing weights in a combined model. Bessler and Brandt examined the two weighting methods and concluded:[10]

1. Forecasts from individual models are not likely to be the most accurate forecasts.
2. Even with no record of prior forecast performance, it may make some sense to combine forecasts using a simple averaging method (i.e., equal weights).
3. If prior forecasting records are available, the user should weight forecasts on the basis of past performance (with the most accurate forecast receiving the highest weight).

At least one other technique is used to combine forecasts in order to improve accuracy. This technique involves the use of a regression analysis in determining the weights. Charles Nelson suggests that if we are trying to weight a portfolio of forecasts in order to minimize the forecast error, an optimal linear composite forecast would be:[11]

$$F^* = b_1 F(1) + b_2 F(2)$$

---

[10] See Bessler and Brandt, "Composite Forecasting," p. 139.

[11] Charles R. Nelson, "A Benchmark for the Accuracy of Econometric Forecasts of GNP," *Business Economics* 19, no. 3 (April 1984), pp. 52–58.

The Ministry of Justice in New Zealand is a relatively new branch of government that serves the Department of Corrections and the New Zealand police by carrying out research on crime and providing statistical studies to the ministers and associate ministers of justice.

Sue Triggs completed such a statistical study titled "Interpreting Trends in Recorded Crime in New Zealand." A portion of this report deals specifically with forecasting recorded crime rates. These "forecasts are required for managing the impacts of crime on the workload of the police, the courts, and the correctional system."

Three separate types of models were used to make crime rate predictions:

- Time-series methods, using information on the past trends in recorded crime rates
- Regression models, using information on statistically related variables
- Judgment methods, using expert opinion

Time-series methods were used because of their inherent simplicity. Regression models were used because they are able to take into account demographic trends and estimate their effect on crime rates. Judgmental forecasts added information on the effect of such factors as policy and legislative changes, which have the potential to cause substantial shifts in trends.

The accuracy of the individual forecasts was estimated using two tools:

- *The in-sample error:* The *fit* of each model to the data was estimated by the mean-squared error (MSE) of the in-sample forecasts.
- *The forecast error:* The forecast *accuracy* of each model was estimated by using only the 1962–1992 data to estimate each model and then estimating "forecasts" for 1993–1995. The forecast error was calculated as the MSE of the 1993–1995 forecasts.

Once individual model forecasts were completed, a forecast for each offense group was calculated by using a combination of the models. Usually a simple average (i.e., equal weighting) was used to combine the models.

Source: Sue Triggs, "Interpreting Trends in Recorded Crime in New Zealand" (1997), Ministry of Justice, http://www.justice.govt.nz/pubs/reports/.

where:

$$F^* = \text{Optimal combined forecast}$$

$$F(1) = \text{First individual forecast}$$

$$F(2) = \text{Second individual forecast}$$

$$b_1 = \text{Weight allocated to the first forecast}$$

$$b_2 = \text{Weight allocated to the second forecast}$$

The actual values of b_1 and b_2 would be calculated by running a regression with the past actual values as the dependent variable and the forecasted values for each individual model as the independent variables. Note that this is not exactly the type of regression we have run before in the text; this regression has no intercept term, and so the equation must be calculated in a manner different from that we have used earlier.

Using this method, if the two (or more) individual forecasts are free of systematic bias, the values of b_1 and b_2 will sum roughly to 1. The *t*-ratios for the regression will essentially answer the question: Does individual forecast 1 add any explanatory power to what is already present in forecast 2? and similarly for forecast 2. If the b_1 value passes the t-test at some reasonable confidence level, we can be assured that the first individual model, $F(1)$, did add explanatory power when combined with the second model, $F(2)$, using the weights calculated by the regression.

To apply this method and to determine the best values for b_1 and b_2, a two-step regression process is used. First, you perform a standard multiple regression of the actual values (dependent variable) on the values predicted from the individual forecasting methods (independent variables in this regression). We can express this as:

$$A = a + b_1F(1) + b_2F(2)$$

The value of the intercept (a) should be (not statistically different from) zero if there is no bias in the combined forecast. A standard t-test can be used to test whether the intercept is significantly different from zero.[12] Note that a two-tailed test would be appropriate here.

Assuming that you conclude that $a = 0$, you then redo the regression, forcing the regression through the origin. Most regression programs provide an option that allows this to be done quite easily. The result of regressing the actual values on the two forecast series, without an intercept, yields the desired result to determine the best weights to be used in combining the forecasts. We have:

$$F^* = b_1F(1) + b_2F(2)$$

Using these values of b_1 and b_2, along with the $F(1)$ and $F(2)$ forecast series, the optimal combined forecast, F^*, is easily determined.

As indicated, the values of b_1 and b_2 should sum roughly to 1. On occasion one of these weights may be negative, in which case interpretation is tenuous. Some forecasters use such a model even if b_1 or b_2 is negative, as long as the RMSE for F^* is lower than for $F(1)$ or $F(2)$ alone. However, we advise using this method only when both weights are positive. It should be noted that this method can be extended to include more than two forecast series in the combination process. Remember, however, that each method should have unique information content.

An Application of the Regression Method for Combining Forecasts

To illustrate the widely used regression method of combining forecasts, we will apply it to the problem of forecasting the sales of a household cleaning product

---

[12] This is one of the few cases for which we are interested in testing to see whether the intercept is different from zero. Normally, we do this test only for the slope terms.

(the product's name is not used because the information is proprietary) using data from 2006M4 through 2008M6. The firm that produces this cleaning product routinely uses a sales-force composite method to tap the information held by the sales force. The column labeled "Sales Force" in Table 8.4 contains these forecasts. Forecasts based on this model will be referred to as "sales force." The RMSE of the sales-force composite method was 3,423.

A Winters' exponential smoothing model for sales was the second forecast estimated and resulted in an RMSE of 6,744. We will refer to the Winters' forecast as "Winters."

TABLE 8.4
Sales of a Household
Cleaning Product
and Three Forecasts
of Sales
(c8t4)

Date	Sales	CFCST	Sales Force	Winters
Apr-06	18,364.00	21,465.21	19,197.19	31,901.94
May-06	30,008.00	32,115.60	32,823.38	30,666.56
Jun-06	34,897.00	34,494.95	34,947.72	34,217.79
Jul-06	54,882.00	48,915.66	53,449.23	32,330.57
Aug-06	34,193.00	29,716.74	30,245.30	28,901.65
Sep-06	33,664.00	31,967.89	32,806.22	29,968.75
Oct-06	38,418.00	37,668.69	38,928.83	34,179.98
Nov-06	27,865.00	24,191.78	22,115.28	33,958.61
Dec-06	35,719.00	35,643.67	37,988.11	27,549.04
Jan-07	22,688.00	21,672.12	20,193.23	28,835.05
Feb-07	25,337.00	22,303.46	20,143.32	32,330.39
Mar-07	29,549.00	36,217.87	37,962.14	30,647.20
Apr-07	30,429.00	27,677.55	28,562.09	25,286.32
May-07	23,545.00	27,118.54	27,800.05	25,546.04
Jun-07	29,014.00	29,649.77	30,072.50	29,271.92
Jul-07	24,875.00	25,291.15	24,824.56	28,410.61
Aug-07	30,204.00	29,098.32	30,847.60	23,175.14
Sep-07	22,406.00	24,702.13	25,333.20	23,226.90
Oct-07	30,648.00	34,249.05	36,338.65	27,149.80
Nov-07	27,307.00	21,919.45	21,074.17	26,457.54
Dec-07	29,730.00	30,095.13	32,335.88	22,173.51
Jan-08	22,598.00	24,035.57	24,803.64	21,959.28
Feb-08	20,590.00	24,561.18	24,415.07	26,313.12
Mar-08	17,858.00	19,309.48	18,202.10	24,816.54
Apr-08	13,971.00	18,215.03	17,931.35	20,243.83
May-08	15,822.00	16,676.25	16,428.36	18,484.41
Jun-08	20,120.00	19,292.93	18,836.49	22,090.75

Sales = Sales of a household cleaning product
CFCST = A combination forecast of sales where sales = 0.799(sales force) + 0.192(Winters)
Sales force = Sales-force composite forecast (a judgmental forecast method)
Winters = Winters' exponential smoothing model

Regressing sales on sales force and Winters, and using the standard method including an intercept term, yields the following results (using 2006M4 to 2008M6):

$$\text{Sales} = -5{,}445 + 0.81(\text{sales force}) + 0.37(\text{Winters})$$

$$(-1.42) \quad (10.22) \qquad\qquad (2.44)$$

The values in parentheses are t-ratios. On the basis of these t-ratios, the intercept $(-5{,}445)$ is not significantly different from zero, but the slope terms are significantly positive. Since the intercept is essentially zero, we conclude that there is no bias in combining these two methods.

Repeating the regression without an intercept yields the following (again using 2006M4 to 2008M6):

$$\text{Sales} = 0.80(\text{sales force}) + 0.20(\text{Winters})$$

$$(9.93) \qquad\qquad (2.26)$$

$$(\text{RMSE} = 3{,}045)$$

We see that the combined RMSE of 3,045 is less than the root-mean-squared error of either the sales-force composite model ($\text{RMSE} = 3{,}423$) or the Winters' model ($\text{RMSE} = 6{,}744$). Notice also that the coefficients sum to 1 ($0.80 + 0.20 = 1$).

Note that the two methods combined in this example contain quite different information. The sales-force composite model includes the expertise of the sales force, while the Winters' model statistically takes into account trend and seasonal components of the time series (but not the collective wisdom of the sales force). Incidentally, the correlation coefficient between the squared errors for the two individual models is –0.18 in this case (quite small, as we would expect).

The values for sales, CFCST (the combined forecast), sales force, and Winters are shown in Table 8.4. Figure 8.2 shows the combined forecast and the actual sales data for the historical period. The forecast values certainly appear reasonable.

FIGURE 8.2

Actual Sales Data and the Combined Forecast (CFCST)
(c8t4)

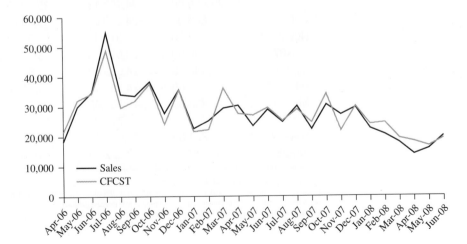

FORECASTING TOTAL HOUSES SOLD WITH A COMBINED FORECAST

We will now apply the forecasting concepts of this chapter to the problem of forecasting total houses sold. We will combine two types of the forecasting models we have presented in previous chapters. The models chosen for combination are a multiple-regression model and a time-series decomposition model. These two models were chosen because they differ in both the variables included and the type of relationship hypothesized.

The multiple-regression model contains information from the mortgage interest rate and the index of consumer sentiment. The regression model estimated was:

$$THS = 106.31 - 10.78(MR) + 0.45(ICS)$$

The root-mean-squared error for this forecasting model is 10.06 in the historical period.

The time-series decomposition model takes both trend and seasonality into account. The root-mean-squared error for the decomposition forecasting model for THS is 3.55 in the historical period.

If we were to simply choose the optimum forecasting model from only these two, we would choose the decomposition model. The RMSE for the decomposition model of 3.55 is less than the RMSE of the regression model. Recall, however, that the objective in combining forecasts is not to choose the optimum forecasting model (forecast optimality) but to improve the forecast (forecast improvement).

Let us see what happens when we combine these forecasts using the regression method of selecting the best set of weights. For notational simplicity we will let THSRF (total houses sold regression forecast) refer to the multiple-regression forecast, and THSDF (total houses sold decomposition forecast) refer to the decomposition forecast. THSCF (total houses sold combined forecast) will be used to represent the combined forecast.

We begin by regressing the actual values of total houses sold (THS) on THSRF and THSDF, using standard regression techniques to determine whether the intercept is essentially equal to zero. See Table 8.5. The results are:

$$THS = -2.54 + 0.06(THSRF) + 0.97(THSDF)$$
$$(-1.2) \quad (1.53) \quad\quad (31.8)$$

where the *t*-ratios are in parentheses. Given a *t*-ratio of −1.2 for the intercept, we would conclude that it is not statistically different from zero at any meaningful significance level.

Next we do the same regression, but this time we force it through the origin by eliminating the constant term (i.e., the intercept). See Table 8.5. The new regression results are:

$$THS = 0.03(THSRF) + 0.97(THSDF)$$
$$(0.96) \quad\quad (31.73)$$

TABLE 8.5   Regression with a Constant Term

Note that the constant term is not statistically significant   (c8t5)

```
Audit Trail--Coefficient Table (Multiple Regression Selected)
```

Series Description	Included in Model	Coefficient	Standard Error	T-test	P-value	F-test	Elasticity	Overall F-test
THS	Dependent	−2.54	2.10	−1.21	0.23	1.46		1,039.99
THSRF	Yes	0.06	0.04	1.53	0.13	2.34	0.06	
THSDF	Yes	0.97	0.03	31.80	0.00	1,011.45	0.97	

```
Audit Trail--Statistics
```

Accuracy Measures	Value	Forecast Statistics	Value
AIC	772.92	Durbin Watson(12)	1.71
BIC	775.89	Mean	67.94
Mean Absolute Percentage Error (MAPE)	4.23%	Max	107.00
R-Square	93.65%	Min	40.00
Adjusted R-Square	93.56%	Sum Squared Deviation	28,071.56
Root Mean Square Error	3.52	Range	67.00
Theil	0.52	Ljung-Box	67.50

Regression without a Constant Term (Constant = 0)—This Regression Is Used for the Combined Forecast

```
Audit Trail--Coefficient Table (Multiple Regression Selected)
```

Series Description	Included in Model	Coefficient	Standard Error	T-test	P-value	F-test	Elasticity	Overall F-test
THS	Dependent	0.00	0.00	0.00	0.00	0.00		1,035.93
THSRF	Yes	0.03	0.03	0.96	0.34	0.93	0.03	
THSDF	Yes	0.97	0.03	31.73	0.00	1,006.76	0.97	

```
Audit Trail--Statistics
```

Accuracy Measures	Value	Forecast Statistics	Value
AIC	774.40	Durbin Watson(12)	1.72
BIC	777.37	Mean	67.94
Mean Absolute Percentage Error (MAPE)	4.20%	Max	107.00
R-Square	93.59%	Min	40.00
Adjusted R-Square	93.49%	Sum Squared Deviation	28,071.56
Root Mean Square Error	3.54	Range	67.00
Theil	0.52	Ljung-Box	66.87

where the *t*-ratios are in parentheses. These results are interesting. First, they show that the coefficients do sum approximately to 1 (0.03 + 0.97 = 1). Second, we see that by far the greatest weight is assigned to the decomposition model, which has an RMSE about one-third the size of the RMSE for the regression model. Third, we see that after accounting for the contribution of the regression model, the

FIGURE 8.3

Total Houses Sold (THS) and Combined Forecast (THSCF) ($000) (c8t5)

This graphic shows actual THS and a combined forecast (THSCF) that is based on a combination of a multiple-regression forecast (THSRF) and a decomposition forecast (THSDF). The combined forecast is:

THS = 0.03(THSRF) + 0.97(THSDF)

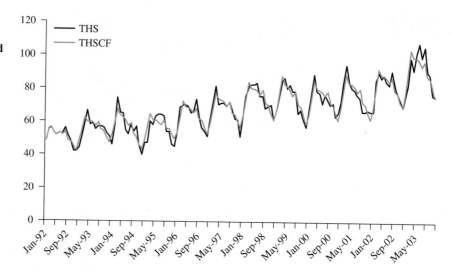

amount of explanatory power added by the decomposition model is substantial (note the large *t*-ratio for THSDF). This is not surprising, since the correlation coefficient between the squared error terms resulting from THSRF and THSDF is quite low. These results suggest that the amount of improvement from combining these models could possibly (but not necessarily) be significant.

Using this set of weights to determine the combined forecast (THSCF), we have:

$$THSCF = 0.03(THSRF) + 0.97(THSDF)$$

The resulting root-mean-squared error of 3.54 shows only a very modest improvement over the 3.55 RMSE based on the decomposition model alone. The forecast values based on THSCF are plotted for the historical period as well as for the forecast horizon, along with actual THS, in Figure 8.3. The data are shown in tabular form in Table 8.6.

TABLE 8.6

Total Houses Sold and Three Forecasts of THS (c8t5)

Date	THS	THSRF	THSDF	THSCF
Jan-1992	48.00	45.48	48.00	48.02
Feb-1992	55.00	42.50	55.00	54.73
Mar-1992	56.00	43.77	56.00	55.74
Apr-1992	53.00	45.27	53.00	52.87
May-1992	52.00	48.10	52.00	51.98
Jun-1992	53.00	50.36	53.00	53.02
Jul-1992	52.00	52.77	51.87	51.99
Aug-1992	56.00	54.16	53.17	53.30
Sep-1992	51.00	54.59	47.88	48.17
Oct-1992	48.00	51.73	47.43	47.65

(continued on next page)

TABLE 8.6
(continued)

Date	THS	THSRF	THSDF	THSCF
Nov-1992	42.00	54.70	44.27	44.66
Dec-1992	42.00	58.21	41.93	42.50
Jan-1993	44.00	59.61	46.52	47.00
Feb-1993	50.00	62.08	53.97	54.32
Mar-1993	60.00	63.70	61.83	62.00
Apr-1993	66.00	63.89	59.31	59.56
May-1993	58.00	61.53	59.60	59.77
Jun-1993	59.00	62.61	59.08	59.30
Jul-1993	55.00	62.87	57.09	57.37
Aug-1993	57.00	64.08	59.40	59.65
Sep-1993	57.00	66.39	54.41	54.87
Oct-1993	56.00	69.50	53.66	54.23
Nov-1993	53.00	65.28	49.53	50.09
Dec-1993	51.00	68.29	46.56	47.30
Jan-1994	46.00	72.19	51.03	51.76
Feb-1994	58.00	70.73	58.97	59.43
Mar-1994	74.00	64.26	67.14	67.18
Apr-1994	65.00	57.85	63.61	63.56
May-1994	65.00	54.92	62.67	62.56
Jun-1994	55.00	56.36	60.33	60.33
Jul-1994	52.00	53.12	57.39	57.37
Aug-1994	59.00	55.40	58.83	58.84
Sep-1994	54.00	53.91	52.02	52.17
Oct-1994	57.00	51.31	50.00	50.14
Nov-1994	45.00	48.24	45.63	45.79
Dec-1994	40.00	49.47	43.04	43.31
Jan-1995	47.00	51.13	48.18	48.36
Feb-1995	47.00	53.46	56.41	56.43
Mar-1995	60.00	55.31	64.46	64.31
Apr-1995	58.00	57.80	61.02	61.04
May-1995	63.00	60.48	60.33	60.45
Jun-1995	64.00	65.98	59.17	59.49
Jul-1995	64.00	66.31	57.21	57.59
Aug-1995	63.00	64.41	60.33	60.57
Sep-1995	54.00	63.53	55.60	55.95
Oct-1995	54.00	65.84	55.18	55.60
Nov-1995	46.00	66.02	51.35	51.88
Dec-1995	45.00	69.21	48.40	49.12
Jan-1996	54.00	70.29	53.43	54.03
Feb-1996	68.00	69.39	62.31	62.63
Mar-1996	70.00	65.89	71.86	71.82
Apr-1996	70.00	62.10	68.64	68.58
May-1996	69.00	59.12	68.43	68.28
Jun-1996	65.00	57.76	67.43	67.27
Jul-1996	66.00	59.54	65.17	65.13
Aug-1996	73.00	62.50	67.67	67.64

Date	THS	THSRF	THSDF	THSCF
Sep-1996	62.00	59.75	61.46	61.52
Oct-1996	56.00	63.90	60.47	60.69
Nov-1996	54.00	68.34	55.64	56.12
Dec-1996	51.00	67.53	52.46	53.01
Jan-1997	61.00	65.38	58.12	58.45
Feb-1997	69.00	68.24	67.31	67.46
Mar-1997	81.00	65.67	76.88	76.69
Apr-1997	70.00	63.71	73.44	73.29
May-1997	71.00	66.67	73.32	73.27
Jun-1997	71.00	69.94	71.90	71.98
Jul-1997	69.00	73.15	69.03	69.28
Aug-1997	72.00	72.16	71.69	71.84
Sep-1997	67.00	73.42	64.84	65.22
Oct-1997	62.00	74.75	63.82	64.26
Nov-1997	61.00	76.32	59.47	60.08
Dec-1997	51.00	75.24	56.56	57.22
Jan-1998	64.00	78.43	62.96	63.54
Feb-1998	75.00	79.58	73.20	73.53
Mar-1998	81.00	76.87	83.59	83.55
Apr-1998	82.00	77.75	79.68	79.77
May-1998	82.00	76.77	79.64	79.70
Jun-1998	83.00	77.87	78.60	78.72
Jul-1998	75.00	78.23	75.87	76.09
Aug-1998	75.00	78.20	78.54	78.68
Sep-1998	68.00	78.80	70.94	71.31
Oct-1998	69.00	77.35	69.58	69.94
Nov-1998	70.00	77.98	64.01	64.55
Dec-1998	61.00	78.62	59.94	60.61
Jan-1999	67.00	79.38	66.11	66.63
Feb-1999	76.00	81.04	76.71	76.98
Mar-1999	84.00	77.49	87.39	87.26
Apr-1999	86.00	78.29	82.68	82.71
May-1999	80.00	76.79	81.37	81.39
Jun-1999	82.00	72.70	78.86	78.83
Jul-1999	78.00	71.26	75.40	75.42
Aug-1999	78.00	67.25	77.97	77.80
Sep-1999	65.00	69.74	70.50	70.61
Oct-1999	67.00	67.64	68.72	68.82
Nov-1999	61.00	70.61	62.76	63.11
Dec-1999	57.00	67.97	58.40	58.80
Jan-2000	67.00	67.68	63.85	64.09
Feb-2000	78.00	66.07	73.54	73.46
Mar-2000	88.00	65.17	83.79	83.39
Apr-2000	78.00	67.08	79.91	79.68
May-2000	77.00	63.76	79.41	79.09

(continued on next page)

TABLE 8.6
(continued)

Date	THS	THSRF	THSDF	THSCF
Jun-2000	71.00	64.32	77.97	77.71
Jul-2000	76.00	66.68	75.27	75.16
Aug-2000	73.00	67.52	78.28	78.10
Sep-2000	70.00	68.60	71.06	71.12
Oct-2000	71.00	69.34	69.89	70.00
Nov-2000	63.00	70.68	64.54	64.85
Dec-2000	65.00	70.57	60.92	61.32
Jan-2001	72.00	72.69	67.40	67.68
Feb-2001	85.00	70.65	77.99	77.92
Mar-2001	94.00	72.13	88.71	88.38
Apr-2001	84.00	69.35	83.75	83.48
May-2001	80.00	70.20	82.88	82.66
Jun-2001	79.00	70.36	81.14	80.98
Jul-2001	76.00	70.59	77.54	77.48
Aug-2001	74.00	72.13	79.78	79.70
Sep-2001	66.00	69.21	71.70	71.76
Oct-2001	66.00	71.77	69.97	70.15
Nov-2001	67.00	71.87	64.65	64.99
Dec-2001	66.00	69.63	61.08	61.46
Jan-2002	66.00	72.26	67.69	67.96
Feb-2002	84.00	72.42	79.23	79.18
Mar-2002	90.00	73.36	91.82	91.45
Apr-2002	86.00	72.37	88.36	88.06
May-2002	88.00	76.05	88.28	88.09
Jun-2002	84.00	75.77	86.64	86.48
Jul-2002	82.00	75.58	83.62	83.54
Aug-2002	90.00	77.51	86.72	86.61
Sep-2002	82.00	79.00	78.39	78.55
Oct-2002	77.00	76.33	77.09	77.21
Nov-2002	73.00	78.37	71.48	71.82
Dec-2002	70.00	79.70	68.26	68.73
Jan-2003	76.00	79.18	76.67	76.89
Feb-2003	82.00	78.93	90.04	89.88
Mar-2003	98.00	78.88	103.70	103.16
Apr-2003	91.00	81.97	99.27	98.94
May-2003	101.00	88.25	98.94	98.81
Jun-2003	107.00	89.88	96.95	96.92
Jul-2003	99.00	86.10	93.25	93.21
Aug-2003	105.00	78.59	96.66	96.31
Sep-2003	90.00	79.06	87.43	87.35
Oct-2003	88.00	82.07	85.73	85.78
Nov-2003	76.00	84.11	79.07	79.37
Dec-2003	75.00	84.16	74.44	74.87

THS = Total houses sold
THSRF = Multiple regression forecast of THS
THSDF = Time-series decomposition forecast of THS
THSCF = A combination forecast of THS where:
THSCF = 0.03(THSRF) + 0.97(THSDF)

DELFIELD

This statement was made by Deborah Allison-Koerber, a product-line manager at the Delfield Company, a leading manufacturer of food-service equipment. Delfield uses a production-planning system consisting of a master production schedule and a corresponding material requirements planning (MRP) system. The MRP system is driven in large part by sales forecasts. For some time, management had been relying on a heavily judgmental sales forecast that started with a three-month moving average, incorporated judgmental factors from an informal "jury of executive opinion," and was finally adjusted by "add factors" provided by the person who was responsible for the MRP system.

According to Ms. Allison-Koerber, the results from this approach to forecasting were unsatisfactory from an operational perspective, and so she started to test some more quantitative forecasting methods. She focused her initial attention on a particular three-door reach-in freezer that represented a large cost when held in inventory, and so accurate forecasts of sales were important. A review of the sales history for this product showed some trend and some seasonality. Thus, Ms. Allison-Koerber believed that a multiple-regression model and a Winters' exponential smoothing model would be good candidates.

For a multiple-regression model she "reviewed a large set of potential causal variables, but settled on GNP and the prime interest rate as the most important." In addition, "dummy variables were used to account for seasonality and a temporary demand surge" that reflected the rollout of new menu items by a large fast-food chain that purchases Delfield food-service equipment. Ms. Allison-Koerber commented,

A regression model based on this information is comprehensive enough to forecast sales of these freezers and yet simple enough to be easily communicated to others in the organization. In addition, the model is desirable because it necessitates having to develop forecasts for only two independent variables.

For the first six months of actual use, this model resulted in an RMSE of 20.185, which compared with an RMSE of 42.821 based on the traditional subjective method.

Ms. Allison-Koerber found a Winters' exponential smoothing forecast to also outperform the subjective forecast by producing an RMSE of 29.081 for the first six months of use. Because the regression model and the Winters' model contain different information, they were combined. The resulting RMSE was 17.198, lower than the regression model (20.185) or the Winters' model (29.081), and much better than the subjective approach (42.821).

However, as Ms. Allison-Koerber commented, it was felt that "the personnel who make the subjective forecasts have good insights about the industry and these insights should be utilized when possible." Thus, she used a regression technique to combine the quantitative and subjective forecasts. Even though the RMSE for the subjective forecast was much higher, the results demonstrated that the subjective method contained information not found in the other models. The results are summarized in the following table:

Model	RMSE
A. Regression	20.185
B. Winters'	29.081
C. Subjective	42.821
D. A and B combined	17.198
E. C and A combined	17.944
F. C and B combined	16.724
G. C and D combined	16.168

These results confirmed for Delfield that the use of quantitative forecasting methods and the combination of subjective and quantitative forecasts can improve results.

Integrative Case

Forecasting The Gap Sales Data with a Combination Model

The sales of The Gap stores for the 88 quarters covering 1985Q1 through 2006Q4 are again shown in the graph below. Recall that The Gap sales data are quite seasonal and are increasing over time. Use the full 1985Q1 through 2006Q4 data to construct your forecast models.

(c8Gap)

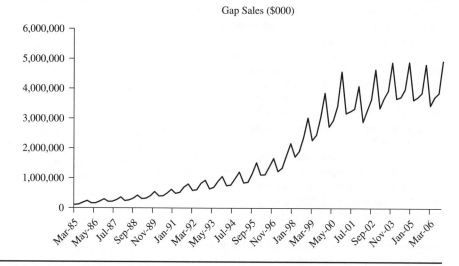

Gap Sales ($000)

Case Questions	1. Assume you would like to use a Winters' model and combine the forecast results with a multiple-regression model. Use the regression technique to decide on the weighting to attach to each forecast.
	2. Combine the two methods (i.e., the Winters' and the multiple-regression models) with the calculated weighting scheme, and construct a combined forecast model.
	3. Calculate the root-mean-squared error for the historical period and comment on any improvement.
Solutions to Case Questions	1. To see if both models may reasonably be used in a combined forecast, run the regression that uses The Gap sales as the dependent variable and the two forecasts (one from the Winters' model and the other from the multiple-regression model) as the explanatory variables. The regression (shown in upper half of Table 8.7) indicates that there is little significance attached to the constant term (because of its t-statistic of 1.08), and so we may reasonably attempt to combine the models.
	2. The two models are combined by running the same regression through the origin (shown in the lower half of Table 8.7). Here the dependent variable is again The Gap sales. Note that the weight on the Winters' forecast (i.e., 0.93) is larger than the weight on the multiple-regression forecast (i.e., 0.07); this seems appropriate because the Winters' forecast alone has a lower RMSE than does the multiple-regression forecast when considered separately.

TABLE 8.7 Regression with a Constant Term

Note that the constant term is not statistically significant (c8Gap)

Audit Trail--Coefficient Table (Multiple Regression Selected)

Series Description	Included in model	Coefficient	Standard error	T-test	Elasticity	Overall F-test
The Gap Sales ($000)	Dependent	10,584.01	17,983.89	0.59		9,161.03
Regression Forecast	Yes	0.11	0.03	3.83	0.11	
Winters Forecast	Yes	0.88	0.03	30.83	0.88	

Audit Trail--Statistics

Accuracy Measures	Value	Forecast Statistics	Value
AIC	2,284.30	Durbin Watson (4)	1.77
BIC	2,286.78	Mean	1,849,629.97
Mean Absolute Percentage Error (MAPE)	5.63%	Standard Deviation	1,533,875.23
R-Square	99.54%	Ljung-Box	39.19
Adjusted R-Square	99.53%		
Root Mean Square Error	103,639.57		
Theil	0.35		

Regression without a Constant Term

Audit Trail--Coefficient Table (Multiple Regression Selected)

Series Description	Included in Model	Coefficient	Standard error	T-test	Elasticity	Overall F-test
The Gap Sales ($000)	Dependent	0.00	0.00	0.00		9,231.01
Regression Forecast	Yes	0.12	0.03	4.07	0.12	
Winters Forecast	Yes	0.88	0.03	30.94	0.88	

Audit Trail--Statistics

Accuracy Measures	Value	Forecast Statistics	Value
AIC	2,284.66	Durbin Watson (4)	1.76
BIC	2,287.14	Mean	1,849,629.97
Mean Absolute Percentage Error (MAPE)	6.19%	Standard Deviation	1,533,875.23

Note the very close association of the forecast with the original data as shown in the graph below:

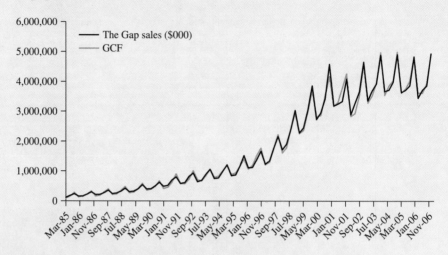

3. The combined forecast and the two candidate models can be compared by using the RMSE of each model:

	RMSE
Winters' model	114,863.59
Regression model	361,694.23
Combination model	103,850.52

Since the lowest RMSE calculated belongs to the combination model, it appears that there may be some support for forecast improvement from the combined model.

Both models we have used here, however, are statistical forecasting models and contain similar (but not identical) information; if we had used two forecasting models employing significantly different types of information, the improvement might have been more substantial for the combined model.

Date	The Gap Sales ($000)	GCF	Date	The Gap Sales ($000)	GCF
Mar-1985	105,715.00	88,109.35	Jun-1987	217,753.00	191,141.14
Jun-1985	120,136.00	90,830.14	Sep-1987	273,616.00	295,356.40
Sep-1985	181,669.00	158,817.14	Dec-1987	359,592.00	397,186.49
Dec-1985	239,813.00	281,134.86	Mar-1988	241,348.00	215,835.30
Mar-1986	159,980.00	133,229.14	Jun-1988	264,328.00	227,889.54
Jun-1986	164,760.00	152,847.97	Sep-1988	322,752.00	345,520.75
Sep-1986	224,800.00	227,183.85	Dec-1988	423,669.00	480,828.85
Dec-1986	298,469.00	333,573.86	Mar-1989	309,925.00	274,272.01
Mar-1987	211,060.00	162,809.32	Jun-1989	325,939.00	298,101.85

(continued)

Date	The Gap Sales ($000)	GCF	Date	The Gap Sales ($000)	GCF
Sep-1989	405,601.00	410,405.94	Jun-1998	1,904,970.00	1,785,360.00
Dec-1989	545,131.00	588,955.81	Sep-1998	2,399,900.00	2,402,008.16
Mar-1990	402,368.00	364,202.07	Dec-1998	3,029,900.00	2,961,212.35
Jun-1990	404,996.00	394,301.04	Mar-1999	2,277,734.00	2,259,675.83
Sep-1990	501,690.00	487,706.24	Jun-1999	2,453,339.00	2,364,295.82
Dec-1990	624,726.00	671,140.93	Sep-1999	3,045,386.00	2,995,946.00
Mar-1991	490,300.00	413,971.79	Dec-1999	3,858,939.00	3,708,533.03
Jun-1991	523,056.00	457,002.96	Mar-2000	2,731,990.00	2,825,320.82
Sep-1991	702,052.00	625,809.86	Jun-2000	2,947,714.00	2,858,814.65
Dec-1991	803,485.00	904,147.59	Sep-2000	3,414,668.00	3,516,435.30
Mar-1992	588,864.00	579,279.74	Dec-2000	4,579,088.00	4,171,367.25
Jun-1992	614,114.00	577,400.07	Mar-2001	3,179,656.00	3,168,953.43
Sep-1992	827,222.00	735,324.67	Jun-2001	3,245,219.00	3,304,442.84
Dec-1992	930,209.00	1,009,992.46	Sep-2001	3,333,373.00	3,784,127.20
Mar-1993	643,580.00	710,725.74	Dec-2001	4,089,625.00	4,265,764.55
Jun-1993	693,192.00	673,211.12	Mar-2002	2,890,840.00	2,831,538.61
Sep-1993	898,677.00	851,604.32	Jun-2002	3,268,309.00	2,922,844.59
Dec-1993	1,060,230.00	1,062,406.52	Sep-2002	3,644,956.00	3,508,458.04
Mar-1994	751,670.00	793,664.22	Dec-2002	4,650,604.00	4,583,655.13
Jun-1994	773,131.00	830,671.04	Mar-2003	3,352,771.00	3,281,668.45
Sep-1994	988,346.00	1,007,662.84	Jun-2003	3,685,299.00	3,517,839.75
Dec-1994	1,209,790.00	1,193,403.01	Sep-2003	3,929,456.00	3,959,315.51
Mar-1995	848,688.00	887,193.34	Dec-2003	4,886,264.00	4,971,833.46
Jun-1995	868,514.00	935,854.67	Mar-2004	3,667,565.00	3,539,330.45
Sep-1995	1,155,930.00	1,158,741.46	Jun-2004	3,720,789.00	3,856,236.87
Dec-1995	1,522,120.00	1,401,021.94	Sep-2004	3,980,150.00	4,029,485.05
Mar-1996	1,113,150.00	1,070,627.21	Dec-2004	4,898,000.00	4,990,248.75
Jun-1996	1,120,340.00	1,193,500.77	Mar-2005	3,626,000.00	3,625,727.23
Sep-1996	1,383,000.00	1,526,410.94	Jun-2005	3,716,000.00	3,755,862.19
Dec-1996	1,667,900.00	1,774,076.90	Sep-2005	3,860,000.00	4,016,741.10
Mar-1997	1,231,186.00	1,212,319.44	Dec-2005	4,821,000.00	4,838,641.30
Jun-1997	1,345,221.00	1,295,312.30	Mar-2006	3,441,000.00	3,611,228.60
Sep-1997	1,765,939.00	1,753,572.57	Jun-2006	3,716,000.00	3,609,175.74
Dec-1997	2,165,479.00	2,224,782.40	Sep-2006	3,856,000.00	3,942,513.79
Mar-1998	1,719,712.00	1,611,794.81	Dec-2006	4,930,000.00	4,896,055.40

Gap Sales = Actual The Gap sales
GCF = The Gap sales combined forecast model

where:
GCF = 0.12(GRF) + 0.88(GWF)
GRF = The Gap sales multiple-regression forecast
GWF = The Gap sales Winters' forecast

USING FORECASTX™ TO COMBINE FORECASTS

As usual, begin by opening your data file in Excel and start ForecastX™. In the **Data Capture** dialog box identify the data you want to use, as shown here. Note that in this case you want a sheet that has the date, the actual values for the series you are forecasting, and then two or more of the forecasts you have developed. Then click the **Forecast Method** tab.

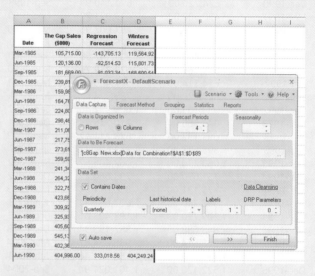

In the **Method Selection** dialog box click the down arrow in the **Forecasting Technique** box and select **Multiple Regression.** Make sure the desired variable is selected as the **Dependent Series,** which is the actual value of **Gapsales** in this example. Then click the **Statistics** tab.

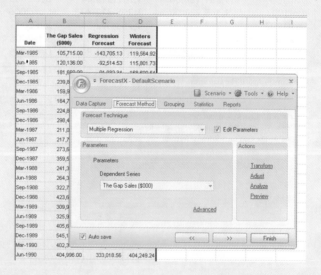

In this dialog box select the statistics that you desire. Remember that there are more choices if you click the **More Statistics** button at the bottom.

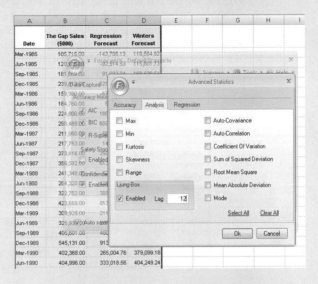

After selecting the statistics you want to see, click the **Reports** tab. In the **Reports** dialog box select those you want. Typical selections might be those shown here. In the **Audit Trail** tab (the active tab shown here) click **Fitted Values Table**.

Then click the **Finish!** button.

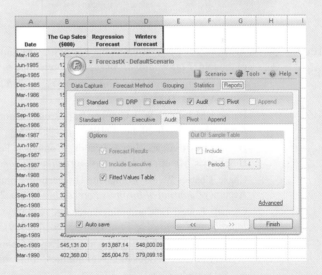

ForecastX™ will automatically apply a time-series method to forecast the independent variables. Check the results to see that the constant term is *not* significantly different than zero. This provides a way to check for systematic bias.

If the constant term *is* essentially zero (the *p*-value is greater than 0.05), you want to redo the regression, forcing the line through the origin. To do this, estimate the regression model again, but this time in the **Method Selection** screen click the **Advanced** button at the bottom. In the dialog box that appears, check the box **Constant is Zero**. The regression coefficients in the resulting model are the optimum weights for the combined forecast, and the fitted values provided by ForecastX™ are the combined forecast values.

Date	The Gap Sales ($000)	Regression Forecast	Winters Forecast
Mar-1985	105,715.00	-143,705.13	119,564.92
Jun-1985	120,136.00	-92,514.53	115,801.73
Sep-1985	181,669.00	91,032.34	168,600.54
Dec-1985	239,813.00	529,162.72	249,938.67
Mar-1986	159,980.00	-67,531.50	160,721.40
Jun-1986	164,760.00	8,273.62	173,896.45
Sep-1986	224,800.00	188,760.78	
Dec-1986	298,469.00	609,420.27	
Mar-1987	211,060.00		
Jun-1987	217,753.00	14,294.07	
Sep-1987	273,616.00	258,436.29	
Dec-1987	359,592.00		
Mar-1988	241,348.00	52,052.16	
Jun-1988	264,328.00	135,574.97	
Sep-1988	322,752.00	387,009.00	
Dec-1988	423,669.00	813,929.89	
Mar-1989	309,925.00	211,101.29	
Jun-1989	325,939.00	207,058.84	
Sep-1989	405,601.00	450,517.56	
Dec-1989	545,131.00	984,097.14	
Mar-1990	402,368.00	265,004.76	379,093.18
Jun-1990	404,996.00	333,018.56	404,249.24

Regression Advanced

☑ Constant is Zero
☐ Use Existing Values
☐ Remove Empty Values

Ok   Cancel

Suggested Readings

Armstrong, J. Scott. "Combining Forecasts: The End of the Beginning or the Beginning of the End?" *International Journal of Forecasting* 5, no. 4 (1989), pp. 585–88.

———. *Long-Range Forecasting from Crystal Ball to Computer.* 2nd ed. New York: John Wiley & Sons, 1985.

Bates, J. M.; and C. W. J. Granger. "The Combination of Forecasts." *Operational Research Quarterly* 20, no. 4 (1969), pp. 451–68.

Bessler, David A.; and Jon A. Brandt. "Composite Forecasting: An Application with U.S. Hog Prices." *American Journal of Agricultural Economics* 63 (1981), pp. 135–40.

Chase, Charles W., Jr. "Composite Forecasting: Combining Forecasts for Improved Accuracy." *Journal of Business Forecasting* 19, no. 2 (Summer 2000), pp. 2, 20–22.

Clemen, Robert T. "Combining Forecasts: A Review and Annotated Bibliography." *International Journal of Forecasting* 5, no. 4 (1989), pp. 559–83.

Collopy, Fred; and J. Scott Armstrong. "Expert Opinions about Extrapolation and the Mystery of the Overlooked Discontinuities." *International Journal of Forecasting* 8, no. 4 (December 1992), pp. 575–82.

Diebold, Francis X. "Forecast Combination and Encompassing: Reconciling Two Divergent Literatures." *International Journal of Forecasting* 5, no. 4 (1989), pp. 589–92.

Flores, Benito E.; David L. Olson; and Christopher Wolfe. "Judgmental Adjustment of Forecasts: A Comparison of Methods." *International Journal of Forecasting* 7, no. 4 (1992), pp. 421–33.

Fullerton, Thomas M., Jr. "A Composite Approach to Forecasting State Government Revenues: Case Study of the Idaho Sales Tax." *International Journal of Forecasting* 5, no. 3 (1989), pp. 373–80.

Goodwin, Paul. "Connect or Combine? Mechanically Integrating Judgmental Forecasts with Statistical Methods." *International Journal of Forecasting* 16, no. 2 (April–June 2000), pp. 261–275.

Hayes, Samuel P., Jr. "The Predictive Ability of Voters." *Journal of Social Psychology* 7 (1936), pp. 183–91.

Hendry, David F.; and Michael P. Clements. "Pooling of Forecasts." *Econometrics Journal* 5 (2002), pp. 1–26.

Hogarth, Robin M. "On Combining Diagnostic 'Forecasts': Thoughts and Some Evidence." *International Journal of Forecasting* 5, no. 4 (1989), pp. 593–97.

Li, Fuchun; and Greg Tkacz. "Combining Forecasts with Nonparametric Kernel Regressions." *Studies in Nonlinear Dynamics & Econometrics* 8, no. 4 (2004), article 2, http://www.bepress.com/snde/vol8/iss4/art2.

Lobo, Gerald I. "Analysis and Comparison of Financial Analysts' Time Series, and Combined Forecasts of Annual Earnings." *Journal of Business Research* 24 (1992), pp. 269–80.

Mahmoud, Essam. "Combining Forecasts: Some Managerial Issues." *International Journal of Forecasting* 5, no. 4 (1989), pp. 599–600.

Makridakis, Spyros. "Why Combining Works." *International Journal of Forecasting* 5 (1989), pp. 601–603.

Nelson, Charles R. "A Benchmark for the Accuracy of Econometric Forecasts of GNP." *Business Economics* 19, no. 3 (April 1984), pp. 52–58.

Swanson, N. R.; and T. Zeng. "Choosing among Competing Econometric Forecasts: Regression-Based Forecast Combining Model Selection." *Journal of Forecasting* 20 (2001), pp. 425–40.

Wilson, J. Holton; and Deborah Allison-Koerber. "Combining Subjective and Objective Forecasts Improve Results." *Journal of Business Forecasting* 11, no. 3 (1992), pp. 3–8.

Winkler, Robert L.; and Robert T. Clemen. "Multiple Experts vs. Multiple Methods: Combining Correlation Assessments." *Decision Analysis* 1, no. 3 (September 2004), pp. 167–76.

Exercises

1. Explain why a combined model might be better than any of the original contributing models. Could there be cases in which a combined model would show no gain in forecast accuracy over the original models? Give an example where this situation might be likely to occur.

2. Outline the different methods for combining forecast models explained in the chapter. Can more than two forecasting models be combined into a single model? Does each of the original forecasts have to be the result of the application of a quantitative technique?

3. *Air Carrier Traffic Statistics Monthly* is a handbook of airline data published by the U.S. Department of Transportation. In this book you will find revenue passenger-miles

(RPM) traveled on major airlines on international flights. Airlines regularly try to predict accurately the RPM for future periods; this gives the airline a picture of what equipment needs might be and is helpful in keeping costs at a minimum.

The revenue passenger-miles for international flights on major international airlines is shown in the accompanying table for the period Jan-1979 to Feb-1984. Also shown is personal income during the same period, in billions of dollars.

Date	RPM	Personal Income	Date	RPM	Personal Income
Jan-1979	4,114,904	1,834.3	Aug-1981	5,465,791	2,443.4
Feb-1979	3,283,488	1,851.4	Sep-1981	4,320,529	2,462.6
Mar-1979	4,038,611	1,872.1	Oct-1981	4,036,149	2,473.5
Apr-1979	4,312,697	1,880.7	Nov-1981	3,272,074	2,487.6
May-1979	4,638,300	1,891.6	Dec-1981	3,514,227	2,492.1
Jun-1979	6,661,979	1,905.1	Jan-1982	3,558,273	2,499.1
Jul-1979	6,221,612	1,933.2	Feb-1982	2,834,658	2,513.8
Aug-1979	6,489,078	1,946.5	Mar-1982	3,318,250	2,518.6
Sep-1979	5,258,750	1,960.1	Apr-1982	3,660,038	2,535.5
Oct-1979	4,720,077	1,979.2	May-1982	4,014,541	2,556.2
Nov-1979	4,037,529	2,000.0	Jun-1982	4,487,598	2,566.3
Dec-1979	4,240,862	2,022.5	Jul-1982	5,088,561	2,588.3
Jan-1980	4,222,446	2,077.2	Aug-1982	5,292,201	2,592.0
Feb-1980	3,540,027	2,086.4	Sep-1982	4,320,181	2,597.2
Mar-1980	4,148,262	2,101.0	Oct-1982	4,069,619	2,611.5
Apr-1980	4,106,723	2,102.1	Nov-1982	3,125,650	2,621.3
May-1980	4,602,599	2,114.1	Dec-1982	3,381,049	2,636.8
Jun-1980	5,169,789	2,127.1	Jan-1983	3,513,758	2,652.6
Jul-1980	5,911,035	2,161.2	Feb-1983	2,876,672	2,650.5
Aug-1980	6,236,392	2,179.4	Mar-1983	3,536,871	2,670.1
Sep-1980	4,700,133	2,205.7	Apr-1983	3,744,696	2,689.0
Oct-1980	4,274,816	2,235.3	May-1983	4,404,939	2,719.3
Nov-1980	3,611,307	2,260.4	Jun-1983	5,201,363	2,732.6
Dec-1980	3,794,631	2,281.5	Jul-1983	5,915,462	2,747.6
Jan-1981	3,513,072	2,300.7	Aug-1983	6,022,431	2,756.4
Feb-1981	2,856,083	2,318.2	Sep-1983	5,000,685	2,781.6
Mar-1981	3,281,964	2,340.4	Oct-1983	4,659,152	2,812.8
Apr-1981	3,694,417	2,353.8	Nov-1983	3,592,160	2,833.1
May-1981	4,240,501	2,367.4	Dec-1983	3,818,737	2,857.2
Jun-1981	4,524,445	2,384.3	Jan-1984	3,828,367	2,897.4
Jul-1981	5,156,871	2,419.2	Feb-1984	3,221,633	2,923.5

a. Build a multiple-regression model for the data to predict RPM for the next month. Check the data for any trend, and be careful to account for any seasonality. You should easily be able to obtain a forecast model with an R-squared of about 0.70 that exhibits little serial correlation.

b. Use the same data to compute a time-series decomposition model, and again forecast for one month in the future.

c. Judging from the root-mean-squared error, which of the models in parts (a) and (b) proved to be the best forecasting model? Now combine the two models, using a weighting scheme like that shown in Table 8.1. Choose various weights until you believe you have come close to the optimum weighting scheme. Does this combined model perform better (according to RMSE) than either of the two original models? Why do you believe the combined model behaves in this way?

d. Try one other forecasting method of your choice on these data, and combine the results with the multiple-regression model. Do you obtain a better forecast (according to RMSE) than with either of your two original models?

4. Estimating the volume of loans that will be made at a credit union is crucial to effective cash management in those institutions. In the table that follows are quarterly data for a real credit union located in a midwestern city. Credit unions are financial institutions similar to banks, but credit unions are not-for-profit firms whose members are the actual owners (remember their slogan, "It's where you belong"). The members may be both depositors in and borrowers from the credit union.

Quarter	Loan Volume	Assets	Members	Prime Rate
Mar-98	2,583,780	4,036,810	3,522	6.25
Jun-98	2,801,100	4,164,720	3,589	6.75
Sep-98	2,998,240	4,362,680	3,632	7.13
Dec-98	3,032,720	4,482,990	3,676	7.75
Mar-99	3,094,580	4,611,300	3,668	8
Jun-99	3,372,680	4,696,720	3,689	8.63
Sep-99	3,499,350	4,844,960	3,705	9.41
Dec-99	3,553,710	4,893,450	3,722	11.55
Mar-00	3,651,870	5,089,840	3,732	11.75
Jun-00	3,832,440	5,185,360	3,770	11.65
Sep-00	4,013,310	5,381,140	3,845	12.9
Dec-00	3,950,100	5,413,720	3,881	15.3
Mar-01	3,925,100	5,574,160	3,923	18.31
Jun-01	3,717,480	5,838,990	3,941	12.63
Sep-01	3,712,300	6,150,350	3,955	12.23
Dec-01	3,677,940	6,133,030	3,943	20.35
Mar-02	3,724,770	6,119,030	3,960	18.05
Jun-02	3,787,760	6,221,090	3,971	20.03
Sep-02	3,981,620	6,229,000	3,993	20.08
Dec-02	3,848,660	6,412,230	4,011	15.75
Mar-03	3,619,830	6,795,830	4,040	16.5
Jun-03	3,623,590	7,538,210	4,103	16.5
Sep-03	3,632,120	8,496,080	4,133	13.5
Dec-03	3,482,000	9,979,390	4,173	11.5
Mar-04	3,378,500	11,475,300	4,218	10.5
Jun-04	3,433,470	12,116,900	4,266	10.5
Sep-04	3,615,430	12,686,500	4,305	11
Dec-04	3,865,780	13,457,600	4,657	11
Mar-05	3,955,270	14,118,300	4,741	11.21
Jun-05	4,394,140	14,448,600	4,826	12.6
Sep-05	4,803,630	14,687,200	4,943	12.97
Dec-05	4,952,740	14,885,800	4,945	11.06
Mar-06	5,249,760	16,106,300	5,007	10.5
Jun-06	5,943,390	17,079,400	5,112	9.78

(continued on next page)

(continued)

Quarter	Loan Volume	Assets	Members	Prime Rate
Sep-06	6,387,000	17,846,800	5,164	9.5
Dec-06	6,435,750	19,435,600	5,210	9.5
Mar-07	6,482,780	19,714,100	5,255	9.1
Jun-07	6,683,800	21,185,800	5,289	8.5
Sep-07	7,094,210	22,716,700	5,391	7.5
Dec-07	7,329,770	23,790,500	5,461	7.5

a. Estimate a multiple-regression model to estimate loan demand and calculate its root-mean-squared error.

b. Estimate a time-series decomposition model to estimate loan demand with the same data and calculate its root-mean-squared error.

c. Combine the models in parts (a) and (b) and determine whether the combined model performs better than either or both of the original models. Try to explain why you obtained the results you did.

5. HeathCo Industries, a producer of a line of skiwear, has been the subject of exercises in several earlier chapters of the text. The data for its sales and two potential causal variables, income (INCOME) and the northern-region unemployment rate (NRUR), are repeated in the following table:

Date	Sales	Income	NRUR
Jan-98	72,962	218	8.4
Apr-98	81,921	237	8.2
Jul-98	97,729	263	8.4
Oct-98	142,161	293	8.4
Jan-99	145,592	318	8.1
Apr-99	117,129	359	7.7
Jul-99	114,159	404	7.5
Oct-99	151,402	436	7.2
Jan-00	153,907	475	6.9
Apr-00	100,144	534	6.5
Jul-00	123,242	574	6.5
Oct-00	128,497	622	6.4
Jan-01	176,076	667	6.3
Apr-01	180,440	702	6.2
Jul-01	162,665	753	6.3
Oct-01	220,818	796	6.5
Jan-02	202,415	858	6.8
Apr-02	211,780	870	7.9
Jul-02	163,710	934	8.3
Oct-02	200,135	1,010	8
Jan-03	174,200	1,066	8
Apr-03	182,556	1,096	8
Jul-03	198,990	1,162	8
Oct-03	243,700	1,178	8.9
Jan-04	253,142	1,207	9.6
Apr-04	218,755	1,242	10.2
Jul-04	225,422	1,279	10.7

Date	Sales	Income	NRUR
Oct-04	253,653	1,318	11.5
Jan-05	257,156	1,346	11.2
Apr-05	202,568	1,395	11
Jul-05	224,482	1,443	10.1
Oct-05	229,879	1,528	9.2
Jan-06	289,321	1,613	8.5
Apr-06	266,095	1,646	8
Jul-06	262,938	1,694	8
Oct-06	322,052	1,730	7.9
Jan-07	313,769	1,755	7.9
Apr-07	315,011	1,842	7.9
Jul-07	264,939	1,832	7.8
Oct-07	301,479	1,882	7.6
Jan-08	**334,271**	**1,928**	**7.6**
Apr-08	**328,982**	**1,972**	**7.7**	← Holdout
Jul-08	**317,921**	**2,017**	**7.5**
Oct-08	**350,118**	**2,062**	**7.4**

a. Develop a multiple-regression model of SALES as a function of both INCOME and NRUR:

$$SALES = a + b_1(INCOME) + b_2(NRUR)$$

Use this model to forecast sales for 2008Q1–2008Q4 (call your regression forecast series SFR), given that INCOME and NRUR for 2004 have been forecast to be:

Quarter	INCOME	NRUR
2008Q1	1,928	7.6
2008Q2	1,972	7.7
2008Q3	2,017	7.5
2008Q4	2,062	7.4

b. Calculate the RMSE for your regression model for both the historical period (1998Q1–2007Q4) and the forecast horizon (2008Q1–2008Q4).

Period	RMSE
Historical	____
Forecast	____

c. Now prepare a forecast through the historical period and the forecast horizon (2008Q1–2008Q4) using Winters' exponential smoothing. Call this forecast series SFW, and fill in the RMSEs for SFW:

Period	RMSE
Historical	____
Forecast	____

    d. Solely on the basis of the historical data, which model appears to be the best? Why?

    e. Now prepare a combined forecast (SCF) using the regression technique described in this chapter. In the standard regression:

$$SALES = a + b_1(SFR) + b_2(SFW)$$

Is the intercept essentially zero? Why? If it is, do the following regression as a basis for developing SCF:

$$SALES = b_1(SFR) + b_2(SFW)$$

Given the historical RMSEs found in parts (*b*) and (*c*), do the values for b_1 and b_2 seem plausible? Explain.

    f. Calculate the RMSEs for SCF:

Period	RMSE
Historical	_____
Forecast	_____

Did combining models reduce the RMSE in the historical period? What about the actual forecast?

6. Your company produces a favorite summertime food product, and you have been placed in charge of forecasting shipments of this product. The historical data below represent your company's past experience with the product.

    a. Since the data appear to have both seasonality and trend, you should estimate a Winters' model and calculate its root-mean-squared error.

    b. You also have access to a survey of the potential purchasers of your product. This information has been collected for some time, and it has proved to be quite accurate for predicting shipments in the past. Calculate the root-mean-squared error of the purchasers' survey data.

    c. After checking for bias, combine the forecasts in parts (*a*) and (*b*) and determine if a combined model may forecast better than either single model.

Date	Shipments ($000)	Purchasers' Survey ($000)	Date	Shipments ($000)	Purchasers' Survey ($000)
Apr-2002	13,838.00	13,920.32	Jun-2003	21,056.00	24,644.20
May-2002	15,137.00	15,052.82	Jul-2003	13,509.00	14,224.17
Jun-2002	23,713.00	26,207.69	Aug-2003	9,729.00	9,194.77
Jul-2002	17,141.00	17,237.59	Sep-2003	13,454.00	12,141.25
Aug-2002	7,107.00	7,687.23	Oct-2003	13,426.00	11,971.93
Sep-2002	9,225.00	9,788.06	Nov-2003	17,792.00	17,654.14
Oct-2002	10,950.00	7,889.46	Dec-2003	19,026.00	15,580.19
Nov-2002	14,752.00	14,679.10	Jan-2004	9,432.00	9,961.98
Dec-2002	18,871.00	17,644.48	Feb-2004	6,356.00	7,368.55
Jan-2003	11,329.00	10,436.45	Mar-2004	12,893.00	11,286.25
Feb-2003	6,555.00	6,304.89	Apr-2004	19,379.00	18,915.33
Mar-2003	9,335.00	9,354.44	May-2004	14,542.00	14,056.06
Apr-2003	10,845.00	11,759.15	Jun-2004	18,043.00	20,699.38
May-2003	15,185.00	14,971.57	Jul-2004	10,803.00	12,892.97

Data Mining

INTRODUCTION[1]

Data mining is quite different from the statistical techniques we have used previously for forecasting. In most forecasting situations you have encountered, for example, in the model imposed on the data to make forecasts has been chosen by the forecaster. For example, in the case of new product forecasting we have assumed that new products "roll out" with a life cycle that looks like an s-curve. With this in mind we chose to use one of three models that create s-curves: the logistic model, the Gompertz model, and the Bass model. When we chose any of these three models we knew we were imposing on our solution the form of an s-curve, and we felt that was appropriate because we had observed that all previous new products followed this pattern. In a sense, we imposed the pattern on the data.

With data mining, the tables are turned. We don't know what pattern or family of patterns may fit a particular set of data or sometimes what it is we are trying to predict or explain. This should seem strange to a forecaster; it's not the method of attacking the data we have been pursuing throughout the text. To begin data mining we need a new mindset. We need to be open to finding relationships and patterns we never imagined existed in the data we are about to examine. To use data mining is to let the data tell us the story (rather than to impose a model on the data that we feel will replicate the actual patterns in the data). Peter Bruce points out, however, that most good data mining tasks have goals and circumscribed search parameters that help reduce the possibility of finding interesting patterns that are just artifacts of chance.

Data mining traditionally uses very large data sets, oftentimes far larger than the data sets we are used to using in business forecasting situations. The tools

[1] The authors would like to thank Professor Eamonn Keogh of the Department of Computer Science & Engineering at the University of California, Riverside, for many of the examples that appear in this chapter. We also want to thank Professors Galit Shmueli of the University of Maryland, Nitin Patel of MIT, and Peter Bruce of Statistics.com for the use of materials they created for their text *Data Mining for Business Intelligence* (John Wiley & Sons, 2007), ISBN 0-470-08485-5. The authors recommend visiting Professor Keogh's website for sample data sets and explanations of data mining techniques. We also recommend the *Data Mining for Business Intelligence* text for an in-depth discussion of all data mining techniques.

we use in data mining are also different from business forecasting tools; some of the statistical tools will be familiar but they are used in different ways than we have used them in previous chapters. The premise of data mining is that there is a great deal of information locked up in any database—it's up to us to use appropriate tools to unlock the secrets hidden within it. Business forecasting is explicit in the sense that we use specific models to estimate and forecast known patterns (e.g., seasonality, trend, cyclicality, etc.). Data mining, on the other hand, involves the extraction of implicit (perhaps unknown) intelligence or useful information from data. We need to be able to sift through large quantities of data to find patterns and regularities that we did not know existed beforehand. Some of what we find will be quite useless and uninteresting, perhaps only coincidences. But, from time to time, we will be able to find true gems in the mounds of data.

The objective of this chapter is to introduce a variety of data mining methods. Some of these methods are simple and meant only to introduce you to the basic concept of how data mining works. Others, however, are full-blown statistical methods commonly employed by data miners to exploit large databases. After completing this chapter you will understand what data mining techniques exist and appreciate their strengths; you will also understand how they are applied in practice. If you wish to experiment with your own data (or that provided on the CD that accompanies this text), we recommend the XLMiner$^©$ software.[2]

DATA MINING

A decade ago one of the most pressing problems for a forecaster was the lack of data collected intelligently by businesses. Forecasters were limited to few pieces of data and only limited observations on the data that existed. Today, however, we are overwhelmed with data. It is collected at grocery store checkout counters, while inventory moves through a warehouse, when users click a button on the World Wide Web, and every time a credit card is swiped. The rate of data collection is not abating; it seems to be increasing with no clear end in sight. The presence of large cheap storage devices means that it is easy to keep every piece of data produced. The pressing problem now is not the generation of the data, but the attempt to understand it.

The job of a data miner is to make sense of the available mounds of data by examining the data for patterns. The single most important reason for the recent interest in data mining is due to the large amounts of data now available for analysis.

---

[2] XLMiner$^©$ is an Excel add-in that works in much the same manner as ForecastX™. Both student and full versions of the software are available from Resample.com (http://www.resample.com/xlminer/). The authors also recommend *Data Mining for Business Intelligence* by Galit Shmueli, Nitin Patel, and Peter Bruce (John Wiley & Sons, 2007).

There is a need for business professionals to transform such data into useful information by "mining" it for the existence of patterns. You should not be surprised by the emphasis on patterns; this entire text has been about patterns of one sort or another. Indeed, men have looked for patterns in almost every endeavor undertaken by mankind. Early men looked for patterns in the night sky, for patterns in the movement of the stars and planets, and for patterns to help predict the best times of the year to plant crops. Modern man still hunts for patterns in early election returns, in global temperature changes, and in sales data for new products. Over the last 25 years there has been a gradual evolution from data processing to what today we call data mining. In the 1960s businesses routinely collected data and processed it using database management techniques that allowed indexing, organization, and some query activity. *Online transaction processing (OLTP)* became routine and the rapid retrieval of stored data was made easier by more efficient storage devices and faster and more capable computing.

Database management advanced rapidly to include very sophisticated query systems. It became common not only in business situations but also in scientific inquiry. Databases began to grow at previously unheard-of rates and for even routine activities. It has been estimated recently that the amount of data in all the world's databases doubles in less than two years. That flood of data would seem to call for analysis in order to make sense of the patterns locked within. Firms now routinely have what are called data warehouses and data marts. *Data warehouse* is the term used to describe a firm's main repository of historical data; it is the *memory* of the firm, it's collective information on every relevant aspect of what has happened in the past. A *data mart*, on the other hand, is a special version of a data warehouse. Data marts are a subset of data warehouses and routinely hold information that is specialized and has been grouped or chosen specifically to help businesses make better decisions on future actions. The first organized use of such large databases has come to be called *online analytical processing (OLAP)*. OLAP is a set of analysis techniques that provides aggregation, consolidation, reporting, and summarization of data. It could be thought of as the direct precursor to what we now refer to as data mining. Much of the data that is collected by any organization becomes simply a historical artifact that is rarely referenced and even more rarely analyzed for knowledge. OLAP procedures began to change all that as data was summarized and viewed from different angles.

Data mining, on the other hand, concerns analyzing databases, data warehouses, and data marts that already exist, for the purpose of solving some problem or answering some pressing question. *Data mining* is the *extraction of useful information from large databases*. It is about the extraction of knowledge or information from large amounts of data.[3] Data mining has come to be referenced

---

[3] D. Hand, H. Mannila, P. Smyth, *Principles of Data Mining* (Cambridge, MA: MIT Press, 2001), ISBN 0-262-08290-X.

by a few similar terms; in most cases they are all much the same set of techniques referred to as data mining in this text:

- Exploratory data analysis
- Business intelligence
- Data driven discovery
- Deductive learning
- Discovery science
- Knowledge discovery in databases (KDD)

Data mining is quite separate from database management. Eamonn Keogh points out that in database management queries are well defined; we even have a language to write these queries (structured query language or SQL, pronounced as "sequel"). A query in database management might take the form of "Find all the customers in South Bend," or "Find all the customers that have missed a recent payment." Data mining uses different queries; they tend to be less structured and are sometimes quite vague. For example: "Find all the customers that are likely to miss a future payment," or "Group all the customers with similar buying habits." In one sense, data mining is like business forecasting in that we are looking forward in an attempt to obtain better information about future likely events.

Companies may be data rich but are often information poor; data mining is a set of tools and techniques that can aid firms in making sense of the mountains of data they already have available. These databases may be about customer profiles and the choices those customers have made in the past. There are likely patterns of behavior exhibited, but the sheer amount of the data will mask the underlying patterns. Some patterns may be interesting but quite useless to a firm in making future decisions, but some patterns may be predictive in ways that could be very useful. For example, if you *know* which of your customers are likely to switch suppliers in the near future, you may be able to prevent them from jumping ship and going with a competitor. It's always less costly to keep existing customers than to enlist new ones. Likewise, if you were to *know* which of your customers were likely to default on their loans you might be able to take preventive measures to forestall the defaults, or you might be less likely to loan to such individuals. Finally, if you *know* the characteristics of potential customers that are likely to purchase your product, you might be able to direct your advertising and promotional efforts better than if you were to blanket the market with advertising and promotions. A well-targeted approach is usually better than a "shotgun" approach. The key lies in knowing where to aim.

What types of patterns would we find useful to uncover with data mining? The answer is quite different from the patterns we expected to find in data with business forecasting methods such as Winters' exponential smoothing. When we applied the Winters' model to time-series data we were looking for specific patterns that we knew had existed in many previously examined data sets (e.g., trend and seasonality). The patterns we might find with data mining techniques, however, are usually unknown to us at the beginning of the process. We may find descriptive patterns in our data; these tell us only the general properties of the database. We may also find predictive patterns in the data; these allow us to make forecasts or predictions in much the same manner as we have been seeing in the preceding chapters.

THE TOOLS OF DATA MINING

Shmueli, Patel, and Bruce use a taxonomy of data mining tools that is useful for seeing the big picture. There are basically four categories of data mining tools or techniques:

1. Prediction
2. Classification
3. Clustering
4. Association

Prediction tools are most like the methods we have covered in previous chapters; they attempt to predict the value of a numeric variable (almost always a continuous rather than a categorical variable). The term *classification* is used when we are predicting the particular category of an observation when the variable is a categorical variable. We might, for example, be attempting to predict the amount of a consumer expenditure (a continuous variable) in a particular circumstance or the amount that an individual might contribute yearly to a particular cause (also a continuous variable). The variable we are attempting to predict in each of these instances is a continuous variable, but the variable to be predicted might also be a categorical variable. For example, we might wish to predict whether an individual will contribute to a particular cause or whether someone will make a certain purchase this year. Prediction then involves both categories of variables: continuous and categorical.

Classification tools are the most commonly used methods in data mining. They attempt to distinguish different classes of objects or actions. For instance, a particular credit card transaction may be either normal or fraudulent. Its correct classification in a timely manner could save a business a considerable amount of money. In another instance you may wish to know which characteristic of your advertising on a particular product is most important to consumers. Is it price? Or, could it be the description of the quality and reliability of the item? Perhaps it is the compatibility of the item with others the potential purchaser already owns. Classification tools may tell you the answer for each of many products you sell, thus allowing you to make the best use of your advertising expenditures by providing consumers with the information they find most relevant in making purchasing decisions.

Clustering analysis tools analyze objects viewed as a class. The classes of the objects are not input by the user; it is the function of the clustering technique to define and attach the class labels. This is a powerful set of tools used to group items that naturally fall together. Whether the clusters unearthed by the techniques are useful to the business manager is subjective. Some clusters may be interesting but not useful in a business setting, while others can be quite informative and able to be exploited to advantage.

Association rules discovery is sometimes called *affinity analysis*. If you have been handed coupons at a grocery store checkout counter your purchasing patterns have probably been subjected to association rules discovery. Netflix will recommend movies you might like based upon movies you have watched and rated in the past—this is an example of association rules discovery.

In this chapter we will examine four techniques from the most used data mining category: classification. Specifically we will examine:

1. k-Nearest Neighbor
2. Naive Bayes
3. Classification/regression trees
4. Logistic regression (logit analysis)

Business Forecasting and Data Mining

In business forecasting we have been seeking verification of previously held hypotheses. That is, we *knew* which patterns existed in the time-series data we tried to forecast and we applied appropriate statistical models to accurately estimate those patterns. When an electric power company looks at electric load demand, for instance, it expects that past patterns, such as trend, seasonality, and cyclicality, will replicate themselves in the future. Thus, the firm might reasonably use time-series decomposition as a model to forecast future electric usage. Data mining, on the other hand, seeks the discovery of new knowledge from the data. It does not seek to merely verify the previously set hypotheses regarding the types of patterns in the data but attempts to discover new facts or rules from the data itself.

Mori and Kosemura[4] have outlined two ways electric demand is forecasted in Japan that exemplify the differences between data mining and standard business forecasting. The first method for forecasting load involves standard business forecasting. ARIMA models are sometimes used because of their ability to match those patterns commonly found in time-series data. However, causal time-series models such as multiple regression are more frequently used because of their ability to take into account local weather conditions as well as past patterns of usage exhibited by individuals and businesses. Multiple regression is a popular and useful technique much used in actual practice in the electric power industry. Data mining tools are beginning to be used for load forecasting, however, because they are able to discover useful knowledge and rules that are hidden among large bodies of electric load data. The particular data mining model that Mori and Kosemura find useful for electric load forecasting is the regression tree; because the data features are represented in regression tree models as visualizations, if-then rules can be created and causal relationships can be acquired intuitively. This intuitive acquisition of rules and associations is a hallmark of data mining and sets it apart methodologically from the standard set of business forecasting tools.

The terminology we use in data mining will be a bit different from that used in business forecasting models; while the terms are different, their meanings are quite similar.

Data Mining	Statistical Terminology
Output variable = Target variable	Dependent variable
Algorithm	Forecasting model
Attribute = Feature	Explanatory variable
Record	Observation
Score	Forecast

Source: Eamonn Keogh.

A DATA MINING EXAMPLE: k-NEAREST-NEIGHBOR

Consider the following data mining example from Eamonn Keogh; while it is not business related, it is easy to see the technique unfold visually. You are a researcher attempting to classify insects you have found into one of two groups (i.e., you are attempting to forecast the correct category for new insects found). The insects you find may be either katydids or grasshoppers. These insects look quite a bit alike, but there are distinct differences. They are much like ducks and geese: many similarities, but some important differences as well.

---

[4] "A Data Mining Method for Short-Term Load Forecasting in Power Systems," *Electrical Engineering in Japan*, Vol. 139, No. 2, 2002, pp. 12–22.

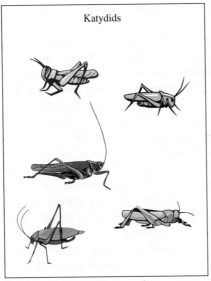

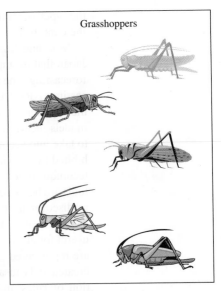

Source: Eamonn Keogh.

You have five examples of insects that you know are katydids and five that you know are grasshoppers. The unknown is thought to be either a katydid or a grasshopper. Could we use this data set to come up with a set of rules that would allow us to classify any unknown insect as either a katydid or a grasshopper? By seeing how this might be done by hand through trial and error we can begin to understand one general process that data mining techniques use.

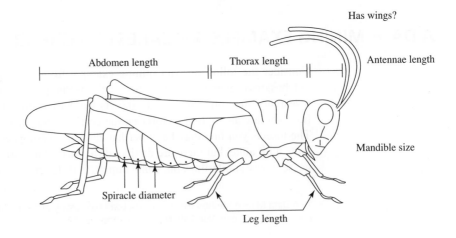

There are many characteristics we could use to aid in our classification. Some of them would include abdomen length, thorax length, leg length, and so on. The 10 insects we have in our database have the following values for the attributes titled abdomen length and antenna length.

Insect ID	Abdomen Length (mm)	Antenna Length (mm)	Insect Class
1	2.7	5.5	Grasshopper
2	8.0	9.1	Katydid
3	0.9	4.7	Grasshopper
4	1.1	3.1	Grasshopper
5	5.4	8.5	Katydid
6	2.9	1.9	Grasshopper
7	6.1	6.6	Katydid
8	0.5	1.0	Grasshopper
9	8.3	6.6	Katydid
10	8.1	4.7	Katydid
Unknown	5.1	7.0	?

The unknown insect is represented by the last row in the table. We have only included two attributes in our table for demonstration purposes. As we have seen in discussing business forecasting techniques, it is usually a good idea to graph the data in order to look for obvious relationships. We can do the same here by placing abdomen length on one axis and antenna length on the other, thus creating a scatterplot of the data.

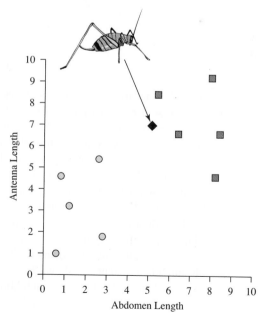

The resulting plot is quite informative; the katydids (shown as squares) cluster in the upper right-hand corner of our plot while the grasshoppers (shown as circles) cluster in the lower left-hand corner of the plot. While neither characteristic by itself would do well in helping our classification, the combination of the two attributes might accurately define unknown insects. This unknown insect appears to fall closest to the katydids. But can we come up with a mechanistic (i.e., rules-based) way of choosing the unknown as a katydid rather than as a grasshopper? One method would be to look at the geographical neighbors of the unknown insect. Which neighbors are the closest to the unknown? We could describe this process by drawing distance lines between the unknown insect and its neighbors.

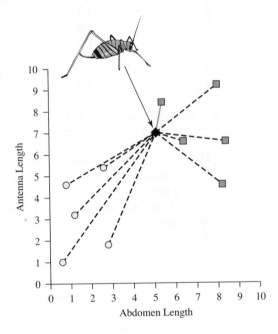

If the distance to the unknown is closest to the katydids (as measured by summing the distance to katydid neighbors and comparing this to the summation of the distances to grasshopper neighbors), then the unknown is likely a katydid. In essence the k-Nearest-Neighbor model of data mining works in just this manner. In actual practice it is not necessary to calculate the distance to every neighbor; only a small subset of the neighbors are used. The "k" in k-Nearest-Neighbor refers to the number of nearest neighbors used in determining a category correctly.

When using k-Nearest-Neighbor we use a subset of the total data we have available (called a *training data* set) to attempt to identify observations in the training data set that are similar to the unknown. Scoring (or forecasting) new unknowns is assigning the unknowns to the same class as their nearest neighbors. While Euclidian distance is shown in the diagrams here, there are other metrics possible that are used to define neighbors and some are used in the various commercial data mining packages. What we are interested in is classifying future unknown insects, not the past performance on old data. We already know the classifications of the insects in the training data set; that's why we call it a training data set. It trains the model to correctly classify the unknowns by selecting closeness to the k-nearest-neighbors. So, the error rate on old data will not be very useful in determining if we have a good classification model. An error rate on a training set is not the best indicator of future performance. To predict how well this model might do in the real world at classifying *of* unknowns we need to use it to classify some data that the model has not previously had access to; we need to use data that was not part of the training data set. This separate data set is called the *validation data*. In one sense, this separation of data into a training data set and a validation data set is much like the difference between "in-sample" test statistics and "out-of-sample" test statistics. The real test of a business forecast was the "out-of-sample" test; the real test of a data mining model will be the test statistics on the validation data, not the statistics calculated from the training data.

In order to produce reliable measures of the effectiveness of a data mining tool researchers *partition* a data set before building a data mining model. It is standard practice to divide the data set into partitions using some random procedure. We could, for instance, assign each instance in our data set a number and then randomly partition the data set into two parts called the training data and the validation data (sometimes researchers also use a third partition called the *test set*). If there is a great deal of data (unlike the simple example of the katydids and grasshoppers), there is little trouble in using 60 percent of the data as a training set and the remaining 40 percent as a validation data set. This will ensure that no effectiveness statistics are drawn from the data used to create the model. Thus an early step in any real data mining procedure is to partition the data. It is common practice to fold the validation data back into the training data and re-estimate the model if the model shows up well in the validation data.

A BUSINESS DATA MINING EXAMPLE: k-NEAREST-NEIGHBOR

What would such a model look like in a business situation? We now turn to examining a data set used by Shmueli, Patel, and Bruce.[5] This data set represents information on the customers a bank has in its data warehouse. These individuals

[5] Galit Shmueli, Nitin Patel, and Peter Bruce, *Data Mining for Business Intelligence,* (John Wiley & Sons, 2007).

TABLE 9.1
Universal Bank (Fictitious) Data
The bank has data on a customer-by-customer basis in these categories

ID	Customer ID
Age	Customer's age in completed years
Experience	No. of years of professional experience
Income	Annual income of the customer ($000)
ZIP code	Home address, ZIP code
Family	Family size of the customer
CC Avg.	Average spending on credit cards per month ($000)
Education	Education level (1) Undergrad; (2) Graduate; (3) Advanced/Professional
Mortgage	Value of house mortgage if any ($000)
Personal loan	Did this customer accept the personal loan offered in the last campaign?
Securities account	Does the customer have a securities account with the bank?
CD account	Does the customer have a certificate of deposit (CD) account with the bank?
Online	Does the customer use Internet banking facilities?
Credit card	Does the customer use a credit card issued by Universal Bank?

have been customers of the bank at some time in the past; perhaps many are current customers in one dimension or another. The type of information the bank has on each of these customers is represented in Tables 9.1 and 9.2.

Universal Bank would like to know which customers are likely to accept a personal loan. What characteristics would forecast this? If the bank were to consider expending advertising efforts to contact customers who would be likely to consider a personal loan, which customers should the bank contact first? By answering this question correctly the bank will be able to optimize its advertising effort by directing its attention to the highest-yield customers.

This is a classification problem not unlike the situation of deciding in what class to place an unknown insect. The two classes in this example would be: (1) those with a high probability of accepting a personal loan (*acceptors*), and (2) those with a low probability of accepting a personal loan (*nonacceptors*). We will be unable to classify customers with certainty about whether they will accept a personal loan, but we may be able to classify the customers in our data into one of these two mutually exclusive categories.

The researcher would begin by first partitioning the Universal Bank data. Recall that partitioning the data set is the first step in any data mining technique. Since each row, or record, is a different customer we could assign a number to each row and use a random selection process to choose 60 percent of the data as a training set. All data mining software has such an option available. Once the data is selected into a training set it would look like Table 9.3. This partial rendition of the table is produced using the XLMiner© software.

TABLE 9.2 Universal Bank Customer Profiles

Data includes both continuous variables such as income, as well as dummy variables like a personal loan

ID	Age	Experience	Income	ZIP Code	Family	CCAvg	Education	Mortgage	Personal Loan	Securities Account	CD Account	Online	Credit card
1	25	1	49	91107	4	1.60	1	0	0	1	0	0	0
2	45	19	34	90089	3	1.50	1	0	0	1	0	0	0
3	39	15	11	94720	1	1.00	1	0	0	0	0	0	0
4	35	9	100	94112	1	2.70	2	0	0	0	0	0	0
5	35	8	45	91330	4	1.00	2	0	0	0	0	0	1
6	37	13	29	92121	4	0.40	2	155	0	0	0	1	0
7	53	27	72	91711	2	1.50	2	0	0	0	0	1	0
8	50	24	22	93943	1	0.30	3	0	0	0	0	0	1
9	35	10	81	90089	3	0.60	2	104	0	0	0	1	0
10	34	9	180	93023	1	8.90	3	0	1	0	0	0	0
11	65	39	105	94710	4	2.40	3	0	0	0	0	0	0
12	29	5	45	90277	3	0.10	2	0	0	0	0	1	0
13	48	23	114	93106	2	3.80	3	0	0	0	0	0	0
14	59	32	40	94920	4	2.50	2	0	0	0	0	1	0
15	67	41	112	91741	1	2.00	3	0	0	1	0	0	0
16	60	30	22	95054	1	1.50	3	0	0	0	0	1	1
17	38	14	130	95010	4	4.70	3	134	1	0	0	0	0
18	42	18	81	94305	4	2.40	1	0	0	0	0	0	0
19	46	21	193	91604	2	8.10	3	0	0	1	0	0	1
20	55	28	21	94720	1	0.50	2	0	0	1	0	0	1

TABLE 9.3 Training Data

This data is a subset of the complete data set

Data

Binneddata1D$20:$R$5019

Data Source

Selected Variables									Personal Loan	Securities Account
Partitioning method	Randomly chosen									
Random Seed	12345									
# training rows	3000									
# validation rows	2000									

ID	Age	Experience	Income	ZIP Code	Family	CCAvg	Education	Mortgage	Personal Loan	Securities Account

Selected Variables

Row Id.	ID	Age	Experience	Income	ZIP Code	Family	CCAvg	Education	Mortgage	Personal Loan	Securities Account	CD Account
1	1	25	1	49	91107	4	1.6	1	0	0	1	0
4	4	35	9	100	94112	1	2.7	2	0	0	0	0
5	5	35	8	45	91330	4	1	2	0	0	0	0
6	6	37	13	29	92121	4	0.4	2	155	0	0	0
9	9	35	10	81	90089	3	0.6	2	104	0	0	0
10	10	34	9	180	93023	1	8.9	3	0	1	0	0
12	12	29	5	45	90277	3	0.1	2	0	0	0	0
17	17	38	14	130	95010	4	4.7	3	134	1	0	0
18	18	42	18	81	94305	4	2.4	1	0	0	0	0
19	19	46	21	193	91504	2	8.1	3	0	1	0	0
20	20	55	28	21	94720	1	0.5	2	0	0	1	0

Note that the "Row ID" in Table 9.3 skips from row 1 to row 4 and then from row 6 to row 9. This is because the random selection process has chosen customers 1, 4, 5, 6, and 9 for the training data set (displayed in Table 9.3) but has placed customers 2, 3, 7, and 8 in the validation data set (not displayed in Table 9.3). Examining the header to Table 9.3, you will note that there were a total of 5,000 customers in the original data set that have now been divided into a training data set of 3,000 customers and a validation data set of 2,000 customers.

When we instruct the software to perform a k-Nearest-Neighbor analysis of the training data the real data mining analysis takes place. Just as in the insect classification example, the software will compare each customer's personal loan experience with the selected attributes. This example is, of course, much more multidimensional since we have many attributes for each customer (as opposed to only the two attributes we used in the insect example). The program will compute the distance associated with each attribute. For attributes that are measured as continuous variables, the software will normalize the distance and then measure it (because different continuous attributes are measured in different scales). For the dummy type or categorical attributes, most programs use a weighting mechanism that is beyond the scope of this treatment.

The accuracy measures for the estimated model will tell if we have possibly found a useful classification scheme. In this instance we want to find a way to classify customers as likely to accept a personal loan. How accurately can we do that by considering the range of customer attributes in our data? Are there some attributes that could lead us to classify some customers as much more likely to accept a loan and other customers as quite unlikely? While the accuracy measures are often produced by the software for both the training data set and the validation data set, our emphasis should clearly be on those measures pertaining to the validation data. There are two standard accuracy measures we will examine: the *classification matrix* (also called the *confusion matrix*) and the *lift chart*. The classification matrix for the Universal Bank data training data is shown in Table 9.4.

When our task is classification, accuracy is often measured in terms of error rate, the percentage of records we have classified incorrectly. The error rate is often displayed for both the training data set and the validation data set in separate tables. Table 9.4 is such a table for the validation data set in the Universal Bank

TABLE 9.4
Classification Matrix (confusion matrix) for the Universal Bank Data
The number of nearest neighbors we have chosen is 3

Validation Data Scoring—Summary Report (for k = 3)

Cut off prob. val. for success (updatable)	0.5

Classification Confusion Matrix

	Predicted Class	
Actual Class	1	0
1	118	76
0	8	1,798

case. The table is correctly called either a *confusion matrix* or a *classification matrix*. In Table 9.4 there were 118 records that were correctly classified as "class 1" (i.e., probable personal loan candidates). They were correctly classified because these records represented individuals that did indeed take out a personal loan. However, eight records were classified as class 1 incorrectly; these were individuals that the model expected to take out a personal loan when, in fact, they did not historically do so. In addition, the table shows 1,798 records predicted to be class 0 (i.e., not probable loan candidates). These records were classified correctly since historically these individuals did not take out personal loans. Finally, 76 records were incorrectly classified as class 0 when they actually were loan acceptors. The table can then be used to compute a *misclassification rate*. This calculation simply shows the percentage of the records that the model has placed in the incorrect category. In this case we have 2,000 records in the validation data set and we have correctly classified 1,916 of them (1,798 + 118). But we have also incorrectly classified 8 records as class 1 when they were actually in class 0. We have also incorrectly classified 76 records as class 0 when they were actually in class 1. Thus we have incorrectly classified 84 records (8 + 76). The misclassification rate is the total number of misclassifications divided by the total records classified (and is usually reported as a percentage). Most packages show the calculation and report it.

In Table 9.5 the misclassification rate is shown in the lower right-hand corner as 4.20 percent (calculated as 84/2,000 and expressed as a percentage). It should be noted that there are two ways in which the error occurred in our example and although some errors may be worse than others, the misclassification rate groups

TABLE 9.5
Classification Matrix (confusion matrix) and Misclassification Rate Calculation for the Universal Bank Data
The number of nearest neighbors has been chosen to be 3

Validation Data Scoring—Summary Report (for k = 3)		
Cut off prob. val. for success (updatable)	0.5	(Updating the value here will NOT update value in detailed report)

Classification Confusion Matrix

	Predicted Class	
Actual Class	1	0
1	118	76
0	8	1,798

Error Report

Class	#Cases	#Errors	%Error
1	194	76	39.14
0	1,806	8	0.44
Overall	2,000	84	4.20

these two types of errors together. While this may not be an ideal reporting mechanism, it is commonly used and displayed by data mining software. Some software also allows placing different costs on the different types of errors as a way of differentiating their impacts. While the overall error rate of 4.2 percent in the validation data is low in this example, the absolute error of classifying an actual loan acceptor incorrectly as a non-loan acceptor (76 cases) is much greater than that of incorrectly classifying an actual nonacceptor as a loan acceptor (only 8 cases).

Notice that in both Tables 9.4 and 9.5 the summary report is for the k = 3 case (see the top of either table), meaning that we have used three neighbors (not three attributes) to classify all the records. The software has taken a "vote" of the three nearest neighbors in order to classify each record as either a loan acceptor or a non-loan acceptor. The software actually varied the number of nearest neighbors used from a small number to a large number and reported only the best results. Usually the researcher may specify the range over which the program searches and the program will respond by choosing the number of neighbors that optimizes the results (in this situation XLMiner© minimized the misclassification error rate).

In Table 9.6 the XLMiner© program provides an easy way to visualize how the number of nearest neighbors has been chosen. The misclassification error rate of 4.20 percent is lowest for three neighbors (it's actually the same for four neighbors but using the principle of parsimony, three nearest neighbors are chosen as the reported optimum).

TABLE 9.6
Validation Error Log for the Universal Bank Data
The best number of nearest neighbors has been chosen to be 3 because this provides the lowest misclassification rate

Value of k	% Error Training	% Error Validation	
	Validation Error Log for Different k		
1	0.00	5.30	
2	1.30	5.30	
3	2.70	4.20	<— Best k
4	2.60	4.20	
5	3.43	4.70	
6	3.27	4.50	
7	3.70	4.85	
8	3.40	4.30	
9	4.47	5.15	
10	4.00	4.85	
11	4.83	5.65	
12	4.33	5.35	
13	5.00	5.60	
14	4.60	5.35	
15	5.20	5.70	
16	4.93	5.40	
17	5.33	5.75	
18	5.23	5.60	
19	5.83	6.00	
20	5.60	5.90	

FIGURE 9.1   **Lift Chart and Decile-wise Lift Chart for the Universal Bank Validation Data Set**

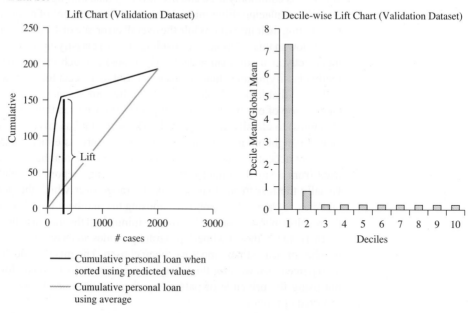

A second way of examining the accuracy and usefulness of a data mining model can be demonstrated with our Universal Bank example. All data mining programs will display a lift chart for any calculated solution; the one for the Universal Bank k-Nearest-Neighbor model is displayed in Figure 9.1.

Lift charts are the most common way (and perhaps the fastest) to compare different classification models. *Lift* is actually a ratio. Lift measures the change in concentration of a particular class when the model is used to select a group from the general population.

Consider why Universal Bank is attempting to classify the records in its database into *acceptors* and *nonacceptors*. Perhaps Universal Bank is considering a direct mailing to individuals in the database in order to solicit new personal loan applications. Based on previous experience, the percentage of individuals who respond favorably and take out a personal loan is 0.2 percent (that is not 2 percent, but two-tenths of 1 percent). Very few of the direct mailing recipients took out a personal loan. What if the bank could identify, before sending the mailing, the most likely *acceptors*? And what if the number of these likely *acceptors* was quite small relative to the size of the entire database? If the bank could successfully classify the database and identify these likely acceptors, then it might pay for the bank to restrict the direct mailing to only those individuals. Mailing and preparation costs would be saved and the bank would receive a *lift* in the percentage of recipients actually accepting a loan. What we may be able to help the bank do is to mail only to those customers with a high probability of loan acceptance, as opposed to mailing to everyone in the database. Remember, most of the people represented in the database are not likely loan acceptors. Only a relatively small number of the records in the database represent acceptors.

The lift curve is drawn from information about what the k-Nearest-Neighbor model predicted in a particular case and what that individual actually did. The lift chart in Figure 9.1 is actually a cumulative gains chart. It is constructed with the records arranged on the *x*-axis left to right from the highest probability to the lowest probability of accepting a loan. The *y*-axis reports the number of true positives at every point (i.e., the *y*-axis counts the number of records that represent loan acceptors).

Looking at the decile-wise lift chart in Figure 9.1, we can see that if we were to choose the top 10 percent of the records classified by our model (i.e., the 10 percent most likely to accept a personal loan) our selection would include approximately seven times as many correct classifications than if we were to select a random 10 percent of the database. That's a dramatic lift provided by the model when compared to a random selection.

The same information is displayed in a different manner in the lift chart on the left-hand side of Figure 9.1. This lift chart represents the cumulative records correctly classified (on the *y*-axis), with the records arranged in descending probability order on the *x*-axis. Since the curve inclines steeply upward over the first few hundred cases displayed on the *x*-axis, the model appears to provide significant lift relative to a random selection of records. Generally a better model will display higher lift than other candidate models. Lift can be used to compare the performance of models of different kinds (e.g., k-Nearest-Neighbor models compared with other data mining techniques) and is a good tool for comparing the performance of two or more data mining models using the same or comparable data. Notice the straight line rising at a 45-degree angle in the lift chart in Figure 9.1—this is a reference line. The line represents how well you might do by classifying as a result of random selection. If the calculated lift line is significantly above this reference line, you may expect the model to outperform a random selection. In the Universal Bank case the k-Nearest-Neighbor model outperforms a random selection by a very large margin.

CLASSIFICATION TREES: A SECOND CLASSIFICATION TECHNIQUE

Our second data mining technique is variously called a classification tree, a decision tree, or a regression tree. As the name implies, it is, like k-Nearest Neighbor, a way of classifying or dividing up a large number of records into successively smaller sets in which the members become similar to one another. Regression trees are used to predict or forecast categories rather than specific quantities. Data miners commonly use a tree metaphor to explain (and to display results from) this technique. Because the term *regression* is most often used to forecast a numeric quantity, when the data mining technique is predicting numeric quantities it is called a *regression tree*. When the technique is classifying by category, it is usually called either a *classification tree* or a *decision tree*.

As a child you may have played a game called "Animal, Mineral, or Vegetable." The origin of the game's name some believe arises from the fifteenth-century belief that all life was either animal or vegetable, while all inanimate objects were mineral. Thus, the three categories could effectively separate all matter into three neat categories. In the game, as you may recall, one player picks any object and other players must try to guess what it is by asking yes or no questions. The object is to ask the least number of questions before guessing the item correctly. In a sense, classification trees are like the game—we begin by knowing virtually nothing about the items we are sorting, but we make up rules along the way that allow us to place the records into different bins with each bin containing like objects. In "Animal, Mineral, or Vegetable," the set of questions you successfully used to determine the object's name would be the set of rules you could again use if the same object were to be chosen by another participant. In the same manner, we create a set of rules from our successful classification attempt, and these rules become the solution to the classification problem.

We now return to our insect classification problem.

In Figure 9.2 we ask first if the abdomen length is greater than 7.1. The vertical line drawn at a value of 7.1 is the graphical representation of this question (or rule). Note that when we draw this line all the known instances to the right of the line are katydids—we have a uniform classification on that side of the line. To the left of the line, however, we have a mix of katydids and grasshoppers in the known instances.

A further question (or rule) is necessary to continue the classification. This time we ask whether the antenna length is greater than six. The horizontal line drawn at a value of six in Figure 9.2 is the graphical representation of this question (or rule). An examination now of the entire set of known instances shows that

FIGURE 9.2
The Insect Classification Problem Viewed as a Classification Tree Exercise

Source: Eamonn Keogh.

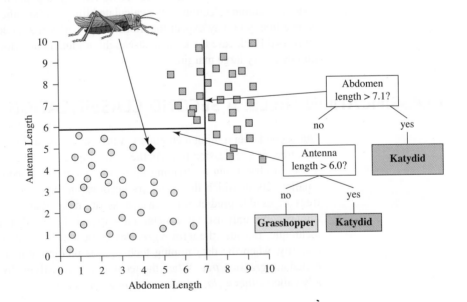

there is homogeneity in each region defined by our two questions. The right-hand region contains only katydids as does the topmost region in the upper left-hand corner. The bottommost region in the lower left-hand corner, however, contains only grasshoppers. Thus we have divided the geometric attribute space into three regions, each containing only a single type of insect.

In asking the two questions to create the three regions, we have also *created* the rules necessary to perform further classifications on unknown insects. Take the unknown insect shown in the diagram with an antenna length of 5 and an abdomen length of 4.5. By asking whether the unknown has an abdomen length of greater than 7.1 (answer = no) and then asking whether the antenna length is greater than 6 (answer = no), the insect is correctly classified as a grasshopper.

In our example we have used only two attributes (abdomen length and antenna length) to complete the classification routine. In a real-world situation we need not confine ourselves to only two attributes. In fact, we can use many attributes. The geometric picture might be difficult to draw but the decision tree (shown on the right-hand side of Figure 9.2) would look much the same as it does in our simple example. In data mining terminology, the two decision points in Figure 9.2 (shown as "abdomen length > 7.1" and "antenna length > 6") are called *decision nodes*. Nodes in XLMiner© are shown as circles with the decision value shown inside. They are called decision nodes because we classify unknowns by "dropping" them through the tree structure in much the same way a ball drops through the Pachinko game. (See Figure 9.3).

The bottom of our classification tree in Figure 9.2 has three leaves. Each *leaf* is a terminal node in the classification process; it represents the situation in which all the instances that follow that *branch* result in uniformity. The three leaves in Figure 9.2 are represented by the shaded boxes at the bottom of the diagram. Data mining classification trees are *upside-down* in that the leaves are at the bottom while the root of the tree is at the top; this is the convention in data mining circles. To begin a *scoring* process all the instances are at the root (i.e., top) of the tree; these instances are partitioned by the rules we have determined with the known instances. The result is that the unknown instances move downward through the tree until reaching a leaf node, at which point they are (hopefully) successfully classified.

At times the classification trees can become quite large and ungainly. It is common for data mining programs to *prune* the trees to remove branches. The unpruned tree was made using the training data set and it probably matches that data perfectly. Does that mean that this unpruned tree will do the best job in classifying new unknown instances? Probably not. A good classification tree algorithm will make the best split (at the first decision node) first followed by decision rules that are made up with successively smaller and smaller numbers of training records. These later decision rules will become more and more idiosyncratic. The result may be an unstable tree that will not do well in classifying new instances. Thus the need for pruning. Each data mining package uses a proprietary pruning algorithm that usually takes into account for any branch the added drop in the misclassification rate versus the added tree complexity. XLMiner© and other data

FIGURE 9.3
Classic Pachinko Game
A ball falls from the top through to the bottom and is guided by an array of pins. The user normally controls only the speed at which the ball enters the playing field. Like a slot machine the game is usually played in hope of winning a payoff.

mining programs use candidate tree formulations with the validation data set to find the lowest validation data set misclassification rate—that tree is selected as the final best-pruned tree. While the actual process is more complicated than we have described here, our explanation is essentially correct for all data mining software.

Classification trees are very popular in actual practice because the decision rules are easily generated and, more importantly, because the trees themselves are easy to understand and explain to others. There are disadvantages as well, however. The classification trees can suffer from overfitting and if they are not pruned well, these trees may not result in good classifications of new data (i.e., they will not score new data well). Attributes that are correlated will also cause this technique serious problems. It is somewhat similar to multicollinearity in a regression model. Be careful not to use features that are very closely correlated one with another.

A Business Data Mining Example: Classification Trees

We can once again use the Universal Bank data from Table 9.2 in an attempt to classify customers into likely or unlikely personal loan clients. The first step, as always, would be to partition the data into training and validation data sets; the training data set was displayed in Table 9.3. Note that while the data miner selects the attributes that are to be used, the data mining software algorithm selects the decision rules and the order in which they are executed. Table 9.7 displays a portion of the classification tree output from XLMiner© for the Universal Bank data. We have used a number of attributes to help in making up the decision rules; most of the attributes can be seen to intuitively affect whether a person is a likely personal loan candidate. Among the attributes used are:

- Customer's age
- Individual's average spending per month on credit cards
- Value of the individual's house mortgage
- Individual's annual income
- And others.

The scoring summary format is identical to the one we saw with the k-Nearest-Neighbor technique. For the classification tree technique the misclassification rate is just 1.80 percent; this is even lower than the 4.20 percent achieved with the k-Nearest-Neighbor model. A scant four individuals were expected to be likely to accept personal loans and yet did not do so.

TABLE 9.7
Scoring Summary Using the Best Pruned Tree on the Validation Data Set of the Universal Bank

Validation Data Scoring—Summary Report (Using Best Pruned Tree)

Cut off prob. val. for success (Updatable)	0.5	(Updating the value here will NOT update value in detailed report)

Classification Confusion Matrix

	Predicted Class	
Actual Class	1	0
1	182	32
0	4	1,802

Error Report

Class	#Cases	#Errors	%Error
1	194	32	16.49
0	1,806	4	0.22
Overall	2,000	36	1.80

FIGURE 9.4 **The Lift Chart and Decile-Wise Lift Chart Using the Best Pruned Tree on the Validation Data Set of the Universal Bank**

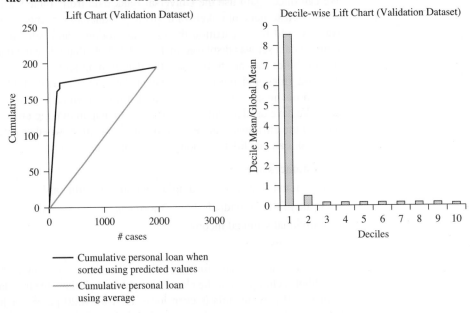

Looking at the decile-wise lift chart on the right-hand side of Figure 9.4, we can see that if we were to choose the top 10 percent of the records classified by our classification tree model (i.e., the 10 percent most likely to accept a personal loan) our selection would include approximately 8.5 times as many correct classifications than if we were to select a random 10 percent of the database. That result is even more striking than the one we obtained with the k-Nearest-Neighbor model.

The lift chart on the left-hand side of Figure 9.4 is a cumulative gains chart. Recall that it is constructed with the records arranged on the x-axis left to right from the highest probability of accepting a loan to the lowest probability of accepting a loan. The y-axis reports the number of true positives at every point (i.e., the y-axis counts the number of records that represent actual loan acceptors). The fact that the cumulative personal loan line jumps sharply above the average beginning on the left side of the chart shows that our model does significantly better than choosing likely loan applicants at random. In other words, there is considerable lift associated with this model.

The actual topmost part of the classification tree that was produced by XLMiner[C] is displayed in Figure 9.5.

The classification tree first divides on the income variable. Is income greater than 100.5? That results in 1,507 of the instances being classified as unlikely to accept a personal loan; these individuals are shown in the leaf node in the upper left-hand corner of the diagram. XLMiner[C] then sorted on the basis of educational

FIGURE 9.5
The Topmost Portion of the Classification Tree Using the Best Pruned Tree on the Validation Data Set of the Universal Bank

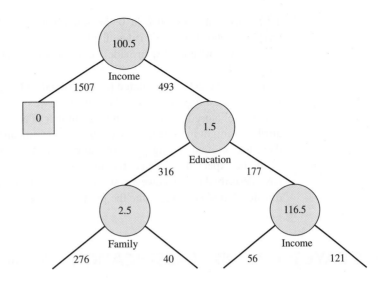

level followed by sorts based upon the family size of the customer (Family) and the annual income of the customer (Income). While examining the tree in Figure 9.5 is useful, it may be more instructive to examine the rules that are exemplified by the tree. Some of those rules are displayed in Table 9.8.

The rules displayed in Table 9.8 represent the same information shown in the diagram in Figure 9.5. Examining the first row of the table shows the split value as 100.5 for the split variable of income. This is the same as asking if the individual had a yearly income greater than 100.5. It is called a decision node because there are two branches extending downward from this node (i.e., it is not a terminal node or leaf). The second row of the table contains the information shown in the leaf on the left-hand side of the classification tree in Figure 9.5; this is called a terminal node or leaf because there are no successors. Row two shows that

TABLE 9.8 The Topmost Portion of the Tree Rules Using the Best Pruned Tree on the Validation Data Set of the Universal Bank

Best Pruned Tree Rules (Using Validation Data)									
#Decision nodes		8				#Terminal nodes		9	
Level	Node ID	Parent ID	Split Var	Split Value	Cases	Left Child	Right Child	Class	Node Type
0	0	N/A	Income	100.5	2,000	1	2	0	Decision
1	1	0	N/A	N/A	1,507	N/A	N/A	0	Terminal
1	2	0	Education	1.5	493	3	4	0	Decision
2	3	2	Family	2.5	316	5	6	0	Decision

1,507 cases are classified at 0, or unlikely to take out a personal loan in this terminal node. It is these rules displayed in this table that the program uses to score new data, and they provide a concise and exact way to treat new data in a speedy manner.

If actual values are predicted (as opposed to categories) for each case, then the tree is called a regression tree. For instance, we could attempt to predict the selling price of a used car by examining a number of attributes of the car. The relevant attributes might include the age of the car, the mileage the car had been driven to date, the original selling price of the car when new, and so on. The prediction would be expected to be an actual number, not simply a category. The process we have described could, however, still be used in this case. The result would be a set of rules that would determine the predicted price.

NAIVE BAYES: A THIRD CLASSIFICATION TECHNIQUE

A third and somewhat different approach to classification uses statistical classifiers. This technique will predict the probability that an instance is a member of a certain class. This technique is based on Bayes' theorem; we will describe the theorem below. In actual practice these Naive Bayes algorithms have been found to be comparable in performance to the decision trees we examined above. One hallmark of the Naive Bayes model is speed, along with high accuracy. This model is called *naive* because it assumes (perhaps naively) that each of the attributes is independent of the values of the other attributes. Of course this will never be strictly true, but in actual practice the assumption (although somewhat incorrect) allows the rapid determination of a classification scheme and does not seem to suffer appreciably in accuracy when such an assumption is made.

To explain the basic procedure we return to our insect classification example. Our diagram may be of the same data we have used before, but we will examine it in a slightly different manner.

The known instances of katydids and grasshoppers are again shown in Figure 9.6, but only a single attribute of interest is labeled on the y-axis: antenna length. On the right-hand side of Figure 9.6 we have drawn a histogram of the antenna lengths for grasshoppers and a separate histogram representing the antenna lengths of katydids.

Now assume we wish to use this information about a single attribute to classify an unknown insect. Our unknown insect has a measured antenna length of 3 (as shown in Figure 9.7). Look on the problem as an entirely statistical problem. Is this unknown more likely to be in the katydid distribution or the grasshopper distribution? A length of 3 would be in the far-right tail of the katydid distribution (and therefore unlikely to be a part of that distribution). But a length of 3 is squarely in the center of the grasshopper distribution (and therefore it is more likely to be a member of that distribution). Of course there is the possibility that the unknown with an antenna length of 3 is actually part of the katydid distribution (and

FIGURE 9.6
Insect Example This has only a single attribute displayed: antenna length abdomen length is still measured on the *x*-axis

Source: Eamonn Keogh.

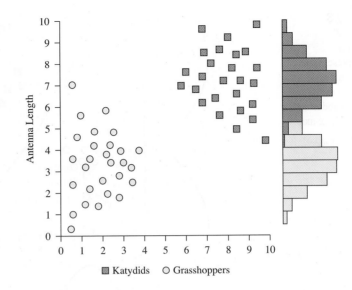

■ Katydids ○ Grasshoppers

FIGURE 9.7
Histograms Representing Antenna Lengths Katydids are on the left, and grasshoppers on the right

Source: Eamonn Keogh.

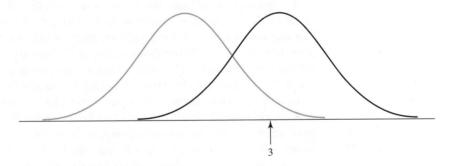

therefore is actually a katydid), but that probability is small as evidenced by a length of 3 being in the small tail of the distribution. It is far more likely that our unknown is part of the grasshopper distribution (and is therefore truly a grasshopper). So far we have used only a single attribute. What if we consider an additional attribute? Would that perhaps help our accuracy in making classifications?

Figure 9.8 represents two attributes (antenna length on the *y*-axis and abdomen length on the *x*-axis) for the known katydids and grasshoppers. By using the two attributes together we effectively create a quadratic boundary between the two classes of known insects. An unknown would be classified by its location above or below the boundary. One of the important features of the Naive Bayes model is that it handles irrelevant features quite well. If an irrelevant feature is included in the attributes list it has little effect on the classifications the model makes (and thus introduces little error).

FIGURE 9.8

Two Sets of Histograms

These represent the antenna lengths of katydids on the *y*-axis, and abdomen lengths on the *x*-axis

Source: Eamonn Keogh.

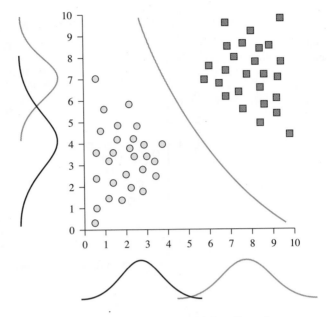

To examine this technique we will use actual data from the passenger list of the HMS *Titanic*. On Sunday evening April 14, 1912, the *Titanic* struck an iceberg. The ship sank a scant two hours and forty minutes later. We have somewhat complete information on 2,201 souls on the ship at the time of the accident. We say the information is "somewhat" complete because this data is based on a report made shortly after the event and the White Star line (the owners of the *Titanic*) kept their records in a peculiar manner.[6] For instance, boys are classified by the title "Master," but girls are not clearly distinguished from women. The data are not without some ambiguity but we can still attempt to ascertain characteristics of the survivors. We are attempting to classify individuals as survivors of the disaster or nonsurvivors (i.e., those who perished). Our data looks like the following:

Age	Sex	Class	Survived
Adult	Male	First	Alive
Adult	Male	First	Alive
Adult	Male	First	Alive
Adult	Male	First	Alive
Adult	Male	First	Alive
Adult	Male	First	Alive
Adult	Male	First	Alive
Adult	Male	First	Alive
Adult	Male	First	Alive

[6] The *Titanic* data set is used by permission of Professor Robert J. MacG. Dawson of Saint Marys University, Halifax, Nova Scotia. See "The Unusual Episode, Data Revisited." Robert J.MacG. Dawson, *Journal of Statistics Education*, vol. 3 no. 3 (1995).

TABLE 9.9
Validation Data
Scoring for the Naive
Bayes Model of
Titanic Passengers
and Crew

Validation Data Scoring—Summary Report		
Cut off prob. val. for success (updatable)	0.5	(Updating the value here will NOT update value in detailed report)

Classification Confusion Matrix

	Predicted Class	
Actual Class	Alive	Dead
Alive	172	123
Dead	107	478

Error Report

Class	#Cases	#Errors	%Error
Alive	295	123	41.69
Dead	585	107	18.29
Overall	880	230	26.14

The data set contains information on each of the individuals on the *Titanic*. We know whether they were adult or child, whether they were male or female, the class of their accommodations (first class passenger, second class, third class, or crew), and whether they survived that fateful night. In our list 711 are listed as alive while 1,490 are listed as dead; thus only 32 percent of the people on board survived.

What if we wished to examine the probability that an individual with certain characteristics (say, an adult, male crew member) were to survive? Could we use the Naive Bayes method to determine the probability that this person survived? The answer is Yes; that is precisely what a Naive Bayes model will do. In this case we are classifying the adult, male crew member into one of two categories: survivor or dead.

The Naive Bayes process begins like our two previous techniques; the data set is divided into a training data set and a validation data set. In Table 9.9 we present the Validation Summary Report for the model as computed in XLMiner©.

The misclassification rate computed by XLMiner© is 26.14 percent but the lift chart and the decile-wise lift chart in Figure 9.9 show that the model does improve on naively selecting a class at random for the result.

The Naive Bayes model rests on Bayes' theorem. Simply stated, *Bayes' theorem* predicts the probability of a prior event (called a posterior probability) given that a certain subsequent event has taken place. For instance, what is the probability that a credit card transaction is fraudulent given that the card has been reported lost? Note that the reported loss preceded the current attempted use of the credit card.

FIGURE 9.9 Lift Chart and Decile-Wise Lift Chart for the Naive Bayes *Titanic* Model

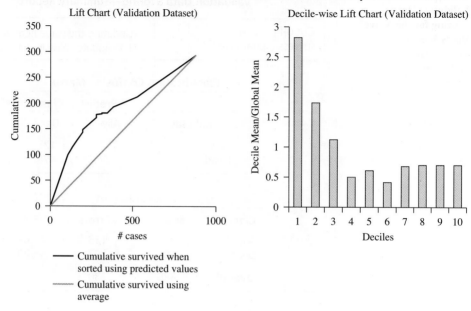

The posterior probability is written as P($A \mid B$). Thus , P($A \mid B$) is the probability that the credit card use is fraudulent given that we know the card has been reported lost. P(A) would be called the prior probability of A and is the probability that any credit card transaction is fraudulent regardless of whether the card is reported lost.

The Bayesian theorem is stated in the following manner:

$$P(A \mid B) = \frac{P(B \mid A)P(A)}{P(B)}$$

where:

P(A) is the prior probability of A. It is *prior* in the sense that it does not take into account any information about B.

P($A \mid B$) is the conditional probability of A, given B. It is also called the *posterior probability* because it is derived from or depends upon the specified value of B. This is the probability we are usually seeking to determine.

P($B \mid A$) is the conditional probability of B given A.

P(B) is the prior probability of B.

An example will perhaps make the use of Bayes' theorem clearer. Consider that we have the following data set showing eight credit card transactions. For each transaction we have information about whether the transaction was fraudulent and whether the card used was previously reported lost (see Table 9.10).

TABLE 9.10
Credit Card
Transaction Data Set

Transaction No.	Fraudulent?	Reported Lost?
1	Yes	Yes
2	No	No
3	No	No
4	No	No
5	Yes	Yes
6	No	No
7	No	Yes
8	Yes	No

Applying Bayes' theorem:

$$P(Fraud \mid Card\ Reported\ Lost) = \frac{P(Lost \mid Fraud)P(Fraud)}{P(Lost)}$$

$$= \frac{\left(\frac{2}{3}\right)\left(\frac{3}{8}\right)}{\frac{3}{8}} = .667$$

and

$$P(NonFraud \mid Card\ Reported\ Lost) = \frac{P(Lost \mid NonFraud)P(NonFraud)}{P(Lost)}$$

$$= \frac{\left(\frac{1}{5}\right)\left(\frac{5}{8}\right)}{\frac{3}{8}} = .333$$

Thus, the probability of a fraudulent transaction if the card has been reported lost is 66.7 percent. The probability of a nonfraudulent transaction if the card has been reported lost is 33.3 percent.

Returning to the *Titanic* data and the Naive Bayes model calculated by XLMiner©, we may now demonstrate the calculation of the posterior probabilities of interest. These are the answers to our question concerning the probability that an adult, male crew member would survive the disaster. XLMiner© produces an additional output for the Naive Bayes model displaying the prior class probabilities and the calculated conditional probabilities. These are displayed in Table 9.11.

To answer our question concerning the survival probability of an adult, male crew member we need once again to apply Bayes' theorem. We first need to calculate the conditional probabilities required in the Bayes' theorem:

Conditional probability of "alive" if you were a crew member, male, and adult:

$$P(alive) = (0.295673077)(.53125)(.9375)(0.314912945) = 0.046373782$$

TABLE 9.11
Prior Class
Probabilities and
Conditional
Probabilities
Calculated in
XLMiner© for
the *Titanic* Data

Prior Class Probabilities

According to relative occurrences in training data

Class	Prob.	
Alive	0.314912945	← Success Class
Dead	0.685087055	

Conditional Probabilities

Input Variables	Alive		Dead	
	Value	Prob	Value	Prob
Age	Adult	0.9375	Adult	0.964640884
	Child	0.0625	Child	0.035359116
Sex	Female	0.46875	Female	0.082872928
	Male	0.53125	Male	0.917127072
Class	Crew	0.295673077	Crew	0.450828729
	First	0.295673077	First	0.071823204
	Second	0.146634615	Second	0.10718232
	Third	0.262019231	Third	0.370165746

Note that we are now multiplying probabilities assuming they are independent. In like manner we calculate the "dead" probability:

Conditional probability of "dead" if you were a crew member, male, and adult:

$$P(dead) = (.450828729)(0.917127072)(0.9640884)(0.685087055) = 0.273245188$$

To compute the actual probabilities, we divide each of these probabilities by their sum:

Posterior probability of "alive" if you were a crew member, male, and adult:

$$= (0.046373782)/(0.046373782 + 0.273245188) = 0.145090831$$

and

Posterior probability of "dead" if you were a crew member, male, and adult:

$$= (0.273245188)/(0.273245188 + 0.046373782) = 0.854909169$$

There are only two possible outcomes here ("dead" or "alive") and the probabilities should (and do) sum to one. Naive Bayes has assumed the attributes have independent distributions. While this is not strictly true, the model seems to work well in situations where the assumption is not grossly violated. Use of larger data sets will all but eliminate the problem of including irrelevant attributes in the model. The effects of these irrelevant attributes are minimized as the data set becomes

FIGURE 9.10

The Naive Bayes Model Applied to the Universal Bank Data

Included are confusion matrix, misclassification rate, and lift charts

Validation Data Scoring—Summary Report		
Cut off prob. val. for success (updatable)	0.5	(Updating the value here will NOT update value in detailed report)

Classification Confusion Matrix

	Predicted Class	
Actual Class	1	0
1	122	72
0	77	1,729

Error Report

Class	#Cases	#Errors	%Error
1	194	72	37.11
0	1,806	77	4.26
Overall	2,000	149	7.45

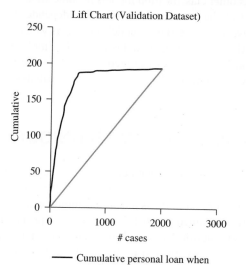

Lift Chart (Validation Dataset)

— Cumulative personal loan when sorted using predicted values

— Cumulative personal loan using average

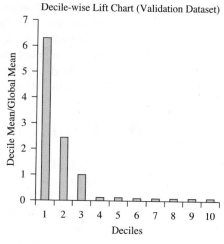

Decile-wise Lift Chart (Validation Dataset)

larger. We can again use the Universal Bank data and apply the Naive Bayes model in order to predict customers that will accept a personal loan. Figure 9.10 displays the Naive Bayes results from XLMiner© for the Universal Bank data.

Once again it is clear that the model performs much better than a naive selection of individuals when we try to select possible loan acceptors. Looking at the decile-wise lift chart on the right-hand side of Figure 9.10, we can see that if we were to choose the top 10 percent of the records classified by our classification tree model (i.e., the 10 percent most likely to accept a personal loan) our selection would include approximately 6.5 times as many correct classifications than if we were to select a random 10 percent of the database. While Naive Bayes models do extremely well on training data, in real-world applications these models tend not to do quite as well as other classification models in some situations. This is likely due to the disregard of the model for attribute interdependence. In many real-world situations, however, Naive Bayes models do just as well as other classification models. While the Naive Bayes model is relatively simple, it makes sense to try the simplest models first and to use them if they provide sufficient results. Clearly data sets that contain highly interdependent attributes will fare poorly with Naive Bayes.

REGRESSION: A FOURTH CLASSIFICATION TECHNIQUE

Our final classification data mining technique is logistic regression or logit analysis (both names refer to the same method). This technique is a natural complement to linear least-squares regression. It has much in common with the ordinary linear regression models we examined in Chapters 4 and 5. Ordinary linear regression provides a universal framework for much of economic analysis; its simplified manner of looking at data has proven useful to researchers and forecasters for decades. Logistic regression serves the same purpose for categorical data. The single most important distinction between logistic regression and ordinary regression is that the dependent variable in logistic regression is categorical (and not continuous). The explanatory variables, or attributes, may be either continuous or categorical (as they were in linear least-squares models). Just like the ordinary linear regression model, logistic regression is able to use all sorts of extensions and sophisticated variants. Logistic regression has found its way into the toolkits of not only forecasters and economists; but also, for example, into those of toxicologists and epidemiologists.

TABLE 9.12
Data on 20 Students and Their Test Performance and Hours of Study

Student No.	Hours of Study	Pass/Fail
1	2.5	0
2	22.6	1
3	17.8	0
4	5.4	0
5	14	0
6	13.3	1
7	26	1
8	33.1	1
9	13.6	0
10	45.3	1
11	1.9	0
12	31.4	1
13	27	1
14	10.1	0
15	2.7	0
16	16.3	1
17	14.5	1
18	4.5	0
19	22.6	1
20	17.1	1

The Universal Bank situation we have been examining provides a case in point. The dependent variable, the item we are attempting to forecast, is dichotomous—either a person accepts a loan or rejects the loan. There is no continuous variable here; it is more like an on/off switch. But why are we unable to use linear least-squares models on this data?

Consider Table 9.12—it contains information about 20 students, the hours they spent studying for a qualifying exam, and their results. If they passed the exam the table shows a 1; if they failed the exam, the table shows a 0.

If we graph this data as a scatterplot (Figure 9.11) we see there are two possible outcomes: pass (shown as 1) and fail (shown as 0).

FIGURE 9.11
Scatterplot of Student Performance

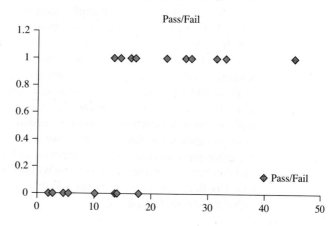

TABLE 9.13   Linear Least-Squares Regression

```
Audit Trail--Coefficient Table (Multiple Regression Selected)
```

Series Description	Included in Model	Coefficient	Standard Error	T-test	P-value	Elasticity	Overall F-test
Hours of Study	Yes	0.03	0.01	4.47	0.00	1.00	
Pass/Fail	Dependent	0.0020532033	0.15	0.01	0.99		20.02

It appears from the scatterplot that students who spent more time studying for the exam had a better chance of passing. We might seek to quantify this perception by running a least-squares regression using "hours of study" as the independent variable and "pass/fail" as the dependent variable. Running this regression results in the output in Table 9.13.

Since the "hours of study" coefficient is positive ($+0.03$), it appears to indicate that more study leads to a higher probability of passing. But, is the relationship correctly quantified? Suppose an individual studies for 100 hours. How well will this individual do on the exam? Substituting into the regression equation we have:

$$\text{Pass/fail} = 0.002053 + (0.032072) \times (100)$$
$$3.209253 = 0.002053 + (0.032072) \times (100)$$

What does this mean? Is the predicted grade 3.209 percent? This doesn't seem to make sense. Examining the regression line estimated and superimposing it on the data scatter may make the problem clear (see Figure 9.12).

The difficulty becomes clearer when examining the diagram. There are only two states of nature for the dependent variable (pass and fail). However, the regression line plotted in Figure 9.12 is a straight line sloping upward to the right and predicting values all along its path. When predicting the outcome from 100 hours of study the regression chooses a number (i.e., 3.209253) that is much greater than the maximum value of 1 exhibited in the data set. Does this mean the individual has passed the test 3.209 times? Or does this mean that the expected score is 3.209 percent? Or does this have any meaningful explanation at all? This confusing result indicates that we have used an inappropriate tool in attempting to find the answer to our question. In earlier chapters we assumed the dependent variable was continuous; this one is not. Linear least-squares regression does not restrict the predictions of the dependent variable to a range of zero to one as we would like in this case.

We would really like to use this same data but predict the probability that an individual would pass the test given a certain number of hours of study. To accomplish this we will modify the linear least-squares model by modifying what we use as the dependent variable. Ordinarily we simply use Y as the dependent variable; in logistic regression we will use a function of Y as the dependent variable instead. This function of the dependent variable will be limited to values between zero and one. The function we use is called a *logit* and that is the reason the technique is called logistic regression.

FIGURE 9.12
Linear Least-Squares Regression Plot

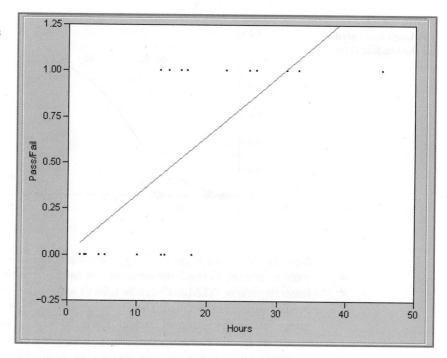

The logit is $\mathrm{Log}(e^{\alpha+\beta_1 X_1+\beta_2 X_2+\cdots+\beta_p X_p})$. You will recognize this as being similar to our explanation of the logistic curve in Chapter 3. In fact the concepts are one and the same. We are going to use some knowledge of how growth works in the real world just as we did in that chapter. Recall that the diffusion models' assumed growth proceeded along an s-curve. When we used these models to predict new product sales we did so in the knowledge that real-world new products almost always follow such a path. We now make the same assumption that real-world probabilities will behave in a similar manner. This assumption has withstood the test of time as logistic regression has proven very predictive and accurate in actual practice.

The logistic regression model will estimate a value for pass/fail as a probability with zero as the minimum and one as the maximum. If we were to look at the entire range of values that a logistic regression would estimate for the student data it would appear like the s-curve in Figure 9.13. Recall that "hours of study" are represented on the x-axis while "pass/fail" is represented on the y-axis. If, for instance, an individual had studied for a scant 10 hours the model would predict a probability of passing somewhere near 10 percent (since the y-axis represents the values from zero to one it can be read directly as the probability of occurrence of the dependent event). However, if the individual in question were to have studied for 30 hours the probability of passing is predicted to be near 90 percent.

Let's examine the Universal Bank data with a logistic regression model and note the difference in the output from the other classification models we have

FIGURE 9.13
The Logit Estimated for the Student Data

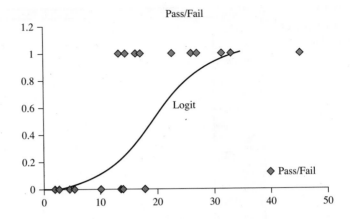

used. As always, we begin by using a partition of the original data set to act as a training data set. In much the same way we used ForecastX to set up an ordinary linear regression, XLMiner© can be used to set up a logistic regression. The dependent variable is specified. The dependent variable in any logistic regression is categorical; in the Universal Bank case it is the personal loan variable that takes on a value of either 1 (if a personal loan is accepted) or 0 (if no personal loan is accepted). The independent variables are also specified just as in ForecastX. Note that unlike the student study example presented above, the Universal Bank logistic regression will include more than one independent variable. In this sense, it is a multiple logistic regression. Table 9.14 shows the output from the XLMiner© program for this data.

The output resembles ordinary linear regression output from ForecastX. There is a constant term, the values of the coefficients are reported, and standard errors

TABLE 9.14
Logistic Regression for the Universal Bank Data

Input Variables	Coefficient	Std. Error	p-value	Odds
		The Regression Model		
Constant term	−12.8019095	2.16737223	0	*
Age	−0.04461157	0.08051153	0.57950926	0.95636886
Experience	0.05816582	0.07969882	0.46549997	1.05989075
Income	0.05698515	0.00351325	0	1.05864012
Family	0.62984651	0.09647165	0	1.87732232
CCAvg	0.11668219	0.05372836	0.02987786	1.12376225
Education	1.80500054	0.15606253	0	6.07997465
Mortgage	0.00141519	0.0007293	0.05232161	1.00141621
Securities Account	−0.8171795	0.37658975	0.03001092	0.44167566
CD Account	3.56768751	0.41729182	0	35.43455887
Online	−0.70467436	0.21116103	0.00084645	0.49426949
CreditCard	−1.10061717	0.26931652	0.00004375	0.33266568

for those coefficients allow *p*-values to be reported. The interpretation of these variables is much the same as it was with ordinary linear regression.

For example, the Family variable represents the family size of the customer. Since the logistic regression coefficient for this variable is positive (i.e., +0.62984651) we would expect that the probability of accepting a personal loan increases with family size. Further, since the *p*-value for this variable is very small (reported as zero in the printout but actually a very small number) we believe that the coefficient is significant at the 99 percent level. That is, we believe that there is very little chance that the real relationship between family size and the acceptance of a personal loan is zero. This ability to examine individual attributes is similar to the manner in which we examined the individual coefficients of an ordinary linear regression.

Table 9.15 displays the validation data set confusion matrix and misclassification rate. This information allows us to judge in part the overall fit of the logistic regression model. The confusion matrix and misclassification rate give an overall sense of fit. In this case the 5.05 percent misclassification rate would indicate how well we believe the model would classify new data into the correct categories.

The validation data set lift charts are also used to judge the overall fit of the model. Examining the right-hand side of Figure 9.14 shows that selecting the top 10 percent of the training data observations (i.e., those persons judged most likely to accept a personal loan) resulted in a better than 7 times result when compared to selecting individual cases at random. The same information is again displayed in the left-hand side of Figure 9.14 in the lift chart. The steep rise in the lift compared to the reference line for a naive selection of cases (i.e., the straight line in the figure) shows significant explanatory power in the model.

TABLE 9.15
Logistic Regression Confusion Matrix and Misclassification Rate

Validation Data Scoring—Summary Report

Cut off prob. val. for success (updatable)	0.5	(Updating the value here will NOT update value in detailed report)

Classification Confusion Matrix

	Predicted Class	
Actual Class	1	0
1	125	69
0	32	1,774

Error Report

Class	#Cases	#Errors	%Error
1	194	69	35.57
0	1,806	32	1.77
Overall	2,000	101	5.05

BusinessWeek related the story of Michael Drosnin, author of a bestselling book, *The Bible Code*. In the book Drosnin claimed to have found references in the Bible to President Bill Clinton, dinosaurs, and the Land of Magog. Peter Coy, the author of the article, pointed out many of the useful tasks to which data mining had been put (e.g., weeding out credit card fraud, finding sales prospects, and discovering new drugs).

But Coy also pointed out that data mining was the method used by Michael Drosnin to make his "discoveries" in the Bible. It seems Drosnin wrote out the Hebrew Bible as a grid of letters and used data mining to look for words on the diagonal, up, down, and across. Not surprisingly he found some recognizable words and references. Cryptic messages appeared according to Coy such as the close juxtaposition of the word dinosaur with the word asteroid. According to Andrew Lo of the Massachusetts Institute of Technology, "Given enough time, enough attempts, and enough imagination, almost any pattern can be teased out of any data set."

The moral to the story is that a formula that fits the data may not have any predictive power at all!

There is always the chance that what a data mining technique "observes" or "discovers" may just be a coincidence in the current data set and not something that is reproducible in the future with other data. The chance of this being true in data mining is more prominent than in the standard business forecasting routines we presented earlier in the text. Most of those techniques relied on proven economic theory as a basis for specifying a particular type of model. With data mining it is the data itself that specifies the model and the analyst should be wary of making the same mistake as Michael Drosnin. Coy gives the example of David J. Leinweber, managing director of First Quadrant Corporation, who sifted through a United Nations CD-ROM and discovered that historically, the single best predictor of the Standard & Poor's 500-stock index was butter production in Bangladesh. Leinweber called this an example of "stupid data miners' tricks."

Source: Peter Coy, "Commentary: He Who Mines Data May Strike Fool's Gold." *BusinessWeek*, June 16, 1997, p. 40.

FIGURE 9.14   **Validation Data Lift Charts for the Logistic Regression Model**

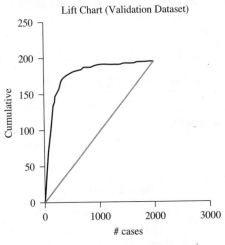

Lift Chart (Validation Dataset)

— Cumulative personal loan when sorted using predicted values

— Cumulative personal loan using average

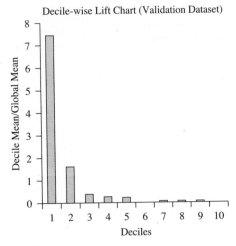

Decile-wise Lift Chart (Validation Dataset)

Summary

In this chapter we have covered four classification techniques that are commonly used by real data miners. Classification, however, is only a single aspect of data mining. In general there is no one best classification technique; the individual data in a particular situation will determine the best technique to use. The diagnostic statistics will lead the researcher to choose an appropriate model; there may be no optimal model.

Data mining also uses other tools such as clustering analysis and neural network analysis. These tools are not covered here but there are excellent resources for those interested in pursuing the study of data mining. The growth in the use of commercial data mining tools rivals the growth in business forecasting software sales; SAS Enterprise Miner and SPSS Clementine have become important additions to the forecaster's toolkit in recent years.

Suggested Readings

Berry, Michael J. A.; and Gordon S. Linhoff. *Data Mining Techniques for Marketing, Sales, and Customer Relationship Management.* Indianapolis: Wiley Publishing, Inc., 2004.

Cramer, J. S. *Logit Models from Economics and Other Fields.* Cambridge: Cambridge University Press, 2003.

Han, Jiawei; and Micheline Kamber. *Data Mining Concepts and Techniques.* San Diego, California: Academic Press, 2001.

Shmueli, Galit; Nitin R. Patel; and Peter C. Bruce. *Data Mining for Business Intelligence.* Hoboken, New Jersey: John Wiley & Sons, Inc., 2007

Witten, Ian H.; and Eibe Frank. *Data Mining: Practical Machine Learning Tools and Techniques.* Amsterdam: Elsevier, 2005.

Exercises

1. A data mining routine has been applied to a transaction dataset and has classified 88 records as fraudulent (30 correctly so) and 952 as nonfraudulent (920 correctly so).

   The decile-wise lift chart for a transaction data model:

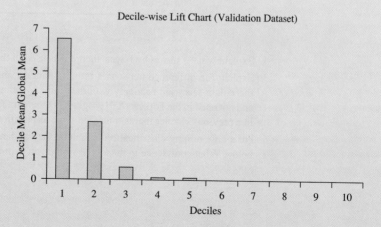

   Interpret the meaning of the bars in this chart.

2. Which of the following situations represents the confusion matrix for the transactions data mentioned in question 1 above? Explain your reasoning.

A

Classification Confusion Matrix

	Predicted Class	
Actual Class	1	0
1	58	920
0	30	32

B

Classification Confusion Matrix

	Predicted Class	
Actual Class	1	0
1	32	30
0	58	920

C

Classification Confusion Matrix

	Predicted Class	
Actual Class	1	0
1	30	32
0	58	920

D

Classification Confusion Matrix

	Predicted Class	
Actual Class	1	0
1	920	58
0	30	32

3. Calculate the classification error rate for the following confusion matrix. Comment on the pattern of misclassifications. How much better did this data mining technique do as compared to a naive model?

	Predict Class 1	Predict Class 0
Actual 1	8	2
Actual 0	20	970

4. Explain what is meant by Bayes' theorem as used in the Naive Bayes model.

5. Explain the difference between a training data set and a validation data set. Why are these data sets used routinely with data mining techniques in the XLMiner© program and not used in the ForecastX™ program? Is there, in fact, a similar technique presented in a previous chapter that is much the same as partitioning a data set?

6. For a data mining classification technique the validation data set lift charts are shown below. What confidence in the model would you express given this evidence?

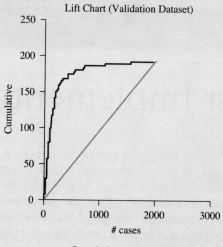

Lift Chart (Validation Dataset)

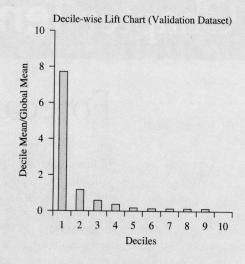

Decile-wise Lift Chart (Validation Dataset)

—— Cumulative personal loan when
     sorted using predicted values

—— Cumulative personal loan
     using average

7. In data mining the candidate model should be applied to a data set that was not used in the estimation process in order to find out the accuracy on unseen data; that unseen data set. What is the unseen data set called? How is the unseen data set selected?

8. Explain what the "k" in the k-Nearest-Neighbor model references.

Forecast Implementation

In this chapter we discuss the forecasting process and provide a framework that will help you get the most out of any forecasting effort. While every forecasting problem has unique features, there is enough commonality in forecasting that guidelines can be helpful in several ways. First, the guidelines we provide will help you come to grips with some of the nuts-and-bolts issues related to data problems. Second, these guidelines will help you in making certain that the effort that goes into forecasting has the desired result in terms of the decision process. Finally, the guidelines discussed in this chapter will help you make logical choices regarding the technique(s) you should use for any particular situation.

KEYS TO OBTAINING BETTER FORECASTS

As part of an ongoing research study that has focused on very practical forecasting issues, a group of researchers led by John Mentzer has identified key elements to improving forecasts.[1] These elements are summarized in Table 10.1. One of the findings of Mentzer's group is that blind reliance on computer-generated quantitative forecasts is not a good management practice. As indicated in Chapter 1 of this text, judgments are important in forecasting even when quantitative methods are used. You have spent considerable time and effort developing a working knowledge of many quantitative techniques and how they can be implemented using a software package. Our own personal experiences, as well as the experiences of others, provide convincing evidence that quantitative forecasting methods tend to outperform qualitative forecasts. However, the best software cannot automatically take into account the specific industry, marketing, and economic knowledge that a business professional may have. To obtain the best forecast outcomes, both quantitative and qualitative information should be valued and, when possible, combined in preparing a forecast.

Both quantitative and qualitative information should be valued and, when possible, combined in preparing a forecast.

The work of Mentzer and others has also helped to clarify the distinction between forecasts, plans, and goals. In a recent discussion, a veteran forecaster in the automobile industry commented: "I prepared what I thought was a logical and well-thought-out forecast, but when it was presented to management the response

[1] Mark A. Moon, John T. Mentzer, Carlo D. Smith, and Michael S. Garver, "Seven Keys to Better Forecasting," *Business Horizons*, September–October 1998, pp. 44–52; and Mark A. Moon and John T. Mentzer, "Improving Salesforce Forecasting," *Journal of Business Forecasting*, Summer 1999, pp. 7–12.

TABLE 10.1 **Seven Keys to Better Forecasting**

Source: Adapted from Mark A. Moon, John T. Mentzer, Carlo D. Smith, and Michael S. Garver, "Seven Keys to Better Forecasting," *Business Horizons,* September–October 1998, p. 45. Reprinted with permission from *Business Horizons* by The Board of Trustees at Indiana University, Kelley School of Business.

Keys	Issues and Symptoms	Actions	Results
Understand what forecasting is and is not	Computer system as focus, rather than management processes and controls Blurring of the distinction between forecasts, plans, and goals	Establish forecasting group Implement management control systems before selecting forecasting software Derive plans from forecasts Distinguish between forecasts and goals	An environment in which forecasting is acknowledged as a critical business function Accuracy emphasized and game playing minimized
Forecast demand, plan supply	Use of shipment history as the basis for forecasting demand rather than actual demand	Identify sources of demand information Build systems to capture key demand data	Improved customer service and capital planning
Communicate, cooperate, and collaborate	Duplication of forecasting effort Mistrust of the "official" forecast Little understanding of the impact throughout the firm	Establish a cross-functional approach to forecasting Establish an independent forecast group that sponsors cross-functional collaboration	All relevant information used to generate forecasts Forecasts trusted by users More accurate and relevant forecasts
Eliminate islands of analysis	Mistrust and inadequate information leading different users to create their own forecasts	Build a single "forecasting infrastructure" Provide training for both users and developers of forecasts	More accurate, relevant, and credible forecasts Islands of analysis eliminated Optimized investments in information and communication systems
Use tools wisely	Relying solely on either qualitative or quantitative methods	Integrate quantitative and qualitative methods Identify sources of improved accuracy and increased error Provide instruction	Process improvement in efficiency and effectiveness
Make it important	No accountability for poor forecasts Developers not understanding how forecasts are used	Training developers to understand implications of poor forecasts Include forecast performance in individual performance plans and reward systems	Developers take forecasting more seriously A striving for accuracy More accuracy and credibility
Measure, measure, measure	Not knowing if the firm is getting better Accuracy not measured at relevant levels of aggregation Inability to isolate sources of forecast error	Establish multidimensional metrics Incorporate multilevel measures Measure accuracy whenever and wherever forecasts are adjusted	Forecast performance can be included in individual performance plans Sources of errors can be isolated and targeted for improvement Greater confidence in forecast process

was that the forecast was wrong and that I should go back and redo it." In this individual's case, what management wanted was a plan (what the company intends to do) or a goal (the company target) rather than an objective projection of what is likely given the current business environment. This scenario is not uncommon. What it points out is a serious confusion on the part of many between a forecast, a plan, and a goal. The forecast should be one piece of objective information that plays a part in the development of plans and/or goals, but it should not be confused with the planning or goal-setting functions.

The forecast should be one piece of objective information that plays a part in the development of plans and/or goals, but it should not be confused with the planning or goal-setting functions.

The emergence of widely available and sophisticated forecasting software has made it possible for people to implement complex forecasting methods quickly and easily. However, there is danger in implementing a technique about which one does not have a reasonable level of understanding. For example, suppose that you are a brand manager who has some forecasting responsibility for certain brands, but that this function is only about 10 percent of your overall workload. In this situation you might be inclined to make relatively simple judgmental forecasts, or if you have come to realize that quantitative methods can improve forecast accuracy, you might be tempted to use an automated forecast "black box" to develop your forecasts. In either case you are likely to have difficulty explaining and/or justifying the forecast to those to whom you report. However, if you have a basic understanding of forecast methods (which you have now developed), you can articulate the reasoning behind your forecast and how the quantitative methods employed are well suited to the type of data that represent sales of your products. You will be able to make qualitative judgments and adjustments to the forecasts and be able to explain why such adjustments may be necessary. You may not be able to derive the formulas for the Winters' exponential smoothing model or for developing an ARIMA forecast, but you know enough about how these methods work to know when they are appropriate.

As we will discuss in more detail later in this chapter, communication, cooperation, and collaboration are important if the forecasting effort is to be as successful as it can be. Many times the people who develop a forecast do so in a vacuum of sorts. They look at the data and prepare a forecast, which is then sent to users who have had little or no input into the forecast process. The forecast may not be in a form that is useful to the end user, or the units forecast may be inappropriate for their use, or they may simply not have enough understanding of the forecast to use it properly.

Often there are two particular groups that need to communicate well: the analysts or number crunchers, and the sales, marketing, and customer service people. Each of these groups may have quite different perspectives on the forecasting process. Sean Reese, demand planner at Ocean Spray Cranberries, Inc., has observed that for collaborative forecasting to be successful, all parties need to work together by treating the perspectives and biases of others as valuable inputs rather than as obstacles to overcome.[2] These days the need for communication,

---

[2] Sean Reese, "The Human Aspects of Collaborative Forecasting," *Journal of Business Forecasting*, Winter 2000–2001, pp. 3–9.

cooperation, and collaboration goes beyond company boundaries. To maximize the benefits to be derived from the forecast process, communication, cooperation, and collaboration should involve the entire supply chain.

Everyone is well aware that inventory is expensive and there may be substantial savings if inventory levels can be reduced. Such reduction was the premise upon which "Just in Time" processes were developed. As Moon reports,

"The more accurate the forecasts, the less inventory that needs to be carried, with all the well-understood cost savings that brings."

> When demand can be predicted accurately, it can be met in a timely and efficient manner, keeping both channel partners and final customers satisfied. Accurate forecasts help a company avoid lost sales or stock-out situations, and prevent customers from going to competitors. . . . Perhaps most important, accurate forecasting can have a profound impact on a company's inventory levels. In a sense, inventory exists to provide a buffer for inaccurate forecasts. Thus, the more accurate the forecasts, the less inventory that needs to be carried, with all the well-understood cost savings that brings.[3]

In Chapter 1 you read an example based on the brake parts company in which *savings of $6 million per month* resulted from an improved forecasting system.[4]

THE FORECAST PROCESS

The forecast process begins with a need to make one or more decisions that depend, at least in part, on the future value(s) of some variable(s) or on the future occurrence of some event. Subjective forecasting methods, such as the Delphi method, are usually the most useful in forecasting future events such as the nature of the home computer market 20 years from now. The quantitative techniques you have studied in this text are widely used in providing forecasts of variables such as sales, occupancy rates, income, inventory needs, and personnel requirements. Regardless of the specific scenario, the forecast is needed to help in making the best possible decision.

Communication, cooperation, and collaboration are critical if forecasting is to have the desired positive effect on decisions.

We have divided the entire forecasting process into the nine steps first introduced in Chapter 2 and shown again in Figure 10.1. These begin and end with communication, cooperation, and collaboration between the managers who use the forecasts and the technicians who prepare them. This communication and cooperation are critical if forecasting is to have the desired positive effect on decisions. Most of the students who study this text will probably be managers and will be better able to communicate with their professional forecasters because they have developed an understanding of the methods that can be used.

---

[3] Moon et al. "Seven Keys to Better Forecasting," p. 44.

[4] John T. Mentzer and Jon Schroeter, "Multiple Forecasting System at Brake Parts, Inc.," *Journal of Business Forecasting*, Fall 1993, pp. 5–9.

FIGURE 10.1
A Nine-Step
Forecasting Process

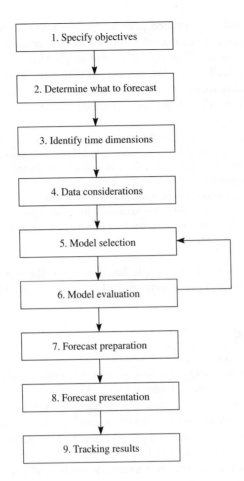

1. Specify objectives

2. Determine what to forecast

3. Identify time dimensions

4. Data considerations

5. Model selection

6. Model evaluation

7. Forecast preparation

8. Forecast presentation

9. Tracking results

Step 1. Specify Objectives

The objectives related to the decisions for which a forecast is important should be stated clearly. Management should articulate the role that the forecast will have in the decision process. If the decision will be the same regardless of the forecast, then any effort devoted to preparing the forecast is wasted. This may sound too obvious to deserve mention. However, it is not uncommon for a manager to request a forecast only to ignore it in the end. One reason that this happens is that the manager does not understand or have faith in the forecast. This issue will be addressed more fully in steps 7, 8, and 9, but a grounding of faith and understanding should begin here in step 1. If the manager who needs the information from a forecast and the technician who prepares the forecast take the opportunity to discuss the objectives and how the forecast will be used, there is increased likelihood that the ultimate forecast will be one that the manager understands and has faith in using.

Step 2. Determine What to Forecast

Once your overall objectives are clear, you must decide exactly what to forecast. For example, it is not sufficient to say that you want a sales forecast. Do you want a forecast of sales revenue or unit sales? Do you want an annual forecast or a quarterly, monthly, or weekly forecast? It is generally better to base sales forecasts on units rather than dollars so that price changes do not cloud actual variations in unit sales. The unit sales forecast can then be converted to a dollar figure easily enough. If the effect of price on sales is important, you may want to use a regression-based technique that incorporates causality. Good communication between forecast user and forecast preparer is important in making certain that the appropriate variables are being forecast.

Step 3. Identify Time Dimensions

There are two types of time dimensions to consider. First, one must establish the length of the forecast horizon. For annual forecasts this might be from one to five years or more, although forecasts beyond a few years are likely to be influenced by unforeseen events that are not incorporated into the model used. Quarterly forecasts are probably best used for one or two years (four to eight quarters), as are monthly forecasts (perhaps as long as 12 to 18 months). The objectives dictate the time interval (year, quarter, and so forth) that is appropriate in preparing the forecast. For inventory control, short time periods are often necessary, whereas an annual forecast may be sufficient for the preparation of an estimated profit-and-loss statement for the coming year.

Second, the manager and the forecaster must agree on the urgency of the forecast. Is it needed tomorrow? Is there ample time to explore alternative methods? Proper planning is appropriate here. If their forecasting process is integrated into ongoing operations, then the forecasting personnel can plan an appropriate schedule, which will contribute to better forecasts.

Step 4. Data Considerations

The data necessary in preparing a forecast may come from within or may be external. Let us first consider internal data. Some people may believe that internal data are readily available and easy to incorporate into the forecasting process. It is surprising how often this turns out to be far from correct. Data may be available in a technical sense yet not readily available to the person who needs them to prepare the forecast. Or the data may be available but not expressed in the right unit of measurement (e.g., in sales dollars rather than units sold).

Data are often aggregated across both variables and time, but it is best to have disaggregated data. For example, data may be kept for refrigerator sales in total but not by type of refrigerator, type of customer, or region. In addition, what data are maintained may be kept in quarterly or monthly form for only a few years and annually thereafter. Such aggregation of data limits what can be forecast and may limit the appropriate pool of forecasting techniques. Communication and cooperation among the personnel involved in database maintenance, forecast

How to Evaluate and Improve a Forecasting Process

1

Mark Walden, Sales Forecasting
Manager, PartyLite Gifts, Inc.

One of the fundamentals of making good forecasts is
to understand exactly what comprises the historical
data to be used in preparing forecasts. Do not accept
the data at face value. In fact, this is one of the reasons why forecasts, and the resulting financial decisions based on those forecasts, can go awry. This may
also be part of the reason a forecast department can

lack credibility. The best statistical model in the world
is only as good as the input data. To provide effective
forecasts and market analyses, one has to fully understand the business. The best way to begin is to in-
quire into the systems that feed your source data.
There is no single answer as to what constitutes the
best data.

Source: *Journal of Business Forecasting* 15, no. 2
(Summer 1996), p. 23.

preparation, and forecast use can help alleviate many unnecessary problems in
this regard.

External data are available from a wide variety of sources, many of which
have been discussed in Chapter 1. Data from national, state, and local government agencies are generally available at low cost. The more local the level of government unit, the more likely it is that the data will not be available as quickly as
you might like or in the desired detail. Other sources of secondary data include
industry or trade associations and private companies, such as some of the major
banks. Often, secondary data are available on computer disk, a CD, or on the
Internet.[5]

Step 5. Model Selection

There are many methods to select from when you set out to make any forecast.
There are subjective or judgmental methods, some of which were reviewed in
Chapter 1, and a growing set of quantitative methods is becoming available. The
most widely used of these quantitative methods have been discussed in the previous chapters. Now, how can you decide which methods are most appropriate for a
particular situation? Some of the things that should be included in making the
selection are:

1. The type and quantity of data available
2. The pattern that the data have exhibited in the past
3. The urgency of the forecast
4. The length of the forecast horizon
5. The technical background of the people preparing and using the forecast

[5] One of the best starting points for finding data on the Internet is http://www.economagic.com.

This issue of selecting the appropriate methods to use is of sufficient importance that we will come back to it in the next section. There we provide specific guidelines for each of the methods discussed in the text.

Step 6. Model Evaluation

Once the methods that we want to use have been selected we need to do some initial evaluation of how well they work. For the subjective or judgmental methods, this step is less appropriate than for the quantitative methods that have been stressed in this text. For those subjective methods, the comparable sixth step would be to organize the process to be used (e.g., setting up procedures for gathering information from a sales force or Delphi panel).

For quantitative methods, we should apply the techniques to historical series and evaluate how well they work in a retrospective sense. We have referred to this as an evaluation of the "fit" of the model. If they do not work well in the historical context, there is little reason to believe that they will perform any better in the unknown domain of the future.

If we have sufficient historical data, a good approach to model testing is to use a "holdout" period for evaluation. For example, suppose we have quarterly data on sales for 10 years. We might use only the earliest nine years (36 data points) and make a forecast for the 10th year. If the model performs well when the forecast values are compared with the known values for the four quarters of year 10, we have reason to believe that the technique may also work well when the forecast period is indeed unknown. Out-of-sample evaluations such as this provide a measure of forecast "accuracy."

Once you are satisfied with a model based on historical and holdout period evaluations, you should respecify the model using all the available data (historical and holdout) and then use it for your actual forecast.

Suppose a technique turns out not to perform well when tested. The purpose of testing is, at least in part, to help us avoid applying a method that does not work well in our unique situation. Therefore, we should go back to step 5 and select another method that is appropriate to the problem at hand. It is not always possible to tell ahead of time how well a particular method will actually perform in a specific forecasting environment. We can apply reasoned judgment to our initial selection, but ultimately the proof is in the pudding. We must apply the method to see whether it performs adequately for the purpose at hand.

Step 7. Forecast Preparation

At this point, some method or set of methods has been selected for use in developing the forecast, and from testing you have reasonable expectations that the methods will perform well. We recommend using more than one forecasting method when possible, and it is desirable for these to be of different types (e.g., a regression model and Holt's exponential smoothing rather than two different regression models). The methods chosen should be used to prepare a range of forecasts. You might, for example, prepare a worst-case forecast, a best-case forecast, and a most-likely forecast. The latter may be based on a combination of forecasts developed by following the procedures suggested in Chapter 8.

Once you are satisfied with a model based on historical and holdout period evaluations, you should respecify the model using all the available data (historical and holdout) and then use it for your actual forecast.

Step 8. Forecast Presentation

For a forecast to be used as intended, it must be presented to management clearly, in a way that provides an understanding of how the numbers were obtained and that elicits confidence in the forecast. It does not matter how much work is put into developing the forecast. It does not matter how confident the preparer is in the results. It does not matter how sophisticated the methodology may be. What matters is whether or not the manager understands and has confidence in the forecast. All too often, quantitative analyses are put on a shelf and do not play the role in decision making that they should, because the results are not effectively presented to management. Mark J. Lawless, who has been involved with forecasting within a number of corporations, including Chrysler, NCR, Ponderosa, and Hanson Industries Housewares Group, has commented that:

"The forecaster must be capable of communicating the findings in language which the functional managers can understand. . . ."

> In communicating the forecast results to management, the forecaster must be capable of communicating the findings in language which the functional managers can understand and which is compatible with the corporate culture.[6]

The forecast should be communicated to management both in written form and in an oral presentation. The written document should be at a level that is appropriate to the reader. In most cases the managers who read the forecast document will have little interest in technical matters. They need just enough information to give them a general understanding of the method used. They do not need the amount of background and detail to be able to prepare the forecast themselves.

Tables should be kept relatively short. Rarely would it be desirable to include an entire history of the data used and historical forecasts. The most recent observations and forecasts are usually sufficient. The long series should, however, be shown graphically and should include both actual and forecast values. In such graphic displays, colors and/or patterns can be used effectively to distinguish actual and forecast values.

The oral presentation should follow the same form and be made at about the same level as the written document. Generous use should be made of flip charts, slides, overheads, or projections of computer displays to heighten interest and involvement in the presentation. This oral presentation provides an excellent opportunity for discussion and clarification, which helps the manager gain a more complete understanding of the forecast and confidence in its usefulness.

Step 9. Tracking Results

Neither the preparer nor the user is done with the forecast after the presentation and incorporation of results into the relevant decisions. The *process* continues. Deviations from the forecast and the actual events should be discussed in an open, objective, and positive manner. The objectives of such discussions should be to understand why errors occurred, to determine whether the magnitude of the errors was sufficient to have made a difference in the decisions that were based on the

---

[6] Mark J. Lawless, "Effective Sales Forecasting: A Management Tool," *Journal of Business Forecasting 9*, no. 1 (Spring 1990), p. 10.

forecast, and to reevaluate the entire process with the intent of improving performance in the next round of forecasts. Input from both managers and technicians is important for the continual refinement of the forecasting process.

It is important to stress once more the critical role that communication and cooperation between managers and technicians play in building and maintaining a successful forecasting process. This is true whether forecasts are prepared "in house" or by outside suppliers. Without a commitment to communication and cooperation, it is not likely that any organization can get a maximum return from the forecasting effort.

CHOOSING THE RIGHT FORECASTING TECHNIQUES

In the spring 1991 issue of the *Journal of Business Forecasting,* Charles W. Chase, Jr. (currently at the SAS Institute), commented that:

"The key task of a practicing forecaster is to determine at the outset the best match possible between the situation and the methods. . . ."

> The key task of a practicing forecaster is to determine at the outset the best match possible between the situation and the methods before doing anything else.[7]

Now that you have an understanding of a variety of forecasting techniques, you need a general framework that will help you determine when to use each method. There are few hard-and-fast rules in this regard, but there are guidelines to assist in making the determination. If you understand how to use the methods discussed in this text, you have a good start toward determining when each method is likely to be useful. For example, if you are preparing a quarterly forecast of sales for a product that exhibits considerable seasonality, you would want to use one of the methods that is designed to handle such seasonal fluctuations.

In this section we evaluate the forecasting methods presented earlier in the text relative to the underlying conditions for which they are most likely to be useful. There are many characteristics of a forecasting situation that might be considered in selecting an appropriate method. We will focus attention on three major areas: data, time, and personnel. For data, we consider the type and quantity of data that are available as well as any pattern that may exist in the data (e.g., trend, cycle, and/or seasonality). The time dimension focuses on the forecast horizon. For personnel we consider the necessary technical background of both the preparer and the user of the forecast. We begin with the methods discussed in Chapter 1 and progress sequentially through the text, ending with the ARIMA technique. Table 10.2 provides a quick reference summary of the data and time issues.

Sales Force Composite (SFC)

In using the sales force composite method, little or no historical data are necessary. The data required are the current estimates of salespeople regarding expected sales for the forecast horizon. Historical data may be considered by the sales

[7] Charles W. Chase, Jr., "Forecasting Consumer Products," *Journal of Business Forecasting* 10, no. 1 (Spring 1991), p. 3.

TABLE 10.2 **A Guide to Selecting an Appropriate Forecasting Method**

Forecasting Method	Data Pattern	Quantity of Historical Data (Number of Observations)	Forecast Horizon
Subjective Methods			
Sales force composite	Any	Little	Short to medium
Customer surveys	Not applicable	None	Medium to long
Jury of executive opinion	Any	Little	Any
Delphi	Any	Little	Long
Naive			
	Stationary[a]	1 or 2	Very short
Moving Averages			
	Stationary[a]	Number equal to the periods in the moving average	Very short
Exponential Smoothing			
Simple	Stationary[a,b]	5 to 10	Short
Adaptive response	Stationary[a,b]	10 to 15	Short
Holt's	Linear trend[b]	10 to 15	Short to medium
Winters'	Trend and seasonality	At least 4 or 5 per season	Short to medium
Bass model	S-curve	Small, 3 to 10	Short, medium, and long
Regression-Based			
Trend	Linear and nonlinear trend with or without seasonality	Minimum of 10 with 4 or 5 per season if seasonality is included	Short to medium
Causal	Can handle nearly all data patterns	Minimum of 10 per independent variable	Short, medium, and long
Time-Series Decomposition			
	Can handle trend, seasonal, and cyclical patterns	Enough to see 2 peaks and troughs in the cycle	Short, medium, and long
ARIMA			
	Stationary[a]	Minimum of 50	Short, medium, and long
Data Mining			
	Any	Used with large databases	Prediction usually for near-term use

[a] Or data that have been transformed to a stationary series.
[b] May be used for seasonal data if the data are first deseasonalized.

force, but not necessarily. Thus, this method may not reflect patterns in the data unless they are obvious to the sales force (e.g., Christmas season sales of jewelry). The method may, however, provide early warning signals of pending change (positive or negative) because of the closeness of the sales force to the customer. SFC is probably best used for short- to medium-term forecasts.[8] The preparation time is relatively short once a system for gathering data from the sales force is in place. This method requires little quantitative sophistication on the part of the preparer or the user, which contributes to its ease of use and to ready acceptance of results.

Customer Surveys (CS)

Forecasts that are based on surveys of buyers' intentions require no historical data, and thus the past plays no explicit role in forecasting the future. Customer surveys are most appropriate for medium- to long-term forecasting. For example, a natural gas utility has used this method to help in long-term planning by gathering survey data on customers' plans for future energy use, including long-term capital expansion plans. The time necessary to develop, conduct, and analyze a survey research project can be relatively extensive. Rarely can such a project be completed in less than two to three months. If the same survey is used year after year, however, this time can be shortened considerably. CS is not a method to consider if there is a sense of urgency in getting the forecast. Those involved in preparing such a forecast need considerable technical expertise in the area of survey research. Users, on the other hand, need not have a sophisticated technical background, as long as they know enough about survey research to interpret the results appropriately.

Jury of Executive Opinion (JEO)

The executives included do not need a formal data set. They need only the body of experience that they have developed to make judgments concerning the most likely value of the forecast variable during the period of interest. Historical data patterns may or may not be reflected in the opinions expressed, although regular patterns such as seasonality are very likely to receive attention, albeit implicit attention. A JEO may be used for any forecast horizon and is generally a relatively quick procedure. This method does not require much quantitative sophistication on the part of either preparers or users, but it does require a substantial base of expertise on the part of the participants.

Delphi Method

The Delphi method does not require a historical data series, other than what is in the knowledge base of the panel members, and therefore does not necessarily reflect patterns that may have existed in the past. It is most often applicable for long-range forecasting but can be applied to medium-term projects as well. In these respects it is much like JEO. However, the time to develop the Delphi forecast can be

---

[8] Short-term, medium-term, and long-term forecasts will be mentioned throughout this section. Short-term forecasts include up to three months, medium-term forecasts cover four months to about two years, and long-term forecasts are for periods longer than two years.

considerable unless the responses of panel members stabilize quickly. Computers can be effectively used to speed the flow of information and thus shorten the time considerably. The Delphi method requires only modest technical sophistication on the part of the preparer, and no particular technical sophistication is necessary for the end user, other than to understand the process through which the forecast was developed. The Delphi approach, as well as a jury of executive opinion and customer surveys, are sometimes useful in forecasting the sales of new products. We will discuss new product forecasting in more detail later in this chapter.

Naive

The basic naive model requires only one historical value as a basis for the forecast. An extended naive model that takes the most recent trend into account requires just two past values. This method is best suited to situations in which the data are stationary or in which any trend is relatively stable. Seasonality can sometimes be accounted for in a reasonably stationary series using a seasonal time lag, such as was demonstrated for total houses sold and The Gap sales in Chapter 1. The naive approach is suited only for very short-term forecasts. Preparation time is minimal, and no technical sophistication is necessary on the part of either the preparer or the user.

Moving Averages

Moving averages are most appropriate when the data are stationary and do not exhibit seasonality. Relatively few historical data are necessary. The number of past observations must be at least equal to the number of periods in the moving average. For example, if a four-period moving average is used, you need at least four historical data points. Moving averages are normally used to forecast just one period ahead and require very little quantitative sophistication.

Simple Exponential Smoothing (SES)

Historical data are necessary to establish the best weighting factor in simple exponential smoothing, but thereafter only the most recent observed and forecasted values are required. Five to ten past values are sufficient to determine the weighting factor. The data series should be stationary (i.e., have no trend and no seasonality) when SES is used. This method is appropriate for short-term forecasting and requires little technical sophistication. While the arithmetic work can be done by hand, a computer can be helpful in determining the best weighting factor. Once the weighting factor is known, forecasts can be developed very quickly.

Adaptive–Response-Rate Single Exponential Smoothing (ADRES)

The adaptive–response-rate single exponential smoothing model may be used when the data are stationary and exhibit no seasonality but have a shift in level. Ten to fifteen historical observations should be available when ADRES is used, and forecasts should be for only a short forecast horizon, typically one or two periods ahead. This method requires a bit more quantitative sophistication by the preparer than does SES, but users need little quantitative background.

Holt's Exponential Smoothing (HES)

As in SES, Holt's exponential smoothing model requires historical data to determine weighting values, but only the very recent past is required to apply the model. It is desirable to have at least 10 to 15 historical observations in determining the two weights. HES can be used effectively with data series that exhibit a positive or negative trend, and thus this method has a much wider scope of application than SES. However, it should not be used when the data contain a seasonal pattern unless the data have been deseasonalized. HES is appropriate for short- and medium-term forecasts and, like SES, can be implemented rapidly once the weights have been selected. Some technical expertise is required of the preparer, but users with little sophistication can understand HES well enough to use it properly. A computer is desirable, but not necessary, for model development.

Winters' Exponential Smoothing (WES)

Sufficient historical data to determine the weights are necessary in using Winters' exponential smoothing model. A minimum of four or five observations per season should be used (i.e., for quarterly data, 16 or 20 observations should be used). Because this method incorporates both trend and seasonal components, it is applicable to a wide spectrum of data patterns. Like HES, this method is most appropriate for short- to medium-term forecasts. Once the weights have been determined, the process of making a forecast moves quickly. The preparer needs some technical expertise, but the nature of the method can be understood by users with little technical sophistication. Use of a computer is recommended for the process of selecting the best values for the weights in the WES model. Even if weights are restricted to one decimal place, the number of combinations that might be evaluated becomes too cumbersome to do by hand.

Regression-Based Trend Models

The data requirement for using a regression-based trend depends to a considerable extent on the consistency in the trend and whether or not the trend is linear. We look for enough data that the *t*-statistic for the slope term (i.e., the trend) is significant (a *t*-value of 2 or more in absolute value is a handy rule of thumb). For a simple linear trend, 10 observations may be quite sufficient. A simple trend model can be effective when the series being forecast has no pattern other than the trend. Such a model is appropriate for short- to medium-term forecasts and can be developed and implemented relatively quickly. The preparer needs to have a basic understanding of regression analysis but does not need a sophisticated background for simple linear trends. More complex nonlinear trends require deeper understanding. Using a computer simplifies preparation of the forecast. The method is sufficiently straightforward that the user needs little technical sophistication.

Regression-Based Trend Models with Seasonality

To include seasonality in a regression-based trend model, it is desirable to have at least four or five observations per season. Thus, for quarterly data a minimum of 16 observations would be appropriate. For monthly data, 48 or more observations

James G. Steen, Forecasting Analyst,
Sensormatic Electronics Corporation

TEAM WORK: KEY TO SUCCESSFUL FORECASTING

Sensormatic Electronics is a manufacturer of electronic surveillance equipment. The most challenging part of our forecasting effort is getting the market management and product development groups together to come up with a consensus forecast. This is important because they are in frequent contact with salespeople, customers, and account managers, and thus have access to information vital for forecasting. But, due to their hectic schedule, the information is often not communicated in a timely manner to be used effectively in preparing forecasts. Because of the lead time of certain products, ample time is needed to plan and manufacture products. We often don't hear of a large order or potential order until the end of our fiscal quarter. At that point, there is little or no time left to react.

Once every quarter we have a meeting in which we discuss, review, and update our forecasts. Such meetings are very helpful but not quite adequate to do the job. Many things change during the period between one meeting and the next. But the information about the changes is often not passed on to those responsible for preparing the forecasts. We are currently working on improving the flow of information from our sales force to those involved in forecasting at our head office.

The "team" approach is the only way we can be successful since no one person has all the necessary information to prepare forecasts. By working together, we can all benefit and keep our customers satisfied.

Source: Adapted from *Journal of Business Forecasting* 11, no. 2 (Summer 1992), p. 22. Reprinted by permission.

should be used. Regular seasonal patterns in the series are often modeled quite well by using dummy variables. As with simple trend models, linear or nonlinear forms can be used; the models are best for short- to medium-term forecasts, and the time necessary for preparation is short. Except when nonlinear models are used, little mathematical sophistication is necessary on the part of either the preparer or the user of the forecast. A computer regression program is a virtual necessity, however.

Regression Models with Causality

The quantity of data required for the development of a causal regression model depends on the number of independent variables in the model and on how much contribution each of those variables makes in explaining variation in the dependent variable. One rule of thumb is that you should expect to have a minimum of 10 observations per independent variable. Thus, for a model with three independent variables you should have at least 30 observations. You can see that developing and maintaining a database for multiple-regression models can be a significant undertaking. The effort may be worthwhile, however, since multiple-regression models are often effective in dealing with complex data patterns and may even help identify turning points. Seasonality can be handled by using dummy variables. Causal regression models can be useful for short-, medium-, or long-term

Debra M. Schramm, Manager, Sales
Forecasting, Parke-Davis

HOW TO SELL FORECASTS
TO MANAGEMENT

One of the universal problems forecasters have is "selling" their forecast to others, especially marketing management. Management is reluctant, at best, to use numbers from a group or individual who is viewed as only able to analyze numbers. They question why our crystal ball should be any better than theirs. Our company was no exception. Five years ago the forecast area was viewed as a department that did something with the sales numbers. No one seemed to know what our role was in the organization or how we meshed with the big picture. Although our forecasts were used to feed manufacturing and distribution, they were not considered in the management review process, which took place each month, to determine the division's sales numbers. It became our goal to change our image or the lack of it.

Today the forecasting department and its forecasts are an integral part of the management process. Our system forecasts are used as the basis for the monthly review, the annual, and longer-term plans. We continue to support marketing with reliable information, anticipating their future needs and experimenting with external data in order to improve the forecasts. There is no point lower than to work at something, then find you are the only one who believes in what you do. If we as forecasters are to raise our image in business, we must be able to prove ourselves and prove the integrity of the data we supply. The process can be long and frustrating, but it is attainable with determination, patience, and perseverance. Once achieved it is immensely rewarding.

Source: Adapted from *Journal of Business Forecasting* 10, no. 4 (Winter 1991–92), p. 22. Reprinted by permission.

forecasts. Because the causal variables must usually be forecast as well, regression models may take more effort to develop. It can take a long time to develop a good causal regression model. Once the model is developed, preparation of a forecast can be done reasonably quickly. In using causal regression models, you should reestimate equations at least once a year so that structural changes are identified in a timely manner. The technician who prepares regression forecasts needs to have a solid background in regression analysis. Managers, on the other hand, can use such forecasts effectively as long as they have a basic understanding of regression methods.

Time-Series Decomposition (TSD)

The quantity of data needed for time-series decomposition should be enough for you to see at least two peaks and two troughs in the cycle factor, if the cycle factor is important. If the cycle factor does not appear important (i.e., has not been far above or below 1.0 during the historical period), then the quantity of data needed should be determined by what is necessary to adequately identify the seasonal pattern. A rule of thumb would be at least four or five observations per season (e.g., for quarterly data you should have at least 16 to 20 observations). TSD is quite good at picking up patterns in the data. The challenge is for the analyst to successfully project the patterns through the forecast horizon. This is generally fairly easy for the trend and seasonal pattern, but is more difficult for the cyclical pattern. TSD is especially appropriate for short-term and medium-term forecasting. If the cycle pattern is not important or if it can be projected with confidence, the method can also be used effectively for long-term forecasts. This method may be one of the best in terms of being able to identify and incorporate turning points. Doing so is dependent on the analyst's ability to correctly interpret when the cycle factor may turn up or down. The preparation time for a TSD forecast is relatively short, and this method does not require much sophistication on the part of the preparer or the user. In fact, most managers find the concepts inherent in the TSD model quite consistent with how they see the world.

ARIMA

A long data series (at least 50 data points—more if data are seasonal) is necessary to make use of the ARIMA models. These models can handle variability in the data as long as the series is stationary or can be transformed to a stationary series. This method can be applied to short-, medium-, or long-term forecast horizons. Because of the complexity of model identification, forecast preparation can take an extended period of time. This complexity also means that the preparer needs a highly sophisticated technical background. Users of ARIMA forecasts must also be quite sophisticated, because even achieving a basic understanding of the method is not easy. It is rare to find a manager who has a good feel for how an ARIMA forecast is developed, and rarer still to find a manager capable of explaining the forecast derivation to others who must use the results. This may be part of the reason that ARIMA models have had relatively low ratings in terms of importance, accuracy, and use by business managers.

SPECIAL FORECASTING CONSIDERATIONS

In the text a number of situations have been discussed for which special forecasting techniques are appropriate. Four of these are (1) situations when we must make forecasts if "events" of some type influence the forecast, (2) situations when we have multiple forecasts, each of which may contain valuable information that we do not want to ignore, (3) situations when we need to forecast a new product for which we have little historical information, and (4) situations in which we need to predict some outcome and we have very large, often somewhat unrelated, databases that hold hidden keys to the likely outcome. Here we review some important aspects of each of these four.

Event Modeling

When forecasting sales or demand in a highly promoted market, using event modeling can often significantly improve forecast accuracy. Event modeling is a feature of some exponential smoothing programs, such as ForecastX™. This feature allows the user to specify the time of one or more special events, such as irregular promotions and natural disasters, in the calibration data. For each type of special event, the effect is estimated and the data adjusted so that the events do not distort the trend and seasonal patterns of the time series.

The method of event modeling follows in the same pattern as the other smoothing models except that the event model adds a smoothing equation for each of the events being considered. Event models are analogous to seasonal models: just as each month is assigned its own index for seasonality, so, too, each event type is assigned its own index. Event adjustments are created through the use of an indicator variable that assigns an integer for each event type to the period during which it recurs. An example of integer value assignment would be that 0 indicates a period where no event has occurred, 1 indicates a period where a free-standing advertising insert was used, 2 indicates a period where instant redeemable coupons were used, and so on. The event indicator variable must be defined for each historical period and future period in the forecast horizon.

Combining Forecasts

Instead of choosing the best model from among two or more alternatives, a more reasoned approach, according to the empirical evidence, is to combine the forecasts in order to obtain a forecast that is more accurate than any of the separate predictions. Any time a particular forecast is ignored because it is not the "best" forecast produced, it is likely that valuable independent information contained in the discarded forecast has been lost. The information lost may be of two types:

1. Some variables included in the discarded forecast may not be included in the "best" forecast.
2. The discarded forecast may make use of a type of relationship ignored by the "best" forecast.

In the first of these cases it is quite possible for individual forecasts to be based on different information; thus, ignoring any one of these forecasts would necessarily exclude the explanatory power unique to the information included in the discarded model. In the second situation, it is often the case that different assumptions are made in different models about the form of the relationship between the variables. Each of the different forms of relationship tested, however, may have some explanatory value. Choosing only the "best" of the relationships could exclude functional information. To prevent this loss of useful information requires some method for combining the two forecasts into a single *better* forecast. We should expect that combinations of forecasts that use very different models are likely to be effective in reducing forecast error.

New-Product Forecasting (NPF)

Most products for which we are likely to have to prepare a sales forecast are products with a substantial amount of sales history for which the methods you have learned in earlier chapters will work quite well. However, often we are faced with new, or substantially altered, products with little sales history. These new products pose particularly difficult issues for a forecaster. You have seen that understanding the concept of a product life cycle (PLC) can be helpful in developing a forecast for a new product. During the introductory stage of the product life cycle, only consumers who are *innovators* are likely to buy the product. Sales start low and increase slowly. Near the end of this stage, sales start to increase at an increasing rate. As the product enters the growth stage of the PLC, sales are still increasing at an increasing rate as *early adopters* enter the market. In this stage the rate of growth in sales starts to decline. Near the end of the growth stage, sales growth starts to level off substantially as the product enters the maturity stage. Businesses may employ marketing strategies to extend this stage; however, all products eventually reach the stage of decline in sales and are, at some point, removed from the market.

Product life cycles are not uniform in shape or duration and vary from industry to industry. Think, for example, about products that are fashion items or fads in comparison with products that have real staying power in the marketplace. Fashion items and products that would be considered fads typically have a steep introductory stage followed by short growth and maturity stages and a decline that is also very steep. High-tech products often have life cycles that are relatively short in comparison with low-technology products. For high-tech electronic products, life cycles may be as short as six to nine months. An example would be a telephone that has a design based on a movie character.

Methods such as analog forecasts, test marketing, and product clinics are often useful for new-product forecasting. The Bass model for sales of new products is probably the most notable model for new-product forecasting. The Bass model was originally developed for application only to durable goods. However, it has been adapted for use in forecasting a wide variety of products with short product life cycles and new products with limited historical data.

Data Mining

Sometimes people think of forecasting only in the context of time-series data. In some manner past data are used to help predict the likely outcomes in the future. These include univariate time-series methods, such as exponential smoothing, as well as causal models, such as multiple regression. We have seen that at times regression models may be useful with cross-sectional data to predict some outcome, such as sales volume. Data mining is another technique that has been developed to help one predict outcomes when there is a great deal of data available that might contain hidden information.

Data mining techniques work often with very large and somewhat unrelated databases. There was a time when decision makers had too little data upon which to base decisions. Now that has changed dramatically and decision makers have so much data that it is difficult to find the information content from the data. This is where data mining becomes a useful tool.

Data mining has become a new application for some types of forecasting in which we have huge amounts of data but we know little about the structural

Mark J. Lawless, Senior Vice President of the Business Group, National Fire Protection Association

FORECASTS MUST BE RELEVANT AND EFFECTIVE

The environment of business is continuing to change at an increasing rate, and the demands on management to create value are increasing with it. The role of forecasters is changing as well, and the value created by the forecaster is very much a consideration in the role which forecasting plays in the management-decision process.

If management must create value for the shareholder, the forecaster must create value for the shareholder as well. Hence, rather than pining for earlier times when things were better for forecasters, we need to adapt to the changing environment as well. We need to be continuously asking: "How can we create value? How can we enhance value? How can we assist others in creating value?" If forecasters will ask themselves these simple questions, and act upon their answers, the ability of forecast functions to be effective and credible will take care of itself. Looking to the needs of the management decisions, using whatever information that is available (imperfect though it may be), and developing the forecasts and recommendations in the context of these management needs are important parts of the forecast function.

To be successful in the future, there are two important ground rules for all forecasters—be relevant and be effective.

Source: Adapted from "Ten Prescriptions for Forecasting Success," *Journal of Business Forecasting* 16, no. 1 (Spring 1997), pp. 3–5.

relationships contained therein. Data mining is a tool that helps us uncover relationships that are often quite unexpected yet useful in making predictions. For example, a California retailer found through data mining that shoppers who buy diapers are also likely to buy beer.[9] Such knowledge would not be likely to be uncovered using more simplistic data analysis but can be useful in predicting sales of both items and in developing new ways to structure marketing communications involving both products.

Suppose you wanted to forecast the number of sports cars an insurance company would insure. It is obvious to us that one factor would be the price (premium) charged for coverage, which in turn would be influenced by the number of claims filed by sports car owners. Conventional wisdom might suggest that sports car owners would have more claims for accidents and/or thefts. However, through data mining, Farmers Group found that sports cars owned by people who also owned another vehicle have fewer insurance claims. As a result they restructured their premiums in these situations with a resulting increase in premium revenue of over $4 million in two years without having a substantial increase in claims.[10] It was only possible to make the prediction about the potential new market by using data mining.

[9] Donald R. Cooper and Pamela S. Schindler, *Marketing Research*, McGraw-Hill/Irwin, 2006, p. 261.
[10] Carl McDaniel and Roger Gates, *Marketing Research Essentials*, 6th ed., John Wiley & Sons, 2008, pp. 79–80.

Summary

The forecasting process begins with the need to make decisions that are dependent on the future values of one or more variables. Once the need to forecast is recognized, the steps to follow can be summarized as follows:

1. Specify objectives.
2. Determine what to forecast.
3. Identify time dimensions.
4. Data considerations.
5. Model selection. ←⏋
6. Model evaluation. ──⏌
7. Forecast preparation.
8. Forecast presentation.
9. Tracking results.

Throughout the process, open communication between managers who use the forecasts and the technicians who prepare them is essential.

You have been introduced to the most widely used forecasting methods and need to know when each is appropriate. The section entitled "Choosing the Right Forecasting Techniques" (page 491) provides a guide to help you in determining when to use each technique and when each should not be used. Table 10.2 also provides a handy summary of that discussion.

Developing a forecast for new products is an especially difficult task. Because little or no historical data are available, we are forced to use methods based on judgments and/or various marketing research methods. Often, looking at the sales history of relatively similar products can provide a basis upon which a forecast for the new product can be built. Information gathered using a survey technique about intention to purchase on the part of potential customers may also provide helpful insight.

In Chapter 9 you have seen that data mining is a relatively new tool that can be used in forecasting when we have such large databases that uncovering relationships can be difficult. A variety of data mining tools were discussed. These tools once were accessible only if one had access to very large computers, but now even personal computers can be used for some data mining applications. In the future we can expect to see data mining become a more common tool in the forecaster's toolbox.

USING PROCAST™ IN FORECASTX™ TO MAKE FORECASTS

As usual, begin by opening your data file in Excel and start ForecastX™. In the **Data Capture** dialog box identify the data you want to use, as shown below. Then click the **Forecast Method** tab.

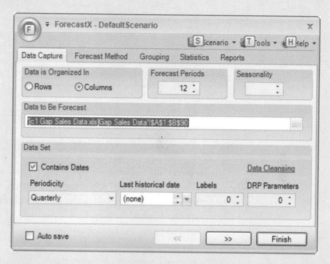

In the **Method Selection** dialog box click the down arrow in the **Forecasting Technique** box and select **ProCast™.** Click the down arrow in the **Error Term** box and select **Root Mean Squared Error** (or another error term you want to use). Then click the **Statistics** tab.

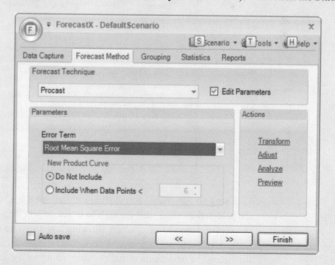

In this dialog box select the statistics that you desire. Remember that there are more statistics choices if you click the **More Statistics** button at the bottom.

After selecting the statistics you want to see, click the **Reports** tab.

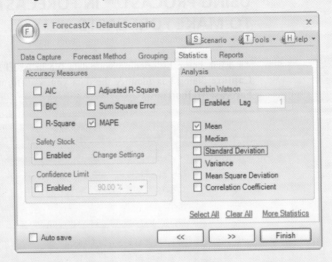

In the **Reports** box select those you want. Typical selections might be those shown here. When you click the **Standard** tab select the **Show Chart** and **Classic.** In the **Audit Trail** tab (the active tab shown here) click the **Fitted Values Table.**

Then click the **Finish!** button. In the Audit Trail output you will find the method that ProCast™ used to make the requested forecast.

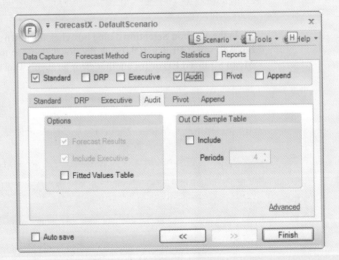

Using an automated forecasting method such as ProCast™ is all right if you understand the selected method well enough to evaluate whether it is truly a logical choice. It is wise to exercise some caution when allowing any software to select a method automatically. By using a software package over a period of time, such as ForecastX™, you may develop confidence in the selections it makes. Then using an automated process may provide considerable time savings—such as in situations where there are hundreds or thousands of items that must be forecast frequently.

Suggested Readings

Armstrong, J. Scott. "Research Needs in Forecasting." *International Journal of Forecasting* 4, no. 3 (1988), pp. 449–65.

Chase, Charles W., Jr. "Business Forecasting: A Process Not an Application." *Journal of Business Forecasting* 11, no. 3 (Fall 1992), pp. 12–13.

Fisher, Marshall; and Kumar Rajaram. "Accurate Retail Testing of Fashion Merchandise: Methodology and Application." *Marketing Science* 19, no. 3 (Summer 2000), pp. 266–78.

Harrington, Lisa H. "Retail Collaboration: How to Solve the Puzzle." *Transportation and Distribution,* May 2003, pp. 33–37.

"The Improved Demand Signal: Benefiting from Collaborative Forecasting." *PeopleSoft White Paper Series.* January 2004. http://www.peoplesoft.com/media/en/pdf/white_paper/improved_demand_signal_wp_0104.pdf (February 9, 2005).

Keating, Barry; and J. Holton Wilson. "Forecasting Practices and Teachings." *Journal of Business Forecasting* 7, no. 4 (Winter 1987–88), pp. 10–13, 16.

Larréché, Jean-Claude; and Reza Moinpour. "Managerial Judgement in Marketing: The Concept of Expertise." *Journal of Marketing Research* 20, no. 2 (May 1983), pp. 110–21.

Lawless, Mark J. "Effective Sales Forecasting: A Management Tool." *Journal of Business Forecasting* 9, no. 1 (Spring 1990), pp. 2–11.

———. "Ten Prescriptions for Forecasting Success." *Journal of Business Forecasting* 11, no. 4 (Spring 1997), pp. 3–5.

LeLee, Gary S. "The Key to Understanding the Forecasting Process." *Journal of Business Forecasting* 11, no. 4 (Winter 1992–93), pp. 12–16.

Lynn, Gary S.; Steven P. Schnaars; and Richard B. Skov. "Survey of New Product Forecasting Practices in Industrial High Technology and Low Technology Businesses." *Industrial Marketing Management* 28 (November 1999), pp. 565–71.

Mentzer, John T.; and Kenneth B. Kahn. "State of Sales Forecasting Systems in Corporate America." *Journal of Business Forecasting* 11, no. 4 (Spring 1997), pp. 6–13.

Moon, Mark A.; and John T. Mentzer. "Improving Salesforce Forecasting." *Journal of Business Forecasting* 18, no. 2 (Summer 1999), pp. 7–12.

Moon, Mark A.; John T. Mentzer; Carlo D. Smith; and Michael S. Garver. "Seven Keys to Better Forecasting." *Business Horizons* (September–October 1998), pp. 44–52.

Pammer, Scott E.; Duncan K. H. Fong; and Steven F. Arnold. "Forecasting the Penetration of a New Product—A Bayesian Approach." *Journal of Business & Economic Statistics* 18, no. 4 (October 2000), pp. 428–35.

Raghunathan, Srinivasan. "Interorganizational Collaborative Forecasting and Replenishment Systems and Supply Chain Implications," *Decision Sciences* 30, no. 4 (Fall 1999), pp. 1053–71.

Reese, Sean. "The Human Aspects of Collaborative Forecasting." *Journal of Business Forecasting* 19, no. 4 (Winter 2000–2001), pp. 3–9.

Reyes, Luis. "The Forecasting Function: Critical Yet Misunderstood." *Journal of Business Forecasting* 14, no. 4 (Winter 1995–96), pp. 8–9.

Szmania, Joe; and John Surgent. "An Application of an Expert System Approach to Business Forecasting." *Journal of Business Forecasting* 8, no. 1 (Spring 1989), pp. 10–12.

Tkacz, Greg. "Neural Network Forecasting of Canadian GDP Growth." *International Journal of Forecasting* 17, no. 1 (January–March 2001), pp. 57–69.

Weitz, Rob R. "NOSTRADAMUS—A Knowledge-Based Forecast Advisor." *International Journal of Forecasting* 2, no. 1 (1986), pp. 273–83.

Wilson, J. Holton; and Hugh G. Daubek. "Marketing Managers Evaluate Forecasting Models." *Journal of Business Forecasting* 8, no. 1 (Spring 1989), pp. 19–22.

Exercises

1. You have read the statement that the forecast process begins with a need to make one or more decisions that depend on the future value of some variable. Think about this as it relates to the daily weather forecast you hear, and write a list of five decisions that might depend on such a forecast.

2. Why do you think communication between the person preparing a forecast and the forecast user is important? Give several specific places in the nine-step forecast process where you think such communication is especially important and explain why.

3. The availability and form of data to be used in preparing a forecast are often seen as especially critical areas. Summarize, in your own words, the database considerations in the forecasting process (step 4).

4. Suppose that you have been asked to recommend a forecasting technique that would be appropriate to prepare a forecast, given the following situational characteristics:

   a. You have 10 years of quarterly data.

   b. There is an upward trend to the data.

   c. There is a significant increase in sales prior to Christmas each year.

   d. A one-year forecast is needed.

   e. You, as the preparer of the forecast, have good technical skills, but the manager who needs the forecast is very nontechnical.

   f. You need to have the forecast done and the presentation ready in just a few days.

   What method(s) would you consider using and why?

5. Write an outline of what you would like to see in a forecast presentation from the perspective of a manager who needs to use the forecast.

6. Explain in your own words how artificial intelligence can be used in a forecasting environment.

7. If you had been assigned the task of forecasting the demand for MP3 players when they were a new product, how might you have approached the problem?

Index